THE NATIONAL UNDERWF

MW00423084

The Advisor's Guide to 401(k) Plans, 2014 Edition
By Bruce A. Tannahill, J.D., CPA/PFS, CLU®, ChFC®, AEP®, and Louis R. Richey, J.D.

The book you hold in your hands provides proven, practice-oriented insights, advice, analysis, and strategy on all key issues related to 401(k) Plans.

Written by two highly respected attorneys who are retirement planning experts, this is a valuable and necessary tool for any retirement planning, pension planning, benefits, HR, or financial planning professional.

With *The Advisor's Guide to 401(k) Plans, 2014 Edition*, you know what rules apply and when—and you're able to find the source for those rules right away.

Look through these pages to find immediate insights into the most critical aspects of:

- Plan Design

- Eligibility Requirements

- Safe Harbor Plans

- Defined Contribution Plan Cross-Testing

- SIMPLE 401(k) Plans

- The Roth Option (including accounts, contributions, conversions, and distributions)

- The Use of Life Insurance in 401(k) Plans

- The Relationship between 401(k) Plans and Defined Benefit Plans

- Complying with Nondiscrimination Rules and Creating Programs that will Comply

- Multiple Employers, Plan Mergers, and Plan Terminations

- Regulatory Matters: Determination Letters, ERISA/IRS Reporting, and Other Matters

The Advisor's Guide to 401(k) Plans helps you understand how to do things right and what to do when things go wrong. This resource also covers:

- Prohibited Transactions

- Administration Problems

- Design Defects

- Plan Correction—full coverage of the recently released IRS and DOL guidelines!

Our respected authors—Bruce A. Tannahill, J.D., CPA/PFS, CLU˚, ChFC˚, AEP˚, and Louis R. Richey, J.D.—deliver proven, practical guidance you can apply immediately.

For anyone advising on 401(k) Plans *The Advisor's Guide to 401(k) Plans, 2014 Edition,* is fully cited to both the tax code and ERISA. So you can quickly get at the source information, support your advice, and communicate confidently with other professionals.

To place additional orders for *The Advisor's Guide to 401(k) Plans, 2014 Edition,* or any of our products, or for additional information, contact Customer Service at 1-800-543-0874.

2014 Edition

The Advisor's Guide to 401(k) Plans

Bruce Tannahill, J.D., CPA, CLU®
Louis R. Richey, J.D.

ISBN 978-1-939829-37-5

THE NATIONAL UNDERWRITER COMPANY

Copyright © 2014

The National Underwriter Company
5081 Olympic Blvd.
Erlanger, KY 41018

About Summit Professional Networks

Summit Professional Networks supports the growth and vitality of the insurance, financial services and legal communities by providing professionals with the knowledge and education they need to succeed at every stage of their careers. We provide face-to-face and digital events, websites, mobile sites and apps, online information services, and magazines giving professionals multi-platform access to our critical resources, including Professional Development; Education & Certification; Prospecting & Data Tools; Industry News & Analysis; Reference Tools and Services; and Community Networking Opportunities.

Using all of our resources across each community we serve, we deliver measurable ROI for our sponsors through a range of turnkey services, including Research, Content Development, Integrated Media, Creative & Design, and Lead Generation.

For more information, go to http://www.SummitProfessionalNetworks.com.

About the National Underwriter Company

For over 110 years, The National Underwriter Company has been the first in line with the targeted tax, insurance, and financial planning information you need to make critical business decisions. Boasting nearly a century of expert experience, our reputable Editors are dedicated to putting accurate and relevant information right at your fingertips. With *Tax Facts, Tools & Techniques, National Underwriter Advanced Markets, Field Guide, FC&S®, FC&S Legal®*, and other resources available in print, eBook, CD, and online, you can be assured that as the industry evolves National Underwriter will be at the forefront with the thorough and easy-to-use resources you rely on for success.

The National Underwriter Company
Update Service Notification

This National Underwriter Company publication is regularly updated to include coverage of developments and changes that affect the content. If you did not purchase this publication directly from The National Underwriter Company and you want to receive these important updates sent on a 30-day review basis and billed separately, please contact us at (800) 543-0874. Or you can mail your request with your name, company, address, and the title of the book to:

The National Underwriter Company
5081 Olympic Boulevard
Erlanger, KY 41018

If you purchased this publication from The National Underwriter Company directly, you have already been registered for the update service.

Summit employs more than 300 employees in ten offices across the United States. For more information, please visit www.summitbusinessmedia.com.

National Underwriter Company Contact Information

To order any National Underwriter Company title, please

- call 1-800-543-0874, 8-6 ET Monday – Thursday and 8 to 5 ET Friday

- online bookstore at www.nationalunderwriter.com, or

- mail to The National Underwriter Company, Orders Department, 5081 Olympic Blvd., Erlanger, KY 41018

Dedication

To my wife, Deanna – for accompanying me wherever my career has taken me

To my sons, Daniel, Andy, and Alex – for helping me understand
the importance of our impact on our children

Bruce Tannahill

Preface

The popularity of 401(k) plans means that most individuals will participate in at least one 401(k) plan during their careers. Business owner clients may not only be participants in their business's plan but may also be the plan administrator and/or plan trustee.

This means that advisors must be familiar with the rules governing 401(k) plans. Clients who participate in a plan often want guidance on distribution options and requirements. Business owners may look to their advisors for help in navigating the rules affecting plan sponsors and administrators. Those rules, including the steps to establish a plan, complying with the nondiscrimination rules, and knowing when distributions *may* be made and when they *must* be made, are often technical, detailed, and involve interpreting varied authorities, including the Internal Revenue Code, ERISA sections, regulations, and guidance from both the Internal Revenue Service and the Department of Labor.

In working with 401(k) plans, we found that 401(k) plan reference books that were detailed enough to answer the questions posed by attorneys, CPAs, and persons involved in administering plans were not written so that financial representatives and other nontechnical people would find them useful. This book is our attempt to provide detailed information for those who need it that is equally as useful for those who want basic information on 401(k) plans. We included citations to the specific authorities that apply to specific requirements so that those who need additional information may easily find it. This also helped us keep the explanations as nontechnical as possible.

We hope that readers, regardless of their background, find this book useful.

Bruce A. Tannahill
Louis R. Richey
December 2013

About the Authors

Bruce A. Tannahill, J.D., CPA/PFS, CLU®, ChFC®, AEP®, is currently Assistant Vice President of Advanced Markets for Global Atlantic Financial Company's Accordia Life Company, located in Des Moines, Iowa. Accordia Life is a leader in indexed universal life products.

Mr. Tannahill is an experienced tax, estate, and business planning attorney and CPA with specific expertise in estate and business planning, qualified plans, IRAs, life insurance, and annuities. He is a nationally recognized author and holds securities and life insurance licenses.

Mr. Tannahill provides technical and informational support to Accordia agents on case design, tax, and technical information concerning employer sponsored retirement plans, estate planning, and business plans. He also acts as a subject matter expert for other Accordia departments, including Legal and Compliance, regarding Advanced Markets issues. This includes tax questions and ownership changes. Mr. Tannahill also participates in the development of marketing concepts and concept packages, maintains existing Advanced Marketing materials, and assists in the creation of regularly-published documents such as tax updates. Prior to beginning in the life insurance industry in 2000 he had practiced law with a large St. Louis law firm, practiced accounting with an international CPA firm, and managed the research and design department for an income tax software company.

He has been the Qualified Plans & Retirement Planning columnist for *the Journal of Financial Service Professionals* since January 2013. Mr. Tannahill has been the author or a coauthor of articles in numerous other publications, including *Trusts & Estates* and *Probate & Property*.

Mr. Tannahill has been a leader in professional and industry organizations. Among other honors, he is a former Director of the Society of Financial Service Professionals; former chair of the Synergy Summit, an organization consisting of ten different financial service organizations; and chair of the LIMRA Advanced Sales Committee. He currently serves as a Trust & Estate Division Vice Chair of the ABA Real Property, Trust & Estate Law Section CLE Committee and chair of the Trust & Estate Division eCLE (webinar) Committee.

He received his Juris Doctor, with distinction, from the University of Missouri at Kansas City, Kansas City, Missouri, and his B.S. of Accounting, Summa Cum Laude, from University of Dayton. He is admitted to practice before the Ohio, Missouri, and Kansas Supreme Courts and the Tax Court.

Mr. Tannahill can be reached at bruce.tannahill@avivausa.com or Bruce.Tannahill@gmail.com.

Louis R. Richey, J.D., is currently Senior Vice President (and counsel) with Infosys McCamish LLC, an Infosys subsidiary located in Atlanta, Georgia. McCamish Systems is one of the nation's leading providers of outsourced administrative and other back-office support Internet platforms & services for life insurance carriers and other major financial services organizations, like banks and brokerage companies. Infosys is a leading global IT and administration BPO company.

Mr. Richey helps lead the Infosys McCamish *Retirement & Employer Sponsored Plans Services Division.* Mr. Richey is the content and support legal expert for all of Infosys McCamish's executive, employee, and qualified and nonqualified pension and other retirement and welfare benefit web-based marketing, design, and plan administration platforms. He also assists with other in-house counsel duties. He is a cocreator of the innovative electronic end-to-end DEFERRAL+® retirement plan Internet platform. He is widely known as a retirement, financial, and executive benefits product and services marketing innovator, attorney, consultant, and author, with special expertise in 409A nonqualified deferred compensation plans and other retirement and executive benefit plans and techniques, especially those involving insurance products. His thirty years of experience in these compensation and benefit areas includes all types and sizes of business organizations, including public, private, and tax exempt organizations. He is also the founder of the Retirement Plans Nexus that consults on retirement plans generally. During his career he was an executive for a life insurance carrier, a major employee benefits consulting firm, a specialty retirement plans brokerage firm, and a major financial services company.

He is a graduate of Wabash College in Indiana, a cum laude graduate of the Indiana University Law School in Indianapolis, and an active member of the Indiana, Georgia, and Federal Bar. He is also a retired Chairman of the Board of Visitors of the Indiana University Law School, Indianapolis. He has been named a Kentucky Colonel and an Arkansas Traveler in recognition of his professional contributions to the legal profession.

Mr. Richey lectures widely on qualified and nonqualified retirement plans (design and planning), the impact and implications of 409A on plans, executive and employee benefit topics, financial services marketing, insurance, and financial planning at major conferences, institutes, and national webinars such as the New York University Federal Tax Institute, Notre Dame Estate Planning Conference, Southeast Federal Tax Conference, Enrolled Actuaries Annual Conference, Knowledge Congress, and LIMRA Retirement and LIMRA Advanced Planning Conferences, as well as at a host of client meetings and conferences. Over his career, Mr. Richey's comments have appeared in *Business Week, The Wall Street Journal, Forbe's Magazine,* and *Investor's Daily,* and he has appeared on the *Financial News Network* for National Public Radio.

He has authored or coauthored a number of books and BNA portfolios, plus more than 300 articles, audios, and videos. Lou's current practice-oriented books include *Section 409A:Answers to 200 Frequently Asked Questions,* available from American Bar Association, 2013 Edition; *The Nonqualified Deferred Compensation Advisor (Covered & Exempt Plans Under 409A), 2014*

Edition; The 401(k) Advisor, 2014 Edition; the deferred compensation sections of *2014 Tax Facts,* all publications which are available from the SBM National Underwriter Company; and BNA Tax Management Portfolios #386 4rd, and #282 2nd, entitled, *Insurance-Related Compensation.* He is also a Special Editor for other sections of the National Underwriter's *Tax Facts Online.*

In the 1980s, the Internal Revenue Service used one of his published articles in training materials for its own estate and gift tax agents and attorneys. Lou's BNA Portfolio was cited in 2012 in a US Tax Court opinion.

Mr. Richey can be reached at Louis_Richey@Infosys.com or LouRichey@aol.com.

About the Editor

Deborah A. Miner, J.D., CLU, ChFC, has been writing and communicating about estate planning, business planning, and retirement planning for over twenty-five years. As Editorial Director of the Tax & Financial Planning Group at The National Underwriter Company from 1991 to 2010, Debbie worked with all the industry greats, writing many sections of *Tax Facts* and editing Steve Leimberg's *Tools & Techniques* series and Don Cady's *Field Guides*. She also spent several years as a Senior Advanced Sales Consultant at a Midwestern life insurance company. She holds a law degree from the Ohio State University College of Law and CLU and ChFC designations from the American College.

Recently, she started her own advanced sales consulting business, designing, writing, and updating advanced markets client and advisor materials and presenting educational seminars for life insurance companies and producer groups. Her company also provides consultative legal, tax, and life sales expertise and analysis on issues concerning large case planning and development and complex insurance strategies, as well as advanced markets phone support.

About the Editorial Director

Diana B. Reitz, CPCU, AAI, is the editorial director of the Professional Publishing Division of The National Underwriter Company. As such she is responsible for the overall integrity of all division publications. She previously was the Director of the Property & Casualty Publishing Department of the Reference Division.

Ms. Reitz has been with The National Underwriter Company since 1998, when she was named editor of the *Risk Financing and Self-Insurance* manuals and associate editor of the *FC&S Bulletins*®. She also is coauthor of the National Underwriter publication, *Workers Compensation Coverage Guide, 1st Edition*, and has edited and contributed to numerous other books and publications, including *The Tools & Techniques of Risk Management and Insurance, Claims* magazine, and *National Underwriter Property & Casualty* magazine.

Prior to joining The National Underwriter she was with a regional insurance broker, concentrating on commercial insurance. She is a graduate of the University of Maryland and St. Francis College.

Editorial Services

Connie L. Jump, Supervisor, Editorial Services

Emily Brunner, Editorial Assistant

Table of Contents

Chapter 1: Background of 401(k) Plans 1

Chapter 2: Fundamentals of 401(k) Plans 7

Chapter 3: Contributions... 19

Chapter 4: Contribution Limits 35

Chapter 5: Passing the Tests – Complying with the Nondiscrimination Rules...................... 47

Chapter 6: Designing the Plan.. 73

Chapter 7: The Roth Option 107

Chapter 8: I Put It In, How Can I Get It Out?... 121

Chapter 9: Plan Investments... 163

Chapter 10: Life Insurance in 401(k) Plans.. 185

Chapter 11: Multiple Employers, Plan Mergers, and Plan Terminations 201

Chapter 12: Regulatory Matters: Determination Letters, ERISA/IRS Reporting
    and Other Matters.. 221

Chapter 13: Preventing and Fixing Broken 401(k) Plans 249

Appendix A: 401(k) Plan Design Checklist 271

Appendix B: Hardship Distribution Checklist.. 275

Appendix C: Plan Loan Checklist.. 277

Appendix D1: Sample Spouse's Consent to Waiver of Qualified Joint and
    Survivor Annuity from Notice 97-10, 1997-1 CB 370 279

Appendix D2: Sample Spouse's Consent to Waiver of Qualified Preretirement
    Survivor Annuity from Notice 97-10, 1997-1 CB 370 285

Appendix E: Model Investment Option Comparative Chart; Appendix to
DOL Reg. 2550.404a-5... 291

Appendix F: Revenue Procedure 2013-4, Procedure for Requesting Private
Letter Rulings, 2013-1 CB 126 295

Appendix G: Revenue Procedure 2013-6, Procedure for Requesting Private
Letter Rulings, 2013-1 CB 198 337

Appendix H: Sample Summary Plan Description, DOL Regs. §2520.102-3t(2)................................... 373

Appendix I: Sample Summary Annual Report, DOL Regs. §2520.104-10(d)(3)................................ 377

Appendix J: Model Section 402(f) Notice for Payments from a Designated
Roth Account from Notice 2009-68, IRB 2009-39.. .381

Appendix K: Model Section 402(f) Notice for Payments NOT from a
Designated Roth Account from Notice 2009-68, IRB 2009-39 391

Appendix L1: Operational Failures and Correction Methods;
Appendix A to Rev. Proc. 2013-12, 2013-4 IRB 313.................................. 401

Appendix L2: Correction Methods and Examples; Earnings Adjustment
Methods and Examples; Appendix B to Rev. Proc. 2013-12, 2013-4 IRB 313 413

Index.. 455

Chapter 1

Background of 401(k) Plans

Introduction

First formally sanctioned in 1978 and permitted in 1980, 401(k) plans have become the most popular employer-sponsored retirement plan in the United States.

For many years, employers offered "thrift savings plans" that allowed employees to make after-tax contributions. The earnings were not subject to income tax until the employee received a distribution from the plan. In addition, employers could make tax-deductible contributions to a profit-sharing plan for employees. A trust held the employer contributions in a trust for the employees and allocated the contributions among the eligible employees. The employees were not subject to income tax on the contributions or earnings until actually received from the plan.

Eventually, some employers offered profit-sharing plans with "cash or deferred arrangements" (hereinafter CODAs or CODA). These plans allowed employees to defer some of the profit-sharing payment into the profit-sharing trust, treating the amount deferred as an employer payment rather than an employee contribution. If the contribution was treated as an employer payment, the constructive receipt doctrine did not apply. This doctrine provides that a payment is treated as received as income in a year if it is set aside for the individual and made available without substantial restriction, even if it is not actually received in that year.

The Internal Revenue Service (IRS) began issuing revenue rulings on these types of plans in 1956. In the first ruling, the IRS held that if the plan was nondiscriminatory, it met the Internal Revenue Code section 401(a) requirements to be a qualified plan.[1] In a 1963 revenue ruling,[2] the IRS held that if an employee chose to receive a profit-sharing plan contribution in trust rather than in cash, the contribution was not taxable until distributed or made available to the employee.

In 1972, the Treasury Department released proposed regulations that would have disallowed cash or deferred treatment for basic or regular salary. As part of the Employee Retirement Income Security Act (ERISA) of 1974, Congress froze the status quo, prohibiting the IRS from disqualifying a CODA adopted before June 27, 1974. At the same time, new plans could only accept after-tax employee contributions. Originally scheduled to end on December 31, 1976, Congress eventually extended the freeze through the end of 1979.

As part of the Revenue Act of 1978, Congress finally enacted Code section 401(k). It provided that any contribution to a qualifying CODA that the participant could have received as cash was not included as income. To qualify for this favorable tax treatment, the CODA had to meet the standard qualification rules applicable to defined contribution plans. In addition, employer contributions could not be distributed until after a minimum period of plan participation or after a specific period of time, and employer contributions attributable to an employee's election must always be nonforfeitable. It also imposed special nondiscrimination rules on plans created under Section 401(k).

The Revenue Act of 1978 also enacted Section 402(a)(8), which provides that amounts an employee elects to have contributed to a 401(k) account are not treated as amounts paid or made available to the employee. This prevents the employee from being taxed on the contributions under the constructive receipt doctrine. The section, after various amendments, is now Section 402(e)(3). It also treats the amounts an employee elects to have contributed to the plan as employer, rather than employee, contributions to the plan.

The new provisions were effective for tax years beginning after 1979. In November 1981, the Treasury Department issued proposed regulations that specifically permitted contributions made from employee salary reductions in addition to profit-sharing payments.

The Rise of 401(k) Plans

With favorable tax treatment of salary reductions now clearly permitted and enabled, employers responded by allowing employees to make pre-tax contributions to their profit-sharing plans, switching from after-tax thrift savings plans to CODAs, or creating plans meeting the rules of new Section 401(k). The formal name of cash or deferred arrangements used in the section was soon dropped and the plans with this feature began to be known as 401(k) plans.

Congress, the Treasury Department, and the IRS have changed the rules numerous times since 1978. Some of these changes applied to 401(k) plans in particular, others to defined contribution or qualified plans in general. At times, the changes made it easier for employers to offer 401(k) plans and for employees to participate; sometimes Congress tried to ensure that highly compensated employees do not receive substantially more benefit from the plan than the rank-and-file employees in the plan; and sometimes the goal was to minimize the revenue loss from the 401(k) plan pre-tax contributions.

These changes included:

- Reducing or freezing the maximum allowable contribution (Tax Equity and Fiscal Responsibility Act of 1982; Tax Reform Act of 1986)

- Requiring Social Security and Medicare (FICA) taxes to be paid on employee contributions (Social Security Amendments Act of 1983)

- Limiting employee deferrals (Tax Reform Act of 1986)

- Imposing stricter nondiscrimination rules (Tax Reform Act of 1986)

- Simplifying nondiscrimination rules (Small Business Job Protection Act of 1996)

- Repealing limits on 401(k) contributions if an employee also participated in a defined benefit plan (Small Business Job Protection Act of 1996)

- Revising rollover rules, including imposing a 20 percent mandatory withholding on all distributions not transferred directly to an IRA or another qualified plan (Unemployment Compensation Amendments Act of 1992)

- Allowing automatic enrollment (Rev. Rul. 98-30, 1998-1 CB 1273; Rev. Rul. 2000-8, 2000-1 CB 617; Pension Protection Act of 2006)

- Increasing employee contribution limits and indexing them for inflation (Economic Growth and Tax Relief Reconciliation Act of 2001; Pension Protection Act of 2006)

- Allowing Roth 401(k) accounts (Economic Growth and Tax Relief Reconciliation Act of 2001; Pension Protection Act of 2006)

- Reducing restrictions on converting regular 401(k) account to Roth 401(k) accounts (American Taxpayer Relief Act of 2012)

The Popularity of 401(k) Plans

Over the past 30 years, 401(k) plans have become the most popular type of employer-sponsored retirement plan. In 2010, of the approximately 701,000 defined benefit and defined contribution plans, almost 519,000 were 401(k)-type plans.[3] These 401(k)-type plans had more than 72 million total participants; more than 60 million active participants;[4] more than $3.14 trillion of assets; and total benefits paid of $245 billion. The 515,900 profit-sharing and thrift-savings plans had more than 70 million total participants; almost 59.5 million active participants; more than $3 trillion of total assets; and paid total benefits of almost $240 billion.

Attractiveness to Employers

401(k) plans have become popular with employers for several reasons.[5] First, the employer does *not* bear the investment risk inherent in a defined benefit (DB) plan. An employer's regular contribution to DB plans is based on the estimated amount required to fund the projected benefits. The current plan assets and expected investment results affect the required annual contribution amounts. Poor investment performance can increase the employer's DB plan contribution in two ways: 1) by reducing the plan's assets; and 2) by reducing the future expected return on those assets and future contributions. Better-than-expected investment performance can substantially reduce or eliminate an employer's DB plan contribution. In addition, in recent years, the IRS has been mandating the funding standards and assumptions for employers to use in calculations of annual contributions and, thereby, imposing mandates on the magnitude of annual contributions to such DB plans.

Second, DB plan administrative costs can be significantly more than 401(k) plan administrative costs. The savings for DB plans of not having to manage the individual accounts required by DC plans may be outweighed by the cost of providing annuities to retirees and hiring actuarial and investment professionals to comply with plan provisions and legal requirements of a DB plan.

Third, terminating an underfunded DB plan can be very expensive. The employer must contribute enough to fully fund the plan as defined by IRS regulations.

Attractiveness to Employees

For employees, 401(k) plans may be more attractive than a DB plan. They may offer more benefits for younger employees or those who anticipate a short employment tenure with a company because the employer benefits are based on their contributions, employer profits, or other factors not tied to their age or length of service, which are typical benefit factors in DB plans. The 401(k) benefit available upon termination may be significantly more than for a DB plan because the benefit is based on the account value, not the present value of the projected DB plan benefits.

Moreover, employees can generally access 401(k) funds through loans or hardship withdrawal. They generally cannot access DB plan funds. Employees may also view 401(k) plans as more secure than DB plans because the employer's bankruptcy does not affect the employee's benefits.

Endnotes

1. Rev. Rul. 56-497, 1956-2 CB 284.

2. Rev. Rul. 63-180, 1963-2 CB 189.

3. Department of Labor (DOL) Employee Benefits Security Administration, *Private Pension Plan Bulletin: Abstract of 2010 Form 5500 Annual Reports*, November 2012, Table of Highlights. Plans included as 401(k)-type are profit-sharing and thrift-savings plans, stock bonus plans, target benefit plans, money purchase plans, 403(b)(1) annuity plans, 403(b)(7) custodial account plans, and other defined contribution plans. Plans covering only one participant, Simplified Employee Pension (SEP) plans, and SIMPLE plans are not included.

4. Active participants are defined as employed workers currently covered by a plan who are earning or retaining credited service, nonvested participants who have not incurred a break in service, and those eligible for employer contributions.

5. This discussion draws on information from *An Evolving Pension System: Trends in Defined Benefit and Defined Contribution Plans*, Employee Benefit Research Institute, September 2002, especially Figure 20, "Comparison of Traditional Defined Benefit Plans with Traditional Defined Contribution Plans."

Chapter 2

Fundamentals of 401(k) Plans

Plan Requirements

The tax benefits of 401(k) plans – deductible employer contributions, pre-tax employee contributions, and tax-deferred growth – are only available if the plan complies with specific requirements laid out in the Internal Revenue Code, ERISA, regulations, and other pronouncements of the Internal Revenue Service (IRS) and the Department of Labor (DOL) upon inception and throughout the life of the plan.

Enforcement Responsibility

ERISA divides the responsibility for ensuring 401(k) plans and other retirement plans meet the requirements between the IRS, the DOL, and the Pension Benefit Guaranty Corporation (PBGC). Under ERISA, the DOL administers Title I of ERISA, concerning reporting and disclosure, vesting, participation, funding, and civil enforcement. The IRS administers Title II, which incorporates similar provisions into the Internal Revenue Code. Title III covers jurisdictional issues and the coordination of responsibility between DOL and IRS. The PGBC administers Title IV, dealing with the insurance of defined benefit plans.

Because the Title I and Title II provisions overlap, in 1978, the agencies divided the responsibilities by functional activity. The result is that the DOL has primary responsibility for reporting, disclosure, and fiduciary requirements. The IRS has primary responsibility for participation, funding, and vesting issues. However, if something materially affects the rights of participants, DOL can intervene, even if the IRS has primary responsibility for that area.

Formal Requirements

ERISA requires that every employee benefit plan, including qualified retirement plans, be established and maintained pursuant to a written instrument that provides for one or more fiduciaries to control and manage the plan.[1] Plan assets must generally be held in trust by one or more trustees.[2]

Treasury Regulations flesh out the formal requirements, specifying that the plan must be "a definite written program and arrangement which is communicated to the employees and which is established and maintained by an employer."[3]

The regulations also spell out the following tests that a plan trust must meet to qualify under Section 401(a):[4]

- It must be created or organized in the U.S. and maintained as a U.S. domestic trust.

- It must be part of a pension, profit-sharing, or stock bonus plan established by an employer for the exclusive benefit of the employer's employees or their beneficiaries.

- Its purpose must be to distribute the trust principal and income according to the terms of the plan. If the plan covers any self-employed individual, the plan's distribution time and method must meet the Required Minimum Distribution (RMD) rules of Section 401(a)(9) for all employees.

- The trust must prohibit any of the trust assets from being used for any purpose other than the exclusive benefit of the employees or their beneficiaries before all liabilities to the employees and beneficiaries are satisfied (the "exclusive benefit" rule).[5]

- It must be part of a nondiscriminatory plan.

- The plan must meet the vesting requirements of Section 411.

- If the plan covers a self-employed individual who is an owner-employee, contributions of the owner-employee must be limited to that individual's earned income from the trade or business that established the plan.

Permanent Plan

The plan must be a permanent program.[6] This does not prohibit employers from changing or terminating the plan or discontinuing plan contributions. However, the regulations state that if a plan is abandoned "for any reason other than business necessity within a few years after it has taken effect," it will be evidence that the plan was not a "bona fide program for the exclusive benefit of employees in general."[7] The IRS and DOL apply a facts-and-circumstances test to determine if a plan is terminated. Profit-sharing plans must make recurring and substantial contributions for the employees.[8] Single or occasional contributions to a profit-sharing plan are not sufficient to constitute a profit-sharing plan.

Established by the Employee

The employer must establish and maintain the plan.[9] The employer does not have to make any contributions to the plan – it can be funded exclusively by employee contributions.[10] In Revenue Ruling 80-306, the IRS restated its position in two earlier rulings that a plan can be a qualified plan even though no employer contributions are made to the plan.

Exclusive Benefit

A plan must be established for the exclusive benefit of employees but does not need to provide benefits for all employees. A plan whose eligibility requirements, contributions, or benefits discriminate in favor of officers, shareholders, managers or supervisors, or highly compensated employees will not qualify as established for the exclusive benefit of employees.[11] As with determining if a plan is a permanent plan, whether a plan is established for the exclusive benefit of employees is based on a facts-and-circumstances test. This evaluation considers both the written plan document and the plan's effects in operation.[12]

Plans may cover former employees or employees on leave (such as in the U.S. Armed Forces) without violating the exclusive benefit rule. An employee's beneficiaries include the employee's estate, dependents, natural objects of the employee's bounty, and the beneficiaries designated by the employee.[13]

Independent contractors and leased employees can create problems for plan sponsors. If an independent contractor or leased employee does not qualify as a common law employee, including them in the plan violates the exclusive benefit rule, disqualifying the plan. Failing to include an independent contractor or leased employee who qualifies as a common law employee in a 401(k) plan may make it difficult for the plan to pass the discrimination and participation tests.

Leased employees may be excluded from the plan of the company for which they perform services (not the company that leases them to the ultimate service recipient). To qualify for the exception, the leasing company must offer a money purchase plan that provides a contribution of at least 10 percent of compensation, immediate participation, and immediate 100 percent vesting.[14]

Communication to Employees

The employer or plan sponsor must communicate the plan to the employees for it to be a qualified plan.[15] In Rev. Rul. 72-509, an arrangement intended to qualify as a profit-sharing plan was reduced to writing and approved by the board of a calendar year taxpayer on December 29, 1970. The employer did not communicate the plan to the employees until March 1, 1971. As a result, the IRS ruled that the plan did not come into existence until the plan was communicated to the employees.[16]

The IRS, in Revenue Ruling 71-90,[17] states that the most effective way to communicate the plan is to furnish each employee with a copy of the plan. While this may have been true in 1971, it is doubtful that it is the most effective way to communicate the existence of a plan and its terms now. With the requirements now imposed by ERISA and subsequent law changes as amplified by regulations, court decisions, revenue rulings, and other guidance, the plan document for a 401(k) or other qualified plan is likely to be difficult for most employees to understand.

Fortunately, the revenue ruling identifies substitutes for providing employees with a copy of the plan if that is not feasible. The ruling mentions a booklet summarizing the plan or a conspicuous notice on the company's bulletin board. The information that the ruling deems necessary to notify employees of the plan are:

- That a plan has been established and the type of plan

- Eligibility requirements

- A synopsis of all benefits provided

- Information about employee contributions

- Vesting provisions

- The employer contribution formula

The notice must also clearly state that the complete plan can be inspected at a designated place on the company's premises during reasonable times. The notice must specify the times the plan is available for inspection.

Of course, in 1971, notifying employees of a plan being established through a company-wide email or posting information on the Internet or a company's internal network was not an option. Most employers today are likely to use electronic communications to notify employees, likely with a summary of the plan and a link to a full copy of the plan available to employees. In 2006, the Treasury provided guidance on using electronic media to notify the plan participants about the plan.[18] (The Summary Plan Description (SPD) is not required to be provided until 120 days after the plan is established and becomes subject to ERISA.[19])

Eligible Employers

Most employers are eligible to offer a 401(k) plan to their employees. The 401(k) plan must be a part of a profit-sharing or stock bonus plan, a pre-ERISA money purchase plan, or a rural cooperative plan,[20] meaning the employer must be eligible to offer one of those plans.

This made the ability of tax-exempt organizations and state and local governments to offer 401(k) plans uncertain. Because they do not issue stock, they cannot offer stock bonus plans. If profits are defined as the excess of revenues over expenses, they could offer a profit-sharing plan that includes a 401(k). Fortunately, the Tax Reform Act of 1986 provided that whether a plan is a profit-sharing plan was determined without regard to the employer's current or accumulated profits and without regard to whether the employer is a tax-exempt organization.[21]

While that would seem to allow tax-exempt organizations to establish a profit-sharing and 401(k) plan, another provision of the Tax Reform Act of 1986 initially prohibited tax-exempt organizations and state and local governments from offering 401(k) plans.[22] It provided an exception for plans in existence before May 7, 1986 for state and local governments or before July 2, 1986 for tax-exempt organizations.[23] Ultimately, the Small Business Job Protection Act of 1996 removed the restriction for tax-exempt organizations that are not part of a state or local government or their subdivisions, agencies, and instrumentalities, effective for plan years beginning after December 31, 1996.[24]

A tax-exempt organization that is also considered a state or local government agency or instrumentality cannot maintain a 401(k) plan.[25] In at least two private letter rulings,[26] the IRS has looked to Rev. Rul. 89-49[27] to determine if a tax-exempt organization is a state or local government agency or instrumentality. That ruling addressed whether a plan was a governmental plan under section 414(d). It stated that "a plan will not be considered a governmental plan merely because a plan's sponsoring organization has a relationship with a governmental unit or a quasi-governmental power." Under the ruling, one of the most important factors to be considered in determining if the sponsoring organization is a governmental agency or instrumentality is the degree of the government's control over the organization's everyday operations. Additional factors are:

- whether specific legislation created the organization;

- the organization's source of funds;

- how the organization's trustees or operating board are selected; and

- whether the governmental unit considers the organization's employees to be its employees.

The ruling states that the determination of whether an organization is a government agency or instrumentality considers all factors and satisfying one or all of them is not necessarily determinative.

Eligible Employees

The Internal Revenue Code defines who must be eligible to participate in a 401(k) plan. As long as a 401(k) plan meets those minimum requirements, it can expand the eligibility to include additional employees.

Under the basic minimum participation standards, a 401(k) plan must cover any employee once they are either 21 or have completed one year of service, whichever occurs later.[28]

Although not considered employees for most purposes, self-employed individuals are generally treated as employees in determining eligibility to participate in a 401(k) or other retirement plan.[29] To qualify as an employee, a self-employed individual must have earned income, defined as net earnings from self-employment under Section 1402(a), computed with various modifications.[30]

Exclusion of certain employees. For purposes of complying with the minimum participation standards, a plan can exclude the following employees who meet the minimum age and years of service tests:

- If a plan provides that an employee is fully vested in the plan benefits after two years of service, the plan can delay eligibility until the later of the employee completing two years of service or becoming 21.[31]

- Plans established by tax-exempt educational institutions can require an employee to be at least 26 rather than 21 if the employee is fully vested after completing one year of service.[32]

- A nonresident alien employee who does not receive any U.S. source income from the employer can be excluded.[33] If all of a nonresident alien employee's U.S. source income is exempt from U.S. income tax under an income tax treaty, the employee can be excluded if all nonresident alien employees whose entire U.S. source income is exempt under a treaty are excluded.

- Union employees can be excluded from a plan that covers only non-union employees if "retirement benefits were the subject of good faith bargaining" between the union and the employer or employers.[34] (Note that the good faith bargaining does not have to result in the actual provision of retirement benefits, just that the bargaining included the benefits.) Plans that cover both union and non-union employees are treated as two separate plans, one for the union employees and one for the non-union employees.[35]

- Former union employees who are participants in a multiemployer plan treated as union employees for the plan year can be excluded.[36]

- An employer that operates different businesses that qualify as separate lines of business can exclude employees of qualified separate lines of business that do not benefit from the plan under consideration.[37]

- Employees who terminate during the plan year if they were eligible to participate but do not receive a benefit or allocation solely because they fail to satisfy the plan's minimum period of service requirement or a requirement that the employee be employed on the last day of the plan year.[38]

- Employees of governmental entities can be excluded if they are prohibited from participating in a 401(k) plan if more than 95 percent of the employer's eligible employees participate in a plan maintained by the governmental entity.[39]

- Employees of tax-exempt entities eligible to participate in a 403(b) plan can be excluded if:

    - No employee of the tax-exempt organization is eligible to participate in the 401(k) plan or a matching plan under Section 401(m) that is part of the 401(k) plan; and

    - At least 95 percent of the employees are eligible to participate. For this purpose, the 95 percent requirement excludes employees who are employees of a tax-exempt organization or are precluded from participating in a 401(k) plan because they are employees of a governmental entity.[40]

    - Former employees can be excluded if they left the employer more than 10 years before January 1 of the year in which the current plan year begins and before any former employee who benefits under the plan left the employer.[41]

Planning Tip: When possible, consider hiring the owner's spouse to work for the business sufficiently to make them eligible to defer into the plan, even if only part time. As a plan participant, the spouse may help with the nondiscrimination testing and create another family deferral account and tax deduction for the business at the same time.

Complying with the Nondiscrimination Tests

One requirement all qualified plans must meet is that they cannot discriminate in favor of highly compensated employees, as defined for the particular plan. Originally, a facts-and-circumstances test was used to determine if a plan discriminated. Today objective tests defined by the Internal Revenue Code and regulations largely determine if a plan discriminates in an impermissible manner. Different tests apply to different types of contributions, based on the source of the contribution and the tax treatment.

Basic requirement for employee elective contributions. For a plan to be qualified, the contributions or benefits cannot discriminate in favor of highly compensated employees.[42] For this purpose, a highly compensated employee is one who was either:

(1) a 5 percent owner at any time during the current or preceding year; or

(2) had compensation from the employer for the preceding year exceeding $80,000, adjusted for inflation ($115,000 for 2014).[43]

The employer can elect to limit the employees included in the second prong of this test to members of the top-paid group, defined as the top 20 percent of employees ranked by compensation.[44] For a full discussion of this requirement, see Chapter 5.

Coverage requirement. The employees covered by the plan must meet one of three requirements designed to ensure that the plan covers at least 70 percent of the non-highly compensated employees. The different tests may result in different numbers of employees being covered by the plan. The first test simply states that the plan must benefit at least 70 percent of employees who are not highly compensated employees.[45] The second test is met if the percentage of non-highly compensated employees who benefit from the plan is at least 70 percent of the percentage of highly compensated employees who benefit from the plan.[46] The plan meets the third test if the classification of employees under the plan is found not to discriminate in favor of highly compensated employees and the average benefit percentage for non-highly compensated employees is at least 70 percent of the average benefit percentage for highly compensated employees.[47] The average benefit percentage is computed by first computing the contribution or benefit provided for each employee as a percentage of that employee's compensation. The benefit percentages of all employees in the group are then averaged[48]. For this purpose, any employee eligible to contribute or have contributions made on their behalf to the plan is considered to benefit from the plan.[49]

Average deferral percentage (ADP) test – employee contributions. The ADP test involves a comparison of the percentage of compensation deferred by eligible highly compensated employees to the percentage of compensation deferred by all other eligible employees. Plans can comply with the test in one of two ways.

1.   The ADP (defined later) for the eligible highly compensated employees does *not* exceed 125 percent of the ADP for all other eligible employees.[50]

2.   The ADP for eligible highly compensated employees does *not* exceed the ADP of all other eligible employees by more than two percentage points and the ADP for the eligible highly compensated employees is not more than double the ADP of all other eligible employees.[51]

Determining the ADP for a group of employees requires the following calculations:

1.   Calculate the ratio of employer contributions for the plan year to the employee's compensation for the plan year.

2.   Average the ratios calculated above.

In making the calculation, the employer contributions include the employee's elective deferral and the employer can elect to include matching contributions and qualified nonelective contributions.[52]

A safe harbor is available for the ADP test.

Complying with the ADP test is discussed in detail in Chapter 5.

Contribution percentage requirement for matching contributions and employee after-tax contributions. The contribution percentage test bears a great deal of similarity to the ADP test for employee deferrals.

The contribution percentage for eligible highly compensated employees for a plan year cannot exceed the greater of:

1.   125 percent of the contribution percentage for the eligible non-highly compensated employees for the preceding plan year; or

2.   the lesser of

   (a)   200 percent of the contribution percentage for non-highly compensated employees; or

   (b)   the contribution percentage of non-highly compensated employees for the preceding plan year plus two percentage points.[53]

Determining the contribution percentage for a group of employees requires the following calculations:

1.   Calculate the ratio of the matching contributions and employee contributions for the plan year to the employee's compensation for the plan year.

2.   Average the ratios calculated above.[54]

An employer may elect to include elective deferrals and qualified nonelective deferrals into account in computing the contribution percentage.[55]

Similar to the ADP tests, safe harbors are available to meet the contribution percentage test. A plan that violates the contribution percentage requirement in a year can distribute the excess contributions and related income before the end of the following plan year.[56]

Availability of benefits related to matching contributions and employee nonelective contributions. To meet the general nondiscrimination rules, a 401(k) plan *must* make each level of matching contributions and other benefits available in a manner that complies with those rules.[57] If a benefit is not available in the same manner to all eligible employees, it is treated as a separate benefit.

Failure to Comply with the Qualification Requirements

If a plan does not meet all these requirements and thereby "qualify," all of the tax benefits provided to qualified plans as to the plan participants and the employer are lost. In the worst case, elective deferrals are taxable to the employee in the year that they otherwise would have been paid to the employee.[58] A profit-sharing plan, stock bonus, pre-ERISA money purchase plan, or rural cooperative plan may be a qualified plan even if it includes a nonqualified cash or deferred arrangement.[59] If the only reason a plan does not qualify is its failure to meet the section 410(b) coverage test, a special rule allows the qualified plan rules to continue to apply to non-highly compensated employees.[60] The IRS has developed correction programs for plans that fail one or more of the qualification tests to cure the failure. Those programs for correction of failure to comply are covered in Chapter 13.

For failed plans, employer contributions also become taxable under Code section 83 rules, using the value of the employee's interest in the trust rather than the property's fair market value.[61] Amounts that are distributed or made available are taxed under the Section 72 rules.

Endnotes

1. ERISA §402(a), codified as 29 USC §1102(a)(1).

2. ERISA §403(a) [29 USC §1103(a)]. Subsection (b) identifies various exceptions, including insurance policies issued by a licensed insurance company or plan assets held by a licensed insurance company, and a plan that includes self-employed individuals.

3. Treas. Reg. §1.401-1(a)(2).

4. reas. Reg. §1.401-1(a)(3).

5. Note the difference here between qualified and typical nonqualified retirement pension plans wherein the assets acquired in connection with the nonqualified deferred compensation plan must remain employer-owned assets and not become ERISA "plan assets" or become funded for income tax purposes (as well as comply with Section 409A) in order to achieve the income tax benefits of deferred taxation, including on earnings, until distribution.

6. Treas. Reg. §1.401-1(b)(2).

7. *Ibid.*

8. *Ibid.* Although the regulation requires that the contributions be made out of profits, the Code no longer requires that profit-sharing plan contributions be made out of profits. IRC Sec. 401(k)(4)(B).

9. IRC Sec. 401(a) refers to a plan of an employer. Treas. Reg. §1.401-1(a)(1) provides that a qualified plan is established and maintained by an employer.

10. Rev. Rul. 80-306, 1980-2 CB 131.

11. Treas. Reg. §1.401-1(b)(3).

12. *Ibid.*

13. Treas. Reg. §1.401-1(b)(4).

14. IRC Sec. 414(n)(5).

15. Treas. Reg. §1.401-1(a)(2).

16. Rev. Rul. 72-509, 1972-2 CB 221.

17. 1971-1 CB 115.

18. Treas. Reg. §1.401(a)-21.

19. ERISA Sec. 102(b) [29 USC §1024(b)].

20. IRC Sec. 401(k)(1).

21. P.L. 99-514, Sec. 1136(a).

22. IRC Sec. 401(k)(4)(B).

23. P.L. 99-514, Sec. 1116(f)(2)(B).

24. P.L. 104-188, Sec. 1426(a).

25. IRC Sec. 401(k)(4)(B)(i).

26. Let. Ruls. 9749014, 200244021.

27. 1989-1 CB 117.

28. IRC Sec. 410(a)(1)(A).

29. IRC Sec. 401(c)(1)(B).

30. IRC Sec. 401(c)(2). For this purpose, net earnings from self-employment is limited to net earnings with respect to a trade or business in which the individual's personal services are a material income-producing factor and excludes items that are not included in gross income and related deductions; income from service as a minister, a member of a religious order, or as a Christian Science practitioner; and income received by certain statutory employees. Earned income for this purpose also includes gains and net income from the sale, disposition, transfer, or licensing of any property by the individual who created the property, excluding capital gains.

31. IRC Sec. 410(a)(1)(B)(i).

32. IRC Sec. 410(a)(1)(B)(ii). An educational institution must choose between requiring two years of service and the employee attaining age 26 to be eligible. It cannot require an employee to be both 26 and complete two years of service. If a plan requires both, the section provides that the minimum age is 21.

33. Treas. Reg. §1.410(b)-6(c).

34. Treas. Reg. §1.410(b)-6(d). Special rules apply if more than two percent of the union employees are professionals.

35. Treas. Reg. §1.410(b)-(7)(c)(4).

36. Treas. Reg. §1.410(b)-6(d)(2)(ii).

37. Treas. Reg. §1.410(b)-6(e). Separate lines of business are defined under IRC Sec. 414(r) and Treas. Reg. §1.414(r)-1(b).

38. Treas. Reg. §1.410(b)-6(f).

39. Treas. Reg. §1.410(b)-6(g)(2).

40. Treas. Reg. §1.410(b)-6(g)(3).

41. Treas. Reg. §1.410(b)-6(h)(2).

42. IRC Sec. 401(a)(4).

43. IRC Sec. 414(q)(1), IRS News Release IR-2012-77, October 18, 2012, Rev. Proc. 2013-35, 2013-35 IRB 167, November 18, 2013. The dollar limitation is adjusted for inflation annually.

44. IRC Sec. 414(q)(3).

45. IRC Sec. 410(b)(1)(A).

46. IRC Sec. 410(b)(1)(B).

47. IRC Sec. 410(b)(2)(A).

48. IRC Sec. 410(b)(2)(B), (C).

49. IRC Sec. 410(b)(6)(E).

50. IRC Sec. 401(k)(3)(A)(i).

51. IRC Sec. 401(k)(3)(A)(ii).

52. IRC Sec. 401(k)(3)(D).

53. IRC Sec. 401(m)(2).

54. IRC Sec. 410(m)(3).

55. IRC Sec. 410(m)(3), flush language.

56. IRC Sec. 410(m)(6).

57. Treas. Reg. §1.401(k)-1(a)(4)(iv)(B).

58. Treas. Reg. §1.401(k)-1(a)(5)(iii).

59. Treas. Reg. §1.401(k)-1(a)(5)(iv).

60. IRC Sec. 402(b)(4)(B).

61. IRC Sec. 402(b)(1).

Chapter 3

Contributions

Introduction

"Employer contributions" is a confusing term when dealing with 401(k) plans. Technically, all contributions to a 401(k) plan are employer contributions because an employee's elective deferrals are considered employer contributions for many purposes and 401(k) plans have their origin as a kind of employer profit-sharing plan. Employer contributions, whether matching or otherwise, are made to a profit-sharing plan that includes the 401(k) plan. For administrative convenience, an employer offering both types of plans will generally combine them into one plan.

Therefore, for purposes of this book, the term "employer contributions" refers to the matching or other contributions an employer makes to the profit-sharing portion of the 401(k) plan and 401(k) plan includes both the profit-sharing plan as well as the 401(k) plan itself.

An employer generally determines its contribution to the 401(k) plan in one of three ways.

1. The first and most common approach is to contribute an amount equal to the employee's elective deferral, up to a limit based on the employee's contributions or a specific dollar amount.

2. The second approach is to contribute an amount that may be based on the employer's profits or on some other determination.

3. Finally, the employer may combine the two approaches, matching employee contributions up to a specified limit and then contributing an additional amount.

Planning Tip. Although optional when designing a plan, employer contributions are frequently an essential part of a 401(k) plan. An employer's offer to match some of an employee's elective deferral is usually designed to entice rank-and-file employees to defer some of their compensation into the 401(k) plan. Without these rank-and-file employee contributions, the plan might fail the required nondiscrimination tests, thereby restricting the amount that highly compensated employees may contribute to the plan. In fact, much of the design work with 401(k) plans is to assure that the plan will pass the tests so as to allow the highly compensated participants to contribute the maximum possible contributions permitted under the contribution limits.

Contribution Limits

Contributions to an employer's defined contribution plans are subject to limits on how much can be contributed to an employee's account and the total amount an employer can deduct. The annual contribution to an employee's account cannot exceed the lesser of:

1. $52,000 for 2014; or

2.   100 percent of the employee's compensation.[1]

The IRS adjusts the dollar limits for inflation annually. The total deduction cannot exceed 25 percent of the participants' compensation for the year[2]. Chapter 4 discusses the computation of the contribution limit.

Allocation Methods

The plan must provide a "definite predetermined formula for allocating the contributions made to the plan among the participants."[3] Thus, the plan *must* maintain separate accounts for each participant. An example of a definite allocation formula provided by the regulations is one that provides for allocation of the contributions in proportion to each participant's basic compensation. The allocations cannot discriminate in favor of officers, shareholders, persons whose principal duties are supervising others, or highly compensated employees.[4]

Maintaining separate accounts is just part of the allocation requirement. For the amounts held for a particular participant to be ascertainable, the plan must also provide that the investments held by the trust are valued at least annually, on a specified date, using a method that is consistently followed and uniformly applied.

The separate account requirement does not mean that the plan assets must actually be segregated into separate accounts for each participant. A plan can comply with the separate account requirement by maintaining records of the amounts contributed by each participant and the allocation of employer contributions, gains, losses, expenses, and forfeitures among the participants. The plan must make the allocation to the accounts on a reasonable and consistent basis.[5]

This requirement does not pose a problem for the many 401(k) plans today that segregate the plan assets among separate accounts for each participant and allow them to choose among investment options offered by the plan and that provide daily valuation. Plans that do not segregate the assets and offer or use other types of investments may find complying with this requirement more difficult. Valuing and allocating trust assets among participants' accounts at infrequent or irregular intervals or using different allocation methods for different participants does not provide a definite formula for allocating and distributing the funds.[6]

Who Is a "Highly Compensated Employee"?

An employee is a "highly compensated employee" if the employee is either:

1.   a 5 percent owner at any time during the current year or preceding year;[7] or

2.   in the preceding year, had compensation from the employer that exceeded a specified amount ($115,000 for 2014) adjusted for inflation. An employer can elect to consider only those employees whose compensation exceeds the specified amount and who were in the top-paid group of employees highly compensated employees.[8]

5 percent owner

An employee is a 5 percent owner of a corporation if they own more than 5 percent of the outstanding stock of the corporation or stock possessing more than 5 percent of the total combined voting power of all stock of the corporation.[9] If the employer is not a corporation, ownership of more than 5 percent of the capital or profits interest in the employer will make an employee a 5 percent owner.[10]

Under the alternative testing, ownership of voting stock carries as much weight as overall stock ownership. If a corporation has voting and non-voting stock or different classes of stock with different voting rights, employees who own less than 5 percent of the outstanding stock can be considered 5 percent owners if the stock they own has disproportionate voting rights.

Section 318 attribution rules. The Section 318 attribution rules apply in determining if an employee is a 5 percent owner, with one modification. Stock or ownership interests owned by the employer will be attributed to the employee if the employee owns 5 percent or more of the employer, rather than the standard 50 percent.[11] However, the aggregation rules concerning controlled groups of corporations under Section 414(b), businesses under common control under Section 414(c), and affiliated service group rules do not apply in determining if an employee is a 5 percent owner.[12]

Top-Paid Group

The top paid group is the top 20 percent of employees ranked by compensation paid during the year.

Compensation

The same definition of compensation used for determining the contribution limits is also used to determine if an employee is a highly compensated employee.[13]

Excluded Employees

In determining the number of employees in the top-paid group, employees who have not completed six months of service, normally work less than 17.5 hours per week, normally work during no more than 6 months during a year, employees under age 21, and employees in a collective bargaining group are excluded.[14] An employer can elect to include employees in this group by using a shorter period of service, fewer hours or months, or a lower age for the amounts specified.[15]

Former Employees

Former employees are considered highly compensated employees if they were a highly compensated employee when they terminated or a highly compensated employee at any time after age 55.[16]

Safe Harbor Discrimination Tests

Either the contributions or the benefits available under a plan *must* be nondiscriminatory in amount. A plan can discriminate as to either contributions or benefits and still qualify as nondiscriminatory as long as it does not discriminate as to the other.[17] Plans that provide uniform allocations of employer contributions can meet one of two safe harbors and be considered nondiscriminatory as to amount. Plans that do not provide qualifying uniform allocations can satisfy a general test. The safe harbor tests focus on the plan's design while the general test is based on the operation of the plan and must be checked each year.

Uniform Allocation Formula

A plan has a uniform allocation formula if it allocates the same percentage of compensation to each employee, the same dollar amount, or the same dollar amount for each uniform unit of service performed by the employee during the plan year. For this purpose, the unit of service cannot exceed one week.[18]

> *Example 1.* Robinson Manufacturing's plan allocates employer contributions to the plan in excess of the matching contributions to an employee's account based on the percentage of the employee's compensation to the total compensation of all participants. All five of the company's employees are participants in the plan.

> For the current year, Robinson Manufacturing contributed $25,000 to the plan in addition to matching employee elective deferrals. The $25,000 is allocated among the participants as shown in the following table.

Name	Compensation	Compensation after limit	Allocation %	Allocation of $25,000
Chris	$300,000	$260,000	46.01%	$11,502
Mary	$100,000	$100,000	17.67	$4,418
Sandra	$75,000	$75,000	13.30	$3,325
Dan	$70,000	$70,000	12.39	$3,097
Dave	$60,000	$60,000	10.63	$2,658
Total	$605,000	$565,000	100.00%	$25,000

Note that only $260,000 of Chris' $300,000 compensation is considered in making the allocation. If an employee's compensation exceeds the compensation limit, the excess is not included.

Example 2. Robinson Manufacturing allocates employer contributions to the plan in excess of the matching contributions to an employee's account based on the number of hours worked, up to a maximum of 50 per week. All five of the company's employees are participants in the plan. The company determines that the per-hour allocation for the current year is $3.50.

Name	Total allowable hours	Allocation
Chris	2,200	$7,700
Mary	2,250	$7,875
Sandra	1,980	$6,930
Dan	1,480	$5,180
Dave	1,860	$6,510
Total	9,770	$34,195

The plan can provide for differences in allocations if the:

(1) plan satisfies the permitted disparity provisions of Section 401(l) in form; and

(2) differences are due to disparities permitted under Treasury Regulation Section 1.401(l)-2(c)(2).[19]

Uniform points allocation formula. Under a uniform points allocation formula, a plan credits each employee with the same number of points for each year of age, each year of service, and each unit of plan compensation. It then allocates the contribution and forfeitures among the participants based on each participant's percentage of the total points. The formula must comply with the following rules for the assignment and allocation of points:

- It must grant points for either age or service. Points may be assigned for both.[20]

- Points do not need to be assigned for compensation units. If they are, the unit must be a single dollar amount for all employees that does not exceed $200.[21]

- The average allocation rate for highly compensated employees cannot exceed the average allocation rate for non-highly compensated employees.[22]

Example. The McDermott Company uses a single allocation formula for all employees. An employee's allocation for the year is the total contributions and forfeitures for the plan year multiplied by a fraction. The numerator of the fraction is the employee's points for the year. The denominator is the total points of all employees for the plan year. An employee receives 10 points for each year of service and one point for each $100 of compensation. For the plan year, the total allocations are $61,200 and the total points for all employees are 6,120. The following table shows the allocation and allocation rate for each employee.

Employee	Years of service	Compensation	Points	Allocation	Allocation rate
Highly compensated employees					
Alex	20	$150,000	1,700	$17,000	11.3%
Bob	10	$150,000	1,600	$16,000	10.7%
Carol	30	$140,000	1,700	$17,000	12.1%
Non-highly compensated employees					
Diane	10	$40,000	500	$5,000	12.5%
Elisa	5	$35,000	400	$4,000	11.4%
Frank	1	$30,000	310	$3,100	10.3%
Totals	–	–	6,210	$62,100	

The average allocation rate of 11.4 percent for the non-highly compensated employees exceeds the average allocation rate for the highly compensated employees of 11.36 percent. The allocation formula does qualify as a uniform points allocation formula.

Additional rules for the use of safe harbors. Including all or any of the following provisions will not prevent a plan from satisfying either safe harbor.

- The plan can provide for one or more entry dates during the plan year, as long as it complies with the provisions of Section 410(a)(4) concerning when an employee begins to participate in the plan.[23]

- The plan can provide that an employee does not receive an allocation unless the employee is employed on the last day of the plan year, completes a minimum number of hours of service during the plan year, or both. The minimum hours of service required cannot exceed 1,000. An exception can be provided for all employees who terminate employment during the year or just for employees who terminate due to retirement, disability, death, or military service.[24]

- The plan can limit allocations to a maximum dollar amount or a maximum percentage of compensation, limit the dollar amount of compensation considered in the allocations, or apply the restrictions of Section 409(n) (concerning sales of stock to an ESOP or eligible worker-owned cooperative) or the Section 415 limits.[25]

- The allocations to highly compensated employees can be less than required under the safe harbors.[26]

- The plan can use multiple formulas if the employee's allocation is either (1) the largest allocations under the formulas or (2) the sum of the allocations under the formulas.[27]

Planning Tip: It is not necessary to place a "stated match" provision into a plan document (example: 50 percent of a participant's salary deferrals up to 6 percent of the participant's annual compensation). In fact, it is probably wiser to make stated matches discretionary on an annual basis in case the company's financial condition makes the stated match financially impossible to make. This situation would require a plan amendment to the plan match provisions to comply properly if the plan is not followed (including even a larger than stated match). Annually executing a company resolution of the match to be applied for the current plan *year prior to the company filing its tax return* under a discretionary match provision will avoid this kind of problem for the plan sponsor.

General Nondiscrimination Test

A plan satisfies the general nondiscrimination test if each rate group under the plan satisfies the minimum participation test of Section 410(b). A rate group is made up of each highly compensated employee and all employees (whether a highly compensated employee or not) who have an allocation rate equal to or higher than the highly compensated employee's allocation rate.[28]

An employee's allocation rate is the sum of the allocations to the employee's account for a plan year.[29] It includes all employer contributions and forfeitures and can be expressed as either a percentage of compensation for the plan year or as a dollar amount.[30] The allocation rate does not include income, expenses, gains, and losses allocated to an employee's account.[31] The regulation allows a plan to group allocation rates within certain ranges.[32]

The minimum participation test of Section 410(b) applies to each rate group as if it were a separate plan covering only the employees in the rate group.[33] In determining if a rate group satisfies that test, special rules govern the application of the nondiscriminatory classification test and average benefit percentage test.[34]

Making Contributions (Timely Deposits)

Employee Contributions

Once an employer has withheld elective deferrals from an employee's wages, the employer must segregate those amounts from the employer's general assets as soon as they can reasonably be segregated. They are considered assets of the plan at that time.[35] As of the effective date of final DOL regulations in 2010, the only safe harbor for plans with less than 100 participants at the beginning of a plan year provides that deposit of employee contributions to the plan must be made within seven business days of the date they would have otherwise been paid to the employee.[36]

The regulation allows an ultimate deposit deadline of the fifteenth business day of the month following the month in which the elective deferral was withheld from a participant's wages.[37] Because this deadline is based on business days, employers may have until the twenty-fifth of the following month, or possibly even later, to segregate the elective deferrals from the employer's general assets. However, under the 2010 final DOL regulations, both the safe harbor and ultimate deadline does not apply to larger employers who are expected to deposit employee contributions as soon as possible based on a facts-and-circumstances basis. The DOL is focused heavily on the timely deposit of employee deposits into plans when auditing plans and believes that employers should be making the deposit as soon as normal business practices will permit, regardless of size, and feels the deadline of the fifteenth day of the month following the month the compensation would have been paid in the absence of the deferral should *not* be a standard practice if contributions could routinely be made as soon as possible following the payroll, and even less than seven business days whenever possible.[38]

However, in special circumstances, an employer can obtain a ten business day extension to make a deposit of employee contributions and segregate the funds to the plan from its general assets. To obtain the extension, the employer must comply with the requirements set out in the regulation. Those include actually making the contribution to the plan (but not segregating it), notifying the employees and the DOL, and providing a performance bond or irrevocable letter of credit guaranteed by a bank. The performance bond or letter of credit must stay in effect for three months after the month in which the extension expires.[39] For many employers, these requirements, especially the bond or letter of credit, may make obtaining the extension impractical, if not impossible. See Chapter 13 for a discussion of the failure to make timely deposits of employee contributions to the plan and how to properly correct the failure to maintain the plan's qualified plan status.

Employer Contributions

The deadline is different for employer contributions. Employer contributions, whether matching or otherwise, may be made until the due date of the employer's federal income tax return, including extensions.[40] A contribution made after the end of the employer's tax year is treated as having been made on the last day of the prior tax year. The employer must actually have obtained an extension of time to file to qualify for the extended deadline, simply being able to obtain one will not extend the deadline.[41] Once the extension has been obtained, the contribution will be considered timely if made before the extended deadline, even if the tax return is filed during the extension period before the contribution is made.[42]

Planning Tip: In the case of a stated match, the plan sponsor should deposit the stated match contributions on the same time basis as the plan actually limits compensation for matching contribution purposes. Otherwise, it may find itself having to attempt to properly "true up" the matching contributions annually to meet the annual compensation limit, especially when the sponsor makes the matching contribution more frequently, like monthly or per payroll and a mismatch is created. The sponsor must comply with the terms of the plan document in all cases.

Vesting

Vesting addresses whether a 401(k) participant can lose the right to the money in his or her 401(k) account. It may occur all at once (known as "cliff vesting") or over a period of time ("graduated vesting"). Whether the participant can access the money in the account is separate from whether the participant is vested in the account. A participant may be fully vested but still have limited ability to access the money until a triggering event occurs or attaining a specified age.

Requiring a certain period of employment before a participant is vested in plan benefits can serve several purposes for employers. First, it provides employees with an incentive to stay with a company, at least until they have completed the vesting period. Knowing that leaving an employer means losing benefits attributable to employer contributions can be an effective incentive to stay with the employer. It can reduce employers' costs by providing that amounts forfeited can be used to pay the plan's reasonable administrative expenses or reduce future contributions.

The vesting requirements for a 401(k) plan can be summarized as follows:

1. A participant is always fully vested in the benefits attributable to elective deferrals and any growth attributable to those deferrals.[43]

2. A participant's normal retirement benefit is fully vested upon attaining normal retirement age.[44]

3. A participant becomes fully vested upon complete discontinuance of contributions under the plan.[45]

4. The plan must provide for either three-year cliff vesting[46] or a graduated vesting schedule providing that the participant becomes 20 percent vested after two years of service and accrues an additional 20 percent vesting for each additional year of service.[47] The graduated vesting schedule results in a participant becoming fully vested after completing six years of service.

A participant's elective deferrals are not considered in determining if the vesting requirements are met for other contributions or benefits.

> *Example.* Roger's employer has a 401(k) plan that includes both elective deferrals and employer contributions. His account includes an accrued benefit of $20,000 attributable to the elective deferrals and a $10,000 accrued benefit attributable to employer contributions. Under the plan's vesting schedule, he is 60 percent vested. If he were to leave the employer, he would be entitled to the full $20,000 accrued benefit attributable to his elective deferrals and 60 percent of the $10,000 accrued benefit attributable to the employer contributions.

Determining the Amount Attributable to Elective Deferrals and Employer Contributions

A plan can maintain separate accounts for elective deferrals and for employer contributions or one account that contains both. If the plan maintains only one account, the accrued benefit attributable to elective deferrals is determined using the following steps:

- Divide the elective deferrals, less any withdrawals, by

- The total of the elective deferrals, less withdrawals, plus employer contributions, less withdrawals.

- Multiply the result by the total accrued benefit.[48]

Only withdrawals distributed to the employee are included in the computations.[49] The balance is the amount attributable to employer contributions.

> *Example.* Jessica has contributed a total of $10,000 to her account. Her employer has contributed $5,000 to the account. Her total accrued benefit is $24,000. She has not taken any withdrawals from the account. The amount attributable to her elective deferrals is determined as follows:
>
> $10,000 / $15,000 = 66.67%
>
> $24,000 * 66.67% = $16,000

The amount attributable to her employer's contributions is $8,000 ($24,000 − 16,000).

Participant's Elective Deferrals and Related Growth

Elective deferrals represent money that participants could have received in cash but deferred into the 401(k) plan. If the participants had not deferred the money, they could have invested it on an after-tax basis without the risk of forfeiting any portion of the deferral. As a result, a participant must always be 100 percent vested in accrued benefits attributable to the participant's contributions. For separate account plans such as 401(k) plans, this is the portion of the account consisting of the participant's contributions and income, expenses, gains, and losses attributable to those contributions.[50] The balance of the account is attributable to employer contributions and subject to the plan's vesting schedule.

Normal Retirement Benefit at Normal Retirement Age

For a 401(k) plan, the normal retirement benefit is the balance in the employee's account at normal retirement age.[51] This makes determining when a participant reaches normal retirement age crucial. A participant reaches normal retirement age for vesting purposes at the earlier of:

1. attaining the plan's normal retirement age, or

2. the later of

    a. age 65, or

    b. the fifth anniversary of becoming a participant in the plan.[52] For this purpose, a participant is treated as beginning participation on the first day of the first year in which the participant began participating.[53]

If the plan or the sponsoring employer requires an employee to retire at a certain age, the normal retirement age cannot exceed the mandatory retirement age. If a plan does not specify a normal retirement age, a participant reaches normal retirement age when their benefits do not increase by attaining a later age or additional service.[54]

This definition can be used to establish the tests for when a participant will reach normal retirement age for vesting purposes shown in Figure 3.1 below.

Figure 3.1. Guide for When a Participant Reaches Normal Retirement Age for Vesting Purposes	
If the plan's normal retirement age is:	*The participant will reach normal retirement age for vesting purposes at:*
65	65
Under 65	The plan's normal retirement age
After 65 and: The participant began participation in the plan before age 60 The participant began participation after age 60	65 The fifth anniversary of becoming a participant in the plan

Complete Discontinuance of Contributions

If a plan completely discontinues contributions, the participants must be fully vested in their accounts. Whether a plan suspends or completely discontinues contributions requires examining all the facts and circumstances without regard to elective deferrals. Among the factors considered in determining if a suspension or discontinuance has occurred are whether: (1) the employer is calling an actual discontinuance a suspension to avoid full vesting or for any other reason;[55] (2) whether contributions are recurring and substantial;[56] or (3) whether there is any reasonable probability that the lack of contributions will continue indefinitely.[57] Depending on the plan, avoiding full vesting allows forfeited amounts to be allocated among the fully vested employees, used to reduce the employer's final contribution to the plan, or used to pay the plan's reasonable administrative expenses.

Three-Year Cliff Vesting

A cliff vesting schedule provides that a participant's vesting status in the portion of the accrued benefits attributable to employer contributions is like a light switch, either unvested or fully vested. Unlike a graduated vesting schedule, cliff vesting requires the employee to scale the cliff by completing the full vesting period. Failure to complete the vesting period, by even a day, results in loss of all benefits attributable to employer contributions. For defined contribution plans, the cliff vesting period cannot exceed three years. Plans can provide for a shorter cliff vesting schedule.

Planning Tip: A start-up company's plan may provide a one or two-year cliff vesting to allow the founders to become fully vested in the employer contributions made in the company's early years. A potential disadvantage is that other plan participants will also become fully vested quickly.

Graduated Vesting

A graduated vesting schedule provides a stair-step approach to full vesting of the accrued benefit from employer contributions. Once participants have two years of service, they are 20 percent vested and are fully vested after six years of service. Figure 3.2 below shows the minimum graduated vesting schedule for defined contribution plans.[58]

Figure 3.2. Minimum Graduated Vesting Schedule for 401(k) Plans	
Years of service	*Percentage vested*
Less than 2	0
2	20
3	40
4	60
5	80
6 or more	100

Graduated vesting creates an incentive for participants to stay with the employer and increase their vested percentage. An employer can provide for a faster graduated vesting schedule, as long as the percentage vested is always at least the amount specified in Figure 3.2.

Comparison of Cliff and Graduated Vesting

Cliff vesting may be less expensive than graduated vesting for employers who have considerable turnover among employees with few years of service because the forfeitures can reduce employer contributions or be used to pay plan expenses. Once an employee has three years of service, full vesting eliminates the incentive to stay with the employer that a graduated vesting schedule can provide. If the number of highly compensated employees who vest is disproportionately high compared to the number of non-highly compensated employees who vest, cliff vesting is more likely to cause a plan to be considered discriminatory in operation. The earlier and more gradual vesting under a graduated schedule is likely to provide less discrimination in operation than cliff vesting.

Year of Service

A year of service measures the length of an employee's service for an employer to determine the vesting credited to the employee. Unless the plan provides for a smaller number, a year of service is a 12-month period designated by the plan in which a participant completes at least 1,000 hours of service.[59] DOL regulations[60] and Treasury regulations[61] provide alternative methods to exact timekeeping of determining if a participant has completed a year of service.

DOL regulations define an hour of service as an hour for which an employee is entitled to be paid:

- for performing services for the employer;

- for vacation, holiday, illness, incapacity, layoff, jury duty, military duty, or leave of absence; or

- for which back pay is awarded or agreed to by the employer.[62]

All of an employee's years of service with the employer maintaining the plan must be considered, except for:

- years of service before age 18;[63]

- years of service during a period that the employee did not contribute to a plan requiring employee contributions;[64]

- years of service with an employer while the employer did not maintain the plan or a predecessor plan;[65]

- service not required to be considered under the break-in-service rules;[66]

- years of service before 1971 unless the employee has had at least three years of service after 1970;[67] or

- years of service after an employer completely or partially withdraws from a multiemployer plan or the multiemployer plan terminates.[68]

Note that a plan may have different definitions for a year of service to determine vesting, benefit accrual, and eligibility to participate.

Endnotes

1. IRC Sec. 415(c)(1).
2. IRC Sec. 404(a)(3).
3. Treas. Reg. §1.401-1(b)(1)(ii).
4. *Ibid.*
5. Treas. Reg. §1.401(k)-1(e)(3)(i).
6. Rev. Rul. 80-155, 1980-1 CB 84.
7. IRC Sec. 414(q)(1)(A).
8. IRC Sec. 414(q)(1)(B)(ii); Rev. Proc. 2013-35, 2013-35 IRB 167, November 18, 2013.
9. IRC Sec. 416(i)(1)(B)(i)(I).
10. IRC Sec. 416(i)(1)(B)(i)(II).
11. IRC Sec. 416(i)(1)(B).
12. IRC Sec. 416(i)(1)(c).
13. IRC Sec. 414(q)(4).
14. IRC Sec. 414(q)(5).
15. IRC Sec. §414(q)(5), flush language.
16. IRC Sec. 414(q)(6).
17. Treas. Reg. §1.401(a)(4)-1(b)(2).
18. Treas. Reg. §1.401(a)(4)-2(b)(2)(i).
19. Treas. Reg. §1.401(a)(4)-2(b)(2)(ii).
20. Treas. Reg. §1.401(a)(4)-2(b)(3)(i)(A).
21. *Ibid.*
22. Treas. Reg. §1.401(a)(4)-2(b)(3)(i)(B).
23. Treas. Reg. §1.401(a)(4)-2(b)(4)(ii).
24. Treas. Reg. §1.401(a)(4)-2(b)(4)(iii).
25. Treas. Reg. §1.401(a)(4)-2(b)(4)(iv).
26. Treas. Reg. §1.401(a)(4)-2(b)(4)(v).
27. Treas. Reg. §1.401(a)(4)-2(b)(4)(vi).
28. Treas. Reg. §1.401(a)(4)-2(c)(1).
29. Treas. Reg. §1.401(a)(4)-2(c)(2)(i)
30. Treas. Reg. §1.401(a)(4)-2(c)(2)(ii).

31. Treas. Reg. §1.401(a)(4)-2(c)(2)(iii).

32. Treas. Reg. §1.401(a)(4)-2(c)(2)(v).

33. Treas. Reg. §1.401(a)(4)-2(c)(3)(i).

34. Treas. Regs. §§1.401(a)(4)-2(c)(3)(ii), 1.401(a)(4)-2(c)(3) (iii).

35. DOL Reg. §2510.3-102(a)(1).

36. DOL Reg. §2510.3-102(a)(2)(i).

37. DOL Reg. §2510.3-102(b)(1).

38. DOL Reg. §2510-102(b)(1), 75 Fed. Reg. 2010 (January 14, 2010). These DOL regulations comprehensively outline the timing for timely deposit and segregation of assets to the plan for ERISA and Internal Revenue Code Purposes.

39. DOL Reg. §2510.3-102(d).

40. IRC Sec. 404(a)(6).

41. *Hydro Molding Co., Inc. v. Comm'r*, 38 TC 312 (1962); Rev. Rul. 56-674, 1956-2 CB 293.

42. Rev. Rul. 66-144, 1966-1 CB 91.

43. IRC Secs. 401(k)(2)(C), 411(a)(1).

44. IRC Sec. 411(a).

45. IRC Sec. 411(d)(3). Because profit-sharing plans and 401(k) plans are not subject to the minimum funding rules of Section 412, full vesting occurs upon complete discontinuance of contributions. Full vesting upon full or partial termination is required for plans subject to the Section 412 minimum funding standard.

46. IRC Sec. 411(a)(2)(B)(ii).

47. IRC Sec. 411(a)(2)(B)(iii).

48. Treas. Reg. §1.411(c)-1(b)(2).

49. Treas. Reg. §1.411(c)-1(b)(2), flush language.

50. IRC Sec. 411(c)(2)(A)(i).

51. IRC Sec. 411(a)(7)(A)(ii).

52. IRC Sec. 411(a)(8).

53. Treas. Reg. §1.411(a)-7(b)(1), flush language. Years that can be disregarded under the breaks in service rule for nonvested participants of Section 410(a)(5)(D) concerning minimum participation can be disregarded for vesting purposes as well.

54. *Ibid.*

55. Treas. Reg. §1.411(d)-2(d)(1)(i).

56. Treas. Reg. §1.411(d)-2(d)(1)(ii).

57. Treas. Reg. §1.411(d)-2(d)(1)(iii).

58. IRC Sec. 411(a)(2)(B)(iii).

59. IRC Sec. 411(a)(5)(A).

60. DOL Regs. §2530.200b-2(a)(2), 2530.200b-3.

61. Treas. Reg. §1.410(a)-7.

62. DOL Reg. §2530.200b-2.

63. IRC Sec. 411(a)(4)(A).

64. IRC Sec. 411(a)(4)(B).

65. IRC Sec. 411(a)(4)(C).

66. IRC Secs. 411(a)(4)(D), 411(a)(4) (F).

67. IRC Sec. 411(a)(4)(E).

68. IRC Sec. 411(a)(4)(G).

Chapter 4

Contribution Limits

Introduction

When first enacted in 1978, the only limits on elective deferrals were the per-employee limits on contributions to a defined contribution plan. If the total of the employer and employee deferrals were less than the maximum, the employee could contribute enough so the per-employee limit was met. However, Congress introduced more stringent limitations on contributions to 401(k) plans to reduce employer tax deductions for contributions to qualified plans in order to raise tax revenues for other purposes, and in an attempt to reduce the shift toward employee-funded qualified plans (which attempt completely failed as we now know).

By 1986, Congress placed a cap on annual contributions, believing it was necessary for the proper operation of the 401(k) nondiscrimination rules.[1] At that time, the total of an employee's elective deferrals and all other additions to the employee's account could not exceed the lesser of $30,000 or 25 percent of the participant's non-deferred compensation.[2]

The Tax Reform Act of 1986 limited the amount employees could defer into a 401(k) plan. Now, contributions to a 401(k) plan, whether from employees' election to defer a portion of their salary or employer's matching or other contributions, are subject to multiple limits. In total, the sum of all contributions to the 401(k) plan cannot exceed the limits specified in Section 415(c).

The overall limit for contributions to an employee's account consists of the following:

- Employee elective deferral limit of $15,000, adjusted for inflation ($17,500 for 2014[3]).

- Catch-up contribution[4] limit of $5,000 for employees who are at least 50, adjusted for inflation ($5,500 for 2014).[5]

- Combined employee and employer contribution limit of $40,000, adjusted for inflation ($52,000 for 2014) or 100 percent of the employee's compensation.[6]

In addition to the per-employee limit, the total deductible contribution to the plan cannot exceed 25 percent of all compensation paid to plan participants during the year. For SIMPLE 401(k) plans, the limit is the greater of 25 percent of all compensation or the amount the employer is required to contribute to the plan for the year.[7]

The per-employee limit is computed without regard to community property laws.[8] Generally, under community property laws, half of the income is considered to be earned by each spouse. Without this provision, a married person could defer the full amount for each spouse even though only one spouse works for the sponsoring employer.

Employers cannot avoid the limit by creating multiple plans and contributing the maximum to each plan. In applying the limit, multiple plans of the same employer are combined and total contributions to all plans cannot exceed the limit.[9]

The limit on an employee's elective deferrals ($17,500 for 2013) catches more than just contributions to a 401(k) plan. This limit also applies to employee deferrals to a Section 403(b) plan, a SIMPLE IRA, a SARSEP, and designated Roth accounts.[10] It does not include contributions to a Section 457(b) plan.[11] This limit on elective deferrals must be monitored by the employee. Employers generally do not have the ability to do so.

Amounts that an employee elects to defer into a 401(k) plan are treated as employer contributions, even though the employee would have otherwise received the amount in cash.[12] In contrast, if a plan allows for after-tax contributions, other than contributions to a Roth account, the regulations specifically provide that it is not a 401(k) plan.[13]

Catch-up contributions for employees who are at least 50 years of age by the end of the calendar year are not subject to either the combined employee and employer contribution limit or the total contribution limit.[14] This allows a total employee and employer contribution in 2014 of $57,500 ($5,500 + 52,000)[15] to the account of an employee who is at least 50 by the end of the year.

Compensation in General

Contributions to a 401(k) plan are subject to two limitations based on compensation. First, the annual per-employee contribution (employee deferrals and employer contributions) cannot exceed 100 percent of the employee's compensation for the year.[16] Second, the overall contribution to the plan cannot exceed 25 percent of all compensation paid or accrued to plan beneficiaries during the year.[17]

In an ideal or even just a simpler world, the definition of compensation for both purposes would be the same. Alas, the tax world we live in is not ideal or simple. While similar, the definition of compensation for these two purposes is different. In addition, compensation can be defined differently for other purposes, such as nondiscrimination testing.

Planning Tip: As indicated, a 401(k) plan measures contributions up against a participant's current compensation. In contrast, a defined benefit plan allows the plan to use historical compensation rather than current compensation. Therefore, if the business objective for major participants (owners) is to "save" at a higher rate and increase employer deductions, a defined benefit plan may be a better qualified retirement plan technique for the situation than a 401(k) plan.

Compensation for the Per-Employee Limit under Section 415

The Code definition of "participant's compensation" simply defines it as the participant's compensation from the employer for the year.[18] A special rule for self-employed individuals defines their compensation as their net earnings from self-employment, determined without the foreign earned income exclusion of Section 911.[19]

This bare-bones definition is fleshed out by Treasury Regulation Section 1.415(c)-2, which specifies types of pay that are included and excluded in determining compensation; provides safe harbor definitions that a plan can use; provides timing rules concerning the plan year for which compensation is considered paid; and provides other rules affecting the definition of compensation.

The following types of payments for services are included in compensation:

1. Wages, salaries, fees for professional services, and other amounts received for personal services provided as an employee of the employer that maintains the plan.[20] This includes commissions on sales or insurance premiums, compensation based on a percentage of profits, tips, bonuses, and reimbursements, or other expense allowances paid under a nonaccountable plan.

2. Amounts that were excluded from income as a result of a Section 125 cafeteria plan election, or a transportation fringe benefit election.[21]

3. Elective deferrals under a 401(k) plan, a SARSEP, a SIMPLE, or a Section 457(b) plan.[22]

4. For self-employed persons, their earned income as determined under Section 401(c)(2) (self-employment income under Section 1402(a) with certain modifications in Section 401(c)(2)) plus the same elective deferral amounts described above.[23]

5. Accident or health insurance payments for personal injuries or sickness described in Section 104(a)(3), Section 105(a), or Section 105(h) to the extent included in the employee's gross income.[24]

6.   Nondeductible moving expense payments or reimbursements.[25]

7.   The value of a nonqualified stock option received from an employer to the extent that the option's value is included in the employee's income for the year of grant.[26]

8.   Income resulting from a section 83(b) election.[27]

9.   Amounts includable in income under either Section 409A or Section 457(f)(1)(A) or because the employee constructively received them.[28]

Compensation does not include the following types of payments:

1.   Non-taxable employer contributions, other than employee elective deferrals, to a qualified or nonqualified deferred compensation plan.[29]

2.   Distributions from a qualified or nonqualified deferred compensation plan, regardless of whether the distributions are included in the employee's gross income. However, the plan may provide that distributions from an unfunded nonqualified deferred plan are considered compensation in the year received to the extent the distributions are included in the employee's income.[30]

3.   Amounts received from exercising a nonqualified stock option or when restricted stock or other property becomes freely transferable or is no longer subject to a substantial risk of forfeiture.[31]

4.   Amounts received from the sale, exchange, or other disposition of stock acquired through a statutory stock option.[32]

5.   Other amounts that receive special tax benefits. The regulation uses the exclusion for group term life insurance premiums under Section 79 as an example but points out that the limit only applies to the extent that the premiums aren't included in the employee's gross income and aren't subject to salary reduction under a Section 125 cafeteria plan.[33]

6.   Payments that are similar to any payments listed above.[34]

Employers and their owners and top employees cannot escape these limits by using multiple businesses. An aggregation rule provides that compensation for individuals who are employees of two or more corporations that are members of a controlled group[35] of corporations includes compensation from all employers that are members of the group.[36] This aggregation rule applies even if the employee's actual employer does not have a qualified plan. It also applies to an employee of two or more trades or businesses that are under common control, an employee of two or more members of an affiliated service group,[37] and an employee of two or more members of a group treated as one employer under Section 414(o). See Chapter 11 for more information about treating multiple companies as one employer for 401(k) plan purposes.

Example. David had the following compensation for the year:

Type of payment	Amount	Included in compensation
Salary	$100,000	Yes
Section 125 plan contributions	7,500	Yes
Section 401(k) plan elective deferrals	10,000	Yes
Section 401(k) plan matching contributions	6,000	No
Income from a Section 83(b) election	3,000	Yes
Nonqualified stock options included in income	10,000	Yes
Proceeds from sale of stock acquired through a statutory (incentive) stock option	5,000	No

David's compensation for purposes of the per-employee limit is $130,500, computed as:

Type of payment	Amount
Salary	$100,000
Section 125 plan contributions	7,500
Section 401(k) plan elective deferrals	10,000
Income from a section 83(b) election	3,000
Nonqualified stock options included in income	10,000
Total	$130,500

Self-Employed Individuals

Compensation for self-employed individuals includes net earnings from self-employment, as defined for self-employment tax purposes, with certain adjustments.[38] The most important adjustment is that the income must be from a trade or business in which the individual's personal services are a material income-producing factor.[39] This prevents a passive investor from making elective deferrals. The special computation of compensation for the 25 percent of compensation deduction limit is discussed below.

Safe Harbors

The regulations provide three safe harbor compensation definitions that a plan can use to automatically satisfy Section 415(c)(3) and authorize the IRS Commissioner to provide additional definitions.

1. Simplified compensation – compensation includes only items 1 and 2 of the included items and none of the excluded items.[40]

2. Section 3401(a) wages – this safe harbor compensation definition includes wages for the income tax withholding purposes under Section 3401(a) plus amounts deferred through a Section 125 cafeteria plan election, a transportation fringe benefit election, or an elective deferral under a 401(k) plan, a SARSEP, a SIMPLE, or a Section 457(b) plan.[41]

3. Wages required to be reported to the employee – compensation can include all amounts considered compensation under the Section 3401(a) wages safe harbor described above, plus all other compensation paid by an employer that must be reported to the employee. The employer may exclude amounts paid or reimbursed to the employee for moving expenses if, at the time of payment, it is reasonable to believe the payments are deductible by the employee.[42]

When Is Compensation Paid?

Once a payment is determined to be compensation, it is included in the limitation for the year of payment. The general rule is that for compensation to be included in computing a year's limitation, it must actually be paid or made available to an employee in the limitation year. Non-taxable amounts that an employee defers into a qualifying retirement plan or qualifying transportation fringe benefits are considered to be received on the date they would have been paid if a deferral election had not been made.[43] Amounts must generally be paid prior to an employee's severance from employment to be considered in the limitation.[44]

Plans can include compensation earned in one year but paid in the next year due to the timing of the pay period and the pay date as paid to the employee in the year earned. To qualify, the compensation must be paid during the "first few weeks of the next" year, the amounts are included on a uniform and consistent basis for all similarly situated employees, and compensation is only included in one year.[45]

> *Example.* Company A's last pay period in Year 1 ends on December 26 and payment is made to employees on January 2, Year 2. Company A can elect to include the compensation

earned for that pay period in calculating either the Year 1 or Year 2 compensation limitation as long as it is applied uniformly and consistently for all similarly situated employees.

A similar rule applies to regular pay[46] paid after an employee's severance from employment. To be included in determining the limitation, the compensation must be paid by the later of:

1. 2½ months after the employee's severance from the employer that maintains the plan, or

2. the end of the plan year in which the employee stopped working for the employer that maintained the plan.[47]

A plan can also provide that payments to a former employee for unused sick leave, vacation, and other leave are includable in compensation if the leave would have been available to the employee if they had continued to work for the employer.[48] Payments from an unfunded nonqualified deferred compensation plan to a former employee are included in compensation for the year if the payment would have been made to the employee at the same time if they had remained with the employer. Only the amount taxable to the employee is included in compensation.[49] To be included in compensation, the payment must be made by the deadline discussed above.

Compensation does not include severance pay or golden parachute payments paid after an individual's employment ends, even if made within the time period described previously. Post-employment payments from an unfunded nonqualified deferred compensation plan are only included if they would have been paid at that time if the individual was still working for the employer.[50]

> *Example.* Marilyn's last day working for Company A was June 1. On June 10, she receives her final regular pay. This payment is included in computing the compensation limit for the year of payment. If the plan year ends on June 30th and the payment was made by August 25, the payment could be included in computing the compensation limit for the plan year. If the plan year ended on December 31, the payment is included in compensation for the year as long as it was made by December 31st.

> If Company A had elected to include payments for unused sick leave, vacation, and other leave or nonqualified deferred compensation payments in computing the compensation limit, any amounts Marilyn received would be included in the compensation limit, if paid within the time limit.

> Any severance pay or golden parachute payments Marilyn receives will not be included in determining compensation for the year.

Special timing rules apply to salary continuation payments received by service members, disabled participants, governmental plans, and back pay.[51]

Treatment of Excess Contributions

An employer cannot deduct contributions that exceed the per-employee contribution limit imposed by Section 415.[52] In addition, excess contributions can disqualify the 401(k) plan. If the plan is disqualified, the employer would not be able to deduct any of the contributions to the plan. A plan can avoid disqualification by taking advantage of correction procedures established under the IRS Employee Plans Compliance Resolution System, discussed in Chapter 13.

Compensation for the Overall Limit

The beginning point for determining compensation for the 25 percent of compensation limit is the per-employee compensation definition limit. It also includes compensation that a permanently and totally disabled individual would have received if they received the same rate of compensation as before they became disabled.[53] Finally, it includes any employee 401(k) or 457 plan elective deferrals, non-taxable cafeteria plan contributions, and qualified transportation fringe benefits (commuter van pools, transit passes, parking, and bicycle reimbursement) that were not included in the employee's taxable income.[54] The maximum amount of compensation for any one employee used to determine the total compensation is limited. This amount is adjusted for inflation annually.[55] For 2014, the maximum amount of compensation per employee is $260,000.

Employee deferrals are not subject to the 25 percent of compensation limit[56] but are included in the definition of compensation in determining the limit.

> *Example.* John contributes $10,000 to his 401(k) and receives cash compensation of $90,000 for 2013. His 401(k) contribution is not subject to the 25 percent of compensation limit. In determining the 25 percent of compensation limit, his employer would include both the $90,000 of cash compensation **and** his $10,000 401(k) contribution. For this purpose, John's compensation is $100,000. If John were the only participant, the employer could contribute $25,000 itself to John's account, making the total contributions to John's account $35,000 (John's $10,000 plus his employer's $25,000) without violating the 25 percent of compensation limit.

Self-employed individuals. For self-employed individuals, two adjustments must be made to compensation before computing the 25 percent of compensation limit. The first is to reduce the net earnings from self-employment by the deductible portion of self-employment tax.[57] The second is to deduct the 401(k) contribution.[58] Because these reductions are interrelated, the IRS's computations use a reduced contribution rate for the plan.[59]

Combined limit for defined benefit and defined contribution plans. Employers may offer multiple plans to their employees. If any employees participate in more than one,[60] the total deduction is limited to the greater of:

1. 25 percent of compensation (the limit discussed previously); or

2. the employer contributions required to satisfy the minimum funding standard of Section 412 for the defined benefit plan.[61]

If the defined benefit plan contributions exceed the minimum funding standard, this limitation means that no current year deduction is allowed for contributions to other plans.

This combined limit is subject to exceptions. It does not apply if only elective deferrals are made to the defined contribution plans.[62] It also does not apply if employer contributions to the defined contribution plans do not exceed 6 percent of compensation. If employer contributions do exceed 6 percent, only the contributions exceeding 6 percent are subject to the limit.[63]

Treatment of excess contributions. If contributions for a plan year exceed the overall limit of 25 percent of participant compensation, the excess contributions are carried over to future years. However, the carryover contributions plus the current year contributions cannot exceed the 25 percent of compensation limit for the current year.[64]

> *Example.* Smith Company makes the contributions shown in the following table to its 401(k) plan. The table also shows the application of excess contributions, assuming the combined plan limit does not apply.

Year	Compensation	Deduction Limit (25% of compensation)	Contribution	Contribution carryover used	Total deduction (including carryovers)	Contribution carryover to next year
2010	$1,000	$250	$200	$0	$200	$0
2011	$600	$150	$200	$0	$150	$50
2012	$800	$200	$175	$25	$200	$25
2013	$900	$225	$225	$0	$225	$25
2014	$960	$240	$215	$25	$240	$0
$000s omitted.						

Endnotes

1. H.Rep. No. 99-426, Part 2, at 95. In part, the House Ways & Means Committee mistakenly thought the caps would stop the trend toward the 401(k) defined contribution plan design in place of DB plans. In addition to the annual deferral limits, the Ways and Means Committee proposed reducing the IRA deduction dollar for dollar by an individual's 401(k) or 403(b) deferrals for the year but did not do so.

2. *Ibid*, page 94.

3. IRC Sec. 402(g)(1)(B), as adjusted for inflation in Notice 2012-67, IRB 2012-50.

4. Catch-up contributions for people who are at least 50 by the end of the taxable year are authorized by IRC Sec. 414(v).

5. IRC Sec. 414(v)(2)(B)(i), as adjusted for inflation in Notice 2012-67, IRB 2012-50.

6. IRC Sec. 415(c)(1), as adjusted for inflation in Notice 2012-67. Any forfeitures added to an employee's account are also included in calculating the annual contribution limit.

7. IRC Sec. 404(a)(3)(A).

8. IRC Sec. 402(g)(5).

9. IRC Sec. 404(a)(3)(A)(iv).

10. IRC Sec. 402(g)(3).

11. IRC Sec. 457e)(15).

12. Treas. Reg. §1.401(k)-1(a)(4)(ii).

13. Treas. Reg. §1.401(k)-1(a)(2)(ii).

14. Treas. Reg. §1.415(c)-1(b)(2)(ii)(B).

15. Adjusted annually by the IRS and usually announced for the coming calendar year in September or October.

16. IRC Sec. 415(c)(1).

17. IRC Sec. 404(a)(3)(A).

18. IRC Sec. 415(c)(3)(A).

19. IRC Sec. 415(c)(3)(B).

20. Treas. Reg. §1.415(c)-2(b)(1).

21. IRC Sec. 415(c)(3)(D)(ii).

22. IRC Sec. 415(c)(3)(D)(i).

23. Treas. Reg. §1.415(c)-2(b)(2).

24. Treas. Reg. §1.415(c)-2(b)(3).

25. Treas. Reg. §1.415(c)-2(b)(4).

26. Treas. Reg. §1.415(c)-2(b)(5).

27. Treas. Reg. §1.415(c)-2(b)(6).

28. Treas. Reg. §1.415(c)-2(b)(7).

29. Treas. Reg. §1.415(c)-2(c)(1).

30. *Ibid.*

31. Treas. Reg. §1.415(c)-2(c)(2).

32. Treas. Reg. §1.415(c)-2(c)(3).

33. Treas. Reg. §1.415(c)-2(c)(4).

34. Treas. Reg. §1.415(c)-2(c)(5).

35. IRC Sec. 1563(a).

36. Treas. Reg. §1.415(c)-2(g)(2).

37. IRC Sec, 414(m).

38. IRC Sec. 401(c)(2).

39. IRC Sec. 401(c)(2)(A)(i).

40. Treas. Reg. §1.415(c)-2(d)(2).

41. Treas. Reg. §1.415(c)-2(d)(3).

42. Treas. Reg. §1.415(c)-2(d)(4).

43. Treas. Reg. §1.415(c)-2(e)(1).

44. Treas. Reg. §1.415(c)-2(e)(2).

45. Treas. Reg. §1.415(c)-2(e)(2).

46. Regular pay is defined by Treas. Reg. §1.415(c)-2(e)(3)(ii) as regular compensation such as salary, commissions, bonuses, and overtime that would have been paid to the employee prior to a severance from employment if the employee had continued to work for the employer.

47. Treas. Reg. §1.415(c)-2(e)(3)(i)

48. Treas. Reg. §1.415(c)-2(e)(3)(iii)(A).

49. Treas. Reg. §1.415(c)-2(e)(3)(iii)(B).

50. Treas. Reg. §1.415(c)-2(e)(3)(iv).

51. Treas. Regs. §§1.415(c)-2(e)(4), 1.415(c)-2(e)(5).

52. IRC Sec. 404(j)(1), as adjusted for inflation in Notice 2012-67, IRB 2012-50.

53. IRC Sec. 415(c)(3)(C).

54. IRC Sec. 404(a)(12).

55. IRC Sec. 404(l)

56. IRC Sec. 404(n).

57. IRC Sec. 401(c)(2)(A)(vi).

58. IRC Sec. 401(c)(2)(A)(v).

59. See the Rate Table for Self-Employed and the Rate Worksheet for Self-Employed in IRS Publication 560.

60. IRC Sec. 404(a)(7)(C)(i).

61. IRC Sec. 404(a)(7).

62. IRC Sec. 404(a)(7)(C)(ii).

63. IRC Sec. 404(a)(7)(C)(iii).

64. IRC Sec. 404(a)(3)(A)(ii).

Chapter 5

Passing the Tests – Complying with the Nondiscrimination Rules

Introduction

An important factor for retirement plans in qualifying for tax-favored treatment and maintaining that qualification is that the plan *cannot* discriminate in favor of highly compensated employees (HCEs). Naturally, Congress decided that the IRS and DOL couldn't take a plan or employer's word for it that the plan doesn't discriminate. The plan has to show both that its:

1.   design doesn't discriminate; and

2.   operation doesn't discriminate either.

Designing a plan to comply with the nondiscrimination rules and the testing required to determine if a plan complies with the nondiscrimination rules creates considerable complexity for plans, plan sponsors, and plan administrators.

In addition to the general nondiscrimination rules for elective deferrals, employer matching contributions and employee after-tax contributions must also meet special nondiscrimination rules.

The elective deferral and the matching contributions parts of a 401(k) plan must meet the nondiscrimination rules both in form and in operation. To meet the form requirement, the plan must provide that the Section 401(k) nondiscrimination rules will be met.[1]

General Nondiscrimination Tests

Contributions to a 401(k) plan must run a gauntlet of three nondiscrimination tests.

1. For the plan to be a qualified plan, it must comply with the Section 401(a)(4) require-
    ment that the plan not discriminate in favor of HCEs.[2] See Chapter 3 for a discussion
    of the two safe harbors and the general test for compliance with this test.

2. It must meet the coverage requirements under Section 410(b), discussed below.

3. The final test for elective deferrals is the average deferral percentage (ADP) test estab-
    lished by Section 401(k)(3). As an alternative to passing the ADP test, the plan can:

    -   qualify as a *SIMPLE* 401(k) plan;[3]

    -   provide minimum employer matching contributions or a minimum
        employer contribution of at least 3 percent, regardless of the employee's
        contributions;[4]

    -   provide an automatic contribution arrangement with minimum deferrals;[5] or

    -   be part of a combined defined benefit and defined contribution plan.[6] For
        matching contributions or employee contributions to the profit-sharing
        portion of the plan, the final test is the actual contribution percentage test
        (ACP) set out in Section 401(m).

In addition to these three tests, a 401(k) plan may have to meet the Section 416 top-heavy rules.

Coverage Requirements

The Internal Revenue Code sets out three ways a plan can meet the Section 410(b) coverage requirements. The plan can:

1. benefit at least 70 percent of non-highly compensated employees (percentage test);[7]

2. benefit a percentage of non-highly compensated employees that is at least 70 percent
    of the HCEs benefiting from the plan (ratio test);[8] or

3. pass the average benefit percentage test. This test looks at whether the average benefit
    percentage for non-highly compensated employees is at least 70 percent of the average
    benefit percentage for HCEs. The testing criteria are discussed later in this chapter.[9]

The Section 410(b) regulations flesh out the coverage requirements. First, they provide that current employees and former employees be tested separately, using different tests. The tests for employees disregard former employees while the test for former employees disregards employees. Second, they combine the percentage test and ratio test into one test, called the "ratio percentage test."

Former Employees

The regulation applies a facts-and-circumstances test to determine if the coverage requirements are met for former employees.[10] A former employee benefits under a plan during the plan year if the former employee receives an allocation or benefit increase during the year based on the person's status as a former employee.[11] In the year a person stops working for the employer, he is treated as an employee for purposes of the employee tests and as a former employee for purposes of the former employee test.

Current Employees

The test to determine if an employee benefits under a plan for a plan year is similar to the test for former employees. A special rule for 401(k) plans provides that employees are considered to benefit under a 401(k) plan for a plan year if they are eligible to make a deferral election.[12] An employee who does not meet the age or service requirements is not considered an eligible employee.[13]

Excludable Employees

Plans may exclude certain employees in applying the coverage tests. This is true even if they are benefiting under the plan, unless an exception applies.[14] The permitted exclusions are:

- employees who do not meet the plan's minimum age and service requirements;[15]

- nonresident aliens who receive no earned income from the employer that is considered income from sources within the U.S.;[16]

- employees who are members of an employee unit covered by a collectively bargained agreement if retirement benefits were the subject of good faith bargaining and if the plan solely benefits employees not covered by the collectively bargained agreement;[17]

- employees of other qualified separate lines of business operated by the employer in testing a plan for one qualified separate line of business of an employer;[18]

- terminating employees if they do not receive a benefit or allocation because they failed to satisfy either the minimum period of service requirement or a requirement to be employed on the last day of the plan year;[19]

- employees of governmental entities precluded from maintaining a 401(k) plan;[20]

- employees of a tax-exempt entity who meet certain requirements;[21]

- former employees who terminated before a specified date or were excludable under another provision in the year that they terminated;[22] and

- former non-highly compensated employees treated as employees solely because of an increase in their accrued benefits under a defined benefit plan after they terminated.[23]

Ratio Percentage Test

A plan's ratio percentage for a plan year must be at least 70 percent.[24] The regulation provides a three-step process to determine a plan's ratio percentage.[25]

1. Divide the number of non-highly compensated employees who benefit under the plan by the total number of the employer's non-highly compensated employees.

2. Divide the number of HCEs who benefit under the plan by the total number of the employer's HCEs.

3. The ratio percentage is then determined by dividing the percentage of non-highly compensated employees who benefit from the plan by the percentage of HCEs who benefit under the plan. This percentage is rounded to the nearest hundredth of a percentage point, e.g., .01.

Example 1. In a plan year, Plan A benefits 70 percent of an employer's non-highly compensated employees and 100 percent of the employer's HCEs. For the year, its ratio percentage is 70 percent/100 percent, or 70 percent. Plan A satisfies the ratio percentage test for the plan year.[26]

Example 2. In a plan year, Plan B benefits 40 percent of an employer's non-highly compensated employees and 60 percent of the employer's HCEs. For the year, its ratio percentage is 66.67 percent (40 percent/60 percent). Plan B does not satisfy the ratio percentage test for the plan year.[27]

Average Benefit Test

The average benefit test has two parts:

1. A nondiscriminatory classification test,

2. An average benefit percentage test.[28]

Nondiscriminatory classification test. The nondiscriminatory classification test itself has two parts – reasonable classification and nondiscriminatory classification. First, it looks to whether the plan benefits employees who qualify under a reasonable classification established by the employer. Second, it looks at whether the classification of employees is nondiscriminatory. The employer's classification is a reasonable classification "if and only if" it is reasonable and established under objective business criteria to identify the category of employees who benefit from the plan.[29]

That regulatory definition seems circular so we are fortunate the regulation provides some examples, stating that "reasonable classifications generally include specified job categories, nature of compensation (e.g., salaried or hourly), geographic location, and similar bona fide business criteria."[30] In contrast, specifying employees by name or other specific criteria that produces substantially the same result as specifying employees by name (e.g., "vice president of marketing hired on January 2, 2013") is not a reasonable classification.[31]

To be considered a nondiscriminatory classification, the group of employees included in the classification must satisfy either a safe harbor test or a facts-and-circumstances test. A plan meets the safe harbor test if its ratio percentage (discussed previously) is equal to or greater than the employer's safe harbor percentage.[32] The safe harbor percentage is 50 percent, reduced by .75 percent for each 1 percent that the non-highly compensated employee (NHCE) concentration percentage exceeds 60 percent.[33] The NHCE concentration percentage is simply the percentage of employees who are NHCEs, excluding any excludable employees.

> *Example 3.* Same facts as *Example 1.* Eighty percent of the employer's employees are non-highly compensated employees. Its ratio percentage is 70 percent and its safe harbor percentage is 35 percent, computed as follows:
>
> 1. 80 percent (NHCE concentration percentage) – 60 percent (threshold) = 20 percent.
>
> 2. 20 percent * .75 = 15 percent.
>
> 3. 50 percent – 15 percent = 35 percent.

Because Plan A's ratio percentage of 70 percent exceeds its safe harbor percentage of 35 percent, it meets the safe harbor test.

The facts-and-circumstances test is satisfied if a plan's ratio percentage is greater than or equal to the unsafe harbor percentage and the classification satisfies the factual determination test.[34] The unsafe harbor percentage is calculated in the same way as the safe harbor percentage, using 40 percent in place of 50 percent. The minimum unsafe harbor percentage is 20 percent. If the ratio percentage does not equal or exceed the unsafe harbor percentage, the plan is discriminatory and it is unnecessary to consider if the factual determination test is met.

> *Example 4.* Same facts as *Example 3.* The unsafe harbor percentage is 25 percent (40 percent – 15 percent).

The factual determination test is met if the IRS determines, based on all relevant facts and circumstances, that the classification is nondiscriminatory.[35] While no one fact is determinative, the regulation identifies the following elements as relevant in determining if a classification is nondiscriminatory:

- The underlying business reason for the classification. The regulation specifically states that reducing the employer's cost of providing retirement benefits is not a relevant business reason.[36]

- The percentage of employees that benefit under the plan.[37]

- If the number of employees in each salary range that benefit from the plan is representative of the number of employees in each salary range.[38]

- The size of the difference between the plan's ratio percentage and the employer's safe harbor percentage.[39]

- The extent to which the plan's average benefit percentage exceeds 70 percent.[40]

The following examples illustrate the computation of the safe harbor rule and the ratio percentage comparison.

> *Example 5.* Employer A has 200 nonexcludable employees, of whom 120 are NHCEs) and 80 are HCEs. Employer A maintains a plan that benefits 60 NHCEs and 72 HCEs. Thus, the plan's ratio percentage is 55.56 percent ([60 (NHCES benefited)/120 (total NHCES)] / [72 (HCEs benefited) / 80 (total HCEs)] = 50 percent/90 percent = 0.5556), which is below the percentage necessary to satisfy the ratio percentage test of Treasury Regulation Section 1.410(b)-2(b)(2). The employer's NHCE concentration percentage is 60 percent (120/200). Employer A's safe harbor percentage is 50 percent and its unsafe harbor percentage is 40 percent. (The safe harbor starting point of 50 percent and the unsafe harbor starting point of 40 percent are not reduced because the NHCE concentration is 60 percent.) Because the ratio percentage of 55.56 percent exceeds the 50 percent safe harbor percentage, the plan's classification satisfies the safe harbor of paragraph (c)(2) of this Section.[41]

> *Example 6.* The facts are the same as in *Example 5*, except that the plan benefits only 40 NHCEs. The plan's ratio percentage is thus 37.03 percent [40 NHCEs/120 NHCEs / [72 HCEs/80 HCEs] = 33.33 percent/90 percent = 0.3703). The plan's ratio percentage is below the unsafe harbor percentage. As a result, the plan fails the facts-and-circumstances test and the plan is considered discriminatory, even if it were to satisfy the factual determination.[42]

> *Example 7.* The facts are the same as in *Example 5*, except that the plan benefits 45 NHCEs. The plan's ratio percentage is thus 41.67 percent ([45 NHCE /120 NHCE] / [72 HCE /80 HCE] = 37.50 percent/90 percent = 0.4167), above the unsafe harbor percentage

(40 percent) and below the safe harbor percentage (50 percent). The Commissioner may determine that the classification is nondiscriminatory after considering all the relevant facts and circumstances.[43]

Average benefit percentage test. The second part of the average benefit test is the average benefit percentage test of Treasury Regulation Section 1.410(b)-5. A plan satisfies it if the average benefit provided to NHCEs for the plan year is at least 70 percent of the benefit provided to HCEs. A special rule applies to collectively bargained plans.[44]

The determination for a plan must include all plans that can be aggregated with the plan.[45] If the plans have different plan years, the testing uses all plan years that end in the same calendar year.[46] Calculating the average benefit percentage for a plan requires calculating an employee benefit percentage for each employee (other than excludable employees) based on the general nondiscrimination test rules under Section 401(a)(4).[47] The employee benefit percentage can be determined on either a benefits or contribution basis,[48] considering only employer-provided contributions and benefits.[49] The regulations include rules for permitted disparity[50] and optional rules for determining employee benefit percentages.[51]

After calculating the employee benefit percentages for all employees, the next step is to determine the actual benefit percentages for the NHCEs and for the HCEs. These are the average of the employee benefit percentages for each group of employees and the actual benefit percentage for the HCEs.[52]

Finally, the average benefit percentage is computed by dividing the actual benefit percentage of the NHCEs by the actual benefit percentage of the HCEs.[53]

> *Example 8.* The actual benefit percentages for the NHCEs of Employer B average to 20 percent and to 25 percent for HCEs, based on each employee's employee benefit percentage. The average benefit percentage is 20 percent/25 percent or 80 percent. The plan satisfies the average benefit percentage test.

> *Example 9.* Same facts as *Example 8* except that the actual benefit percentage for the non-highly compensated employees is 16 percent. The average benefit percentage is 16 percent/25 percent, or 64 percent. The plan does not satisfy the average benefit percentage.

Actual Deferral Percentage (ADP) Test for Elective Deferrals

To prevent HCEs from contributing significantly more to a plan than the NHCEs, HCEs' elective deferrals cannot be disproportionate to the NHCEs' elective deferrals. Since the HCEs are more likely to be able to contribute larger amounts than NHCEs are, the test is based on the percentage of compensation deferred, rather than the amount deferred.

The plan document must specify the method it will use to satisfy the ADP requirements. If that method provides employer options, it must also specify which options apply.[54]

The actual deferral percentage (ADP) test requires the plan to meet one of two tests.

- 1.25 times test – The ADP for the eligible HCEs does not exceed 1.25 times the ADP for all other eligible employees.[55]

- 2 + 2 test – The ADP for eligible HCEs does not exceed the ADP for all other eligible employees by more than two percentage points and the ADP for eligible HCEs does not exceed two times the ADP of all other eligible employees.[56]

Computing the ADP. Determining whether a plan meets the ADP test requires the following steps.

1. Compute the ratio of employer contributions actually paid to the plan for an employee for the plan year to the employee's compensation for the plan year, known as the actual deferral ratio (ADR).[57]

2. Determine the ADP for HCEs by averaging the ADRs for the HCEs.

3. Determine the ADP for all other employees by averaging the ADRs for all other employees.

4. Compare the ADP for HCEs to the ADP for all other employees using each ADP test.

Plan's choice of current year or prior year to determine the ADP for NHCEs. A plan has the choice of determining the ADP for eligible NHCEs using the prior-year testing method or the current-year testing method.[58] The plan document must specify its choice of the current-year or prior-year testing methods.[59]

The basics of these methods are self-explanatory. The prior-year testing method uses the ADP for NHCEs from the plan year immediately before the plan year being tested. It uses the eligible employees who were NHCEs in that year, regardless of whether they were eligible employees or NHCEs in the plan year being tested. The current-year method uses the ADP for the eligible NHCEs in the plan year being tested. Both methods use the current year ADP for HCEs.[60]

Unless the plan is a successor to another plan, in its first year, a plan that elects the prior-year testing method is allowed to use either its ADP in that first plan year or 3 percent as its ADP.[61]

A plan can change from the prior-year testing method to the current-year testing method for any year.[62] Plans wanting to change to the prior-year testing method must meet certain requirements set out in the regulations. One of the general requirements is that the plan must have used the current-year testing method for each of the five plan years preceding the year of change or, if less, the number of years the plan has been in existence.[63]

A plan that uses the prior-year testing method and has a change in the group or groups of eligible employees during a plan year may be required to use special rules to calculate the ADP for NHCEs.[64] For the special rules to apply, the change must be due to (1) the establishment or amendment of a plan; (2) a plan merger, consolidation, or spinoff; (3) a change in the way plans are combined under the permissive aggregation rules; (4) a reclassification of employees that has the same effect as a plan amendment; or (5) a combination of these.[65] In addition, the change must affect more than 10 percent of the NHCEs. If it does not, the plan can provide that it will use the ADP for the eligible NHCEs for the prior plan year.[66]

Planning Tip. The benefit of using the prior-year testing method is that the ADP for the NHCEs for the prior year is known early in the current plan year. The employer and plan administrator can then calculate the ADP limit for HCEs for the current plan year. They can then monitor the ADP for HCEs and reduce the likelihood that the plan will fail the ADP test. Because HCEs may leave the employer, new ones may become participants, change their contributions, their compensation may change or other occurrences can change their ADR, it is unlikely that a plan can determine if it satisfied the ADP test until the end of the plan year.

Example 9. Employer X has three employees, A, B, and C. It sponsors a profit-sharing plan that includes a 401(k) plan. Employee A is an HCE. Employees B and C are NHCEs. The plan uses the current-year testing method and includes elective contributions in compensation.

The following table shows their compensation and elective deferrals.

Employee	Compensation	Elective Deferrals	ADR
A	$100,000	$5,770	5.77%
B	60,000	2,860	4.77%
C	45,000	1,250	2.78%

The ADP for the HCEs (Employee A) is 5.77 percent. The ADP for the NHCEs is 3.78 percent ((4.77 percent + 2.78 percent)/2).

1.25 times test: The limit is 4.73 percent (3.78 percent * 1.25). The ADP for HCEs of 5.77 exceeds the limit, so *FAILED.*

2 and 2 test: 1. The 5.77 percent ADP for the highly compensated employees is less than 5.78 percent (the NHCEs' ADP of 3.78 percent plus 2 percent). 2. The 5.77 percent

ADP for the HCEs is less than 7.56 percent (the NHCEs' ADP of 3.78 percent multiplied by 2 percent.), so *PASSED.*

Because the plan satisfies one of the two tests, it satisfies the ADP test.[67]

Example 10. Plan T is a profit-sharing plan that includes a 401(k) plan. It uses the prior-year testing method. Employees D and E are HCEs. The following table shows their compensation, elective contributions, and ADRs for the current plan year.

Employee	Compensation	Elective Deferrals	ADR
D	$100,000	$10,000	10%
E	95,000	4,750	5%

The ADP for the HCEs is 7.5 percent (10 percent + 5 percent)/2.

Employees F through L were eligible NHCEs for the prior year. The following table shows their compensation, elective contributions, and ADRs for the prior plan year.

Employee	Compensation	Elective Deferrals	ADR
F	$60,000	$3,600	6%
G	40,000	1,600	4%
H	30,000	1,200	4%
I	20,000	600	3%
J	20,000	600	3%
K	10,000	300	3%
L	5,000	150	3%

The ADP for the NHCEs is 3.71 percent (the sum of their ADRs for the prior year, 26 percent, divided by 7 employees).

1.25 times test: The limit is 4.64 percent (3.71 percent * 1.25 percent). The HCEs' ADP of 7.5 percent exceeds the limit, so *FAILED.*

2 + 2 test: The HCEs' ADP of 7.5 percent exceeds the ADP of the NHCEs by more than 2 percentage points, so *FAILED.*

Figure 5.1. Guide to Maximum ADP for HCE	
ADP for NHCE	**Maximum ADP for HCE**
0 – 2%	2 times ADP of NHCE
2 – 8%	ADP of NHCE plus 2 percentage points
8% or more	ADP of NHCE times 1.25

Because the plan does not satisfy either ADP test, it is not a qualified 401(k) plan unless the plan corrects the ADP failure.[68]

Figure 5.1 provides a guide to the application of the 1.25 times test and the 2 +2 test, based on the ADP for the highly compensated employees.

Determining compensation. The Section 414(s) definition of "compensation" is used for Section 401(k) purposes.[69] Section 414(s), for its part, generally looks to the definition of compensation in Section 415(c)(3), which provides several safe harbor rules for the definition of compensation. These safe harbor rules include the definition of wages under Section 3401(a) for income tax withholding purposes[70] and amounts included on an employee's Form W-2 for the year.[71] Compensation also includes an employee's elective deferrals to the 401(k) plan as well as Section 125 (cafeteria) plan deferrals, qualified transportation fringes, and deferrals to a Section 457 plan.[72]

An employee's compensation used to compute the ADR cannot exceed the compensation limit of Section 401(a)(17), as adjusted for inflation. For 2014, the limit is $260,000.[73]

Planning Tip. Using a broad definition of compensation reduces the ADRs, which produces a lower ADP. For example, a plan that excludes irregular or additional compensation such as overtime pay and shift differentials under Treasury Regulation Section 1.414(s)-1(d)(2)(ii) will have lower total compensation for an employee who receives that type of compensation than if the plan included such compensation.

Using qualified nonelective contributions (QNECs) and qualified matching contributions (QMACs) to comply. A plan can include employer contributions that qualify as QMACs and QNECs in addition to elective deferrals in calculating an employee's ADR. A QMAC is a matching contribution that is subject to the same vesting and distribution rules as elective deferrals. A QNEC is an employer contribution other than an elective deferral or matching contribution that is subject to the same vesting and distribution rules as elective deferrals. This means that QMACs and QNECs are immediately vested and cannot be distributed before the employee's death, disability, severance from employment, attainment of age 59½, hardship, or termination of the plan.[74]

An employer *must* contribute a QNEC or QMAC by the end of the 12-month period after the plan year or applicable year. If the plan uses the prior-year testing method, this means that the contributions for NHCEs must be made by the end of the plan year being tested. For example, if a plan uses QNECs or QMACs to help pass the ADP test for the 2014 plan year, the prior-year testing method requires that QNECs or QMACs must be allocated to the plan for the accounts of the NHCEs for the 2013 plan year by the end of 2014. In contrast, the allocation must be made by the end of 2015 for HCEs.[75]

If the plan treats QMACs or QNECs as elective contributions to satisfy the ADP test, they cannot be used in determining if a plan meets the ACP test or the ADP test for the same or any other plan or for any other year.[76]

Special rules. The Code and regulations set out the following special rules for determining if a plan violates the ADP test.

- An employee's elective deferrals are considered employer contributions.[77]

- An employer may elect to include matching contributions and qualified non-elective contributions in computing the ADP test if the requirements set out in the regulations are met.[78]

- In a plan's first year, the ADP for NHCEs is 3 percent unless the employer elects to use the ADP for the NHCEs determined for the plan year.[79]

- If all eligible employees in a plan year are HCEs, the plan is deemed to satisfy the ADP test for that plan year.[80]

- Elective deferrals made for a partner or sole proprietor are treated as if they are allocated to the partner's account on the last day of the proprietor's or partnership's tax year.[81]

- Elective deferrals of HCEs include any excess contributions, even if the excess deferrals are distributed.[82]

- A participant's catch-up contributions are subtracted from the participant's elective deferrals for the plan year in determining the participant's ADR.[83]

Alternative methods to meet the ADP test. A plan can meet the ADP test by satisfying one of two contribution requirements and a notice requirement.[84]

Matching contribution. The plan meets the matching contribution requirement for NHCEs if it matches:[85]

- 100 percent of the employee's elective contributions, up to 3 percent of the employee's compensation; plus

- 50 percent of the employee's elective contributions between 3 and 5 percent of compensation.

In addition, the matching contribution rate for HCEs cannot exceed the rate for NHCEs.[86] If a plan's matching contribution rate does not satisfy the previously mentioned rates, the plan can still satisfy this alternative if its matching rate does not increase as an employee's contribution rate increases and its total matching contributions are at least as much as they would be using the matching rates.[87] This allows a plan to satisfy the alternative test by matching contributions up to 4 percent of compensation.

Nonelective contributions. If a plan makes a contribution of at least 3 percent of compensation for every eligible NHCE, the alternative test is met.[88]

Notice requirement. A plan meets the notice requirement if it provides a notice to eligible employees that is "sufficiently accurate and comprehensive" to inform the employees of their rights and obligations under the plan and is written so it can be understood by an average eligible employee.[89]

Nondiscrimination Tests for the Profit-Sharing Portion of the Plan

Matching contributions and after-tax employee contributions to the profit-sharing portion of a 401(k) plan must meet the same nondiscrimination tests of Section 401(a)(4) and the coverage test of Section 410(b) as the 401(k) portion. Instead of the ADP test, they must satisfy an actual contribution percentage (ACP) test, which is similar to the ADP test. The ACP test is based on the percentage of matching contributions and employee contributions to compensation for the NHCEs and HCEs for the year.[90] Any employee who is eligible to make an employee contribution or to receive a matching contribution is considered an eligible employee for purposes of the ACP test.[91]

Matching contributions. The Code defines a matching contribution as:

- any employer contribution made to a defined contribution plan for an employee based on a contribution made by the employee (other than an elective deferral);[92]

- any employer contribution made to a defined contribution plan for an employee based on the employee's elective deferral;[93] and

- any forfeiture allocated on the basis of employee contributions, matching contributions, or elective deferrals.[94]

To be included in the actual contribution ratio for an eligible employee, each of the following requirements must be met:[95]

- The matching contribution must be allocated to the employee's account as of a date within the year being considered.

- The matching contribution is made or allocated based on the employee's elective deferrals or contributions for the year.

- The matching contribution is actually paid to the trust by the end of the 12-month period immediately following the year that includes the allocation date.

The regulation also specifies certain employee contributions and matching contributions that are not taken into account under the ACP test. These include matching contributions that do not meet the requirements previously discussed. Instead, those contributions must satisfy the general nondiscrimination test of Section 401(a)(4).[96] Other contributions not included in the ACP test are disproportionate matching contributions, qualifying matching contributions used to satisfy the ADP test, and matching contributions considered under safe harbor provisions.[97]

Employee contributions. Under the regulations, employee contributions are contributions treated as after-tax employee contributions and allocated to an individual account for each eligible employee. An employer treats contributions as after-tax employee contributions by subjecting them to withholding.[98] The definition of employee contributions excludes certain amounts paid to a plan on a participant's behalf, including designated Roth contributions, loan repayments, rollover contributions, and employee contributions transferred from another plan.[99] Matching contributions made for self-employed persons are not considered elective employee contributions.[100] Employee contributions also include contributions applied to the purchase of whole life insurance protection or survivor benefit protection and excess contributions and related income recharacterized as employee contributions to satisfy the ADP test.[101]

Satisfying the ACP test. The determination of whether a plan satisfies the ACP test uses the 1.25 and 2 + 2 tests in a very similar way to the determination of whether a plan satisfies the ADP test. While the testing methods do not have to be consistent between an employer's 401(k) plan and its profit-sharing plan, the following restrictions generally make using different methods unattractive:

- The plans cannot correct excess contributions for a plan year by using the recharacterization method.

- They cannot elect to consider elective contributions under the ACP test instead of the ADP test.

- The option to take qualified matching contributions into account under the ADP test instead of the ACP test is not available.[102]

Alternative way to meet the ACP test. Instead of satisfying the standard 1.25 and 2 + 2 tests, a plan can satisfy the ACP test by meeting the alternative ADP test and limiting any matching contributions.[103] The matching contributions (1) cannot exceed 6 percent of compensation, (2) cannot increase as an employee's contributions or elective deferrals increase, and (3) the matching rate for a HCE cannot exceed the matching rate for any NHCE.[104]

A plan's options if it fails the ACP test are discussed later in this chapter.

Top Heavy Rules

As if the previous tests aren't complex and complicated enough, plans may also need to comply with the top-heavy rules. These rules are an additional protection against discrimination in favor of "key employees." If a plan is top heavy, it must meet specific vesting and minimum benefit requirements.

Practice Tip: A 401(k) plan is not subject to the top-heavy rules if it meets the alternative tests for elective deferrals and matching contributions previously discussed.

If a plan is top heavy, the top-heavy rules require it to provide an employer contribution for non-key employees of at least 3 percent of compensation, including matching contributions.[105] Section 416 also requires the plan to provide the same vesting schedule that is normally required.[106]

A 401(k) plan is top-heavy if the aggregate of the key employees' accounts exceeds 60 percent of the accounts of all employees covered by the plan.[107]

The definition of key employee looks much like the definition of an HCE. A key employee is defined as:[108]

- an officer of the employer with an annual compensation greater than $130,000 ($170,000 for 2014[109]);

- a 5 percent owner of the employer; or

- a 1 percent owner with annual compensation from the employer greater than $150,000 (not adjusted for inflation).

Aggregation or Disaggregation of Plans

The Code and regulations include anti-abuse provisions to prevent employers from manipulating the plans and participants to satisfy the nondiscrimination rules while maximizing the contributions for HCEs and minimizing the contributions for NHCEs. These provisions include requiring employers to treat parts of a plan as separate plans and permitting or requiring them to aggregate plans.

Planning Tip. If an employer has multiple entities or its owners are owners of more than one entity and the plan is not intended to cover all entities of the employer or owners, the planning process should include examining how the aggregation affects the plan.

The regulations[110] set out situations where plans must be separated into separate portions (disaggregated) in determining if a plan satisfies the coverage requirements. These include requiring that a plan that includes a 401(k) plan, permits matching and employee contributions, and other contributions will be treated as three separate plans for purposes of the coverage tests.[111]

Subject to the disaggregation rule discussed earlier, if an employer sponsors multiple plans that have the same plan year, it can elect to treat the plans as one plan for purposes of the ratio percentage and nondiscriminatory classification tests.[112] This means that if an employer sponsors two plans that receive the same type of contributions, such as two 401(k) plans, they can be aggregated to satisfy those tests.

If any HCE participates in more than one 401(k) plan of the same employer that have the same plan year, the plans are treated as one plan in determining the employee's deferral percentage.[113] Similarly, if a highly compensated employee is eligible to participate in more than one plan to which matching contributions or employee contributions are made, all contributions to any of the plans are considered as made to the plan being tested.[114]

An employer that treats two or more plans as one plan for purposes of satisfying the coverage requirements of Section 410(b) must also treat the plans as one plan for satisfying the ADP and ACP tests.

The Plan Fails the General Nondiscrimination Test or Coverage Requirements – What's Next?

A plan that fails the general nondiscrimination test of Section 401(a)(4) or the coverage requirements of Section 410(b) is disqualified and loses the benefits provided to qualified plans. The plan's assets become subject to tax and the plan is governed by the rules applicable to nonqualified plans – Section 83, Section 402(b)(1), and Section 409A. Employees must recognize income when they become substantially vested in the benefits. Employers cannot deduct contributions to the plan. Rather, their deduction is delayed until benefits are paid to participants. This can create a mismatch between when the employee includes the benefits in income and when the employer can deduct them.

A special rule allows the qualified plan rules to continue to apply to NHCEs if the only reason the plan is disqualified is its failure to meet the Section 410(b) coverage test.[115]

A disqualified plan may attempt to correct the failure that caused the disqualification through the Employee Plans Compliance Resolution System (EPCRS), discussed in Chapter 13.

The Plan Fails the ADP Test – What's Next?

If a plan fails the ADP test, it must correct the failure in one of five ways.

1.   Make QNECs or QMACs that are considered in determining if the plan meets the ADP test.[116]

2. Limit elective contributions in a manner intended to prevent excess contributions.[117]

3. Distribute the excess contributions.[118]

4. Recharacterize the excess contributions as employee after-tax contributions, if those are allowed by the plan.[119]

5. Combine any of these methods.[120] If a combination of methods is used, the use of QNECs or QMACs are considered before distributions or recharacterizations.

These are the only permissible correction methods. A plan cannot leave the excess contributions unallocated, allocate them to a suspense account, or correct them using the retroactive correction rules under Treasury Regulation Section 1.401(a)(4)-11(g).[121]

A plan can allow an HCE to elect whether to have excess contributions recharacterized or distributed. If a highly compensated employee made both pre-tax contributions and Roth contributions, the plan can allow them to elect whether the excess contributions are attributed to the pre-tax contributions or Roth contributions.[122]

Distributing or recharacterizing excess contributions. If a plan still fails the ADP test after any QNECs and QMACs are considered and attempting to prevent excess contributions, the plan is left with distributing the excess contributions or, if the plan allows employee after-tax contributions, the excess contributions can be recharacterized as employee contributions.

Determining the excess contributions. The amount of excess contributions is the excess of the total employer contributions for HCEs for the plan year over the maximum amount of HCEs' contributions permitted if the plan meets the ADP test.

Example 11. Plan Z, Employer E's 401(k) plan, has three HCEs. Their elective deferrals for the current plan year are:

Employee	Compensation including deferrals	Elective Deferrals	Actual Deferral Ratio
1	$120,000	$9,000	7.5%
2	$110,000	$8,250	7.5%
3	$80,000	$10,000	12.5%

The ADP for the NHCEs is 4.0 percent. This means the maximum ADP for the HCEs is 6.0 percent. The HCEs' ADP, before any corrective action, is 9.17 percent.

The excess contributions for an individual HCE are the amount that the HCE's contributions must be reduced to equal the highest permitted ADR under the plan. The procedure set out in the regulations is to start with the HCE who has the highest ADR and reducing his or her ADR to equal the ADR of the HCE with the next highest ADR. If the ADP test can be met with a smaller reduction, the smaller reduction is used. The process continues until the ADRs have been reduced enough for the HCEs' ADP to meet either the 1.25 test or the 2 + 2 test. While this procedure is used to determine the excess contributions, it is not used to determine the required reduction in each HCE's contribution.

In *Example 11*, Employee 3's ADR would be reduced to 7.5 percent, reducing his or her contributions to $6,000. This reduces the ADP to 7.5 percent, still above the 6 percent allowable. The ADPs for all three employees must then be reduced to 6 percent each, reducing their contributions to $7,200, $6,600, and $4,800, respectively. The maximum allowable contribution for the HCEs is $18,600. The excess contributions are $8,650 ($27,250 total contributions minus $18,600).

The same result should be produced by multiplying the HCEs' compensation by the maximum ADP for the HCEs. In Example 11, this would involve multiplying the maximum ADP of 6 percent by $310,000, the total compensation for the HCEs. This also produces a maximum contribution for the HCEs of $18,600 and excess contributions of $8,650.

Allocating the excess contributions among HCEs. This excess is allocated to the HCEs based on the amount of contributions by or for each employee. This means that the contributions of the HCEs with the largest contributions are reduced first until reaching the amount of contributions of the HCE with the next most contributions. The order of reduction is based on the amount of contributions and ignores the ADR. A smaller amount can be allocated if sufficient to allocate all of the excess contributions. Once the reduced contributions of the HCEs with the largest contributions equal the contributions of the HCEs with the next highest contribution, the reduction applies to the contributions of all HCEs at that contribution level. If a HCE makes elective contributions to more than one plan of the employer, the allocation is limited to the amount that HCE actually contributed to the plan during the year. The process continues until all of the excess contributions have been allocated among the HCEs.[123]

Example 12. Same facts as *Example 11*. To allocate the $8,650 of excess contributions, Plan Z first reduces Employee 3's contributions by $1,000, to $9,000. It then reduces both Employee 1 and Employee 3's contributions by $750 each, to $8,250. Finally, it must reduce the contributions of all three employees by $2,050 each, to $6,200.

Employee	Compensation including deferrals	Elective Deferrals after Distribution	Actual Deferral Ratio
1	$120,000	$6,200	5.17%
2	$110,000	$6,200	5.64%
3	$80,000	$6,200	7.75%

The highly compensated employees' ADP is not retested after the excess contributions are distributed, even though the revised ADP of 6.17 percent still exceeds the maximum allowable ADP of 6.0 percent.

Allocating plan income to excess contributions. In addition to the excess contributions, the plan must also determine and distribute the income allocable to the excess contributions. For this purpose, only the income on the excess contributions allocable to the plan year must be distributed. The plan does not have to distribute income attributable to the excess contributions earned between the end of the plan year and the date of distribution. The regulations allow plans to use any reasonable method to compute the income allocable to the excess contributions, if the method:

- does not violate the nondiscrimination rules of Section 401(a)(4);

- is applied consistently for all participants and all corrective distributions under the plan for the plan year; and

- is used by the plan for allocating income to participants' accounts.[124]

The income allocable to excess contributions must be determined no more than seven days before the distribution.[125]

The regulation provides an alternative method. A plan using that method would first determine the income for the plan year allocable to elective contributions and amounts treated as elective contributions. It would then multiply that income by a fraction, using the employee's excess contributions for the plan year as the numerator and the beginning of the year plan balance of elective contributions and amounts treated as elective contributions plus any additional contributions for the plan year as the denominator.

Example 13. The plan determines that the income allocable to the excess contributions is $5,000. At the beginning of the year, an HCE's account balance is $100,000 and the employee made $8,000 of elective contributions, including $1,000 found to be an excess contribution. Under the alternative method, the allocable income is:

$$\$5,000 \times (\$1,000/(\$100,000 + \$8,000)) = \$46.30$$

Distributing excess contributions. To avoid disqualification, the plan must distribute the excess contributions allocated to each HCE and the related income within 12 months after the end of the plan year. The plan may make the corrective distribution without regard to any other provision of the law.[126] The employer must designate the distribution as a corrective distribution. If an HCE receives a distribution of his or her entire account before the corrective distribution is made, a portion of the distribution is deemed a corrective distribution to the extent one would have been made to that employee.[127]

If the plan completely terminates in the year an excess contribution occurs, the corrective distribution must be made as soon as administratively feasible after the date of the plan termination. It must occur no later than 12 months after the date of the plan termination.[128]

The corrective distribution does not require any consent from the employee or the employee's spouse.[129] They are treated as employer contributions for purposes of Section 404 and Section 415.[130] If the plan makes a partial distribution to an HCE, it is treated as a pro rata distribution of the excess contributions and allocable income.[131]

Tax treatment of correction distributions. Corrective distributions are included in the HCE's income for the year distributed. The 10 percent penalty of Section 72(t) does not apply.[132] Designated Roth contributions distributed as part of a corrective distribution are not included in income but the allocable income is.[133]

Recharacterizing excess contributions. A plan may allow HCEs to elect to have the excess contributions treated as having been distributed to them and then contributed to the plan.[134] If the plan does not allow employee contributions, the excess contributions cannot be recharacterized. A recharacterization causes the excess contributions to be treated as employee contributions for purposes of Section 72, the nondiscrimination rules under Section 401(a)(4) and Section 401(m) and Treasury Regulation Section 1.401(k)-2 and the distribution limitation of Treasury Regulation Section 1.401(k)-1(d). The recharacterization must be reported as employee contributions.[135] For all other purposes, they are treated as employer contributions.

The recharacterization is deemed to have occurred on the date that the last HCE with excess contributions to be recharacterized receives the required notice that the recharacterization was treated as employee contributions. The recharacterization must be made within 2½ months after the end of the plan year. The total of the recharacterized excess contributions and the HCE's employee contributions cannot exceed the maximum amount of employee contributions permitted for the plan year in which the excess contributions were made. For this purpose, the maximum amount is computed before the actual contribution percentage limit is applied.[136]

Applicability of the 10 percent Excise Tax on Excess Contributions. The plan must meet the deadline of the end of the following plan year to distribute excess contributions to avoid disqualification. To avoid the Section 4979 10 percent excise tax on excess contributions imposed on the employer, the excess contributions must be distributed within 2½ months after the end of the plan year. In addition, QNECs or QMACs do not need to be made within the 2½ month period if they are timely made. This period is extended to six months if the plan includes an eligible automatic contribution arrangement.[137] The six-month period applies only if all HCEs and NHCEs are covered by the plan for the entire plan year (or the portion for which they are eligible to participate).[138]

The Plan Fails the ACP Test – What's Next?

If a plan fails the ACP test, its options are very similar to those available if it fails the ADP test. The plan may (1) make additional contributions considered for purposes of the ACP test; (2) distribute or forfeit the "excess aggregate contributions" by the end of the following plan year;[139] or (3) a combination of these methods. In addition, it may limit employee contributions or matching contributions to prevent excess aggregate contributions from being made. If a plan chooses a combination of these methods, it must first consider the additional contributions made before making any distributions or forfeitures.[140] "Excess aggregate contributions" are the excess of the total matching contributions and employee contributions (and any QNECs or elective contribution included in computing the ACP) actually made for HCEs for the plan year less the maximum contributions permitted under the ACP test.[141]

Corrections cannot be made by forfeiting vested matching contributions, distributing nonvested matching contributions, recharacterizing matching contributions, or not making required matching contributions. In addition, the excess aggregate contributions cannot remain unallocated or be allocated to a suspense account for future allocation. The retroactive correction rules of Treasury Regulation Section 1.401(a)(4)-11(g) are not available.[142]

If a plan chooses to make corrective distributions, the same method used to allocate distributions made to correct a failed ADP test among the HCEs is used to allocate the distributions made to correct a failed ACP test.

If a plan provides for the forfeiture of matching contributions, they are treated as employer contributions, even if distributed from the plan. Any forfeitures reallocated to other participants' accounts are included in determining if the annual contribution limits are met.[143]

As with corrective distributions for the ADP test, a plan's distribution of excess aggregate contributions may be made without regard to any other provision of the law[144] or any notice or consent that would otherwise be provided.[145] The tax treatment for corrective distributions made to correct a failed ACP test is the same as the tax treatment for corrective distributions for a failed ADP test. If a corrective distribution of designated Roth contributions is made, those distributions are not taxable but the income allocable to them is.[146] Corrective distributions are not considered in determining if a plan meets the required minimum distribution (RMD) requirements.[147]

Endnotes

1.   Treas. Reg. §1.401(k)-1(e)(7).
2.   IRC Sec. 401(a)(4).
3.   IRC Sec. 401(k)(11).
4.   IRC Sec. 401(k)(12).
5.   IRC Sec. 401(k)(12).

6. IRC Sec. 414(x)

7. IRC Sec. 410(b)(1)(A).

8. IRC Sec. 410(b)(1)(B).

9. IRC Sec. 410(b)(2).

10. Treas. Reg. §1.410(b)-2(c).

11. Treas. Reg. §1.410(b)-3(b)(1).

12. Treas. Reg. §1.410(b)-3(a)(2).

13. Treas. Reg. §1.410(b)-3(a)(3), Example 2.

14. Treas. Reg. §1.410(b)-6(a)(1).

15. Treas. Reg. §1.410(b)-6(b)(1). Under Section 410(a)(1), the plan cannot require an employee to complete a period of service beyond the later of attaining age 21 or completing one year of service.

16. Treas. Reg. §1.410(b)-6(c). All non-resident alien employees who receive earned income that is considered income from sources within the U.S. may be excluded if all of the earned income is exempt from U.S. income tax under an income tax treaty.

17. Treas. Reg. §1.410(b)-6(d).

18. Treas. Reg. §1.410(b)-6(e). This exclusion is not available to satisfy the nondiscrimination classification requirement of Section 410(b)(5)(B). A qualified separate line of business is defined in Treas. Reg. §1.414(r)-1(b).

19. Treas. Reg. §1.410(b)-6(f).

20. Treas. Reg. §1.410(b)-6(g)(2).

21. Treas. Reg. §1.410(b)-6(g)(3).

22. Treas. Reg. §1.410(b)-6(h).

23. Treas. Reg. §1.410(b)-6(i).

24. Treas. Reg. §1.410(b)-2(b)(2).

25. Treas. Reg. §1.410(b)-9.

26. Treas. Reg. §1.410(b)-2(b)(2)(ii), Example 1.

27. Treas. Reg. §1.410(b)-2(b)(2)(ii), Example 2.

28. Treas. Reg. §1.410(b)-2(b)(3).

29. Treas. Reg. §1.410(b)-4(b).

30. *Ibid.*

31. *Ibid.*

32. Treas. Reg. §1.410(b)-4(c)(2).

33. Treas. Reg. §1.410(b)-4(c)(4)(i).

34. Treas. Reg. §1.410(b)-4(c)(3).

35. Treas. Reg. §1.410(b)-4(c)(3)(ii).

36. Treas. Reg. §1.410(b)-4(c)(3)(ii)(A).

37. Treas. Reg. §1.410(b)-4(c)(3)(ii)(B).

38. Treas. Reg. §1.410(b)-4(c)(3)(ii)(C).

39. Treas. Reg. §1.410(b)-4(c)(3)(ii)(D).

40. Treas. Reg. §1.410(b)-4(c)(3)(ii)(E).

41. Treas. Reg. §1.410(b)-4(c)(5), Example 1.

42. Treas. Reg. §1.410(b)-4(c)(5), Example 2.

43. Treas. Reg. §1.410(b)-4(c)(5), Example 3.

44. Treas. Reg. §1.410(b)-5(a).

45. Treas. Reg. §1.410(b)-5(d)(3)(i).

46. Treas. Reg. §1.410(b)-5(d)(3)(ii).

47. Treas. Reg. §1.410(b)-5(d).

48. Treas. Reg. §1.410(b)-5(d)(4).

49. Treas. Reg. §1.410(b)-5(d)(2).

50. Treas. Reg. §1.410(b)-5(d)(6).

51. Treas. Reg. §1.410(b)-5(d)(7).

52. Treas. Reg. §1.410(b)-5(c).

53. Treas. Reg. §1.410(b)-5(b).

54. Treas. Reg. §1.401(k)-1(e)(7).

55. IRC Sec. 401(k)(3)(A)(ii)(I).

56. IRC Sec. 401(k)(3)(A)(ii)(II).

57. IRC Sec. 401(k)(3)(B).

58. Treas. Reg. §1.401(k)-2(a)(2)(ii).

59. Treas. Reg. §1.401(k)-1(e)(7).

60. Treas. Reg. §1.401(k)-2(a)(2)(ii).

61. Treas. Reg. §1.401(k)-2(c)(2).

62. Treas. Reg. §1.401(k)-2(c)(1)(i).

63. Treas. Reg. §1.401(k)-2(c)(1)(ii).

64. Treas. Reg. §1.401(k)-2(c)(4).

65. Treas. Reg. §1.401(k)-2(c)(4)(iii)(A).

66. Treas. Reg. §1.401(k)-2(c)(4)(ii).

67. Treas. Reg. §1.401(k)-2(a)(7), Example 2.

68. Treas. Reg. §1.401(k)-2(a)(7), Example 3.

69. IRC Sec. 401(k)(9); Treas. Reg. §1.401(k)-6.

70. Treas. Reg. §1.415-2(d)(3).

71. Treas. Reg. §1.415-2(d)(4).

72. IRC Sec. 415(c)(3)(D).

73. IR 2013-86, October 31, 2013.

74. Treas. Regs. §§1.401(k)-6, 1.401(k)-1(c), 1.401(k)-1(d).

75. Treas. Reg. §1.401(k)-2(a)(6)(i).

76. Treas. Reg. §1.401(k)-2(a)(6)(vi).

77. IRC Sec. 401(k)(3)(D)(i).

78. IRC Sec. 401(k)(3)(D)(ii); Treas. Reg. §1.401(k)-2(a)(6).

79. IRC Sec. 401(k)(3)(E).

80. Treas. Reg. §1.401(k)-2(a)(1)(ii).

81. Treas. Reg. §1.401(k)-2(a)(4)(ii).

82. Treas. Reg. §1.401(k)-2(a)(4)(ii).

83. Treas. Reg. §1.414(v)-1(d)(2)(i).

84. IRC Sec. 401(k)(12)(A).

85. IRC Sec. 401(k)(12)(B).

86. IRC Sec. 401(k)(12)(B)(ii).
87. IRC Sec. 401(k)(12)(B)(iii).
88. IRC Sec. 401(k)(12)(C).
89. IRC Sec. 401(k)(12)(D).
90. Treas. Reg. §1.401(m)-2.
91. IRC Sec. 401(m)(5)(A).
92. IRC Sec. 401(m)(4)(A)(i).
93. IRC Sec. 401(m)(4)(A)(ii).
94. Treas. Reg. §1.401(m)-1(a)(2)(C).
95. Treas. Reg. §1.401(m)-2(a)(4)(iii).
96. Treas. Reg. §1.401(m)-2(a)(5).
97. *Ibid.*
98. Treas. Reg. §1.401(m)-1(a)(3).
99. Treas. Reg. §1.401(m)-1(a)(3)(ii).
100. IRC Sec. 402(g)(8).
101. Treas. Reg. §1.401(m)-1(a)(3).
102. Treas. Reg. §1.401(m)-2(c)(3).
103. IRC Sec. 401(m)(11)(A).
104. IRC Sec. 401(m)(11)(B).
105. IRC Sec. 416(c)(2).
106. IRC Sec. 416(b).
107. IRC Sec. 416(g).
108. IRC Sec. 416(i)(1)(A).
109. IR 2013-86, October 31, 2013.
110. Treas. Regs. §§1.410(b)-7, 1.401(k)-2(a)(3)(ii), 1.401(m)-1(b)(4), 1.401(m)-2(a)(3)(ii).
111. Treas. Reg. §1.410(b)-7(c)(1).
112. Treas. Regs. §§1.410(b)-7(d)(1), 1.410(b)-7(d)(5).
113. IRC Sec. 401(k)(3)(A), flush language.
114. Treas. Reg. §1.401(m)-2(a)(3)(ii)(A).
115. IRC Sec. 402(b)(4)(B).
116. Treas. Reg. §1.401(k)-2(b)(1)(i)(A).
117. Treas. Reg. §1.401(k)-2(b)(1)(ii).
118. Treas. Reg. §1.401(k)-2(b)(1)(i)(B).
119. Treas. Reg. §1.401(k)-2(b)(1)(i)(C).
120. Treas. Reg. §1.401(k)-2(b)(1)(ii).
121. Treas. Reg. §1.401(k)-2(b)(1)(iii).
122. Treas. Reg. §1.401(k)-2(b)(1)(ii).
123. Treas. Reg. §1.401(k)-2(b)(2).
124. Treas. Reg. §1.401(k)-2(b)(2)(iv).
125. *Ibid.*
126. IRC Sec. 401(k)(8) flush language.

127. Treas. Reg. §1.401(k)-2(b)(2)(v).

128. *Ibid.*

129. Treas. Reg. §1.401(k)-2(b)(2)(vii)(A).

130. Treas. Reg. §1.401(k)-2(b)(2)(vii)(B).

131. Treas. Reg. §1.401(k)-2(b)(2)(vii)(D).

132. Treas. Reg. §1.401(k)-2(b)(2)(vi)(A).

133. Treas. Reg. §1.401(k)-2(b)(2)(vi)(C).

134. IRC Sec. 401(k)(8)(A)(ii).

135. Treas. Reg. §1.401(k)-2(b)(3)(ii).

136. Treas. Reg. §1.401(k)-2(b)(3)(iii)(C).

137. IRC Sec. 4979(f).

138. Treas. Reg. §54.4979-1(c).

139. IRC Sec. 401(m)(6)(A); Treas. Reg. §1.401(m)-2(b)(1).

140. Treas. Reg. §1.401(m)-2(b)(1)(ii).

141. IRC Sec. 401(m)(6)(B).

142. Treas. Reg. §1.401(m)-2(b)(1)(iii).

143. Treas. Reg. §1.401(m)-2(b)(3)(ii).

144. IRC Sec. 401(m)(6)(A).

145. Treas. Reg. §1.401(m)-2(b)(3)(i).

146. Treas. Reg. §1.401(m)-2(b)(2)(vi).

147. Treas. Reg. §1.401(m)-2(b)(3)(iii).

Chapter 6

Designing the Plan

Introduction

All qualified plans, including 401(k) plans, must be in writing. To establish a 401(k) plan, the employer can use a volume submitter plan with the guidance of a consultant who prepared the plan; adopt a master and prototype plan offered by an institution such as a mutual fund company, life insurance company, or stock brokerage or have a custom-designed plan prepared especially for it by an attorney. Naturally, a custom-designed plan is generally the most expensive and offers the most design flexibility while a master and prototype plan is generally the least expensive while sacrificing design flexibility with a volume submitter plan generally falling in the middle on both cost and design flexibility.

An employer that offers a 401(k) plan can design the plan to meet its objectives, as long as the plan design complies with the guidelines set out in the Code and regulations. Surprisingly, these guidelines still offer considerable flexibility for the plan to meet the nondiscrimination tests. If an employer wants, the plan design can skew the employer contributions toward the owner and other highly compensated employees (HCEs), especially in the case of closely-held businesses, to make it more attractive to put a 401(k) plan in place. Appendix A provides a checklist for use in designing a 401(k) plan.

Common Plan Design Factors

Choices made in designing the plan will affect employee participation, which impacts the plan's ability to meet the nondiscrimination tests. Unlike most defined benefit plans, in which eligible employees automatically become participants and cannot opt out, 401(k) plans traditionally have required participants to affirmatively elect to contribute to the plan, how much to contribute, and how their contributions will be invested.

Law changes since 2001 have allowed employers to select plan designs that automate the plan participation process. Automatic enrollment, automatic increases in contribution rates, and default investments make it more likely that many employees will participate in the employer's 401(k) plan.

Eligibility

Plans generally have to allow employees who are at least age 21 and have completed one year of service to participate in the plan. Reducing or eliminating those requirements can increase a plan's participation rate. A Deloitte survey conducted in 2012 reported that 44 percent of 401(k) plans had no minimum age requirement, 24 percent limited eligibility to employees who were at least age 18, and 32 percent required employees to be at least 21.[1] Only 9 percent required an employee to complete one year of service before becoming eligible, with 58 percent offering immediate eligibility, 28 percent offering eligibility within three months, and 5 percent offering eligibility between four and six months.[2]

Automatic enrollment and escalation

Almost half (48 percent) of plans that use automatic enrollment use 3 percent as the default deferral percentage.[3] Almost the same percentage (49 percent) includes an escalating contribution feature, with 18 percent of plans tying it to the Automatic Enrollment feature and 31 percent as a separate feature.[4] Most plans (61 percent) provided a 1 percent default increase with 35 percent allowing the employee to choose.[5] Allowing the employee the choice could defeat the purpose of the automatic escalation, unless the plan provided a default increase if the employee did not make an election.

In 82 percent of the plans, the default investment election for automatic enrollment was a lifecycle or target date fund.[6] More than 7 of 10 plans offered a Qualified Default Investment Alternative (QDIA) but only 16 percent had a Qualified Automatic Contribution Arrangement (QACA).[7]

Roth 401(k)

In that 2012 Deloitte study, slightly more than half (53 percent) of plans offer a Roth 401(k) feature.[8] The attractiveness of the pre-tax nature of regular 401(k) plan contributions is shown in the percentage of participants who choose to make contributions to a Roth 401(k). Sixty-three percent of the plans reported 5 percent or less of participants make contributions to Roth 401(k) accounts.[9]

Matching Contributions

The overwhelming number of plans (94 percent) offer some form of employer contributions. The most popular were matching contributions, offered by 67 percent of plans; followed by 23 percent of plans offering both matching and profit-sharing contributions; and 4 percent offering solely profit-sharing contributions.[10] Employers use a variety of matching formulas, with 21 percent matching 50 percent of the first 6 percent of the employee's contribution and 10 percent matching 100 percent of the first 6 percent. No other formula was used by more than 10 percent of the respondents.[11]

Eighty-three percent of the plans used the same matching formula for all employees.[12] The same percentage calculated and deposited the match each pay period.[13] Matching contribution forfeitures were used to reduce employer contributions by 64 percent of the plans.[14]

Vesting

The 2011 Hewitt Trends and Experience Survey reported that 43 percent of plans vest employer contributions immediately. For plans with vesting schedules, the most common was 3-year cliff vesting, used by 18 percent of plans and 5-year graduated vesting, used by 16 percent of plans.[15]

Plan Loans

Access to plan contributions if necessary while working is an important consideration for many plan participants. The Hewitt survey found that 94 percent of the surveyed plans offered loans, with 98 percent offering general purpose loans and 82 percent offering home loans.[16] Plans generally limit participants to no more than two outstanding loans.[17] However, we suggest that plan sponsors consider limiting loans to one outstanding loan at a time, to be repaid by salary deduction to simplify administration for both plan and participant.

Hardship Withdrawals

Hardship withdrawals offer participants with another way to access the funds in their 401(k) account, although on a much more restrictive basis than plan loans. The Hewitt survey showed 93 percent of plans offer hardship withdrawals.[18]

Safe Harbor Plans

According to the IRS, 43 percent of 401(k) plans are safe harbor plans.[19] These plans automatically meet the nondiscrimination requirements so the employer does not have to conduct nondiscrimination testing. Plans can choose from several options to qualify as a safe harbor plan.

Types of Plan Documents

Master and Prototype (M&P) Plans

M&P plans consist of a basic plan document, an adoption agreement, and a trust or custodial agreement. The trust or custodial agreement may be included in the basic plan document. The only difference between a master plan and a prototype plan is that a master plan uses the same trust or custodial account for the joint use of all adopting employers while a prototype plan provides a separate trust or custodial account for each employer.[20]

The "basic plan document"[21] contains the non-elective provisions that apply to all adopting employers. It cannot include any options or blanks to be completed unless it is a "flexible plan." Flexible plans can contain optional provisions in the basic plan document or the adoption agreement.[22] Any option must be offered to all adopting employers.[23] The options are limited to:

- Investment provisions describing the plan methods of investing the trust or custodial funds, including funding options, the availability of loans and self-directed investments[24]

- Administrative provisions such as how responsibilities are allocated among fiduciaries, the resignation or replacement of fiduciaries, claims procedures, and record-keeping requirements[25]

- CODAs[26]

The IRS will issue "opinion letters" to sponsors or M&P mass submitters concerning whether the M&P plan meets the qualification requirements.

The M&P plan can be either "standardized" or "non-standardized." A standardized plan is designed to satisfy the qualification requirements. The employer may generally rely on the opinion letter provided to the M&P plan sponsor as a determination letter.[27] A non-standardized plan provides adopting employers choices that do not automatically comply with the nondiscrimination requirements. As a result, the employer may not rely on a favorable opinion letter as a determination letter.[28]

A mass submitter is an individual or business that has an established place of business where it is accessible every business day and submits advisory letter applications on behalf of at least 30 unaffiliated practitioners that each sponsor, on a word-for-word identical basis, the same specimen plan. The 30 unaffiliated practitioners include the mass submitter. Whether a practitioner is affiliated is determined under the same rules that apply to controlled groups of employers, discussed in Chapter 11. In addition, a law firm, accounting firm, consulting firm, or similar firm is considered affiliated with its partners, members, associates, etc. The mass submitter must have 30 unaffiliated practitioners for each specimen plan to qualify as a mass submitter for that plan.[29] "Word-for-word" does not mean that the plans must be identical. Minor changes are allowed if the changes do not require an in-depth technical review.[30]

An advantage of using a mass submitter is that it usually has reduced procedural requirements and receives expedited treatment from the IRS. This reflects the large number of sponsors it represents and the number of identical or near-identical plans it submits to the IRS.[31]

Adopting an M&P plan is generally the least expensive option for an employer, both in terms of set-up costs and ongoing administrative costs. In exchange for a lower cost compared to other types of plans, the employer generally gives up flexibility in plan design. In addition, the M&P sponsor generally limits the participants' investment options to those offered by the M&P sponsor.

Planning Tip: Make certain all the plan design choices in the adoption agreement are complete and conform to the guidance under the statutes, IRS regulations, and notices and that the adoption agreement itself is then properly executed when a master or prototype plan document is used.

Volume Submitter (VS) Plans

A VS plan is a plan prepared by a VS practitioner. It can be either a specimen plan of a VS submitter or a plan of a VS practitioner that is substantially similar to the VS practitioner's approved specimen plan.[32] The IRS issues advisory letters to VS practitioners or VS mass submitters on the acceptability of a specimen plan's form and any related or custodial account documents under Section 401(a).[33]

A VS plan includes the specimen plan document, and a trust or custodial account. The specimen plan document provides employers with options for different provisions of the plan document, such as the eligibility and vesting requirements. The employer then chooses the provisions that will apply to its plan. It may also include an adoption agreement that allows the employer to choose additional elective provisions.

A VS practitioner is an individual or business that has an established place of business where it is accessible every business day and that represents to the IRS that it has at least 30 employer-clients that are all reasonably expected to adopt a plan that is substantially similar to the VS practitioner's specimen plan.[34]

A business can also qualify as a mass submitter of a VS plan. As with mass submitters of M&P plans, VS mass submitters usually have reduced procedural requirements and receive expedited treatment from the IRS.

The fees charged by the VS practitioner that sponsors the plan will generally be substantially less than the cost of having an individually designed plan drafted. The administration expenses can also be less than those for an individually designed plan.

Custom-Designed Plans

A custom-designed plan can be based on a VS or M&P plan and modified by an attorney from the original to accomplish the client's objectives or a document that is prepared specifically for the client. As long as the plan complies with the statutory requirements for a qualified plan, the employer can design the plan to meet its goals. The employer is responsible for ensuring that the plan document is amended when necessary to remain in compliance with the applicable law. A custom-designed plan requires a custom-designed summary plan description (SPD).

Planning Tip: The cost of having a custom-designed plan drafted and administered can be substantial. As a result, employers normally use custom-designed plans only if they cannot accomplish their plan goals in any other way.

Designing with Eligibility Requirements

The plan *must* comply with the minimum participation standards set out in Section 410(a) to be a qualified plan. As long as it meets those requirements, employers can use the eligibility requirements to limit the number of employees who can participate and thereby benefit from the plan. These eligibility requirements were discussed in detail in Chapter 2.

The eligibility requirements can be combined with the vesting requirements of Section 411 to reduce the number of employees who can actually participate and benefit from a plan.

Planning Tip: An employer's decision to use a *safe harbor plan design* to satisfy the nondiscrimination test will limit its ability to reduce the employees who participate and can benefit from the plan. Therefore, use of a safe harbor design involves a series of trade-offs.

Two of the most common exclusions are:

1. for employees who are under age 21 or

2. who have less than one year of service.

Employees under 21 need not be covered, even if they have completed one year of service. An employer whose workforce includes many workers in either or both of these categories may want to exclude those workers from participation in its 401(k) plan. Also, because these workers are not eligible employees, they are not included in the nondiscrimination testing. An employer may extend the one year of service requirement to two years if it is willing to provide 100 percent vesting at the end of two years.[35]

A plan and employer receives three benefits by excluding employees who do not meet the minimum participation standards.

1. No employer contributions need to be made to accounts for those employees.

2. The employer does not have to provide excluded employees with any notices or other information that must be provided to participants, whether it is a notice of eligibility, SPD, or summary annual report.

3. Because the plan does not have to set up an account for the employee, it will not incur any plan fees charged on a per-account basis.

Example 1. Company B operates a restaurant and has 30 employees. It experiences significant turnover. Twenty of the employees are under age 21, have less than one year of service, or both. By providing that an employee does not become eligible until the later of the employee becoming age 21 or completing one year of service, those employees can be excluded. Company B only needs to include the remaining 10 employees in its plan.

New companies that want to offer a 401(k) plan so the owners and key employees can make contributions may want to use a shorter minimum participation requirement. If the plan allows employees who have at least three months of service to contribute, once an employee has three months of service, they can contribute and also become eligible for any employer matching contributions.

Example 2. Company C began operations on April 1. Its owners and key employees want to begin making contributions to a 401(k) plan as quickly as possible. The plan allows employees who have completed at least three months of service to make contributions. On July 1, all employees who were with the company when it started become eligible to make contributions.

Designing Using Safe Harbor 401(k) Plans

Safe harbor plans offer plans and employers a trade-off. In return for the employer making the required contributions and complying with other rules, the plan can dispense with the nondiscrimination tests and all the recordkeeping necessary to do that testing. Employees benefit by having access to a 401(k) plan and a specified level of employer contributions, regardless of their personal contribution.

Four safe harbor designs are available for plans to choose, depending on the employer's objectives.

1. *Section 401(k)(12) safe harbor.* Plans offering minimum matching contributions or nonelective contributions;[36]

2. *Section 401(k)(13) safe harbor.* Plans offering qualified automatic contribution arrangements with a minimum matching contribution or nonelective contribution;[37]

3. *Section 414(x) safe harbor.* Combined defined benefit plans and 401(k) plans (so-called "DB/k Plans");[38] or

4. *SIMPLE 401(k) plans.*

Section 401(k)(12) Plans Offering Minimum Matching Contributions or Nonelective Contributions

Overview

The traditional safe harbor 401(k) plan requires the employer to make specified contributions for non-highly compensated employees (NHCEs), meet withdrawal and vesting restrictions, and notify eligible employees of their rights and obligations under the plan. If it does, it satisfies the ADP test (discussed in Chapter 5).[39] If it meets those requirements and complies with limits on matching contributions, it will also satisfy the ACP test for matching contributions.[40] There is no provision for satisfying the ACP test for employee after-tax contributions using this safe harbor. The safe harbor contributions must be fully vested and subject to the same distribution restrictions as elective deferrals.[41]

Contribution Requirement

A plan can meet the contribution requirement in one of two ways.

1. Matching contributions for NHCEs

2. Nonelective contributions for NHCEs of at least 3 percent

Safe harbor compensation. Determining compensation for purposes of the safe harbor requires a trip through the Code and regulations. The safe harbor regulation, Treasury Regulation Section 1.401(k)-3(b)(2), sends you to the Treasury Regulation Section §1.401-6 definition of compensation, leading you to Section 414(s) and Treasury Regulation Section 1.414(s)-1, without the provision in the last sentence of a paragraph within that regulation. That regulation provides several different definitions that a plan can use. The gist of the regulation is that a plan's definition of compensation for purposes of the safe harbor cannot by design favor HCEs, must be reasonable (as defined in the regulation) and must satisfy the regulation's nondiscrimination test.[42] It cannot exclude compensation above a specified amount.[43] It is possible for a plan to use a different definition of compensation to compute the contribution limit and the safe harbor contribution.

Matching contributions. The regulations provide both a basic matching formula and an enhanced matching formula. The basic matching formula provides matching contributions that are:

*   100 percent of the employee's elective deferrals, up to 3 percent of compensation; plus

*   50 percent of the employee's elective deferrals between 3 percent and 5 percent of compensation.[44]

This formula produces a maximum 4 percent of compensation matching contribution. In addition, contributions cannot be made to any HCE at a higher rate than for a NHCE.[45]

The plan can also provide an enhanced matching formula. The enhanced matching formula provides a matching contribution that is always at least the matching contributions that would be provided under the basic matching formula.

> *Example 3.* Plan D provides a matching contribution of 100 percent of an employee's elective deferrals up to 4 percent of compensation. Plan D's formula is an enhanced matching formula. It satisfies the safe harbor contribution requirement because the matching contributions are always at least equal to the matching contributions provided under the basic formula.[46]

> *Example 4.* Plan E provides a matching contribution of 100 percent of an employee's elective deferrals up to 2 percent of compensation and 50 percent of elective deferrals up to 6 percent of compensation. This formula does not qualify as a safe harbor matching contribution. An employee who contributes more than 2 percent of compensation but less than 6 percent of compensation will receive a matching contribution that is less than provided under the basic formula.

A plan can match both elective deferrals and employee contributions if the plan either treats both the elective deferrals and employee contributions equally for matching contributions or the matching contributions on elective deferrals are not affected by the amount of employee contributions.[47] If the safe harbor matching contributions are made to the plan by the last day of the next plan year quarter, the contributions can be made separately for each payroll period or for all periods ending with or within each month or quarter of a plan year.[48]

Under the safe harbor, the plan can only impose restrictions on elective contributions by NHCEs that fall into one of the following categories:

- The plan may limit when an eligible employee can make or change a plan election. The employee must have a reasonable opportunity to make or change an election, including a reasonable time after receipt of the required notice about the plan's safe harbor matching contribution. Thirty days is considered a reasonable period for making or changing an election.[49]

- A plan can restrict the amount of an employee's elective deferrals, as long as the permitted deferrals are enough to receive the maximum matching contributions for the year or any lesser amount. The plan can require that the deferral election be made in whole percentages or whole dollar amounts.[50]

- The plan can limit the types of compensation that an eligible employee may defer, as long as the definition of compensation qualifies as a reasonable definition of compensation under Treasury Regulation Section 1.414(s)-1(d)(2).[51]

- The plan can limit an eligible employee's elective contributions to comply with the limitations on contributions or because the employee took a hardship distribution and cannot make elective contributions for six months under Treasury Regulation Section 1.401(k)-1(d)(3)(iv)(E).[52]

Nonelective contribution requirement. The plan meets this entire requirement if the employer must make an annual contribution of at least 3 percent of the employee's safe harbor compensation.[53]

Planning Tip: A 3 percent safe harbor nonelective employer contribution into a 401(k) plan can help the plan with three important issues as to HCEs: 1) enable the plan to pass the ADP test; 2) help it pass the contribution allocation discrimination test; and 3) help it to meet the top-heavy plan contribution requirement.

Notice Requirement

Each year the plan must notify each eligible employee in writing of the employee's rights and obligations under the plan. The plan may provide the notice electronically if the plan complies with the rules in Treasury Regulation Section 1.401(a)-21. The notice must be sufficiently accurate and comprehensive to inform the employee of his or her rights and obligations under the plan and be written in a way that is calculated to be understood by the average eligible employee.[54]

To be sufficiently accurate and comprehensive, the notice must accurately describe:

1. The matching contribution or nonelective contribution formula used by the plan, including the levels of matching contributions, if any, under the plan.

2. Any other contributions under the plan or matching contributions to another plan based on elective contributions or employee contributions under the plan, including potential discretionary matching contributions, and when such contributions are made.

3. The plan to which the contributions will be made, if different than the 401(k) plan.

4. The type and amount of compensation that may be deferred.

5. How to make a deferral election, including any administrative requirements.

6. When an election can be made.

7. Withdrawal and vesting provisions.

8. Information that makes it easy to obtain additional information about the plan, including telephone numbers, addresses, and e-mail addresses.[55]

The notice can refer to the portions of the plan's SPD that address items 2 through 4 if the SPD has been provided to the employees or is made available with the notice.

The plan must make the notice available within a reasonable time before the beginning of the plan year. In the year an employee becomes eligible, it must be made available within a reasonable time before the employee becomes eligible. Whether a notice is provided on a timely basis is based on a facts-and-circumstances test. Fortunately, the regulations provide that a notice is deemed timely if it's provided at least 30 days but no more than 90 days before the beginning of the plan year. For an employee who becomes eligible less than 90 days before the beginning of the plan year, the notice is timely if it is provided before the employee becomes eligible but no more than 90 days before.[56]

Plan Year Requirements

A plan must generally adopt the safe harbor provisions before the beginning of the plan year and those provisions remain in effect for an entire 12-month period. The initial plan year can be less than 12 months, as long as it is at least three months. A newly established employer may use a shorter period if it establishes the plan as soon as administratively feasible. A plan can have a short year and not violate the 12-month requirement because it changes its plan year as long as the plan qualified as a safe harbor plan for the previous plan year and the next plan year. If the next plan year is less than 12 months, the plan must qualify as a safe harbor plan for the 12 months following the end of the year of the change. The plan's final year can be less than 12 months if the plan qualifies as a safe harbor plan through the date of termination and meets additional requirements.[57]

Plan Amendments

With limited exceptions, a safe harbor plan cannot be amended during the plan year to make changes to the safe harbor provisions of the plan for the current plan year.[58] One exception allows a plan that is using the current year testing method to adopt safe harbor nonelective contributions for the current year no later than 30 days before the end of the plan year. A plan can only change to the safe harbor nonelective contributions if the notice, as provided to employees, states that the plan may be amended to adopt that method and that a follow-up notice will be provided if the plan is amended rather than stating the safe harbor contributions. If the plan does adopt the safe harbor nonelective contribution method, the follow-up notice concerning the adoption is timely if it is provided at least 30 days before the end of the plan year.[59]

Reduction or suspension of safe harbor matching contributions. An employer can amend the plan to reduce or suspend safe harbor matching contributions on future contributions during the plan year and still meet the nondiscrimination requirements of Section 401(k)(3) if the following requirements are met:

- The plan must provide all eligible employees a supplemental notice explaining the consequences of the suspension or reduction of matching contributions, how to change the amount they are contributing to the plan, and the effective date of the amendment.

- The reduction or suspension cannot take effect until the earlier of 30 days after the notice is provided and the date the amendment is adopted.

- Eligible employees must have a reasonable opportunity before the effective date to change their contributions.

- The plan is amended to provide that the ADP test is met for the plan year of the change using the current year testing method.

- The plan qualifies as a safe harbor plan through the effective date of the amendment.

Additional Rules

A safe harbor contribution must be made within 12 months after the end of the plan year. Safe harbor nonelective contributions may be used to satisfy the safe harbor requirements and to determine if a plan meets the general nondiscrimination test of Section 401(a)(4) but not to satisfy the Section 401(l) rules on permitted disparity. They also are not subject to the prohibition on using qualified nonelective contributions (QNECs) to satisfy more than one nondiscrimination test (see Chapter 5 for the rules on QNECs).[60]

The safe harbor contributions can be made either to the plan that includes the 401(k) plan or to another defined contribution plan. If the contributions are made to another plan, both plans must have the same plan year and same eligibility requirements.[61] Even though the safe harbor contributions can be made to a different plan, they cannot be used as safe harbor contributions for more than one plan.[62]

The plan cannot limit the safe harbor contributions to the accounts of employees who were employed on the last day of the plan year.[63] Such a limitation would mean that the plan would not be required to make contributions to all eligible NHCEs.

Additional Employer Contributions

A plan may allow an employer to make contributions that exceed the required safe harbor contributions. Any such contributions are subject to the nondiscrimination tests that apply to non-safe harbor plans discussed in Chapter 5. To maintain their safe harbor status, safe harbor plans are subject to some additional requirements.

Matching contributions based on elective deferrals or employee contributions cannot exceed 6 percent of an employee's safe harbor compensation. In addition, discretionary matching contributions cannot exceed 4 percent of the employee's safe harbor compensation.[64] The rate of the match cannot increase as an employee's elective deferrals and employee contributions increase and the matching contribution rate for HCEs cannot exceed the rate for NHCEs.[65] HCEs can participate in multiple plans of the same employer that provide for matching contributions as long as they aren't eligible to participate in multiple plans simultaneously during the plan year and the matching contributions are based on only compensation the HCEs earned while participating in the plan.[66]

A safe harbor plan is not subject to the top-heavy rules if only safe harbor employer contributions are made to the plan.[67] If the employer makes additional contributions, the plan will be subject to the top-heavy rules.[68] However, if a plan permits discretionary nonelective contributions but none are made, the top-heavy rules do not apply.

Section 401(k)(13) Plans Offering Qualified Automatic Contributions with Safe Harbor Contributions

Overview

The Pension Protection Act of 2006 allows employers to establish a qualified automatic contribution arrangement (QACA). A QACA allows an employer to automatically enroll employees in the plan and establish a minimum contribution level. The goal of automatic enrollment is to help employees increase their retirement savings by eliminating the need for them to make an affirmative election to participate in the plan with a default percentage contributed. Instead, they must opt out of participating or for a lower contribution. A plan that includes a QACA must include safe harbor matching or non-elective contributions and meet certain other requirements. If it does, it will satisfy both the ADP and ACP tests. A QACA can also include an eligible automatic contribution arrangement (EACA) discussed below.

Automatic Contributions

Unless an employee opts out, the employee is treated as having elected to make specific contributions to the plan. It begins to apply after the employee has had a reasonable time to opt out after receipt of the notice that describes the QACA. The default election does not apply if the employee has elected either a different elective contribution or to opt out of any elective contributions. A plan can elect not to apply the default contribution percentage to an employee who was eligible to participate in the plan prior to the QACA effective date and had already made an election concerning the plan.[69]

Contribution Percentage

The contribution percentage must be uniform for all employees (with certain exceptions discussed later) and cannot exceed 10 percent. It must satisfy the minimum percentage rules:[70]

QACA Minimum Contribution Percentages	
Period	**Contribution percentage**
Initial period	3%
Second year	4%
Third year	5%
Subsequent years	6%

The initial period starts when the employee becomes eligible to participate and ends on the last day of the first plan year beginning after the first elective deferral is made for the employee.[71]

> *Example 5.* Plan K includes a QACA and uses the calendar year as its plan year. Employee 1's first elective deferral of 3 percent is made on July 1, Year 0. The 3 percent rate elective deferral continues through December 31, Year 1. For year 2, Employee 1's elective deferral automatically increases to 4 percent unless Employee 1 has made an affirmative election to change it.

Once the initial period starts, an employee's eligibility to make contributions does not affect the computation of the minimum percentage contribution.

> *Example 6.* Employee 2 cannot make contributions for six months due to a hardship withdrawal. During that period, the minimum percentage increases. When Employee 2 can resume contributions, the contribution percentage must be increased to the new minimum.

If an employee leaves the employer and then returns, they may not start over at the minimum 3 percent rate. If an employee did not have any contributions for an entire plan year, the plan can provide that it will disregard prior participation in determining the minimum contribution percentage.[72] Otherwise, the time would continue to run as if the employee was still a participant during that period.

This treatment can be important for both the employee and the employer. For the employee, it may mean a larger elective deferral. If the plan provides for employer matching contributions, it may require the employer to make a larger employer contribution because the contribution percentage will be higher.

> *Example 7.* Company Y's plan includes a QACA that uses the minimum contribution percentages and matching contributions. Employee 3 began work for the employer in 2013 and terminated in 2014. In late 2015, Employee 3 was rehired. Because 2013 is considered the second year, the default contribution percentage is 4 percent. Company Y must match the first 1 percent of Employee 3's contributions at 100 percent and

50 percent of the next 2 percent contribution. If Employee 3 had been rehired in early 2016 and the plan disregards prior participation, Employee 3's contribution percentage would be 3 percent and the company would only have to match 1 percent at 100 percent plus 50 percent of the next 2 percent (unless the employee elected to contribute a higher percentage.)

The regulations permit the following exceptions to the uniformity requirement:[73]

- The percentage can vary based on the number of years since the employee became eligible to participate.

- The contribution rate in effect immediately before the effective date of the default percentage exceeded the default percentage and was not reduced.

- The elective contribution rate was limited to comply with the applicable compensation limits.

- The employee is not permitted to make contributions due to a hardship distribution.

The first exception allows the plan to provide "automatic escalation." Automatic escalation automatically increases the contribution percentage each year until it reaches a specific percentage. The increase can occur on a date other than the first day of a plan year without violating the uniformity requirement.[74]

Employer Contributions

A plan that includes a QACA requires employer contributions, computed in a manner similar to those of a traditional safe harbor plan. The employer must make either matching contributions or minimum nonelective contributions.[75]

The matching contributions for NHCEs must be 100 percent of the first 1 percent of compensation plus 50 percent of the next 50 percent of compensation. This produces a 3.5 percent match for an employee who contributes at least 6 percent of compensation. This is slightly less than the 4 percent match required for a traditional safe harbor plan (100 percent of the first 3 percent plus 50 percent on the next 2 percent). As with a traditional safe harbor plan, the rate of the match cannot increase as an employee's elective deferrals and employee contributions increase and the matching contribution rate for HCEs cannot exceed the rate for NHCEs.[76]

An employee must be fully vested in the employer contributions once the employee has completed two years of service. The plan cannot distribute employer contributions until an employee's elective deferrals could be distributed.[77]

Notice Requirements

As with a traditional safe harbor plan, each year the plan must notify each eligible employee in writing of the employee's rights and obligations under the plan. The plan may provide the notice electronically if it complies with the rules in Treasury Regulation Section 1.401(a)-21. The notice must be sufficiently accurate and comprehensive to inform employees of their rights and obligations under the plan and be written in a way that is calculated to be understood by the average eligible employee.

In addition to the information required for a traditional safe harbor plan, the notice for a QACA must explain:

- the level of elective contributions that will be made for the employee unless the employee makes an affirmative election;

- the employee's right to elect not to have elective contributions made or to elect a different amount or percentage; and

- how the contributions will be invested unless the employee makes an investment election.[78]

The plan must provide the notice early enough that the employee has reasonable time to make the elections on whether to have a different amount or percentage contributed or no contribution made and how any contributions made are to be invested. The default election cannot become effective sooner than the earlier of the pay date for the second payroll period beginning after the date the notice is provided and the first pay date that is at least 30 days after the notice is provided.[79]

> *Example 8.* An employer pays its employees on the first and fifteenth of every month. On July 1, the first day of the pay period ending on July 15th, it provides the required notice concerning the QACA and how to change the default elections. The default election cannot become effective until August 15th. [80]

Traditional or QACA Safe Harbor

With both safe harbors, the plan is relieved of complying with the ADP and ACP tests. The major difference between the two safe harbors is that the QACA safe harbor imposes minimum contribution percentages. A traditional safe harbor can have an automatic contribution arrangement that does not meet the QACA minimum percentages and is not subject to the uniformity requirement. However, the employer contributions under a traditional safe harbor plan must immediately be fully vested while a QACA safe harbor plan can use a vesting schedule. The QACA safe harbor also requires a slightly lower employer match requirement. If an employee contributes 5 percent, the traditional safe harbor results in a 4 percent employer match while the QACA safe harbor produces a 3.5 percent match.

Qualified Default Investment Alternatives

If an employee becomes a participant through a QACA or EACA, elective deferrals and contributions may be made before the individual has chosen how the funds should be invested. If the plan fiduciary invests the funds in a Qualified Default Investment Alternative (QDIA), the participant is considered to have exercised control over the investment of the account assets and the fiduciary is not liable for their performance. For a discussion of QDIAs, see Chapter 9.

Eligible Automatic Contribution Arrangements

An Eligible Automatic Contribution Arrangement (EACA) can be part of a safe harbor 401(k) plan or a QACA. It can be applied to all employees or only to employees who become eligible to participate in the plan after the EACA's effective date.

Adopting an EACA provides the plan with two advantages over other automatic contribution arrangements. First, participants can get their contributions back by making an election within 90 days of when the first elective contribution is made.[81] This allows participants who did not realize the impact of automatic enrollment on their paychecks to get their money out and the plan to avoid the costs associated with maintaining accounts with small balances.

Second, plans have six months after the end of the plan year to withdraw excess contributions to correct excess contributions that violate the ADP test and excess aggregate contributions that violate the ACP test, rather than the 2½ months that applies to other plans.[82] Because participants can withdraw contributions up to 90 days after the first contribution, a plan may not know if it has violated the ADP test and excess contributions must be withdrawn until after the end of the 2½ month period. This extension is only available if all HCEs and NHCEs are covered employees under the EACA and the EACA was in effect for the entire plan year.[83]

Uniformity requirement. The default elective contribution must be a uniform percentage of compensation. The percentage can vary based on the same factors permitted for QACAs.[84] In applying the uniformity requirement, all automatic contribution arrangements in a plan intended to be EACAs are aggregated. For example, for a plan covering employees in separate divisions, if the default elective contribution in one division is 3 percent and 5 percent in the second, it does not qualify as an EACA.[85]

Notice requirement. The plan administrator must provide each covered employee with written notice of the employee's rights and obligations under the EACA. It must be sufficiently accurate and comprehensive to apprise the employee of such rights and obligations and written in a manner calculated to be understood by the average employee to whom the arrangement applies.[86]

The notice must include the information required for a traditional safe harbor plan that applies to the EACA. In addition, it must also accurately describe:[87]

- The default elective contributions which will be made on the employee's behalf if the employee does not make an affirmative election

- The employee's rights to elect out of the default elective contributions or to have contributions based on a different percentage of compensation or different amount of contribution

- How contributions made will be invested if the employee does not make any investment election

- The employee's rights to make a permissible withdrawal, if applicable, and the procedures to elect such a withdrawal

Permissive withdrawals. Employees must elect a permissive withdrawal within 90 days after the first default elective contribution under the EACA.[88] The first default elective contribution is the date that the employee would have received the compensation if it had been paid in cash.[89] It must be effective not later than the earlier of:

- the pay date for the second payroll period that begins after the date the election is made; and

- the first pay date that occurs at least 30 days after the election is made.[90]

An employee who did not have any default elective contributions made for an entire plan year is treated as not having any contributions made in any previous plan year. If that employee later becomes eligible for a default elective contribution, they can be treated as not having had any default elective contributions made for any prior year.[91] This allows an employee who separated from service and is then rehired to make a permissive withdrawal election.

Amount and timing of distributions. The distribution must be the total default elective contributions made under the EACA through the date of the permissive withdrawal election, adjusted for allocable gains or losses to the date of distribution. If the plan separately accounts for those contributions in the participant's account, it must distribute the account total. If it does not separately account for the default elective contributions, the allocable gains and losses must be determined under rules similar to those used for the distribution of excess contributions under Treasury Regulation Section 1.401(k)-2(b)(2)(iv).[92]

The plan may reduce the amount distributed by any generally applicable fees. Any distribution fee charged cannot exceed the fee charged for other cash distributions.[93]

Consequences of permissive withdrawals. The withdrawal is taxable in the tax year that the distribution is made, even if the contribution occurred in a previous year. Any portion of a distribution attributable to a designated Roth contribution is not taxable. Only the default elective contributions are considered in determining the participant's basis. The 10 percent early withdrawal penalty does not apply to the permissive withdrawal. The amount withdrawn is not included in determining the elective deferral limitation.[94]

Employer matching contributions allocable to the withdrawn amount, adjusted for gains or losses, must be forfeited. The plan can provide that any matching contributions will not be made for any amount withdrawn prior to the date the match would have been allocated. This eliminates the need for an employer to make a matching contribution that will shortly be forfeited and handled according to the plan's procedures for forfeited amounts.[95] The plan does not have to provide the spousal notice or obtain the consent generally required for plan distributions.[96]

Designing with Section 414(x) Combination Defined Benefit and 401(k) Plans (DB/k Plans)

Overview

For plan years beginning after 2009, a small employer (as defined for this purpose) may offer its employees a combination of a defined benefit and 401(k) plan (a so-called DB/k plan).[97] The purpose of a DB/k plan is to encourage employers to offer both a defined benefit plan and a defined contribution plan that includes a 401(k) plan. To do so, a DB/k plan offers simplified administration for both the DB and 401(k) portions of the plan.

Except to the extent provided under the DB/k plan rules, the defined benefit portion and the 401(k) portion are subject to the same requirements as if they were not part of a DB/k plan. If the DB/k plan terminates, each portion is terminated separately.[98]

If a qualified employer offers a DB/k plan, the plan's assets are held in a single trust, the 401(k) portion of the plan qualifies for safe harbors for the ACP and ADP tests, and is not subject to the top-heavy rules. The defined benefit plan portion and 401(k) plan portion are subject to the normal defined benefit and 401(k) plan rules, unless a special rule applies for DB/k plans.[99] This means that the contribution and benefit limits are applied separately to contributions to the 401(k) plan portion of the DB/k plan and to the benefits offered by the DB portion of the DB/k plan. The DB plan funding rules apply to the DB portion of the DB/k plan, including the limits on investing in employer securities or real property. The 401(k) portion of the plan must maintain separate participant accounts, and earnings or losses allocated to participants' accounts are based on the earnings or losses of the 401(k) portion.

DB/k Plan Required Elements

A *DB/k plan* (referred to in the Code as an "eligible combined plan") is a plan:

1. maintained by a small employer (as of the time the plan is established);

2. made up of a defined benefit plan and a defined contribution plan that includes a 401(k) plan (an "applicable defined contribution plan");

3. whose assets are held in a single trust and clearly identified and allocated to the DB and 401(k) portions as needed under the Code and ERISA; and

4. that meets benefit, contribution, vesting, and nondiscrimination requirements.[100]

DB/k Small Employer

An employer is a small employer if (1) it had at least two but not more than 500 employees on business days during the preceding calendar year; and (2) at least two employees on the first day of the plan year.[101] Whether an employer that was not in business during all of the previous year is a small employer is based on the average number of employees the employer is reasonably expected to employ on business days during the current calendar year.[102] Predecessors to the current employer are considered in determining if the employer is a small employer.[103]

DB/k Single Trust Requirement

The assets of a DB/k plan must be held in a single trust. They must be clearly identified and allocated to the appropriate portion of the plan as necessary.

DB/k Requirements for the Defined Benefit Portion

Under the defined benefit portion of a DB/k plan, participants must receive an annual benefit based on a percentage of their final average pay. The percentage is the lesser of:

1. one percent multiplied by their years of service; or

2. 20 percent.[104]

Example 9. John retired after working eight years for the employer sponsoring a DB/k plan. His annual defined benefit is 8 percent of his final average pay.

Example 10. Abigail retired after working twenty-three years for the employer sponsoring a DB/k plan. Her annual benefit is 20 percent of her final average pay.

Final average pay. Final average pay is a misnomer. The average used in the computation is based on the consecutive year period during which the participant has the greatest aggregate compensation. For this purpose, the period used cannot exceed five years.[105]

If the defined benefit portion is an applicable defined benefit plan under Section 411(a) (13)(c),[106] the plan meets the benefit requirement if each participant receives a pay credit for each plan year that is at least the percentage of compensation shown here.

Pay Credits for Applicable Defined Benefit Plans	
Participant's age at beginning of year	*Percentage of Compensation*
30 or less	2
Over 30, less than 40	4
Over 40, less than 50	6
50 or over	8

A participant does not have to make elective deferrals to the 401(k) portion of the DB/k plan to receive the required benefit under the defined benefit portion.[107]

DB/k Requirements for the 401(k) Portion

The defined contribution portion of a DB/k plan must meet automatic enrollment and matching requirements. The 401(k) portion must qualify as an automatic contribution arrangement and treat eligible employees as having elected to defer 4 percent of their compensation, unless an employee opts out or elects a different percentage.[108]

The employer must match 50 percent of the employee's elective contributions up to 4 percent of compensation. In addition, the same matching rules that apply to a traditional safe harbor plan apply to a DB/k plan. First, the matching rate for any HCE cannot exceed the matching rate for a NHCE. Second, the plan can use a different matching rate if the rate does not increase as the rate of elective contributions increases and the total matching contributions it provides are at least equal to the amount that would be provided under the standard formula (50 percent of contributions up to 4 percent).[109]

The employer can also make nonelective contributions but those contributions are not considered in determining if the required matching contributions are made.[110]

DB/k automatic contribution requirement. For the 401(k) portion to qualify as an automatic contribution arrangement, it must:

1. provide for elective deferrals of 4 percent of compensation unless the employee specifically elects no contributions or a different percentage; and

2. meet a notice requirement. The employee must specifically elect not to have contributions made or a different rate of contributions.

DB/k notice requirement. The notice requirement has three components. Eligible employees must:

1.   receive a notice that explains their rights to opt out of the automatic contribution or to choose a different contribution rate;

2.   have a reasonable time after receiving the notice to make that election; and

3.   receive an annual notice of their rights and obligations within a reasonable period before the year begins.[111]

The notice must be sufficiently accurate and comprehensive to inform employees of their rights and obligations under the plan and be written in a way that is calculated to be understood by the average eligible employee.[112]

DB/k Vesting Requirements

All benefits provided under the defined benefit portion must be fully vested after three years.[113] An employee is always fully vested in their contributions and any matching contributions, including matching contributions that exceed the required matching contributions. Once an employee has three years of service, they are fully vested in the benefits attributable to the employer's nonelective contributions.[114]

DB/k Other Rules

The ADP test for the 401(k) portion of the DB/k plan is satisfied if the DB/k plan requirements are met.[115] Similarly, the ACP test is satisfied for matching contributions. However, nonelective contributions are subject to the general ACP test. Both portions of a DB/k plan are treated as meeting the top-heavy requirements.[116] A DB/k plan must stand on its own in satisfying the nondiscrimination tests. All contributions, benefits, rights, and features under a defined benefit or 401(k) plan must be provided uniformly to all participants.[117] This applies even if the plans could provide non-uniform contributions, benefits, or other rights or features without violating the nondiscrimination rules. A plan does not violate the uniformity requirement simply because it protects benefits accrued before a defined benefit or a 401(k) plan became part of a DB/k plan.[118]

The rules for hybrid plans under Section 414(k) do not apply to DB/k plans.[119]

A DB/k plan is treated as a single plan for annual reporting purposes. The Form 5500 filed for the plan must include all information required for a defined benefit plan and for a 401(k) plan. The plan must only provide one summary annual report to participants.[120]

SIMPLE 401(k) Plans

Overview

By adopting a 401(k) plan that qualifies as a SIMPLE Plan, an employer is treated as meeting the ADP tests of Section 401(k))(3)(A)(ii) and the ACP test of Section 401(m)(2).[121] By limiting employer contributions to only the matching contributions or the nonelective contributions, the SIMPLE 401(k) plan also satisfies the top-heavy requirements.[122] The SIMPLE IRA definitions also apply to SIMPLE 401(k) plans.[123] While establishing a SIMPLE 401(k) plan relieves the plan of satisfying certain nondiscrimination provisions, it is still subject to the other qualification provisions. These include:

- The contribution limits of Section 415

- The compensation limits of Section 401(a)(17)

- The distribution restrictions of Section 401(k)(2)(B)

- The restriction of Section 401(k)(4)(B) on state and local governments maintaining a 401(k) plan[124]

SIMPLE 401(k) Eligible Employers

Any eligible employer may establish a SIMPLE 401(k) plan if it paid $5,000 in earnings to 100 employees or less in the preceding year.[125] Once an eligible employer has more than 100 employees who receive $5,000 in compensation, it can be treated as an eligible employer for a grace period of two years after the last year it has no more than 100 eligible employees.[126]

Compensation for purposes of SIMPLE 401(k) plans includes wages, tips, and other compensation from the employer subject to federal income tax withholding plus any elective contributions and elective deferrals under any plan other than the SIMPLE 401(k) that must be reported on the employee's Form W-2.[127] For self-employed individuals, it means net earnings from self-employment for SE tax purposes, before any contributions to the SIMPLE 401(k) for the self-employed person.[128]

The employer aggregation rules under Section 414 are applied to SIMPLE 401(k) plans, causing related employers to be treated as one employer. Leased employees are treated as employed by the company that receives the services (the lessee employer).[129]

SIMPLE 401(k) Eligible Employees

A SIMPLE 401(k) plan *must* include all employees who received at least $5,000 in compensation during any two preceding calendar years and are reasonably expected to receive at least $5,000 of compensation during the current calendar year.[130] An employer can exclude employees that can be excluded from coverage under Section 410(b)(3),[131] as described in Chapter 5. If an acquisition, disposition, or similar transaction during a year or the following calendar year is the only reason an employee would be eligible to participate, an employer can exclude those employees.[132]

As with the eligibility requirements under traditional 401(k) plan designs, an employer can provide more generous eligibility requirements by eliminating or reducing the prior year compensation requirements, the current year compensation requirements, or both. It cannot impose any other conditions.[133]

Although the SIMPLE 401(k) must be the only plan offered for the participant by the employer during the year, an employee may participate in both the employer's SIMPLE 401(k) plan and another employer's plan. The total employee contributions to an employer's plans cannot exceed the contribution limit imposed by Section 402(g), $17,500 for 2014 plus the $5,500 catch-up.[134] Because the limit on contributions to SIMPLE IRA and 401(k) plans is $12,000 plus a $2,500 catch-up for 2014, an employee can contribute the maximum to a SIMPLE 401(k) and still be able to contribute to another type of plan.

> *Example 11.* Craig, 45, works for Company A, which offers a SIMPLE 401(k) plan. He also works for Company B, which offers a traditional 401(k) plan. For 2014, Craig can contribute $12,000 to Company A's SIMPLE 401(k) plan plus $5,500 to Company B's traditional 401(k) plan.

SIMPLE 401(k) Exclusive Plan Requirement

The SIMPLE 401(k) plan must be the exclusive plan for each participant during the plan year. To qualify as the exclusive plan, there can be no contributions made or benefits accrued for services during the plan year for any participant in the SIMPLE 401(k) under any other qualified plan of the employer.[135] Qualified plans include not only plans qualified under Section 401(a) but also:

- A Section 403(a) annuity plan

- A plan set up by a federal, state, or local government

- A Section 403(b) annuity

- A Simplified Employee Pension (SEP)

- A SIMPLE IRA

- A Section 501(c)(18) employee funded pension trust[136]

A SIMPLE 401(k) plan will not violate the exclusive plan rule just because another plan of the employer allocates forfeitures to a SIMPLE 401(k) plan participant.[137]

SIMPLE 401(k) Contributions and Employer Deductions

Contributions to a SIMPLE 401(k) plan are limited to employee elective deferrals, employer contributions, and rollovers from a qualified plan or IRA.[138]

Employee contributions. An employee may elect to contribute up to $10,000 annually, adjusted for inflation ($12,000 in 2014).[139] Employees who are at least age 50 at the end of the calendar year may make catch-up contributions of $2,500, indexed for inflation ($2,500 in 2014).[140]

Employer contributions. An employer may either match contributions made by employees, up to 3 percent of annual compensation, or make a nonelective contribution of 2 percent of compensation. Unlike a SIMPLE IRA, an employer cannot reduce its matching contribution to a SIMPLE 401(k) plan below 3 percent. The nonelective contribution does not depend on whether an eligible employee's contribution is at least 3 percent of compensation but can be limited to eligible employees who receive at least $5,000 of qualifying compensation during the year.[141]

Employer deductions. A special exception allows an employer to deduct the amount it must contribute to a SIMPLE 401(k) plan if it exceeds the 25 percent of compensation limit under Section 404(a)(3)(A)(i).[142]

SIMPLE 401(k) Vesting Requirement

An employee must always be 100 percent vested in the entire SIMPLE 401(k) account.[143]

SIMPLE 401(k) Plan Year, Notice Requirements, and Employee Elections Requirements

Plan year. SIMPLE 401(k) plans must use the calendar year as their plan year. The first plan year can begin as late as October 1. An employer created after October 1 may establish a plan as soon as administratively feasible.

Notice requirements. Eligible employees must receive notice within a reasonable time before the election period or on the day that the election period starts that they can elect to defer some of their compensation or modify their prior deferral election. The notice must specify whether the employer will make the 2 percent nonelective contribution or the 3 percent matching contribution.[144]

For the first plan year an employee is eligible, the employee must be able to elect to participate in the SIMPLE 401(k) plan during a 60-day period that includes either the day the employee becomes eligible or the day before. In subsequent years, the election period is the 60-day period immediately preceding the plan year.[145] Because plan years must begin on January 1, this means that the election period must begin on November 1.

Employee elections. During an election period, eligible employees may modify their election without restrictions. In the year that the employee becomes eligible to participate, the employee must be able to start contributions as soon as he or she is eligible, even if the 60-day period has not ended.[146] An election may be either a percentage of compensation or a specific dollar amount. The employer may not restrict an employee's deferrals, other than to provide that the deferrals may not exceed the amount permitted by law.[147]

An employee can terminate elective deferrals at any time. The plan can provide that an employee who terminates a deferral election during the year cannot resume deferrals for the remainder of the plan year.[148]

Defined Contribution Plan Cross-Testing or New Comparability

Cross testing

Cross-testing provides a way for a defined contribution plan like a 401(k) to satisfy the general nondiscrimination tests based on equivalent employer-provided benefits. Defined benefit plans can satisfy those tests based on equivalent employer-provided contributions. Cross-tested plans are sometimes known as "age-weighted plans" because older employees generally receive higher contribution rates without failing the nondiscrimination tests.

The ability to use cross-testing originates in the Section 401(a)(4) requirement that a plan's benefits or contributions cannot discriminate in favor of HCEs in amount. Treasury Regulation Section 1.401(a)(4)-1 clarifies this requirement, stating that a plan does not have to show that "both the benefits and contributions provided are nondiscriminatory in amount, but only that either the contributions alone or the benefits alone are nondiscriminatory in amount."[149]

Treasury Regulation Section 1.401(a)(4)-8(b) sets out the following tests for a defined contribution plan to provide nondiscriminatory benefits. First, the plan must satisfy the general test for contribution allocation under Treasury Regulation Section 1.401(a)(4)-2(c)(1) if an equivalent accrual rate was used instead of an employee's allocation rate in determining the rate groups.[150] Second, the plan must satisfy one of the following requirements for the plan year:[151]

1. It has broadly available allocation rates

2. It has age-based allocation rates based either on a gradual age or service schedule or a target benefit allocation

3. It must satisfy the minimum allocation gateway

Planning Tip: A cross-tested 401(k) plan (or cash balance plan) can be used as a solution for the situation where there are multiple owners but only a portion of them are interested in making contributions to a qualified plan. Cross testing can allow plan contributions to be tailored to the owner participants to the greatest extent permitted under the rules.

Determination of an Equivalent Accrual Rate

The equivalent accrual rate is the average increase in a participant's account balance during a period, expressed either as a percentage of the participant's pay or as a dollar amount. The measurement period cannot include future years.[152]

The increase does not include income, expenses, gains, or losses during the measurement period attributable to the beginning account balance. It does include any distributions that would have been included in the account balance. If the current year is used as the measurement period, an employer can disregard income, expenses, gains, and losses for the current year attributable to the current year's account balance increase. This results in the account balance being increased by only the employer contributions and forfeitures allocated to an employee's account for the current year. An employer can also disregard distributions to an NHCE and distributions to any employee in plan years beginning before a selected date that is January 1, 1986 or earlier.[153]

An employer can determine an employee's equivalent accrual rate using the optional rules in Treasury Regulation Section 1.401(a)(4)-3(d)(3) by substituting the employee's equivalent accrual rate for the employee's normal accrual rate.[154] The determination of equivalent accrual rates must be consistent for all employees for a plan year. This requires use of the same measurement periods and standard interest rates. Any options used must be applied consistently.[155]

Broadly Available Allocation Rates

A plan has broadly available allocation rates if each allocation rate is currently available during the plan year to a group of employees that satisfies the minimum coverage requirements, without regard to the average benefit percentage test. If Treasury Regulation Section 1.401(a)(4)-4(d) (4) allows two allocation rates to be aggregated, they can be treated as a single allocation rate in determining if the plan has broadly available allocation rates.[156]

Age-Based Allocation Rates

A plan can satisfy the age-based allocation rates using either a gradual age or service schedule or a uniform target benefit allocation.

Gradual age or service schedule. To qualify as a gradual age or service schedule, the allocation formula must use a single schedule of allocation rates with bands based solely on age, years of service, or points based on the sum of age and service. Allocations to all employees within the same band must use the same allocation rate. The allocation rates must increase smoothly at regular intervals.[157]

Allocation rates increase smoothly if the allocation rate for each band does not exceed the allocation rate for the immediately preceding band by more than five percentage points. The allocation rate for any band cannot increase by more than twice the allocation rate for the immediately preceding band or exceed the ratio of the immediately preceding bands to the next preceding band.[158]

A schedule has regular intervals if each band, other than the highest band, is the same length (number of years of age, years of service, or age and service points). For a schedule based on age, the first band is treated as the same length as the other bands if it ends at or before age 25. If it ends after age 25, the starting age of the first band can be treated as age 25 or any age earlier than 25. If the schedule is based on age and service points, the previous tests are applied using the age and service points applicable to age 25. Schedules based on years of service can provide that the starting service for the first band can be one year of service or a lesser amount.[159]

The regulation also permits a schedule that provides a minimum allocation rate for all employees or provides a minimum benefit if the schedule meets specific conditions.[160]

Example 12. Plan N, a defined contribution plan, provides a single schedule based on age to determine the allocation rates for all employees. The schedule used is shown here.

Age	Allocation Rate	Ratio of Band's Allocation Rate to Allocation Rate for Immediately Preceding Band
Under 25	3.0%	n/a
25–34	6.0%	2.00
35–44	9.0%	1.50
45–54	12.0%	1.33
55–64	16.0%	1.33
65 or older	21.0%	1.31

The allocation rates increase smoothly because they do not increase by more than 5 percentage points between bands, and the ratio of the allocation rate for any band is not more than twice the allocation rate for the immediately preceding band and does not increase. The bands are considered to be the same length (because the first band ends prior to age 25, it is considered to be the same length as the others) so the increases occur at regular intervals.

Because Plan N's allocation rates increase smoothly at regular intervals, it has a gradual age or service schedule.[161]

If a target benefit plan fails the safe harbor test for target benefit plans, it can satisfy the age-based allocation test if its rates are based on a uniform target benefit allocation and it failed the safe harbor test for certain reasons.[162]

Minimum Allocation Gateway

A plan may use the cross-testing rules if each NHCE has an allocation rate that is at least 1/3 of the allocation rate of the HCE with the highest allocation rate.[163] It is deemed to satisfy the minimum allocation gateway if each NHCE receives an allocation of at least 5 percent of compensation.[164]

Solutions When HCEs Cannot Get Any Meaningful Amounts into the 401(k) Plan

In some cases, plan participation by NHCE is always so poor and there are so many HCEs in proportion to the eligible NHCEs who want to and actually participate that all the plan feature techniques for increasing NHCE participation will not make a difference as to the HCEs ability to make a contribution, except by using a safe harbor 401(k) with its mandatory employer contribution. Often, the costs of using a safe harbor 401(k) are unacceptable to the employer. For instance, restaurant and poultry processing businesses are frequently unable to attract sufficient NHCEs into a plan regardless of the employer's match so a safe harbor might be the only approach that might be possible to enable HCEs to contribute into the plan in any meaningful way.

In such cases, it is possible to carve out ALL the HCEs from the 401(k) plan and use another nonqualified plan technique to provide the retirement plan for ONLY these key management and highly compensated employees. This so-called Section 410(g) nonqualified plan for the HCEs may then take the form of a pre-tax nonqualified deferred compensation plan under Section 409A (similar in nature to a 401(k)) as to plan participants but with substantially more flexibility as to employer matching and profit-sharing contributions. In the alternative, it may employ a "Roth-like" after-tax bonus life insurance or annuity technique. The after-tax techniques work less well in these deferral situations, unless the HCEs are few (and perhaps owner-operators) so recharacterizing income is easy to accomplish.

However, the pre-tax nonqualified Section 409A technique can be an ideal solution to this problem of getting the bulk of the benefit to the desired participants if the business entity is a C Corp.[165] The happy result using this approach is that the employer may design the 410(k) plan for the general employee base with broad flexibility to add or not add employer contributions (and select the size of the match if one is still desired) in the absence of major HCE participation. Moreover, the creative planning toward HCEs for performance-based employer profit-sharing rewards, other employer matching with the desired golden handcuff-type vesting provisions, and even a different and more complex set of investment choices better suited to an executive group can generally be drafted into a nonqualified plan.[166]

Even if the employer does not want to take ALL the HCEs out of the 401(k) plan, the employer may consider a nonqualified top hat ERISA exempted "excess benefit" or "select group of management" plan (both often referred to as a "401(k) mirror" plan). However, an ERISA exempt nonqualified excess benefit plan technically usually only replaces those benefits (chance for employee and employer contributions) otherwise missed in the 401(k). The ERISA select group exemption allows the employer to make up any and all of these lost 401(k) contributions, but to go beyond the 401(k)'s limits and caps entirely to establish a unique pre-tax plan for its HCEs, subject only to Section 409A requirements imposed on nonqualified deferred compensation plans. Employees are at risk for the claims of the employer's creditors in bankruptcy, which is the major difference for participants under qualified and nonqualified plans, and there are other differences for both the employee and employer that need to be considered. However, these nonqualified plan types are used commonly to help achieve the desired deferral levels for executives and other HCEs, and good qualified plan administrators now offer an opportunity to add an unlimited per the design (not just excess benefit) nonqualified plan on top of the 401(k) plan.[167]

Endnotes

1. Deloitte Annual 401(k) Benchmarking Survey (2012) (hereinafter "Deloitte survey"), Exhibit 3.10.
2. Ibid, Exhibit 3.1.
3. Ibid, Exhibit 3.3.
4. Ibid, Exhibit 3.4.
5. Ibid, Exhibit 3.6.
6. Ibid, Exhibit 3.7.
7. Ibid, Exhibit 3.8.
8. Ibid, Exhibit 4.1.
9. Ibid, Exhibit 4.2.
10. Ibid, Exhibit 4.4.
11. Ibid, Exhibit 4.5.
12. Ibid, Exhibit 4.14.
13. Ibid, Exhibit 4.17.
14. Ibid, Exhibit 4.16.
15. AON Hewitt 2011 Trends & Experience in Defined Contribution Plans, (hereinafter "Hewitt survey"), p. 4.
16. Ibid, p. 11.
17. Deloitte survey, Exhibit 7.10.
18. Hewitt survey, p. 11.
19. Internal Revenue Service (IRS) Section 401(k) Compliance Check Questionnaire, Final Report (March 2013), p. 50.
20. Rev. Proc. 2011-49, IRB 2011-44, Secs. 4.01, 4.02.
21. Ibid, Sec. 4.03.
22. Ibid, Sec. 12.03(1)(a).

23. Ibid, Sec. 12.03(1)(b).

24. Ibid, Sec. 12.03(b)(1)(i).

25. Ibid, Sec. 12.03(b)(1)(ii).

26. Ibid, Sec. 12.03(b)(1)(iii).

27. Ibid, Sec. 19.01.

28. Ibid, Sec. 19.02.

29. Ibid, Sec. 13.06.

30. Ibid, Sec. 12.03(d)(2).

31. http://www.irs.gov/Retirement-Plans/Determination,-Opinion-and-Advisory-Letter-for-Retirement-Plans—Pre-Approved-Plans, last reviewed August 30, 2013.

32. Rev. Proc. 2011-49, IRB 2011-44, Sec. 13.01.

33. Ibid, Sec. 13.03.

34. Ibid, Sec. 13.05.

35. IRC Sec. 410(a)(1)(B)(i).

36. IRC Sec. 401(k)(12).

37. IRC Sec. 401(k)(13).

38. IRC Sec. 414(x).

39. IRC Sec. 401(k)(12).

40. IRC Sec. 401(m)(11)(A).

41. IRC Sec. 401(k)(12)(E)(i).

42. Treas. Reg. §1.414(s)-1(d)(1).

43. Treas. Reg. §1.401(k)-3(b)(2).

44. IRC Sec. 401(k)(12)(B)(i).

45. IRC Sec. 401(k)(12)(B)(ii).

46. Treas. Reg. §1.401(k)-3(c)(7), Example 2.

47. Treas. Reg. §1.401(k)-3(c)(5)(i).

48. Treas. Reg. §1.401(k)-3(c)(5)(ii).

49. Treas. Reg. §1.401(k)-3(c)(6)(ii).

50. Treas. Reg. §1.401(k)-3(c)(6)(iii).

51. Treas. Reg. §1.401(k)-3(c)(6)(iv).

52. Treas. Reg. §1.401(k)-3(c)(6)(v).

53. Treas. Reg. §1.401(k)-3(b)(1).

54. Treas. Reg. §1.401(k)-3(d)(i). In audits, the IRS has found that failure to give this annual required Notice is a common error among safe harbor plans. It can be corrected. See Chapter 13 for the IRS correction procedure for a failure to give notice as required.

55. Treas. Reg. §1.401(k)-3(d)(2)(ii).

56. Treas. Reg. §1.401(k)-3(d)(3).

57. Treas. Reg. §1.401(k)-3(e).

58. Treas. Reg. §1.401(k)-3(e)(1).

59. Treas. Reg. §1.401(k)-3(f).

60. Treas. Reg. §1.401(k)-3(h).

61. Treas. Reg. §1.401(k)-3(h)(4).

62. Treas. Reg. §1.401(k)-3(h)(5).

63. Treas. Reg. §1.401(k)-3(c)(7), Example 4.

64. Treas. Reg. §1.401(m)-3(d)(3).

65. Treas. Reg. §1.401(m)-3(d)(4).

66. Treas. Reg. §1.401(m)-3(d)(5).

67. IRC Sec. 416(g)(4)(H).

68. Rev. Rul. 2004-13, IRB 2004-7.

69. IRC Sec. 401(k)(13)(Treas. Reg. §1.401k)-3((j)(1)(iii).

70. IRC Sec. 401(k)(13)(C)(iii).

71. IRC Sec. 401(k)(13)(C)(iii)(I).

72. Treas. Reg. §1.401(k)-3(j)(2)(iv).

73. Treas. Reg. §1.401(k)-3(j)(2)(iii).

74. Rev. Rul. 2009-30, IRB 2009-39.

75. IRC Sec. 401(k)(13)(D)(i).

76. IRC Sec. 401(k)(13)(D)(ii).

77. IRC Sec. 401(k)(13)(D)(iii).

78. Treas. Reg. §1.401(k)-3(k)(4).

79. Treas. Reg. §1.401(k)-3(k)(4)(iii).

80. The pay date for the first payroll period after the notice is provided is July 31. The pay date for the second payroll period after the notice is provided is August 15. The pay date that is at least 30 days after notice is provided is also August 15.

81. IRC Sec. 414(w)(2).

82. IRC Sec. 4979(f)(1).

83. Treas. Reg. §54.4979-1(c)(1).

84. See the discussion at footnote 69 above.

85. Treas. Reg. §1.414(w)-1(b)(2).

86. Treas. Reg. §1.414(w)-1(b)(3)(i).

87. Treas. Reg. §1.414(w)-1(b)(3)(ii).

88. Treas. Reg. §1.414(w)-1(c)(2)(i).

89. Treas. Reg. §1.414(w)-1(c)(2)(ii).

90. Treas. Reg. §1.414(w)-1(c)(2)(iii).

91. Treas. Reg. §1.414(w)-1(c)(2)(iv).

92. Treas. Reg. §1.414(w)-1(c)(3)(i).

93. Treas. Reg. §1.414(w)-1(c)(3)(ii).

94. Treas. Reg. §1.414(w)-1(d)(1).

95. Treas. Reg. §1.414(w)-1(d)(2).

96. Treas. Reg. §1.414(w)-1(d)(3).

97. IRC Sec. 414(x), added by the Pension Protection Act of 2006, P.L. 109-280, Sec. 903.

98. IRC Sec. 414(x)(1).

99. Ibid.

100. IRC Sec. 414(x)(2).

101. IRC Sec. 414(x)(2)(A), flush language; Sec. 4980D(d)(2)(A).

102. IRC Sec. 4980D(d)(2)(B).

103. IRC Sec. 4980D(d)(2)(C).

104. IRC Sec. 414(x)(2)(B)(ii).

105. IRC Sec. 414(x)(2)(B)(i).

106. IRC Sec. 414(x)(2)(B)(iii). An applicable defined benefit plan is defined by Sec. 411(a)(13)(C) as a defined benefit plan that determines any portion of the benefit as either the balance of a hypothetical account for the participant or as an accumulated percentage of the participant's final average compensation.

107. IRC Sec. 414(x)(2)(B)(iv).

108. IRC Sec. 414(x)(2)(C)(i).

109. Ibid.

110. IRC Sec. 414(x)(2)(C)(ii).

111. IRC Sec. 414(x)(5)(B).

112. IRC Sec. 414(x)(5)(B), flush language.

113. IRC Sec. 414(x)(2)(D)(i).

114. IRC Sec. 414(x)(2)(D)(ii).

115. IRC Sec. 414(x)(3).

116. IRC Sec. 414(x)(4).

117. IRC Sec. 414(x)(2)(E).

118. Joint Committee on Taxation Technical Explanation of the Pension Protection Act of 2006, p. 238.

119. IRC Sec. 414(x)(6)(A).

120. IRC Sec. 414(x)(6)(B).

121. IRC Secs. 401(k)(11)(A), 401(m)(10).

122. IRC Sec. 401(k)(11)(D)(ii)

123. IRC Sec. 401(k)(11)(D)(i).

124. Rev. Proc. 97-9, Sec. 2.06, 1997-1 CB 624.

125. IRC Sec. 408(p)(2)(C)(i)(I); Treas. Reg. §1.401(k)-4(b)(1).

126. IRC Sec. 408(p)(2)(C)(i)(II); Treas. Reg. §1.401(k)-4(b)(2).

127. Treas. Reg. §1.401(k)-4(e)(5).

128. Ibid.

129. Notice 98-4, 1998-1 CB 269, Q&A, B-5.

130. Notice 98-4, 1998-1 CB 269, Q&A, C-1.

131. Ibid.

132. Ibid.

133. Notice 98-4, 1998-1 CB 269, Q&A, C-2.

134. Notice 98-4, 1998-1 CB 269, Q&A, C-3.

135. Treas. Reg. §1.401(k)-4(c)(1).

136. IRC Sec. 219(g)(5).

137. Treas. Reg. §1.401(k)-4(c)(2).

138. Treas. Reg. §1.401(k)-4(e)(1).

139. IRC Sec. 408(p)(2)(E); as adjusted for inflation in Notice 2012-67, IRB 2012-50.

140. IRC Sec. 414(v)(2)(B)(ii), as adjusted for inflation in IR 2013-86, October 31, 2013.

141. Treas. Reg. §1.401(k)-4(e)(4).

142. IRC Sec. 404(a)(3)(A)(i).

143. IRC Sec. 401(k)(11)(A)(iii), referencing the vesting requirements of Section 408(p)(3); Treas. Reg. §1.401(k)-4(f).

144. Treas. Reg. §1.401(k)-4(d)(3).

145. Treas. Reg. §1.401(k)-4(d (2).

146. Notice 98-4, 1998-1 CB 269, Q&A, E-1.

147. Notice 98-4, 1998-1 CB 269, Q&A, D-2.

148. Treas. Reg. §1.401(k)-4(d (2)(iii).

149. Treas. Reg. §1.401(a)(4)-1(b)(2)(i).

150. Treas. Reg. §1.401(a)(4)-8(b)(1)(i)(A).

151. Treas. Reg. §1.401(a)(4)-8(b)(1)(i)(B).

152. Treas. Reg. §1.401(a)(4)-8(b)(2).

153. Treas. Reg. §1.401(a)(4)-8(b)(2)(ii)(A).

154. Treas. Reg. §1.401(a)(4)-8(b)(2)(iii).

155. Treas. Reg. §1.401(a)(4)-8(b)(2)(iv).

156. Treas. Reg. §1.401(a)(4)-8(b)(1)(iii). The permissive aggregation assumes that the allocation rates were treated as benefits, rights, or features.

157. Treas. Reg. §1.401(a)(4)-8(b)(1)(iv)(A).

158. Treas. Reg. §1.401(a)(4)-8(b)(1)(iv)(B).

159. Treas. Reg. §1.401(a)(4)-8(b)(1)(iv)(C).

160. Treas. Reg. §1.401(a)(4)-8(b)(1)(iv)(D).

161. Treas. Reg. §1.401(a)(4)-8(b)(1)(vii), Example 3.

162. Treas. Reg. §1.401(a)(4)-8(b)(1)(v).

163. Treas. Reg. §1.401(a)(4)-8(b)(1)(vi)(A).

164. Treas. Reg. §1.401(a)(4)-8(b)(1)(v)(B).

165. It can work for tax-pass-through companies too if the participants to be benefitted are NOT owner-operators since there is no tax-deferral for them if the entity is a tax pass-through like a partnership or limited liability company.

166. See generally, Richey, Baier & Phelan, The Nonqualified Deferred Compensation Plan Advisor, Plans Covered & Exempt from Section 409A, 5th Ed., Summit Business Media/National Underwriter Company, 2013. This volume provides a practitioner with all the detail needed as to nonqualified deferred compensation plans, especially those covered by Section 409A.

167. Ibid.

Chapter 7

The Roth Option

Introduction

Traditional 401(k) plans allow employees to make elective deferrals on a pre-tax basis. The price for this preferential income tax treatment is two-fold. First, distributions are subject to ordinary income tax. Second, required minimum distributions (RMDs) must generally begin shortly after the employee turns 70½.

When Roth IRAs became available in 1998, many 401(k) participants wanted to make contributions to their 401(k) that offered the same income tax treatment as Roth IRAs – no up-front income tax deduction but no taxation on qualified distributions and no RMDs. The income limits on Roth IRA contributions prevented many of these employees from establishing Roth IRAs. The income limits on Roth IRA conversions in effect until 2009 often prevented them from establishing a non-deductible IRA and then converting it to a Roth IRA. Because 401(k) contributions are not subject to an income limit, the ability to contribute to a Roth-like 401(k) account was especially attractive to these employees.

The 2001 Economic Growth and Tax Relief Reconciliation Act (EGTRRA)[1] added Section 402A that allowed 401(k) (and 403(b)) plans to add Roth accounts for years beginning after 2005. Employers were generally slow to add Roth 401(k) accounts to their plans because EGTRRA was scheduled to sunset on December 31, 2010 and the sunset meant that the accounts would only be available for five years if it expired. Further, EGTRRA's sunset provision stated that once EGTRRA expired, it was to be as if it had never been enacted.[2] This raised questions about how Roth accounts would be treated after EGTRRA's sunset, so employers were not anxious to step into such an uncertain situation by adding a Roth feature to their plans. However, once the Pension Protection Act of 2006[3] made the pension and IRA provisions of EGTRRA permanent, many employers began to add Roth 401(k) accounts to their 401(k) plans.

Employees who direct some of their elective deferrals to a designated Roth account and some to a traditional pre-tax account will end up with a 401(k) account subject to three different sets of rules: the Roth portion; the traditional pre-tax contribution portion; and the employer contribution portion.

Comparison of Roth IRAs and Roth 401(k)s

Roth IRAs and Roth 401(k)s are similar in many ways but some of the differences can be a trap for the unwary.

Figure 7.1 summarizes how Roth IRAs and Roth 401(k)s compare. The subsequent sections discuss these in more detail.

Figure 7.1. Comparison of Roth IRAs and Roth 401(k)s		
Description	**Roth IRA**	**Roth 401(k)**
Contributions made from after-tax money	Yes	Yes
Earnings grow tax-deferred	Yes	Yes
Qualifying distributions not subject to federal income tax	Yes	Yes
Ability to make contributions limited by income	Yes	No
Subject to annual contribution limits	Yes	Yes
RMDs required for account owner	No	Yes
RMDs required for beneficiaries	Yes	Yes
May convert pre-tax account to Roth account	Yes	Yes
5-year participation period begins with first contribution to a Roth account	Yes	No
Special distribution ordering rules apply	Yes	No
Qualifying distributions include distributions for first-time homebuyer	Yes	No

Including a Designated Roth Account in a 401(k) Plan

A Roth 401(k) feature (referred to as a "qualified Roth contribution program" under the Code[4]) can be included in the initial plan design or added to an existing plan. The IRS provided a sample plan amendment for use by employers in Notice 2006-44.[5] A plan that offers a Roth 401(k) feature does not fail to meet any qualified plan requirement solely because it includes a Roth 401(k) feature.[6] It must establish separate accounts, known as "designated Roth accounts" for each employee's designated Roth contributions and the earnings allocable to those contributions.[7]

An employee's designated Roth contributions cannot exceed the maximum elective deferrals for the year less any regular contributions to a 401(k) plan.[8] For example, if an employee under age 50 makes a $7,500 pre-tax elective deferral to a 401(k) plan for 2014, the maximum the employee can designate as a Roth contribution is $10,000.

Plan Design

A 401(k) plan does not have to include a qualified Roth contribution program and permit designated Roth contributions. If it does, an employee's designation of elective deferrals as designated Roth contributions rather than pre-tax contributions is irrevocable.[9]

Impact on Nondiscrimination Testing

A designated Roth contribution must satisfy the requirements applicable to elective deferrals.[10] Since qualified Roth contributions are treated as elective deferrals, the after-tax nature of the contributions should not affect the plan's nondiscrimination testing. The right to make a qualified Roth contribution must be available on a nondiscriminatory basis because it is considered a right, or feature of the plan subject to the nondiscrimination requirement of Section 401(a)(4).[11]

Designated Roth Contribution

To qualify as a designated Roth contribution, an elective deferral must meet three requirements:

1. It must be irrevocably designated at the time of the election as a designated Roth contribution in lieu of some or all of the pre-tax contributions an employee may make.

2. It must be treated by the employer as not excludable from gross income.

3. It must be maintained by the plan in a separate account.[12]

The portion of an employee's elective deferral designated as a Roth contribution is known as a "designated Roth contribution."[13] It is treated as an elective deferral for all purposes, other than the exclusion from gross income.[14]

Treatment of Contributions as not Excludable from Gross Income

The employer treats an elective deferral designated as a qualified Roth contribution as not excludable from an employee's gross income by treating it as wages subject to income tax withholding. Self-employed persons treat it as not excludable by not claiming a deduction.[15]

Separate Account Requirement

The plan must maintain a designated Roth account with separate recordkeeping for each employee who makes a designated Roth contribution. The plan must maintain the account from the time the employee makes the first designated Roth contribution until the designated Roth account is completely distributed. The account reflects an employee's contributions and withdrawals as well as a reasonable and consistent allocation of gains, losses, and other charges and credits. The only contributions allowed are employee contributions and rollover contributions. The plan cannot allocate employer contributions or forfeitures to the account. The plan must keep a record of the employee's investment in the contract (the employee's undistributed designated Roth contributions) for the designated Roth account.[16]

Any transaction or accounting methodology that has the effect of a direct or indirect transfer of value from another account into a designated Roth account, other than the conversion of a pre-tax account to a designated Roth account, violates the separate accounting treatment rules under Section 402A(b)(2). An exchange of investments between accounts at fair market value does not violate the separate accounting requirement.[17]

Elections

An employee must have the ability to make or change a 401(k) election, including the amount of a designated Roth contribution, at least once each plan year.[18] Once made, the designation is irrevocable.[19] Plans that provide the default election to participate in the 401(k) plan must specify whether the default contributions are pre-tax, qualified designated Roth contributions, or how the default contributions are divided between pre-tax and qualified Roth contributions.[20]

Rollovers to a Qualified Roth Contribution Program

An eligible rollover distribution from a designated Roth account may be made to a designated Roth account as a direct (trustee-to-trustee) rollover. A 60-day rollover from one account to another is not available. If a distribution is made directly to the employee, the employee may roll over some or all of the distribution to a Roth IRA within 60 days.[21]

Roth 401(k) Conversions

Originally there was no easy way to convert pre-tax 401(k) accounts into a Roth account. They could not be converted to a Roth 401(k) with the same plan. An employee who wanted to convert a pre-tax 401(k) account to a Roth account could only do so by taking a distribution from the 401(k) plan and rolling it into a Roth IRA. Until simplified by the Pension Protection Act, this required a two-step process. The money first had to be rolled over to a traditional IRA and that IRA then converted to a Roth IRA.

The Small Business Jobs Act of 2010 allowed employees to roll pre-tax 401(k) accounts over to a Roth 401(k) account if the employee was eligible to receive a distribution under the plan.[22] The American Taxpayer Relief Act of 2012, enacted at the beginning of 2013, broadened participants' ability to convert their pre-tax account to a designated Roth account by removing the requirement that the employee must be eligible for an in-service distribution, effective for conversions after December 31, 2012.[23]

A conversion, known as an "in-plan Roth rollover," may be elected by the employee, a surviving spouse who is the beneficiary, or an alternate payee under a qualified domestic relations order (QDRO) who is a spouse or former spouse. It can be accomplished either by a direct rollover (an "in-plan Roth direct rollover") or by a distribution to the individual who then rolls over the funds to a designated Roth account in the plan within 60 days (an "in-plan Roth 60-day rollover").

In-Plan Roth Roll-Over Requirements

A participant may rollover any vested amount to a designated Roth account in the same plan, if the plan permits the rollover.[24] Unlike a Roth IRA conversion, an in-place Roth rollover cannot be recharacterized.[25]

To be eligible for an in-plan Roth rollover, an amount must qualify as an eligible rollover distribution under Section 402(c)(4). This means that the following distributions cannot be subject to an in-plan Roth rollover:

- Distributions included in a series of substantially equal periodic payments for the life or life expectancy of the employee or the joint lives (or joint life expectancies) of the employee and beneficiary or for a specified period of 10 years or more

- Required minimum distributions

- Hardship distributions[26]

A plan must have a qualified Roth contribution program in place at the time the in-plan Roth rollover is made. A qualified Roth contribution program is considered to be in place if employees could elect to make designated Roth contributions to the plan on that date.[27]

The plan must include a description of the in-plan Roth rollover in the written explanation it provides to individuals who receive an eligible rollover description. Notice 2010-84 provides guidance on the information a plan must provide about the in-plan Roth rollover option.[28]

An in-plan Roth rollover simply changes the account in which the amounts rolled over are held and how they are treated for tax purposes. It is not treated as a distribution for the following purposes:

- Section 72 (plan loans) – a plan loan transferred in an in-plan Roth rollover is not treated as a new loan unless the repayment schedule is changed.[29]

- Section 401(a)(11) (spousal annuities) – a married participant does not have to obtain spousal consent to make an in-plan Roth rollover.[30]

- Section 411(a)(11) (participant consent for an immediate distribution of more than $5,000) – the determination of whether a participant's accrued benefit exceeds $5,000 includes the amount rolled over and the in-plan Roth rollover does not trigger a notice of the participant's right to defer receipt of the distribution.[31]

- Section 411(d)(6)(B)(ii) (right to optional forms of benefits) – a distribution right, such as the right to an immediate distribution of the rollover amount, cannot be eliminated due to an in-plan Roth rollover.[32]

Tax Consequences

The participant must include the taxable amount of the in-plan Roth rollover in gross income. The taxable amount is the fair market value of the distribution reduced by the participant's basis in the distribution, determined as if the distribution had been rolled into a Roth IRA.[33] The taxable amount is includible in gross income in the taxable year in which the distribution occurs.[34]

An in-plan Roth rollover is not subject to the 20 percent mandatory withholding[35] or to the 10 percent early distribution penalty under section 72(t).[36] If any of the in-plan Roth rollover is taxable, the participant may need to increase his or her withholding or make estimated tax payments to avoid an underpayment penalty.

However, if any portion of the rollover amount is distributed within a five-year period, it will be subject to the 10 percent penalty. For this purpose, the five-year period begins on the first day of the participant's taxable year in which the rollover occurs and ends on the last day of the fifth taxable year in the period.[37]

> *Example.* Ron withdraws an amount that includes $6,000 allocable to the taxable amount of an in-plan Roth rollover made within the preceding 5 years. For tax purposes, the $6,000 is treated as includable in Ron's gross income for purposes of applying section 72(t) to the distribution. Ron owes an additional tax of $600 unless an exception under Section 72(t)(2) applies.[38]

Roth 401(k) Distributions

The Roth 401(k) plan distribution rules have some similarities to the rules for Roth IRAs but also have some significant differences. A qualified distribution is not includable in income.[39]

Qualified Distributions

For a distribution to be a "qualified distribution" and not be subject to income tax on the earnings, it must meet both a triggering event requirement and a participation requirement. An employee satisfies the triggering event requirement if the payment or distribution is:

- made on or after the employee becomes 59 ½;

- made to a beneficiary or the employee's estate on or after the employee's death; or

- attributable to the employee being disabled, as defined by Section 72(m)(7).[40]

This is the same as the triggering events for Roth IRA purposes except that distributions for a first-time home purchase are not included for Roth 401(k)s.[41]

The participation requirement is not met if the distribution is made during the five consecutive taxable years beginning within:

- the first taxable year that the individual made a designated Roth contribution to any designated Roth account under the same plan; or

- if the designated Roth account includes a rollover from a Roth account with a different plan, the first taxable year for which a designated Roth contribution was made to that account.[42]

The 5-year participation period is determined separately for each Roth 401(k) plan in which an employee participates. If an employee makes designated Roth contributions to two or more Roth 401(k) plans, they will probably have different 5-year participation periods for each plan.[43] This differs from contributory Roth IRAs, which are treated as having the same participation period, even if different accounts were opened in different years.

Planning Tip. If employees make designated Roth contributions to a Roth 401(k) and stop working for the plan sponsor, they can avoid starting a new participation period with a new Roth 401(k) plan. To do so, they need to roll over the designated Roth account from the previous plan to their new Roth 401(k) plan. This option needs to be carefully evaluated. While a rollover to the new Roth 401(k) plan allows use of the participation period from the previous Roth 401(k), it also means that the rollover amount becomes part of the new plan for all purposes. They must choose from the investment options offered by the new plan and may only receive distributions when permitted under the new plan. Another option may be to rollover the Roth 401(k) balance to a Roth IRA, as discussed next.

Once the participation period starts for an employee's designated Roth account under a plan, subsequent events do not end it or cause it to be suspended. For example, if an employee's entire designated Roth account is distributed during the participation period, a new participation period does not begin if the employee makes additional designated Roth contributions to the plan.[44]

In addition, a distribution to a beneficiary due to the employee's death or to an alternate payee under a QDRO does not start a new participation period. The employee's age, death, or disability is used to determine if the distribution is qualified. Alternate payees or spousal beneficiaries can roll the distribution into their own designated Roth account. If they do, their own age, death, or disability is used to determine if a distribution from that account is qualified. If the rollover is done with a direct rollover (also known as a trustee-to-trustee transfer), their participation period begins on the earlier of the employee's participation period or the recipient's participation period under the plan.[45]

Any excess deferral attributable to a designated Roth contribution that is not distributed by April 15th of the taxable year after the year in which the excess deferral occurred is included in gross income for the year in which the excess deferral is distributed.[46]

Distributions from a designated Roth account and other distributions and payments from the 401(k) plan that includes a Roth 401(k) are treated separately in determining their tax treatment.[47]

Nonqualified Distributions

The regulations provide that a distribution that is not a qualified distribution is taxed under Section 402, which provides that Section 72 applies. The designated Roth account is treated as a separate contract under Section 72, ignoring pre-tax elective deferral accounts and after-tax employee contributions.[48] The amount taxable is computed by determining the ratio of the investment in the contract to the account balance and then multiplying that ratio by the amount of the distribution. The result is the amount of the investment in the contract attributable to the distribution.[49]

> *Example 1.* Juliet received a $10,000 distribution from her qualified Roth account. Her contributions were $60,000 and the account balance prior to the distribution was $100,000, producing a ratio of 60 percent. Sixty percent of the distribution, or $6,000, is attributable to her investment in the contract. The remaining $4,000 is taxable. Her remaining investment in the contract is $54,000.

If a nonqualified distribution is not a direct rollover and only a portion is rolled over, the first portion that is rolled over is considered to be the amount includable in income under Section 72(e)(8).[50] This means that if the amount rolled over is at least equal to the income amount, none of the distribution is taxable.

> *Example 2.* Employee B receives a $14,000 eligible rollover distribution that is not a qualified distribution from B's designated Roth account. It consists of $11,000 of investment in the contract and $3,000 of income. Within 60 days of receipt, Employee B rolls over $7,000 of the distribution into a Roth IRA. Because the first portion of the rollover amount is considered to be the amount of income, the $3,000 of income is considered to be

rolled over first. The remaining $4,000 of the rollover is deemed to consist of investment in the contract. Since the $3,000 of the distribution that could be includable in gross income is rolled over, none of the distribution is includable in Employee B's gross income.[51]

Tax treatment of rollovers. As discussed previously, a designated Roth account can be rolled over directly from one Roth 401(k) plan to another without taxation. A distribution made directly to the employee cannot be rolled into another Roth 401(k) plan. It can be rolled into a Roth IRA within 60 days after the employee receives the distribution.[52] A direct rollover and any amount paid directly to an employee are treated as separate distributions.[53]

A Roth 401(k) rollover can be rolled over to a Roth IRA even if the distributee cannot make regular contributions to a Roth IRA.[54]

When a rollover contribution is made to a designated Roth account in a direct rollover, the investment in the contract is the amount that would have been excluded from income if the distribution had not been rolled over. For qualified distributions, this means that the entire amount of the rollover will be allocated to the investment in contract.[55] If the entire balance of a designated Roth account is rolled over to another designated Roth account and the investment in the contract exceeds the account balance, the investment in the contract in the distributing plan is added to the investment in the contract for the recipient plan.[56]

These two provisions make sense. If an employee would not have been taxed on a distribution from Plan 1 and contributes the distribution to a designated Roth account under Plan 2, the tax-status of the Plan 1 distribution should carry over to the Plan 2 account. Similarly, if an entire designated Roth account is rolled over from Plan 1 to Plan 2 and there is no gain in the account, the employee should receive the benefit of the investment in Plan 1 when taking distributions from Plan 2.

Similar rules apply in determining the portion of a rollover to a Roth IRA that is treated as contributions. All of a qualified distribution rolled over to a Roth IRA is treated as a regular contribution.[57] If (1) the entire balance of a designated Roth account is distributed; (2) only a portion of the distribution is rolled over; and (3) the investment in the contract exceeds the balance in the account at the time of the distribution, the excess of the investment in the contract over the amount used to determine the taxable portion of the distribution is treated as a regular contribution to the Roth IRA.[58]

With Roth IRAs, the participation period begins when the first Roth IRA contribution is made. A rollover from a Roth 401(k) does not carry its participation period with it to a Roth 401(k). Instead, the participation period begins with the earlier of the beginning of the participation period for the Roth IRA or the year that the Roth 401(k) rollover occurs.[59] If the Roth IRA has existed for at least five years, this can be a way to take qualified distributions attributable to a Roth 401(k) account earlier than possible if no rollover occurs.

Example 3. Employee D began making designated Roth contributions under his employer's 401(k) plan in 2006. Employee D, who is over age 59 ½, takes a distribution from D's designated Roth account in 2008, prior to the end of the participation period for the designated Roth account. The distribution is an eligible rollover distribution and D rolls it over in accordance with Section 402(c) and Section 402A(c)(3) to D's Roth IRA, which was established in 2003. Any subsequent distribution from the Roth IRA of the amount rolled in, plus earnings thereon, would be a qualified distribution within the meaning of Section 408A(d)(2). None of the distribution would be includable in gross income.[60]

Example 4. Same facts as in Example 3, except that the Roth IRA is D's first IRA, established with the 2008 rollover. No other contributions are made to the Roth IRA. The Roth IRA participation period begins in 2008, the year that the Roth IRA was established with the rollover. Any distribution from the Roth IRA before the end of the participation period will not be a qualified distribution. If any of the distribution exceeds the portion of the rollover contribution that consists of investment in the contract it is includable in D's gross income.[61]

Example 5. Same facts as in Example 4, except that the distribution from the Roth 401(k) and the rollover occur in 2011. At the time of the distribution and rollover, the distribution is a qualified distribution from a Roth 401(k) plan. However, because the participation period for rollovers to Roth IRAs begins at the earlier of the Roth IRA participation period or the year in which a rollover contribution is made to a Roth IRA, the Roth IRA participation period begins in 2011. This means that distributions from the Roth IRA will be taxable to the extent that the distribution exceeds the amount of the rollover.[62]

Rollovers between Roth 401(k)s and Roth IRAs are a one-way street. Distributions from Roth 401(k)s may be rolled over to a Roth IRA but Roth IRAs cannot be rolled over to a Roth 401(k).[63]

Computing the Investment in the Contract Remaining after a Qualified Distribution

If a disabled employee takes any distributions after satisfying the participation period, the entire distribution is qualified and non-taxable. If he or she takes a distribution later when no longer disabled, some of the distribution may be nonqualified unless he or she has attained the age of 59½. In those situations, the investment in the contract attributable to the qualified distribution will affect how much of the nonqualified distribution is taxable.

In this case, the investment in the contract is computed in the same way that it is for nonqualified distributions – the ratio of the investment in the contract to the account balance is computed and then multiplied by the amount of the distribution. This result is then subtracted from the investment in the contract to determine the remaining investment in the contract.

Hardship Distributions

Designated Roth contributions are included in an employee's elective deferrals to determine the amount available for a hardship distribution. The amount that is taxable is determined under the general rules of Section 72.[64]

Reporting and Recordkeeping Requirements

A companion to the complicated rollover rules for Roth 401(k) accounts are detailed requirements for reporting and recordkeeping for those accounts.

Recordkeeping for the Participation Period and Investment in the Contract

Responsibility for tracking each employee's five taxable year period of participation and investment in the contract falls on the plan administrator or other responsible party ("plan administrator"). Plan administrators can assume that employees use the calendar year as their taxable year unless they actually know that the employee uses a different taxable year. Similarly, if a plan receives a direct rollover from another Roth 401(k) account, the plan administrator of the receiving plan can rely on reasonable representations made by the plan administrator of the plan that is making the rollover.[65]

Additional Information Required for Rollovers

When a plan makes a rollover distribution, the plan administrator for a distributing plan must provide a statement with specific information. The statement must be provided within a reasonable time after the direct rollover or the employee's request, but no more than 30 days after the direct rollover or request.[66]

If the rollover is to a designated Roth account under another plan, the plan administrator of the distributing plan must provide the plan administrator of the receiving plan either (1) a statement showing the first year of the participation period and the portion of the distribution attributable to the investment in the contract; or (2) a statement that the distribution is a qualified distribution.[67]

If the distribution is not a direct rollover to a designated Roth account under another plan, at the employee's request, the plan administrator must provide the employee the same information described previously. The statement does not have to indicate the first year of the participation period.[68]

Report of Rollover to the IRS

The recipient plan must file a Form 1099-R, "Distributions from Pensions, Annuities, Retirement or Profit-Sharing Plans, IRAs, Insurance Contracts, etc." The regulation requires the employee's name and Social Security number, amount of the rollover, year that the rollover contribution was made, and other information as prescribed in the form and instructions.[69] If an employee converts some or all of a pre-tax Roth account to a designed Roth account and then receives a distribution within five years from the beginning of the tax year in which the conversion was made, the plan must report the total amount that is allocable to the in-plan Roth rollover.[70] The instructions also include specific directions on how to report a direct rollover from a designated Roth account to a Roth IRA and how to report a direct rollover from a 401(k) plan to a designated Roth account in the same plan.[71]

Endnotes

1. P.L. 107-16.
2. P.L. 107-16, Sec. 901.
3. P.L. 109-280, Sec. 811.
4. IRC Sec. 402A(a).
5. IRB 2006-20.
6. IRC Sec. 402A(a)(2).
7. IRC Sec. 402A(b)(2).
8. IRC Sec. 402A(c)(2).
9. Treas. Reg. §1.401(k)-1(f)(1)(i).
10. Treas. Reg. §1.401(k)-1(f)(4).
11. Treas. Reg. §1.401(k)-1(a)(4)(iv).
12. Treas. Reg. §1.401(k)-1(f)(1).
13. IRC Sec. 402A(c)(1).
14. IRC Sec. 402A(a)(1).
15. Treas. Reg. §1.401(k)-1(f)(2).
16. IRC Sec. 402A(b)(2)(B); Treas. Reg. §1.401(k)-1(f)(3).
17. Treas. Reg. §1.402A-1, A-13.
18. Treas. Reg. §1.401(k)-1(f)(5)(i).
19. Treas. Reg. §1.401(k)-1(f)(1)(i).
20. Treas. Reg. §1.401(k)-1(f)(5)(ii)(A).
21. Treas. Reg. §1.402A-1, A-5.
22. IRC Sec. 402A(c)(4), added by P.L. 111-240, Sec. 2112.
23. IRC Sec. 402A(c)(4)(E), added by P.L. 112-240, Sec. 902(a).
24. Notice 2010-84, IRB 2010-51, November 29, 2010, A-2.
25. Notice 2010-84, A-6.
26. IRC Sec. 402(c)(4).
27. Notice 2010-84, A-19, A-20.
28. Notice 2010-84, A-5.
29. Notice 2010-84, A-3(a).
30. Notice 2010-84, A-3(b).
31. Notice 2010-84, A-3(c).

32. Notice 2010-84, A-3(d).
33. Notice 2010-84, A-7. Notice 2009-75, 2009-39 IRB 436 discusses the tax consequences of a rollover from a 401(k) plan to a Roth IRA.
34. Notice 2010-84, A-9.
35. Notice 2010-84, A-8.
36. IRC Sec. 402A(c)(4)(A)(ii).
37. Notice 2010-84, A-12.
38. Ibid.
39. IRC Sec. 402A(d)(1).
40. IRC Sec. 402A(d)(2)(A), referencing Section 408A(d)(2)(A).
41. IRC Sec. 402A(d)(2)(A).
42. IRC Sec. 402A(d)(2)(B).
43. Treas. Reg. §1.402A-1, A-4.
44. Treas. Reg. §1.402A-1, A-4(c).
45. Treas. Reg. §1.402A-1, A-4(d).
46. IRC Sec. 402A(d)(3).
47. IRC Sec. 402A(d)(4).
48. Treas. Reg. §1.402A-1, A-3.
49. IRC Sec. 72(e)(8).
50. Treas. Reg. §1.402A-1, A-5(c).
51. Treas. Reg. §1.402A-1, A-5(d).
52. IRC Sec. 402(c)(3); Treas. Reg. §1.408a-10, A-1.
53. Treas. Reg. §1.402A-1, A-5(a).
54. Treas. Reg. §1.408A-10, A-2. The income limitations on Roth IRA contributions could prevent a distributee from making regular contributions to a Roth IRA.
55. Treas. Reg. §1.402A-1,A-6(a).
56. Treas. Reg. §1.402A-1, A-6(b).
57. Treas. Reg. §1.408A-10, A-3(a).
58. Treas. Reg. §1.408A-10, A-3(b).
59. Treas. Reg. §1.408A-10, A-4(a).
60. Treas. Reg. §1.408A-10, A-4(b), Example 1.
61. Treas. Reg. §1.408A-10, A-4(b), Example 2.
62. Treas. Reg. §1.408A-10, A-4(b), Example 3.
63. Treas. Reg. §1.408A-10, A-5.
64. Treas. Reg. §1.402A-1, A-8.
65. Treas. Reg. §1.402A-2, A-1.
66. Treas. Reg. §1.402A-2, A-2(b).
67. Treas. Reg. §1.402A-2, A-2(a)(1).
68. Treas. Reg. §1.402A-2, A-2(a)(2).
69. Treas. Reg. §1.402A-2, A-3.
70. 2013 Instructions for Forms 1099-R and 5498, p.2.
71. Ibid, p. 5.

Chapter 8

I Put It In, How Can I Get It Out?

Introduction

Once contributions are made to a 401(k) plan, a participant can only get the money out when allowed by the law and the terms of the plan. The law specifies both when the plan must make distributions and when distributions can be made without penalty to the recipient. As long as the terms of the plan comply with the requirements imposed by law, it can provide other distribution rules.

Plan Requirements

Permissible Benefit Events

The terms of a plan *must* provide that, unless the participant elects otherwise, benefit payments under the plan begin within 60 days after the end of the plan year in which the last of the following events occurs:[1]

- The date on which the participant attains the earlier of age 65 or the plan's normal retirement age

- The tenth anniversary of the year in which the participant commenced participation in the plan

- The participant terminates service with the employer

Late Start Date

The plan may, but is not required to, allow a participant to elect a later start date. To elect a later date, the participant must submit a signed, written statement to the plan administrator that describes the benefit and the start date for the benefit.[2]

A plan must also provide that the entire interest of each participant must either:

- be distributed to the participant not later than the required beginning date; or

- be distributed over the life of the participant or the lives of the participant and a designated beneficiary or a period that does not extend beyond the life expectancy of the participant or the participant and the designated beneficiary.[3]

Elective Deferral Distributions

A participant's elective deferrals and the earnings related to them cannot be distributed before:

- the participant's death, disability, or termination from employment;[4]

- the participant becoming age 59½;[5]

- termination of the plan;[6] or

- the participant's hardship.[7]

A special provision allows members of the military reserve to take distributions from employee elective deferrals and related earnings. To qualify, the reservist must be called up for at least 179 days or an indefinite period and take the distribution during the period beginning with their order or call to active duty and ending when the active duty period ends.[8]

The right to distributions cannot be based just on a participant completing a specific period of participation or the lapse of a fixed number of years.[9]

Severance from employment. A severance of employment occurs when a participant ceases to be an employee of the employer maintaining the plan. However, if the new employer maintains the same plan with respect to the employee, an employee does not have a severance from employment. A new employer can maintain a plan with respect to a participant by continuing or assuming sponsorship of the plan or by accepting a transfer of plan assets and liabilities with respect to the participant.[10] Thus, if Company A buys Company B and transfers the 401(k) plan assets for the Company B participants who remain with Company A, those participants do not have a severance from employment.

Required Minimum Distributions

The price for the ability to make contributions to a 401(k) plan on a pre-tax basis (if desired) and tax-deferred growth is two-fold.

1. A participant has only a limited ability to access the account before reaching age 59½ or the occurrence of certain events.

2. A participant must begin to take distributions upon reaching age 70½ unless they are still working for the plan sponsor and do not own more than 5 percent of the sponsor.

To be a qualified plan, a plan must provide that a participant's entire interest will either be distributed to the participant no later than the Required Beginning Date (RBD) or distributions to the participant meeting specific computational requirements will start no later than the RBD.[11] It must also provide that if a participant dies after their RBD but before the distribution of their entire account, the remaining balance must be distributed at least as rapidly as the method of distributions being used at the participant's death.[12] If a participant dies before RMDs begin and any portion is payable to a designated beneficiary, that portion is distributed over the life or life expectancy of the beneficiary.[13] Any portion not payable to a designated beneficiary must be distributed within five years of the participant's death.[14] Special rules apply if the participant's surviving spouse is the designated beneficiary.[15]

Required Beginning Date

The Required Beginning Date (RBD) is April 1 of the calendar year following the later of:

- the calendar year in which the participant attains age 70½; or

- the participant retires from working for the employer maintaining the plan.[16]

A plan can provide that the RBD for all participants is April 1 of the calendar year after the participant attains age 70½, even if the participant is not a 5 percent owner.[17]

Example 1. Sandra retired at age 66. Her birthday is June 29. She will turn 70½ on December 29 of 2014. Her required beginning date is April 1 of 2015.

Example 2. Jackie retired at age 67. Her birthday is July 15. She will turn 70½ on January 15, 2015. Her RBD is April 1, 2016.

Example 3. In Year 1, Rita turned 70½. In Year 3, she retired from Company A at age 72. She had a 401(k) plan sponsored by Company A and a 401(k) plan sponsored by Company B, which she left at age 60. Her RBD for the Company A 401(k) plan is April 1 of Year 4 after she retired from Company A. Her RBD for Company B 401(k) plan is April 1, Year 2.

Exception for 5 percent owners. For participants who own more than 5 percent of the employer in the year they attain age 70½, their RBD is April 1 of the year after they turn 70½.[18]

A person is deemed to turn 70½ six calendar months after the 70th anniversary of their birth.[19]

> *Example 4.* Karen's date of birth was June 30, 1944. The 70th anniversary of her birth is June 30, 2014. She attains age 70 ½ on December 30, 2014. Her RBD is April 1, 2015.

> *Example 5.* If Karen's date of birth had been July 1, 1944, the 70th anniversary of her birth would be July 1, 2014. She would attain age 70½ on January 1, 2015. Her RBD would be April 1, 2016.

Designated Beneficiary

Not all beneficiaries, even if designated in the beneficiary designation form on file with the plan, qualify as Designated Beneficiaries. The existence of a Designated Beneficiary (DB) affects lifetime RMDs only if the DB is the participant's spouse who is more than ten years younger than the participant. In contrast, whether a DB exists and who the DB is can have a significant impact on RMDs after the participant's death.

To qualify as a DB, the beneficiary must be: (1) an individual; and (2) designated as a beneficiary by the participant.[20] It is sufficient if the individual is designated as the beneficiary under the terms of the plan; it does not have to be an actual designation by the participant. The DB does not have to be identified by name if the individual who is to be the beneficiary is identifiable. For example, a designation of "my spouse" should be sufficient to identify the person intended to be the beneficiary. The members of a class of beneficiaries will be treated as identifiable if it is possible to identify the class member with the shortest life expectancy.[21]

A designation under a will or otherwise that the participant's interest passes to a specific individual is not sufficient to make the individual a DB unless the individual is designated as a beneficiary under the plan.[22] Thus, if no beneficiary designation is filed with a plan and the plan provides that the beneficiary is the participant's estate if there is no named beneficiary, the individuals named under the participant's will to receive the account are not DBs.

To be a DB, an individual must first be a beneficiary as of the date of death. They must also be a beneficiary as of September 30 of the year after the year of the participant's death. If an individual is not a beneficiary as of the date of death, they cannot become a beneficiary between the date of death and September 30 of the year after death and qualify as a DB. This allows individuals who receive their full benefit by that September 30 to be ignored in determining the DB.

Planning Tip. A charity or other entity that was named as a beneficiary by the participant is ignored in determining the DBs if the entity receives its interest by the September 30 deadline.

Similarly, a named beneficiary who makes a qualified disclaimer by that September 30 is also disregarded in determining the DB.[23]

Planning Tip: A disclaimer results in the disclaiming beneficiary being treated as dying before the participant. As a result, the beneficiaries who become entitled to the disclaimed share are treated as beneficiaries as of the date of death.

If the surviving spouse is the DB and dies before distributions begin, the spouse is treated as the participant so the plan DB is the surviving spouse's DB.[24] However, if the surviving spouse remarries before dying, the new spouse is not treated as the deceased participant's surviving spouse and cannot delay distributions until the participant would have attained age 70½.[25] Any other beneficiary who dies prior to September 30 of the year after the participant's death continues to be treated as a beneficiary on that September 30 to determine the distribution period for RMDs.[26]

Trust as Defined Beneficiary

Although a trust is not an individual, its beneficiaries may be treated as the participant's DBs in determining RMDs if specific requirements are met.[27] Those requirements are:

- The trust is valid under state law, or would be but for the fact it does not have any principal.

- The trust is irrevocable or will, by its terms, become irrevocable upon the participant's death.

- The trust beneficiaries who are beneficiaries of the trust's interest in the plan are identifiable, as defined at footnote 21.

- The required documentation has been provided to the plan administrator.[28]

If the trust has multiple beneficiaries, the oldest beneficiary's age will be used to determine the life expectancy in calculating the RMDs.[29] If a participant's interest in the plan is divided into separate accounts, the treatment depends on whether the separate accounts have different beneficiaries. If they do not, all of the separate accounts are aggregated. If they do, the separate accounts are treated separately for purposes of determining the RMDs for each separate account if the separate accounts are established by December 31 of the year after the participant's death.[30] The regulations define separate accounts as separate portions of a participant's benefit reflecting the separate interests of the beneficiaries and for which separate accounting is maintained.[31] If a trust is the only beneficiary and the spouse is the sole trust beneficiary, the spouse will be treated as the sole beneficiary of the participant's account if the trust requirements are met.

Documentation required for RMDs before the participant's death. The documentation that must be provided to the plan administrator is either:

- a copy of the trust agreement (and the participant must agree to provide the plan administrator any trust amendment within a reasonable time of the amendment);[32] or

- the following information in lieu of the trust agreement and agreement to provide a copy of any amendments.

  - A list of all beneficiaries, including contingent and remainder beneficiaries with a description of the conditions on their entitlement sufficient to show the spouse is the sole beneficiary

  - A certification that, to the best of the participant's knowledge, the list is correct and complete and that the trust meets the first three requirements outlined in the previous section

  - An agreement to provide the plan administrator corrected certifications within a reasonable time of a trust amendment that changes any information in a previous certification

  - An agreement to provide a copy of the trust instrument to the plan administrator upon demand[33]

Documentation required for RMDs after the participant's death. The following documentation must be provided to the trust administrator by October 31 of the year after death:

- A copy of the trust document for the trust named as a beneficiary[34]

- The following information in lieu of the trust agreement and agreement to provide a copy of any amendments:

  - A final list of all beneficiaries, including contingent and remainder beneficiaries with a description of the conditions on their entitlement as of September 30 of the year after death

  - A certification that, to the best of the trustee's knowledge, the list is correct and complete and that the trust meets the first three requirements outlined in the previous section

  - An agreement to provide a copy of the trust instrument to the plan administrator upon demand[35]

If the plan administrator reasonably relies on the information provided in determining RMDs but that information is inconsistent with the actual trust agreement, the plan is treated as complying with the RMD requirements if RMDs for years after discovery of the error are based on the actual trust terms.[36]

If the discrepancy causes the beneficiary to receive less than the correct RMD based on the actual trust terms, the beneficiary does not receive the same relief. The Section 4974 fifty percent excise tax on the amount not distributed is computed using the correct information.[37]

Lifetime RMDs

A participant must begin taking distributions when they reach their RBD. The RMD is determined by dividing the account balance by a joint life expectancy, referred to as the applicable distribution period. An RMD must be taken for the year of the participant's death. The calculation assumes that the participant lived for the entire year. Any RMD for the year of death that was not distributed to the participant must be distributed to a beneficiary.[38]

Account value used to determine the RMD. Determining the account value used in the RMD calculation begins with the account balance on the last valuation date of the calendar year. That value is then increased by any contributions or forfeitures allocated to the account balance during the year and after the valuation date. The plan can exclude contributions allocated after the valuation date but not actually made during that year. The account value is decreased by any distributions made in that calendar year but after the valuation date.[39]

RMDs cannot be rolled over to another qualified plan or an IRA.[40] Amounts distributed that exceed the RMD may be rolled over or transferred from one plan to another. In that case, the receiving plan's account balance for the year of the rollover or transfer includes the amount rolled over or transferred, even if received in a different calendar year.[41] This decreases the RMD for the distributing plan and increases it for the receiving plan.

Calculating the joint life expectancy. For most participants, the joint life expectancy is calculated using the *IRS Uniform Lifetime Table* shown in Figure 8.1, based on the participant's age on their birthday in the year for which a distribution is being made.[42]

Planning Tip. Because the distribution is always greater than one, RMDs will never fully deplete the account.

If the spouse is the sole designated beneficiary and is more than ten years younger than the participant, the joint life expectancy is determined using the participant and spouse's ages as of their birthdays during the year. To be the sole designated beneficiary, the spouse must be the sole beneficiary of the participant's entire interest at all times during the year.[43] The spouse is

Figure 8.1. IRS Uniform Lifetime Table	
Participant's age	**Distribution period**
70	27.4
71	26.5
72	25.6
73	24.7
74	23.8
75	22.9
76	22.0
77	21.2
78	20.3
79	19.5
80	18.7
81	17.9
82	17.1
83	16.3
84	15.5
85	14.8
86	14.1
87	13.4
88	12.7
89	12.0
90	11.4
91	10.8
92	10.2
93	9.6
94	9.1
95	8.6
96	8.1
97	7.6
98	7.1
99	6.7
100	6.3
101	5.9
102	5.5

Figure 8.1. IRS Uniform Lifetime Table (Cont'd)	
103	5.2
104	4.9
105	4.5
106	4.2
107	3.9
108	3.7
109	3.4
110	3.1
111	2.9
112	2.6
113	2.4
114	2.1
115+	1.9
Treas. Reg. §1.401(a)(9)-9, A-2.	

considered the sole beneficiary if the participant and spouse are married on January 1 but divorce or either the participant or the spouse die during the year.[44]

Use of an annuity to satisfy the RMD requirement. Alternatively, the RMD can be satisfied by using the participant's entire account to purchase an annuity from an insurance company. The first payment period for the annuity must begin on or before the purchase date and the payment for each payment period must be made before the end of the payment period. For example, for monthly payments, the first month must begin no later than the date the annuity was purchased. Each payment must be made before the end of the month that the payment applies to.[45] If the annuity is purchased after the RBD, the payments will satisfy the RMD requirements of section 401(a)(9) for years after the year of purchase if the annuity payments satisfy Treasury Regulation Section 1.401(a)(9)-6.[46]

A participant can also use a portion of the account to purchase an annuity, leaving a portion in the account. In that case, each portion is examined separately to determine if the RMD requirements are met. The annuity must satisfy the requirements of Treasury Regulation Section 1.401(a)(9)-6. The balance of the account must be distributed based on the regular rules for RMDs from defined contribution plans.[47]

RMDs after the Participant's Death

The rules for RMDs after the participant's death depend on whether the participant died before or after their RBD and whether the beneficiary is a designated beneficiary. Special rules apply if the spouse is the beneficiary.

If the Participant Dies before Their RBD

If a participant dies before their RBD, Section 401(a)(9)(B)(ii) requires that the entire interest of the participant be distributed within five years after the participant's death (the "5-year rule"). However, an exception in the Code treats distributions made over a DB's life expectancy as distributed on the date that the distributions begin. To qualify for this exception, the distribution must be made over the DB's life expectancy or a period that does not extend beyond the DB's life expectancy and begin no later than one year after the participant's death or a later date specified in regulations.[48]

Although the Code treats the 5-year rule as the default and life expectancy distributions as an exception, the regulations reverse this treatment if the participant has named a DB and the plan does not provide otherwise.[49] In that case, the life expectancy method is the default RMD method unless the plan specifies otherwise.

The regulations simplify the 5-year rule by allowing it to be satisfied if the entire interest in the account is distributed by the end of the calendar year that contains the fifth anniversary of the participant's death. The plan does not have to distribute the entire interest by the fifth anniversary of the participant's death. If a participant dies on January 1, 2015, the deadline for distributing the entire interest is December 31, 2020, not January 1, 2020, which is the fifth anniversary of the participant's death.[50]

Surviving spouse. A surviving spouse does not have to start taking RMDs until the end of the calendar year in which the participant would have attained age 70½, if later than December 31 of the year after the participant's death.[51] Note that this rule does not allow the surviving spouse to wait until April 1 of the year after the participant would have attained age 70½, which would have been the participant's RBD. In Example 4, if Karen died in 2010, a nonspouse beneficiary would have to begin RMDs by December 31, 2011. If her surviving spouse was the sole DB, they could delay taking distributions until December 31, 2013. In Example 5, the surviving spouse could have delayed taking distributions until December 31, 2014.

If the surviving spouse is the participant's sole DB and dies after the participant but before distributions have begun, distributions are made as if the surviving spouse was the participant, substituting the surviving spouse's date of death for the participant's. If the surviving spouse had remarried, leaving a surviving spouse, the surviving spouse of the deceased participant's surviving spouse cannot delay RMDs until the deceased surviving spouse would have become 70½.[52] Distributions to a surviving spouse are considered to begin on the date on which they are required to begin, even if distributions were made before that date.[53]

Plan provisions. The plan may specify that the 5-year rule applies to certain distributions, even if the participant has a DB. It may also specify that all distributions will be made using the 5-year rule. The plan can have different distribution methods and satisfy the distribution requirements.[54]

Participant elections. A plan can allow participants or their beneficiaries to elect either the 5-year rule or the life expectancy method for distributions after the participant's death. The election for the life expectancy method must be made before December 31 of the year after the participant's death. The election for the 5-year rule must be made by the end of the year that contains the fifth anniversary of the participant's death. The election becomes irrevocable on the last date for making the election and binds all subsequent beneficiaries. A plan that permits an election can specify the distribution method that applies if no election is made. If neither the participant nor the beneficiary makes an election and the plan does not specify a method, the life expectancy method applies if there is a DB. If there is not a DB, the 5-year rule applies.[55]

If the Participant Dies after His RBD

When a participant dies after her RBD, the Code requires that distributions be made "at least as rapidly" as under the distribution method used before the participant's death.[56] The regulations provide guidance on how to ensure that the distributions meet that requirement.

If the participant has a DB as of September 30 of the year after the participant's death, the applicable distribution period is the longer of:

- the DB's remaining life expectancy; or

- the participant's remaining life expectancy.[57]

This allows a DB who was older than the participant to use the participant's longer remaining life expectancy to determine their RMDs.

If the participant does not have a DB as of September 30 of the year after the participant's death, the applicable distribution period is the participant's remaining life expectancy.[58] The participant's remaining life expectancy is determined by their age on their birthday in the year after their death, reduced by one for each year after their death.[59]

Spouse as DB. If the sole designated beneficiary is the participant's surviving spouse, the spouse's life expectancy is determined using the Single Life Table (shown in Figure 8.2) and the spouse's age as of their birthday each year. This recalculates the surviving spouse's life expectancy every year. After the year of the spouse's death, the life expectancy is calculated using the Single Life Table and the spouse's age in the year of death, reduced by one for each year after the year the spouse died.[60]

Figure 8.2. IRS Single Life Table

Age	Life Expectancy	Age	Life Expectancy	Age	Life Expectancy
0	82.4	38	45.6	76	12.7
1	81.6	39	44.6	77	12.1
2	80.6	40	43.6	78	11.4
3	79.7	41	42.7	79	10.8
4	78.7	42	41.7	80	10.2
5	77.7	43	40.7	81	9.7
6	76.7	44	39.8	82	9.1
7	75.8	45	38.8	83	8.6
8	74.8	46	37.9	84	8.1
9	73.8	47	37.0	85	7.6
10	72.8	48	36.0	86	7.1
11	71.8	49	35.1	87	6.7
12	70.8	50	34.2	88	6.3
13	69.9	51	33.3	89	5.9
14	68.9	52	32.3	90	5.5
15	67.9	53	31.4	91	5.2
16	66.9	54	30.5	92	4.9
17	66.0	55	29.6	93	4.6
18	65.0	56	28.7	94	4.3
19	64.0	57	27.9	95	4.1
20	63.0	58	27.0	96	3.8
21	62.1	59	26.1	97	3.6
22	61.1	60	25.2	98	3.4
23	60.1	61	24.4	99	3.1
24	59.1	62	23.5	100	2.9
25	58.2	63	22.7	101	2.7
26	57.2	64	21.8	102	2.5
27	56.2	65	21.0	103	2.3
28	55.3	66	20.2	104	2.1
29	54.3	67	19.4	105	1.9
30	53.3	68	18.6	106	1.7
31	52.4	69	17.8	107	1.5
32	51.4	70	17.0	108	1.4

Figure 8.2. IRS Single Life Table (Cont'd)					
33	50.4	71	16.3	109	1.2
34	49.4	72	15.5	110	1.1
35	48.5	73	14.8	111 & older	1.0
36	47.5	74	14.1		
37	46.5	75	13.4		
Treas. Reg. §1.401(a)(9)-9, A-1.					

Example 6. Josh's spouse turned 75 in the year of death. Josh was 80 in that year. For purposes of determining the RMD for the year after the death of Josh's spouse, the applicable distribution period is 12.7 years. This is the longer of 9.7, Josh's life expectancy in the year after death, and 12.7, his spouse's life expectancy in the year after death. In the next year, it is the longer of 9.1, Josh's recomputed life expectancy, and 11.7, his spouse's life expectancy in the year after death, reduced by one.

Recalculating the surviving spouse's life expectancy results in it being reduced by less than one year every year. The deceased spouse's life expectancy is reduced by one each year. This means it is possible for the deceased spouse's life expectancy to be longer than the surviving spouse's initially but for the surviving spouse's life expectancy to eventually become longer.

Nonspouse DB. For nonspouse DBs, the life expectancy is computed using the Single Life Table and the DB's age on their birthday in the year after the participant's death, reduced by one for each year after the year after the participant's death.[61]

Example 7. Steve is the nonspouse beneficiary of an account and turned 50 in the year after the participant's death. The participant died at age 75. The RMD is determined using 34.2 years, Steve's life expectancy in the year after the participant's death, instead of the life expectancy of the participant, 12.7 years.

With nonspouse DBs, once the appropriate life expectancy is determined, the same person's life expectancy will be used consistently. Because both life expectancies are reduced by one, it is not possible for the DB's life expectancy to become longer than the participant's remaining life expectancy in subsequent years.

No DB. If the participant does not have a DB, the participant's remaining life expectancy is measured by using the *IRS Single Life Table* shown in Figure 8.2 and the participant's age as of their birthday in the year of death. This age is reduced by one for each year after the year of the participant's death.

Distributions Other than RMDs

Hardship Withdrawals

Section 401(k)(2)(B)(i)(IV) specifically allows hardship distributions to be made from 401(k) plans. A hardship distribution must be due to an immediate and heavy financial need of the employee and be necessary to satisfy the financial need. The plan must have nondiscriminatory and objective standards set out in the plan to determine an immediate and heavy financial need.

The total amount that can be distributed as a hardship withdrawal is the employee's elective deferrals as of the date of the distribution, reduced by the amount of elective deferrals previously distributed. It does not include earnings, qualified nonelective contributions, or qualified matching contributions.[62] In other words, a hardship distribution allows participants to get their own contributions back but nothing else.

The amount distributed is taxable to the participant. In addition, it is subject to the 10 percent early distribution penalty unless an exception applies.

The plan can increase the maximum distributable amount by any amounts credited to a participant's account as of a date that is not later than December 31, 1988, or the end of the last plan year that ended before July 1, 1989.[63]

Immediate and heavy financial need. The existence of an immediate and heavy financial need is based on all the facts and circumstances. The need to pay funeral expenses of a family member would generally qualify while a distribution for the purchase of a boat or television would generally not. As the following examples show, a financial need may be immediate and heavy even if it was reasonably foreseeable or voluntarily incurred.[64]

A distribution is for an immediate and heavy financial need if it is for:

- expenses for (or necessary to obtain) medical care that would qualify as deductible medical expenses (without regard to the adjusted gross income floor) or are incurred for the participant's primary beneficiary under the plan;[65]

- costs directly related to the purchase of the participant's principal residence, not including mortgage payments;[66]

- payment of tuition, related educational fees, and room and board for up to the next 12 months of post-secondary education for the participant or their spouse, children, dependents (as defined in section 152), or the participant's primary beneficiary under the plan;[67]

- payments necessary to prevent the participant from being evicted from their principal residence or to prevent a foreclosure on that mortgage;[68]

- payments for burial or funeral expenses for the participant's deceased parent, spouse, children, dependents (as defined in Section 152, without regard to the earnings test), or the participant's primary beneficiary under the plan;[69] or

- expenses to repair damage to the participant's principal residence that qualifies for a casualty loss deduction, without regard to the 10 percent of adjusted gross income limitation.[70]

Distribution necessary to satisfy financial need. The distribution is necessary to satisfy a participant's immediate and heavy financial need only to the extent of the amount required to satisfy the need. Amounts necessary to pay any federal, state, or local income taxes or penalties reasonably anticipated to result from the distribution may be included in the amount required to satisfy the financial need.[71]

If the participant has other resources reasonably available to satisfy the need, a distribution is not considered to satisfy an immediate and heavy financial need. This determination uses a facts-and-circumstances test. A participant's resources include those of their spouse and minor children reasonably available to the participant. Property held for a child in an irrevocable trust or UTMA account is not considered a resource. The regulation also suggests that a vacation home owned by the participant and the participant's spouse will be generally considered an available resource.[72]

Employee representation. An employer may rely on a participant's representation in writing that the immediate and heavy financial need cannot be relieved from other reasonably available resources:[73]

- through reimbursement or compensation by insurance or otherwise;

- by liquidation of the participant's assets;

- by stopping contributions to the plan;

- by other currently available distributions and nontaxable loans from the plan of any employer; or

- by borrowing enough to satisfy the need from a commercial lender on reasonable commercial terms.

If one of these methods would increase the amount of the need, it does not reasonably relieve the need. For example, if the participant needs funds to purchase a principal residence, a plan loan that would disqualify the participant from other financing would not reasonably relieve the need.[74]

Satisfaction of immediate and heavy financial need. A distribution is deemed necessary to satisfy the participant's immediate and heavy financial need if:

- the participant has obtained all other currently available distributions and nontaxable loans under the plan and all other plans maintained by the employer; and

- the participant is prohibited by the plan terms or a legally enforceable agreement from making any contributions to the plan and all other plans of the employer for at least six months after receiving the hardship distribution.[75] This prohibits the participant from making contributions to stock option, stock purchase or similar plans.[76]

Other plans. Other plans of the employer include all qualified and nonqualified plans maintained by the employer. Excluded from the definition are mandatory employee contributions to a defined benefit plan or health or welfare plan.[77]

Planning Tip. The definition of financial hardship is different for nonqualified deferred compensation plans under Section 457(b) and Section 457(f) for tax exempts (which are now subject to Section 457(f) and Section 409A), and also for such nonqualified plans for profit-making entities under Section 409A. A financial hardship for either type of nonqualified plans may not qualify as a hardship for 401(k) plan purposes. There are special rules to be followed to claim a hardship for nonqualified plans subject to either of these two Code sections (that even includes nonqualified plans "linked" to the 401(k) plan (i.e., an "excess benefit plan"). Therefore, administration of a 401(k) and a nonqualified plan for a participant must be handled separately according to the applicable rules to properly comply.

Plan amounts attributable to employer matching and nonelective contributions. The restrictions on hardship withdrawals described previously apply only to elective contributions and QNECs and QMACs. A plan sponsor can provide that the portion of a participant's account that is not subject to the hardship withdrawal restrictions may be available for hardship withdrawals on more liberal terms than those described previously. If the plan does so, hardship withdrawals are benefits of the plan that must not discriminate in favor of Highly Compensated Employees (HCEs).

See Appendix B for a checklist that can be used in determining if a participant complies with the requirements for a 401(k) hardship withdrawal.

Plan Loans

Another way for participants to access their money is through a plan loan, *if permitted by the plan.* Plan loans do not have the same restrictions as hardship withdrawals of the participant's contributions. If a plan offers hardship withdrawals from other contributions, they may be subject to even fewer restrictions than loans. However, the hardship withdrawal rules require the participant to generally take the maximum amount of plan loans available before taking a hardship withdrawal. The price for plan loans is two-fold.

1. They must carry a reasonable rate of interest.

2. They must be repaid. The repayment obligation makes them riskier than hardship withdrawals – failure to repay them results in a deemed distribution from the plan to repay the loan. The deemed distribution is taxable and, if the participant is under 59½ at the time of the deemed distribution, subject to a 10 percent penalty.

Plan loans, unless structured carefully, will create problems for the plan. These problems can include violating the nondiscrimination rules and the antiassignment requirement, both of which would disqualify the plan, and violating the prohibited transaction rules, which would subject the plan administrator to excise taxes. See Appendix C for a 401(k) plan loan checklist.

Planning Tip: In audits, the IRS is finding that errors in loan administration (collection and reporting of defaults for failure to repay) are one of the most frequent 401(k) plan operational errors. For this reason, employers should consider whether they want to allow loans in the first instance. However, if the plan will allow loans, to reduce problems with this feature and simplify administration, a plan should consider only allowing *one loan* at a time. This will simplify administration of the repayment for both the plan Third-Party Administrator (TPA) as well as the plan participant. Loan repayment should also be done solely through payroll reduction for the same reason. Finally, plan loan provisions should treat a termination of employment as a deemed and automatic default that causes reporting to deal with this issue in the simplest fashion possible.[78]

Treatment of loans, assignments, or pledges. Unless a plan loan meets the requirements set out in Section 72(p), it is deemed to be a distribution from the plan to the borrower.[79] Any assignment, agreement to assign, pledge, or agreement to pledge any portion of an interest in a qualified plan is treated as a loan from the plan (these transactions are included in "plan loans" for purposes of this book). They must also meet the Section 72(p) requirements to avoid loan treatment.[80]

Loans not treated as distributions. Section 72(p) provides that a plan loan is not treated as a distribution if the following requirements are met:

- The total loans outstanding cannot exceed *the lesser of* $50,000, reduced by the excess (if any) of:

    - the highest loan balance during the one-year period ending on the day before the loan was made over;

- the outstanding balance of plan loans on the date the loan was made; or

- the greater of (a) one-half of the participant's vested plan balance or (b) $10,000.[81]

- The loan must be repayable within five years, except for loans made to purchase a residence that will be used as the participant's principal residence within a reasonable time.[82] The plan has discretion to establish a repayment schedule as long as it is not applied in a way that discriminates in favor of HCEs.

- The loan must require substantially level amortization with at least quarterly payments.[83] This prevents the use of an interest-only loan with a balloon payment.

- The loan must be evidenced by a legally enforceable agreement whose terms show compliance with Section 72(p) and Treasury Regulation Section 1.72(p)-1. The agreement must be set out in either a written paper document or a document delivered electronically that meets the requirements of Treasury Regulation Section 1.401(a)-21. It does not have to be signed if the applicable law provides it is enforceable without being signed.[84]

All plan loans to a participant are aggregated for purposes of applying the loan limit. Limiting the amount of any new loan to the $50,000 less any loan repayments made in the year before the date of the new loan prevents a participant from reborrowing the payments made on a loan to bring the total loan back up to $50,000.

Participants cannot deduct any interest paid on a plan loan that would otherwise be allowable if they are a key employee or the loan is secured by amounts attributable to elective deferrals.

A plan loan used to refinance a loan on a principal residence does not qualify for the extended repayment period available for a principal residence loan.[85]

Home refinancing plan loans. The regulations permit a participant to refinance a plan loan and/or borrow additional amounts from the plan if the loans together satisfy the amount limitations, term requirements, and level amortization requirement.[86] When a loan is refinanced and the term of the new loan ends after the date that is five years (or the maximum term allowed for a primary residence loan) from the date of the original loan, both the replacement loan and the replaced loan are considered outstanding on the date of the new loan. If the original loan term was less than maximum term, the replacement loan can have a term that extends beyond the original loan term without having the two loans treated as outstanding on the date of the new loan. A deemed distribution occurs when the two loans are treated as outstanding on the date of the new loan and their total exceeds the maximum loan allowable.

This can be avoided if the replacement loan is treated as two separate loans, the replaced loan and the new loan. The replaced loan must be amortized in substantially equal payments over a period that ends no later than the last of the permissible term for the replaced loan. The new loan must be amortized in substantially equal payments over a period that ends no later than the last of the permissible term for the new loan. [87]

Loan not treated as a prohibited transaction. Section 4975(d) sets out the rules a loan must meet so it is not treated as a prohibited transaction:

- It must be available to all participants or beneficiaries on a reasonably equivalent basis.

- It is not available to HCEs in an amount greater than the amount made available to other employees.

- It complies with specific plan provisions concerning plan loans.

- It bears a reasonable rate of interest.

- It is adequately secured.[88]

A loan is available to all participants and beneficiaries on a reasonably equivalent basis if:

- such loans are available to all plan participants and beneficiaries without regard to an individual's race, color, religion, sex, age, or national origin;

- the only factors considered in making a loan are those that would be considered in a normal commercial setting by an entity in the business of making similar loans (those factors can include an applicant's creditworthiness and financial need); and

- an evaluation of all relevant facts and circumstances indicates that loans are not reasonably withheld from any applicant.[89]

Loans are not considered to be made available to HCEs, officers, or shareholders in an amount greater than the amount made available to other employees if, based on all the relevant facts and circumstances, the plan does not operate to exclude large numbers of plan participants from receiving loans. The plan can set either a maximum dollar limitation or a maximum percentage of vested accrued benefit that may be borrowed.[90]

The plan must include specific plan provisions concerning participant loans, including explicit authorization for the plan fiduciary responsible for investing plan assets to establish a participant loan program. The written provisions must include:

- the identity of the person or positions authorized to administer the program;

- a procedure for applying for loans;

- the basis for approving or denying loans;

- any limitations on the types and amount of loans offered;

- the program's procedure for determining a reasonable rate of interest; and

- events constituting a default and how plan assets will be preserved after a default.[91]

Reasonable rate of interest and security. A loan has a reasonable rate of interest if it provides the plan with a return commensurate with the interest rates charged by lenders under similar circumstances.[92] A loan is considered to be adequately secured if the security for the loan is pledged to the plan so it can be disposed of upon default and has enough value and liquidity that it may be reasonably anticipated that no loss of principal or interest will result from the loan. The adequacy of the security is determined based on the type and amount of security required in a commercial setting for an arms-length loan. No more than 50 percent of a participant's vested accrued plan benefit can be used as security for all of the participant's plan loans.[93]

Effect of a default. The failure to make any installment payment when due violates the level amortization requirement under Section 72(p)(2)(C), causing a default and a deemed distribution. The plan may allow a cure period. If the payment is made during the cure period, the level amortization requirement will not be considered to have been violated. The cure period cannot extend beyond the end of the calendar quarter following the due date of the missed payment.[94]

When a deemed distribution occurs, the amount is the entire outstanding loan balance plus accrued interest at the time of the deemed distribution. The taxable amount of the deemed distribution and the 10 percent early distribution excise tax are determined as if it were an actual distribution.[95]

A deemed distribution is not treated as an actual distribution for purposes of the Section 401 qualification requirements, the Section 402 distribution requirements, the distribution restrictions of Section 401(k)(2)(b) or the vesting requirements of Treasury

Regulation Section 1.411(a)-7(d)(5).[96] It does not negate the participant's obligation to repay the loan. A failure to repay that is not reported as a taxable distribution at the time of the failure is an operational failure requiring a correction process if the administrator seeks any other solution but the proper deemed taxable distribution. See Chapter 13 for details on correcting such an operational failure under one of the IRS' correction programs.[97]

Plan loan offset. A plan can enforce its security interest in the loan by offsetting the participant's accrued benefit to repay the loan. The amount offset would be treated as an actual distribution, which may be prohibited under Section 401(a) or Section 401(k)(2)(B) as a distribution to an active employee.[98]

Net Unrealized Appreciation

Qualifying distributions of employer securities can qualify for special tax treatment referred to as Net Unrealized Appreciation (NUA) if the participant or beneficiary elects. If the distribution includes assets other than the employer securities, the employer securities can receive the special treatment and the other assets receive the normal distribution tax treatment. A participant or beneficiary can elect out of the special treatment either by paying tax on the fair market value of the employer securities received or by rolling the distribution over to another qualified account.

Electing NUA results in the following treatment:

- The portion of the distribution that represents the plan's cost or other basis will be taxable to the participant as ordinary income and subject to the 72(t) penalty, unless an exception applies.

- When the stock is sold or disposed of, the accumulated appreciation on the stock at the time of the distribution will be taxed as long-term capital gain.

- Appreciation on the stock after the distribution will be taxed as long-term or short-term capital gain, depending on the holding period after the distribution.

Determining the amount of NUA. NUA is the excess of the market value of the employer securities at the time of the distribution over the plan's cost or other basis in the securities. This means that if some of the securities distributed had appreciation and some had depreciation, the NUA is the net increase in value of all of the securities issued. All distributions to a distributee in a taxable year are treated as one distribution.[99]

The regulations outline four methods for how the cost or basis is determined. Method (A) uses the security's actual cost or basis if the security was earmarked to a participant's account at the time it was purchased by or contributed to the trust.[100]

Method (B) applies if the trust allocates the cost of securities acquired during a year or other period of 12 consecutive months among the accounts of all participants investing in employer securities. In that situation, the basis is the average cost to the trust of securities of the same type allocated to a participant's account.[101]

If neither method (A) nor (B) applies, method (C) applies if the entire trust or a specific portion of it is invested in one particular type of employer security and the plan did not sell any securities during the period except to pay benefits or exercise rights the trust accrued. In that situation, the cost or basis is the total amount credited to the distributee's account reduced by the amount available for investment in employer securities but not yet invested.[102]

Method (D) is used if none of these methods applies. It computes the basis based on the trust's average cost or basis of all employer securities of the type the distributee received, based on a specified inventory date. The inventory date cannot be more than 12 months before the date of distribution. The securities' average cost must be based on the actual cost of the securities. The computation must either consider the securities most recently purchased to be on hand (a LIFO method) or by using a moving average of the cost of the shares on hand.[103]

Although normally considered in regard to employer stock, NUA also applies to an employer's bonds or debentures issued with interest coupons or in registered form.[104]

Spousal Rights in 401(k) Plan Distributions

Qualified retirement plan assets can be a major part of many couples' assets. Frequently, one spouse has a much larger plan balance than the other. Because the husband commonly has a longer work history and higher earnings, his is often the larger account. How the account is distributed can have a significant impact on the couple's retirement income and then on the survivor's income.

ERISA required plans to provide a qualified joint and survivor annuity to retirees unless the participant chose to receive a different form of benefit. The plan also had to provide benefits to a surviving spouse if the participant died before retirement, but only if the participant elected that their survivor would receive retirement benefits.

To provide pension protection for surviving spouses, in the Retirement Equity Act of 1984 (REA)[105] Congress required qualified plans to provide automatic survivor benefits and allowed waiver of survivor benefits only with consent of both the participant and spouse.

Impact of Same-Sex Marriages on Spousal Rights

Spouses in legal same-sex marriages are entitled to the same spousal rights as individuals in traditional marriages. The United States Supreme Court in *United States v. Windsor*[106] held Section 3 of the 1996 Defense of Marriage Act (DOMA) deprived individuals of the equal liberty protected by the Fifth Amendment. That Section provided that that for federal law purposes, marriage was limited to opposite sex couples. Section 2 of DOMA, which provides that states do not have to recognize same sex marriages performed in other states, territories, or countries, was not at issue in *Windsor*. The Supreme Court's decision left many questions on its practical impact to be answered by the IRS and other federal agencies. Among those questions were:

- if the terms "spouse," "husband and wife," "husband," and "wife" include someone married to a person of the same sex if they are lawfully married under state law;

- if "marriage" includes a legal marriage between individuals of the same sex;

- whether individuals who were legally married in a state that authorizes same-sex marriage but live in a state that does not recognize those marriages are considered married for federal purposes;

- if individuals who are part of registered domestic partnerships, civil unions, or similar formal relationships recognized under a state law are treated as married; and

- the effective date of the *Windsor* holding.

In Rev. Rul. 2013-17,[107] the IRS answered the tax questions for tax purposes, including employee benefit plans. First, it stated that the terms "spouse," "husband and wife," "husband," and "wife" include someone married to a person of the same sex if they are lawfully married under state law. Second, "marriage" includes a legal marriage between individuals of the same sex. Third, it recognized same-sex marriages if they were validly married under the laws of the state where the marriage was performed, even if the couple is domiciled in a state that does not recognize same-sex marriages. Fourth, this recognition does not apply to individuals (whether same-sex or opposite sex) who are part of a registered domestic partnership, civil union, or similar formal relationship, even if it is valid under their state of domicile. Finally, the ruling applies prospectively as of September 16, 2013, and for any returns and claims for refund or credit if the statute of limitations has not expired.

The *Windsor* ruling and Rev. Rul. 2013-17 mean that the rules concerning spousal rights in qualified plans apply to all married couples, whether same-sex or opposite sex.

Requirement to Provide a Joint and Survivor Annuity and Preretirement Survivor Annuity

As a condition of qualification, a defined contribution plan must provide that the normal benefit provided to a vested participant upon reaching the annuity starting date is a qualified joint and survivor annuity.[108] If a vested participant dies before the annuity starting date, the normal benefit is a qualified preretirement survivor annuity.[109]

Qualified joint and survivor annuity. A Qualified Joint and Survivor Annuity (QJSA) means an annuity for the participant's life with a survivor annuity for the spouse's life that is at least 50 percent but not more than 100 percent of the participant's annuity. The QJSA must be actuarially equivalent to a single annuity for the participant's life.[110]

Qualified preretirement survivor annuity. For defined contribution plans, a Qualified Preretirement Survivor Annuity (QPSA) is an annuity for the survivor's life that is actuarially equivalent to at least 50 percent but not more than 100 percent of the participant's vested account balance as of the participant's date of death.[111]

Exception for Certain Defined Contribution Plans

Defined contribution plans, other than those subject to the minimum funding standards of Section 412, can be designed so they do not have to provide a QJSA or a QPSA as the default distribution method. To do this, the following requirements must be met:

- The plan provides that the vested account balance is payable in full to the surviving spouse or if there is no surviving spouse or the surviving spouse consents to a designated beneficiary.

- The participant does not elect for the benefits to be paid as a life annuity.

- The plan did not receive a direct or indirect transfer from a defined benefit plan or a defined contribution plan required to provide a QJSA or QPSA for the participant. If the plan separately accounts for the transferred assets and related income, only those assets are subject to the QJSA and QPSA requirements.[112]

Spousal Consent Requirement

A plan cannot distribute any portion of a participant's benefit until the consent requirements are met unless the distribution is a QJSA.[113] This requirement applies both to plan distributions as well as plan loans.[114]

Time of consent. The consent must be given during the period that begins 90 days before the annuity starting date and ends on the annuity starting date.[115] The plan must also provide participants with a written explanation of the QJSA at least 30 days before the annuity starting date but no more than 90 days before the annuity starting date.[116] The IRS provided sample language in Notice 97-10,[117] which can be found in Appendices D1 (for a QJSA) and D2 (for a QPSA). Once the explanation has been provided and the participant (and spouse, if necessary) consent, the annuity can start less than 30 days after the explanation was provided if the following conditions are met:

- The plan administrator clearly indicates to the participant that the participant has a right to at least 30 days to consider whether to waive the QJSA and consent to a different form of distribution.

- The participant can revoke an affirmative distribution election until at least the annuity starting date or, if later, any time before the end of the 7-day period beginning the day after the QJSA explanation is provided to the participant.

- The annuity starting date is after the date that the QJSA explanation is provided to the participant.

- Distribution does not begin before the end of the 7-day period beginning the day after the explanation of the QJSA is provided to the participant.[118]

Content of the consent. For a spouse's consent to be valid, it must:

- be in writing;

- designate a beneficiary or a form of benefits that cannot be changed without spousal consent (or expressly permits the participant to make future designations without the spouse's additional consent);

- acknowledges the effect of the election; and

- is witnessed by a plan representative or a notary public.[119]

No consent is required if the plan representative is satisfied that there is no spouse, the spouse cannot be located, or for other reasons provided in regulations.[120]

Effect of Windsor. Under Rev. Rul. 2013-17, a same-sex spouse's consent is required to any distribution that is not a QJSA. In *Cozen O'Connor, P.C. v. Tobits,*[121] less than five weeks after the *Windsor* decision, a federal district court applied *Windsor* to provide that a same-sex spouse was the deceased participant's surviving spouse and entitled to death benefits because she had not waived her spousal rights.

Qualified Domestic Relations Orders

The significance of qualified plan assets in many couple's net worth and the common disparity between the spouses' accounts are important factors in dividing assets as part of a divorce. As a result, the division of assets as part of a divorce often requires a transfer of qualified retirement plan assets from one spouse to another. Originally, this created problems for the plan and the participant involved since qualified plan benefits generally cannot be assigned or alienated.[122] Another provision of the Retirement Equity Act (REA) of 1984 dealt with the division of qualified retirement plan assets in a divorce. REA provided a process for the division of qualified retirement plan assets between spouses that does not violate the antialienation and assignment or distribution rules and provides an exception to the ERISA preemption of state laws. Qualified Domestic Relations Orders (QDROs), permitted under Section 414(p), provide a method for benefits to be transferred from one person to another without violating the antialienation and assignment or distribution rules. Figure 8.3 shows the process for a QDRO.

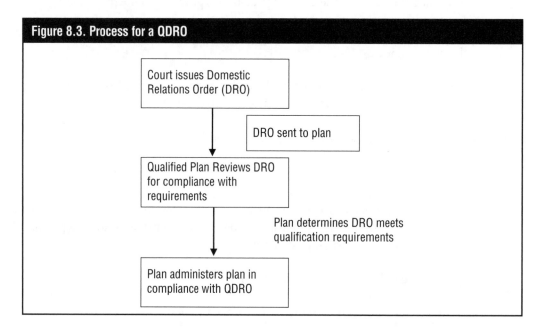

Figure 8.3. Process for a QDRO

Court issues Domestic Relations Order (DRO)

DRO sent to plan

Qualified Plan Reviews DRO for compliance with requirements

Plan determines DRO meets qualification requirements

Plan administers plan in compliance with QDRO

If the plan determines that the DRO does not meet the qualification requirements, it returns the order to the court or drafting attorney for necessary revisions.

Domestic Relations Order

A QDRO starts with a Domestic Relations Order (DRO) that either creates or recognizes the right of someone other than the plan participant (an alternate payee) to all or some of the participant's benefits under a plan. A DRO is a judgment, decree, or order that:

- relates to the provision of child support, alimony payments, or marital property rights to a spouse, former spouse, child, or other dependent of a participant; and

- is made pursuant to a State domestic relations law, including a community property law.[123]

Approval of a property settlement agreement qualifies as a DRO if it meets the other requirements.[124]

Facts a DRO must specify. A DRO must clearly specify the following information:

- The name and last known mailing address (if any) of the participant and the name and last known mailing address of each alternate payee covered by the order

- The amount or percentage of the participant's benefits to be paid by the plan to each alternate payee or how the amount or percentage is to be determined

- The number of payments or period to which the order applies

- Each plan to which the order applies[125]

Impact of DRO on benefits. A DRO cannot:

- require a plan to provide any type or form of benefit or any option that it does not otherwise provide;

- require a plan to provide increased benefits (based on their actuarial value); or

- require benefits to be paid to an alternate payee if they are required to be paid to a different alternate payee under a previous QDRO.[126]

A DRO may require that payments be made to an alternate payee once the participant attains the "earliest retirement age," even though the participant has not retired as of that time.[127] For this purpose, "earliest retirement age" is the earlier of:

- the date on which the participant is entitled to receive a distribution under the plan; or

- the later of:

  - the date that the participant attains age 50 or

  - the earliest date that the participant could begin receiving benefits if the participant separated from service.[128]

The DRO may provide that a former spouse will be treated as a surviving spouse for purposes of the survivor annuity requirements under Section 401(a)(11) and Section 417. If the spouses were married for at least one year, the surviving former spouse is treated as married throughout the one-year period ending on the earlier of the participant's annuity starting date or the date of the participant's death.[129] If a QDRO includes this provision, the participant's future spouse is not included as a surviving spouse.

Plan Handling of the DRO

When the plan administrator receives a DRO, the participant and each alternate payee must be notified that the plan has received the order and of its procedures to determine whether it is qualified. Within a reasonable time after receiving the order, the plan administrator must determine if it is a QDRO and notify the participant and each alternate payee of its determination.[130]

Plan procedures for handling QDROs. A plan must establish reasonable procedures to determine whether DROs are qualified and to administer distributions required by QDROs.[131] The procedures must be: (1) in writing; (2) provide for prompt notification of each person specified in the DRO as entitled to benefits of the plan's procedures; and (3) permit an alternate payee to designate a representative for receipt of copies of notices concerning the DRO. The notifications to persons specified in the DRO are to be sent to the address included in the DRO.[132]

DOL suggests that the procedures should also include:

- an explanation of the information about the plan and benefits available to assist in preparing DROs;

- a description of time limits set by the plan administrator for making determinations;

- a description of the steps that will be taken to protect and preserve plan assets or benefits upon receipt of a DRO; and

- a description of the plan's process for obtaining a review of the plan administrator's determination as to whether a DRO qualifies as a QDRO.[133]

The DOL takes the position that prospective alternate payees should have access to plan and participant information sufficient to prepare a QDRO. This information could include the summary plan description, relevant plan documents, and a statement of the participant's benefit entitlements. The plan administrator can require prospective alternate payees to provide sufficient information to reasonably establish that the disclosure request is being made in connection with a domestic relations proceeding.[134]

A 401(k) plan administrator may assess reasonable expenses attributable to a QDRO determination to a participant's account.[135]

Plan review of QDROs. A plan does not have to reject a DRO because the factual identifying information is incomplete. If the plan administrator can clearly determine the correct or missing information from its records or by communicating with the prospective alternate payee or participant, it should supplement the order with the appropriate information.[136]

Once the plan administrator makes its determination whether the order constitutes a QDRO, it must notify the participant and each alternate payee of its determination. The notice should be in writing and provided promptly after the determination.

If the plan administrator determines that the DRO is not qualified, its notice should include the following information:

- The reasons why the order is not a QDRO

- References to the plan provisions on which the plan administrator's determination is based

- An explanation of any time limits that apply to rights available to the parties under the plan (such as the duration of any protective actions the plan administrator will take)

- A description of any additional material, information, or modifications necessary for the order to be a QDRO and an explanation of why such material, information, or modifications are necessary[137]

Once a DRO is determined to be a QDRO, the plan administrator must act in accordance with its provisions as if the QDRO were part of the plan. The alternate payee must be able to exercise any right that the plan provides to participants, such as the right to elect the form of benefit payments.[138] The alternate payee is considered a beneficiary receiving benefits under the plan. They must automatically have the summary plan description, summaries of material plan changes, and the plan's summary annual report furnished to them.[139]

Segregation of amounts during DRO review. While the qualification of a DRO is being determined, the plan administrator must separately account for amounts (segregated amounts) that would be payable to the alternate payee if the order is determined to be a QDRO. If the determination method is made within 18 months after the date that the first payment would be required to be made under the QDRO, the segregated amounts plus any interest must be paid to the person or persons entitled to them. If it is determined not to be a QDRO or the qualification is not resolved, the segregated amounts and any interest must be paid to the person entitled to them as if there was no order. Any determination that the order is qualified that is made after the end of the 18-month period applies prospectively only.[140]

Planning Tip. Practitioners should note that a DRO (not a QDRO) can now be done on a Section 409A nonqualified deferred compensation plan, like a 401(k) excess benefit plan, if it so provides in the nonqualified plan. However, the two orders are not the same since a nonqualified deferred compensation plan has no ERISA plan asset, like under a 401(k) plan, for the order to attach to. Although Section 409A requires a DRO similar to a QDRO, the orders should therefore be different and the plan administrator (who may handle both plans) should not generally accept a standard QDRO for both the 401(k) and any linked nonqualified 409A excess benefit or other top hat plan.

How Distributions under QDROs Are Taxed

An alternate payee who is the spouse or former spouse of a participant is taxed on the payments made pursuant to the QDRO.[141] The spouse or former spouse alternate payee can also rollover any payment or distribution under the QDRO if the participant could roll it over.[142] The investment in the contract is divided between the present value of the distribution or payment to an alternate payee and the present value of all other benefits payable to the participant.[143]

The Code does not specifically address the tax treatment of distributions to alternate payees who are not a spouse or former spouse. Section 402(a) provides that distributions are taxable to the distributee. Code section 402(e)(1)(A) provides that a spouse or nonspouse alternate payee is treated as the distributee of any distribution or payment received under a QDRO. Notice 89-25 states that distributions to a nonspouse alternate payee during the participant's lifetime are included in the participant's gross income.[144] Nonspousal alternate payees are not eligible to rollover plan distributions. Distributions to a nonspousal alternate payee are not subject to the 20 percent withholding on eligible rollovers required by Section 3405(c).[145]

Payments to any alternate payee, regardless of whether a spouse, former spouse, or nonspouse, are specifically excluded from the 10 percent penalty tax.[146]

Withholdings on Distributions

Any amount distributed as an annuity or similar periodic payment is subject to income tax withholding as if the payment were wages paid to an employee, unless the employee elects out of withholding.[147] Any other amount distributed is subject to 10 percent withholding, unless the participant opts out of withholding.[148]

Rollover distributions. A special rule requires the plan to withhold 20 percent of any distribution that is an eligible rollover distribution.[149] It can be avoided by doing a direct transfer of the distribution to an eligible retirement plan.[150] A participant cannot opt out of this withholding[151] but can elect to have more than 20 percent withheld.[152] If a portion of the distribution is paid in a direct rollover (sometimes called a trustee-to-trustee transfer) to an eligible retirement plan and the participant receives the balance, the 20 percent withholding requirement only applies to the portion that the participant actually receives.[153]

If the distribution includes property other than cash, employer securities, or plan offsets, the plan administrator must apply Treasury Regulation Section 35.3405-1T, Q&A F-2 and may apply Treasury Regulation Section 35.3405-1T, Q&A F-3 in determining how to satisfy the withholding requirements.[154] The plan administrator can determine the property value as of the last valuation date before the distribution, as long as the valuation is made at least annually.[155] Treasury Regulation Section §35.3405-1T, Q&A F-2 requires that the plan administrator satisfy the withholding obligation, even if it must sell some or all of the property and distributing any cash proceeds remaining after the withholding. The plan administrator may allow the payee to pay the plan administrator or payor sufficient cash to satisfy the withholding requirement. Any property included in the disposition that is not included in a designated distribution, such as U.S. Savings Bonds or an annuity contract does not need to be sold or redeemed to meet the withholding obligation.[156] The plan does not have to withhold tax from each type of property proportionately.[157]

If a nonperiodic distribution is less than $200, no withholding is required. The $200 threshold includes all amounts distributed within one taxable year of the payee. The plan administrator does not know if the total distributions for a year will exceed $200, it is not required to withhold from the first payment.[158]

The plan administrator is responsible for withholding and paying the withheld tax unless it transfers its responsibility to the payor of a designated distribution.[159] To transfer its responsibility, the plan administrator must: (1) direct the payor in writing to withhold the tax; and (2) provide the payor with any required information. The direction is presumed to continue until revoked in writing by the plan administrator.[160] The required information is all information necessary to correctly compute the withholding tax liability and the information reportable on the Form W-2P or 1099R or that information does not apply to a particular payee or payments.[161]

Minimum withholding information requirement. The minimum information required to transfer the plan administrator's withholding liability is:

- the name, address, and social security number of the payee and the payee's spouse or other beneficiary if applicable;

- the existence and amount of any employee contributions,

- the amount of accumulated deductible employee contributions, if any,

- the payee's cost basis in any employer securities and the current fair market value of the securities,

- the existence and amount of any premiums paid for the current cost of life insurance that were previously includable in income,

- a statement of the reason (*e.g.*, death, disability, retirement) for the payment or distribution,

- the date on which payments commence and the amount and frequency of payments,

- the age of the payee and of the payee's spouse or designated beneficiary if applicable, and

- any other information required by Form W-2P or 1099R.[162]

The plan administrator is not required to determine the amount to be withheld if it transfers the withholding responsibility. If it does compute the amount to be withheld, the payor may rely on the plan administrator's computation of the amount to be withheld unless the payor knows or has reason to know that the computations are wrong.[163]

Section 72(t) Early Distribution Penalty and Exceptions

Even if a participant can get money out of a 401(k) plan, tax penalties may apply. The general rule is that the taxable portion of a distribution from a 401(k) plan is subject to a penalty tax of 10 percent.

However, the general rule is subject to a myriad of exceptions, some that are useful in planning and some that are not. A distribution is not subject to the penalty if it is:

- made on or after the date the participant attains age 59½;[164]

- made to a beneficiary or the participant's estate on or after the death of the employee;[165]

- attributable to the employee being disabled (as defined in section 72(m)(7);[166]

- part of a series of substantially equal periodic payments;[167]

- made to a participant after separation from service after attaining age 55:[168]

- a dividend paid on ESOP stock;[169]

- made in response to an IRS levy on the plan;[170]

- a payment under a composite retirement annuity or a phased retirement annuity.[171]

- made to the participant to the extent that the distributions do not exceed the amount allowable as medical expenses, without regard to whether the participant itemizes deductions for the taxable year;[172]

- a payment to an alternate payee under a QDRO;[173] and

- a distribution to an unemployed individual for health insurance premiums.[174]

The plan administrator or payor does not have to withhold any amount for the 10 percent penalty.[175] Because it is considered income tax, a participant may want to consider it in setting up their income tax withholdings or estimated taxes.

Distributions Due to the Participant's Disability

Definition of disability. Section 72(m)(7) provides that an individual is considered disabled if "he is unable to engage in any substantial gainful activity by reason of any medically determinable physical or mental impairment which can be expected to result in death or to be of long-continued and indefinite duration." In determining whether an individual meets that definition, the regulation states that primary consideration is to be given to the nature and severity of the impairment. Other factors considered include the individual's education, training, and work experience. While the Code refers to any substantial gainful activity, the regulation states that the substantial gainful activity referred to is the activity, or a comparable activity, that the individual customarily engaged in prior to the disability or prior to retirement if the individual was retired at the time of the disability.[176]

Indefinite impairment. Whether a specific individual's impairment constitutes a disability depends on the facts of the case. The regulation lists nine examples of impairments that would ordinarily be considered as preventing substantial gainful activity. It then cautions that having one of the listed impairments or an impairment of greater severity, by itself, will not always result in an individual being disabled under Section 72(m)(7). The test is whether the actual impairment prevents the individual from engaging in their customary or a comparable substantial gainful activity.[177]

An impairment is considered indefinite if it cannot reasonably be anticipated that the impairment will, in the foreseeable future, improve to the point that it no longer prevents substantial gainful activity. A condition that initially is not sufficient for the individual to be disabled can eventually result in disability. For example, an individual who has a bone fracture that prevents them from working for an extended period of time will not be considered disabled if recovery can be expected in the foreseeable future. If the fracture persistently does not heal, the individual would ordinarily be considered disabled.[178]

If an impairment can be diminished with reasonable effort and safety to the individual so that it does not prevent the individual from engaging in their customary or any comparable substantial gainful activity, it will not constitute a qualifying disability.[179]

Separation from Service after Attaining Age 55

The IRS relaxed the application of this exception by providing that the 10 percent penalty does not apply if a participant separates from service in the calendar year that they turn 55. The separation can occur before their fifty-fifth birthday as long as it occurs in the year that the individual turns 55.[180] To qualify, the distribution itself must be after the separation from service. The participant does not have to retire for this exception to apply. They can return to work for the same or different employer as long as they did, in fact, separate from service.[181]

Planning Tip. For clients who separate from service after age 55 but before reaching age 59½, leaving money with that employer's 401(k) plan allows them access to the money without being subject to the 10 percent penalty. If the money is rolled over to an IRA, it cannot be withdrawn without a 10 percent penalty unless a different exception applies. Similarly, rolling the 401(k) account to a new employer's plan subjects the rollover amount to the same restrictions as contributions to the plan and the 10 percent penalty.

A client who retires between age 55 and 59½ and plans to use some of the 401(k) account for living expenses may want to leave enough in the 401(k) account to pay their anticipated living expenses. Amounts the client does not expect to need before age 59½ could be rolled over to an IRA.

Medical Expenses Incurred

This exception applies to distributions made to the participant to reimburse the participant for medical expenses paid during the year. It is limited to the amount allowable as a deduction under Section 213. The participant can qualify for this exception without itemizing deductions for the year. Because only medical expenses that exceed 10 percent of adjusted gross income qualify as deductible, this exception is of limited utility. (Although the limit for individuals over 65 remains at 7.5 percent through 2016 for someone over 65 at the end of the year, those individuals qualify for the exception for people over 59½). In addition, other exceptions may be available that apply to the entire distribution.

Distributions to Unemployed Individuals for Health Insurance Premiums

If a person has received unemployment compensation for 12 consecutive weeks due to a separation from employment, the 10 percent penalty does not apply to distributions that do not exceed the amount paid during the year for medical insurance for the individual, their spouse, and dependents. The distributions can occur in either the year in which the unemployment compensation was paid or the succeeding year. The distribution must be made no more than 60 days after the individual is reemployed. A self-employed individual qualifies for the exemption if they would have qualified to receive unemployment compensation if they had been an employee rather than self-employed.[182]

Exceptions That Do Not Apply to 401(k) Plans

One of the confusing things about the exceptions under Section 72(t) is that different exceptions apply to different types of retirement accounts. IRA owners can take distributions for first-time homebuyer expenses and qualified higher education expenses without penalty while 401(k) participants cannot. The distinction may turn on the participant's ability to access the funds through another method without penalty. Because most qualified plans, especially defined contribution plans, allow plan loans, the participant has access to some of the funds without being subject to the penalty. Because IRAs do not permit loans, IRA owners have few options to access the funds without penalty for a first-time home purchase or qualified higher education expenses.

Plan Cashouts and Automatic Rollovers

Maintaining participant accounts with a small balance for participants who are no longer employed by a plan sponsor can be expensive for the plan sponsor and result in a participant losing track of the account. Distribution of a small account directly to a participant may result in the account being cashed out, tax and any penalty paid, and the balance used for purposes other than qualified retirement savings.

To deal with the concerns, Section 401(a)(31) requires that plans provide an automatic rollover for any mandatory distribution that is more than $1,000.[183] A mandatory distribution is a distribution made without the participant's consent before the participant attains the later of 62 or normal retirement age. It does not include distributions to a surviving spouse or alternate payee.[184]

If a participant's account value is at least $5,000, the plan cannot distribute the balance to the participant without the participant's consent.[185] However, the plan may make an automatic rollover of an account balance that exceeds $5,000 because the automatic rollover is available for any account with a balance in excess of $1,000.[186] If the account value is more than $1,000 and less than $5,000, the plan must make any distribution to an IRA unless the participant elects to have it transferred to another eligible retirement plan or to receive it directly. No spousal consent is required if the account balance is less than $5,000.[187]

Process for making an automatic rollover. Prior to making a mandatory distribution, the plan must provide the participant with the notice required by Section 402(f).[188] The notice must state that the account balance will automatically be rolled over to an IRA unless the participant chooses to either receive the distribution directly or have it transferred directly to an eligible retirement plan.[189]

Establishment of an IRA by the plan administrator. The plan administrator may execute the necessary documents to establish an IRA for the participant who has not made an election concerning the mandatory distribution. The plan administrator can select the financial institution where the IRA will be established and use the participant's most recent mailing address in its records. Once the IRA is established, the trustee or issuer or the IRA must provide the disclosure statement to the participant and a revocation period required in Treasury Regulation Section 1.408-6.[190] It will not be treated as failing to satisfy the disclosure requirements merely because the disclosure statements were returned by the U.S. Postal Service as undeliverable after being mailed to the participant's last known address according to the records of the employer and plan administrator.[191]

A plan administrator that sets up an IRA for a participant still has fiduciary duties with respect to the investment of the automatic rollover. DOL regulations provide plan administrators with a safe harbor for satisfying their fiduciary duties concerning the selection of an IRA provider and the investment of the funds.[192]

The safe harbor requirements are met if: [193]

- The amount of the mandatory distribution does not exceed the maximum amount under Section 401(a)(31)(B) of the Code

- The mandatory distribution is to an IRA

- In connection with the distribution, the fiduciary enters into a written agreement with an IRA provider that provides:

  - the funds shall be invested in a product designed to preserve principal and provide a reasonable rate of return, whether or not such return is guaranteed, consistent with liquidity;

  - the investment selected seeks to maintain, over the term of the investment, the amount invested in the product by the individual retirement plan;

  - the investment product must be offered by a bank or savings association insured by the FDIC or NCUA, an insurer whose products are protected by a State guaranty association, or a mutual fund;

  - all fees and expenses for the IRA do not exceed the fees and expenses charged by the IRA for comparable individual retirement plans established for reasons other than the receipt of an automatic rollover; and

- the participant on whose behalf the fiduciary makes an automatic rollover has the right to enforce the terms of the contractual agreement establishing the IRA against the IRA provider.

- The participant has been furnished a summary plan description or statement of material modifications describing the plan's automatic rollover provisions meeting the requirements set out in DOL Regulation Section 2550.404a-2(c)(4)

- Both the fiduciary's selection of an IRA and the investment of funds would not result in a prohibited transaction, unless covered by a prohibited transaction exemption

Endnotes

1. IRC Sec. 401(a)(14).
2. Treas. Reg. §1.401(a)-14(b).
3. IRC Sec. 401(a)(9).
4. IRC Sec. 401(k)(2)(B)(i)(I).
5. IRC Sec. 401(k)(2)(B)(i)(III).
6. IRC Sec. 401(k)(10).
7. IRC Sec. 401(k)(2)(B)(i)(IV).
8. IRC Sec. 401(k)(2)(B)(i)(v), referencing Section 72(t)(2)(G)(iii).
9. IRC Sec. 401(k)(2)(B)(i).
10. Treas. Reg. §1.401(k)-1(d)(2).
11. IRC Sec. 401(a)(9)(A).
12. IRC Sec. 401(a)(9)(B)(i).
13. IRC Sec. 401(a)(9)(B)(iii).
14. IRC Sec. 401(a)(9)(B)(ii).
15. IRC Sec. 401(a)(9)(B)(iv).
16. IRC Sec. 401(a)(9)(C)(i); Treas. Reg. §1.401(a)(9)-2, A-2(a).
17. Treas. Reg. §1.401(a)(9)-2, A-2(e).
18. IRC Sec. 401(a)(9)(C)(ii)(I); Treas. Reg. §1.401(a)(9), A-2(c). The rules of Section 416(i)(1)(B(i) are applied to determine if a participant is a 5 percent owner.
19. Treas. Reg. §1.401(a)(9)-2, A-3.
20. IRC Sec. 401(a)(9)(E).
21. Treas. Reg. §1.401(a)(9)-4, A-1.
22. Ibid.
23. Treas. Reg. §1.401(a)(9)-4, A-4(a).
24. Treas. Reg. §1.401(a)(9)-4, A-4(b).
25. Treas. Reg. §1.401(a)(9)-3, A-5.
26. Treas. Reg. §1.401(a)(9)-4, A-4(c).
27. Treas. Reg. §1.401(a)(9)-4, A-5(a).
28. Treas. Reg. §1.401(a)(9)-4, A-5(b).

29. Treas. Reg. §1.401(a)(9)-5, A-7(a)(1).

30. Treas. Reg. §1.401(a)(9)-8, A-2(a)(2).

31. Treas. Reg. §1.401(a)(9)-8, A-3.

32. Treas. Reg. §1.401(a)(9)-4, A-6(a)(1).

33. Treas. Reg. §1.401(a)(9)-4, A-6(a)(2).

34. Treas. Reg. §1.401(a)(9)-4, A-6(b)(1).

35. Treas. Reg. §1.401(a)(9)-4, A-6(b)(2).

36. Treas. Reg. §1.401(a)(9)-4, A-6(c)(1).

37. Treas. Reg. §1.401(a)(9)-4, A-6(c)(2).

38. Treas. Reg. §1.401(a)(9)-5, A-4(a).

39. Treas. Reg. §1.401(a)(9)-5, A-3.

40. IRC Sec. 402(c)(4)(B).

41. Treas. Reg. §1.401(a)(9)-7, A-2.

42. Treas. Reg. §1.401(a)(9)-5, A-4.

43. Treas. Reg. §1.401(a)(9)-5, A-4(b)(1).

44. Treas. Reg. §1.401(a)(9)-5, A-4(b)(2).

45. Treas. Reg. §1.401(a)(9)-5, A-1(e), referencing Treas. Reg. §1.401(a)(9)-6, A-4.

46. Treas. Reg. §1.401(a)(9)-5, A-1(e).

47. Treas. Reg. §1.401(a)(9)-8, A-2(a)(3).

48. IRC Sec. 401(a)(9)(B)(iii).

49. Treas. Reg. §1.401(a)(9)-3, A-4(a).

50. Treas. Reg. §1.401(a)(9)-3, A-2.

51. IRC Sec. 401(a)(9)(B)(iv).

52. Treas. Reg. §1.401(a)(9)-3, A-5.

53. Treas. Reg. §1.401(a)(9)-3, A-6.

54. Treas. Reg. §1.401(a)(9)-3, A-4(b).

55. Treas. Reg. §1.401(a)(9)-3, A-4(c).

56. IRC Sec. 401(a)(9)(B)(i).

57. Treas. Reg. §1.401(a)(9)-5, A-5(a).

58. Treas. Reg. §1.401(a)(9)-5, A-5(b).

59. Treas. Reg. §1.401(a)(9)-5, A-5(a)(1)(ii).

60. Treas. Reg. §1.401(a)(9)-5, A-5(c)(2).

61. Treas. Reg. §1.401(a)(9)-5, A-5(c)(1).

62. Treas. Reg. §1.401(k)-1(d)(3)(ii)(A).

63. Treas. Reg. §1.401(k)-1(d)(3)(ii)(B). Additional grandfather rules apply to collectively bargained plans.

64. Treas. Reg. §1.401(k)-1(d)(3)(iii)(A).

65. Treas. Reg. §1.401(k)-1(d)(3)(iii)(B)(1); Pension Protection Act of 2006 (PPA 2006), P.L. 109-280, Sec. 826; Notice 2007-7, IRB 2007-5, A-5(a).

66. Treas. Reg. §1.401(k)-1(d)(3)(iii)(B)(2).

67. Treas. Reg. §1.401(k)-1(d)(3)(iii)(B)(3); PPA 2006,, Sec. 826; Notice 2007-7, IRB. 2007-5, A-5(a). Dependent for this purpose includes dependents of another taxpayer, married dependents who file a joint return with their spouse, and individuals who do not qualify as dependents because their income exceeds the income limit.

68. Treas. Reg. §1.401(k)-1(d)(3)(iii)(B)(4).

69. Treas. Reg. §1.401(k)-1(d)(3)(iii)(B)(5); PPA 2006, Sec. 826; Notice 2007-7, IRB 2007-5, A-5(a).

70. Treas. Reg. §1.401(k)-1(d)(3)(iii)(B)(6).

71. Treas. Reg. §1.401(k)-1(d)(3)(iv)(A).

72. Treas. Reg. §1.401(k)-1(d)(3)(iv)(B).

73. Treas. Reg. §1.401(k)-1(d)(3)(iv)(C).

74. Treas. Reg. §1.401(k)-1(d)(3)(iv)(D).

75. Treas. Reg. §1.401(k)-1(d)(3)(iv)(E).

76. Treas. Reg. §1.401(k)-1(d)(3)(iv)(F).

77. Ibid.

78. Putting rigorous structure around plan loans will help the plan sponsor administer the plan properly. However, the plan should be confident the plan TPA can handle even this simplified structure properly, and communicate clearly to participants how loans will be handled, before a loan is authorized to reduce later complaints about required plan loan repayment processes.

79. IRC Sec. 72(p)(1)(A).

80. IRC Sec. 72(p)(1)(B).

81. IRC Sec. 72(p)(2)(A).

82. IRC Sec. 72(p)(2)(B).

83. IRC Sec. 72(p)(2)(C).

84. Treas. Reg. §1.72(p)-1, A-3(b).

85. Treas. Reg. §1.72(p)-1, A-8(a).

86. Treas. Reg. 1.72(p)-1, A-20(a)(1).

87. Treas. Reg. 1.72(p)-1, A-20(a)(2).

88. IRC Sec. 4975(d)(1).

89. DOL Reg. §2550.408b-1(b).

90. DOL Reg. §2550.408b-1(c).

91. DOL Reg. §2550.408b-1(d).

92. DOL Reg. §2550.408b-1(e).

93. DOL Reg. §2550.408b-1(f).

94. Treas. Reg. §1.72(p)-1, A-10(a).

95. Treas. Reg. §1.72(p)-1, A-11.

96. Treas. Reg. §1.72(p)-1, A-12.

97. In audits, the IRS has found this failure to repay plan loans a common operational error.

98. Treas. Reg. §1.72(p)-1, A-13.

99. Treas. Reg. §1.402-1(b)(2)(i).

100. Treas. Reg. §1.402-1(b)(2)(ii)(A).

101. Treas. Reg. §1.402-1(b)(2)(ii)(B).

102. Treas. Reg. §1.402-1(b)(2)(ii)(C).

103. Treas. Reg. §1.402-1(b)(2)(ii)(D).

104. IRC Sec. 402(e)(4)(E).

105. P.L. 98-397.

106. 570 U.S. ____, 133 S.Ct. 2675 (2013).

107. 2013 - __ I.R.B., ___, released August 29, 2013.

108. IRC Sec. 401(a)(11)(A)(i).

109.IRC Sec. 401(a)(11)(A)(ii).

110.IRC Sec. 417(b).

111.IRC Sec. 417(c)(2).

112.IRC Sec. 401(a)(11)(B)(iii).

113.Treas. Reg. §1.417(e)-1(b)(1).

114.Treas. Reg. §1.401(a)-20, A-24.

115.Treas. Reg. §1.417(e)-1(b)(3)(i).

116.Treas. Reg. §1.417(e)-1(b)(3)(ii).

117.1997-1 CB 370.

118.Ibid.

119.IRC Sec. 417(a)(2)(A).

120.IRC Sec. 417(a)(2)(B).

121.2013-2 U.S.T.C. ¶50,453 (E.D. Pa. 2013)

122.IRC Sec. 401(a)(13).

123.IRC Sec. 414(p)(1)(B).

124.Ibid.

125.IRC Sec. 414(p)(2).

126.IRC Sec. 414(p)(3).

127.IRC Sec. 414(p)(4).

128.IRC Sec. 414(p)(4)(B).

129.IRC Sec. 414(p)(5).

130.IRC Sec. 414(p)(6)(A).

131.IRC Sec. 414(p)(6)(B).

132.ERISA Sec. 206(d)(3)G)(ii).

133.U.S. Department of Labor, QDROs – The Division of Retirement Benefits through Qualified Domestic Relations Orders", Q&A 2-5.

134.U.S. Department of Labor, QDROs – The Division of Retirement Benefits through Qualified Domestic Relations Orders", Q&A 2-1.

135.U.S. Department of Labor, QDROs – The Division of Retirement Benefits through Qualified Domestic Relations Orders", Q&A 2-6.

136.U.S. Department of Labor, QDROs – The Division of Retirement Benefits through Qualified Domestic Relations Orders", Q&A 2-9.

137.U.S. Department of Labor, QDROs – The Division of Retirement Benefits through Qualified Domestic Relations Orders", Q&A 2-14.

138.U.S. Department of Labor, QDROs – The Division of Retirement Benefits through Qualified Domestic Relations Orders", Q&A 2-15.

139.U.S. Department of Labor, QDROs – The Division of Retirement Benefits through Qualified Domestic Relations Orders", Q&A 2-16.

140.IRC Sec. 414(p)(7).

141.IRC Sec. 402(e)(1).

142.IRC Sec. 402(e)(2).

143.IRC Sec. 72(m)(10).

144.Notice 89-25, 1989-1 CB 662, A-3, A-4.

145. Treas. Reg. §1.402(c)-2, A-12(b).

146. IRC Sec. 72(t)(2)(C).

147. IRC Sec. 3405a).

148. IRC Sec. 3405(b).

149. IRC Sec. 3405(c).

150. IRC Sec. 3405(c)(2).

151. Treas. Reg. §31.3405-1, A-2.

152. Treas. Reg. §31.3405-1, A-3.

153. Treas. Reg. §31.3405-1, A-6.

154. Treas. Reg. §31.3405-1, A-9.

155. Treas. Reg. §35.3405-1T, F-1.

156. Treas. Reg. §35.3405-1T F-2.

157. Treas. Reg. §35.3405-1T, F-3.

158. Treas. Reg. §35.3405-1T, F-6.

159. IRC Sec. 3405(d).

160. Treas. Reg. §35.3405-1T, E-2.

161. Treas. Reg. §35.3405-1T, E-3.

162. Ibid.

163. Treas. Reg. §35.3405-1T, A-34.

164. IRC Sec. 72(t)(2)(A)(i).

165. IRC Sec. 72(t)(2)(A)(ii).

166. IRC Sec. 72(t)(2)(A)(iii).

167. IRC Sec. 72(t)(2)(A)(iv).

168. IRC Sec. 72(t)(2)(A)(v).

169. IRC Sec. 72(t)(2)(A)(vi).

170. IRC Sec. 72(t)(2)(A)(vii).

171. IRC Sec. 72(t)(2)(A)(viii).

172. IRC Sec. 72(t)(2)(B).

173. IRC Sec. 72(t)(2)(C).

174. IRC Sec. 72(t)(2)(D).

175. Notice 87-13, A-20, 1987-1 CB 432.

176. Treas. Reg. §1.72-17A(f)(1).

177. Treas. Reg. §1.72-17A(f)(2).

178. Treas. Reg. §1.72-17A(f)(3).

179. Treas. Reg. §1.72-17A(f)(4).

180. Notice 87-13, A-20, 1987-1 C.B.432.

181. Joint Committee on Taxation, General Explanation of the Tax Reform Act of 1986, P.L. 99-514, p. 717.

182. IRC Sec. 72(t)(2)(D).

183. IRC Sec. 401(a)(31)(B).

184. Notice 2005-5, I.R.B. 2005-3, A-2.

185. IRC Sec. 411(a)(11)(A).

186.Notice 2005-5, 2005-1 CB 337, A-2.

187.Notice 2005-5, 2005-1 CB 337, A-13.

188.Notice 2005-5, 2005-1 CB 337, A-3.

189.IRC Sec. 402(f)(1)(A).

190.Notice 2005-5, 2005-1 CB 337, A-10.

191.Ibid.

192.DOL Reg. §2550-404a-2(b).

193.DOL Reg. §2550-404a-2(c).

Chapter 9

Plan Investments

Introduction

Participants in a 401(k) plan bear the investment risk: the value of their account determines their retirement benefit. Most plans allow participants to allocate their account balance among various investment choices, including guaranteed income contracts providing a fixed return similar to certificates of deposit, mutual fund-type accounts, index funds, and employer stock. Some plans also offer totally self-directed options that allow participants to invest directly in stocks, bonds, and other investments through a brokerage account. Other plans pool the investments and then allocate the contributions, gains, losses, and expenses among the participants' accounts.

Fiduciary Responsibilities

ERISA spells out specific responsibilities for fiduciaries for employee benefit plans, which include employee pension benefit plans and pension funds. It defines those as a plan fund, or program established by an employer or an employer organization or both that, either by its express terms or as a result of surrounding circumstances, provides retirement income to employees or results in a deferral of income by employees until the end of covered employment or beyond.[1] The method of calculating contributions to the plan, benefits under the plan, or distributing benefits under the plan does not affect the plan's classification.

ERISA bases its definition of a fiduciary on the relationship to the plan. A fiduciary can be an individual or an entity such as a partnership, corporation, trust, estate, or employee association.[2] A person is a fiduciary with respect to a plan to the extent they:

- exercise any discretionary authority or control over the plan's management or the management or disposition of its assets;

- render investment advice for a fee or any direct or indirect compensation with respect to any plan property or has any authority or responsibility to do so; or

- have any discretionary authority or responsibility in the administration of the plan.[3]

Collectively these are referred to as "fiduciary functions".

An investment company, its investment adviser, or principal underwriter *does not* become a plan fiduciary simply because plan assets are invested in securities issued by the investment company.[4] And, in general, do not want to become plan fiduciaries and usually seek to avoid this in both their contracts and their conduct in connection with a plan.

Exercise of Discretionary Authority or Control over the Plan or Its Assets

However, this definition of fiduciary clearly includes a plan's administrator and trustees because they have authority or control over the plan or its assets. Other persons, regardless of their formal role, might become fiduciaries by exercising the required discretionary authority or control. Under this provision, a person does not need to receive a fee or compensation to be classified as a fiduciary.

Rendering of Investment Advice for a Fee or Any Compensation

A person can be a fiduciary even if they do not have or exercise authority or control over the plan or its assets but provide investment advice for a fee or compensation. For ERISA purposes, a person renders investment advice to the plan by:

- providing advice on the value of securities or other property or making recommendations on investing in, purchasing, or selling securities or other property;[5] and

- rendering any advice about the value of securities or other property on a regular basis under a mutual agreement, or understanding between the person and the plan or a plan fiduciary that:

    - the services will be a primary basis for plan investment decisions;

    - such services will serve as a primary basis for investment decisions concerning plan assets; and

- the person will provide individualized investment advice to the plan based on its particular needs concerning such things as investment policies or strategy, overall portfolio composition, or diversification of plan investments.

The agreement does not have to be in writing.[6]

A person is only considered a fiduciary over those assets that it has or exercises discretionary authority, control, or responsibility over. They may still be liable for fiduciary breaches by other fiduciaries under ERISA section 405(a).[7]

The current DOL regulations do not provide guidance on what is a fee. Regulations proposed on October 22, 2010 would define a fee or other compensation received from rendering investment advice as any fee or compensation received from any source and any fee incident to the transaction in which the investment advice was rendered. It specifically includes commissions from brokerage, mutual fund, and insurance sales and fees and commissions based on multiple transactions involving different parties.[8] After proposed regulations caused an uproar, the DOL announced in September 2011 that it was going to repropose the regulation.[9] Although the announcement stated that the new proposed rule was expected to be issued in early 2012, no new proposal had been released as of late July 2013.

Discretionary Authority or Responsibility for Plan Administration

A person who performs purely ministerial functions such as applying the eligibility rules for determination of benefits, calculating service and compensation credits for benefits, calculating benefits, collecting and applying contributions, and making recommendations to others for plan administration is not a fiduciary.[10] A person who has discretion over these matters would be considered a fiduciary.

Holding certain positions automatically makes the person holding them a fiduciary. For example, the position of plan administrator or trustee provides discretionary authority or responsibility in the administration of the plan, making those persons fiduciaries. A person's title is not always dispositive of whether the holder in the position is a fiduciary.

Example 1. A plan employee has the title of "benefit supervisor" with the responsibility to calculate the benefit a participant is entitled to receive using a mathematical formula. Based on the results of the calculation, the plan administrator authorizes payment to a particular participant. The benefit supervisor does not perform any of the functions described previously. As a result, they are not a plan fiduciary.[11]

Example 2. The "benefit supervisor" for a different plan has final authority to authorize or deny benefit payments in disputed cases. This benefit supervisor is a plan fiduciary.[12]

Limits on Fiduciary Responsibility

A person is not considered a fiduciary over any assets for which that person does not have discretionary authority, control, or responsibility over plan assets, does not exercise any authority or control, does not render investment advice for a fee or other compensation, or have any authority or responsibility to do so.[13] A fiduciary that is not a named fiduciary is only a fiduciary to the extent that they perform a fiduciary function.

If a plan has two or more trustees, one is responsible for a breach by the other if:

- they knowingly participate in, or knowingly attempt to conceal, an act or omission of the other that is known to be breach;

- failing to comply with their responsibilities under ERISA section 404(a)(1) enables the other fiduciary to commit a breach; or

- they have knowledge of a breach by the other fiduciary, unless they make reasonable efforts under the circumstance to remedy the breach.[14]

Designation of nonnamed fiduciaries. Named fiduciaries remain liable for their fiduciary functions carried out by a nonnamed fiduciary, unless the plan sets out procedures for the named fiduciary to designate a nonnamed fiduciary to carry out fiduciary responsibilities. If the plan does not provide a procedure for a named fiduciary to designate nonnamed fiduciaries to carry out fiduciary responsibilities, the named fiduciary remains responsible for the acts and omissions of the designated persons.[15]

Delegation of responsibility for management and control of plan assets. Fiduciaries cannot delegate responsibility or discretion over the management or control of plan assets.[16] They can, however, delegate that authority and discretion to investment managers or employ others to assist the named fiduciary by providing advice to the named fiduciary in carrying out their investment responsibilities. An investment manager is defined as a fiduciary other than a trustee or named fiduciary who meets the following requirements:[17]

- has the power to manage, acquire, or dispose of any plan assets;

- who:

  - is a registered investment adviser under the Investment Advisors Act of 1940 (the "1940 Act");

  - qualifies for an exception from registration under the 1940 Act and is registered as an investment adviser with the state where it maintains its principal office and place of business and filed the most recent state registration form with the DOL secretary;

- is a bank as defined under the 1940 Act; or

- is an insurance company qualified to manage, acquire, or dispose of plan assets under the laws of more than one state; and

- has acknowledged in writing that it is a fiduciary for the plan.

Proper delegation to an investment manager relieves trustees and named fiduciaries from liability for the acts or omissions of the investment manager and the obligation to manage assets managed by the investment manager.[18]

Open Architecture

An "open architecture 401(k)" refers to a 401(k) plan whose administrator offers the employer the ability to choose from an investment menu of mutual funds, exchange-traded funds, or other investments. The investment options may include proprietary funds sponsored by the administrator. The funds chosen may affect the administrative fees paid by the employer, because some investment options may provide revenue sharing payment to the plan to offset plan expenses.

Participant or Beneficiary Control

The potential liability to plan fiduciaries for investment decisions that do not work out can be enormous. A participant or beneficiary and their lawyer have the benefit of hindsight and can allege that whoever made investment decisions for the plan should have known that a specific investment was not prudent. For example, after the 2008 financial crisis, a participant might have claimed that the fiduciary should have seen the problems that would trap AIG, Bear Sterns, Merrill Lynch, or any of numerous companies.

For that reason, to provide employees discretion over how the funds in their account are invested, and to potentially increase employees' participation in the plan, a 401(k) plan can permit a participant or beneficiary to control the assets in their account. Allowing participants to control how the assets in their account are invested creates concerns about how the fiduciary rules apply. Does a participant who has control over their account become a fiduciary for ERISA purposes? Are the named fiduciaries liable for delegating the investment management to the participant? If the participant's account loses money or doesn't match a benchmark, can the participant hold the plan or the named fiduciaries liable for the difference?

ERISA section 404(c) and the related regulations resolve those questions and others. A participant or beneficiary is not a fiduciary because they exercise control over the assets in their account.[19] No fiduciary under any provision of ERISA is liable for any loss resulting from a participant or beneficiary's exercise of control.[20] Fiduciaries are liable for a loss or breach incurred during a blackout period unless the fiduciary meets the ERISA requirements for authorizing and implementing the blackout period.[21]

Allowing participant control does not relieve fiduciaries of ERISA 404(c) Plans from their duty to prudently select and monitor the plan's service providers and the designated investment alternatives offered under the plan.[22]

ERISA section 404(c) plans. Plans that qualify for this relief are known as "ERISA section 404(c) Plans." To qualify as an ERISA section 404(c) Plan, the plan must:

1. provide an opportunity for a participant or beneficiary to exercise control over assets in their individual account; and

2. allow the participant or beneficiary an opportunity to choose how some or all of the assets are invested from a broad range of investment opportunities.[23]

A plan offers a broad range of investment alternatives if the investment alternatives provide the participant or beneficiary a reasonable opportunity to:

- materially affect the potential return on the amounts that they have the ability to control and the degree of risk to which the amounts are subject; and

- choose from at least three diversified investment alternatives that each have materially different risk and return characteristics, allowing for diversification of the overall portfolio with aggregate risk and return characteristics appropriate for them.[24]

Opportunity to Exercise Control

A participant or beneficiary has an opportunity to exercise control only if:

- they have a reasonable opportunity to give investment instructions to an identified plan fiduciary who must comply with the instructions unless an exception applies; and

- they receive or can obtain sufficient information to make informed investment decisions about the plan's investment options and ownership rights related to those investments.[25]

A participant or beneficiary is considered to have sufficient information if they are provided the following information:

- that the plan is designed to be an ERISA 404(c) Plan and that the plan fiduciaries may be relieved of liability for losses that are the direct and necessary result of the participant or beneficiary's investment instructions;

- specified general plan information, including administrative expense information and individual expense information; and

- investment-related information.

A plan can impose charges for the reasonable expenses if it has procedures to periodically inform participants and beneficiaries of actual expenses incurred with respect to their own accounts.[26] A fiduciary may decline to implement investment instructions if they would result in a prohibited transaction or generate taxable income for the plan.[27]

The plan may impose reasonable restrictions on how frequent investment instructions may be provided. However, the frequency for each investment alternative must be reasonable based on the alternative's reasonably expected market volatility. At least three investment alternatives providing a broad range of investment alternatives must permit investment instructions at least once within any three-month period. One of those three investment alternatives must permit investment instructions to be given more frequently than once within any three months.[28]

General Plan Information

The plan must provide information about the participant or beneficiary's rights concerning the control of plan investments and the plan expenses. It must be provided on or before a participant or beneficiary can direct their investments and at least annually thereafter. Financial professionals, financial publications, and others began to focus on the impact of fees and expenses on a participant's actual return. It was often difficult or impossible to identify fees. For plan years beginning on or after November 1, 2011, DOL requires plans to make specific disclosures concerning fees.

The following general information must be provided:

- An explanation of when a participant or beneficiary may give investment instructions

- An explanation of any specified limits on the instructions, including restrictions on transfers to or from a designated investment alternative (a designated investment alternative is any investment alternative designated by the plan available for participants and beneficiaries to use, other than "brokerage windows," "self-directed brokerage accounts," or similar arrangements that allow the selection of investments other than those designated by the plan)[29]

- A description of or reference to plan provisions concerning the exercise of voting, tender, and similar rights related to a designated investment alternative and any restrictions on such rights

- An identification of any designated investment alternatives offered by the plan

- An identification of any designated investment managers

- A description of any "brokerage windows," "self-directed brokerage accounts," or similar arrangements enabling the selection of investments other than those offered by the plan[30]

Administrative expenses. The plan must provide the following information about its administrative expenses.

- On or before a participant or beneficiary can direct their investments and at least annually thereafter:

  - an explanation of fees and expenses for general plan administrative expenses such as legal, accounting, and recordkeeping expenses that may be charged against individual accounts and are not included in the total annual operating expenses of a designated investment alternative; and

  - how the charges will be allocated or affect the balance of each individual account.

- At least quarterly, provide a statement including:

  - the dollar amount of the administrative fees and expenses that were actually charged during the preceding quarter;

  - a description of the services provided for the charges; and

  - an explanation that other administrative expenses for the preceding quarter were paid from operating expenses of one or more of the plan's designated investment alternatives.[31]

Individual expenses. The plan must provide the following information that may be charged against an individual's account instead of on a plan-wide basis and are not reflected in any designated investment alternative's expenses. These can include fees related to processing loans, QDROs, investment advice, brokerage windows, and optional rider charges for annuity contracts. In addition, it must provide a statement at least quarterly that includes:

- the dollar amount of the administrative fees and expenses that were actually charged during the preceding quarter; and

- a description of the services provided for the charges.[32]

The most recent annual disclosure and any updates can be used to furnish the information required to be provided on or before the first investment.[33]

If a change occurs in any of the general plan, administrative expense, or individual expense information, the plan must provide participants and beneficiaries a description of the changes at least 30 but no more than 90 days in advance. If the plan administrator cannot provide the required advance notice due to unforeseeable events or things beyond its control, the notice must be provided as soon as reasonably practicable.[34]

Investment-Related Information

The plan must provide specific investment-related information on or before a participant or beneficiary can direct their investments and at least annually thereafter.[35]

Identifying information. The plan must provide the name of each designated investment alternative and the type or category of the investment, such as money market fund, balanced fund, large-cap stock fund, high-yield bond fund, etc.[36]

Performance data. If the investment's return is not fixed, the average annual total return for the one, five, and ten calendar year period ending on December 31 of the previous calendar year. If the designated investment alternative has not existed for the full ten-year period, its average annual total return for its life must be provided. In addition, it must include the standard statement that an investment's past performance is not necessarily an indication of how it will perform in the future.[37]

For designated investment alternative with a fixed or stated return, both the fixed or stated annual return and the term of the designated investment alternative must be disclosed. If the issuer has the right to adjust the fixed or stated rate prospectively during the term, the plan must disclose it and the current rate, any minimum guaranteed rate, and how participants can obtain the most recent rate of return.[38]

Benchmarks. For designated investment alternatives whose return is not fixed, the plan must disclose the name and returns of an appropriate broad-based securities market index over periods comparable to those used for the investment. The benchmark cannot be administered by an affiliate of the investment issuer, its investment adviser, or a principal underwriter, unless the index is widely recognized and used.[39]

Fee and expense information. Detailed fee and expense information must be provided for designated investment alternatives.

If the return is not fixed, the following information must be provided:[40]

- A description and amount of each shareholder-type fee and a description of any restriction or limitation that may apply to a purchase, transfer, or withdrawal of the designated investment alternative in whole or in part. A shareholder-type fee is a fee charged directly against a participant or beneficiary's designated investment alternative that is not included in the designated investment alternative total annual operating expenses.

- An expense ratio based on the total annual operating expenses, calculated as directed in the regulation.

- The total annual operating expenses of the designated investment alternative for a one-year period, expressed as a dollar amount for a $1,000 investment, based on the expense ratio described above and assuming no returns.

- A statement that expenses and fees are only one of several factors that should be considered when making investment decisions.

- A statement that the cumulative effect of fees and expenses can substantially reduce the growth of a retirement account and that participants and beneficiaries can visit the Employee Benefit Security Administration's website for an example that demonstrates the long-term effect of fees and expenses.

If the investment return is fixed for the term of the designated investment alternative, the plan must provide the amount and a description of any shareholder-type fees and describe any restriction or limitation that may apply to a purchase, transfer, or withdrawal of the designated investment alternative in whole or in part.[41]

Website information. The plan must provide a website address that provides access to the following information about the designated investment alternative:

- The name of the issuer

- A description of the designated investment alternative 's objectives or goals that is consistent with Securities and Exchange Commission (SEC) Form N-1A or N-3

- The principal strategies, including a general description of the types of assets held by the designated investment alternative, and principal risks consistent with the SEC forms mentioned previously

- The designated investment alternative's portfolio turnover rate, in a manner consistent with the SEC forms described previously

- The designated investment alternative's performance data described above, updated at least quarterly, or more frequently if required by other applicable law

- The designated investment alternative's fee and expense information described previously[42]

Glossary. The plan must provide either a general glossary of terms to assist participants and beneficiaries in understanding the designated investment alternatives or the address of a website that provides access to such a glossary and a description of the purpose of the address.[43]

Employer securities and annuity options. If participants have the option to invest in employer securities or an annuity, the regulation sets out additional information that the plan must provide.[44]

Format for the information. The plan must provide the required information in a format designed to make it easy to compare the information for each designated investment alternative option. An appendix to the regulation provides a comparative format a plan can use. A plan that follows the format and completes it accurately will be considered to have complied with the requirement.[45] This appendix is reproduced as Appendix E. It must also include:

- the name, address, and telephone number of the person to contact for information required to be provided upon request;

- a statement that additional information, including more current performance information, is available at the websites specified; and

- how to obtain paper copies of information required to be available on a website at no charge.[46]

Information concerning rights in the designated investment alternative. After investment in a designated investment alternative, the plan must provide a participant or beneficiary with information on any voting, tender, or other rights related to the designated investment alternative passed through to the participant.[47]

Qualified Change in Investment Options

A change in investment options offered by a plan may occur for numerous reasons, including a change in the plan provider, poor performance of an investment option, and lack of investment in an option. A participant will still be treated as exercising control over the account assets after a change in investment options that causes a reallocation of a participant's account among other investment options if the change is a qualified change in investment options and certain notice and additional requirements are met.

To be a qualified change in investment options, the account must be allocated among one or more investment options offered in lieu of investment options available immediately prior to the effective date of the change. As of immediately after the change, the stated characteristics of the accounts to which the funds are reallocated, including risk and rate of return, are reasonably similar to those of the existing investment options immediately before the change.[48]

The notice and additional requirements are:[49]

- The plan administrator provides the participants and beneficiaries with written notice of the change at least 30 days but no more than 60 days before the effective date of the change that includes the following information.

    - A comparison of the existing and new investment options

    - An explanation of how the account will be invested after the change unless the participant or beneficiary provides other investment instructions

- Before the effective date of the change, the participant or beneficiary does not provide the plan administrator with affirmative investment instructions that are different from the change.

- The participant or beneficiaries had exercised their control over the account to choose how the plan assets were invested immediately before the effective date of the change.

Providing Investment Advice to Plan Participants

Making investment decisions is difficult for most people. Even people successful in their occupations and professions are often unable to invest successfully over a long period of time. Most 401(k) plans give the participants and beneficiaries the right to control how their accounts are invested. The potential liability under the fiduciary responsibility and prohibited transaction rules limit the plans' ability to aid participants and beneficiaries in making investment decisions. The large number of investment options available makes it harder for participants and beneficiaries to choose among those options.

A DOL regulation provides guidelines that allow a plan to provide four categories of information and materials on investment-related matters to its participants and beneficiaries without being considered to have provided investment advice. For this purpose, it does not matter whether the information and materials are provided by the plan sponsor, a plan fiduciary, or a service provider, how frequently the information is provided, the form in which the information is provided, or whether one category of information and materials is provided alone or with other categories of information and materials.[50]

Categories of information and Materials

Plan information. This category includes information and materials on:

- the benefits of plan participation, the benefits of increasing plan contributions, the impact of early withdrawals, the plan terms, or the plan's operations; or

- information such as that described in DOL Regulation 2550.404c-1(b)(2)(i) that describes investment alternatives under the plan, including investment objectives and philosophies, risk and return characteristics, historical return information, or related prospectuses.[51]

General financial and investment information. This category includes information and materials on:

- general financial and investment concepts, including risk and return, diversification, dollar cost averaging, compounded return, and tax-deferral;

- historic differences in the rates of returns between different asset classes;

- the impact of inflation;

- estimating retirement income needs;

- determining investment time horizons; and

- assessing risk tolerance.[52]

Asset allocation models. Information and materials that provide a participant or beneficiary with models of asset allocation portfolios for hypothetical individuals with different time horizons and risk profiles, subject to the following guidelines:

- The models must be based on generally accepted investment theories that considered the historic returns of different asset classes.

- All material facts and assumptions used in the models are disclosed.

- If an asset allocation model identifies specific investment alternatives available under the plan, it must be accompanied by a statement that other investment alternatives with similar risk and return characteristics may be available under the plan and where information on those alternatives may be found.

- A statement that participants or beneficiaries should consider their other assets, income, and investments in addition to their interest in the plan in applying asset allocation models to their personal situations.

- Providing an asset allocation model is not investment advice, even if a plan offers only one investment alternative in a particular asset class shown in an asset allocation model.[53]

Interactive investment materials. A plan can make questionnaires, worksheets, software, and similar materials available to provide a participant or beneficiary the ability to estimate future retirement income needs and assess how different asset allocations will affect retirement income. The tools made available must meet these guidelines:

- Be based on generally accepted investment theories that consider the historic returns of different asset classes over defined periods of time

- Have an objective correlation between the asset allocations generated and the information and data supplied by the participant or beneficiary

- Disclose all material facts and assumptions that may affect a participant's or beneficiary's assessment of the different asset allocations or use information specified by the participant or beneficiary

- If an asset allocation model identifies specific investment alternatives available under the plan, it must be accompanied by a statement that other investment alternatives with similar risk and return characteristics may be available under the plan and where information on those alternatives may be found

- State that participants or beneficiaries should consider their other assets, income, and investments in addition to their interest in the plan in applying asset allocation models to their personal situations[54]

The regulation points out that the selection of a person or persons to provide investment educational services or investment advice to participants and beneficiaries is an exercise of discretionary authority or control with respect to the plan management. This means that whoever makes the designation must act prudently and solely in the interests of the participants and beneficiaries, both in making the designation and in continuing it. For an ERISA 404(c) Plan, neither the designation of someone to provide education nor the designation of a fiduciary to provide investment advice, by itself, creates fiduciary liability for a loss that is the direct and necessary result of a participant's or beneficiary's exercise of independent control. If a participant or beneficiary chooses an educator or advisor and the plan sponsor did not select, endorse, or make arrangements for the educator or advisor to provide education or investment advice, the plan sponsor or fiduciary has no fiduciary responsibility or liability with respect to the actions of the educator or advisor chosen.[55]

Qualified Default Investment Alternative (QDIA)

With a QACA or EACA (discussed later), the default contributions and employer contributions must be invested. It is also possible that a participant must make an investment choice for other reasons, such as their current choice is no longer available. If the participant does not choose how the funds are invested, it falls to the plan fiduciary to make that choice. This could expose the fiduciary to liability based on the performance of the chosen investment.

Fortunately, relief is available if the fiduciary complies with provisions in ERISA section 404(c) (5) and the related regulations. The participant will be treated as having exercised control over the account assets so the fiduciary is not liable for any loss that results from investing all or part of a participant's or beneficiary's account in a QDIA or investment decisions made by the QDIA manager.[56] A fiduciary must prudently select and monitor the QDIA for this relief to be available.

The relief is available if the following requirements are met.[57]

- The assets are invested in a QDIA.

- The participant had the opportunity to direct the investment of the assets but failed to do so.

- The fiduciary provides the participant with a notice meeting the following requirements:

  - at least 30 days before the participant becomes eligible for the plan or the date of the first investment in a QDIA or on or before the date the participant becomes eligible to participate in the plan if the participant can make a permissive withdrawal (as discussed in Chapter 6); and

  - at least 30 days in advance of each subsequent plan year.

- A fiduciary provides information concerning the QDIA specified in DOL Regulations 2550-404c-1(b)2)(i)(B)(1)(viii), 2550-404c-1(b)2)(i)(B)(1)(ix), and §2550-404c-1(b)(2)(i)(B)(2).

- The participant can transfer the funds out of the QDIA as specified in 2 in the following section.

- The plan complies with DOL Regulation Section 2550.404c-1(b)(3) in offering a broad range of investment alternatives.

Requirements to Be a QDIA

For an investment alternative offered by a plan to be a QDIA, it must meet the following requirements:

1. It cannot hold or permit the purchase of employer securities, unless one of two limited exceptions apply.[58]

2. The participant has the ability to change from the default investment to another investment alternative at least every three months. In the first 90 days, they must be able to make the transfer without any restrictions or financial penalties and after 90 days are only subject to the fees and restrictions that apply to any participant invested in that QDIA.[59]

3. It must be managed by an investment manager or mutual fund.[60]

4. It is diversified to minimize the risk of large losses using one of three types of investment products:[61]

    a. A mix of equity and fixed income exposures based on the participant's age, target retirement date (e.g., a life-cycle or targeted date fund)

    b. A mix of equity and fixed income exposures consistent with a target level of risk appropriate for participants of the plan as a whole (e.g., a balanced fund)

    c. A managed portfolio that is diversified so as to minimize the risk of large losses and change their asset allocations and associated risk levels for an individual account over time with the objective of becoming more conservative (i.e., decreasing risk of losses) with increasing age (e.g., a managed account)

Notice Requirement

The plan must provide the participant with a notice that is written in a manner calculated to be understood by the average plan participant, containing the following information:[62]

*   The circumstances when a participant's account may be invested in a QDIA

*   When elective contributions may be made on behalf of a participant, the percentage of the contributions, and the participant's right to elect out of the contributions or to elect a different percentage or amount

*   An explanation of the participant's right to direct the investment of the assets in their accounts

- A description of the QDIA, including its investment objectives, risk and return characteristics (if applicable), and the fees and expenses of the investment alternative

- A description of the right of a participant invested in a QDIA to direct the investment to any of the plan's other investment alternatives, including any restrictions, fees, or expenses connected with the transfer

- An explanation of where the participant can obtain investment information about the plan's other investment alternatives

Prohibited Transaction Exemption for Investment Advice Tailored to Participants and Beneficiaries

The Code provides a Prohibited Transaction Exemption (PTE) for investment advice provided to a participant or beneficiary of a 401(k) or other individual account plan. To qualify, the investment advice must be provided by a fiduciary adviser who is regulated under the applicable banking, insurance, or securities law.[63]

The investment advice must be provided under an arrangement that either:

- provides any fees for investment advice or concerning the sale, holding, or acquisition of plan assets are not affected by the investment option chosen;[64] or

- uses a computer model certified prior to its use by an eligible investment expert that it:

  - complies with generally accepted investment theories;

  - considers relevant information about the participant;

  - uses objective criteria to provide asset allocation portfolios from the plan's investment options;

  - is not biased in favor of investments offered by the fiduciary adviser or an affiliated person; and

  - considers all plan investment options and is not inappropriately weighted with respect to any investment option.[65]

The Code spells out additional requirements to qualify for the exemption.[66] These include that: the arrangement must be expressly authorized by a separate plan fiduciary; any investment transaction must occur solely at the direction of the participant; the arrangement is subject to an annual independent audit; proper disclosures are made to the participant or beneficiary; and records concerning the arrangement are kept for at least six years.

Employer Securities

The collapse of Enron and its employees' loss of 401(k) account values invested in Enron stock highlighted the problems associated with investing 401(k) accounts in employer stock or an employer making its matching contributions in employer stock and limiting a participant's ability to diversify into other investments.

The Pension Protection Act of 2006 addressed this by adding Section 401(a)(35), which requires plans that hold publicly-traded employer securities allowing participants to diversify out of the employer securities.[67] The requirement does not apply to:

- ESOPs that do not include any elective deferrals, matching contributions, or employee contributions;[68] and

- one participant plans, defined as a plan that, on the first day of a plan year covers only:

  - a 100 percent owner of the plan sponsor or the owner and the owner's spouse; or

  - one or more partners (or partners and their spouses) in the plan sponsor.[69]

A plan and investment option is not treated as holding employer securities held indirectly as part of a broader fund such as a mutual fund, common or collective trust fund or pooled investment fund, an investment fund for a multiemployer plan, or any other investment fund designated by the IRS.[70] To qualify for the exception, the fund must have stated investment objectives and the investment is independent of the employer (or employers) and any affiliate thereof.[71] If the fund owns employer securities that exceed 10 percent of the total value of all of the fund's investments as of the end of the previous plan year, an investment in employer securities is not considered to be independent of the employer or employers.[72]

Elective deferrals and employee contributions. For any elective deferrals, employee contributions, or rollover contributions invested in employer securities, a participant, alternate payee, or beneficiary of a deceased participant must be able to divest the employer securities and invest an equivalent amount in other investment options at least quarterly.[73]

Employer nonelective contributions. Unlike elective deferrals and employee contributions, an individual must qualify to be able to divest employer securities attributable to employer nonelective contributions and reinvest in other investments. An individual qualifies if they are:

- a participant who completed at least three years of service;

- an alternate payee whose account relates to a participant who has completed at least three years of service; or

- a beneficiary of a deceased participant.

A participant is treated as completing three years of service on the last day of the plan's vesting computation period that constitutes the completion of the third year of service under Section 411(a)(5). If the plan uses the elapsed time method of crediting service or provides for immediate vesting, the three years of service is completed on the day immediately preceding the third anniversary of the participant's hire date.[74]

Restrictions on investment in employer securities. A plan cannot impose restrictions, directly or indirectly, on the investment of employer securities that are not imposed on the investment of other assets in the plan. Restrictions may be a restriction on an individual's right to divest an investment in employer securities that is not imposed on other investments or a benefit conditioned on being invested in employer securities.[75] An indirect restriction or condition would include a restriction on the ability to invest in employer securities for a period of time after divesting employer securities. It does not include tax consequences that result from divesting employer securities, such as the loss of the special treatment for net unrealized appreciation. It also does not include a prohibition on investing divested amounts in the same employer securities account if they can be invested in another employer securities account where the only relevant difference is the trust's basis in the shares.[76]

A plan can impose restrictions on divesting employer securities that are either required to ensure compliance with applicable securities laws or are reasonably designed to ensure compliance with those laws. It can also restrict the application of the diversification requirements for up to 90 days after the plan becomes an applicable defined contribution plan or after a mutual fund or similar fund stops being independent of the employer.[77]

The following indirect restrictions on investments in employer securities are permitted:

- A limit on the amount an individual's account can invest in employer securities, if it applies regardless of whether the individual previously divested employer securities

- Reasonable restrictions on the timing and number of elections to invest in employer securities designed to limit short-term trading in the securities

- The imposition of fees on other investment options that are not imposed on investments in employer securities or on divesting employer securities

- Permitting transfers into or out of a stable value or similar fund more frequently than a fund that invests in employer securities, if the plan otherwise does not impose impermissible restrictions.

- Permitting transfers out of a QDIA more frequently than an employer securities fund

- Prohibitions on further investments in employer securities[78]

Investment options. The plan must offer three investment options other than employer securities. Each must be diversified and have materially different risk and return characteristics. Investment options that comply with DOL Regulation Section 2550.404c1(b)(3) satisfy this requirement.

Endnotes

1. ERISA Sec. 3(2)(A). ERISA Sec. 3(3) defines "employee benefit plan" or "plan" to include employee pension benefit plans, employee welfare benefit plan, or a plan that is both an employee welfare benefit plan and an employee pension benefit plan.

2. ERISA Sec. 3(9).

3. ERISA Sec. 3(21)(A).

4. ERISA Sec. 3(21)(B).

5. DOL Reg. §2510.3-21(c)(1)(i).

6. DOL Reg. §2510.3-21(c)(1)(ii).

7. DOL Reg. §2510.3-21(c)(2).

8. DOL Prop. Reg. §2510.3-21(c)(3), published in 75 Fed. Reg. 65263 (10/22/10).

9. DOL Release No. 11-1382-NAT (09/19/2011).

10. DOL Reg. §2509.75-8, D-2.

11. DOL Reg. §2510.75-8, D-3.

12. Ibid.

13. DOL Reg. §2510.3-21(c)(2).

14. ERISA Sec. 405(a).

15. DOL Reg. §2510.75-8, FR-14.

16. DOL Reg. §2510.75-8, FR-15; ERISA Sec. 405(c)(1).

17. ERISA Sec. 3(38).

18. ERISA Sec. 405(d)(1).

19. ERISA Sec. 404(c)(1)(A)(i).

20. ERISA Sec. 404(c)(1)(A)(ii).

21. ERISA Secs. 404(c)(1)(A)(ii), 404(c)(1)(B). A blackout period, as defined in ERISA Section 101(i)(7), is a period when a participant or beneficiary's ability to make changes to the investments in their account is temporarily suspended, limited, or restricted for more than three consecutive business days.

22. DOL Reg. §2550.404a-5(f).

23. DOL Reg. §2550.404c-1(b)(1).

24. DOL Reg. §2550.404c-1(b)(3).

25. DOL Reg. §2550.404c-1(b)(2).

26. DOL Reg. §2550.404c-1(b)(2)(ii)(A).

27. DOL Reg. §2550.404c-1(b)(2)(ii)(B).

28. DOL Reg. §2550.404c-1(b)(2)(ii)(C).

29. DOL Reg. §2550.404a-5(h)(4).

30. DOL Reg. §2550.404a-5(c)(1).

31. DOL Reg. §2550.404a-5(c)(2)(ii).

32. DOL Reg. §2550.404a-5(c)(3)(ii).

33. DOL Reg. §2550.404a-5(c)(4).

34. DOL Regs. §§2550.404a-5(c)(1)(ii), 2550.404a-5(c)(2)(i)(B), 2550.404a-5(c)(3)(i)(B).

35. DOL Reg. §2550.404a-5(d)(1).

36. DOL Reg. §2550.404a-5(d)(1)(i).

37. DOL Reg. §2550.404a-5(d)(1)(ii)(A).

38. DOL Reg. §2550.404a-5(d)(1)(ii)(B).

39. DOL Reg. §2550.404a-5(d)(1)(iii).

40. DOL Reg. §2550.404a-5(d)(1)(iv)(A).

41. DOL Reg. §2550.404a-5(d)(1)(iv)(B).

42. DOL Reg. §2550.404a-5(d)(1)(v).

43. DOL Reg. §2550.404a-5(d)(1)(vi).

44. DOL Regs. §§2550.404a-5(d)(1)(vii), 2550.404a-5(i)(1), 2550.404a-5(i) (2).

45. DOL Reg. §2550.404a-5(e)(3).

46. DOL Reg. §2550.404a-5(d)(2)(i).

47. DOL Reg. §2550.404a-5(d)(3).

48. ERISA Sec. 404(c)(4)(B).

49. ERISA Sec. 404(c)(4)(C).

50. DOL Reg. §2509.96-1(d).

51. DOL Reg. §2509.96-1(d)(1).

52. DOL Reg. §2509.96-1(d)(2).

53. DOL Reg. §2509.96-1(d)(3).

54. DOL Reg. §2509.96-1(d)(4).

55. DOL Reg. §2509.96-1(e).

56. DOL Reg. §2550.404c-5(b)(1).

57. DOL Reg. §2550.404c-5(c).

58. DOL Reg. §2550.404c-5(e)(1).

59. DOL Reg. §2550.404c-5(e)(2).

60. DOL Reg. §2550.404c-5(e)(3).

61. DOL Reg. §2550.404c-5(e)(4).

62. DOL Reg. §2550.404c-5(d).

63. IRC Sec. 4975(f)(8)(J)(i).

64. IRC Sec. 4975(f)(8)(B).

65. IRC Sec. 4975(f)(8)(C).

66. IRC Secs. 4975(f)(8)(D), 4975(f)(8)(E), 4975(f)(8)(F), 4975(f)(8)(G), 4975(f)(8)(H), 4975(f)(8)(I).

67. IRC Sec. 401(a)(35)(A).

68. IRC Sec. 401(a)(35)(E)(ii).

69. IRC Sec. 401(a)(35)(E)(iii).

70. Treas. Reg. §1.401(a)(35)-1(f)(3)(ii)(A).

71. Treas. Reg. §1.401(a)(35)-1(f)(3)(ii)(B).

72. Treas. Reg. §1.401(a)(35)-1(f)(3)(ii)(C).

73. Treas. Reg. §1.401(a)(35)-1(b).

74. Treas. Reg. §1.401(a)(35)-1(c).

75. Treas. Reg. §1.401(a)(35)-1(e)(1)(i).

76. Treas. Reg. §1.401(a)(35)-1(e)(1)(ii).

77. Treas. Reg. §1.401(a)(35)-1(e)(1)(iii).

78. Treas. Reg. §1.401(a)(35)-1(e)(3).

Chapter 10

Life Insurance in 401(k) Plans

Introduction

Life insurance can be a very powerful financial tool. Owning it in a 401(k) plan can increase its power. The death benefit can supplement the retirement benefits accumulated in the 401(k) plan. For the plan and the insured to get the most out of life insurance owned by a 401(k) plan (and avoid problems for the plan), compliance with IRS and DOL guidelines is essential.

If a 401(k) plan purchases life insurance on a plan participant, the participant can provide life insurance protection at a significantly lower cost than if the participant paid the premiums directly. Figure 10.1 illustrates the difference.

As explained next, a significant difference between the two situations is that if the plan owns the policy, only the pure life insurance portion of the death benefit and the cumulative imputed income is received income tax-free by the beneficiaries. If the participant pays the premiums, none of the death proceeds are generally subject to income tax.

Benefits of insurance in plan. A plan's purchase of life insurance offers the following benefits to the insured participant.

- The plan pays the premiums using pre-tax plan contributions or assets. The participant may not be eligible for plan distributions that could be used to pay the premiums or may not want to incur the income tax and potential 10 percent early withdrawal penalty on the distributions.

- The current cost to the participant may be significantly less than the actual premiums.

Figure 10.1. Participant's Potential Cash Flow Savings		
	Premiums Paid by 401(k) Plan	**Premiums Paid by Participant**
Premium Amount*	$10,000	$10,000
Contribution/income required to pay premiums (assumes 40% effective tax rate)	$10,000	$16,667
Imputed income to participant, based on 50 year old participant, $1,000,000 coverage, $50,000 cash surrender value ($2.30/1,000 of coverage)	N/A	$2,185
Tax on imputed income at 40%	N/A	$874
Cash flow savings	N/A	$15,793

*Premium is for illustrative purposes and does not reflect any specific life insurance product.

- The participant's beneficiaries will receive a portion of the death benefit income-tax free.

Disadvantages of insurance in plan. There are also downsides to using plan assets to purchase life insurance:

- The participant's taxable estate includes the policy death benefit because the participant has incidents of ownership in the policy. Many participants may not view this as a problem, either because they do not expect their estate, including the life insurance death benefits, to exceed the applicable exclusion amount ($5,250,000 in 2013 and indexed for inflation) or because their spouse is the beneficiary of the life insurance benefit. In that case, the marital deduction may protect the death benefit from tax in the participant's estate.

- The incidental benefit rule (discussed next) may limit the amount of coverage that the plan can purchase on the participant.

- The participant must pay tax on the value of the life insurance protection each year.

- The plan cannot own life insurance on the participant after the participant retires. If the participant wants to continue the policy, the plan must transfer it to the participant (a taxable event) or the participant must purchase it from the plan (which could be costly).

In addition, the plan must allow for purchase of life insurance by the plan. Plans frequently do not permit the use of plan contributions or assets to pay life insurance premiums. For plan administrators, the purchase of life insurance can create a substantial administrative burden.

Complying with the Incidental Benefit Rule

Because a 401(k) plan is designed to provide retirement benefits, any life insurance must be incidental to the retirement benefits.[1] Subject to certain exceptions, the IRS guidance provides that whether a life insurance benefit is incidental depends on what percentage of contributions is used to provide life insurance benefits.

Percentage Test

Beginning in Rev. Rul. 54-51,[2] the IRS has ruled that life insurance is incidental if the aggregate premiums for life insurance on a participant are less than 50 percent of the contributions allocated to the participant. It also required that, at or before the participant's retirement, the policy's entire value be converted to provide periodic income and no portion used to continue life insurance coverage. The IRS considers the use of plan contributions or funds for current benefits, including life insurance protection, as a distribution from the plan.[3]

In Rev. Rul. 61-164,[4] the IRS established the following guidelines.

- For ordinary (whole) life insurance, the premiums must be less than 50 percent of the contributions for the participant.

- If the plan provides both ordinary life insurance and health insurance, the total of the health insurance premiums plus 50 percent of the ordinary life insurance premiums cannot exceed 25 percent of the contributions for the participant.

Based on these guidelines, the IRS has consistently ruled that a plan could use 50 percent of the contributions for whole life policies, 25 percent for term policies,[5] or 25 percent for a combination of the two using half of the whole life premiums and the term premiums. The IRS equated 50 percent of the contributions used to purchase whole life protection with 25 percent of the contribution used to purchase term insurance.[6] It also applied the 25 percent limit to a decreasing whole life policy.[7]

Universal life policies (which led to variable universal life and indexed universal life policies) were developed after publication of this guidance. As a result, how the guidance applied to UL and its variants was unanswered. The only guidance provided by the IRS is FSA 1999-633, which concludes that the 25 percent test applies to UL policies.

Seasoned Money

The percentage test does not apply if a profit-sharing plan uses money that has been in the plan long enough. A plan can distribute accumulated funds after a fixed number of years, attaining a specified age, or the prior occurrence of an event such as layoff, illness, disability, retirement, death, or severance of employment.[8] In Rev. Rul. 54-231, the IRS defined "fixed number of years" as at least two years.[9]

If the participant has participated in the plan for at least five years, the rules are even more liberal. Not only does the percentage test not apply but all contributions can be used to pay life insurance premiums, including those made within the last 24 months.[10]

The IRS guidance on the use of seasoned money by profit-sharing plans to pay life insurance premiums predates the enactment of Section 401(k). It has not issued any guidance on the use of elective deferrals and matching contributions to pay life insurance premiums. Until it does, prudence would dictate that a plan either pay premiums only from other employer contributions or obtain advice from its ERISA counsel that such use is permitted.

Figure 10.2 summarizes the incidental benefit limit.

Figure 10.2. Incidental Benefit Rule	
Defined Contribution Plans	
Type of Insurance Coverage	**Percentage of Contributions Permitted to Pay Life Insurance Premiums**
Whole Life Insurance	Less than 50%
Other Insurance	Less than 25%
Combination	50% of whole life premiums plus 100% of other premiums must be less than 25% of contributions
Profit-Sharing Plans	
Funds held in the plan for at least two years used to pay premiums	No limit on seasoned money to pay premiums
Participant has participated for at least 5 years	No limit on either seasoned money or contributions to pay premiums

Income Tax Consequences

Congress and the IRS have been consistent in treating the receipt of life insurance protection to the insured by someone else as subject to income tax or gift tax. This holds true when a qualified plan purchases life insurance on a participant. In addition, getting the policy out of the plan may have income tax consequences. Those may vary, depending on whether the plan distributes the policy to the insured or the plan sells the policy to the insured.

Income Tax on Value of Life Insurance Protection

Section 72(m) specifically provides that the life insurance benefit received by a plan participant is taxable if the policy proceeds are payable directly or indirectly to the participant or a beneficiary of the participant.[11] Proceeds are payable indirectly to a participant's beneficiary if the trustee is the named beneficiary but the plan terms require the trustee to pay all of the proceeds to the participant's beneficiary.[12] If only a portion of the proceeds are payable to the participant's beneficiary, it is unlikely that the value of the portion payable to the participant's beneficiary is taxable to the participant.

The amount includable in income is based on the life insurance protection provided by the policy, based on the amount of the proceeds that exceed the policy's cash surrender value.[13] Table 2001, shown in Figure 10.3, is generally used to determine the cost of the insurance protection.[14] Until the IRS issues further guidance, the value can also be determined by using the insurer's published premium rates available to all standard risks for initial issue one-year term contracts. To qualify as available to all standard risks, the insurer must:

- generally make the availability of such rates known to persons who apply for term insurance; and

- regularly sell term insurance at such rates to those who apply for term insurance through the insurer's normal distribution channels.[15]

Example 1. Monica, 43, is covered by $100,000 of life insurance coverage offered through her employer's 401(k) plan. The policy's cash surrender value at the end of the calendar year is $10,000, making the net insurance provided $90,000. Under IRS Table 2001 in Figure 10.3, the value of life insurance for a 43-year old is $1.29 per thousand of coverage. Monica must recognize income of $116.10 for the value of the life insurance protection ($100,000 – 10,000)/1,000 × 1.29 = 90 × 1.29 = 116.10. This creates $116.10 of basis in the policy.

If the insurer offered qualifying term rates that were lower than $1.29 per thousand, Monica could use that rate to determine the value of the life insurance protection.

Amount Included in Income Creates Basis

The life insurance value included in a participant's taxable income creates basis in the contract.[17] The participant recovers the basis without income tax if the policy is surrendered or distributed to the participant.

Example 2. Jonathan received a distribution of a life insurance policy from a 401(k) plan, valued at $65,000. He has paid tax on $5,000 as the value of the life insurance protection provided under the policy. The taxable amount is $60,000 ($65,000 – 5,000).

Figure 10.3. IRS Table 2001 Interim Table of One-Year Term Premiums For $1,000 of Life Insurance Protection[16]					
Attained Age	Section 79 Extended and Interpolated Annual Rates	Attained Age	Section 79 Extended and Interpolated Annual Rates	Attained Age	Section 79 Extended and Interpolated Annual Rates
0	$0.70	34	$0.98	68	$16.92
1	$0.41	35	$0.99	69	$18.70
2	$0.27	36	$1.01	70	$20.62
3	$0.19	37	$1.04	71	$22.72
4	$0.13	38	$1.06	72	$25.07
5	$0.13	39	$1.07	73	$27.57
6	$0.14	40	$1.10	74	$30.18
7	$0.15	41	$1.13	75	$33.05
8	$0.16	42	$1.20	76	$36.33
9	$0.16	43	$1.29	77	$40.17
10	$0.16	44	$1.40	78	$44.33
11	$0.19	45	$1.53	79	$49.23
12	$0.24	46	$1.67	80	$54.56
13	$0.28	47	$1.83	81	$60.51
14	$0.33	48	$1.98	82	$66.74
15	$0.38	49	$2.13	83	$73.07
16	$0.52	50	$2.30	84	$80.35
17	$0.57	51	$2.52	85	$88.76
18	$0.59	52	$2.81	86	$99.16
19	$0.61	53	$3.20	87	$110.40
20	$0.62	54	$3.65	88	$121.85
21	$0.62	55	$4.15	89	$133.40
22	$0.64	56	$4.68	90	$144.30
23	$0.66	57	$5.20	91	$155.80
24	$0.68	58	$5.66	92	$168.75
25	$0.71	59	$6.06	93	$186.44
26	$0.73	60	$6.51	94	$206.70
27	$0.76	61	$7.11	95	$228.35
28	$0.80	62	$7.96	96	$250.01
29	$0.83	63	$9.08	97	$265.09
30	$0.87	64	$10.41	98	$270.11
31	$0.90	65	$11.90	99	$281.05
32	$0.93	66	$13.51		
33	$0.96	67	$15.20		

Tax Treatment of Policy Proceeds Received on the Participant/Insured's Death

If the participant/insured dies before retirement, the life insurance proceeds are paid to the participant's beneficiary. For income tax purposes, the beneficiary is considered to have received two different types of payments. The first type is the portion that represents pure life insurance protection, determined by subtracting the cash surrender value from the total death benefit. It is exempt from income tax under Code section 101(a). The second type is the cash surrender value, which is considered part of the 401(k) plan retirement benefit, not a life insurance death benefit. As such, it is not excludable under Section 101(a).[18] The basis created by paying tax on the value of the life insurance benefit reduces the beneficiary's taxable amount. Figure 10.4 nicely summarizes the taxation of life insurance inside a pension plan.

Figure 10.4	
Income Tax Consequences for Life Insurance Held in Qualified Retirement Plans	
Income Taxation While Participating in Plan	Participant taxed annually on economic benefit costs of "Net Death Benefit" for life insurance held in qualified plan. Cost of life insurance protection if measured using IRS Table 2001 or, if appropriate under IRS Notice 2002-8, the insurance carrier's published one-year term rates.
Income Taxation of Death Benefits	The portion of the death benefit equal to the cash value of the policy immediately prior to death – minus the aggregate economic benefits recognized as income – will be taxed as income in respect of a decedent for "IRD". The remaining death benefits received income tax-free.
Income Taxation of Policy Distribution	Fair market value of policy – minus the aggregate economic benefits recognized as income – taxed to the participant as ordinary income.
Income Taxation of Policy Sale	If the sale's price is less than the policy's fair market value, the participant recognizes as ordinary income the difference between the sale's price and the fair market value of the policy (minus the aggregate economic benefits recognized as income).
Source: ING White Paper: *Using Life Insurance as an Asset in Qualified Retirement Plans*, July 2012. Copyright 2012-2013. Used by permission of ING U.S.	

Example 3. Same facts as Example 1, except that Monica dies when the cash surrender value is $10,000 and her basis from paying tax on the life insurance protection is $1,000. The $90,000 of the death proceeds that exceed the $10,000 cost basis is exempt

from income tax under section 101(a). The $10,000 cash value is considered a taxable distribution to her beneficiary. Monica's $1,000 cost basis reduces the taxable amount to $9,000.

Options at Retirement or Termination

The plan cannot own a policy on a participant after the participant stops working for the plan sponsor. The plan's options are to distribute the policy to the participant, sell the policy to the participant or a third party, or surrender the policy.

Distribution to the Participant

If the participant has terminated service with the plan sponsor, the participant can receive the policy as a distribution. Because IRAs cannot own life insurance policies, the policy cannot be rolled over to an IRA.[19] The fair market value of the policy, reduced by the participant's basis and any nondeductible contributions,[20] is income to the participant.[21]

Sale of the Policy

The sale of plan assets to a participant or other disqualified person is generally a prohibited transaction under ERISA and the Code.[22] This subjects the disqualified person to an excise tax that can reach up to 100 percent of the amount involved in the transaction.[23]

Fortunately, the DOL provided guidelines on how to avoid the treatment of a sale of a policy to a disqualified person as a prohibited transaction. To qualify for the exemption, a two-pronged test must be met.

First, the sale must be to:

- a plan participant;

- a relative of a plan participant who is the beneficiary;

- an employer of an employee covered by the plan;

- another employee benefit plan;[24] or

- a trust established by or for the benefit of a plan participant or one or more relatives of the plan participant that is the beneficiary.[25]

Second, the following conditions must be met:

- The participant is the insured

- The policy would, but for the sale, be surrendered by the plan

- The consideration received for the policy must be at least equal to the amount necessary to put the plan in the same cash position as if it had surrendered the policy and made any distributions owed to the participant for their vested interest in the plan

- The plan must not discriminate in favor of participants who are officers, shareholders, or highly compensated employees

- If the sale is to someone other than the participant:

  - the participant is informed of the proposed sale and given the opportunity to purchase the contract from the plan; and

  - if the participant elects not to purchase the policy, provides a written statement to the plan that they:

    - elect not to purchase the policy, and

    - consent to the plan's sale of the policy to the proposed purchaser.[26]

Fair Market Value of the Policy

When a plan distributes a policy to a participant, the taxable amount is the fair market value of the life insurance policy. Similarly, the fair market value can determine if the consideration received is sufficient to put the plan in the same cash position as if it had surrendered the policy and made any required distributions to the participant.

In Rev. Proc. 2005-25,[27] the IRS established safe harbors for determining the fair market value of life insurance policies. The fair market value is the greater of:

- the sum of the interpolated terminal reserve and any unearned premiums plus a pro rata portion of a reasonable estimate of dividends expected to be paid for that policy year based on company experience; and

- the product of the Premiums, Earnings, and Reasonable Charges (PERC) amount and the applicable Average Surrender Factor.

Determining the Interpolated Terminal Reserve. The Interpolated Terminal Reserve is used to determine the fair market value for gifts of life insurance policies. The gift tax regulations provide the following example of how it is calculated.[28]

Example 4. A gift is made four months after the last premium due date of an ordinary life insurance policy issued nine years and four months prior to the gift thereof by the insured, who was thirty-five years of age at date of issue. The gross annual premium is $2,811. The computation follows:

Terminal reserve at end of tenth year	$14,601.00
Terminal reserve at end of ninth year	12,965.00
Increase	$1,636.00
One-third of such increase (the gift having been made four months following the last preceding premium due date), is	$545.33
Terminal reserve at end of ninth year	12,965.00
Interpolated terminal reserve at the date of gift	$13,510.33
Two-thirds of gross premium ($2,811)	1,874.00
Value of the gift	$15,384.33

Determining PERC. Calculation of the PERC amount depends on whether the policy is a variable or nonvariable product.

For nonvariable policies, the PERC amount is the total of:

- premiums paid through the valuation date, without reduction for dividends used to pay premiums; PLUS

- dividends used to purchase paid-up insurance before the valuation date; PLUS

- any amounts credited or made available to the policyholder, including interest and similar income items (whether made to the policy or some other account); but excluding dividends used to offset premiums or purchase paid-up insurance; MINUS

- explicit or implicit reasonable mortality charges and other charges actually charged on or before the valuation date and not expected to be refunded or rebated, reversed later; MINUS

- any distributions, withdrawals, or partial surrenders prior to the valuation date.[29]

For variable policies, the PERC amount is the total of:

- premiums paid through the valuation date, without reduction for dividends used to pay premiums; PLUS

- dividends used to increase the value of the policy, including dividends used to purchase paid-up insurance, before the valuation date; PLUS

- all adjustments that reflect the investment return and the market value of separate accounts (whether made to the policy or some other account); MINUS

- explicit or implicit reasonable mortality charges and other charges actually charged on or before the valuation date and not expected to be refunded or rebated, reversed later; MINUS

- any distributions, withdrawals, or partial surrenders prior to the valuation date.[30]

Average Surrender Factor. If a policy distributed from a qualified plan provides for explicit surrender charges, the Average Surrender Factor is the unweighted average of the applicable surrender factors over the ten years beginning with the policy year of the distribution or sale. The applicable surrender factor for a policy year is the greater of 0.70 and a fraction. The numerator of the fraction is the projected cash value available if the policy was surrendered on the first day of the policy year. For the year that the policy is sold or distributed, the applicable surrender factor is the actual cash available on the first day of the policy year). The denominator is the projected (or actual) PERC amount on the first day of the policy year. The applicable surrender factor is 1.0 if no surrender charge applies for the year.[31]

Example 5. Bill transfers a policy in its fifth year. It carried a 100 percent surrender charge in the first year. In the next two years, it is reduced by 5 percent each year. Starting in the fourth year, the surrender charge is reduced by 10 percent per year. The Average Surrender Factor is determined by the following chart:

Year	Applicable Surrender Factor	Policy Surrender Charge
5	0.7	70%
6	0.7	60%
7	0.7	50%
8	0.7	40%
9	0.7	30%
10	0.7	20%
11	0.7	10%
12	1.0	0%
13	1.0	0%
14	1.0	0%
The Average Surrender Factor is 0.79.		

Unisex Rates Requirement

Under Title VII of the Civil Rights Act, an employer cannot discriminate against any person with respect to the compensation, terms, conditions, or privileges of employment.[32] Premiums for most life insurance policies differ based on the insured's sex, even if all other factors are the same.

In *Arizona Governing Committee v. Norris*,[33] the U.S. Supreme Court considered an Arizona deferred compensation plan that offered annuities issued by life insurance offering lower retirement benefits to a woman than a man who has made the same contributions. The Court held that the plan discriminated against women because it provided a woman lower benefits based on the same contributions. It did not dispute that women, as a class, live longer than men do. However, that does not allow an individual woman to receive lower benefits under the plan.

No court has applied *Norris* to require that life insurance policies held by a qualified plan be issued on a unisex basis. Life insurance provided under a qualified plan is a term, condition, or privilege of employment. It is widely accepted that *Norris* does prohibit a plan from owning gender-based policies. Some have suggested that gender-based policies could be used if a plan provides the insurance company a letter acknowledging the existence of the *Norris* decision and assuming any liability for the plan being found to discriminate based on the use of gender-based policies. The number of companies that would accept a "*Norris* letter" and issue a gender-based policy to a qualified plan is unknown.

Prohibited Transactions

Anyone working with a qualified plan needs to determine whether their activities concerning the plan causes them to be considered a plan fiduciary, subject to the ERISA rules on fiduciary responsibility. Whether an insurance agent who sells a life insurance policy to a 401(k) plan is considered a fiduciary depends on the relationship between the agent and the plan, its trustees, and its sponsor.

The DOL issued PTE 84-24, which provides guidance on how an agent can avoid being classified a fiduciary as a result of receiving a commission or a plan's purchase of a life insurance contract. The agent must provide an independent fiduciary for the plan the information listed in writing and in a form designed to be understood by a plan fiduciary without special expertise in insurance matters.

- The nature of the agent's relationship or affiliation with the insurance company that issues the contract and any limitation on the agent's ability to recommend insurance or annuity contracts that results from an agreement with the company.

- The sales commission that will be paid to the agent in connection with the purchase of the contract. The commission must be expressed as a percentage of gross annual premiums for the first year and each renewal year.

- A description of any charges, fees, discounts, penalties, or adjustments that may be imposed under the recommended contract.[34]

The independent fiduciary must provide a written receipt for such information and approve the transaction for the plan. The fiduciary may be an employer whose employees are covered by the plan but cannot be an insurance agent or broker, pension consultant, or insurance company involved in the transaction. In addition, the fiduciary cannot receive any compensation or other consideration for its own account from any party dealing with the plan in connection with the transaction.[35] If the plan makes additional purchases of insurance or annuity contracts, the written disclosures are not required unless:

- it has been at least three years since disclosure was made for the same kind of contract; or

- the contract recommended or the commission is materially different from that previously approved by the fiduciary.[36]

The following information must be retained for six years by the insurance agent or broker (or insurance company if designated by the agent or broker) or pension consultant:

- The information required to be disclosed

- Any additional information or documents provided to the fiduciary concerning the transaction

- The written acknowledgement from the independent fiduciary[37]

Fee Disclosures

Beginning on July 1, 2012, "covered service providers" must disclose specific information to a plan fiduciary about compensation received for providing services to the plan. A covered service provider is anyone who enters into a contract or arrangement with a plan and reasonably expects to receive direct or indirect compensation of $1,000 or more in connection with providing services to the plan. For this purpose, services include insurance services.[38] Thus, a life insurance agent who makes a commission on the sale of a life insurance policy must provide the required disclosure.

The information that must be disclosed includes:

- a description of the services to be provided;[39]

- whether the services will be provided as a fiduciary under ERISA;[40] and

- a description of the direct compensation (paid by the plan) and indirect compensation (paid by others) reasonably expected to be received in connection with the plan.[41]

A covered service provider must generally make the disclosure reasonably in advance of the date the contract is entered into, extended, or renewed. The covered service provider must disclose changes concerning fiduciary services, recordkeeping, and brokerage services annually. Other changes must be disclosed as soon as practical but no more than 60 days after the covered service provider is informed of the change.[42]

The regulation provides a sample fee disclosure that plans can use as guidance in determining the format for providing the required information. The sample is part of the Model Investment Option Comparative Chart shown in Appendix E.

Endnotes

1. Treas. Reg. §1.401-1(b)(ii). The plan can also provide health insurance benefits that are incidental to the retirement benefits.

2. 1954-1 CB 147, amplified by Rev. Rul. 57-213, 1957-1 CB 157 and Rev. Rul. 60-84, 1960-1 CB 159.

3. Rev. Rul. 60-83, 1960-1 C.B. 157.

4. 1961-2 CB 99.

5. Rev. Rul. 70-611, 1970-2 CB 89.

6. Ibid. See also Rev. Rul. 66-143, 1966-1 CB 79; Rev. Rul. 73-501, 1973-2 CB 127; Rev. Rul. 74-307, 1974-2 CB 126.

7. Rev. Rul. 76-353, 1976-2 CB 112.

8. Treas. Reg. §1.401-1(b)(1)(ii).

9. 1954-1 CB 150. This ruling was superseded and its holding restated in Rev. Rul. 71-295, 1971-2 CB 184.

10. Rev. Rul. 68-24, 1968-1 CB 150. The ruling actually states 60 months.

11. IRC Sec. 72(m)(3).

12. Treas. Reg. §1.72-16(b)(1), flush language.

13. Treas. Reg. §1.72-16(b)(3).

14. IRS Notice 2002-8, 2002-1 CB 398.

15. Ibid., Sec. III.3.

16. Id.

17. Treas. Reg. §1.72-16(b)(4).

18. Treas. Reg. §1.72-16(c)(2)(ii).

19. IRC Sec. 408(a)(3).

20. Treas. Reg. §1.72-16(c)(3), Example 2; PLR 7922109.

21. Treas. Reg. §1.402(a)-1(a)(2).

22. IRC Sec. 4975(c)(1)(A).

23. IRC Sec. 4975(b); ERISA Sec. 406.

24. PTE 92-6, Sec. I(a).

25. PTE 92-6, Sec. I(b). The relative must fall within the definition of "relative" under ERISA section 3(15), "member of the family" under Section 4975(e)(6) of the Code, or Section II(b) of PTE 92-6.

26. PTE 92-6, Sec. II.

27. IRB 2005-17.

28. Treas. Reg. §25.2512-6(a), Example 4.

29. Rev. Proc. 2005-25, Sec. 3.02.

30. Rev. Proc. 2005-25, Sec. 3.03.

31. Rev. Proc. 2005-25, Sec. 3.04.

32. 42 USC Sec. 2000e-2(a)(1).

33. 463 U.S. 1073 (1983).

34. PTE 84-24, Sec. V(b)(1).

35. PTE 84-24, Sec. V(b)(2).

36. PTE 84-24, Sec. V(d).

37. PTE 84-24, Sec. V(e).

38. DOL Reg. §2550.408b-2(c)(1)(iii)(C).

39. DOL Reg. §2550.408b-2(c)(1)(iv)(A).

40. DOL Reg. §2550.408b-2(c)(1)(iv)(B).

41. DOL Reg. §2550.408b-2(c)(1)(iv)(C).

42. DOL Reg. §2550.408b-2(c)(1)(v).

Chapter 11

Multiple Employers, Plan Mergers, and Plan Terminations

Introduction

When you look under the hood of many businesses, you find different entities that operate as and appear to be one business. Common situations include a retail chain that operates each location as a separate entity, a manufacturer whose operating business leases its equipment from an entity with identical ownership, and a professional practice whose Highly Compensated Employees (HCEs) work for one entity and whose Nonhighly Compensated Employees (NHCEs) work for another entity.

These business structures may be established for many different reasons including liability protection and tax benefits. Business owners may want to take advantage of these types of structures to provide retirement and other employee benefits to owners and HCEs without providing benefits to NHCEs.

To prevent the use of multiple entities to avoid the nondiscrimination rules, the nondiscrimination rules are applied to qualified plans of employers with common control as if all employees worked for the same employer.

Controlled Group Rules

All employees of all employers that are members of a controlled group of corporations or other entities that are under common control are treated as employed by a single employer for the following purposes:

- All Section 401 requirements

- The minimum participation standards under Section 410

- The minimum vesting standards of Section 411

- The benefit and contribution limits of Section 415

- The top-heavy rules of Section 416[1]

The rules of Section 1563(a), with slight modifications, determine if a controlled group exists. A controlled group can be either a parent-subsidiary controlled group or a brother-sister controlled group.

Planning Tip. Whenever the plan sponsor has any ownership connection with any other business or its owners have any interest in any other business, the plan sponsor should consult its tax advisor to determine if the controlled group or affiliated group rules apply. Further, how the rules apply should be reexamined after any change in the plan sponsor's ownership or affiliation with other businesses.

Parent-Subsidiary Controlled Groups

A parent-subsidiary controlled group involves vertically connected entities, starting with a common parent organization. It exists if one or more chains of entities are connected through a common parent that directly owns a controlling interest in at least one of the other entities. Except for the common parent, an entity within the group must directly own a controlling interest in each of the other entities.[2] The entities must be conducting trades or businesses for a controlled group to exist. For purposes of determining if a controlling interest exists, any option to acquire an interest in an entity is treated as if the option had been exercised.[3]

A controlling interest is generally 80 percent of the entity, determined as follows.

- For corporations, ownership of stock possessing at least 80 percent of the total combined voting power of all of the corporation's voting stock or at least 80 percent of the total value of all classes of the corporation's stock[4]

- For trusts or estates, ownership of an actuarial interest of at least 80 percent of the trust or estate[5]

- For partnerships, ownership of at least 80 percent of the profits interest or capital interest[6]

- For sole proprietorships, ownership of the sole proprietorship[7]

The actuarial interest of a beneficiary of a trust or estate is determined by assuming the fiduciary's maximum exercise of discretion in favor of the beneficiary and the estate tax rules under Treasury Regulation Section 20.2031-7.[8]

Example 1. ABC partnership owns 80 percent of the total combined voting power of all classes of the voting stock of X corporation. This makes ABC partnership the common parent of a parent-subsidiary group of trades or businesses under common control consisting of the ABC partnership and X Corporation.[9]

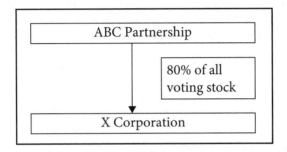

Example 2. Same facts as in Example 1. X Corporation owns 80 percent of the profits interest in the DEF Partnership. The controlled group consists of ABC Partnership, X Corporation, and DEF Partnership, with ABC Partnership as the common parent. If the interest in DEF Partnership was owned by ABC Partnership, the result would be the same.[10]

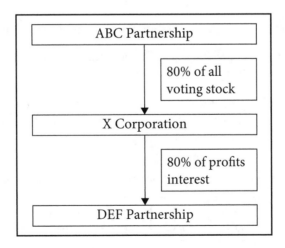

Brother-Sister Controlled Groups

A brother-sister controlled group involves horizontally connected entities, rather than the vertical connection found in a parent-subsidiary controlled group. It requires that: (1) the same five or fewer individuals, trusts, or estates directly own a controlling interest in each entity; and

(2) considering a person's ownership only to the extent they have the same ownership in each entity, the group has effective control of the organization. The same group of five or fewer persons must both own a controlling interest and have effective control.[11] As with a parent-subsidiary controlled group, in determining if a controlling interest exists, any option to acquire an interest in an entity is treated as if the option had been exercised.[12]

The definition of controlling interest used for parent-subsidiary controlled groups is used for brother-sister controlled groups. Thus, the same group of five or fewer individuals, trusts, or estates must own an 80 percent or more controlling interest AND have effective control. Whether a group of individuals has a controlling interest looks at their full ownership interest in each entity. In contrast, the effective control is determined using the smallest ownership interest each person has in the entities under consideration.

For a group of persons to have effective control of an organization, the following requirements apply:

- For corporations, they own stock possessing at least 50 percent of the total combined voting power of all of the corporation's voting stock or at least 50 percent of the total value of all classes of the corporation's stock[13]

- For trusts or estates, ownership of an actuarial interest of at least 50 percent of the trust or estate[14]

- For partnerships, ownership of at least 50 percent of the profits interest or capital interest[15]

- For sole proprietorships, ownership of the sole proprietorship[16]

The same definition of actuarial interest applies for brother-sister controlled groups as it does for parent-subsidiary controlled groups.

This means that a sole proprietorship can only be a member of a brother-sister controlled group with another entity in which the sole proprietor has a controlling interest.

Example 3.[17] Unrelated individuals Alex, Bob, Carol, Dave, and Emily own interests in the following entities. Each corporation only has one class of stock.

Owner	A	GHI	M Corp	W Corp	X Corp	Y Corp	Z Corp
Alex	100%	50%	100%	60%	40%	20%	60%
Bob		40%		15%	40%	50%	30%
Carol					10%	10%	10%
Dave				25%		20%	
Emily		10%			10%		
Frank							

The following brother-sister controlled groups exist:

- A and M – both are wholly owned by Alex. If Alex owned at least 80 percent of another entity, that entity would also be part of a brother-sister controlled group with A and M.

- GHI, X and Z – Combined, Alex and Bob own 90 percent of GHI; 80 percent of X Corporation; and 90 percent of Z Corporation, giving them a controlling interest in each. Determination of their effective control uses Alex's 40 percent interest in X and Bob's 30 percent in Z, their identical ownership interests in the three entities. This gives them a combined 70 percent effective control of each entity. Y Corporation is not a member because Alex and Bob's combined ownership of 70 percent does not give them a controlling interest. Their combined identical interest in all of the entities (using Alex's 20 percent interest in Y and Bob's 30 percent interest in Z) does not exceed 50 percent.

- X, Y, and Z – Alex, Bob, and Carol together own at least 80 percent of each entity. Their combined identical interest is 60 percent in each, giving them effective control.

- W and Y – Alex, Bob, and Dave together own 100 percent of W Corporation and 90 percent of Y Corporation. They also have effective control of each, based on Alex's 20 percent identical interest in both; Bob's 15 percent identical interest in both; and Dave's 20 percent identical interest in both.

Combined Groups

A combined group consists of at least one parent-subsidiary controlled group and at least one brother-sister controlled group. A group of three or more entities qualifies as a combined group if:

- each entity is a member of either a parent-subsidiary controlled group or a brother-sister controlled group; and

- at least one entity is the common parent of a parent-subsidiary controlled group and a member of a brother-sister controlled group.

Example 4. Amy owns a controlling interest in ABC Partnership and DEF Partnership. ABC owns a controlling interest in X Corporation. They are members of the same controlled group because:

- ABC, DEF, and X are all members of either a parent-subsidiary controlled group or a brother-sister controlled group; and

- ABC is the common parent of the parent-subsidiary controlled group consisting of ABC and X and a member of the brother-sister controlled consisting of ABC and DEF.[18]

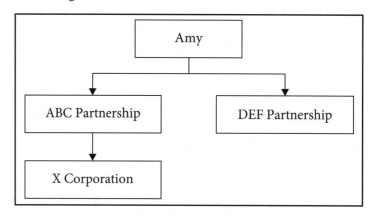

Attribution Rules

Treasury Regulation Section 1.414(c)-4 outlines attribution rules used to determine constructive ownership of an entity.

Attribution from partnerships. A partner who owns at least a 5 percent interest in the profits or capital of a partnership is considered to own a pro rata share of any interest in an entity owned by a partnership. If a partner's profits and capital interest in the partnership are not the same, whichever is greater is used to determine the pro rata share in the interest owned by the partnership.[19]

Example 5. Alice, Barb, and Colin—unrelated individuals—are partners in the ABC Partnership. The following table shows their interests in the capital and profits.

Partner	Capital	Profits
Alice	36	25
Barb	60	71
Colin	4	4

ABC owns all of the 100 shares of N corporation. Alice's constructive ownership in N is the greater of the stock owned by ABC in proportion to her interest in capital

(36 percent) or profits (25 percent). As a result, she is considered to own 36 shares of N. Barb's 71 percent profits interest exceeds her 60 percent capital interest so she is considered as owning 71 shares of N. Colin has less than a 5 percent interest in the profits and capital of ABC so no shares of N stock are attributed to him.[20]

Attribution from estates and trusts. A beneficiary who has an actuarial interest of 5 percent or more in an estate or trust is considered to own a pro rata share of any entity interest owned by the estate or trust. In determining a beneficiary's actuarial interest, the fiduciary is assumed to exercise the maximum amount of discretion in favor of the beneficiary and the maximum use of the estate or trust's interest in the entity to satisfy the beneficiary's rights.

If there are no circumstances where the beneficiary can receive any part of the estate or trust's interest in the entity, including proceeds from its disposition, none of the estate or trust's interest is attributed to the beneficiary. This can occur if stock owned by an estate is specifically bequeathed to other beneficiaries.

An income beneficiary who can receive income from an entity interest but cannot receive the interest itself has an actuarial interest in the entity interest. The actuarial interest of a beneficiary of a trust or estate is determined by assuming the fiduciary's maximum exercise of discretion in favor of the beneficiary and the estate tax rules under Treasury Regulation Section 20.2031-7.[21]

An estate is considered to own property that is subject to the administration by the estate fiduciary for purposes of paying claims against the estate and expenses of administration, even if local law provides that legal title vests in the decedent's heirs, legatees, or devisees immediately upon death.[22]

Attribution from corporations. The same general rule applies to a business interest owned by a corporation as for other entities. A person who owns 5 percent or more of a corporation's stock value is deemed to own a pro rata share of the corporation's interest in the entity.[23]

> *Example 6.* Rick owns 60 percent of P Corporation's only class of stock outstanding, Sally owns 4 percent, and T Corporation owns 36 percent. P owns 100 shares of D Corporation. Rick is deemed to own 60 shares of D Corporation and T Corporation is deemed to own 36 shares. Because Sally owns less than 5 percent of P's stock, she is not considered to own any of the D Corporation stock.[24]

Spousal attribution. An individual is treated as owning interests directly or indirectly by their spouse unless they are legally separated.[25] A spouse's indirect interest in an entity is not attributed to their spouse if the requirements of Treasury Regulation Section 1.414(c)-4(b)(5) (ii) are met.

Attribution from other family members. If a child is under 21, an interest that they own, directly or indirectly, is attributed to their parents and any interest owned directly or indirectly by their parents is attributed to them.[26] Individuals in direct effective control of an entity are considered to own an interest in the entity that is owned directly or indirectly by their parents, grandparents, grandchildren, and children who are at least 21.[27]

Operating rules. An interest treated as constructively owned by a person through the attribution rules is treated as actually owned by the person.[28] An exception provides that an interest attributed to an individual through their spouse or other family members is not treated as owned by the individual for purposes of reattributing it to another person.[29]

An interest that is attributed to a person through option attribution and another attribution rule is treated as constructively owned through the option.[30]

Affiliated Service Group

The affiliated service group rules are designed to treat businesses that operate as one economic entity as one employer for retirement plan purposes. They cover both affiliated service groups and management organizations. An employer must determine if it is a member of an affiliated service group. If it is, it must determine if its plans comply with Section 401(a). If not, it must take any action necessary to comply.[31]

Employees of affiliated service group members are treated as employed by a single employer for the following purposes:[32]

- Minimum participation standards under Section 410

- Determination of highly compensated employees under Section 414(q)

- Minimum vesting requirements under Section 411

- Contribution and benefit limits of Section 415

- Annual compensation limit of Section 401(a)(17) ($260,000 for 2014, adjusted for inflation)

- Additional participation requirements under Section 401(a)(26)

- Top heavy rules under Section 416

An affiliated service group consists of an entity (described in proposed regulations as a First-Service Organization (FSO)) and one or more other entities that perform services for the FSO if certain ownership requirements are met or a management organization and a recipient organization.

First Service Organization

An FSO is an organization whose principal business is the performance of services.[33] The proposed regulation provides two tests for determining whether the principal business of an organization is the performance of services.

Noncapital intensive business. An entity's principal business will be considered the performance of services if capital is not a material income-producing factor. Whether capital is a material income-producing factor is based on a facts-and-circumstances test. The regulations state that capital is a material income-producing factor if a substantial portion of the business' gross income comes from the use of capital in the business, such as substantial investment in inventories and depreciable assets. It is also a material income-producing factor for banks and similar institutions. Capital is not a material income-producing factor if the gross income is principally fees, commissions, or other compensation for an individual's personal services.[34]

Specific fields. An entity engaged in any one or more of the following fields is automatically a service organization:

- Health

- Law

- Engineering

- Architecture

- Accounting

- Actuarial science

- Performing arts

- Consulting

- Insurance[35]

A corporation other than a professional service corporation is not considered an FSO.[36] A professional service corporation is a corporation established for the principal purpose of providing professional services and has at least one shareholder who is licensed or otherwise legally authorized to render that type of service. Professional services means services performed by:

- certified or other public accountants;

- actuaries;

- architects;

- attorneys;,

- chiropodists;

- chiropractors;

- medical doctors;

- dentists;

- professional engineers;

- optometrists;

- osteopaths;

- podiatrists;

- psychologists; and

- veterinarians.[37]

"A Organizations"

An "A Organization" is a service organization that is a partner or shareholder in the FSO and regularly performs services for the FSO or is regularly associated with the FSO in performing services for third persons.[38] Any ownership interest in the FSO is sufficient to meet the ownership requirement. Constructive ownership is determined using the rules of Section 267(c).[39] Whether a service organization regularly performs services for the FSO depends on the facts and circumstances. According to the regulation, the amount of earned income the service organization derives from performing services for the FSO or for third persons in association with the FSO is a relevant factor.[40]

"B Organizations"

A service organization is classified as a "B Organization" if it meets the following tests:

- A significant portion of its business is performing services for an FSO, for one or more A Organizations determined with respect to the FSO, or for both.

- The services are historically performed by employees in the service field of the FSO or the A Organization.

- Ten percent or more of the interests in the organization are held by persons who are designated group members of the FSO or of the A Organizations.[41]

Significant portion. A facts-and-circumstances test determines if a significant portion of an organization's business is performing services for an FSO, A Organization(s), or both. The regulations do provide two safe harbors. The Service Receipts safe harbor requires that the performance of services for an FSO, A organization(s), or both produces 5 percent or more of the organization's gross receipts from performing services. The Total Receipts threshold test requires that the performance of services for an FSO, A organization(s), or both produce at least 10 percent of the organization's gross receipts.[42]

Historically performed. Services are considered to be of a type historically performed by employees in a particular service field if it was not unusual for them to be performed by employees of organizations in that service field in the U.S. on December 13, 1980.[43] As that date gets farther and farther away, it may become more difficult to determine if this test is met.

Designated group. The designated group consists of the officers, HCEs, and common owners of an organization. A common owner is an owner of an FSO or an A Organization if at least 3 percent of the interests in the FSO or A Organization, in the aggregate, is held, directly or indirectly, by owners of the potential B Organization.[44]

Application of the rules. The 10 percent test is applied using the direct and constructive ownership of all designated group members of the FSO and the designated group members of the A Organizations.[45] It is not necessary for the 10 percent test to be met by a single person or single class within the designated group members. An organization does not have to qualify as a service organization to be a B Organization.[46]

Example 7. R is a service organization that has eleven partners. Each partner of R owns one percent of the stock in Corporation D. Corporation D provides services to R of a type historically performed by employees in the partnership's service field. A significant portion of D's business consists of providing services to the partnership.

Considering R as a First Service Organization, D is a B Organization because:

- a significant portion of the business of the corporation is the performance of services for the partnership of a type historically performed by employees in the service field of the partnership; and

- more than 10 percent of the interests in the corporation are held, in the aggregate, by the designated group members (consisting of the eleven common owners of the partnership).

Accordingly, R and D are an affiliated service group.

R and D would also be an affiliated service group if no more than 8 percent of the 11 percent ownership in D was held by R's HCEs who were not owners of R (even though no one group owns 10 percent or more of the stock of Corporation D).[47] When the ownership of R's HCEs is added to the 3 percent of R's partners who own D, together they qualify as a designated group.

Management Organizations

A second type of affiliated service group consists of a management organization and a recipient organization.

A management organization is an organization whose principal business is performing management functions for one organization (or one organization and organizations related to that organization) on a regular and continuous basis.[48] The recipient organization is the organization and any related organizations for which the management organization performs functions.[49]

Plan Mergers

When an employer that sponsors a 401(k) plan is involved in a merger or acquisition, what happens to the plan becomes part of the negotiations and is a matter of significant interest for the plan participants and beneficiaries. The plan can be terminated or merged, the assets transferred from one plan to another, the assets distributed to the participants or beneficiaries (if the plan allows), or separate plans maintained (if they can continue to qualify under Section 401(a)).

A plan merger results in the individual accounts maintained under each plan becoming part of the same plan. The merged plan must continue to meet all of the qualification requirements. In addition, the merger must not result in a participant losing any accrued benefits.[50] The analysis considers both direct and indirect provisions, including provisions relating to years of service and compensation.[51] The protected benefits, known as "Section 411(d)(6) protected benefits" are:

- accrued benefits;

- early retirement benefits and retirement-type subsidies (such as a subsidized early retirement benefit and a subsidized qualified joint and survivor annuity); and

- optional forms of benefit such as different payment schedules, election rights, eligibility requirements, or the portion of the alternative to which the distribution alternative applies.[52]

A plan can eliminate a form of distribution that had been available to any participant if a single payment is available at the same time or times as the form of distribution being eliminated and that payment is based on the same or greater portion of the participant's account as the form of distribution being eliminated.[53] Treasury Regulation Section 1.411(d)-4 sets out when Section 411(d)(6) benefits can be reduced or eliminated. These exceptions apply to 401(k) plans:

- A change in statutory requirements, to the extent necessary to allow the plan to continue to be a qualified plan.[54]

- Replacing the ability to receive an in-kind distribution of marketable securities, other than employer securities, with cash or limiting the property that the participant can receive as an in-kind distribution. The plan cannot eliminate the right to receive employer stock.[55]

- If the plan terminates, it can eliminate the ability to receive in-kind distributions, unless it also maintains another plan that allows distributions of the specified property.[56]

- The plan is amended to eliminate or restrict a participant's ability to receive their accrued benefits under an optional form of benefit for distributions that start after the date the amendment is adopted if the participant can receive a single-sum distribution that is otherwise identical to the optional benefit eliminated or restricted. A single-sum distribution is otherwise identical in all respects to the benefit that was restricted or eliminated except with respect to the timing of benefits. A benefit is also treated as otherwise identical if the only difference is that it provides greater rights.[57] For example, the elimination of a right to receive a distribution in the form of an annuity contract is not a violation of Section 411(d)(6) if the participant is entitled to receive a single-sum distribution of their vested account balance on any date that the annuity contract would have been distributed.[58]

A direct rollover of assets from one plan to another is not considered a taxable distribution to the affected participants if it is an eligible rollover distribution paid directly to an eligible retirement plan for the benefit of the distributee.[59]

If a participant elects to have their entire benefit transferred between qualified defined contribution plans and their protected Section 411(d)(6) benefits are reduced, the transfer does not violate Section 411(d)(6) if:

- The transferring plan provides that the transfer is conditioned upon the participant's voluntary, fully-informed election to transfer the participant's entire benefit to the other qualified defined contribution plan. The participant must be offered the alternative of retaining the participant's Section 411(d)(6) protected benefits under the plan. If the plan is terminating, the participant must be offered any optional form of benefit for which the participant is eligible under the plan as required by Section 411(d)(6)).[60]

- To the extent the benefits being transferred are part of a qualified cash or deferred arrangement under Section 401(k), the benefits must be transferred to a qualified cash or deferred arrangement under Section 401(k).[61]

- The transfer must be made either in connection with an asset or stock acquisition, merger, or other similar transaction involving a change in employer of the employees of a trade or business (i.e., an acquisition or disposition within the meaning of Treasury Regulation Section 1.410(b)-2(f)) or in connection with the participant's change in employment status to an employment status with respect to which the participant is not entitled to additional allocations under the transferor plan.[62]

- If the plan qualifies under this exception, it still must satisfy all other applicable qualification requirements.[63]

Plan Terminations

Terminating a 401(k) plan has significant ramifications for the plan sponsor and participants. Unless the employer sponsoring the plan is going through a merger, divestiture, or similar transaction, it should only be undertaken after carefully analyzing the costs involved and any available alternatives. Potential alternatives include reducing or eliminating the employer match, changing plan administrators, restricting eligibility for plan participation, or lengthening the vesting schedule. If any of these methods are chosen, the plan sponsor must be careful not to violate the rules on Section 411(d)(6) protected benefits or plan qualification. Plan changes such as those discussed in the previous sentence may reduce participation by NHCEs and make it harder for the plan to satisfy the ADP test, ACP test, or both.

Planning Tip. Obtaining a favorable determination letter helps assure the employer and plan participants that plan distributions will receive the expected favorable tax treatment. If any problems are found during the determination letter process, the plan has an opportunity to correct them.

A plan may experience a partial termination if benefits are reduced or the plan experiences a substantial reduction in the number of employees covered by the plan. A partial plan termination results in the terminated employees becoming fully vested in their plan benefits.[64] Similarly, if contributions under the plan are completely discontinued, the participants become fully vested.[65]

Occurrence of a partial termination. Under the regulations, a facts-and-circumstances test determines if a partial termination occurs and the time of the partial termination. The facts and circumstances include a plan amendment or severance by the employer of a group of employees previously covered by the plan and plan amendments that adversely affect the rights of employees to vest in plan benefits.[66] As a comparison, a defined benefit plan reports to the Pension Benefit Guarantee Corporation if the plan's participation drops by 20 percent in one year or 25 percent over two years.[67] In a 2004 case, *Matz v. Household International Tax Reduction Investment Plan,*[68] Judge Richard Posner, writing for the Seventh Circuit Court of Appeals, thoroughly examined the IRS rulings, case law, and other guidance on when a partial termination occurs.

Based on that analysis, the Seventh Circuit created a rebuttable presumption that a 20 percent or greater reduction in plan participants is a partial termination while a lesser reduction is not. The decision indicates that consideration of tax motives or consequences can be used to rebut that percentage. It further states that if the reduction is less than 10 percent, the reduction in coverage should be conclusively presumed not to be a partial termination while a reduction in coverage above 40 percent should be conclusively presumed to be a partial termination.[69] In Rev. Rul. 2007-43,[70] the IRS included *Matz* in its summary of the law concerning partial terminations. Without expressly acknowledging that it was following Matz, the IRS stated that there is a presumption that a partial plan termination occurs if the turnover rate is at least 20 percent. It also examined whether the turnover rate is routine for the employer, based on the extent to which terminated employees were actually replaced, whether new employees performed the same functions, had the same job classification or title, and received comparable compensation.

Occurrence of a complete discontinuance of contributions. The regulations provide more guidance on when a complete discontinuance of contributions occurs. As with partial terminations, the regulation states whether a complete discontinuance of contributions occurs requires examining all of the facts and circumstances in the case. For this purpose, employee contributions to the plan are ignored.[71] Unlike the partial termination situation, the regulations provide some factors to be considered in making the determination.

- Whether the employer is calling an actual discontinuance of contributions a suspension to avoid the required full vesting or for any other reason

- Whether contributions are recurring and substantial

- Whether there is any reasonable probability that the lack of contributions will continue indefinitely[72]

The Code provides that a complete discontinuance occurs on the day that the plan administrator notifies the IRS of the discontinuance.[73]

IRS Reporting Requirements

When a plan terminates, it should comply with specific notice and reporting requirements. Terminating plans are not required to obtain a determination as to whether the plan meets the requirements for qualification when it terminates.

As part of the termination process, a 401(k) plan may need to file certain forms with the IRS, including:

- Form 5310, Application for Determination upon Termination. This form is used to request a determination that the plan meets all of the qualified plan requirements as of the plan termination. This form is open to public inspection if the plan has more than 25 participants. Along with the form, the plan must submit the following documents concerning the plan:

  - The plan document

  - All amendments made since the last determination letter

  - A statement explaining how the amendments affect or change the plan or any other plan maintained by the employer

  - The plan's latest determination letter, if any

  - A copy of the latest opinion letter for a standardized master or prototype plan, if any

  - A copy of the latest opinion or advisory letter for a master or prototype plan or volume submitter plan on which the employer is entitled to rely, if any

  - Copies of all records or all actions taken to terminate the plan

  - Copies of all required attachments and statement[74]

- Form 8717, User Fee for Employee Plan Determination Letter Request. This form is the transmittal form for the user fee charged for the determination letter request.

- Form 5300, Schedule Q, Elective Determination Requests. Schedule Q indicates if the plan wants its determination letter request to be evaluated using certain qualification requirements for minimum participation, coverage, and nondiscrimination.

- Form 5500, Annual Return/Report of Employee Benefit Plan (with 100 or more participants) or Form 5500-SF, Short Form Annual Return/Report of Small Employee Benefit Plan (used generally by plans with less than 100 participants). The plan's annual return must be filed with the DOL indicating that the plan is being terminated.

As part of the determination letter process, the plan must provide interested parties of its application for a determination letter and provide the IRS with satisfactory evidence that the required notice was given.[75] The requirements are discussed in Chapter 12.

Endnotes

1. IRC Secs. 414(b), 414(c).
2. IRC Sec. 1563(a)(1); Treas. Reg. §1.414(c)-2(b)(1).
3. Treas. Reg. §1.414(c)-4(b)(1).
4. Treas. Reg. §1.414(c)-2(b)(2)(i)(A).
5. Treas. Reg. §1.414(c)-2(b)(2)(i)(B).
6. Treas. Reg. §1.414(c)-2(b)(2)(i)(C).
7. Treas. Reg. §1.414(c)-2(b)(2)(i)(D).
8. Treas. Reg. §1.414(c)-2(b)(2)(ii).
9. Treas. Reg. §1.414(c)-2(e), Example 1(a).
10. Treas. Reg. §1.414(c)-2(e), Example 1(b).
11. Treas. Reg. §1.414(c)-2(c)(1).
12. Treas. Reg. §1.414(c)-4(b)(1).
13. Treas. Reg. §1.414(c)- 2(c)(2)(i).
14. Treas. Reg. §1.414(c)-2(c)(2)(ii).
15. Treas. Reg. §1.414(c)-2(c)(2)(iii).
16. Treas. Reg. §1.414(c)-2(c)(2)(iv).
17. Treas. Reg. §1.414(c)-2(e), Example 4.
18. Treas. Reg. §1.414(c)-2(e), Example 6.
19. Treas. Reg. §1.414(c)-4(b)(2)(i).
20. Treas. Reg. §1.414(c)-4(b)(2)(ii).
21. Treas. Reg. §1.414(c)-4(b)(3)(i).
22. Treas. Reg. §1.414(c)-4(b)(3(ii).
23. Treas. Reg. §1.414(c)-4(b)(4)(i).
24. Treas. Reg. §1.414(c)-4(b)(4)(ii).
25. Treas. Reg. §1.414(c)-4(b)(5)(i).
26. Treas. Reg. §1.414(c)-4(b)(6)(i).
27. Treas. Reg. §1.414(c)-4(b)(6)(Ii).

28. Treas. Reg. §1.414(c)-4(c)(1).
29. Treas. Reg. §1.414(c)-4(c)(2).
30. Treas. Reg. §1.414(c)-4(c)(3).
31. Rev. Proc. 2011-6, IRB 2011-1, 195, Sec. 14.05.
32. IRC Sec. 414(m)(4).
33. IRC Sec. 414(m)(3).
34. Treas. Reg. §1.414(m)-2(f)(1).
35. Treas. Reg. §1.414(m)-2(f)(2).
36. Treas. Reg. §1.414(m)-1(c).
37. Ibid.
38. Prop. Treas. Reg. §1.414(m)-2(b)(1).
39. Prop. Treas. Reg. §1.414(m)-2(d)(1).
40. Prop. Treas. Reg. §1.414(m)-2(b)(2).
41. Prop. Treas. Reg. §1.414(m)-2(c).
42. Prop. Treas. Reg. §1.414(m)-2(c)(2).
43. Prop. Treas. Reg. §1.414(m)-2(c)(3).
44. Prop. Treas. Reg. §1.414(m)-2(c)(4).
45. Prop. Treas. Reg. §1.414(m)-2(c)(6).
46. Prop. Treas. Reg. §1.414(m)-2(c)(7).
47. Prop. Treas. Reg. §1.414(m)-2(c)(8), Example 1.
48. IRC Sec. 414(m)(5)(A).
49. IRC Sec. 414(m)(5)(B).
50. IRC Sec. 411(d)(6).
51. Treas. Reg. §1.411(d)-3(a)(2).
52. Treas. Reg. §1.411(d)-4, A-1(a).
53. IRC Sec. 411(d)(6)(E).
54. Treas. Reg. §1.411(d)-4, A-2(b)(2)(i)
55. Treas. Reg. §1.411(d)-4, A-2 (b)(2)(iii)(A).
56. Treas. Reg. §1.411(d)-4, A-2 (b)(2)(iii)(C).
57. Treas. Reg. §1.411(d)-4, A-2(e)(2).
58. Treas. Reg. §1.411(d)-4, A-2(e)(3).
59. Treas. Reg. §1.411(d)-4, A-3(a)(4).
60. Treas. Reg. §1.411(d)-4, A-3(b)(1)(i).
61. Treas. Reg. §1.411(d)-4, A-3(b)(1)(ii).
62. Treas. Reg. §1.411(d)-4, A-3(b)(1)(iii).
63. Treas. Reg. §1.411(d)-4, A-3(b)(2).
64. Treas. Reg. §1.411(d)-2(b)(3).
65. IRC Sec. 411(d)(3).
66. Treas. Reg. §1.411(d)-2(b)(1).
67. ERISA Sec. 4043(c)(3).
68. 388 F.3d 570 (7th. Cir. 2004), 2004-2 USTC ¶50,403.

69. Ibid.

70. IRB 2007-28.

71. Treas. Reg. §1.411(d)-2(d)(1).

72. Ibid.

73. IRC Sec. 411(d)(3).

74. Instructions for Form 5310 (Rev. April 2006).

75. Treas. Reg. §1.7476-1(a)(1).

Chapter 12

Regulatory Matters: Determination Letters, ERISA/IRS Reporting and Other Matters

Introduction

401(k) plans receive special tax treatment: the employer receives a tax deduction for its contributions, the employee can make contributions before tax (unless they elect to make the contributions to a designated Roth account), and the accounts accumulate on a tax-deferred basis. The price for this special tax treatment includes ordinary income tax treatment for the non-Roth portion of the account, compliance with the qualification requirements, amending the plan when necessary to comply with law changes, filing annual reports with the IRS, and providing plan participants with required information.

A plan that complies with the qualification requirements does *not* have to file plan documents or other information to document its compliance. However, if the IRS or DOL finds that the plan does not comply, the results can be devastating: These can include immediate taxation of all plan participants, loss of the employer's deduction for all contributions to the plan, liability of the trustee for violating fiduciary duties, and liability of the trustee, plan sponsor, or other disqualified person for engaging in prohibited transactions involving the plan. Preventing and fixing broken 401(k) plans is discussed in detail in Chapter 13.

In this chapter, we will discuss how a plan obtains a determination from the IRS that the 401(k) plan, as established, meets the qualification requirements; how to amend the plan to reflect law changes, changes in the plan's design, or other changes; and the filing and reporting requirements. Of course, meeting the formal qualifications is just the first step. The plan must also be operated in compliance with the terms of its governing documents.

Obtaining a Determination Letter

The IRS examines a determination letter request to determine if the plan complies with the plan provisions required to qualify under Section 401(a). For terminating plans, it applies the requirements effective on the date of termination.[1]

The review process includes whether the plan satisfies the Section 401(k) requirements and the requirements for matching contributions or employee contributions.[2]

The determination letter process generally does not cover whether the plan satisfies the following requirements:

- Section 401(a)(4)'s nondiscrimination requirements

- Section 401(a)(26)'s minimum participation requirements

- Section 410(b)'s minimum coverage requirements[3]

The employer can elect to have the determination letter include whether:

- the plan satisfies either the safe harbor for plans with a uniform allocation formula or a uniform points allocation formula;[4]

- the employer is a member of an affiliated service group; or

- if a partial termination has occurred with respect to the plan and, if it has, the impact on plan qualification.[5]

Effect of a Determination Letter

It is important to remember that an IRS determination letter is its opinion as to whether the plan meets the Section 401 requirements and its trust meets the Section 501(a) requirements. The letter reflects the facts and demonstrations (illustrations of how the plan satisfies the numerical requirements) included with the application for a Determination Letter. It cannot be relied upon after a change in a material fact or the effective date of a law change, unless otherwise provided. A plan's ability to rely on its determination letter may be reduced or eliminated if the plan fails to disclose or misrepresents a material fact or does not accurately provide any of the required information. The IRS cautions that failure to retain copies of the data submitted with the Determination Letter request (and, implicitly, any underlying data used to develop the submitted data) may limit the amount a plan may rely on its determination letter.[6]

Because a plan must comply with the qualification requirements in both form and operation, a Determination Letter is *not* a guarantee that the plan will be considered qualified upon examination. In fact, the IRS states that a favorable determination letter may serve as a basis for determining employer contributions to a plan but is not an indication that the contributions are deductible. That requires an examination of the employer's tax return and applying Section 404.[7]

Revocation or Modification of a Determination Letter

The IRS may modify or revoke a determination letter at any time. If it does, the revocation or modification applies to all open years unless the IRS limits the retroactive effect of the revocation or modification.

The revocation or modification may result from:

- a notice to the taxpayer to whom the letter ruling was issued;

- the enactment of legislation or ratification of a tax treaty;

- a decision of the U.S. Supreme Court;

- the issuance of temporary or final regulations; or

- the issuance of a revenue ruling, revenue procedure, notice, or other statement published in the Internal Revenue Bulletin.[8]

Publication of a notice of proposed rulemaking containing a proposed regulation does not affect the application of the determination letter.[9]

The publication of a revenue ruling, revenue procedure, or other IRS administrative pronouncement will not adversely affect the prior qualification of a plan if:

- the plan received a favorable determination letter and the request for that letter contained no misstatement or omission of material facts;

- the facts subsequently developed are not materially different from the facts on which the determination letter was based;

- there has been no change in the applicable law; and

- the employer that established the plan acted in good faith in reliance on the determination letter.[10]

The plan must be amended to comply with the IRS guidance for subsequent years.[11] Plans that have received favorable determination letters do not need to request new determination letters solely because annual amendments are made to reflect cost-of-living adjustments to plan amounts.[12]

The Determination Letter Process

Revenue Procedure 2013-6[13] sets out the general procedure for requesting a determination letter. In addition, the provisions of Revenue Procedure 2013-4[14] also generally apply. Copies of these important Revenue Procedures are included as Appendix F and G, respectively. Combined, these procedures provide a comprehensive roadmap to preparing, completing, and filing a determination letter request on a 401(k) plan to the IRS. They include such information as:

- the IRS forms to submit;

- the proper font to use in competing the determination letter form;

- the mailing address; and

- the documents to submit.

User fees. Form 8717, *User Fee for Employee Plan Determination Letter Request*, must be submitted as part of the determination letter request package. As of February 2013, the user fee for a determination letter that a plan or plan amendment is qualified or that a terminating plan is qualified is $2,500. If multiple employer plans are involved, the cost for less than 100 forms is $3,000. For 100 or more plans, the cost is $15,000. The fee for submitting a determination letter request for adopting a master or prototype plan is $300.

Planning Tip. There are many trade-offs to using a custom drafted plan versus a volume submitter plan versus a master or prototype plan. However, clearly one of the reasons that master and prototype plans have been popular is the lower legal fees to have them reviewed and submitted for a determination letter. In fact, most of the plans based upon a master or prototype plan are probably not submitted for a determination letter currently. Plan sponsors should be provided a list of the trade-offs (like for correction processes) before making a business decision on the matter.

Determination based on the administrative record. The decision as to whether a plan is qualified or not is based solely on the facts in the administrative record.

The administrative record consists of:

- the request for determination, the retirement plan, and any related trust instruments, and any written modifications or amendments made by the applicant during the proceedings with the IRS;

- all other documents submitted to the IRS by, or on behalf of, the applicant with respect to the request for determination;

- all written correspondence between the IRS and the applicant with respect to the request for determination and any other documents issued to the applicant from the IRS;

- all written comments submitted to the IRS pursuant to Sections 17.01(2), (3), and (4) of Rev. Proc. 2013-6, and all correspondence relating to comments submitted between the IRS and persons (including the Pension Benefit Guaranty Corporation (PBGC) and the DOL) submitting comments pursuant to such sections; and

- in any case in which the IRS makes an investigation regarding the facts as represented or alleged by the applicant in the request for determination or in comments submitted pursuant to Sections 17.01(2), (3), and (4) of Rev. Proc. 2013-6, a copy of the official report of such investigation.[15]

Any oral representation or modification of the facts included in the determination letter request or an interested party's comment must be reduced to writing to become a part of the administrative record. If it is not reduced to writing, it does not become part of the administrative record and considered in determining the plan's qualified status.[16]

Figure 12.1. Tradeoffs between Custom Drafted Plans, Volume Submitter Plans, and Master and Prototype Plans			
	Custom Drafted Plans	*Volume Submitter Plans*	*Master and Prototype Plans*
Plan design flexibility (subject to qualification rules)	Unlimited	Some	Limited
Set-up costs (legal fees, determination letter costs)	High	Moderate	Low
Administrative costs	High	Moderate	Low
Plan amendments	Employer may be responsible for monitoring need for plan amendments and adopting them on a timely basis	VS sponsor should monitor need for plan amendments and adoption	M&P sponsor should monitor need for plan amendments and adoption
Investment options	May offer a wide variety	Employer may be able to pick among a menu	Generally limited to those offered by M&P sponsor

Closing of the administrative record. The administrative record is closed on the earlier of the following events:

- The date of mailing of a notice of the IRS's final determination

- The filing of a petition with the Tax Court for a declaratory judgment concerning the plan[17]

Conferences. If the application has been pending at least 270 days, the plan can request a conference with the Employee Plans Determinations Manager about the status of the request. The conference is limited to issues concerning the processing of the application. It will not involve any substantive discussion of technical issues and no party can make a verbatim recording. Additional status conferences can be requested if at least 90 days have passed since the previous status conference.[18]

Upon the plan's request, Employee Plan Determinations can grant a conference if it determines that the conference would be warranted in facilitating the review and determination when the determination letter request is formally submitted. The request must show that a substantive plan, amendment, termination, etc. has been developed for submission to the IRS but that special problems or issues are involved.[19]

Withdrawal of request. The plan may withdraw its determination letter request at any time before an adverse determination letter is issued. If an appeal of a proposed adverse determination letter is filed, the determination letter request may be withdrawn at any time before the proposed adverse action is forwarded to the Chief Appeals Office. Once the request has been withdrawn, the IRS will not issue any determination. That failure to issue a determination letter will not allow the plan to request a declaratory judgment under Section 7476. Information submitted in connection with the withdrawn request may be considered in a subsequent examination. The user fee will generally not be refunded if the request is withdrawn.[20]

Notice to Interested Parties

As part of the determination letter process, the plan must provide notice to interested parties of its application for a determination letter and provide the IRS with satisfactory evidence that the required notice was given.

Interested parties. If a plan requests a determination letter concerning a plan termination, the interested parties include:

- all present employees with accrued benefits;

- all former employees with vested benefits; and

- all beneficiaries of deceased employees currently receiving benefits under the plan.[21]

The plan decides the date used to determine whether a person is an interested party and a present employee or former employee. However, the date must fall within a five business day window. The window begins five business days before the first date that the plan provides notice of the determination letter request to interested parties and ends on the date that the notice is given.[22] The controlled group rules of Section 414(b) and Section 414(c) apply in determining if someone is an employer's employee.[23] Self-employed individuals are considered employees.[24]

Notice timing. The notice must be given at least days but not more than 24 days prior to the date that the determination letter request is filed.[25] A determination letter request is deemed to be filed when it is received by the IRS district director or the DOL.[26] The notice is deemed to be given when it is given in person, posted, or received in the mail.[27]

Notice content. The notice must contain the following information:[28]

- A brief description identifying the class or classes of interested parties to whom the notice is addressed

- The name of the plan, the plan identification number, and the name of the plan administrator

- The name and taxpayer identification number of the applicant (plan sponsor)

- That an application for a determination as to the qualified status of the plan is to be made to the IRS relating to an initial qualification, a plan amendment, or a plan termination, and the address of the district director to whom the application will be submitted

- A description of the class of employees eligible to participate under the plan;

- If the IRS has issued a previous determination as to the qualified status of the plan

- A statement concerning the right of any interested party to submit, or request the DOL to submit, to the district director, a comment on whether the plan meets the plan qualification requirements; that two or more such persons may join in a single comment or request; and that if the DOL declines to submit a comment on one or more matters raised in the request, the person or persons so requesting may submit a comment to the district director on those matters

- The procedures for submitting a comment to the district director or a request to the DOL

- The procedure for obtaining the additional information required to be made available to interested parties, unless the notice includes that information

The procedure for making the additional information available can include:

- making such material available for inspection and copying by interested parties at a place or places reasonably accessible to them; or

- supplying the material by using a method of delivery or a combination thereof that is reasonably calculated to ensure that all interested parties will have access to the materials.

Whatever procedure is chosen must be immediately available to all interested parties and designed to allow them to have the information in time to pursue their rights on a timely basis. The information must be available until a declaratory judgment action is filed under Section 7476 concerning the plan qualification or the ninety-second after the notice of final determination is sent to the plan.[29]

An updated copy of the plan, related trust agreement, the determination letter request and any additional document must be included in the information made available to interested parties unless they are included in the notice. If the plan includes less than twenty-six participants, the plan may provide a summary of the plan meeting specific requirements instead. For this purpose, participants includes retired employees, beneficiaries of deceased employees with vested rights, and employees eligible to participate when they make mandatory employee contributions. Once the final determination is received, the plan must make available an updated copy of the plan and trust to any interested party and their designated representative. Information concerning an individual's compensation and trade secrets may be withheld.[30]

Method of providing the notice. The plan may provide the notice using any method reasonably calculated to ensure each interested party is notified that a determination letter request is being filed. A plan that covers union employees must also notify the union. A facts-and-circumstances test applies in determining if the plan provided the notice in a satisfactory manner. The regulation envisions that it may be necessary to use more than one delivery method to provide all interested parties with timely and adequate notice.[31] The notice can be provided electronically if the electronic system used satisfies the applicable notice requirements of Treasury Regulation Section 1.401(a)-21.[32]

Based on the examples in the regulation, a plan provides reasonable notice to present employees by using the same method that it customarily uses for its notices to employees concerning employment and employee benefit matters. Electronic notification through the employer's website satisfies the notification requirement if employees have reasonable access to computers at their worksites and the employer normally notifies employees of employment and employee benefit matters through the website. Use of email satisfies the requirement for interested parties for whom the employer has an email address. If the employer does not have an e-mail address for an interested party, sending the notice to the interested party to their last known address satisfies the notice requirement.[33]

Plan Amendments

A plan may be amended due to changes in the plan's terms made by the plan sponsor. Plan amendments should be adopted in the manner prescribed by the plan document. Unless the amendment qualifies for the remedial amendment procedure, the plan should consider obtaining a new determination letter, using the procedures discussed previously.

Remedial Amendments

A plan may also need to be amended due to changes in the Internal Revenue Code and regulations. Keeping the plan documents updated for those changes and requesting new determination letters can pose a significant burden on plan sponsors, administrators, and trustees.

To simplify the process, the IRS established a system of cyclical remedial amendment periods so plans generally only need to apply for new determination letters every five years. Plans that fail the Section 401(a) qualification requirements solely because of a disqualifying provision do not need to be amended until the last day of the remedial amendment period, if the amendment is effective retroactively to the beginning of the remedial amendment period.[34]

Remedial amendment cycles. An individually designed plan has a five-year remedial amendment cycle. A plan's cycle is based on the last digit in its employer identification number. For master and prototype plans and volume submitter plans, the remedial amendment cycle is six years rather than five. Sponsors, practitioners[35] and adopters of preapproved plans generally need to apply for new opinion, advisory, or determination letters only once every six years. The same six-year cycle applies to all preapproved defined contribution plans. The correction process for failure to make the required remedial amendments is discussed in Chapter 13.

Disqualifying Provisions

A disqualifying provision is:[36]

1. a provision of a new plan, the absence of a provision from a new plan, or an amendment to an existing plan that causes the plan to fail the qualification requirements as of the date the plan or amendment is effective; or

2. a plan provision that the IRS designates in guidance published in the Internal Revenue Bulletin as a disqualifying provision that either:

    a. causes the plan to fail the qualification requirements due to a change in those requirements; or

    b. is integral to a qualification requirement that has been changed.

For purposes of item 2, a disqualifying provision includes the absence of a plan provision needed for the plan to meet the qualification requirements.[37]

IRS and DOL Reporting Requirements

ERISA requires employers or plan administrators who maintain a funded plan of deferred compensation to file an annual return with the DOL and IRS, reporting information concerning the plan's qualification, financial condition, and operations.[38] The report is filed on one of the Form 5500 series forms; the specific form used depends on the number of employees.

- Form 5500, Annual Return/Report of Employee Benefit Plan is generally used for employee benefit plans, including 401(k) plans that have 100 or more participants.

- Form 5500-SF, Short Form Annual Return/Report of Small Employee Benefit Plan can be used by plans that meet the following requirements:

    - Qualify as a small plan; a plan qualifies if it had less than 100 participants at the beginning of the current plan year

    - Not hold any employer securities at any time during the year

    - Not be required to have an annual audit

    - All of its assets held for investment purposes were invested in assets that have a readily determinable fair market value

    - Is not a multiemployer plan[39]

- Form 5500-EZ, Annual Return of One Participant (Owners and Their Spouses) Retirement Plan is generally used by plans that cover only the business owner and their spouse or only partners and their spouses and does not provide benefits for anyone else. If the total plan assets of the plan and any other one-participant plan maintained by the employer are less than $250,000 at the end of the plan year and it is not the plan's final plan year, no return needs to be filed. If the total assets exceed $250,000, Form 5500-EZ must be filed for all of the employer's one-participant plans, regardless of the amount of a plan's assets.

A special rule allows plans that have between 80 and 120 participants as of the beginning of a plan year to file the same 5500 series form that it filed the previous year.[40]

Form 5500

A 401(k) plan that covers 100 or more participants can elect a limited exemption or alternative method of compliance.[41] If a plan does not elect a limited exemption or alternative method of compliance, the following information must be provided:

- Financial statements, providing the detail specified in ERISA section 103(b)(3) and an accountant's opinion.[42] The financial statement must include:[43]

    - a statement of assets and liabilities,

    - a statement of changes in net assets available for plan benefits, including details of revenues and expenses and other changes aggregated by general source and application; and

    - in the notes, ERISA directs the accountant to consider disclosures concerning such things as significant changes to the plan during the period and their impact on benefits; the funding policy and any changes to the policy; contingent liabilities; agreements and transactions with persons known to be parties in interest; whether a tax ruling or determination letter has been obtained; and any other matters necessary to fully and fairly present the financial statements.

- The number of employees covered by the plan[44]

- The name and address of each fiduciary[45]

- The name of each person who rendered services to the plan and received compensation from the plan directly or indirectly, the amount of the compensation, and details about the services provided, the relationship to the employer or covered employees, and any other relationship with any party in interest[46]

- The reason for any change in plan trustee, accountant, insurance carrier, administrator, investment manager, or custodian[47]

- Any financial and actuarial information that the Secretary requires, including the financial statement information described above[48]

- 401(k) and other profit sharing plans do not have to provide actuarial information[49]

- If any benefits under the plan are purchased or guaranteed by an insurance company, the insurer must provide a report with specific information[50]

Plans that elect the limited exemption or alternative method of compliance must include the following information.

Form 5500 and any statement or schedules required to be attached,[51] including:

- Schedule A (Insurance Information)

- Schedule C (Service Provider Information)

- Schedule D (Direct Filing Entity (DFE)/Participating Plan Information)

- Schedule G (Financial Transaction Schedules)

- Schedule H (Financial Information)

- Schedule R (Retirement Plan Information)

- The following financial schedules:[52]

    - Assets held for investment

    - Assets acquired and disposed within the plan year

    - Party in interest transactions

    - Obligations in default

    - Leases in default

    - Reportable transactions

- separate financial statements (in addition to those described above) if any are prepared for the audit and notes to the financial statement, complying with the requirements of DOL Regulation Sections 2520.103-1(b)(3) and 2520.103-1(b) (4).[53]

- Financial statements for the account or trust (if some or all of the plan's assets are held in a pooled separate account maintained by an insurance company or a common or collective trust)[54]

- The opinion of an independent qualified accountant[55] that states:

    - if the audit was made in accordance with generally accepted auditing standards;[56]

    - any omitted auditing procedures deemed necessary and the reason for their omission;[57]

    - whether the accounting principles were consistently applied between the current year and the preceding year;[58]

    - any changes in principles that have a material effect on the financial statements;[59] and

- a clear identification of any matters to which the accountant takes exception, clearly specifying the exception and the effect of the matters subject to the exception on the financial statements, and whether the matters are the result of DOL regulations or otherwise.[60]

Schedule A – Insurance Information

Schedule A is used to report information concerning benefits that are purchased from and guaranteed by an insurance company, insurance service, or other similar organization. These benefits may include a life insurance policy or annuity. Schedule A must provide the following information for the plan year:

1. The premium rate or subscription charge and the total premium or subscription charges paid to each insurer and the approximate number of persons covered by each class of such benefits

2. The total amount of premiums received, the approximate number of persons covered by each class of benefits, and the total claims paid by the carrier

3. The dividends or retroactive rate adjustments, commissions, and administrative service or other fees or other specific acquisition costs paid by the insurer

4. Any amounts held to provide benefits after retirement and the remainder of such premiums

5. The names and addresses of persons to whom commissions or fees were paid, the amount paid to each, and for what purpose

If an insurer does not maintain separate experience records covering the specific groups it serves, instead of the information in items 2-5, the report must include the basis of its premium rate or subscription charge, the total amount of premiums or subscription charges received from the plan, and a copy of the financial report of the insurer. If the insurer incurs specific costs in connection with the acquisition or retention of any particular plan or plans, Schedule A must include a detailed statement of such costs.[61]

The commissions and fees that must be reported on Schedule A include all commissions and fees directly or indirectly attributable to a contract or policy between a plan and an insurer.

Schedule C – Service Provider Information

Schedule C must be completed and attached to a Form 5500 to report persons who rendered services to or who had transactions with the plan during the reporting year if the person received, directly or indirectly, $5,000 or more in reportable compensation in connection with services rendered or their position with the plan.[62] The following persons are exempt from reporting:

1.   Employees of the plan whose only compensation in relation to the plan was less than $25,000 for the plan year

2.   Employees of the plan sponsor or other business entity where the plan sponsor or business entity is reported on the Schedule C as a service provider, provided the employee did not separately receive reportable direct or indirect compensation in relation to the plan

3.   Persons whose only compensation in relation to the plan consists of insurance fees and commissions listed in a Schedule A filed for the plan

4.   Payments made directly by the plan sponsor that are not reimbursed by the plan. In the case of a multiemployer or multiple-employer plan, where the plan sponsor would be the joint board of trustees for the plan, payments by contributing employers, directly or through an employer association, or by participating employee organizations, should be treated the same as payments by a plan sponsor.

Form 5500-SF

Plans that qualify to file Form 5500-SF must complete that form and attach any required statements or schedules. One participant plans can file a Form 5500-SF instead of a Form 5500-EZ if they meet the following requirements.

- The plan is a one-participant plan. This means either:

  - the plan only covers the owner (or the owner and their spouse) and the owner (or the owner and their spouse) own the entire business (which may be incorporated or unincorporated); or

  - the plan only covers one or more partners (or partner(s) and spouse(s)) in a business partnership.

- The plan does not provide benefits for anyone except the owner or the owner and their spouse, or one or more partners and their spouses.

- The plan covered fewer than 100 participants at the beginning of the plan year.

- A plan that does not meet ALL the listed conditions is not a one-participant plan filer eligible to file Form 5500-SF instead of Form 5500-EZ. It must file a paper

Form 5500-EZ with the IRS if it meets the first two conditions but does not meet the third condition.

Eligible one-participant plans need complete only the basic questions about the plan, its finances, and operation.[63]

Filing Requirements & Timing

The plan must file Form 5500, 5500-SF, or 5500-EZ by the last day of the seventh month following the end of the plan year.[64] The plan can obtain a 2½ month extension by filing Form 5558, Application for Extension of Time to File Certain Employee Plan Returns with the IRS' Ogden, Utah Service Center.[65] Failure to do so subjects the plan to a $25 per day penalty, up to a maximum of $15,000 per return.[66] In addition, the DOL can impose a penalty of $1,100 per day for a failure or refusal to file the appropriate Form 5500.[67]

Electronic filing. For plan years beginning on or after January 1, 2009, Form 5500 or 5500-SF and all statements and schedules must be filed electronically.[68] Form 5500-EZ is still filed on paper with the IRS as of the date of this publication.

Information Provided to Participants and Beneficiaries

In addition to filing the Form 5500 series report with the DOL or IRS, the plan administrator must also provide certain information to plan participants. ERISA requires three different types of disclosures. First, certain material must be provided to participants at stated times or if certain events occur. Second, the plan administrator must provide certain material to participants upon request. Finally, the plan administrator must make certain material available to participants for inspection at reasonable times and places.[69]

The information that must be provided to participants at stated times or upon certain events consists of:

- a summary plan description;

- a statement of material modifications;[70] and

- a summary annual report.[71]

The following material must be available upon request or for inspection:

- The latest annual report

- The instruments under which the plan is established or operated, including the bargaining agreement, trust agreement, contract, or other instruments[72]

Methods of Complying with the Disclosure Requirements

If reports, statements, notices, and other documents are required to be furnished, either automatically or upon request, the documents must be current, readily accessible, and clearly identified. Sufficient copies must be available to accommodate the expected number of inquiries.

The documents do not have to be maintained at each employer establishment, union hall, or office but must be available at any such location within 10 calendar days after the day on which a request for disclosure is made. A plan administrator that sets out a procedure to request such plan documents and communicates it to plan participants does not have to comply with requests that do not follow that procedure. The procedure must allow requests to be made in a reasonably convenient manner to the plan administrator and at each location where the documents must be made available. If a reasonable procedure has not been established, a good faith effort to request examination of plan documents will be considered a request to the plan administrator.[73]

For other documents required to be furnished to plan participants, the plan administrator must use measures reasonably calculated to ensure actual receipt of the material by plan participants, beneficiaries, and other specified individuals. Materials required to be furnished to all participants and beneficiaries receiving benefits must be sent by a method likely to result in full distribution. In-hand delivery to an employee at their worksite is sufficient while simply placing copies in a location frequented by participants is not.[74] If a participant makes a written request for materials, they must be mailed to an address provided by the requesting participant or beneficiary or personally delivered to the participant or beneficiary.[75]

Electronic delivery. An administrator can provide the documents electronically if it complies with the procedures outlined in the DOL regulations. Those procedures include the following actions.

- Ensuring that the system for furnishing documents:

    - results in actual receipt of transmitted information, such as using return-receipt or notice of undelivered electronic mail features, conducting periodic reviews or surveys to confirm receipt of the transmitted information; and

    - protects the confidentiality of personal information relating to the individual's accounts and benefits;

- Preparing and furnishing the electronically delivered documents in a manner that is consistent with the style, format, and content requirements applicable to the particular document

- Providing notice when a document is furnished electronically, in electronic or nonelectronic form, that informs the individual of the significance of the document when it is not otherwise reasonably evident as transmitted and of the right to request and obtain a paper version of such document

- Providing, upon request, a paper version of the electronically furnished documents[76]

Electronic delivery can only be provided to individuals who fall into one of two categories.

1. Participants who have the ability to effectively access the electronic documents at their work location and whose access to the employer's or plan sponsor's internet or intranet is an integral part of their duties[77]

2. A participant, beneficiary, or other person entitled to documents who meets certain requirements, including:[78]

   - affirmatively consented to receiving the documents electronically and has not withdrawn their consent;

   - consented electronically in a way that reasonably demonstrates their ability to access information in the form that will be used;

   - provided an email address for the receipt of the electronic documents;

   - was provided a statement about the electronic delivery of documents that included the types of documents covered by the consent, how to withdraw consent, and how to change the email address used, and the right to obtain a paper version, and any hardware or software requirements;

   - any changes to the hardware or software requirements that create a material risk that the individual will not be able to access or retain the documents require a new notice to the individual and new consent and the ability to withdraw the previous consent without charge or any condition or consequence not disclosed at the time of the initial consent.

Summary Plan Description (SPD)

ERISA requires that participants and beneficiaries receive a Summary Plan Description (SPD) that includes specific information about the plan. The statute requires plan administrators to perform a difficult balancing act. The SPD must be written in a manner calculated to be understood by the average plan participant while being sufficiently accurate and comprehensive to reasonably apprise the participants and beneficiaries of their rights and obligations under the plan.[79] The plan administrator is to "exercise considered judgment and discretion" by considering factors such as the level of comprehension and education of typical participants and the complexity of the plan.[80]

If a plan provides different benefits for different classes of participants and beneficiaries, the plan may provide different SPDs for different classes of benefits. The SPD for each class can be limited to the information relevant to that class and omit information that is not relevant to that class. It must clearly identify on the first page of the text the class of participants and beneficiaries for which it has been prepared and the plan's coverage of other classes. If the classes covered by the plan are too numerous to be listed adequately on the first page of the SPD's text, they may be listed elsewhere in the text if the first page of the text refers to the page or pages in the text that contain this information.[81]

When an SPD must be provided. The SPD must be provided to each participant and beneficiary on or before the later of:

- 90 days after an employee becomes a participant or a beneficiary first receives benefits; or

- within 120 days after the plan becomes subject to ERISA's reporting and disclosure requirements.[82] This is generally the first day an employee is credited with an hour of service. Special rules apply to plans that have prospective or retroactive effective dates.[83]

An updated SPD must be provided every five years if any plan amendments were made since the last SPD was provided.[84] Even if no amendments were made to the plan, a new SPD must be provided every 10 years.[85]

Style and format. The SPD must not be formatted in a way to be misleading, misinforming, or failing to inform participants and beneficiaries. It cannot describe exceptions, limitations, reductions, and other restrictions of plan benefits in a way that minimizes them, renders them obscure, or otherwise makes them appear unimportant. They must be described or summarized in a manner that is as prominent as the description or summary of the plan benefits. The advantages and disadvantages of the plan cannot exaggerate the benefits or minimize the limitations. The restrictions do not need to be disclosed in the SPD near the description or summary of benefits, if the page on which the restrictions are described is noted adjacent to the benefit description.

If a significant number of plan participants are only literate in a language other than English, the English SPD must include a prominent notice to those individuals in their own language. The notice must be prominently displayed and offer those individuals assistance and the procedures to follow to obtain the assistance. The assistance provided does not have to be in writing. It must be given in their native language and calculated to provide a reasonable opportunity to learn about their rights and obligations under the plan.[86]

A plan must provide this notice and assistance if:

- it covers fewer than 100 participants at the beginning of a plan year, and in which 25 percent or more of all plan participants are literate only in the same nonEnglish language; or

- it covers 100 or more participants at the beginning of the plan year, and in which the lesser of (i) 500 or more participants, or (ii) 10 percent or more of all plan participants are literate only in the same non-English language.[87]

Content of the SPD. The SPD must accurately reflect the plan contents as of the date not more than 120 days before the date of the SPD. Although the SPD is not intended to be a complete description of the plan terms, its description should be accurate and consistent with the plan document. The sample Summary Plan Description set out in the DOL regulations is found in Appendix H.

It must include the following information.

- The name of the plan and, if different, the name by which the plan is commonly known by its participants and beneficiaries.[88]

- The name and address of the employer or employee organization maintaining the plan.[89]

- The name, business address, and business phone number of the plan administrator.[90]

- For a collectively-bargained plan established or maintained by one or more employers and one or more employee organizations, detailed information about the employers and organizations involved and that additional information will be provided upon written request and is available for inspection.[91]

- In the case of a plan established or maintained by two or more employers, the association, committee, joint board of trustees, parent or most significant employer of a group of employers all of which contribute to the same plan, or other similar representative of the parties who established or maintain the plan, and how additional information can be obtained.[92]

- The plan's Employer Identification Number (EIN) and the plan number assigned by the plan sponsor.[93]

- The type of pension plan—defined benefit, defined contribution, 401(k), cash balance, money purchase, profit-sharing, ERISA section 404(c) plan, etc.[94]

- The type of administration of the plan, e.g., contract administration, insurer administration, etc.[95]

- The plan's designated agent for service of legal process, and the address at which process may be served on such person, and, a statement that service of legal process may be made upon a plan trustee or the plan administrator.[96]

- The name, title, and address of the principal place of business of each trustee of the plan.[97]

- If a plan is maintained pursuant to one or more collective bargaining agreements, a statement that the plan is so maintained, and how a copy of any such agreement may be obtained or examined by participants and beneficiaries.[98]

- The plan's requirements for eligibility for participation and for benefits, including any conditions that must be met before a participant is eligible to receive benefits and circumstances that could result in the participant not receiving benefits they might expect based on the SPD's description of benefits.[99]

- Any joint and survivor benefits provided under the plan, including any requirement that an election is required to select or reject the joint and survivor annuity.[100]

- The participant's right to self-direct the investment of their account and whether the plan is designed to qualify for the exception to the ERISA fiduciary duties for accounts directed by the participant.[101]

- A statement that the plan benefits are not insured by the Pension Benefit Guaranty Corporation and the reason why.[102]

- A description and explanation of the plan provisions for determining years of service for eligibility to participate, vesting, and breaks in service, and years of participation for benefit accrual. It must include the service required to accrue full benefits and the manner in which accrual of benefits is prorated for employees failing to complete full service for a year.[103]

- The sources of contributions to the plan—for example, employer, employee organization, employees—and the method by which the amount of contribution is calculated.[104]

- The identity of any funding medium used for the accumulation of assets through which benefits are provided. The SPD must identify any insurance company, trust fund, or any other institution, organization, or entity that maintains a fund on behalf of the plan or through which the plan is funded or benefits are provided.[105]

- The date that the plan's fiscal year ends.[106]

- The procedures governing claims for benefits, including filing claim forms, providing notifications of benefit determinations, and reviewing denied claims, time limits, and remedies for appealing denied claims.[107]

- A statement of ERISA rights, containing information included in a model statement provided in the regulations. It may include an explanatory and descriptive provision in addition to the model statement provisions. The statement must comply with the SPD style and format rules. The plan may mention certain rights elsewhere in the SPD but the statement of ERISA rights must appear as one consolidated statement.[108]

The complete model statement set out in the regulations is shown in Appendix L2. A plan may delete items that do not apply.[109]

Summary of Material Modifications (SMM)

SPDs only have to be updated for plan changes every five years. If a plan is amended during the five-year period, the SPD could be misleading. Even if there are no plan amendments, other plan information can change during the five-year, such as the name and/or address of the plan administrator or trustee. As a result, the plan administrator must provide a summary description of any material modification to the plan and any change in the SPD information to participants and beneficiaries. As with the SPD, the SMM must be written in a manner calculated to be understood by the average plan participant.[110]

Time for providing an SMM. The SMM must be provided within 210 days after the close of the plan year in which the modification or change occurred, regardless of the change's effective date. Changes that are retroactive to a prior plan year do not affect the disclosure date. An SMM is not required if the material modification or change does not take effect, whether it is rescinded or otherwise.[111]

Example 1. A calendar year adopts a material modification in April 2014 that applies retroactively to the 2013 plan year. The SMM is timely if it is provided on or before July 29, 2015 (210 days after the end of 2014, the year in which the modification was adopted).

Example 2. The material modification in Example 1 is rescinded before the end of 2014. No SMM is required.

If the plan incorporates the material modification or changes in a timely SPD, no SMM is required.[112]

When a SPD is furnished, it must be accompanied by all SMMs that are required to be included in the SPD but that are not reflected in the SPD furnished.[113]

Summary Annual Report (SAR)

While the Form 5500 series can include a great deal of information about the plan, it is unintelligible for many participants. Rather than require the plan to provide that information to participants and beneficiaries, ERISA and the DOL require that plans provide them with a copy of the statements and schedules and a summary of the most recent Form 5500 series.[114]

Time to furnish. A SAR must be furnished within nine months after the close of the plan's year. If the IRS granted the plan an extension of time to file its Form 5500 series, the SAR must be furnished within two months after the end of the extended filing period.[115]

> *Example 3.* A calendar year plan receives an extension of time to October 15, 2015 to file its 2014 Form 5500. It must provide participants and beneficiaries with the SAR by December 15, 2015.

Contents, style, and format. The DOL has prescribed a format for pension plans that must be completed using the information in the most recent Form 5500 series filed with the DOL.[116] The format is reproduced in Appendix I. The plan may omit any portion of the form that is not applicable or that requires information not required to be reported on the plan's Form 5500.[117] If the plan administrator determines that additional information is needed to fairly summarize the Form 5500, it should be provided after the required form and headed "Additional Explanation".[118]

Foreign languages. Plans required to include a foreign language notice in its SPD that assistance is available to certain persons who are literate in a nonEnglish language must include a similar notice in their SAR. As with the SPD, the notice offering assistance must clearly set forth the procedure that must be followed to obtain such assistance. The assistance does not have to involve written materials but must be given in the nonEnglish language common to the participants.[119]

Requests for additional information. A plan administrator must promptly provide any additional documents requested by a plan participant or beneficiary that follows the plan procedures or rights set out in the SAR.[120]

Notice Concerning Distributions from a 401(k) Plan

401(k) plan distributions can be a significant amount for many participants. The Code provides them with various options for the distributions and prescribes certain tax effects, including mandatory withholding, depending on the option chosen. Without appropriate information, a distributee may make a choice that not only reduces their potential retirement income but may result in the imposition of significant income tax and penalty. So participants about to receive a distribution have information to use in their decision, Code section 402(f) requires plan administrators to provide participants with a written explanation of their rights and the effect of the exercise of those rights (a "Section 402(f) notice"). The IRS provided separate sample Section 402(f) notices for rollover distributions from accounts other than designated Roth accounts and distributions from designated Roth accounts in Notice 2009-68.[121] The sample notices are reproduced in Appendix J (for designated Roth accounts) and Appendix K (for accounts other than designated Roth accounts).

Content of the Section 402(f) notice. As with other notices to participants, the Section 402(f) notice must be designed to be easily understood and explain:

- the rules that allow a distributee to elect a direct rollover (also known as a trustee-to-trustee transfer) to an eligible retirement plan;

- the rules requiring a mandatory 20 percent withholding of tax if the distribution is not paid in a direct rollover;

- the rules that allow the distributee to defer tax on the distribution if it is rolled over to an eligible retirement plan within 60 days of the distribution; and

- if applicable, the special rules concerning averaging of lump sum distributions and treatment of net unrealized appreciation.[122]

The IRS is authorized to provide a model Section 402(f) notice. A plan administrator that provides the applicable model Section 402(f) notice is deemed to comply with the content requirement for a Section 402(f) notice.[123]

When the Section 402(f) notice must be provided. The Section 402(f) notice must satisfy either 1 or 2:

1. The notice must be provided to the distributee at least 30 days but no more than 180,[124] days before the date of a distribution.

    a. If the distributee receives the Section 402(f) notice and then elects a distribution, the distribution can be made within 30 days of when the notice was provided if the plan administrator clearly indicates to the distributee that the distributee has the right to consider whether to elect a direct rollover for at least 30 days after the notice is provided. The plan administrator can use any method reasonably designed to attract the distributee's attention to inform them of the relevant time period. It could be provided in the Section 402(f) notice or in a separate document provided at the same time as the notice (e.g., attached to the election form).

b. The plan administrator can use the annuity starting date for the date of distribution.[125]

2. This paragraph is satisfied by the plan administrator:

a. providing a distributee with the Section 402(f) notice;[126]

b. providing the distributee with a summary of the notice within the time period described in paragraph 1a; [127] and

c. upon the distributee's request after receiving the summary Section 402(f) notice, providing another Section 402(f) notice without charge and at least 30 days before the date of a distribution (or the annuity starting date). The distributee can waive the 30-day period.[128]

The summary Section 402(f) notice must:

- set forth the principal provisions of the Section 402(f) notice;

- refer the distributee to the most recent version of the Section 402(f) notice;

- if the notice was provided in a document that contained information other than the notice, identify that document and include a reasonable indication of where the notice is located in that document, such as by index reference or section heading; and

- must advise the distributee that, upon request, a copy of the Section 402(f) notice will be provided without charge.[129]

Endnotes

1. Rev. Proc. 2013-6, IRB 2013-1, 198; Sec. 5.02.
2. Rev. Proc. 2013-6, IRB 2013-1, 198; Sec. 5.03.
3. Ibid.
4. Ibid.
5. Rev. Proc. 2013-6, IRB 2013-1, 198; Sec. 5.08.
6. Rev. Proc. 2013-6, IRB 2013-1, 198; Sec. 21.01.
7. Rev. Proc. 2013-6, IRB 2013-1, 198; Sec. 21.04.
8. Rev. Proc. 2013-4, IRB 2013-1, 126; Sec. 13.04.
9. Ibid.
10. Rev. Proc. 2013-6, IRB 2013-1, 198; Sec. 21.03.
11. Ibid.
12. Notice 2004-72, IRB 2004-46, 840.

13. IRB 2013-1, 198

14. IRB 2013-1, 126.

15. Rev. Proc. 2013-6, IRB 2013-1, 198; Sec. 19.03(1).

16. Rev. Proc. 2013-6, IRB 2013-1, 198; Sec. 19.03(3).

17. Rev. Proc. 2013-6, IRB 2013-1, 198; Sec. 19.03(2).

18. Rev. Proc. 2013-6, IRB 2013-1, 198; Sec. 6.18.

19. Rev. Proc. 2013-6, IRB 2013-1, 198; Sec. 19.02.

20. Rev. Proc. 2013-6, IRB 2013-1, 198; Sec. 6.17.

21. Treas. Reg. §1.7476-1(b)(5).

22. Treas. Reg. §1.7476-1(c)(1).

23. Treas. Reg. §1.7476-1(c)(2).

24. Treas. Reg. §1.7476-1(c)(3).

25. Treas. Reg. §601.201(o)(3)(xv).

26. Treas. Reg. §601.201(o)(3)(xxi).

27. Ibid.

28. Treas. Reg. §601.201(o)(3)(xvi).

29. Treas. Reg. §601.201(o)(3)(xvii).

30. Treas. Regs. §§601.201(o)(3)(xviii), 601.201(o)(3)(xix).

31. Treas. Reg. §1.7476-2(c)(1).

32. Treas. Reg. §1.7476-2(c)(2).

33. Treas. Reg. §1.7476-2(d).

34. Rev. Proc. 2007-44, IRB 2007-28, Sec. 2.02.

35. Rev. Proc. 2005-16, IRB 2005-10, Sec. 13.04 defines a practitioner as a volume submitter with an established place of business in the U.S. where it is accessible during every business day and has at least 30 employer-clients reasonably expected to timely adopt a plan that is substantially similar to the practitioner's specimen plan.

36. Treas. Reg. §1.401(b)-1(b). Also included in the disqualifying provision definition are plan provisions that fail the qualification requirements due to a change made by ERISA, the Tax Equity and Fiscal Responsibility Act of 1982 (TEFRA), or effective before the first day of the first plan year beginning after December 31, 1989 and affected by the Tax Reform Act of 1986, the Omnibus Budget Reconciliation Act of 1986, or the Omnibus Budget Reconciliation Act of 1987.

37. Treas. Reg. §1.401(b)-1(c)(1).

38. IRC Sec. 6058(a); Treas. Reg. §301.6058-1(a); ERISA Secs. 101(b)(1), 103, 104.

39. DOL Reg. §2520.103-1(c)(2)(ii).

40. DOL Reg. §2520.103-1(d).

41. DOL Reg. §2520.103-1(a).

42. ERISA Sec. 103(a)(1)(B).

43. ERISA Sec. 103(b)(2).

44. ERISA Sec. 103(c)(1).

45. ERISA Sec. 103(c)(2).

46. ERISA Sec. 103(c)(3).

47. ERISA Sec. 103(c)(4).

48. ERISA Sec. 103(c)(5).

49. ERISA Sec. 103(d)(A).

50. ERISA Sec. 103(e).

51. DOL Reg. §2520.103-1(b)(1).

52. DOL Reg. §2520-103-10(b).

53. DOL Regs. §§2520.103-1(b)(2), 2520.103-1(b) (3).

54. DOL Reg. §2520.103-1(b)(4).

55. DOL Reg. §2520-103-1(b)(5).

56. DOL Reg. §2520.103-1(b)(5)(ii).

57. Ibid.

58. DOL Reg. §2520.103-1(b)(5)(iii).

59. Ibid.

60. DOL Reg. §2520.103-1(b)(5)(iv).

61. ERISA Sec. 103(e).

62. Instructions to 2012 Form 5500 Schedule C; DOL FAQs About the 2009 Schedule C, available at http://www.dol.gov/ebsa/faqs/faq_scheduleC.html and DOL Supplemental FAQs About the 2009 Schedule C, available at http://www.dol.gov/ebsa/faqs/faq-sch-C-supplement.html. Updated FAQs have not been issued.

63. Instructions for 2012 Form 5500-SF.

64. IRC Sec. 6058; Instructions for 2012 Form 5500, 5500-SF, and 5500-EZ.

65. Treas. Reg. §1.6081-11(a); 2012 Form 5558 instructions.

66. IRC Sec. 6652(e).

67. ERISA Sec. 502(c)(2); DOL Reg. §2575.502c-2.

68. DOL Reg. §2520-104a-2.

69. DOL Reg. §2520.104b-1(a).

70. ERISA Sec. 104(b)(1).

71. ERISA Sec. 104(b)(3).

72. ERISA Sec. 104(b)(2).

73. DOL Reg. §2520.104b-1(b)(3).

74. DOL Reg. §2520.104b-1(b)(1)

75. DOL Reg. §2520.104b-1(b)(2).

76. DOL Reg. §2520.104b-1(c)(1).

77. DOL Reg. §2520.104b-1(c)(2)(i).

78. DOL Reg. §2520.104b-1(c)(2)(ii).

79. ERISA Sec. 102(a).

80. DOL Reg. §2520.102-2(a).

81. DOL Reg. §2520.102-4.

82. DOL Reg. §2520.104b-2(a)(3).

83. Ibid.

84. DOL Reg. §2520.104b-2(b)(1).

85. DOL Reg. §2520.104b-2(b)(2).

86. DOL Reg. §2520.104b-2(c).

87. Ibid.

88. DOL Reg. §2520.102-3(a).

89. DOL Reg. §2520.102-3(b).

90. DOL Reg. §2520.102-3(f).

91. DOL Reg. §2520.102-3(b)(3).

92. DOL Reg. §2520.102-3(b)(4).

93. DOL Reg. §2520.102-3(c).

94. DOL Reg. §2520.102-3(d).

95. DOL Reg. §2520.102-3(e).

96. DOL Reg. §2520.102-3(g).

97. DOL Reg. §2520.102-3(h).

98. DOL Reg. §2520.102-3(i). For the purpose of this paragraph, a plan is maintained pursuant to a collective bargaining agreement if such agreement controls any duties, rights, or benefits under the plan, even though such agreement has been superseded in part for other purposes.

99. DOL Regs. §§2520.102-3(j), 2520.102-3(l).

100. DOL Reg. §2520.102-3(k).

101. DOL Reg. §2550.404c-1(b)(2)(i)(B).

102. DOL Reg. §2520.102-3(m).

103. DOL Reg. §2520.102-3(n).

104. DOL Reg. §2520.102-3(p).

105. DOL Reg. §2520.102-3(q).

106. DOL Reg. §2520.102-3(r).

107. DOL Reg. §2520.102-3(s). The plan may furnish its claims procedures as a separate document if it satisfies the style and format rules applicable to SPDs. The SPD must state that the plan's claim procedures are furnished automatically as a separate document, without charge.

108. DOL Reg. §2520.102-3(t)(1).

109. DOL Reg. §2520.102-3(t)(2).

110. DOL Reg. §2520.104b-3(a).

111. Ibid.

112. DOL Reg. §2520.104b-3(b).

113. DOL Reg. §2520.104b-3(c).

114. ERISA Sec. 104(b)(3); DOL Regs. §2520-104b-10(a).

115. DOL Reg. §2520-104b-10(c).

116. DOL Reg. §2520-104b-10(d).

117. DOL Reg. §2520-104b-10(d)(1).

118. DOL Reg. §2520-104b-10(d)(2).

119. DOL Reg. §2520-104b-10(e).

120. DOL Reg. §2520-104b-10(f).

121. IRB 2009-39.

122. Treas. Reg. §1.402(f)-1, A-1(a).

123. Treas. Reg. §1.402(f)-1, A-1(b).

124. P.L. 109-280, Sec. 1102(a)(1)(B), directing the Treasury to amend Reg. §1.402(f)-1 by substituting 180 days for 90 days for plan years beginning after 2006. Prop. Reg. §1.402(f)-1 makes this change but the regulation has not been finalized as of the date of writing.

125. Treas. Reg. §1.402(f)-1, A-2(a).

126. Treas. Reg. §1.402(f)-1, A-2(b)(1).

127. Treas. Reg. §1.402(f)-1, A-2(b)(2).

128. Treas. Reg. §1.402(f)-1, A-2(b)(3).

129. Ibid.

Chapter 13

Preventing and Fixing Broken 401(k) Plans

Introduction

As we have noted in prior chapters, a qualified 401(k) plan is a defined contribution retirement plan that by its nature will likely run decades. It might be expected to continue beyond current management and maybe even current ownership in the case of family-owned, closely-held companies. And, as we have discussed, in order to obtain and maintain the desired tax and other qualified plan benefits of a 401(k) plan for the participants (primarily income tax deferral and tax-free growth of earnings) and for the sponsoring company (business expense deduction for employee and employer contributions to the 401(k), the plan must be properly documented and then operate according to the plan-documented 401(k) design and required legal terms for the life of the plan. That compliance period extends until the plan is officially terminated under the Internal Revenue Code and ERISA requirements. In summary, the plan must always be in both (1) form and (2) operational compliance, including demographic eligibility compliance, with the terms of the plan document for the life of the 401(k) plan in order to claim the benefits granted to a qualified plan.

Why Comply

As noted, there is the possibility of the 401(k) plan losing its qualified plan status, resulting in immediate taxation of all plan participants as well as the loss of the employer's business expense deduction for all contributions made to the 401(k) plan. These negative tax consequences are bad enough in themselves for the employer sponsor and the plan participants. However, even worse consequences can occur. As we have already discussed, the sponsor and its designated officials in charge of the plan take on certain personal fiduciary duties and other legal responsibilities with regard to the plan and, with this duty, assume certain legal liabilities if they do not assure proper qualified 401(k) plan compliance. For example, the DOL has instituted a special program to track down and recover from the fiduciaries on certain plans the employee salary reduction contributions that should have been made to a 401(k) by the employer and were not.[1] The liability for these missed employee contributions (or misdirected and misused contributions due the plan) is not avoided by either corporate or personal bankruptcies. In effect they are like income tax obligations owed; they may not be avoided. Moreover, if there is evidence of intentionality in the actions, even criminal charges may be applied, and have been.

Who Is an ERISA Fiduciary?

According to ERISA, "every employee benefit plan shall be established and maintained pursuant to a written instrument (plan document). Such instrument shall provide for one or more *named fiduciaries* (emphasis added) who jointly or severally shall have authority to control and manage the operation and administration of the plan."[2] The statute adds, "For purposes of this title, the term 'named fiduciary' means a fiduciary who is named in the plan instrument, or who, pursuant to a procedure specified in the plan, is identified as a fiduciary (A) by a person who is an employer or employee benefit organization with respect to the plan or (B) by such an employer and such an employee benefit organization acting jointly."[3] Further, ERISA details that:

> A person is a fiduciary with respect to a plan to the extent (i) he exercises any discretionary authority or discretionary control respecting management or disposition of its assets, (ii) he renders investment advice for a fee or other compensation, direct or indirect, with respect to any moneys or the property of such plan, or has any authority or responsibility to do so, or (iii) he has any discretionary authority or discretionary responsibility in the administration of such plan.[4]

An employer is going to be a fiduciary because of its authority and responsibility to administer the plan. Fiduciary duties include some of the following: proper processing and remittance of employee contributions; providing plan participants with sufficient investment information to make an informed decision regarding their investment alternatives; and avoiding a lengthy list of "Prohibited Transactions" (for example, loans to a plan sponsor or any affiliate of the sponsor) that a fiduciary must decline to carry out.[5] As noted, in many, if not most of these cases, these are duties that cannot be delegated, avoided, or shed. Certain fiduciary duties tied to the responsibility to see that contributions are made and made timely to the plan and kept in the plan for the exclusive benefit of the plan participants and their beneficiaries or to defray reasonable plan administration costs cannot even be shed or extinguished in bankruptcy. It is therefore important for plan sponsors and designated responsible officials to first fully understand these fiduciary duties and responsibilities under the Code and ERISA.

Second, they need to structure the plan sponsor's business processes and internal audit controls (in conjunction with any third party administrators) to see that these duties and responsibilities are met according to the statutes and regulations provided by the IRS and the DOL governing qualified plans generally and 401(k) defined contribution plans specifically.

Moreover, the IRS and the DOL have both stepped up audit programs to increase and assure compliance. The IRS is currently—as of the date of this publication—conducting audits based upon the 401(k) questionnaire it has been sending out to plan sponsors and fiduciaries. A nonresponse to the questionnaire will cause an automatic IRS audit on the nonresponder. Otherwise, the IRS is zeroing in on common problems identified by the responses as the focus of its selected compliance program audits. For instance, recently it has been targeting those companies with safe harbor plans that are failing to provide the required annual safe harbor plan notice to participants, as apparently identified from the questionnaire. The IRS has also been more broadly examining plan sponsors generally for documented internal control procedures to prevent and identify errors and violations on 401(k) plans. For its part, the DOL also has a current project to target 401(k) plans with higher than average fees. The plan fee issue and disclosure of plan fees to plan participants has a high focus in the press and by the public currently, as well as the DOL.

And, while many errors offer the opportunity for self-correction under the IRS and DOL correction programs, higher penalties will normally apply if the IRS identifies the problem and takes action on the violation before the plan sponsor. With the advent of the electronic filing of Form 5500, the IRS is likely to discover noncompliance and violations in a plan more quickly than in the past. In this regard, it is valuable to understand the errors and mistakes most commonly made by plan sponsors and fiduciaries with regard to 401(k) plans so that preventative process and procedure measures might be installed from the outset to avoid or reduce the incidence of errors and violations. We will identify and discuss those common errors and violations that make a 401(k) plan noncompliant later in this chapter.

Planning Tip. It should be noted that the use of third party vendors to help with the ongoing administration of the plan is important and will help most plan sponsors and designated officials comply with the Code and ERISA requirements for such plans. However, such TPAs and other plan service providers usually are not and by contract (and conduct) will seek to specifically avoid being deemed ERISA fiduciaries for the plan. This alone should convince plan sponsors and those persons clearly identified as the plan's fiduciaries to recognize the requirements for compliance as important, and treat them accordingly in their day-to-day operations. In addition, some critical plan tasks, like timely and correct remittance of elected contributions to the qualified plan trust, will always remain in the hands of the employer and its designated officials. Currently there is also extraordinary discussion about the fiduciary duties with respect to the investment choices to be provided in 401(k) plans and those parties in interest who provide assistance with fund selections for the plan.[6]

Finally, it is unreasonable to assume that such a complex retirement plan with substantial initial and ongoing compliance requirements will never experience an error in its documentation or violation in its operation. In fact, realistic practitioners will say that some errors in connection with qualified 401(k) plans are 100 percent certain to happen given enough time. Fortunately, even the IRS and the DOL have recognized this reality. Therefore, both agencies have adopted extensive programs for the correction of nonegregious qualified plan errors; that is, those made accidentally and without intent to avoid compliance. They have recently even updated and expanded them in Revenue Procedure 2013-12 to make it easier for plan sponsors and their designated officials on the plans to make the necessary corrections.

Moreover, practitioners have indicated that the IRS has demonstrated an unexpected flexibility in applying these correction programs in practice, thereby making the programs attractive for plan sponsors to utilize.[7] In many cases, the corrections can be made without penalty or even notice to the IRS or DOL using the IRS Self Correction Program (SCP), so it is important to identify and correct unintentional plan errors as quickly as possible. We will discuss the IRS and DOL correction programs and their availability to correct errors and violations of required documentary and operational administrative processes in detail in this chapter. Finally, note that these correction programs *do not* cover Section 409A nonqualified deferred compensation plans, even excess benefit plans linked to the 401(k) plan, except for the ability to cure the failure to make a "top hat" plan filing to the DOL, which is discussed along with nonqualified plan correction later in this chapter as well.[8]

Common 401(k) Plan Compliance Errors

Introduction

According to the IRS,[9] the most common errors in connection with qualified plans, and specifically a 401(k) defined contribution plan, are as follows:

1. Failure to update the required plan document to reflect required mandatory law changes governing 401(k) plans

2. Failure to follow the terms of the plan document in operation, generally as to those common errors that hereafter follow

3. Failure to use the SAME plan definition of "compensation" correctly for handling all deferral elections and allocations in the plan

4. Failure to make employer matching contributions to all the appropriate employees

5. Failure to apply the 401(k) ADP and ACP nondiscrimination test results to HCE contributions resulting in excess HCE contributions in the plan

6. Failure to include all the employees in the plan eligible to make a deferral election resulting in lost deferral opportunity (i.e., exclusion of eligible employees)

7. Failure to limit amounts in the plan under Section 402(g) for a calendar year and failure to make the required distribution of those deferrals (excess deferrals) that exceeded this limit back to the affected participants

8. Failure to routinely deposit employee elective deferral amounts on a timely basis

9. Failure of participant loans to conform to both the requirements of the document and Section 72(p) in operation

10. Failure to handle financial hardship distributions properly, including cessation of deferrals for the balance of the plan year as required

11. Failure to make the required minimum employer contributions to the plan when the plan is "top heavy"[10]

12. Failure to file the required annual Form 5500 return or distribute the annual Summary Plan Description to plan participants

IRS EPCRS and DOL 401(k) Correction Programs

IRS Correction Programs

The current IRS EPCRS actually consists of three separate programs as follows:

1. Self-Correction Program (SCP). This IRS correction program generally allows plan sponsors to make corrections as to nonegregious operational failures in the plan. It allows the sponsor to make the correction without notifying the IRS of the correction, and without paying any penalty fee. While the SCP is targeted to address insignificant plan violations, some significant plan violations can also be corrected under the program so long as they are corrected by the end of the second plan year following the year of the violation. Unfortunately, the determination as to whether a violation is significant or insignificant is subjective and is based upon a variety of factors like the percentage of assets and/or contributions involved, number of plan years involved, as well as the percentage of participants affected. However, the determination is not necessarily limited to just these factors alone.

2. Voluntary Correction Program (VCP). This IRS correction program allows a sponsor to make a correction at any time prior to an audit by: (a) submitting an application; (b) paying a more limited penalty fee; and then (c) receive IRS "official" approval on the sponsor's proposed correction method presented in the application.

3.   Audit Closing Agreement Program (Audit CAP). This IRS correction program allows a plan sponsor to correct an error or violation that has been identified during an audit or letter determination review and pay a penalty fee (usually higher than in the VCP), based upon the nature, scope, and severity of the error or violation.

According to the IRS, the goal of the EPCRS is: (a) to preserve tax deferred benefits for plan participants in 401(k) plans;[11] and (b) to provide income tax and excise tax relief for Section 72 loans, 72(t) early distributions, 4974 minimum distributions, 4972/4973 excess contributions, and 4979 ADP/ACP test failures. Under Section 6 of Revenue Procedure 2013-12,[12] the guiding principles for making 401(k) plan corrections are:

1.   Full correction must include all taxable years, whether or not the taxable year is already closed.

2.   The correction method used should restore the plan and its participants to the position that they would have been in absent the error or violation.

3.   The correction must be reasonable and appropriate for the error or violation.

With regard to this requirement for a reasonable and appropriate solution, use of the corrections outlined in Appendix A/B of Revenue Procedure 2013-12 is deemed to be reasonable by the IRS (see Appendix L1 and L2 for a copy of current Appendix A/B). Solutions that are consistent with the Code, provide benefits to the NHCEs, and keep assets in the plan are also factors suggesting a reasonable and appropriate correction solution.

The 401(k) plan must generally have a determination letter and compliance procedures in place to qualify to use the IRS' SCP. Also, it is important to check the total number of participants affected, the level of the mistake, and the plan years in which the violation occurred when considering using the SCP to determine if the error or violation qualified as insignificant or insignificant under the SCP. In the case of certain significant operational failures, special deadlines allow the correction to be made under the SCP. Often it is better to opt for the IRS' VCP program anyway to achieve the maximum protection for the plan sponsor and fiduciary, since the IRS must approve the correction method as part of the mandated process. The VCP is available for a broad variety of correction activities so long as the IRS has not yet identified the violation in an audit or as part of letter determination review. Following Revenue Procedure 2013-12, the VCP covers common violations like failure to follow deferral limitation requirements, failure to include eligible participants, failure to provide a deferral opportunity, failure to withhold the right amount of deferral, overpayments, and failures in connection with plan loans, just to name a few.

If the error or violation has been discovered on audit, or if caught by an IRS reviewer during a letter determination review, the Audit CAP will be the only available option for correction. The plan sponsor can expect higher penalties to be applied than under the VCP (as an acknowledgement of the severe tax consequences if the plan were to be disqualified). However, resolution and correction of the error or violation with the IRS under the Audit CAP guidelines will usually be preferable to litigating the issue in light of the courts' usual support of the IRS in these situations.[13]

Revenue Procedure 2013-12

Revenue Procedure 2013-12[14] was released on December 31, 2012. Revenue Procedure 2008-50 was modified and superseded by this revenue procedure. Major changes were incorporated into Revenue Procedure 2013-12, but most of the changes encompassed the correction of Section 403(b) plans and so are not applicable to Section 401(k) plans. The most significant changes to the Employee Plans Compliance Resolution System (ERCRS) include:

- expanded corrections for 403(b) plan failures as noted and not discussed in this book;

- revised submission procedures for the VCP;

- rules for plans subject to Code section 436 restrictions;

- changes to safe harbor correction methods and fee structures.

New submission procedures.

- *Forms 8950 and 8951* – These are the new VCP application forms and must accompany all VCP submissions made under Revenue Procedure 2013-12.

- VCP mail submissions now go to the IRS Service Center in Covington, KY – Under Revenue Procedure 2013-12, VCP submissions should go to Covington, KY rather than to Washington, DC.

- *Appendices C, D & F (from old Revenue Procedure 2008-50)* – These are substantially revised. The old Appendices D and F are now Appendix C in Revenue Procedure 2013-12. Appendix C is revised to consist of two parts:

  a. A Model VCP Submission Compliance Statement

  b. Various Schedules (formerly Appendix F Schedules) containing standardized failure descriptions and correction methods[15]

The optional Acknowledgement Letter (which was formerly Appendix E). It has been revised and is the new Appendix D in Revenue Procedure 2013-12.

- *Appendix F Schedules* – All former Appendix F Schedules are now known as Appendix C Part II Schedules that may be used with the Appendix C Model VCP Submission Compliance Statement.

- *Anonymous VCP submissions* – The individual representing the plan sponsor must now satisfy the power of attorney requirements and provide a statement to that effect under penalty of perjury.[16]

Locating lost participants. As of August 31, 2012, the IRS letter Forwarding Program is no longer available as a search method for locating lost plan participants who are owed additional retirement benefits. The new procedure revises the reasonable actions that a plan sponsor must take to locate lost plan participants who are owed additional retirement benefits. It provides a limited extension of the SCP correction period and the VCP 150-day correction period for certain plan sponsors taking action to locate lost participants.[17]

Safe harbor correction methods.

- *Missed deferrals* – Appendix A now includes consistent safe harbor correction methods for certain missed deferrals in safe harbor 401(k) plans.[18]

- *Qualified Nonelective Contributions (QNECs)* – Appendix A clarifies that QNEC contributions must satisfy the definition of QNEC in Treasury Regulation Section 1.401(k)-6 when used to correct a failed ADP, ACP, or multiple-use test under the safe harbor correction method. Under current IRS regulations, this means that forfeitures *cannot* be used to fund QNEC contributions.

Self-correction of Section 415(c) failures. Plan sponsors can now use the SCP to correct certain recurring excess annual additions if they take certain actions within a specified time.[19]

Section 436 restricted defined benefit plans. These plans can correct operational failures related to noncompliance with applicable IRC section 436 restrictions. Plan sponsors also need to consider the effect of section 436 restrictions when making corrective distributions and/or corrective plan amendments. Plan sponsors may be required to make an additional corrective contribution.[20]

VCP fees.

- *Late adoption of proposed amendments* – A reduced fee may apply if a plan's sole failure is late adoption of a proposed plan amendment associated with a favorable determination letter.[21] Specific conditions must be met in order to qualify for the reduced fee.

- *Multiple failures* – may be eligible for reduced fees.[22]

Miscellaneous.

- *Plan overpayments* – Correction principles for defined contribution (and defined benefit plans as well) were clarified and listed in separate subsections.[23]

- *Reduced Audit CAP sanctions* – Reduced fees apply for certain late amender failures found during the determination letter application process.[24]

Effective date.

- Revenue Procedure 2013-12 is generally effective as of April 1, 2013.

- Plan sponsors were allowed to elect to apply provisions on or after December 31, 2012.

DOL Correction Programs

The Employee Benefits Security Agency (EBSA) in the DOL has two voluntary self-correction programs for plan sponsor administrators who need help in correcting ERISA errors and failure of requirements for 401(k) plans:

1. Delinquent Filer Voluntary Compliance Program (DFVCP) – This DOL program assists plan sponsors who are late or missed filing Form 5500 in coming up to date with corrected filings. Participation in the DFVCP is a two-part process. The EBSA provides all the information, including a calculator to help accurately determine the penalty payment needed to participate in the DFVCP as well as an option of paying the penalty electronically.[25] Support for this correction program is currently in EBSA's Office of the Chief Accountant at the DOL.[26]

2. Voluntary Fiduciary Correction Program (VFCP) – This DOL program affords plan sponsors and officials the chance to identify and fully correct certain transactions such as prohibited purchases, sales and exchanges, improper loans, delinquent participant contributions, and improper plan expenses. The VFCP currently covers nineteen specific prohibited transactions. The VFCP also provides immediate relief from payment of excise taxes under a class exemption that currently covers six prohibited transactions. Violations can be fully and correctly resolved in four easy steps.

   Sponsors and their advisors can go online for a complete list of violations and safe harbor corrective actions, along with the current addresses of EBSA Regional Offices that can help with correction applications.[27] There are also a number of tools online to assist plan sponsors and their advisors in using the VFCP, including an online calculator, a model application, and a very useful and required checklist. The checklist is used to ensure submission of a complete VFCP application. The applicant must actually sign and date the checklist and include it with the application. The checklist requires a "Yes," "No," or "N/A" next to each item. According to the instructions for the checklist, a "No" answer or the failure to include a completed checklist will delay review of the VFCP application until all required items are received by EBSA.

Figure 13.1 contains examples of common errors and the proper DOL or IRS (or both) correction programs that can be used to bring a 401(k) plan back into compliance. Note the overlap between the common errors highlighted by the IRS and the DOL.

As Figure 13.1 suggests, plan sponsors or fiduciaries may, generally speaking, self-correct unintentional (nonegregious) qualification errors and violations under the IRS' SCP. They can also use the IRS' VCP to make corrections, if the error or violation has not yet been identified either on audit or during the course of a determination letter filing. They must use the IRS' Audit CAP should the IRS catch the violation problem first.

And, in the case of certain ERISA requirements, they can use EBSA's DFVCP to resolve late or missed Form 5500s (and failure to file the one-time "top hat" nonqualified deferred compensation plan notice). The caps under the DFVCP on penalties, $1,500 per small plan and $4,000 per large plan maximum on multiple year filing corrections, are reasonable and so is an attractive correction solution. Of note, this DOL DFVCP can still be used even if an IRS notice has been issued noting the late or nonfiling of the Form 5500. EBSA's other correction program, the VFCP, does not allow self-correction. It requires an application to be made to the EBSA. However, the VFCP can be used to resolve late contributions as well as certain enumerated fiduciary prohibited transaction violations, like loans to parties in interest or asset sales or purchases from the plan. The VFCP requires that the fiduciary make a complete correction to

Figure 13.1

Plan Error or Violation	*Utilize*
Form 5500: Late or Missed Filing	DFVCP
Late or Missed Deposits of Employee Salary Reduction Contributions	VFCP
Participant Loan Failures (for example, loans that exceed the maximum permitted dollar amount)	EPCRS VFCP (for certain failures – after using the EPCRS)
Failure to Timely Amend Plan to Keep it Updated with Changes in the Law or Discretionary Changes	EPCRS
Plan Operational Errors arising from the failure to follow plan terms (for example, an employee who meets the plan's eligibility requirements but is not allowed to participate)	EPCRS
Specified Plan Prohibited Transactions (for example, sales or loans between the plan and a party in interest)	VFCP

included restoration of any principal, any lost profits or earnings, and transaction costs as well, and may even require notice be given to plan participants. There is an online calculator to assist the plan sponsor and fiduciaries to determine the necessary correction amounts. However, correction under the VFCP does provide relief from excise taxes imposed on the prohibited transactions violated.

Investment Fee Disclosures

In 2012, the DOL released new regulations that require plan fiduciaries to receive service provider fee disclosure by July 1, 2012 or to give notice of the provider's noncompliance to the DOL. Failure to comply with this process was deemed an ERISA prohibited transaction requiring replacement of the service provider. The process was tied to the Form 5500 question: "Were there any nonexempt transactions with any party in interest?" to identify compliance or noncompliance by the plan fiduciary. Except for the collection of missing employee and employer contributions owed by plan sponsors to plans, enforcing proper plan fee disclosure is at the top of the list of the DOL's 401(k) priorities as of the date of this this publication.

Errors & Violations Not Covered

It is important to note that that the IRS and DOL correction programs do _not_ cover all errors and violations that may occur in connection with a 401(k) plan. In general, they only cover those listed. For example, the DOL VFCP covering fiduciary error and violations covers _only_ some nineteen specifically enumerated errors and violations (although thankfully the most common) as of the date of this publication. If a prohibited transaction is not covered by the VFCP correction program, the fiduciary must still make a correction of the prohibited transaction but must pay the penalty excise tax as well.[28] Likewise, scrivener's errors, that is, drafting errors in the plan documents (e.g., "… the plan will match 5 percent of a participant's contributions up to the first 6 percent of compensation….", but meant to draft 3 percent rather than 5 percent) are also not covered by the correction programs. As the reader might imagine, such errors, especially in the calculation of benefits, can create enormous problems in a plan and may not be easy to solve. It may actually be necessary for the plan sponsor to go into court to seek an equitable reformation of the contract to cure such drafting errors when grievous enough, and litigation with participants can sometime occur as a consequence.[29]

Correction Procedures under IRS' EPCRS & EBSA's Programs

Documentation Error Correction

Overview. The primary problem in the area of plan documentation is the failure to provide or demonstrate the existence of plan authorization and approval. The plan sponsor's file needs to contain a signed copy of the plan document, and then of any mandatory or discretionary amendments made to the plan during its existence.

New plans. In the case of a new plan, the sponsor's file should reflect corporate authorization for the plan prior to the time that deferrals are withheld from plan participants' salaries and are deposited in the plans trust.

Mandatory & Discretionary Plan Amendments

Mandatory amendments. In the case of amendments to the plan required because of changes in the law, these amendments must be incorporated into the plan as directed by the IRS during the Remedial Amendment Period (RAP). There is now an SCP self-correction procedure for the late adoption of these required amendments *after* expiration of the remedial amendment period. However, Revenue Procedure 2013-12 has new forms and procedures to accomplish this documentary correction under the SCP.

Discretionary amendments. In the case of other amendments to the plan, the general rule is that corporate authorization must occur before the last day of the plan year in which the change is to take effect. In the case of "take away" amendment changes, the authorization must be immediately before the change.

According to the IRS, a review of the documentation would include:

1. the original plan document;

2. subsequent amendments or restatements;

3. adoption agreements;

4. Opinion Letter or Advisory Letter issued by the IRS;

5. Determination Letter issued by the IRS;

6. Board of Director resolutions and minutes with reference to the plan; and

7. the Summary Plan Description (SPD).

Corrective action. Corrections to errors in the plan documentation would generally involve two steps:

1. adoption of the necessary amendments to properly confirm the plan document; and

2. VCP submission to the IRS.

As to the VCP submission, the IRS has indicated that Appendix C, Schedule 1 is available for interim amendments if the extended RAP has not expired. Appendix C Schedule 2 is available for nonamenders where the extended RAP for mandatory law changes has already expired. Finally a determination letter application is required if correction is made on an individually designed plan.[30]

Planning Tip. To avoid plan document mistakes plan sponsor should use the following quick checklist.

____ 1) Maintain plan document records

____ 2) Have periodic but frequent interaction with service providers on the plan

____ 3) Maintain a calendar with deadlines for the adoption of mandatory and any discretionary amendments.

____ 4) Maintain the consistency between the plan and the Summary Plan Description (SPD), and any other communication materials, as amendments occur.

Operational Error Corrections

In general. When a 401(k) plan is not operated in compliance with the plan's terms, it must seek to correct the error or violation under one of the programs offered by the IRS under the EPCRS or the DOL's DFVCP or VFCP administered by the EBSA. The question whether the plan fiduciary or sponsor administratively is following the terms of the plan is more complex. In general, the 401(k) plan must always operate in agreement with the plan's terms unless compliance is tied to a change in the tax law during the remedial amendment period (the RAP). However, the fiduciary is not required to follow the plan's terms, if compliance would involve a breach of a fiduciary duty by the plan fiduciary.

The IRS recommends that plan sponsors identify and avoid operational plan errors with their 401(k) plan by:

1. making certain that the employer, employees, and all service providers on the plan are familiar with its terms, including special communication as necessary to make certain that the proper definition of "compensation" is used for determining elective deferrals to the payroll;

2. conducting a periodic review of plan operations up against current plan terms, including reviews of various systems and processes, such as automatic enrollment and auto-escalation; and

3. making use of checklists geared to the plan sponsor's plan (the IRS provides an Operational Checklist[31] that may be used to create a custom checklist for the plan sponsor.[32]

Missed deferral opportunity for excluded employees (including employer matches). This failure usually occurs when an employee is not provided with a timely notification of their eligibility to participate in a plan. More recently it has been occurring because the plan excludes the employee from an automatic enrollment for some period of time. Finally, it also occurs when the employer fails to process a participant's election to defer in a timely manner. The employee or participant may also miss employer matches as a consequence of the delayed participation.

To correct, the employer usually makes a *Qualified Nonelective Contribution* (QNEC) in an amount equal to 50 percent of the employee's or participant's missed deferral opportunity (40 percent for a missed after-tax contribution) applying the participant's elected deferral amount, or the plan's average deferral percentage rate, whichever is applicable or appropriate. To this, the employer must include the missed match, which must be calculated using 100 percent (not 50 percent or 40 percent) of the missed deferral or after-tax opportunity, as well as applicable earnings. However, under Revenue Procedure 2013-12, the missed match contribution now need not be a QNEC, which requires immediate vesting, withdrawal restrictions, and an inability to fund with forfeitures, unless the plan is a safe harbor 401(k) plan. The missed contributions may now be made as a nonQNEC employer corrective contribution that follows the vesting schedule in the employer's plan. Corrections for this violation are also now available for 401(k) safe harbor plans under 401(k)(13).[33]

The correction process for 401(k)(12) plans was carried forward into Revenue Procedure 2013-12, which says that a missed deferral is deemed equal to the greater of 3 percent or the maximum deferral percentage rate that is at least as favorable as 100 percent of the elective deferral made by the employee.[34] Note that if the failure occurs for a period that does not extend past the first day of the first plan year that begins after the date on which the first deferral would have been made (but for the failure), then the missed deferral is deemed equal to 3 percent. However, if the failure occurs during a period subsequent to this, the missed deferral for each subsequent plan year will be deemed equal to the qualified percentage specified in the plan document in order to comply with Section 401(k)(13(C)(iii).[35] If any contribution error affects a terminated participant, the employer can apply the *di minimis* distribution rule (differences of $75 or less may be disregarded) to any corrective *contribution*.[36] This is unique since the *de minimis* rule is normally limited to corrective distributions only—not contributions.

Too early participation opportunity. If an employee is allowed to participate in a plan before the proper eligibility date there is an operational violation. The correction is to return the improper contributions to the employee, and to forfeit any employer matches and earnings attributable to them.

Missed or late contributions. In general, payroll salary deductions and loan repayments must be remitted to the plan trust on a timely basis. The DOL recently released new guidance on timely remittance of these amounts, and they are very stringent. While the regulations require remittance to the plan's trust within an "administratively reasonable" time period, the latest date for remittance is the fifteenth day of the month immediately following the month in which the plan contribution was withheld or payable by the plan sponsor-employer. However, the safe harbor for timely deposits in companies with less than 100 employees is a mere seven days.[37] The failure to make consistent and timely deposits in these time frames over an extended time period is considered a breach of fiduciary duty that requires corrective action under a DOL (not IRS EPCRS) correction program.

Excess contributions. A plan violation occurs when a plan allows a participant to contribute more than the Section 402(g) maximum annual amount permitted ($17,500 in 2014, unless over age 50 and eligible for a catch-up contribution), or more than that permitted applying ADP and/ or ACP tests in any given plan year. To correct, the excess contributions must be distributed to the plan participant. Any employer contributions made on account of these excess contributions are transferred to the plan's forfeiture account and then the plan follows the plan's rules for disposition of forfeitures, which usually is to pay plan expenses or reduce employer future contributions. In the event of a terminated participant, an effort must be made to collect back the excess amount involved.

A violation also occurs if the employer contributes an amount for the employee that is in excess of the deferral amount elected by the participant. To correct, merely return the excess amount to the employee and report the amount on a Form 1099-R as a corrective distribution not subject to a rollover.[38]

Overpayments. The employer must take reasonable steps to have the overpayment amount, as adjusted for the earnings at the plan's earnings rate from the date of distribution to the date of repayment, returned by the participant or beneficiary under the plan. To the extent the amount of the overpayment as adjusted by earnings is not repaid to the plan, the employer or another person must contribute the difference to the plan. However, the employer does NOT have to contribute the difference if "the failure arose solely because a payment was made from the plan to a participant or beneficiary in the absence of a distributable event [but was otherwise determined in accordance with the terms of the plan (e.g., an impermissible inservice distribution)].[39] If the overpayment has already been rolled over to an IRA, the employer must notify the terminated employee of the amounts rolled that are *not* eligible for a tax-free rollover and the taxable consequences of the situation[40]—immediate normal income taxation and perhaps imposition of the premature distribution penalty if the participant is not yet age 59½.

Plan limit violations. This violation occurs when a plan participant exceeds the deferral contribution plan limits specified in the plan document. This violation and its correction are not addressed directly in the EPCRS. However, according to one major 401(k) plan provider, two correction approaches have been used by plans and their legal counsel that rest upon the general principles of restoring the participant and the plan to the same position they would have occupied if the violation had not occurred. The two approaches are: (a) have the participant forfeit the excess contributions (see previous paragraph entitled Excess contributions), and have the employer make the participant whole for the amounts outside the plan (special bonus); or (b) distribute the excess participant deferrals from the plan to the participant. In either approach, the participant would forfeit any associated employer matches as well.[41]

Financial hardship distributions. This violation generally occurs when a participant qualifies for and receives a hardship distribution, and should have his/her elective pre-tax and after-tax deferrals suspended for the balance of the plan year following the hardship distribution, but the contributions are not suspended as required. This violation is not directly addressed in the EPCRS. However, the IRS has indicated that the plan must distribute the participant's elective deferrals made during the suspension period, any associated match should be forfeited, and any applicable earnings attributable to either. This is essentially the same correction procedure imposed on a Plan Limit Violation.

Loan repayments. Failure to report a loan as taxable income because of a participant's failure to repay plan loans in accordance with the terms of the plan is a violation of operational requirements. By regulation, the failure to repay a plan loan should result in deemed taxable income to the participant in the amount of the unpaid loan in the tax year of the first missed repayment. Under Revenue Procedure 2008-50, the only correction to avoid this result was to file under the IRS' VCP and get the IRS' approval to correct without reporting income. If this violation was the result of an operational failure, correction required the employer to have the participant: (a) make a lump sum repayment equal to the repayments that the participant would have made if there had been no failure to repay, and add to it interest as accrued on the missed repayments; OR (b) reamortize the outstanding balance on the loan, including accrued interest, over the remaining payment schedule of the term of the loan or the period remaining had the loan been amortized over the maximum period (normally five years) that complies with Section 72(p)(2)(B), measuring from the original date of the loan, OR (c) any combination of (a) or (b). The IRS has clearly indicated that if the loan repayments are not remitted to the plan by the end of the maximum period of correction, the loan cannot be reamortized, so remains in default and the violation continues.[42]

Revenue Procedure 2013-12 has not added any new corrective alternatives to this corrective process that would allow a plan sponsor to use the IRS' SCP for loan violations,[43] so currently the IRS'VCP filing is still the only IRS correction program available to make a loan violation correction (assuming it is not already under audit). If the failure to repay was not a result of the employer's operational failure, the employer can choose to treat the defaulted loans as taxable in the tax year in which the failure occurred or, alternatively, treat the loan as taxable to the participant in the year of the correction. However, the ability of an employer to treat the defaulted loan as taxable in the current year of correction still requires filing under IRS' VCP to receive approval for this correction method by the IRS.

Roth violations. Revenue Procedure 2013-12 contains a correction procedure for the error of allowing a plan participant to make an after-tax Roth contribution to a plan that has no provision for Roth contributions under the terms of the plan. In some cases, correction may require complete removal of the Roth feature. In plans properly authorizing Roth contributions, there are three options for correction under Revenue Procedure 2013-12 when a participant's after-tax Roth contributions are accidentally placed in a pre-tax account. The three all involve unwinding the error, moving the contribution from the pre-tax account to the after-tax Roth account, and then correcting the participant's W-2.[44]

EPCRS VCP Submissions

If the plan sponsor cannot file for correction under the SCP, then a VCP correction submission must be made. Guidance for assembling a VCP submission can be found in Section 11.14 of the Revenue Procedure 2013-12. As of the date of this publication, this guidance requires the submission package to be organized in the following order:

1. New Form 8951, plus attach the check and photocopy of the check for the fee to the front of the form

2. Signed new Form 8950

3. Form 2848 (Power of Attorney) or Form 8821 (Tax Information Authorization) attached to Form 8950

4. Narrative information as follows–

   a. Descriptions of the failures.

   b. Explanation of the how and why for the failures.

   c. Description of the method proposed for curing the failures (and earnings methodology and supporting calculations if appropriate).

   d. Description of method(s) utilized to find and notify any former employees or beneficiaries affected by the failures or proposed corrections. The narrative information here should affirmatively state there are no former employees or beneficiaries affected by the failures or proposed corrections if this is, in fact, the stated case.

   e. Description of the administrative procedural changes to be implemented to avoid the listed failures in the future.

   f. Whether the correction request seeks to have participant loans corrected so as not to be treated as deemed distributions under Section 72(p) with the supporting reasoning for the request. If not, the narrative should state that the request with respect to loan correction is made on the basis that loans will be treated as Section 72(p) deemed distributions in the year of correction.

    g.   Whether the relief is being sought from excise taxes under Code sections 4972, 4973, 4974, or 4979, or from the 10 percent excise tax under Section 72(t), along with the supporting reasoning for such relief.

1. Include any required information and enclosures and any schedules necessary if the Model Compliance Statement or any Appendix C Schedule is made part of the VCP submission.

2. Acknowledgement Letter in Appendix D.

3. Copies of any IRS opinion, advisory, or determination letter when applicable.

4. Relevant plan document or plan document language; and a second copy of the plan document or plan document amended language if the VCP submission includes a determination letter application.[45]

5. All other items that may be pertinent to the VCP submission.

6. The determination letter application with all required documentation when appropriate.

Recall that this submission does not now go to Washington, D.C. under Rev. Proc. 2013-12, but should now be sent to:

Internal Revenue Service
P.O. Box 12192
Covington, KY 41011

When using express mail or a private delivery service, the address is:[46]

Internal Revenue Service
201 W. Rivercenter Blvd.
Attn: Extracting Stop 312
Covington, KY 41011

Nonqualified Deferred Compensation Plans & Error Corrections

A nonqualified deferred compensation plan can be created separately without the existence of a 401(k) plan. However, a so-called top hat "excess benefit" or "select group" (named for the two available ERISA exemptions) nonqualified deferred compensation plan is often created in conjunction with a qualified 401(k) plan to allow HCEs, who are otherwise capped by the Section 402(g) annual limit ($17,500 in 2014), to defer amounts above these caps on a pre-tax basis in a manner similar to their monies going into the qualified 401(k) plan as to individual income taxation. These nonqualified plans have very different tax and ERISA requirements than 401(k) plans and so must comply separately according to the laws and regulations governing these top hat nonqualified plans.

Most excess benefit or select group nonqualified deferred compensation plans associated or linked to a qualified 401(k) plan are generally subject to their own special form and operational requirements under Code section 409A. They must meet these Section 409A requirements in order to achieve income tax deferral until distributed, and avoid immediate taxation and the imposition of a special 20 percent excise tax as well as a punitive penalty AFR interest rate that may be applied all the way back to date of original deferral. These Section 409A penalties are applied to the individual plan participant rather than the plan sponsor. These nonqualified plans specifically cannot follow the timing of deferral elections and plan distribution elections of the 401(k) plan, since the rules are totally different.

If an error or violation occurs as to Section 409A form (documentation) or operational (administrative) requirements for a "top hat" nonqualified deferred compensation plan, corrections are not made under the IRS or DOL's qualified plan correction programs heretofore discussed. As mentioned, the sole exception is that the DFVCP may be used to correct a failure to file the required alternative one-time reporting notice to the DOL. The correction requires filing the notice for each "top hat" plan and paying the fee. This can be done online, like other corrections under the DOL's DFVCP.[47] The IRS has constructed two correction programs created especially for Section 409A plans to correct documentation and operational errors of Section 409A requirements. Documentation errors are corrected according to the guidelines in IRS Notice 2010-6 and Notice 2010-80. Operational errors are corrected under IRS Notice 2008-113. Both reduce the penalties that would accrue in the worst case Section 409A violation scenario, but do require filing notices with the IRS and the affected participants in most cases.

Unfortunately, these Section 409A correction programs for nonqualified deferred compensation plans are very narrow and restrictive as to the violations that may be corrected when compared to the programs for qualified 401(k) plans. As a consequence, legal practitioners have considered possible alternative correction approaches based on the premise that Section 409A is "additive" income tax law; therefore, prior concepts and techniques for correction of errors ought to be available for corrections of current plan errors and violations.[48] The IRS, with its strict constructionist view of Section 409A, is unlikely to agree. In any event, these "other" correction techniques would certainly remain applicable to plans grandfathered from Section 409A, or excepted from Section 409A coverage.

Conclusion

In General

401(k) plans offer substantial tax benefits to both the plan participants and the plan sponsor that are worth protecting. Both the IRS and the DOL have provided corrective programs to cure violations in both documentation and operation of a 401(k) plan. The best approach is to establish a set of internal controls and plan documentation files that support correct documentation and operation from inception to termination of the plan in the distant future. Plan sponsors and plan fiduciaries should acquaint themselves with the most common violations that may occur with their 401(k) plan and establish internal plan controls and procedures to help prevent these violations in the first instance. They may also help surface and identify operational and fiduciary prohibited transaction violations early if they should occur despite the controls and procedures. Use of a knowledgeable and experienced qualified plan administrator can assist in this important process of compliance.

However, with the aid of its legal advisors, the plan sponsor should move quickly to ascertain the best available IRS or DOL program to cure the violation once a documentation or operational violation has been identified. It should then move forward to make the necessary correction under the selected program at the earliest date in order to protect the plan's income tax benefits for all concerned. And, this action to correct a form or operational error may also protect the fiduciaries and plan sponsor from penalties for any fiduciary failures in connection with the 401(k) plan.

Endnotes

1. See e.g., Seth D. Harris, Acting Secretary of the DOL v. Mark A. Cottone, Cougar Package Designers Inc.; Cougar Packaging Solutions Inc., successor to Cougar Packaging Designers Inc.; Cougar Packaging Designers Inc. Profit-Sharing Plan, Civil Action No. 1:13-cv-05078 (Fed. Dist. Ct. Northern Ill. 2013).

2. ERISA Sec. 402(a)(1).

3. ERISA Sec. 402(a)(2).

4. ERISA Sec. 3(21)(A).

5. See generally, Chapter 23, pgs. 517-548, of Abramson, *The Advisors Guide to Qualified Plans*, SBM National Underwriter Company, 2012 for an excellent extended discussion of fiduciaries and fiduciary duties in connection with a qualified plan of any type. This area of the law is in significant transition right now as the SEC and DOL seem intent on generating a common definition of "fiduciary" for purposes of both U.S. securities laws and ERISA, so it is important for practitioners to keep current on these developments with both federal agencies, especially those who work with employer plan sponsors in the acquisition and development of the investment fund set in 401(k) plans.

6. See e.g., Perez v. Hofmeister, Et. al., Civil Action Nos. 5:12-cv-00250-KKC; 5:13-cv-00156-KKC and 5:13-cv-00158-KKC (Fed. Dist. Ct. Eastern KY, 2013); John Hancock Life Insurance Company, acting as a service provider, was held not to be a fiduciary in connection with service provider fees or revenue sharing payments it charged to its 401(k) plans since all were disclosed and negotiated at arms-length; and just offering a menu of investments did not make it as a service provider a fiduciary. Santomenno v. John Hancock Life Ins. Co., No. 2:10-cv-01655), 2013 WL 3864395 (Fed. Dist. Ct. NJ 2013).

7. See generally, comments by Ilene Ferenczy, attorney, and Janet Mak in news article, "EPCRS Magic: Let Me Fix That for You," ASPPA News from the Field, 2013 Benefits Conference of the South, Atlanta, dated May 30, 2013, found on ASPPA web site at www.ASPPAnews.org.

8. See Richey, Baier & Phelan, *The Nonqualified Deferred Compensation Plan Advisor: Plans Covered and Exempt from Section 409A*, SBM National Underwriter Company, 2013, for more details on correcting 409A nonqualified deferred compensation plan errors. This book is available for purchase on-line at www.nationalunderwriter.com under the heading "Bookstore." As of the date of this publication, source information on correction of operational and documentation errors of nonqualified deferred compensation plans can be found on the IRS website at www.IRS.gov. by keyword searching "Notice 2008-113" for operational errors and "Notice 2010-10" and also "Notice 2010-80" for documentation errors.

9. For a current update of *The 401(k) Fix-It Guide*, see www.IRS.gov/401(k)Fix-ItGuide.

10. See Chapter 5, infra, for a discussion of top heavy plans and issues.

11. The EPCRS also applies to 403(b) tax sheltered annuity plans, 408(k) SEPs and SARSEPs, and 408(p) SIMPLE IRAs.

12. 2013- 4 IRB 313 (01/22/2013).

13. See e.g., *Christy & Swan Profit Sharing Plan v. Comm'r*, TC Memo 2011-62 (March 15, 2011); and *Michael C. Hollen, DDS v. Comm'r*, TC Memo (Jan. 4, 2011) involving ESOP.

14. A copy (137 pages) of IRS Rev. Proc. 2013-12 may be found on-line at www.IRS.gov/pub/irs-drop/rp-13-12.pdf or www.IRS.gov/Retirement-Plans/New-Revenue-Procedure-Updates-EPCRS.

15. See Secs. 11.01, 11.02 and Appendix C in Rev. Proc. 2013-12 for instructions.

16. See Secs. 10.10 and 11.08(2) in Rev. Proc. 2013-12.

17. See Sec. 6.02(5)(d) of Rev. Proc. 2013-12.

18. This also applies to Section 403(b) and SIMPLE IRAs.

19. See Sec. 4.04 of Rev. Proc. 2013-12.

20. See Sec. 6.02(4)(e) of Rev. Proc. 2013-12.

21. See Sec. 12.03 of Rev. Proc. 2013-12.

22. See Sec. 12.04 of Rev. Proc. 2013-12.

23. See Sec. 6.06 of Rev. Proc. 2013-12.

24. See Sec. 14.04(4) of Rev. Proc. 2013-12.

25. Go to www.dol.gov/ebsa and select "Correction Programs" for more detail.

26. As of the date of this publication, a call to EBSA's Office of the Chief Accountant could be made at 202-693-8360, which is not a toll-free number.

27. Go to www.dol.gov/ebsa and select "Correction Programs" for more detail.

28. Ibid.

29. See e.g., *Young v. Verizon's Bell Atlantic Cash Balance Plan*, 615 F. 2nd 808 (7th Cir. 2010), which involved significant and historic litigation that involved scrivener errors over the calculation of certain plan benefits when the clear scrivener's error favored the participants. Although resolved favorably to the plan sponsor, the litigation was both protracted and costly.

30. IRS Webinar, Plan Corrections: The Employee Plans Compliance Resolution System ("EPCRS"), Slides 14-17, 8-1-2013.

31. The most current version of the IRS Operational Checklist in Figure 13.2 may be found at www.IRS.gov/pub/irs-pdf/p4531.pdf.

32. IRS Webinar, Plan Corrections: The Employee Plans Compliance Resolution System ("EPCRS"), Slide 18, 8-1-2013.

33. See Rev. Proc. 2013-12, Appendix A, Section .05 and related examples in Appendix B. Also see IRS Webinar, Plan Corrections: The Employee Plans Compliance Resolution System ("EPCRS"), Slides 7-9, 8-1-2013.

34. IRS Webinar, Plan Corrections: The Employee Plans Compliance Resolution System ("EPCRS"), Slides 8 and 9, 8-1-2013.

35. Ibid. pg. 9.

36. Comments made by IRS speaker during IRS Webinar, Plan Corrections: The Employee Plans Compliance Resolution System ("EPCRS"), 8-1-2013.

37. See Final DOL Reg. §2510.3-102 and specifically (a)(1) and (f)(1), as to timely 401(k) plan timely deposits, which subsections were amended with amendments becoming effective on 7-14-2010.

38. Comments made by IRS speaker during IRS Webinar, Plan Corrections: The Employee Plans Compliance Resolution System ("EPCRS"), 8-1-2013.

39. IRS Webinar, Plan Corrections: The Employee Plans Compliance Resolution System ("EPCRS"), Slide 11, 8-1-2013.

40. Comments made by IRS speaker during IRS Webinar, Plan Corrections: The Employee Plans Compliance Resolution System ("EPCRS"), 8-1-2013.

41. See Regulatory Brief 2008-6, Vanguard, October 2008, pg. 4. This violation and the correction suggestions would appear to remain valid after Rev. Proc. 2013-12.

42. Comments made by IRS speaker during IRS Webinar, Plan Corrections: The Employee Plans Compliance Resolution System ("EPCRS"), 8-1-2013.

43. See Regulatory Brief: IRS updates plan correction program, Vanguard, July 2013, pg. 3.

44. Comments made by IRS speaker during IRS Webinar, Plan Corrections: The Employee Plans Compliance Resolution System ("EPCRS"), 8-1-2013.

45. More information on the requirements for submission when a determination letter application is to be included with the VCP submission may be found at Section 11.14(1) of Rev. Proc. 2013-12.

46. Section 11.12 of Rev. Proc. 2013-12.

47. See Richey, Baier & Phelan, The Nonqualified Deferred Compensation Plan Advisor: Plans Covered & Exempt under Section 409A, 5th Edition, SBM National Underwriter Company, 2013.

48. See generally, Barker, 409A Failures: Correcting with and without the IRS Formal Correction Programs, 46th Annual Southern Federal Tax Institute, Sept. 19-23, 2011, Outline N.

Appendix A
401(k) Plan Design Checklist

	Yes	No
Type of Plan Document		

Custom-designed
     Will a determination letter be obtained?
Master and prototype
     IRS opinion letter issued concerning the plan document
Volume submitter
     IRS advisory letter issued concerning the plan document		

Eligibility		

Employees must become eligible at the later of:
  • Attaining age 21 or
  • 1 year of service unless plan provides for full vesting at the later of two years of service or attaining age 21
  • *Certain exceptions may apply.*		

Vesting		

Plan must provide for:
  • Immediate vesting in elective deferrals and related growth
  • Full vesting at normal retirement age
  • Full vesting upon complete discontinuance of plan contributions
  • Three-year cliff vesting or qualifying graduated vesting		

Employee Contributions (Elective Deferrals)		

In addition to pre-tax contributions, does the plan permit:
  • Catch-up contributions?
  • Roth contributions (either regular or catch-up)?
  • After-tax contributions to the profit-sharing portion of the plan?
  • Rollover contributions from eligible plans?		

Employer Contributions		

Does the plan
  • Allow discretionary matching contributions?
  • Allow discretionary profit-sharing contributions?
  • Require safe harbor matching contributions?		

	Yes	No
Employers Included in the Plan		

• Is the employer part of a controlled group?
  • Is the employer part of an affiliated service group?
  • If yes to either question above, will all employees of group members be eligible to participate in the plan?		

Aggregation or Disaggregation Rules		
• Does the employer have multiple plans? • Do the aggregation or disaggregation rules apply?		

Contribution Limits
Plan must provide for the following per-participant contribution limits:
  • Employee elective deferral limited to maximum annual amount announced by IRS
  • Catch-up contributions, if allowed, limited to maximum annual amount announced by IRS
  • Combined employee and employer contributions limited to lesser of maximum annual amount announced by IRS or 100% of employee's compensation
Total deductible contribution cannot exceed 25% of all compensation paid to plan participants.		

Compensation		
• Does plan use one of the safe harbor compensation definitions to satisfy Section 415(c)(3)? • If not, does the plan's definition satisfy Section 415(c)(3)?		
Automatic Enrollment and Contribution Increases Will the plan provide for automatic enrollment? Does it qualify as a Qualified Automatic Contribution Arrangement (QACA)? Does it qualify as an Elective Automatic Contribution Arrangement (EACA)? Will the plan provide for automatic contribution increases?		
Qualified Default Investment Alternatives		
Has the plan established a Qualified Default Investment Alternative (QDIA)?		

Safe Harbor Plans
To avoid the nondiscrimination and top-heavy testing, is the plan designed to meet one of the following safe harbors:
  • Traditional safe harbor 401(k) (Section 401(k)(12)) offering minimum matching or nonelective contribution?
  • SIMPLE 401(k)?
  • QACA (Section 401(k)(13)) with minimum matching or nonelective contribution?
  • Defined benefit/401(k)?		

	Yes	No
Plan Distributions		
Does the plan provide distributions must begin within 60 days of the end of the plan year in which the last of the following events occurs, unless the participant elects otherwise: • The date on which the participant attains the earlier of age 65 or the plan's normal retirement age? • The 10th anniversary of the year in which the participant commenced participation in the plan? or • The participant terminates service with the employer? Does the plan provide that a participant's elective deferrals and related earnings cannot be distributed before: • The participant's death, disability, or termination from employment? • The participant becoming age 59 ½? • Termination of the plan? or • The participant's hardship? Does the plan comply with the RMD requirements? Does the plan require an automatic rollover for mandatory distributions exceeding $1,000?		
Spousal Rights		
Is the plan required to provide a Qualified Joint & Survivor Annuity (QJSA) or a Qualified Preretirement Survivor Annuity? Does the plan require spousal consent for any distribution that is not a QJSA? Does the plan provide for the division of a participant's account as required by a Qualified Domestic Relations Order (QDRO)?		
Hardship Withdrawals		
Does the plan permit hardship withdrawals? If so, does it require an employee representation concerning the need for the withdrawal?		
Plan Loans		
Does the plan allow for loans? If so, does it provide for loan terms that comply with the requirement for plan loans?		
Plan Investments		
Does the plan qualify as an ERISA Section 404(c) plan? Does the plan provide the required information concerning plan investment alternatives and fees in an approved format? If the plan holds publicly-traded employer securities, are the diversification requirements met?		

	Yes	No
Life Insurance		
Does the plan allow the purchase of life insurance within the plan? Does the amount of insurance comply with the incidental benefit rules? Is the value of the life insurance to the participant determined and reported to the participant annually? If the policy is transferred to the participant, is the fair market value of the policy at the time of the transferred reported to the participant?		

Appendix B
Hardship Distribution Checklist

Step 1 – Does an immediate and heavy financial need exist?

	Yes	No
Deductible medical expenses for participant, qualifying dependent, or beneficiary* Name _____		
Costs directly related to the purchase of participant's principal residence		
Payment necessary to prevent participant from being evicted from their principal residence or a foreclosure on that mortgage		
Payment for burial or funeral expenses for participant's deceased parent, spouse, children, dependents, or primary beneficiary under the plan		
Expenses to repair damage to participant's principal residence qualifying for a casualty loss deduction*		
Amounts needed to pay taxes expected from the distribution		

*Determined without regard to the AGI limitation

Step 2 – Are other funds reasonably available?

	Yes	No
Reimbursement or compensation by insurance or otherwise		
From liquidating assets		
By stopping plan contributions		
Using other currently available distributions and nontaxable loans from an employer plan		
Borrowing sufficient funds from a commercial lender on reasonable commercial terms		

Step 3 – How much is available for hardship withdrawal ("distributable amount")?

Elective deferrals to the plan	
Less: Previous distributions of elective deferrals	–
Plus: Plan earnings credited to account through December 31, 1988	+
Distributable amount	=

Step 4 – Obtain Participant Verification

	Yes	No
Sufficient to determine a hardship exists		
Sufficient other funds not reasonably available		
No elective deferrals can be made for 6 months		

Appendix C

Plan Loan Checklist

Step 1 – Determine Participant's Eligibility for a Loan

	Yes	No
Is the participant eligible for a loan under the plan terms?		

Step 2 – Determine Loan Terms

	Yes	No
Does loan interest rate qualify as reasonable by providing an interest rate similar to that charged by lenders under similar circumstances?		
Is the loan adequately secured?		
Loan does not exceed 50% of plan balance		
Outside collateral is adequately secured		
General purpose loan – term does not exceed 5 years		
Primary residence loan – loan term complies with plan provisions		
Verification received that loan is for participant's principal residence		
Refinancing loan – loan term complies with special rules for refinanced loans		
Loan provides for substantially equal payments at least quarterly		

Step 3 – Does Loan Amount Comply With Requirements?

Requested loan amount	$
Participant's vested account balance	$
Limited to 50% of vested account balance	× .50
Vested account balance available as loan security	$
Maximum loan amount (lesser of 2b, amount shown on 4c below, or $50,000)	
Reduction if participant has outstanding loan	
Highest outstanding balance of all of participant's loans outstanding during 12-month period ending on day before new loan	$
Less outstanding balance of all of participant's loans outstanding during 12-month period ending on date of new loan	–
Amount of reduction	$
Minimum loan amount specified in plan (if any)	$
Does line 1 equal or exceed line 5? If no, loan is not permitted. Loan must be at least the amount in line 5. If yes, is line 1 equal to or less than line 3? If yes, loan amount meets requirements. If no, loan amount is limited to line 3.	
If refinancing, does loan amount satisfy refinanced loan limit?	

Step 4 – Loan Documentation Requirements

	Yes	No
Loan is evidenced by a legally enforceable agreement that shows compliance with: Repayment term		
Level amortization		
Spousal consent requirements satisfied		

Appendix D1

Sample Spouse's Consent to Waiver of Qualified Joint and Survivor Annuity from Notice 97-10, 1997-1 CB 370

Instruction: The sample language does not address the one-year-of-marriage rule under Section 417(d); if a plan applies the one-year rule, the sample language should be modified to explain this rule.

The sample language contains language in brackets that pertains to a participant's selection of a non-spouse beneficiary to receive death benefits. The bracketed language should be deleted if the plan provides death benefits only to the participant's surviving spouse.

1. What is a Qualified Joint and Survivor Annuity (QJSA)?

Federal law requires the (name of plan) to pay retirement benefits in a special payment form unless your spouse chooses a different payment form and you agree to that choice. This special payment form is often called a "qualified joint and survivor annuity" or "QJSA" payment form. The QJSA payment form gives your spouse a (insert period of QJSA payment, e.g., monthly) retirement payment for the rest of his or her life. This is often called an "annuity." Under the QJSA payment form, after your spouse dies, each (insert period of QJSA payment, e.g., month) the plan will pay you (insert survivor percentage for the QJSA form under the plan) percent of the retirement benefit that was paid to your spouse. The benefit paid to you after your spouse dies is often called a "survivor annuity" or a "survivor benefit." You will receive this survivor benefit for the rest of your life.

Example

Pat Doe and Pat's spouse, Robin, receive payments from the plan under the QJSA payment form. Beginning after Pat retires, Pat receives $600 each month from the plan. Pat then dies. The plan will pay Robin

$ (insert applicable dollar amount for the QJSA) a month for the rest of Robin's life.

2. How Can Your Spouse Change the Way Benefits Are Paid?

Your spouse and you will receive benefits from the plan in the special QJSA payment form required by federal law unless your spouse chooses a different payment form and you agree to the choice. If you agree to change the way the plan's retirement benefits are paid, you give up your right to the special QJSA payments.

3. Do You Have to Give Up Your Right to the QJSA Benefit?

Your choice must be voluntary. It is your personal decision whether you want to give up your right to the special QJSA payment form.

4. What Other Benefit Forms Can My Spouse Choose?

Instruction: The plan administrator may make additions to the paragraph below to explain the plan's optional forms of benefits. For example, the plan administrator could list all optional forms of benefits or provide a cross-reference to a description of benefit options provided to participants. The examples following the paragraph are common optional forms of benefits. The examples should be modified to be consistent with the plan's optional forms of benefits. The plan administrator may give additional examples to explain other available optional forms.

If you agree, your spouse can choose to have the retirement benefits paid in a different form. Other payment forms may give your spouse larger retirement benefits while he or she is alive, but might not pay you any benefits after your spouse dies.

Example of Single Life Annuity Payment Form

If Pat and Robin Doe receive retirement benefits in the special QJSA payment form, Pat would receive retirement benefits of $600 each month from the plan until Pat dies and Robin would receive $ (insert applicable dollar amount for the QJSA) a month for the rest of Robin's life. Pat and Robin Doe agree not to receive retirement benefits in the special QJSA payment form and decide instead to receive payments only during Pat's life. After Pat retires, Pat will receive more than $600 each month from the plan until Pat's death. Robin will not receive any payments from the plan after Pat's death.

Example of Lump Sum Payment Form

Pat and Robin Doe agree not to receive the special QJSA payments and decide instead that Pat will receive a single payment equal to the value of all of Pat's retirement benefits. In this case, no further payments will be made to Pat or Robin.

[If you agree, your spouse can name someone other than you to receive all or a part of the survivor benefits from the plan after your spouse dies. The person your spouse selects to receive all or part of the survivor benefits is often called a "beneficiary." If you agree to let your spouse name someone else as the beneficiary for all of the survivor benefits, you will not receive any payments from the plan after your spouse dies. If you agree to let your spouse name someone else as the beneficiary for a part of the survivor benefits, your survivor benefits will be less than you would have received under the special QJSA payment form.

Example of Naming a Beneficiary Who Is Not the Spouse

Pat and Robin Doe select a payment form that has a survivor benefit of $200 a month payable after Pat dies. Pat and Robin agree that ½ of the survivor benefit will be paid to Robin and ½ will be paid to Pat and Robin's child, Chris. After Pat dies, the plan will pay $100 a month to Robin for the rest of Robin's life. Chris will also receive payments from the plan as long as Chris lives. Chris will receive less than $100 a month because Chris, being younger than Robin, is expected to receive payments over a longer period.]

5. Can Your Spouse Make Future Changes if You Sign this Agreement?

Instruction: The plan administrator should select Option A if the agreement is a "specific consent," that is, the spouse agrees to the participant's choice of a particular form of benefit and beneficiary. The plan administrator should select Option B if the agreement is a "general consent," that is, the spouse agrees to allow the participant to choose any form of benefit and any beneficiary without telling the spouse the selection.

Option A

If you sign this agreement, you agree that benefits under the plan will be paid in the form stated in this agreement. [You also agree that the beneficiary named in this agreement will receive all or a part of the survivor benefits from the plan after your spouse has died]. Your spouse cannot change the payment form [or the beneficiary] unless you agree to the change by signing a new agreement. However, your spouse can change to the special QJSA payment form without getting your agreement.

Option B

If you sign this agreement, you agree that your spouse can choose the form of payments that he or she will receive from the plan without telling you and without getting your agreement. [Your spouse can also choose the beneficiary who will receive any survivor benefits from the plan after your spouse dies without telling you and without getting your agreement.] Your spouse does not need to tell you or get your agreement to any future changes in the form of payments [or the beneficiary].

You may limit your agreement to a particular payment form [and a particular beneficiary]. If you want to allow your spouse to select only a particular payment form [and a particular beneficiary], do not sign this form. In that case, contact the plan administrator for more information and to get a new agreement that lets you state the particular payment form [and the particular beneficiary] that you will allow your spouse to select.

6. Can You Change Your Mind After You Sign this Agreement?

Instruction: The plan administrator should select Option A if the plan does not allow a spouse to revoke his or her consent. The plan administrator should select Option B if the plan allows a spouse to revoke his or her consent. The language in double brackets in Options A and B applies only to general consent forms. For an explanation of a specific consent and a general consent, see the Instruction to section 5.

Option A

You cannot change this agreement after you sign it. Your decision is final [[even if your spouse later chooses a different type of retirement benefit or beneficiary]].

Option B

You can change this agreement until (date). After that date, you cannot change the agreement [[even if your spouse later chooses a different type of retirement benefit or beneficiary]]. If you change your mind, you must notify the plan administrator by (insert the plan procedure for revoking consent).

7. What Happens to this Agreement if You Become Separated or Divorced?

Legal separation or divorce may end your right to survivor benefits from the plan even if you do not sign this agreement. However, if you become legally separated or divorced, you might be able to get a special court order (which is called a qualified domestic relations order or "QDRO") that would give you rights to receive retirement benefits even if you sign this agreement. If you are thinking about separating or getting a divorce, you should get legal advice on your rights to benefits from the plan.

8. What Should You Know Before Signing this Agreement?

Instruction: The plan administrator should modify the language below to reflect the plan's administrative procedures and insert the appropriate address or telephone number.

This is a very important decision. You should think very carefully about whether you want to sign this agreement. Before signing, be sure that you understand what retirement benefits you may get and what benefits you will no longer be able to receive.

Your spouse should have received information on the types of retirement benefits available from the plan. If you have not seen this information, you should get it and read it before you sign this agreement. For additional information, you can contact (name of person or department, such as the Human Resources Department) at the following address (or telephone number).

9. Your Agreement

Instruction: The plan administrator should select Option A if the agreement is a specific consent. The plan administrator should select Option B if the agreement is a general consent. For an explanation of a specific consent and a general consent, see the Instruction to section 5.

Option A

I, (name of participant's spouse), am the spouse of (name of participant). I understand that I have the right to have (name of plan) pay my spouse's retirement benefits in the special QJSA payment form and I agree to give up that right. I understand that by signing this agreement, I may receive less money than I would have received under the special QJSA payment form and I may receive nothing after my spouse dies, depending on the payment form [or beneficiary] that my spouse chooses.

I agree that my spouse can receive retirement benefits in the form of a (insert form of benefit selected). [I also agree to my spouse's choice of (name of beneficiary) as the beneficiary who will receive (insert percentage of survivor benefit that will be paid to the beneficiary) of the survivor benefits from the plan after my spouse dies.] I understand that my spouse cannot choose a different form of retirement benefits [or a different beneficiary] unless I agree to the change.

I understand that I do not have to sign this agreement. I am signing this agreement voluntarily.

I understand that if I do not sign this agreement, then my spouse and I will receive payments from the plan in the special QJSA payment form.

Instruction: The plan administrator should add a line for the spouse's signature and a place for the witness' acknowledgment.

Option B

I, (name of participant's spouse), am the spouse of (name of participant). I understand that I have the right to have (name of plan) pay my spouse's retirement benefits in the special QJSA payment form, and I agree to give up that right. I understand that by signing this agreement, I may receive less money than I would have received under the special QJSA payment form and I may receive nothing after my spouse dies depending on the payment form [or beneficiary] that my spouse chooses.

I understand that by signing this agreement, my spouse can choose any retirement benefit form [and any beneficiary] that is allowed by the plan without telling me and without getting my agreement. I also understand that my spouse can change the retirement benefit form selected [or the name of a beneficiary] at any time before retirement benefits begin without telling me and without getting my agreement.

I understand that I can limit my spouse's choice to a particular retirement benefit form [and a particular beneficiary who will receive payments from the plan after the death of my spouse] and that I am giving up that right.

I understand that I do not have to sign this agreement. I am signing this agreement voluntarily.

I understand that if I do not sign this agreement, then my spouse and I will receive payments from the plan in the special QJSA payment form.

Instruction: The plan administrator should add a line for the spouse's signature and a place for the witness' acknowledgment.

Appendix D2

Sample Spouse's Consent to Waiver of Qualified Preretirement Survivor Annuity from Notice 97-10, 1997-1 CB 370

Instruction: The sample language does not address the one-year-of-marriage rule under Section 417(d); if a plan applies the one-year rule, the sample language should be modified to explain this rule.

1. What is a Qualified Preretirement Survivor Annuity (QPSA)?

Instruction: The final sentence of the sample language before the example addresses situations where a plan pays the survivor benefit in a lump sum if the value of the survivor benefit is $3,500 or less. That sentence should be deleted if the plan pays survivor benefits with a value of $3,500 or less as an annuity.

Your spouse has an account in *(name of plan)*. The money in the account that your spouse will be entitled to receive is called the vested account. Federal law states that you will receive a special death benefit that is paid from the vested account if your spouse dies before he or she begins receiving retirement benefits (or, if earlier, before the beginning of the period for which the retirement benefits are paid). You have the right to receive this *(insert period of QPSA payment, e.g., monthly)* payment for your life beginning after your spouse dies. The special death benefit is often called a "qualified preretirement survivor annuity" or "QPSA" benefit. (The plan will pay this death benefit in a lump sum, rather than as a QPSA, if the value of the death benefit is $3,500 or less.)

2. Can Your Spouse Choose Other Beneficiaries to Receive the Account?

Your right to the QPSA benefit provided by federal law cannot be taken away unless you agree to give up that benefit. If you agree, your spouse can choose to have all or a part of the death benefits paid to someone else. The person your spouse chooses to receive the death benefits is usually called the "beneficiary." For example, if you agree, your spouse can have the death benefits paid to his or her children instead of you.

Example

Pat and Robin Doe agree that Robin will not receive the QPSA benefit. Pat and Robin also decide that ½ of the death benefits that are paid from Pat's vested account will be paid to Robin and ½ of the death benefits will be paid to Pat and Robin's child, Chris. The total death benefits are $200 per month. After Pat dies, the plan will pay $100 a month to Robin for the rest of Robin's life. Chris will also receive payments from the plan as long as Chris lives. Chris will receive less than $100 a month because Chris, being younger than Robin, is expected to receive payments over a longer period.

3. Do You Have to Give Up Your Right to the QPSA Benefit?

Your choice must be voluntary. It is your personal decision whether you want to give up your right to the special QPSA payment form.

4. Can Your Spouse Change the Beneficiary in the Future if You Sign this Agreement?

Instruction: Option A is for use in a "specific consent agreement," that is, where the spouse agrees to the participant's waiver of the QPSA and to the participant's choice of a specific beneficiary to receive death benefits. Option B is for use in a "general consent agreement," that is, where the spouse agrees to the participant's waiver of the QPSA and to allow the participant to select any other beneficiary to receive the death benefits.

Option A

If you sign this agreement, your spouse cannot change the beneficiary named in this agreement unless you agree to the new beneficiary by signing a new agreement. If you agree, your spouse can change the beneficiary at any time before your spouse begins receiving benefits or dies. You do not have to agree to let your spouse change the beneficiary. However, your spouse can select the QPSA benefit for you without getting your agreement.

Option B

If you sign this agreement, your spouse can choose the beneficiary who will receive the death benefits without telling you and without getting your agreement. Your spouse can change the beneficiary at any time before he or she begins receiving benefits or dies.

You have the right to agree to allow your spouse to select only a particular beneficiary. If you want to allow your spouse to select only a particular beneficiary, do not sign this form. In that case, contact the plan administrator for more information and to get a new agreement that lets you state the particular beneficiary that you will allow your spouse to select.

5. Can You Change Your Mind After You Sign this Agreement?

Instruction: The plan administrator should select Option A if the plan does not allow a spouse to revoke his or her consent. The plan administrator should select Option B if the plan allows a spouse to revoke his or her consent. The bracketed language in Options A and B applies only to general consent forms. For an explanation of a specific consent and a general consent, see the Instruction to section 4.

Option A

You cannot change this agreement after you sign it. Your decision is final [even if your spouse later chooses a different beneficiary].

Option B

You can change this agreement until (date). After that date, you cannot change the agreement [even if your spouse later chooses a different beneficiary]. If you change your mind, you must notify the plan administrator by (the plan procedure for revoking consent).

6. What Happens to this Agreement if You Become Separated or Divorced?

You may lose your right to the QPSA benefit if your spouse and you become legally separated or divorced even if you do not sign this agreement. However, if you become legally separated or divorced, you might be able to get a special court order (which is called a qualified domestic relations order or "QDRO") that specifically protects your rights to receive the QPSA benefit or that gives you other benefits under this plan. If you are thinking about separating or getting a divorce, you should get legal advice on your rights to benefits from the plan.

7. Your Agreement

Instruction: The plan administrator should select Option A if the agreement is a specific consent. The plan administrator should select Option B if the agreement is a general consent. For an explanation of a specific consent and a general consent, see the Instruction to section 4.

The final sentence in the first and last paragraphs of the sample language in this section address situations where a plan pays the survivor benefit in a lump sum if the value of the death benefit is $3,500 or less. These sentences should be deleted if the plan pays death benefits with a value of $3,500 or less as an annuity.

Option A

I, (name of participant's spouse), am the spouse of (name of participant). I understand that I have a right to the QPSA benefit from (name of plan) if my spouse dies before he or she begins receiving retirement benefits (or, if earlier, before the beginning of the period for which the retirement benefits are paid). I also understand that if the value of the QPSA benefit is $3,500 or less, the plan will pay the benefit to me in one lump sum payment.

I agree to give up my right to (insert percentage) percent of the QPSA benefit and instead to have that benefit paid to the following beneficiaries:

Name of Beneficiary

Percent of QPSA

I understand that my spouse cannot select a different beneficiary unless I agree to the change.

I understand that by signing this agreement, I may receive less money than I would have received under the special QPSA payment form and I may receive nothing from the plan after my spouse dies.

I understand that I do not have to sign this agreement. I am signing this agreement voluntarily.

I understand that if I do not sign this agreement, then I will receive the QPSA benefit if my spouse dies before he or she begins to receive retirement benefits (or, if earlier, before the beginning of the period for which the retirement benefits are paid). I also understand that if the value of the QPSA benefit is $3,500 or less, the plan will pay the benefit to me in one lump sum payment.

Instruction: The plan administrator should add a line for the spouse's signature and a place for the witness' acknowledgment.

Option B

I, (name of participant's spouse), am the spouse of (name of participant). I understand that I have a right to the QPSA benefit from (name of plan) if my spouse dies before he or she begins receiving retirement benefits (or, if earlier, before the beginning of the period for which the retirement benefits are paid). I also understand that if the value of the QPSA benefit is $3,500 or less, the plan will pay the benefit to me in one lump sum payment.

I agree to give up my right to (insert percentage) percent of the QPSA benefit and to allow my spouse to choose any beneficiary to receive that benefit. I understand that by signing this agreement, my spouse can choose the beneficiary without telling me and without getting my agreement. I also understand that my spouse can change the beneficiary at any time before retirement benefits begin without telling me and without getting my agreement.

I understand that I can limit my spouse's choice to a particular beneficiary who will receive payments from the plan after the death of my spouse and that I am giving up that right.

I understand that by signing this agreement, I may receive less money than I would have received under the special QPSA payment form and I may receive nothing from the plan after my spouse dies.

I understand that I do not have to sign this agreement. I am signing this agreement voluntarily.

I understand that if I do not sign this agreement, then I will receive the QPSA benefit if my spouse dies before he or she begins to receive retirement benefits (or, if earlier, before the beginning of the period for which the retirement benefits are paid). I also understand that if the value of the QPSA benefit is $3,500 or less, the plan will pay the benefit to me in one lump sum payment.

Instruction: The plan administrator should add a line for the spouse's signature and a place for the witness' acknowledgment.

Note to plan administrator: A participant in a plan subject to the survivor annuity requirements of Section 401(a)(11) generally may waive the QPSA benefit with spousal consent only on or after the first day of the plan year in which the participant attains age 35. However, a plan may provide for an earlier waiver with spousal consent, provided that a written explanation of the QPSA is given to the participant and that the waiver executed prior to age 35 becomes invalid upon the beginning of the plan year in which the participant's thirty-fifth birthday occurs. If a new waiver and spousal consent is not executed on or after that date, QPSA benefit must be provided.

Appendix E

Model Investment Option Comparative Chart; Appendix to DOL Reg. 2550.404a-5

ABC Corporation 401k Retirement Plan
Investment Options – January 1, 20XX

This document includes important information to help you compare the investment options under your retirement plan. If you want additional information about your investment options, you can go to the specific Internet Web site address shown below or you can contact [insert name of plan administrator or designee] at [insert telephone number and address]. A free paper copy of the information available on the Web site[s] can be obtained by contacting [insert name of plan administrator or designee] at [insert telephone number].

Document Summary

This document has 3 parts. Part I consists of performance information for plan investment options. This part shows you how well the investments have performed in the past. Part II shows you the fees and expenses you will pay if you invest in an option. Part III contains information about the annuity options under your retirement plan.

Part I. Performance Information

Table 1 focuses on the performance of investment options that do not have a fixed or stated rate of return. Table 1 shows how these options have performed over time and allows you to compare them with an appropriate benchmark for the same time periods. Past performance does not guarantee how the investment option will perform in the future. Your investment in these options could lose money. Information about an option's principal risks is available on the Web site[s].

Table 1—Variable Return Investments								
Name/ Type of Option	Average Annual Total Return as of 12/31/XX				Benchmark			
	1yr.	5yr.	10yr.	Since Inception	1yr.	5yr.	10yr.	Since Inception
Equity Funds								
A Index Fund/ S&P 500 www. website address	26.5%	.34%	-1.03%	9.25%	26.46%	.42% S&P 500	-.95%	9.30%
B Fund/ Large Cap www. website address	27.6%	.99%	N/A	2.26%	27.80%	1.02% US Prime Market 750 Index	N/A	2.77%
C Fund/ Int'l Stock www. website address	36.73%	5.26%	2.29%	9.37%	40.40%	5.40% MSCI EAFE	2.40%	12.09%
D Fund/ Mid Cap www. website address	40.22%	2.28%	6.13%	3.29%	46.29%	2.40% Russell Midcap	-.52%	4.16%
Bond Funds								
E Fund/ Bond Index www. website address	6.45%	4.43%	6.08%	7.08%	5.93%	4.97% Barclays Cap. Aggr. Bd.	6.33%	7.01%
Other								
F Fund/ GICs	.72%	3.36%	3.11%	5.56%	1.8%	3.1%	3.3%	5.75%

www. website address					3-month US T-Bill Index			
G Fund/ Stable Value www. website address	4.36%	4.64%	5.07%	3.75%	1.8% 3.1% 3.3% 4.99% 3-month US T-Bill Index			
Generations 2020/ Lifecycle Fund www. website address	27.94%	N/A	N/A	2.45%	26.46% N/A N/A 3.09% S&P 500			
					23.95% N/A N/A 3.74% Generations 2020 Composite Index*			

*Generations 2020 composite index is a combination of a total market index and a US aggregate bond index proportional to the equity/bond allocation in the Generations 2020 Fund.

Table 2 focuses on the performance of investment options that have a fixed or stated rate of return. Table 2 shows the annual rate of return of each such option, the term or length of time that you will earn this rate of return, and other information relevant to performance.

Table 2—Fixed Return Investments			
Name/ Type of Option	Return	Term	Other
H 200X/ GIC www. website address	4%	2 Yr.	The rate of return does not change during the stated term.
I LIBOR Plus/ Fixed-Type Investment Account www. website address	LIBOR +2%	Quarterly	The rate of return on 12/31/xx was 2.45%. This rate is fixed quarterly, but will never fall below a guaranteed minimum rate of 2%. Current rate of return information is available on the option's Web site or at 1-800-yyy-zzzz.
J Financial Services Co./ Fixed Account Investment www. website address	3.75%	6 Mos.	The rate of return on 12/31/xx was 3.75%. This rate of return is fixed for six months. Current rate of return information is available on the option's Web site or at 1-800-yyy-zzzz.

Part II. Fee and Expense Information

Table 3 shows fee and expense information for the investment options listed in Table1 and Table 2. Table 3 shows the Total Annual Operating Expenses of the options in Table 1. Total Annual Operating Expenses are expenses that reduce the rate of return of the investment option. Table 3 also shows Shareholder-type Fees. These fees are in addition to Total Annual Operating Expenses.

Table 3—Fees and Expenses			
Name / Type of Option	Total Annual Operating Expenses As a % / Per $1000		Shareholder-Type Fees
Equity Funds			
A Index Fund/ S&P 500	0.18%	$1.80	$20 annual service charge subtracted from investments held in this option if valued at less than $10,000.
B Fund/ Large Cap	2.45%	$24.50	2.25% deferred sales charge subtracted from amounts withdrawn within 12 months of purchase.
C Fund/ International	0.79%	$7.90	5.75% sales charge subtracted from amounts invested.

Stock			
D Fund/ Mid Cap ETF	0.20%	$2.00	4.25% sales charge subtracted from amounts withdrawn.
Bond Funds			
E Fund/ Bond Index	0.50%	$5.00	N/A
Other			
F Fund/ GICs	0.46%	$4.60	10% charge subtracted from amounts withdrawn within 18 months of initial investment.
G Fund/ Stable Value	0.65%	$6.50	Amounts withdrawn may not be transferred to a competing option for 90 days after withdrawal.
Generations 2020/ Lifecycle Fund	1.50%	$15.00	Excessive trading restricts additional purchases (other than contributions and loan repayments) for 85 days.
Fixed Return Investments			
H 200X / GIC	N/A		12% charge subtracted from amounts withdrawn before maturity.
I LIBOR Plus/ Fixed-Type Invest Account	N/A		5% contingent deferred sales charge subtracted from amounts withdrawn; charge reduced by 1% on 12-month anniversary of each investment.
J Financial Serv Co. / Fixed Account Investment	N/A		90 days of interest subtracted from amounts withdrawn before maturity.

The cumulative effect of fees and expenses can substantially reduce the growth of your retirement savings. Visit the Department of Labor's Web site for an example showing the long-term effect of fees and expenses at http://www.dol.gov/ebsa/publications/401k employee.html. Fees and expenses are only one of many factors to consider when you decide to invest in an option. You may also want to think about whether an investment in a particular option, along with your other investments, will help you achieve your financial goals.

Part III. Annuity Information

Table 4 focuses on the annuity options under the plan. Annuities are insurance contracts that allow you to receive a guaranteed stream of payments at regular intervals, usually beginning when you retire and lasting for your entire life. Annuities are issued by insurance companies. Guarantees of an insurance company are subject to its long-term financial strength and claims-paying ability.

Table 4—Annuity Options			
Name	Objectives / Goals	Pricing Factors	Restrictions / Fees
Lifetime Income Option www. website address	To provide a guaranteed stream of income for your life, based on shares you acquire while you work. At age 65, you will receive monthly payments of $10 for each share you own, for your life. For example, if	The cost of each share depends on your age and interest rates when you buy it. Ordinarily the closer you are to retirement, the more it will cost you to buy a share.	Payment amounts are based on your life expectancy only and would be reduced if you choose a spousal joint and survivor benefit. You will pay a 25%

	you own 30 shares at age 65, you will receive $300 per month over your life.	The cost includes a guaranteed death benefit payable to a spouse or beneficiary if you die before payments begin. The death benefit is the total amount of your contributions, less any withdrawals.	surrender charge for any amount you withdraw before annuity payments begin. If your income payments are less than $50 per month, the option's issuer may combine payments and pay you less frequently, or return to you the larger of your net contributions or the cash-out value of your income shares.
Generations 2020 Variable Annuity Option www. website address	To provide a guaranteed stream of income for your life, or some other period of time, based on your account balance in the Generations 2020 Lifecycle Fund. This option is available through a variable annuity contract that your plan has with ABC Insurance Company.	You have the right to elect fixed annuity payments in the form of a life annuity, a joint and survivor annuity, or a life annuity with a term certain, but the payment amounts will vary based on the benefit you choose. The cost of this right is included in the Total Annual Operating Expenses of the Generations 2020 Lifecycle Fund, listed in Table 3 above. The cost also includes a guaranteed death benefit payable to a spouse or beneficiary if you die before payments begin. The death benefit is the greater of your account balance or contributions, less any withdrawals.	Maximum surrender charge of 8% of account balance. Maximum transfer fee of $30 for each transfer over 12 in a year. Annual service charge of $50 for account balances below $100,000.

> **Please visit www.ABCPlanglossary.com for a glossary of investment terms relevant to the investment options under this plan. This glossary is intended to help you better understand your options.**

BILLING CODE 4510–29–C

Appendix F

Revenue Procedure 2013-4, Procedure for Requesting Private Letter Rulings, 2013-1 CB 126

26 CFR 601.201: Rulings and determination letters.

Rev. Proc. 2013–4

TABLE OF CONTENTS

SECTION 1. WHAT IS THE PURPOSE OF THIS REVENUE PROCEDURE? 129

SECTION 2. WHAT CHANGES HAVE BEEN MADE TO REV. PROC. 2012–4? 129

SECTION 3. IN WHAT FORM IS GUIDANCE PROVIDED BY THE COMMISSIONER, TAX EXEMPT AND
       GOVERNMENT ENTITIES DIVISION? 129
  .01 In general 129
  .02 Letter ruling 130
  .03 Closing agreement 130
  .04 Determination letter. 130
  .05 Opinion letter 130
  .06 Information letter. 130
  .07 Revenue ruling 131
  .08 Oral advice 131
      (1) No oral rulings, and no written rulings in response to oral requests 131
      (2) Discussion possible on substantive issues 131
      (3) Oral guidance is advisory only, and the Service is not bound by it. 131
  .09 Nonbank trustee requests 132
  .10 Compliance Statement 132
  .11 Advisory letter 132

SECTION 4. ON WHAT ISSUES MAY TAXPAYERS REQUEST WRITTEN GUIDANCE UNDER THIS
       PROCEDURE? 132

SECTION 5. ON WHAT ISSUES MUST WRITTEN GUIDANCE BE REQUESTED UNDER DIFFERENT
       PROCEDURES? 132
  .01 Determination letters 132
  .02 Master and prototype plans and volume submitter plans 132
  .03 Closing agreement program for defined contribution plans that purchased GICs or GACs 133
  .04 Employee Plans Compliance Resolution System 133
  .05 Chief Counsel 133
  .06 Alcohol, tobacco, and firearms taxes 133

SECTION 6. UNDER WHAT CIRCUMSTANCES DOES TE/GE ISSUE LETTER RULINGS? 133
  .01 In exempt organizations matters 133
  .02 In employee plans matters 133
  .03 In qualifications matters 134
  .04 Request for extension of time for making an election or for other relief under § 301.9100–1 of the
      Procedure and Administration Regulations 134
  .05 Issuance of a letter ruling before the issuance of a regulation or other published guidance 135
  .06 Issues in prior return 135
  .07 Generally not to business associations or groups 135
  .08 Generally not to foreign governments 135
  .09 Generally not on federal tax consequences of proposed legislation 135
  .10 Not on certain matters under § 53.4958–6 of the Foundation and Similar Excise Taxes Regulations 135
  .11 Not on stock options 136
  .12 Generally not on EO joint venture with a for-profit organization 136
  .13 Not on qualification of state run programs under § 529 136
  .14 Not on UBIT issues involving certain investments of a charitable lead trust 136
  .15 Not on issues under § 4966 or § 4967 136
  .16 Not on issues under § 507, § 4941 or § 4945 136
  .17 Generally not to partnerships or limited liability companies 136

.18 Not on self-dealing issues involving the issuance of a promissory note by a disqualified person during the administration of an estate or trust.. 136

SECTION 7. UNDER WHAT CIRCUMSTANCES DOES EP OR EO DETERMINATIONS ISSUE DETERMINATION LETTERS?.. 136
.01 Circumstances under which determination letters are issued 136
.02 In general 136
.03 In employee plans matters 137
.04 In exempt organizations matters 137
.05 Circumstances under which determination letters are not issued 138
.06 Requests involving returns already filed 138
.07 Attach a copy of determination letter to taxpayer's return 138
.08 Review of determination letters 138

SECTION 8. UNDER WHAT CIRCUMSTANCES DOES THE SERVICE HAVE DISCRETION TO ISSUE LETTER RULINGS AND DETERMINATION LETTERS? 138
.01 Ordinarily not in certain areas because of factual nature of the problem 138
.02 No "comfort" letter rulings 138
.03 Not on alternative plans or hypothetical situations 138
.04 Ordinarily not on part of an integrated transaction 139
.05 Not on partial terminations of employee plans 139
.06 Law requires letter ruling... 139
.07 Issues under consideration by PBGC or DOL 139
.08 Cafeteria plans 139
.09 Determination letters 139
.10 Domicile in a foreign jurisdiction 139
.11 Employee Stock Ownership Plans 139
.12 Governmental Plans 139

SECTION 9. WHAT ARE THE GENERAL INSTRUCTIONS FOR REQUESTING LETTER RULINGS AND DETERMINATION LETTERS? 140
.01 In general 140
.02 Certain information required in all requests 140
   (1) Complete statement of facts and other information 140
   (2) Copies of all contracts, wills, deeds, agreements, instruments, plan documents, and other documents... 140
   (3) Analysis of material facts... 140
   (4) Statement regarding whether same issue is in an earlier return............................. 140
   (5) Statement regarding whether same or similar issue was previously ruled on or requested, or is currently pending.. 141
   (6) Statement of supporting authorities. 141
   (7) Statement of contrary authorities. 141
   (8) Statement identifying pending legislation.. 142
   (9) Statement identifying information to be deleted from copy of letter ruling or determination letter for public inspection. 142
   (10) Signature by taxpayer or authorized representative.. 143
   (11) Authorized representatives... 143
   (12) Power of attorney and declaration of representative....................................... 145
   (13) Penalties of perjury statement.. 145
   (14) Applicable user fee. 145
   (15) Number of copies of request to be submitted.. 146
   (16) Sample format for a letter ruling request.. 146
   (17) Checklist for letter ruling requests.. 146
.03 Additional information required in certain circumstances 146
   (1) To request separate letter rulings for multiple issues in a single situation.................. 146
   (2) Recipient of original of letter ruling or determination letter................................ 146
   (3) To request expedited handling.. 147
   (4) To receive a letter ruling or submit a request for a letter ruling by facsimile transmission (fax). 148
   (5) To request a conference 148

.04 Address to send the request 148
    (1) Requests for letter rulings 148
    (2) Requests for information letters 148
    (3) Requests for determination letters 149
.05 Pending letter ruling requests 149
.06 When to attach letter ruling to return 149
.07 How to check on status of request 149
.08 Request may be withdrawn or EP or EO Technical may decline to issue letter ruling 150
.09 Compliance with Treasury Department Circular No. 230 150

SECTION 10. WHAT SPECIFIC, ADDITIONAL PROCEDURES APPLY TO CERTAIN REQUESTS? 150
.01 In general 150
.02 Exempt Organizations 150
.03 Employee Plans 150

SECTION 11. HOW DOES EP OR EO TECHNICAL HANDLE LETTER RULING REQUESTS? 151
.01 In general 151
.02 Is not bound by informal opinion expressed 151
.03 Tells taxpayer if request lacks essential information during initial contact 151
.04 Requires prompt submission of additional information requested after initial contact............................ 151
.05 Near the completion of the ruling process, advises taxpayer of conclusions and, if the Service will
    rule adversely, offers the taxpayer the opportunity to withdraw the letter ruling request....................... 152
.06 May request draft of proposed letter ruling near the completion of the ruling process 152

SECTION 12. HOW ARE CONFERENCES SCHEDULED? 153
.01 Schedules a conference if requested by taxpayer 153
.02 Permits taxpayer one conference of right 153
.03 Disallows verbatim recording of conferences 153
.04 Makes tentative recommendations on substantive issues 153
.05 May offer additional conferences 154
.06 Requires written confirmation of information presented at conference 154
.07 May schedule a pre-submission conference 154
.08 Under limited circumstances, may schedule a conference to be held by telephone 154
.09 Conference rules for EO determination letters not subject to § 7428 or § 501 or § 521 155

SECTION 13. WHAT EFFECT WILL A LETTER RULING HAVE? 155
.01 May be relied on subject to limitations 155
.02 Will not apply to another taxpayer 155
.03 Will be used by TE/GE in examining the taxpayer's return.. 155
.04 May be revoked or modified if found to be in error 155
.05 Not generally revoked or modified retroactively 156
.06 Retroactive effect of revocation or modification applied only to a particular transaction 156
.07 Retroactive effect of revocation or modification applied to a continuing action or series of actions 156
.08 May be retroactively revoked or modified when transaction is completed without reliance on the
    letter ruling 156
.09 Taxpayer may request that retroactivity be limited 156
    (1) Request for relief under § 7805(b) must be made in required format...................................... 156
    (2) Taxpayer may request a conference on application of § 7805(b). 157

SECTION 14. WHAT EFFECT WILL A DETERMINATION LETTER HAVE? 157
.01 Has same effect as a letter ruling 157
.02 Taxpayer may request that retroactive effect of revocation or modification be limited 158
    (1) Request for relief under § 7805(b) must be made in required format...................................... 158
    (2) Taxpayer may request a conference on application of § 7805(b). 158
    (3) Taxpayer steps in exhausting administrative remedies. 158

SECTION 15. UNDER WHAT CIRCUMSTANCES ARE MATTERS REFERRED BETWEEN
              DETERMINATIONS AND TECHNICAL?.. 158
.01 Requests for determination letters 158

.02 No-rule areas 159
.03 Requests for letter rulings 159

**SECTION 16. WHAT ARE THE GENERAL PROCEDURES APPLICABLE TO INFORMATION LETTERS
     ISSUED BY THE HEADQUARTERS OFFICE?** 159
.01 Will be made available to the public 159
.02 Deletions made under the Freedom of Information Act 159
.03 Effect of information letters 159

SECTION 17. WHAT IS THE EFFECT OF THIS REVENUE PROCEDURE ON OTHER DOCUMENTS? 159

SECTION 18. EFFECTIVE DATE 159

SECTION 19. PAPERWORK REDUCTION ACT 160

DRAFTING INFORMATION 160

INDEX 161

APPENDIX A—SAMPLE FORMAT FOR A LETTER RULING REQUEST 162

APPENDIX B—CHECKLIST FOR A LETTER RULING REQUEST 164

APPENDIX C—ADDITIONAL CHECKLIST FOR ROTH IRA RECHARACTERIZATIONS 167

APPENDIX D—ADDITIONAL CHECKLIST FOR GOVERNMENT PICK-UP PLANS 168

APPENDIX E—ADDITIONAL CHECKLIST FOR CHURCH PLANS 169

SECTION 1. WHAT IS THE PURPOSE OF THIS REVENUE PROCEDURE?

This revenue procedure explains how the Internal Revenue Service gives guidance to taxpayers on issues under the jurisdiction of the Commissioner, Tax Exempt and Government Entities Division. It explains the kinds of guidance and the manner in which guidance is requested by taxpayers and provided by the Service. A sample format of a request for a letter ruling is provided in Appendix A.

SECTION 2. WHAT CHANGES HAVE BEEN MADE TO REV. PROC. 2012–4?

.01 This revenue procedure is a general update of Rev. Proc. 2012–4, 2012–1 I.R.B. 125 which contains the Service's general procedures for employee plans and exempt organizations letter ruling requests. In addition to minor revisions, such as updating citations to other revenue procedures, the following changes have been made:

.02 Section 6.02(3) changed the reference from section 412(m)(5) to section 430(j)(4) pursuant to the Pension Protection Act of 2006;

.03 Section 9.01 is revised to add language regarding submission of requests and documents in support of requests in English;

.04 Section 9.03 is revised to conform to Form 2848 as revised (Mar. 2012);

.05 Section 10.02 is revised to remove the reference to Notice 2011–43.

.06 Applicable sections are revised to refer to sections 412(c)(7)(B)(i), 412(d)(2) and ERISA section 302(d)(2).

SECTION 3. IN WHAT FORM IS GUIDANCE PROVIDED BY THE COMMISSIONER, TAX EXEMPT AND GOVERNMENT ENTITIES DIVISION?

In general

.01 The Service provides guidance in the form of letter rulings, closing agreements, compliance statements, determination letters, opinion letters, advisory letters, information letters, revenue rulings, and oral advice.

Letter ruling

.02 A "letter ruling" is a written statement issued to a taxpayer by the Service's Employee Plans Technical office or Exempt Organizations Technical office that interprets and applies the tax laws or any nontax laws applicable to employee benefit plans and exempt organizations to the taxpayer's specific set of facts. Once issued, a letter ruling may be revoked or modified for any number of reasons, as explained in section 13 of this revenue procedure, unless it is accompanied by a "closing agreement."

Closing agreement

.03 A "closing agreement" is a final agreement between the Service and a taxpayer on a specific issue or liability. It is entered into under the authority in § 7121 and is final unless fraud, malfeasance, or misrepresentation of a material fact can be shown.

A closing agreement prepared in an office under the responsibility of the Commissioner, TE/GE, may be based on a ruling that has been signed by the Commissioner, TE/GE, or the Commissioner, TE/GE's delegate that says that a closing agreement will be entered into on the basis of the ruling letter.

A closing agreement may be entered into when it is advantageous to have the matter permanently and conclusively closed, or when a taxpayer can show that there are good reasons for an agreement and that making the agreement will not prejudice the interests of the Government. In appropriate cases, taxpayers may be asked to enter into a closing agreement as a condition to the issuance of a letter ruling.

If, in a single case, a closing agreement is requested for each person in a class of taxpayers, separate agreements are entered into only if the class consists of 25 or fewer taxpayers. However, if the issue and holding are identical for the class and there are more than 25 taxpayers in the class, a "mass closing agreement" will be entered into with the taxpayer who is authorized by the others to represent the class.

In appropriate cases, a closing agreement may be made with sponsors of master and prototype plans.

A closing agreement may also be entered into with respect to retirement plan failures corrected under the Audit Closing Agreement Program of the Employee Plans Compliance Resolution System (EPCRS), as set forth in Rev. Proc. 2008–50, 2008–2 C.B. 464, as updated.

Determination letter

.04 A "determination letter" is a written statement issued to a taxpayer by the Service's EO Determinations or EP Determinations office that applies the principles and precedents previously announced to a specific set of facts. It is issued only when a determination can be made based on clearly established rules in the statute, a tax treaty, or the regulations, or based on a conclusion in a revenue ruling, opinion, or court decision published in the Internal Revenue Bulletin that specifically answers the questions presented.

The Manager, EP Determinations, issues determination letters involving §§ 401, 403(a), 409, and 4975(e)(7) as provided in Rev. Proc. 2013–6, page 198, this Bulletin.

Opinion letter

.05 An "opinion letter" is a written statement issued by the Service to a sponsor or M&P mass submitter as to the acceptability of the form of an M&P plan under § 401(a) or § 403(a), and, in the case of a master plan, the acceptability of the master trust under § 501(a), or as to the conformance of a prototype trust, custodial account, or individual annuity with the requirements of § 408(a), (b), (k) or (p) or 408A, as applicable. *See* Rev. Proc. 2011–49, 2011–44 I.R.B. 608. *See also* Rev. Proc. 87–50, 1987–2 C.B. 647; Rev. Proc. 91–44, 1991–2 C.B. 733; Rev. Proc. 92–38, 1992–1 C.B. 859; Rev. Proc. 97–29, 1997–1 C.B. 689; Rev. Proc. 98–59, 1998–2 C.B. 727; Rev. Proc. 2002–10, 2002–1 C.B. 401, and Rev. Proc. 2010–48, 2010–50, I.R.B. 828, as modified by Rev. Proc. 2013–8, page 237, this Bulletin.

Information letter

.06 An "information letter" is a statement issued either by the Director, Employee Plans Rulings and Agreements or the Director, Exempt Organizations Rulings and Agreements. It calls attention to a well-established interpretation or principle of tax law (including a tax treaty) without applying it to a specific set of facts. To the extent resources permit, an information letter may be issued if the taxpayer's inquiry indicates a need for general information or if the taxpayer's request does not meet the requirements of this revenue procedure and the Service thinks general information will help the taxpayer. The taxpayer should provide a daytime telephone number with the taxpayer's request for an information letter. Requests for information letters should be sent to the address stated in section 9.04(2) of this revenue procedure. The requirements of section 9.02 of this revenue procedure are not applicable to information letters. An information letter is advisory only and has no binding effect on the Service.

Revenue ruling

.07 A "revenue ruling" is an interpretation by the Service that has been published in the Internal Revenue Bulletin. It is the conclusion of the Service on how the law is applied to a specific set of facts. Revenue rulings are published for the information and guidance of taxpayers, Service personnel, and other interested parties.

Because each revenue ruling represents the conclusion of the Service regarding the application of law to the entire statement of facts involved, taxpayers, Service personnel, and other concerned parties are cautioned against reaching the same conclusion in other cases unless the facts and circumstances are substantially the same. They should consider the effect of subsequent legislation, regulations, court decisions, revenue rulings, notices, and announcements. *See* Rev. Proc. 89–14, 1989–1 C.B, 814, as amended by Announcement 89–36, 1989–11 I.R.B. 32, which states the objectives of and standards for the publication of revenue rulings and revenue procedures in the Internal Revenue Bulletin.

Oral advice

.08 Oral guidance is advisory only, and the Service is not bound to recognize it.

(1) No oral rulings and no written rulings in response to oral requests.

The Service does not orally issue letter rulings or determination letters, nor does it issue letter rulings or determination letters in response to oral requests from taxpayers. Service employees ordinarily will discuss with taxpayers or their representatives inquiries about whether the Service will rule on particular issues and about procedural matters regarding the submission of requests for letter rulings or determination letters, or requests for recognition of exempt status for a particular organization.

(2) Discussion possible on substantive issues.

At the discretion of the Service and as time permits, Service employees may also discuss substantive issues with taxpayers or their representatives. Such a discussion will not bind the Service or the Office of Chief Counsel, and it cannot be relied upon as a basis for obtaining retroactive relief under the provisions of § 7805(b).

Service employees who are not directly involved in the examination, appeal, or litigation of particular substantive tax issues will not discuss those issues with taxpayers or their representatives unless the discussion is coordinated with Service employees who are directly involved. The taxpayer or the taxpayer's representative ordinarily will be asked whether an oral request for advice or information relates to a matter pending before another office of the Service or before a Federal court.

If a tax issue is not under examination, in appeals, or in litigation, the tax issue may be discussed even though the issue is affected by a nontax issue pending in litigation.

A taxpayer may seek oral technical guidance from a taxpayer service representative in a Field office or Service Center when preparing a return or report.

The Service does not respond to letters seeking to confirm the substance of oral discussions, and the absence of a response to such a letter is not a confirmation

(3) Oral guidance is advisory only, and the Service is not bound by it.

Oral guidance is advisory only, and the Service is not bound by it, for example, when examining the taxpayer's return.

Nonbank trustee requests	.09 In order to receive approval to act as a nonbank custodian of plans qualified under § 401(a) or accounts described in § 403(b)(7), and as a nonbank trustee or nonbank custodian for individual retirement arrangements (IRAs) established under § 408(a), (b), or (h), or for a Coverdell educational savings account established under § 530 or an Archer medical savings account established under § 220, or a Health Savings Account under § 223, a written application must be filed that demonstrates how the applicant complies with the requirements of § 1.408–2(e)(2) through (5) of the Income Tax Regulations.

The Service must have clear and convincing proof in its files that the requirements of the regulations are met. If there is a requirement that the applicant feels is not applicable, the application must provide clear and convincing proof that such requirement is not germane to the manner in which the applicant will administer any trust or custodial account. *See* § 1.408–2(e)(6).

The completed application should be sent to:

Internal Revenue Service
Commissioner, TE/GE
Attention: SE:T:EP:RA
P.O. Box 27063
McPherson Station
Washington, DC 20038

Section 6.01(10) of Rev. Proc. 2013–8 imposes a user fee for anyone applying for approval to become a nonbank trustee or custodian.

Compliance Statement	.10 A "compliance statement" is a binding written agreement between the Service and a taxpayer with respect to certain retirement plan failures identified by a taxpayer in a voluntary submission under the Voluntary Correction Program of the EPCRS (*see* Rev. Proc. 2008–50, as updated). The compliance statement addresses the failures identified in the VCP submission, the terms of correction, including any revision of administrative procedures, and the time period within which proposed corrections must be implemented. A compliance statement is conditioned on (i) there being no misstatement or omission of material facts in connection with the submission, and (ii) the implementation of the specific corrections and satisfaction of any other conditions in the compliance statement. *See* Rev. Proc. 2008–50, as updated.
Advisory letter	.11 An "advisory letter" is a written statement issued by the Service to a VS practitioner or VS mass submitter as to the acceptability of the form of a specimen plan and any related trust or custodial account under § 401(a) or § 403(a). *See* Rev. Proc. 2011–49, 2011–44 I.R.B. 608.
SECTION 4. ON WHAT ISSUES MAY TAXPAYERS REQUEST WRITTEN GUIDANCE UNDER THIS PROCEDURE?	Taxpayers may request letter rulings, information letters and closing agreements on issues within the jurisdiction of the Commissioner, Tax Exempt and Government Entities Division under this revenue procedure. The Service issues letter rulings to answer written inquiries of individuals and organizations about their status for tax purposes and the tax effects of their acts or transactions when appropriate in the interest of sound tax administration.

Taxpayers also may request determination letters that relate to Code sections under the jurisdiction of the Commissioner, Tax Exempt and Government Entities Division. *See* Rev. Proc. 2013–6, this Bulletin.

SECTION 5. ON WHAT ISSUES MUST WRITTEN GUIDANCE BE REQUESTED UNDER DIFFERENT PROCEDURES?	
Determination letters	.01 The procedures for obtaining determination letters involving §§ 401, 403(a), 409, and 4975(e)(7), and the status for exemption of any related trusts or custodial accounts under § 501(a) are contained in Rev. Proc. 2013–6, this Bulletin.
Master and prototype plans and volume submitter plans	.02 The procedures for obtaining opinion letters for master and prototype plans and any related trusts or custodial accounts under §§ 401(a), 403(a) and 501(a) and advisory letters for

volume submitter plans are contained in Rev. Proc. 2011–49. The procedures for obtaining opinion letters for prototype trusts, custodial accounts or annuities under § 408(a), (b), (k) or (p) or 408A, are contained in Rev. Proc. 87–50; Rev. Proc. 91–44; Rev. Proc. 92–38; Rev. Proc. 97–29; Rev. Proc. 98–59; Rev. Proc. 2002–10, and Rev. Proc. 2010–48, as modified by Rev. Proc. 2013–8.

Closing agreement program for defined contribution plans that purchased GICs or GACs

.03 Rev. Proc. 95–52, 1995–1 C.B. 439, restates and extends for an indefinite period the closing agreement program for defined contribution plans that purchased guaranteed investment contracts (GICs) or group annuity contracts (GACs) from troubled life insurance companies.

Employee Plans Compliance Resolution System

.04 The procedures for obtaining compliance statements, etc., for certain failures of plans qualified under § 401(a), § 403(b) plans, SEPs and § 457 plans under the Employee Plans Compliance Resolution System (EPCRS) are contained in Rev. Proc. 2008–50, as updated.

Chief Counsel

.05 The procedures for obtaining rulings, closing agreements, and information letters on issues within the jurisdiction of the Chief Counsel are contained in Rev. Proc. 2013–1, page 1, this Bulletin, including tax issues involving interpreting or applying the federal tax laws and income tax treaties relating to international transactions.

Alcohol, tobacco, and firearms taxes

.06 The procedures for obtaining letter rulings, etc., that apply to federal alcohol, tobacco, and firearms taxes under subtitle E of the Internal Revenue Code are under the jurisdiction of the Alcohol and Tobacco Tax and Trade Bureau within the Treasury Department.

SECTION 6. UNDER WHAT CIRCUMSTANCES DOES TE/GE ISSUE LETTER RULINGS?

In exempt organizations matters

.01 In exempt organizations matters, the Exempt Organizations Technical Office issues letter rulings on proposed transactions and on completed transactions if the request is submitted before the return is filed for the year in which the transaction that is the subject of the request was completed. Exempt Organizations Technical issues letter rulings involving:

(1) Organizations exempt from tax under § 501, including private foundations;

(2) Organizations described in § 170(b)(1)(A) (except clause (v));

(3) Political organizations described in § 527;

(4) Qualified tuition programs described in § 529 other than state run programs;

(5) Trusts described in § 4947(a);

(6) Other matters including issues under §§ 501 through 514, 4911, 4912, 4940 through 4948, 4955, 4958, 4976, 6033, 6104, 6113, and 6115;

(7) Harassment campaign rulings described in § 6104(d).

In employee plans matters

.02 In employee plans matters, the Employee Plans Technical Office issues letter rulings on proposed transactions and on completed transactions either before or after the return is filed. Employee Plans Technical issues letter rulings involving:

(1) §§ 72, 101(d), 219, 381(c)(11), 402, 403(b) (except with respect to whether the form of a plan satisfies the requirements of § 403(b) as noted in Ann. 2009–89), 404, 408, 408A, 412, 414(e), 419, 419A, 511 through 514, 4971, 4972, 4973, 4974, 4978, 4979, and 4980;

(2) Waiver of the minimum funding standard (*See* Rev. Proc. 2004–15, 2004–1 C.B. 490), and changes in funding methods and actuarial assumptions under §§ 412, 430 or 431;

(3) Waiver of the liquidity shortfall (as that term is defined in § 430(j)(4)) excise tax under § 4971(f)(4);

(4) Waiver under § 4980F(c)(4) of all or part of the excise tax imposed for failure to satisfy the notice requirements described in § 4980F(e);

(5) Whether a plan amendment is reasonable and provides for only *de minimis* increases in plan liabilities in accordance with §§ 401(a)(33) and 412(c)(7)(B)(i) of the Code (*See* Rev. Proc. 79–62, 1979–2 C.B. 576);

(6) A change in the plan year of an employee retirement plan and the trust year of a tax-exempt employees' trust (*See* Rev. Proc. 87–27, 1987–1 C.B. 769);

(7) The tax consequences of prohibited transactions under §§503 and 4975;

(8) Whether individual retirement accounts established by employers or associations of employees meet the requirements of § 408(c). (*See* Rev. Proc. 87–50; Rev. Proc. 92–38; Rev. Proc. 98–59; Rev. Proc. 2002–10, and Rev. Proc. 2010–48, as modified by Rev. Proc. 2013–8);

(9) With respect to employee stock ownership plans and tax credit employee stock ownership plans, §§ 409(l), 409(m), and 4975(d)(3). Other subsections of §§ 409 and 4975(e)(7) involve qualification issues within the jurisdiction of EP Determinations.

(10) Where the Commissioner, Tax Exempt and Government Entities Division has authority to grant extensions of certain periods of time within which the taxpayer must perform certain transactions (for example, the 90-day period for reinvesting in employer securities under § 1.46–8(e)(10) of the regulations), the taxpayer's request for an extension of such time period must be postmarked (or received, if hand delivered to the headquarters office) no later than the expiration of the original time period. Thus, for example, a request for an extension of the 90-day period under § 1.46–8(e)(10) must be made before the expiration of this period. However, see section 6.04 below with respect to elections under § 301.9100–1 of the Procedure and Administration Regulations.

In qualifications matters

.03 The Employee Plans Technical office ordinarily will not issue letter rulings on matters involving a plan's qualified status under §§ 401 through 420 and § 4975(e)(7). These matters are generally handled by the Employee Plans Determinations program as provided in Rev. Proc. 2013–6, this Bulletin, Rev. Proc. 93–10 and Rev. Proc. 93–12. Although the Employee Plans Technical office will not ordinarily issue rulings on matters involving plan qualification, a ruling may be issued where, (1) the taxpayer has demonstrated to the Service's satisfaction that the qualification issue involved is unique and requires immediate guidance, (2) as a practical matter, it is not likely that such issue will be addressed through the determination letter process, and (3) the Service determines that it is in the interest of good tax administration to provide guidance to the taxpayer with respect to such qualification issue.

Request for extension of time for making an election or for other relief under § 301.9100–1 of the Procedure and Administration Regulations

.04 Employee Plans Technical or Exempt Organizations Technical will consider a request for an extension of time for making an election or other application for relief under § 301.9100–1 of the Procedure and Administration Regulations even if submitted after the return covering the issue presented in the § 301.9100–1 request has been filed and even if submitted after an examination of the return has begun or after the issues in the return are being considered by an appeals office or a federal court. In such a case, EP or EO Technical will notify the Director, EP or EO Examinations.

Except for those requests pertaining to applications for recognition of exemption, § 301.9100–1 requests, even those submitted after the examination of the taxpayer's return has begun, are letter ruling requests and therefore should be submitted pursuant to this revenue procedure, and require payment of the applicable user fee, referenced in section 9.02(14) of this revenue procedure. In addition, the taxpayer must include the information required by § 301.9100–3(e).

However, an election made pursuant to § 301.9100–2 is not a letter ruling and does not require payment of any user fee. *See* § 301.9100–2(d). Such an election pertains to an automatic extension of time under § 301.9100–1.

Issuance of a letter ruling before the issuance of a regulation or other published guidance

.05 Unless the issue is covered by section 8 of this procedure, a letter ruling may be issued before the issuance of a temporary or final regulation or other published guidance that interprets the provisions of any act under the following conditions:

(1) Answer is clear or is reasonably certain. If the letter ruling request presents an issue for which the answer seems clear by applying the statute to the facts or for which the answer seems reasonably certain but not entirely free from doubt, a letter ruling will be issued.

(2) Answer is not reasonably certain. The Service will consider all letter ruling requests and use its best efforts to issue a letter ruling even if the answer does not seem reasonably certain where the issuance of a letter ruling is in the best interest of tax administration.

(3) Issue cannot be readily resolved before a regulation or any other published guidance is issued. A letter ruling will not be issued if the letter ruling request presents an issue that cannot be readily resolved before a regulation or any other published guidance is issued.

Issues in prior return

.06 The Service ordinarily does not issue rulings if, at the time the ruling is requested, the identical issue is involved in the taxpayer's return for an earlier period, and that issue:

(1) is being examined by the Director, EP or EO Examinations;

(2) is being considered by an appeals office;

(3) is pending in litigation in a case involving the taxpayer or related taxpayer; or

(4) has been examined by the Director, EP or EO Examinations or considered by an appeals office, and the statutory period of limitation has not expired for either assessment or filing a claim for a refund or a closing agreement covering the issue of liability has not been entered into by the Director, EP or EO Rulings and Agreements or by an appeals office.

If a return dealing with an issue for a particular year is filed while a request for a ruling on that issue is pending, EP or EO Technical will issue the ruling unless it is notified by the taxpayer that an examination of that issue or the identical issue on an earlier year's return has been started by the Director, EP or EO Examinations. *See* section 9.05. However, even if an examination has begun, EP or EO Technical ordinarily will issue the letter ruling if the Director, EP or EO Examinations agrees, by memorandum, to permit the ruling to be issued.

Generally not to business associations or groups

.07 EP or EO Technical does not issue letter rulings to business, trade, or industrial associations or to similar groups concerning the application of the tax laws to members of the group. But groups and associations may submit suggestions of generic issues that would be appropriately addressed in revenue rulings. *See* Rev. Proc. 89–14, 1989–1 C.B. 814, as amended by Announcement 89–36, 1989–11 I.R.B. 32, which states objectives of, and standards for, the publication of revenue rulings and revenue procedures in the Internal Revenue Bulletin.

EP or EO Technical, however, may issue letter rulings to groups or associations on their own tax status or liability if the request meets the requirements of this revenue procedure.

Generally not to foreign governments

.08 EP or EO Technical does not issue letter rulings to foreign governments or their political subdivisions about the U.S. tax effects of their laws. However, EP or EO Technical may issue letter rulings to foreign governments or their political subdivisions on their own tax status or liability under U.S. law if the request meets the requirements of this revenue procedure.

Generally not on federal tax consequences of proposed legislation

.09 EP or EO Technical does not issue letter rulings on a matter involving the federal tax consequences of any proposed federal, state, local, municipal, or foreign legislation. EP or EO Technical, however, may provide general information in response to an inquiry.

Not on certain matters under § 53.4958–6 of the Foundation and Similar Excise Taxes Regulations

.10 EO Technical does not issue letter rulings as to whether a compensation or property transaction satisfies the rebuttable presumption that the transaction is not an excess benefit transaction as described in § 53.4958–6 of the Foundation and Similar Excise Taxes Regulations.

Not on stock options

.11 EP Technical does not issue letter rulings on the income tax (including unrelated business income tax) or excise tax consequences of the contribution of stock options to, or their subsequent exercise from, plans described in Part I of Subchapter D of Subtitle A of the Code.

Generally not on EO joint venture with a for-profit organization

.12 With the exception of when the issue is present in an initial application for recognition of exemption, EO Technical does not issue letter rulings as to whether a joint venture with a for-profit organization affects an organization's exempt status or results in unrelated business income.

Not on qualification of state run programs under § 529

.13 EO Technical will not issue letter rulings as to whether a state run tuition program qualifies under § 529.

Not on UBIT issues involving certain investments of a charitable lead trust

.14 EO Technical will not issue letter rulings pertaining to unrelated business income tax issues arising when charitable lead trust assets are invested with charitable organizations.

Not on issues under § 4966 or § 4967

.15 EO Technical will not issue letter rulings under § 4966 or § 4967, as added by section 1231 of the Pension Protection Act of 2006, before the issuance of temporary or final regulations or other published guidance that interprets these provisions.

Not on issues under § 507, § 4941 or § 4945

.16 EO Technical will not issue letter rulings under § 507, § 4941 or § 4945 pertaining to the tax consequences of the termination of a charitable remainder trust (as defined in § 664) before the end of the trust term as defined in the trust's governing instrument in a transaction in which the trust beneficiaries receive their actuarial shares of the value of the trust assets.

Generally not to partnerships or limited liability companies

.17 EO Technical will not issue letter rulings to a partnership, limited liability company or other similar entity unless such entity may be liable for tax imposed by Chapter 42 of the Internal Revenue Code.

EO Technical may, however, issue letter rulings to a partner or member of a partnership or limited liability company if the request meets the requirements of this revenue procedure and the partner or member is under the jurisdiction of the Commissioner, Tax Exempt and Government Entities Division.

Not on Self-Dealing Issues Involving the Issuance of a Promissory Note by a Disqualified Person During the Administration of an Estate or Trust

.18 EO Technical will not issue letter rulings pertaining to the exception to § 4941 for transactions during the administration of an estate or trust set forth in Treas. Reg. § 53.4941(d)–1(b)(3) in cases in which a disqualified person issues a promissory note in exchange for property of an estate or trust.

SECTION 7. UNDER WHAT CIRCUMSTANCES DOES EP OR EO DETERMINATIONS ISSUE DETERMINATION LETTERS?

Circumstances under which determination letters are issued

.01 Employee Plans or Exempt Organizations Determinations issues determination letters only if the question presented is specifically answered by a statute, tax treaty, or regulation, or by a conclusion stated in a revenue ruling, opinion, or court decision published in the Internal Revenue Bulletin.

In general

.02 In employee plans matters, the EP Determinations office issues determination letters in response to taxpayers' written requests on completed transactions. However, *see* section 13.08 of this revenue procedure. A determination letter usually is not issued for a question concerning a return to be filed by the taxpayer if the same question is involved in a return under examination.

In situations involving continuing transactions, such as whether an ongoing activity is an unrelated trade or business, EP Technical would issue a ruling covering future tax periods and periods for which a return had not yet been filed.

EP Determinations does not issue determination letters on the tax consequences of proposed transactions, except as provided in sections 7.03 and 7.04 below.

Under no circumstances will EP Determinations issue a determination letter unless it is clearly shown that the request concerns a return that has been filed or is required to be filed.

In employee plans matters   .03 In employee plans matters, the Employee Plans Determinations office issues determination letters on the qualified status of employee plans under §§ 401, 403(a), 409 and 4975(e)(7), and the exempt status of any related trust under § 501. *See* Rev. Proc. 2013–6, this Bulletin.

In exempt organizations matters   .04 In exempt organizations matters, the Exempt Organizations Determinations office issues determination letters involving:

(1) Initial qualification for exempt status of organizations described in §§ 501 and 521 to the extent provided in Rev. Proc. 2013–9, the next Bulletin (including reinstatement of organizations that have been automatically revoked pursuant to § 6033(j) and subordinate organizations included in a group exemption letter that have been revoked pursuant to that provision);

(2) Updated exempt status letter to reflect changes to an organization's name or address, or to replace a lost exempt status letter, but not to approve or disapprove any completed transaction or the effect of changes in activities on exempt status, except in the situations specifically listed in paragraphs (3) through (12) below;

(3) Classification of private foundation status as provided in 2013–10, the next Bulletin;

(4) Reclassification of private foundation status, including operating foundation status described in § 4942(j)(3) and exempt operating foundation status described in § 4940(d), as provided in Rev. Proc. 2013–10, the next Bulletin;

(5) Recognition of unusual grants to certain organizations under §§ 170(b)(1)(A)(vi) and 509(a)(2);

(6) Requests for relief under § 301.9100–1 of the Procedure and Administration Regulations in connection with applications for recognition of exemption;

(7) Terminations of private foundation status under § 507(b)(1)(B);

(8) Request for a determination that a public charity described in § 509(a)(3) is described in § 509(a)(3)(i), (ii), or (iii), including whether or not a Type III supporting organization is functionally integrated. *See* Rev. Proc. 2013–10, the next Bulletin;

(9) Advance approval of certain set-asides described in § 4942(g)(2);

(10) Advance approval under § 4945 of organizations' grant making procedures;

(11) Advance approval of voter registration activities described in § 4945(f);

(12) Whether an organization is exempt from filing annual information returns under § 6033 as provided in Treas. Reg. § 1.6033–2(g)(1) and Rev. Procs. 95–48, 1995–2 C.B. 418, and 96–10, 1996–1 C.B. 577 (an organization that claims exemption from filing but is not on record with the Service as having established such exemption, by way of a determination letter under this section 7.04(12) or otherwise, may have its tax exempt status or determination letter revoked pursuant to § 6033(j) if it fails to file annual information returns);

(13) Determination of foundation status under § 509(a)(3) of non-exempt charitable trusts described in § 4947(a)(1), as provided in Rev. Proc. 2013–10, next Bulletin; and

(14) Government entity voluntary termination of § 501(c)(3) recognition (must include documentation of tax-exempt status other than under § 501(a)).

Circumstances under which determination letters are not issued	.05 EP or EO Determinations will not issue a determination letter in response to any request if—

(1) it appears that the taxpayer has directed a similar inquiry to EP or EO Technical;

(2) the same issue involving the same taxpayer or a related taxpayer is pending in a case in litigation or before an appeals office;

(3) the determination letter is requested by an industry, trade association, or similar group on behalf of individual taxpayers within the group (other than subordinate organizations covered by a group exemption letter); or

(4) the request involves an industry-wide problem.

Requests involving returns already filed

.06 A request received by the Service on a question concerning a return that is under examination, will be, in general, considered in connection with the examination of the return. If a response is made to the request before the return is examined, it will be considered a tentative finding in any later examination of that return.

Attach a copy of determination letter to taxpayer's return

.07 A taxpayer who, before filing a return, receives a determination letter about any transaction that has been consummated and that is relevant to the return being filed should attach a copy of the determination letter to the return when it is filed.

Review of determination letters

.08 Determination letters issued under sections 7.02 through 7.04 of this revenue procedure are not generally reviewed by EP or EO Technical before they are issued. If a taxpayer believes that a determination letter of this type is in error, the taxpayer may ask EP or EO Determinations to reconsider the matter or to request technical advice from EP or EO Technical as explained in Rev. Proc. 2013–5, page 170, this Bulletin.

(1) In employee plans matters, the procedures for review of determination letters relating to the qualification of employee plans involving §§ 401 and 403(a) are provided in Rev. Proc. 2013–6.

(2) In exempt organizations matters, the procedures for the review of determination letters relating to the exemption from federal income tax of certain organizations under §§ 501 and 521 are provided in Rev. Proc. 2013–9.

SECTION 8. UNDER WHAT CIRCUMSTANCES DOES THE SERVICE HAVE DISCRETION TO ISSUE LETTER RULINGS AND DETERMINATION LETTERS?

Ordinarily not in certain areas because of factual nature of the problem

.01 The Service ordinarily will not issue a letter ruling or determination letter in certain areas because of the factual nature of the problem involved or because of other reasons. The Service may decline to issue a letter ruling or a determination letter when appropriate in the interest of sound tax administration or on other grounds whenever warranted by the facts or circumstances of a particular case.

No "comfort" letter rulings

.02 No letter ruling will be issued with respect to an issue that is clearly and adequately addressed by statute, regulations, decision of a court of appropriate jurisdiction, revenue ruling, revenue procedure, notice or other authority published in the Internal Revenue Bulletin. Instead of issuing a letter ruling, the Service may, when it is considered appropriate and in the best interests of the Service, issue an information letter calling attention to well-established principles of tax law.

Not on alternative plans or hypothetical situations

.03 A letter ruling or a determination letter will not be issued on alternative plans of proposed transactions or on hypothetical situations.

Ordinarily not on part of an integrated transaction

.04 The Service ordinarily will not issue a letter ruling on only part of an integrated transaction. If, however, a part of a transaction falls under a no-rule area, a letter ruling on other parts of the transaction may be issued.

Before preparing the letter ruling request, a taxpayer should call the office having jurisdiction for the matters on which the taxpayer is seeking a letter ruling to discuss whether the Service will issue a letter ruling on part of the transaction.

Not on partial terminations of employee plans

.05 The Service will not issue a letter ruling on the partial termination of an employee plan. Determination letters involving the partial termination of an employee plan may be issued.

Law requires ruling letter

.06 The Service will issue rulings on prospective or future transactions if the law or regulations require a determination of the effect of a proposed transaction for tax purposes.

Issues under consideration by PBGC or DOL

.07 A letter ruling or determination letter relating to an issue that is being considered by the Pension Benefit Guaranty Corporation (PBGC) or the Department of Labor (DOL), and involves the same taxpayer, shall be issued at the discretion of the Service.

Cafeteria plans

.08 The Service does not issue letter rulings or determination letters on whether a cafeteria plan satisfies the requirements of § 125. *See also* Rev. Proc. 2013–3, also in this Bulletin, for areas under the jurisdiction of the Division Counsel/ Associate Chief Counsel (Tax Exempt and Government Entities) involving cafeteria plans in which advance rulings or determination letters will not be issued.

Determination letters

.09 *See* section 3.02 of Rev. Proc. 2013–6 for employee plans matters on which determination letters will not be issued.

Domicile in a foreign jurisdiction

.10

(1) The Service is ordinarily unwilling to rule in situations where a taxpayer or a related party is domiciled or organized in a foreign jurisdiction with which the United States does not have an effective mechanism for obtaining tax information with respect to civil tax examinations and criminal investigations, which would preclude the Service from obtaining information located in such jurisdiction that is relevant to the analysis or examination of the tax issues involved in the ruling request.

(2) The provisions of subsection 8.10(1) above shall not apply if the taxpayer or affected related party (a) consents to the disclosure of all relevant information requested by the Service in processing the ruling request or in the course of an examination to verify the accuracy of the representations made and to otherwise analyze or examine the tax issues involved in the ruling request, and (b) waives all claims to protection of bank and commercial secrecy laws in the foreign jurisdiction with respect to the information requested by the Service.

In the event the taxpayer's or related party's consent to disclose relevant information or to waive protection of bank or commercial secrecy is determined by the Service to be ineffective or of no force and effect, then the Service may retroactively rescind any ruling rendered in reliance on such consent.

Employee Stock Ownership Plans

.11

(1) The Service does not issue a letter ruling on whether or not the renewal, extension or refinancing of an exempt loan satisfies the requirements of § 4975(d)(3) of the Internal Revenue Code.

(2) The Service does not issue a letter ruling on whether the pre-payment of ESOP loans satisfies the requirements of § 4975(d)(3) other than with respect to plan termination.

Governmental Plans

.12 The Service does not issue a letter ruling on whether or not a plan is a governmental plan under § 414(d).

SECTION 9. WHAT ARE THE GENERAL INSTRUCTIONS FOR REQUESTING LETTER RULINGS AND DETERMINATION LETTERS?

In general

.01 This section explains the general instructions for requesting letter rulings and determination letters on all matters. Requests for letter rulings and determination letters require the payment of the applicable user fee discussed in section 9.02(14) of this revenue procedure. In addition to payment of the applicable user fee, exempt organizations determinations requests described in section 7.04(3), (4), (5), (7), (8), (9), (10), (11), (12), and (13) of this revenue procedure must be accompanied by Form 8940.

Specific and additional instructions also apply to requests for letter rulings and determination letters on certain matters. Those matters are listed in section 10 of this revenue procedure followed by a reference (usually to another revenue procedure) where more information can be obtained.

All requests must be submitted in English. All documents submitted in support of such requests must be in English, or accompanied by an English translation. For EO submissions only, *see* Forms 1023 and 1024 Instructions.

Certain information required in all requests

.02

Facts

(1) **Complete statement of facts and other information.** Each request for a letter ruling or a determination letter must contain a complete statement of all facts relating to the transaction. These facts include—

(a) names, addresses, telephone numbers, and taxpayer identification numbers of all interested parties. (The term "all interested parties" does not mean all shareholders of a widely held corporation requesting a letter ruling relating to a reorganization, or all employees where a large number may be involved.);

(b) a complete statement of the business reasons for the transaction; and

(c) a detailed description of the transaction.

The Service will usually not rule on only one step of a larger integrated transaction. *See* section 8.04 of this revenue procedure. However, if such a letter ruling is requested, the facts, circumstances, true copies of relevant documents, etc., relating to the entire transaction must be submitted.

Documents

(2) **Copies of all contracts, wills, deeds, agreements, instruments, plan documents, and other documents.** All documents that are pertinent to the transaction (including contracts, wills, deeds, agreements, instruments, plan documents, trust documents, and proposed disclaimers) must be submitted with the request.

Original documents **should not be submitted** because they become part of the Service's file and will not be returned to the taxpayer. Instead, true copies of all such documents should be submitted with the request. Each document, other than the request, should be labeled alphabetically and attached to the request in alphabetical order.

Analysis of material facts

(3) **Analysis of material facts.** All material facts in documents must be included rather than merely incorporated by reference, in the taxpayer's initial request or in supplemental letters. These facts must be accompanied by an analysis of their bearing on the issue or issues, specifying the provisions that apply.

Same issue in an earlier return

(4) **Statement regarding whether same issue is in an earlier return.** The request must state whether, to the best of the knowledge of both the taxpayer and the taxpayer's representatives, the same issue is in an earlier return of the taxpayer (or in a return for any year of a

related taxpayer within the meaning of § 267, or of a member of an affiliated group of which the taxpayer is also a member within the meaning of § 1504).

If the statement is affirmative, it must specify whether the issue—

(a) is being examined by the Service;

(b) has been examined and if so, whether or not the statutory period of limitations has expired for either assessing tax or filing a claim for refund or credit of tax;

(c) has been examined and if so, whether or not a closing agreement covering the issue or liability has been entered into by the Service;

(d) is being considered by an appeals office in connection with a return from an earlier period;

(e) has been considered by an appeals office in connection with a return from an earlier period and if so, whether or not the statutory period of limitations has expired for either assessing tax or filing a claim for refund or credit of tax;

(f) has been considered by an appeals office in connection with a return from an earlier period and whether or not a closing agreement covering the issue or liability has been entered into by an appeals office;

(g) is pending in litigation in a case involving the taxpayer or a related taxpayer; or

(h) in employee plans matters, is being considered by the Pension Benefit Guaranty Corporation or the Department of Labor.

Same or similar issue previously submitted or currently pending

(5) **Statement regarding whether same or similar issue was previously ruled on or requested, or is currently pending.** The request must also state whether, to the best of the knowledge of both the taxpayer and the taxpayer's representatives—

(a) the Service previously ruled on the same or similar issue for the taxpayer (or a related taxpayer within the meaning of § 267, or a member of an affiliated group of which the taxpayer is also a member within the meaning of § 1504) or a predecessor;

(b) the taxpayer, a related taxpayer, a predecessor, or any representatives previously submitted the same or similar issue to the Service but withdrew the request before a letter ruling or determination letter was issued;

(c) the taxpayer, a related taxpayer, or a predecessor previously submitted a request involving the same or a similar issue that is currently pending with the Service; or

(d) at the same time as this request, the taxpayer or a related taxpayer is presently submitting another request involving the same or a similar issue to the Service.

If the statement is affirmative for (a), (b), (c), or (d) of this section 9.02(5), the statement must give the date the request was submitted, the date the request was withdrawn or ruled on, if applicable, and other details of the Service's consideration of the issue.

Statement of authorities supporting taxpayer's views

(6) **Statement of supporting authorities.** If the taxpayer advocates a particular conclusion, an explanation of the grounds for that conclusion and the relevant authorities to support it must also be included. Even if not advocating a particular tax treatment of a proposed transaction, the taxpayer must still furnish views on the tax results of the proposed transaction and a statement of relevant authorities to support those views.

In all events, the request must include a statement of whether the law in connection with the request is uncertain and whether the issue is adequately addressed by relevant authorities.

Statement of authorities contrary to taxpayer's views

(7) **Statement of contrary authorities.** The taxpayer is also encouraged to inform the Service about, and discuss the implications of, any authority believed to be contrary to the position

advanced, such as legislation (or pending legislation), tax treaties, court decisions, regulations, revenue rulings, revenue procedures, notices or announcements. If the taxpayer determines that there are no contrary authorities, a statement in the request to this effect would be helpful. If the taxpayer does not furnish either contrary authorities or a statement that none exists, the Service in complex cases or those presenting difficult or novel issues may request submission of contrary authorities or a statement that none exists. Failure to comply with this request may result in the Service's refusal to issue a letter ruling or determination letter.

Identifying and discussing contrary authorities will generally enable Service personnel to understand the issue and relevant authorities more quickly. When Service personnel receive the request, they will have before them the taxpayer's thinking on the effect and applicability of contrary authorities. This information should make research easier and lead to earlier action by the Service. If the taxpayer does not disclose and distinguish significant contrary authorities, the Service may need to request additional information, which will delay action on the request.

Statement identifying pending legislation

(8) Statement identifying pending legislation. At the time of filing the request, the taxpayer must identify any pending legislation that may affect the proposed transaction. In addition, if applicable legislation is introduced after the request is filed but before a letter ruling or determination letter is issued, the taxpayer must notify the Service.

Deletions statement required by § 6110

(9) Statement identifying information to be deleted from copy of letter ruling or determination letter for public inspection. The text of certain letter rulings and determination letters is open to public inspection under § 6110. The Service makes deletions from the text before it is made available for inspection. To help the Service make the deletions required by § 6110(c), a request for a letter ruling or determination letter must be accompanied by a statement indicating the deletions desired ("deletions statement"). If the deletions statement is not submitted with the request, a Service representative will tell the taxpayer that the request will be closed if the Service does not receive the deletions statement within 30 calendar days. *See* section 11.03 of this revenue procedure.

(a) Format of deletions statement. A taxpayer who wants only names, addresses, and identifying numbers to be deleted should state this in the deletions statement. If the taxpayer wants more information deleted, the deletions statement must be accompanied by a copy of the request and supporting documents on which the taxpayer should bracket the material to be deleted. The deletions statement must indicate the statutory basis under § 6110(c) for each proposed deletion.

If the taxpayer decides to ask for additional deletions before the letter ruling or determination letter is issued, additional deletions statements may be submitted.

(b) Location of deletions statement. The deletions statement must not appear in the request, but instead must be made in a separate document and placed on top of the request for a letter ruling or determination letter.

(c) Signature. The deletions statement must be signed and dated by the taxpayer or the taxpayer's authorized representative. A stamped or faxed signature is not permitted.

(d) Additional information. The taxpayer should follow the same procedures above to propose deletions from any additional information submitted after the initial request. An additional deletions statement, however, is not required with each submission of additional information if the taxpayer's initial deletions statement requests that only names, addresses, and identifying numbers are to be deleted and the taxpayer wants only the same information deleted from the additional information.

(e) Taxpayer may protest deletions not made. After receiving from the Service the notice under § 6110(f)(1) of intention to disclose the letter ruling or determination letter (including a copy of the version proposed to be open to public inspection and notation of third-party communications under § 6110(d)), the taxpayer may protest the disclosure of certain information in the letter ruling or determination letter. The taxpayer must send a written statement within 20 calendar days to the Service office indicated on the notice of intention to disclose. The statement must identify those deletions that the Service has not made and that the taxpayer believes should have been made. The taxpayer must also submit a copy of the version of the letter ruling or determination letter and bracket the deletions proposed that have not been made by the Service. Generally, the Service will not consider deleting any material that the taxpayer did not propose to be deleted before the letter ruling or determination letter was issued.

Within 20 calendar days after the Service receives the response to the notice under § 6110(f)(1), the Service will mail to the taxpayer its final administrative conclusion regarding the deletions to be made. The taxpayer does not have the right to a conference to resolve any disagreements concerning material to be deleted from the text of the letter ruling or determination letter. However, these matters may be taken up at any conference that is otherwise scheduled regarding the request.

(f) Taxpayer may request delay of public inspection. After receiving the notice under § 6110(f)(1) of intention to disclose, but within 60 calendar days after the date of notice, the taxpayer may send a request for delay of public inspection under either § 6110(g)(3) or (4). The request for delay must be sent to the Service office indicated on the notice of intention to disclose. A request for delay under § 6110(g)(3) must contain the date on which it is expected that the underlying transaction will be completed. The request for delay under § 6110(g)(4) must contain a statement from which the Commissioner of Internal Revenue may determine that there are good reasons for the delay.

Section 6110(l)(1) states that § 6110 disclosure provisions do not apply to any matter to which § 6104 applies. Therefore, letter rulings, determination letters, technical advice memoranda, and related background file documents dealing with the following matters (covered by § 6104) are not subject to § 6110 disclosure provisions—

(i) An approved application for exemption under § 501(a) as an organization described in § 501(c) or (d), or notice of status as a political organization under § 527, together with any papers submitted in support of such application or notice;

(ii) An application for exemption under § 501(a) with respect to the qualification of a pension, profit-sharing or stock bonus plan, or an individual retirement account described in § 408 or § 408A, whether the plan or account has more than 25 or less than 26 participants, or any application for exemption under § 501(a) by an organization forming part of such a plan or an account;

(iii) Any document issued by the Internal Revenue Service in which the qualification or exempt status of a plan or account is granted, denied, or revoked or the portion of any document in which technical advice with respect thereto is given;

(iv) Any application filed and any document issued by the Internal Revenue Service with respect to the qualification or status of EP master and prototype plans; and

(v) The portion of any document issued by the Internal Revenue Service with respect to the qualification or exempt status of a plan or account of a proposed transaction by such plan or account.

Signature on request

(10) Signature by taxpayer or authorized representative. The request for a letter ruling or determination letter must be signed and dated by the taxpayer or the taxpayer's authorized representative. Neither a stamped signature nor a faxed signature is permitted. Special rules apply in the case of a request for a determination letter made by filing Form 1023; please see the instructions to that Form for who may sign the application on behalf of an organization.

Authorized representatives

(11) Authorized representatives. To sign the request or to appear before the Service in connection with the request, the representative must be:

Attorney

(a) An attorney who is a member in good standing of the bar of the highest court of any state, possession, territory, commonwealth, or the District of Columbia and who is not currently under suspension or disbarment from practice before the Service. He or she must file a written declaration with the Service showing current qualification as an attorney and current authorization to represent the taxpayer;

Certified public accountant

(b) A certified public accountant who is qualified to practice in any state, possession, territory, commonwealth, or the District of Columbia and who is not currently under suspension or disbarment from practice before the Service. He or she must file a written declaration with the Service showing current qualification as a certified public accountant and current authorization to represent the taxpayer;

Enrolled agent

(c) An enrolled agent who is a person, other than an attorney or certified public accountant, that is currently enrolled to practice before the Service and is not currently under suspension or disbarment from practice before the Service, including a person enrolled to practice only for employee plans matters. He or she must file a written declaration with the Service showing current enrollment and authorization to represent the taxpayer. Either the enrollment number or the expiration date of the enrollment card must be included in the declaration. For the rules on who may practice before the Service, *see* Treasury Department Circular No. 230;

Enrolled actuary

(d) An enrolled actuary who is a person enrolled as an actuary by the Joint Board for the Enrollment of Actuaries pursuant to 29 U.S.C. 1242 and qualified to practice in any state, possession, territory, commonwealth, or the District of Columbia and who is not currently under suspension or disbarment from practice before the Service. He or she must file a written declaration with the Service showing current qualification as an enrolled actuary and current authorization to represent the taxpayer. Practice as an enrolled actuary is limited to representation with respect to issues involving the following statutory provisions: §§ 401, 403(a), 404, 412, 413, 414, 419, 419A, 420, 430, 431, 432, 436, 4971, 4972, 6057, 6058, 6059, 6652(d), 6652(e), 6692, 7805(b), former § 405 and 29 U.S.C. 1083;

Enrolled Retirement Plan Agent

(e) An enrolled retirement plan agent (ERPA) is an individual who has earned the privilege to practice before the Service. The ERPA program is established under Circular 230 of the U.S. Department of the Treasury and is administered by the Office of Professional Responsibility (the "OPR"). The Director of the OPR may grant enrollment as an ERPA to an applicant who demonstrates special competence in qualified retirement plan matters (by either passing a written examination or by virtue of past service and technical experience with the Service) and who has not engaged in any conduct that would justify the censure, suspension or disbarment of the practitioner. An ERPA must apply for enrollment with the Service, have been issued an enrollment card and satisfy renewal and continuing education requirements.

Practice as an ERPA is limited to representation with respect to issues involving the following programs: Employee Plans Determination Letter program; Employee Plans Compliance Resolution System; and Employee Plans Master and Prototype and Volume Submitter program. In addition, ERPAs are generally permitted to represent taxpayers with respect to Form 5300 series and Form 5500 filings, but not with respect to actuarial forms or schedules. For eligibility, application and enrollment information, see §§ 10.4, 10.5 and 10.6 of Circular 230;

A person with a "Letter of Authorization"

(f) Any other person, including a foreign representative who has received a "Letter of Authorization" from the Director, Office of Professional Responsibility under section 10.7(d) of Treasury Department Circular No. 230. A person may make a written request for a "Letter of Authorization" to: Office of Director, Office of Professional Responsibility, Internal Revenue Service, 1111 Constitution Avenue, N.W., Washington, DC 20224. Section 10.7(d) of Circular No. 230 authorizes the Commissioner to allow an individual who is not otherwise eligible to practice before the Service to represent another person in a particular matter. For additional information, see section 9.02(12) below;

Employee, general partner, bona fide officer, administrator, trustee, etc.

(g) The above requirements do not apply to a regular full-time employee representing his or her employer, to a general partner representing his or her partnership, to a *bona fide* officer representing his or her corporation, association, or organized group, to a trustee, receiver, guardian, personal representative, administrator, or executor representing a trust, receivership, guardianship, or estate, or to an individual representing his or her immediate family. A preparer of a return (other than a person referred to in paragraph (a), (b), (c), (d) or (e) of this section

9.02(11)) who is not a full-time employee, general partner, a *bona fide* officer, an administrator, trustee, etc., or an individual representing his or her immediate family may not represent a taxpayer in connection with a letter ruling, determination letter or a technical advice request. *See* section 10.7(c) of Treasury Department Circular No. 230;

Foreign representative

(h) A foreign representative (other than a person referred to in paragraph (a), (b), (c), (d) or (e) of this section 9.02(11)) is not authorized to practice before the Service and, therefore, must withdraw from representing a taxpayer in a request for a letter ruling or a determination letter. In this situation, the nonresident alien or foreign entity must submit the request for a letter ruling or a determination letter on the individual's or entity's own behalf or through a person referred to in paragraph (a), (b), (c), (d) or (e) of this section 9.02(11).

Power of attorney and declaration of representative

(12) Power of attorney and declaration of representative. Any authorized representative, whether or not enrolled to practice, must also comply with the conference and practice requirements of the Statement of Procedural Rules (26 C.F.R. § 601.501–601.509 (*2005*)), which provide the rules for representing a taxpayer before the Service. In addition, an unenrolled preparer must file a Form 8821 (Rev. August 2008), *Tax Information Authorization*, for certain limited employee plans matters.

Form 2848 (Rev. March 2012), *Power of Attorney and Declaration of Representative*, must be used to provide the representative's authorization (Part I of Form 2848, Power of Attorney) and the representative's qualification (Part II of Form 2848, Declaration of Representative). The name of the person signing Part I of Form 2848 should also be typed or printed on this form. A stamped signature is not permitted. An original, a copy, or a facsimile transmission (fax) of the power of attorney is acceptable so long as its authenticity is not reasonably disputed. For additional information regarding the power of attorney form, *see* section 9.03(2) of this revenue procedure.

For the requirement regarding compliance with Treasury Department Circular No. 230, *see* section 9.09 of this revenue procedure.

Penalties of perjury statement

(13) Penalties of perjury statement.

(a) Format of penalties of perjury statement. A request for a letter ruling or determination letter and any change in the request submitted at a later time must be accompanied by the following declaration: **"Under penalties of perjury, I declare that I have examined this request, or this modification to the request, including accompanying documents, and, to the best of my knowledge and belief, the request or the modification contains all the relevant facts relating to the request, and such facts are true, correct, and complete."** See section 11.04 of this revenue procedure for the penalties of perjury statement applicable for submissions of additional information.

(b) Signature by taxpayer. The declaration must be signed and dated by the taxpayer, not the taxpayer's representative. Neither a stamped signature nor a faxed signature is permitted.

The person who signs for a corporate taxpayer must be an officer of the corporate taxpayer who has personal knowledge of the facts, and whose duties are not limited to obtaining a letter ruling or determination letter from the Service. If the corporate taxpayer is a member of an affiliated group filing consolidated returns, a penalties of perjury statement must also be signed and submitted by an officer of the common parent of the group.

The person signing for a trust, a state law partnership, or a limited liability company must be, respectively, a trustee, general partner, or member-manager who has personal knowledge of the facts.

Applicable user fee

(14) Applicable user fee. Section 7528 of the Code requires taxpayers to pay user fees for requests for rulings, opinion letters, determination letters, and similar requests. Rev. Proc. 2013–8 contains the schedule of fees for each type of request under the jurisdiction of the Commissioner, Tax Exempt and Government Entities Division and provides guidance for administering the user fee requirements. If two or more taxpayers are parties to a transaction and each requests a letter ruling, each taxpayer must satisfy the rules herein and additional user fees may apply.

Number of copies of request to be submitted

(15) **Number of copies of request to be submitted.** Generally a taxpayer needs only to submit one copy of the request for a letter ruling or determination letter. If, however, more than one issue is presented in the letter ruling request, the taxpayer is encouraged to submit additional copies of the request

Further, two copies of the request for a letter ruling or determination letter are required if—

(a) the taxpayer is requesting separate letter rulings or determination letters on different issues as explained later under section 9.03(1) of this revenue procedure;

(b) the taxpayer is requesting deletions other than names, addresses, and identifying numbers, as explained in section 9.02(9) of this revenue procedure. (One copy is the request for the letter ruling or determination letter and the second copy is the deleted version of such request.); or

(c) a closing agreement (as defined in section 3.03 of this revenue procedure) is being requested on the issue presented.

Sample of a letter ruling request

(16) **Sample format for a letter ruling request.** To assist a taxpayer or the taxpayer's representative in preparing a letter ruling request, a sample format for a letter ruling request is provided in Appendix A. This format is not required to be used by the taxpayer or the taxpayer's representative. If the letter ruling request is not identical or similar to the format in Appendix A, the different format will neither defer consideration of the letter ruling request nor be cause for returning the request to the taxpayer or taxpayer's representative.

Checklist

(17) **Checklist for letter ruling requests.** The Service will be able to respond more quickly to a taxpayer's letter ruling request if it is carefully prepared and complete. The checklist in Appendix B of this revenue procedure is designed to assist taxpayers in preparing a request by reminding them of the essential information and documents to be furnished with the request. The checklist in Appendix B must be completed to the extent required by the instructions in the checklist, signed and dated by the taxpayer or the taxpayer's representative, and placed on top of the letter ruling request. If the checklist in Appendix B is not received, a group representative will ask the taxpayer or the taxpayer's representative to submit the checklist, which may delay action on the letter ruling request. A photocopy of this checklist may be used.

Additional information required in certain circumstances

.03

Multiple issues

(1) **To request separate letter rulings for multiple issues in a single situation.** If more than one issue is presented in a request for a letter ruling, the Service generally will issue a single ruling letter covering all the issues. However, if the taxpayer requests separate letter rulings on any of the issues (because, for example, one letter ruling is needed sooner than another), the Service will usually comply with the request unless it is not feasible or not in the best interests of the Service to do so. A taxpayer who wants separate letter rulings on multiple issues should make this clear in the request and submit two copies of the request. Additional checklists are solely for the specific issues designated.

In issuing each letter ruling, the Service will state that it has issued separate letter rulings or that requests for other letter rulings are pending.

Power of attorney

(2) **Recipient of original letter ruling or determination letter.** The Service will send the original of the letter ruling or determination letter to the taxpayer and a copy of the letter ruling or determination letter to the taxpayer's representative. In this case, the letter ruling or determination letter is addressed to the taxpayer. A Form 2848, *Power of Attorney and Declaration of Representative* (Rev. March 2012), must be used to provide the representative's authorization except in certain employee plans matters. *See* section 9.02(12) of this revenue procedure.

Copies of letter ruling or determination letter sent to multiple representatives

(a) To have copies sent to multiple representatives. When a taxpayer has more than one representative, the Service will send the copy of the letter ruling or determination letter to any representative with a check in the box in the name and address block on Form 2848 to indicate they are to receive notices and communications. Copies of the letter ruling or determination letter, however, will be sent to no more than two representatives.

Copy of letter ruling or determination letter sent to taxpayer's representative

(b) To have copy sent to taxpayer's representative. A copy of the letter ruling or determination letter will be sent to any representative with a check in the box in the name and address block on Form 2848 to indicate they are to receive notices and communications

Expedited handling

(3) To request expedited handling. The Service ordinarily processes requests for letter rulings and determination letters in order of the date received. Expedited handling means that a request is processed ahead of the regular order. Expedited handling is granted only in rare and unusual cases, both out of fairness to other taxpayers and because the Service seeks to process all requests as expeditiously as possible and to give appropriate deference to normal business exigencies in all cases not involving expedited handling.

A taxpayer who has a compelling need to have a request processed ahead of the regular order may request expedited handling. This request must explain in detail the need for expedited handling. The request must be made in writing, preferably in a separate letter with, or soon after filing, the request for the letter ruling or determination letter. If the request is not made in a separate letter, then the letter in which the letter ruling or determination letter request is made should say, at the top of the first page: **"Expedited Handling Is Requested. See page ___ of this letter."**

A request for expedited handling will not be forwarded to the appropriate group for action until the check or money order for the user fee in the correct amount is received.

Whether the request will be granted is within the Service's discretion. The Service may grant a request when a factor outside a taxpayer's control creates a real business need to obtain a letter ruling or determination letter before a certain time in order to avoid serious business consequences. Examples include situations in which a court or governmental agency has imposed a specific deadline for the completion of a transaction, or a transaction must be completed expeditiously to avoid an imminent business emergency (such as the hostile takeover of a corporate taxpayer), provided that the taxpayer can demonstrate that the deadline or business emergency, and the need for expedited handling, resulted from circumstances that could not reasonably have been anticipated or controlled by the taxpayer. To qualify for expedited handling in such situations, the taxpayer must also demonstrate that the taxpayer submitted the request as promptly as possible after becoming aware of the deadline or emergency. The extent to which the letter ruling or determination letter complies with all of the applicable requirements of this revenue procedure, and fully and clearly presents the issues, is a factor in determining whether expedited treatment will be granted. When the Service agrees to process a request out of order, it cannot give assurance that any letter ruling or determination letter will be processed by the time requested. The scheduling of a closing date for a transaction or a meeting of the board of directors or shareholders of a corporation, without regard for the time it may take to obtain a letter ruling or determination letter, will not be considered a sufficient reason to process a request ahead of its regular order. Also, the possible effect of fluctuation in the market price of stocks on a transaction will not be considered a sufficient reason to process a request out of order.

Because most requests for letter rulings and determination letters cannot be processed ahead of their regular order, the Service urges all taxpayers to submit their requests well in advance of the contemplated transaction. In addition, in order to facilitate prompt action on letter ruling requests taxpayers are encouraged to ensure that their initial submissions comply with all of the requirements of this revenue procedure (including the requirements of other applicable guidelines set forth in section 10 of this revenue procedure), and to provide any additional information requested by the Service promptly.

Facsimile transmission (fax)

(4) To receive a letter ruling or submit a request for a letter ruling by facsimile transmission (fax).

(a) To receive a letter ruling by fax. A letter ruling ordinarily is not sent by fax. However, if the taxpayer requests, a copy of a letter ruling may be faxed to the taxpayer or the taxpayer's authorized representative. A letter ruling, however, is not issued until the ruling is mailed. *See* § 301.6110–2(h).

A request to fax a copy of the letter ruling to the taxpayer or the taxpayer's authorized representative must be made in writing, either as part of the original letter ruling request or prior to the approval of the letter ruling. The request must contain the fax number of the taxpayer or the taxpayer's authorized representative to whom the letter ruling is to be faxed.

The Service will take certain precautions to protect confidential information. For example, the Service will use a cover sheet that identifies the intended recipient of the fax and the number of pages transmitted. The cover sheet, if possible, will not identify the specific taxpayer by name, and it will be the first page covering the letter ruling being faxed.

(b) To submit a request for a letter ruling by fax. Original letter ruling requests sent by fax are discouraged because such requests must be treated in the same manner as requests by letter. For example, the faxed letter ruling request will not be forwarded to the applicable office for action until the check for the user fee is received.

Requesting a conference

(5) To request a conference. A taxpayer who wants to have a conference on the issues involved should indicate this in writing when, or soon after, filing the request. *See also* sections 12.01, 12.02, and 13.09(2) of this revenue procedure.

Address to send the request   .04

Requests for letter rulings

(1) Requests for letter rulings should be sent to the following offices (as appropriate):

> Internal Revenue Service
> Attention: EP Letter Rulings
> P.O. Box 27063
> McPherson Station
> Washington, D.C. 20038

> Internal Revenue Service
> Attention: EO Letter Rulings
> P.O. Box 27720
> McPherson Station
> Washington, D.C. 20038

Hand delivered requests must be marked RULING REQUEST SUBMISSION. The delivery should be made between the hours of 8:30 a.m. and 4:00 p.m.; where a receipt will be given:

> Courier's Desk
> Internal Revenue Service
> Attention: SE:T:EP:RA [for employee plans] or
> SE:T:EO:RA [for exempt organizations]
> 1111 Constitution Avenue, N.W. — NCA
> Washington, D.C. 20224

Requests for information letters

(2) Requests for information letters on either employee plans matters or exempt organizations matters should be sent to Employee Plans or Exempt Organizations (as appropriate):

Internal Revenue Service
Commissioner, TE/GE
Attention: SE:T:EP:RA or SE:T:EO:RA
1111 Constitution Avenue, N.W. — NCA
Washington, D.C. 20224

Requests for determination letters

(3) Requests for either (i) EP determination letters or (ii) EO determination letters that **are subject to a user fee** should be sent to:

Internal Revenue Service
P.O. Box 12192
Covington, KY 41012–0192

Requests for EO determination letters that are **not subject to a user fee** should be sent to:

Internal Revenue Service
P.O. Box 2508
Rm. 4024
Cincinnati, OH 45201

Requests for EO determination letters described in section 7.04(14) should be sent to:

Internal Revenue Service
Attn: Correspondence Unit
P.O. Box 2508
Cincinnati, OH 45201

For user fees required with determination letter requests, see section 6 of Rev. Proc. 2013–8.

Pending letter ruling requests

.05

(1) Circumstances under which the taxpayer must notify EP or EO Technical. The taxpayer must notify EP or EO Technical if, after the letter ruling request is filed but before a letter ruling is issued, the taxpayer knows that—

(a) an examination of the issue or the identical issue on an earlier year's return has been started by an EP or EO Examinations office;

(b) in employee plans matters, the issue is being considered by the Pension Benefit Guaranty Corporation or the Department of Labor; or

(c) legislation that may affect the transaction has been introduced (*see* section 9.02(8) of this revenue procedure).

(2) Taxpayer must notify EP or EO Technical if return is filed and must attach request to return. If the taxpayer files a return before a letter ruling is received from EP or EO Technical concerning the issue, the taxpayer must notify EP or EO Technical that the return has been filed. The taxpayer must also attach a copy of the letter ruling request to the return to alert the EP or EO Examinations office and thereby avoid premature EP or EO Examinations office action on the issue.

When to attach letter ruling to return

.06 A taxpayer who receives a letter ruling before filing a return about any transaction that is relevant to the return being filed must attach a copy of the letter ruling to the return when it is filed.

How to check on status of request

.07 The taxpayer or the taxpayer's authorized representative may obtain information regarding the status of a request by calling the person whose name and telephone number are shown on the acknowledgement of receipt of the request.

Request may be withdrawn or EP or EO Technical may decline to issue letter ruling

.08

(1) In general. A taxpayer may withdraw a request for a letter ruling or determination letter at any time before the letter ruling or determination letter is signed by the Service. However, withdrawal in exempt organization matters is limited by section 6 of Rev. Proc. 2013–9, next Bulletin. Correspondence and exhibits related to a request that is withdrawn or related to a letter ruling request for which the Service declines to issue a letter ruling will not be returned to the taxpayer. *See* section 9.02(2) of this revenue procedure. In appropriate cases, the Service may publish its conclusions in a revenue ruling or revenue procedure.

A request for a letter ruling will not be suspended in EP or EO Technical at the request of a taxpayer.

(2) Notification of Director, EP or EO Examinations. If a taxpayer withdraws a request for a letter ruling or if EP or EO Technical declines to issue a letter ruling, EP or EO Technical will notify the Director, EP or EO Examinations and may give its views on the issues in the request to the Director, EP or EO Examinations to consider in any later examination of the return.

(3) Refunds of user fee. The user fee will not be returned for a letter ruling request that is withdrawn. If the Service declines to issue a letter ruling on all of the issues in the request, the user fee will be returned. If the Service, however, issues a letter ruling on some, but not all, of the issues, the user fee will not be returned. *See* section 10 of Rev. Proc. 2013–8 for additional information regarding refunds of user fees.

Compliance with Treasury Department Circular No. 230

.09 The taxpayer's authorized representative, whether or not enrolled, must comply with Treasury Department Circular No. 230, which provides the rules for practice before the Service. In those situations when EP or EO Technical believes that the taxpayer's representative is not in compliance with Circular No. 230, EP or EO Technical will bring the matter to the attention of the Director, Office of Professional Responsibility.

For the requirement regarding compliance with the conference and practice requirements, see section 9.02(12) of this revenue procedure.

SECTION 10. WHAT SPECIFIC, ADDITIONAL PROCEDURES APPLY TO CERTAIN REQUESTS?

In general

.01 Specific revenue procedures and notices supplement the general instructions for requests explained in section 9 of this revenue procedure and apply to requests for letter rulings or determination letters regarding the Code sections and matters listed in this section.

Exempt Organizations

.02 If the request is for the qualification of an organization for exemption from federal income tax under § 501 or 521, *see* Rev. Proc. 72–5, 1972–1 C.B. 709, regarding religious and apostolic organizations; Rev. Proc. 80–27, 1980–1 C.B. 677, concerning group exemptions; Rev. Proc. 2013–9, next Bulletin, regarding applications for recognition of exemption, determinations for which § 7428 applies, and conference protest and appeal rights; Rev. Proc. 2013–10, next Bulletin, regarding determinations of private foundation status; and Notice 2011–44, 2011–25 I.R.B. 883, regarding applications for reinstatement of tax-exempt status and requesting retroactive reinstatement under § 6033(j) of the Code.

Employee Plans

.03

(1) For requests to obtain approval for a retroactive amendment described in § 412(d)(2) of the Code and section 302(d)(2) of the Employee Retirement Income Security Act of 1974 (ERISA) that reduces accrued benefits, see Rev. Proc. 94–42, 1994–1 C.B. 717.

(2) For requests for a waiver of the minimum funding standard, see Rev. Proc. 2004–15, 2004–1 C.B. 490.

(3) For requests for a waiver of the 100 percent tax imposed under § 4971(b) of the Code on a pension plan that fails to meet the minimum funding standards of § 412, see Rev. Proc. 81–44, 1981–2 C.B. 618.

(4) For requests for a determination that a plan amendment is reasonable and provides for only *de minimis* increases in plan liabilities in accordance with §§ 401(a)(33) and 412(c)(7)(B)(i), see Rev. Proc. 79–62, 1979–2 C.B. 576.

(5) For requests to obtain approval for an extension of an amortization period of any unfunded liability in accordance with §§ 431(d) of the Code and 304(d) of ERISA, see Rev. Proc. 2010–52, 2010–52 I.R.B. 927.

(6) For requests by administrators or sponsors of a defined benefit plan to obtain approval for a change in funding method, see Rev. Proc. 2000–41, 2000–2 C.B. 371.

(7) For requests for the return to the employer of certain nondeductible contributions, see Rev. Proc. 90–49, 1990–2 C.B. 620 (as modified by Rev. Proc. 2013–8).

(8) For requests for determination letters for plans under §§ 401, 403(a), 409, and 4975(e)(7), and for the exempt status of any related trust under § 501, see Rev. Proc. 2013–6, Rev. Proc. 93–10, 1993–1 C.B. 476 and Rev. Proc. 93–12, 1993–1 C.B. 479.

(9) For requests under § 414(e) relating to church plans, see Rev. Proc. 2011–44, 2011–39, I.R.B. 446.

SECTION 11. HOW DOES EP OR EO TECHNICAL HANDLE LETTER RULING REQUESTS?

In general

.01 The Service will issue letter rulings on the matters and under the circumstances explained in sections 4 and 6 of this revenue procedure and in the manner explained in this section and section 13 of this revenue procedure.

Is not bound by informal opinion expressed

.02 The Service will not be bound by the informal opinion expressed by the group representative or any other authorized Service representative under this procedure, and such an opinion cannot be relied upon as a basis for obtaining retroactive relief under the provisions of § 7805(b).

Tells taxpayer if request lacks essential information during initial contact

.03 If a request for a letter ruling or determination letter does not comply with all the provisions of this revenue procedure, the request will be acknowledged and the Service representative will tell the taxpayer during the initial contact which requirements have not been met.

Information must be submitted within 30 calendar days

If the request lacks essential information, which may include additional information needed to satisfy the procedural requirements of this revenue procedure, as well as substantive changes to transactions or documents needed from the taxpayer, the Service representative will tell the taxpayer during the initial contact that the request will be closed if the Service does not receive the information within 30 calendar days unless an extension of time is granted. *See* section 11.04 of this revenue procedure for information on extension of time and instructions on submissions of additional information.

Letter ruling request mistakenly sent to EP or EO Determinations Processing

A request for a letter ruling sent to EP/EO Determinations Processing that does not comply with the provisions of this revenue procedure will be returned by EP/EO Determinations Processing so that the taxpayer can make corrections before sending it to EP or EO Technical.

Requires prompt submission of additional information requested after initial contact

.04 Material facts furnished to the Service by telephone or fax, or orally at a conference, must be promptly confirmed by letter to the Service. This confirmation and any additional information requested by the Service that is not part of the information requested during the initial contact must be furnished within 21 calendar days to be considered part of the request.

Additional information submitted to the Service must be accompanied by the following declaration: **"Under penalties of perjury, I declare that I have examined this information, including accompanying documents, and, to the best of my knowledge and belief, the information contains all the relevant facts relating to the request for the information, and such facts are true, correct, and complete."** This declaration must be signed in accordance with the requirements in section 9.02(13)(b) of this revenue procedure. A taxpayer who submits additional factual information on several occasions may provide one declaration subsequent to all submissions that refers to all submissions.

Encourage use of fax

(1) To facilitate prompt action on letter ruling requests, taxpayers are encouraged to submit additional information by fax as soon as the information is available. The Service representative who requests additional information can provide a telephone number to which the information can be faxed. A copy of this information and a signed perjury statement, however, must be mailed or delivered to the Service.

Address to send additional information

(2) Additional information should be sent to the same address as the original letter ruling request. *See* section 9.04. However, the additional information should include the name, office symbols, and room number of the Service representative who requested the information and the taxpayer's name and the case control number (which the Service representative can provide).

Number of copies of additional information to be submitted

(3) Generally, a taxpayer needs only to submit one copy of the additional information. However, in appropriate cases, the Service may request additional copies of the information.

30-day or 21-day period may be extended if justified and approved

(4) An extension of the 30-day period under section 11.03 or the 21-day period under section 11.04, will be granted only if justified in writing by the taxpayer and approved by the manager of the group to which the case is assigned. A request for extension should be submitted before the end of the 30-day or 21-day period. If unusual circumstances close to the end of the 30-day or 21-day period make a written request impractical, the taxpayer should notify the Service within the 30-day or 21-day period that there is a problem and that the written request for extension will be coming soon. The taxpayer will be told promptly, and later in writing, of the approval or denial of the requested extension. If the extension request is denied, there is no right of appeal.

If taxpayer does not submit additional information

(5) If the taxpayer does not follow the instructions for submitting additional information or requesting an extension within the time provided, a letter ruling will be issued on the basis of the information on hand, or, if appropriate, no letter ruling will be issued. When the Service decides not to issue a letter ruling because essential information is lacking, the case will be closed and the taxpayer notified in writing. If the Service receives the information after the letter ruling request is closed, the request may be reopened and treated as a new request. However, the taxpayer may be required to pay another user fee before the case can be reopened.

Near the completion of the ruling process, advises taxpayer of conclusions and, if the Service will rule adversely, offers the taxpayer the opportunity to withdraw the letter ruling request

.05 Generally, after the conference of right is held before the letter ruling is issued, the Service representative will inform the taxpayer or the taxpayer's authorized representative of the Service's final conclusions. If the Service is going to rule adversely, the taxpayer will be offered the opportunity to withdraw the letter ruling request. If the taxpayer or the taxpayer's representative does not promptly notify the Service representative of a decision to withdraw the ruling request, the adverse letter will be issued. The user fee will not be refunded for a letter ruling request that is withdrawn. *See* section 10 of Rev. Proc. 2013–8.

May request draft of proposed letter ruling near the completion of the ruling process

.06 To accelerate issuance of letter rulings, in appropriate cases near the completion of the ruling process, the Service representative may request that the taxpayer or the taxpayer's representative submit a proposed draft of the letter ruling on the basis of discussions of the issues. The taxpayer, however, is not required to prepare a draft letter ruling in order to receive a letter ruling.

The format of the submission should be discussed with the Service representative who requests the draft letter ruling. The representative usually can provide a sample format of a letter ruling and will discuss the facts, analysis, and letter ruling language to be included.

The typed draft will become part of the permanent files of the Service. If the Service representative requesting the draft letter ruling cannot answer specific questions about the format, the questions can be directed to Donzell Littlejohn at (202) 283–9606 (Employee Plans), or Dave Rifkin at (202) 283–8952 or Matt Perdoni at (202) 283–9924 (Exempt Organizations) (not toll-free calls).

The proposed letter ruling should be sent to the same address as any additional information and contain in the transmittal the information that should be included with any additional information (for example, a penalties of perjury statement is required). *See* section 11.04 of this revenue procedure.

SECTION 12. HOW ARE CONFERENCES SCHEDULED?

Schedules a conference if requested by taxpayer

.01 A taxpayer may request a conference regarding a letter ruling request. Normally, a conference is scheduled only when the Service considers it to be helpful in deciding the case or when an adverse decision is indicated. If conferences are being arranged for more than one request for a letter ruling involving the same taxpayer, they will be scheduled so as to cause the least inconvenience to the taxpayer. As stated in section 9.03(5) of this revenue procedure, a taxpayer who wants to have a conference on the issue or issues involved should indicate this in writing when, or soon after, filing the request.

If a conference has been requested, the taxpayer will be notified by telephone, if possible, of the time and place of the conference, which must then be held within 21 calendar days after this contact. Instructions for requesting an extension of the 21-day period and notifying the taxpayer or the taxpayer's representative of the Service's approval or denial of the request for extension are the same as those explained in section 11.04 of this revenue procedure regarding providing additional information.

Permits taxpayer one conference of right

.02 A taxpayer is entitled, as a matter of right, to only one conference, except as explained under section 12.05 of this revenue procedure. This conference normally will be held at the group level and will be attended by a person who, at the time of the conference, has the authority to sign the ruling letter in his or her own name or for the group manager.

When more than one group has taken an adverse position on an issue in a letter ruling request, or when the position ultimately adopted by one group will affect that adopted by another, a representative from each group with the authority to sign in his or her own name or for the group manager will attend the conference. If more than one subject is to be discussed at the conference, the discussion will constitute a conference on each subject.

To have a thorough and informed discussion of the issues, the conference usually will be held after the group has had an opportunity to study the case. However, at the request of the taxpayer, the conference of right may be held earlier.

No taxpayer has a right to appeal the action of a group to any other official of the Service. *But see* section 12.05 of this revenue procedure for situations in which the Service may offer additional conferences.

Disallows verbatim recording of conferences

.03 Because conference procedures are informal, no tape, stenographic, or other verbatim recording of a conference may be made by any party.

Makes tentative recommendations on substantive issues

.04 The senior Service representative present at the conference ensures that the taxpayer has the opportunity to present views on all the issues in question. A Service representative explains the Service's tentative decision on the substantive issues and the reasons for that decision. If the taxpayer asks the Service to limit the retroactive effect of any letter ruling or limit the revocation or modification of a prior letter ruling, a Service representative will discuss the recommendation concerning this issue and the reasons for the recommendation. However, the representatives will not make a commitment regarding the conclusion that the Service intends to adopt.

May offer additional conferences	.05 The Service will offer the taxpayer an additional conference if, after the conference of right, an adverse holding is proposed, but on a new issue, or on the same issue but on different grounds from those discussed at the first conference. There is no right to another conference when a proposed holding is reversed at a higher level with a result less favorable to the taxpayer, if the grounds or arguments on which the reversal is based were discussed at the conference of right.

The limit on the number of conferences to which a taxpayer is entitled does not prevent the Service from offering additional conferences, including conferences with an official higher than the group level, if the Service decides they are needed. Such conferences are not offered as a matter of course simply because the group has reached an adverse decision. In general, conferences with higher level officials are offered only if the Service determines that the case presents significant issues of tax policy or tax administration and that the consideration of these issues would be enhanced by additional conferences with the taxpayer.

Requires written confirmation of information presented at conference

.06 The taxpayer should furnish to the Service any additional data, reasoning, precedents, etc., that were proposed by the taxpayer and discussed at the conference but not previously or adequately presented in writing. The taxpayer must furnish the additional information within 21 calendar days from the date of the conference. *See* section 11.04 of this revenue procedure for instructions on submission of additional information. If the additional information is not received within that time, a ruling will be issued on the basis of the information on hand or, if appropriate, no ruling will be issued.

Procedures for requesting an extension of the 21-day period and notifying the taxpayer or the taxpayer's representative of the Service's approval or denial of the requested extension are the same as those stated in section 11.04 of this revenue procedure regarding submitting additional information.

May schedule a pre-submission conference

.07 Sometimes it will be advantageous to both the Service and the taxpayer to hold a conference before the taxpayer submits the letter ruling request to discuss substantive or procedural issues relating to a proposed transaction. These conferences are held only if the identity of the taxpayer is provided to the Service, only if the taxpayer actually intends to make a request, only if the request involves a matter on which a letter ruling is ordinarily issued, and only at the discretion of the Service and as time permits. For example, a pre-submission conference will not be held on an income tax issue if, at the time the pre-submission conference is requested, the identical issue is involved in the taxpayer's return for an earlier period and that issue is being examined. *See* section 6 of this revenue procedure. Generally, the taxpayer will be asked to provide before the pre-submission conference a statement of whether the issue is an issue on which a letter ruling is ordinarily issued and a draft of the letter ruling request or other detailed written statement of the proposed transaction, issue, and legal analysis. If the taxpayer's representative will attend the pre-submission conference, a power of attorney form is required. A Form 2848, *Power of Attorney and Declaration of Representative*, must be used to provide the representative's authorization.

Any discussion of substantive issues at a pre-submission conference is advisory only, is not binding on the Service, and cannot be relied upon as a basis for obtaining retroactive relief under the provisions of § 7805(b). *See* section 3.08(2) of this procedure. A letter ruling request submitted following a pre-submission conference will not necessarily be assigned to the group that held the pre-submission conference.

Under limited circumstances, may schedule a conference to be held by telephone

.08 A taxpayer may request that their conference of right be held by telephone. This request may occur, for example, when a taxpayer wants a conference of right but believes that the issue involved does not warrant incurring the expense of traveling to Washington, DC. If a taxpayer makes such a request, the group manager will decide if it is appropriate in the particular case to hold the conference of right by telephone. If the request is approved by the group manager, the taxpayer will be advised when to call the Service representatives (not a toll-free call).

Conference rules for EO determination letters not subject to § 7428 or § 501 or § 521

.09 The procedures for requesting a conference for determination letters that are not subject to § 7428 or § 501 or § 521 are the same as described in this section, except that generally conferences will be held by telephone.

SECTION 13. WHAT EFFECT WILL A LETTER RULING HAVE?

May be relied on subject to limitations

.01 A taxpayer ordinarily may rely on a letter ruling received from the Service subject to the conditions and limitations described in this section.

Will not apply to another taxpayer

.02 A taxpayer may not rely on a letter ruling issued to another taxpayer. *See* § 6110(k)(3).

Will be used by the Director, EP or EO Examinations in examining the taxpayer's return

.03 When determining a taxpayer's liability, the Director, EP or EO Examinations must ascertain whether—

(1) the conclusions stated in the letter ruling are properly reflected in the return;

(2) the representations upon which the letter ruling was based reflected an accurate statement of the material facts;

(3) the transaction was carried out substantially as proposed; and

(4) there has been any change in the law that applies to the period during which the transaction or continuing series of transactions were consummated.

If, when determining the liability, the Director, EP Examinations finds that a letter ruling should be revoked or modified, unless a waiver is obtained from EP Technical, the findings and recommendations of the Director, EP Examinations will be forwarded to EP Technical for consideration before further action is taken by the Director, EP Examinations. Such a referral to EP Technical will be treated as a request for technical advice and the procedures of Rev. Proc. 2013–5 will be followed. Otherwise, the letter ruling is to be applied by the Director, EP Examinations in determining the taxpayer's liability. Appropriate coordination with EP Technical will be undertaken if any field official having jurisdiction over a return or other matter proposes to reach a conclusion contrary to a letter ruling previously issued to the taxpayer.

In certain exempt organizations cases, section 4.04 of Rev. Proc. 2013–5 provides that a request for a TAM is mandatory.

May be revoked or modified if found to be in error

.04 Unless it was part of a closing agreement as described in section 3.03 of this revenue procedure, a letter ruling found to be in error or not in accord with the current views of the Service may be revoked or modified. If a letter ruling is revoked or modified, the revocation or modification applies to all years open under the statute of limitations unless the Service uses its discretionary authority under § 7805(b) to limit the retroactive effect of the revocation or modification.

A letter ruling may be revoked or modified due to—

(1) a notice to the taxpayer to whom the letter ruling was issued;

(2) the enactment of legislation or ratification of a tax treaty;

(3) a decision of the United States Supreme Court;

(4) the issuance of temporary or final regulations; or

(5) the issuance of a revenue ruling, revenue procedure, notice, or other statement published in the Internal Revenue Bulletin.

Consistent with these provisions, if a letter ruling relates to a continuing action or a series of actions, it ordinarily will be applied until any one of the events described above occurs or until it is specifically withdrawn.

Publication of a notice of proposed rulemaking will not affect the application of any letter ruling issued under this revenue procedure.

Not generally revoked or modified retroactively

.05 Except in rare or unusual circumstances, the revocation or modification of a letter ruling will not be applied retroactively to the taxpayer for whom the letter ruling was issued or to a taxpayer whose tax liability was directly involved in the letter ruling provided that—

(1) there has been no misstatement or omission of material facts;

(2) the facts at the time of the transaction are not materially different from the facts on which the letter ruling was based;

(3) there has been no change in the applicable law;

(4) the letter ruling was originally issued for a proposed transaction; and

(5) the taxpayer directly involved in the letter ruling acted in good faith in relying on the letter ruling, and revoking or modifying the letter ruling retroactively would be to the taxpayer's detriment. For example, the tax liability of each employee covered by a ruling relating to a qualified plan of an employer is directly involved in such ruling. However, the tax liability of a member of an industry is not directly involved in a letter ruling issued to another member and, therefore, the holding in a revocation or modification of a letter ruling to one member of an industry may be retroactively applied to other members of the industry. By the same reasoning, a tax practitioner may not extend to one client the non-retroactive application of a revocation or modification of a letter ruling previously issued to another client.

If a letter ruling is revoked or modified by letter with retroactive effect, the letter will, except in fraud cases, state the grounds on which the letter ruling is being revoked or modified and explain the reasons why it is being revoked or modified retroactively.

Retroactive effect of revocation or modification applied only to a particular transaction

.06 A letter ruling issued on a particular transaction represents a holding of the Service on that transaction only. It will not apply to a similar transaction in the same year or any other year. And, except in unusual circumstances, the application of that letter ruling to the transaction will not be affected by the later issuance of regulations (either temporary or final), if conditions (1) through (5) in section 13.05 of this revenue procedure are met.

However, if a letter ruling on a transaction is later found to be in error or no longer in accord with the position of the Service, it will not protect a similar transaction of the taxpayer in the same year or later year.

Retroactive effect of revocation or modification applied to a continuing action or series of actions

.07 If a letter ruling is issued covering a continuing action or series of actions and the letter ruling is later found to be in error or no longer in accord with the position of the Service, the Commissioner, Tax Exempt and Government Entities Division, ordinarily will limit the retroactive effect of the revocation or modification to a date that is not earlier than that on which the letter ruling is revoked or modified.

May be retroactively revoked or modified when transaction is completed without reliance on the letter ruling

.08 A taxpayer is not protected against retroactive revocation or modification of a letter ruling involving a completed transaction other than those described in section 13.07 of this revenue procedure, because the taxpayer did not enter into the transaction relying on a letter ruling.

Taxpayer may request that retroactivity be limited

.09 Under § 7805(b), the Service may prescribe any extent to which a revocation or modification of a letter ruling or determination letter will be applied without retroactive effect.

A taxpayer to whom a letter ruling or determination letter has been issued may request that the Commissioner, Tax Exempt and Government Entities Division, limit the retroactive effect of any revocation or modification of the letter ruling or determination letter.

Format of request

(1) Request for relief under § 7805(b) must be made in required format.

Sec. 13.04
January 2, 2013

A request to limit the retroactive effect of the revocation or modification of a letter ruling must be in the general form of, and meet the general requirements for, a letter ruling request. These requirements are given in section 9 of this revenue procedure. Specifically, the request must also—

(a) state that it is being made under § 7805(b);

(b) state the relief sought;

(c) explain the reasons and arguments in support of the relief requested (including a discussion of the five items listed in section 13.05 of this revenue procedure and any other factors as they relate to the taxpayer's particular situation); and

(d) include any documents bearing on the request.

A request that the Service limit the retroactive effect of a revocation or modification of a letter ruling may be made in the form of a separate request for a letter ruling when, for example, a revenue ruling has the effect of revoking or modifying a letter ruling previously issued to the taxpayer, or when the Service notifies the taxpayer of a change in position that will have the effect of revoking or modifying the letter ruling. However, when notice is given by the Director, EP or EO Examinations during an examination of the taxpayer's return or by an Appeals Area Director, or the Appeals Domestic Operations Director, during consideration of the taxpayer's return before an appeals office, a request to limit retroactive effect must be made in the form of a request for technical advice as explained in section 19 of Rev. Proc. 2013–5.

When germane to a pending letter ruling request, a request to limit the retroactive effect of a revocation or modification of a letter ruling may be made as part of the request for the letter ruling, either initially or at any time before the letter ruling is issued. When a letter ruling that concerns a continuing transaction is revoked or modified by, for example, a subsequent revenue ruling, a request to limit retroactive effect must be made before the examination of the return that contains the transaction that is the subject of the letter ruling request.

Consideration of relief under § 7805(b) will be included as one of the taxpayer's steps in exhausting administrative remedies only if the taxpayer has requested such relief in the manner described in this revenue procedure. If the taxpayer does not complete the applicable steps, the taxpayer will not have exhausted the taxpayer's administrative remedies as required by § 7428(b)(2) and § 7476(b)(3) and will, thus, be precluded from seeking a declaratory judgment under § 7428 or § 7476. Where the taxpayer has requested § 7805(b) relief, the taxpayer's administrative remedies will not be considered exhausted until the Service has had a reasonable time to act upon the request.

Request for conference

(2) Taxpayer may request a conference on application of § 7805(b).

A taxpayer who requests the application of § 7805(b) in a separate letter ruling request has the right to a conference in EP or EO Technical as explained in sections 12.01, 12.02, 12.03, 12.04 and 12.05 of this revenue procedure. If the request is made initially as part of a pending letter ruling request or is made before the conference of right is held on the substantive issues, the § 7805(b) issue will be discussed at the taxpayer's one conference of right as explained in section 12.02 of this revenue procedure. If the request for the application of § 7805(b) relief is made as part of a pending letter ruling request after a conference has been held on the substantive issue and the Service determines that there is justification for having delayed the request, the taxpayer is entitled to one conference of right concerning the application of § 7805(b), with the conference limited to discussion of this issue only.

SECTION 14. WHAT EFFECT WILL A DETERMINATION LETTER HAVE?

Has same effect as a letter ruling

.01 A determination letter issued by EP or EO Determinations has the same effect as a letter ruling issued to a taxpayer under section 13 of this revenue procedure.

If the Director, EP or EO Examinations proposes to reach a conclusion contrary to that expressed in a determination letter, he or she need not refer the matter to EP or EO Technical. However, the Director, EP or EO Examinations must refer the matter to EP or EO Technical if the Director, EP or EO Examinations desires to have the revocation or modification of the determination letter limited under § 7805(b).

Taxpayer may request that retroactive effect of revocation or modification be limited

.02 The Director, EP or EO Examinations does not have authority under § 7805(b) to limit the revocation or modification of the determination letter. Therefore, if the Director, EP or EO Examinations proposes to revoke or modify a determination letter, the taxpayer may request limitation of the retroactive effect of the revocation or modification by asking EP or EO Determinations to seek technical advice from EP or EO Technical. *See* section 19 of Rev. Proc. 2013–5.

Format of request

(1) Request for relief under § 7805(b) must be made in required format.

A taxpayer's request to limit the retroactive effect of the revocation or modification of the determination letter must be in the form of, and meet the general requirements for, a technical advice request. *See* section 18.06 of Rev. Proc. 2012–5. The request must also—

(a) state that it is being made under § 7805(b);

(b) state the relief sought;

(c) explain the reasons and arguments in support of the relief sought (including a discussion of the five items listed in section 13.05 of this revenue procedure and any other factors as they relate to the taxpayer's particular situation); and

(d) include any documents bearing on the request.

Request for conference

(2) Taxpayer may request a conference on application of § 7805(b).

When technical advice is requested regarding the application of § 7805(b), the taxpayer has the right to a conference in EP or EO Technical to the same extent as does any taxpayer who is the subject of a technical advice request. *See* section 11 of Rev. Proc. 2013–5.

Exhaustion of administrative remedies

(3) Taxpayer steps in exhausting administrative remedies.

Consideration of relief under § 7805(b) will be included as one of the taxpayer's steps in exhausting administrative remedies only if the taxpayer has requested such relief in the manner described in this revenue procedure. If the taxpayer does not complete the applicable steps, the taxpayer will not have exhausted the taxpayer's administrative remedies as required by § 7428(b)(2) and § 7476(b)(3) and will, thus, be precluded from seeking a declaratory judgment under § 7428 or § 7476. Where the taxpayer has requested § 7805(b) relief, the taxpayer's administrative remedies will not be considered exhausted until the Service has had a reasonable time to act upon the request.

SECTION 15. UNDER WHAT CIRCUMSTANCES ARE MATTERS REFERRED BETWEEN DETERMINATIONS AND TECHNICAL?

Requests for determination letters

.01 Requests for determination letters received by EP or EO Determinations that, under the provisions of this revenue procedure, may not be issued by EP or EO Determinations, will be forwarded to EP or EO Technical for reply. EP Determinations or EO Technical will notify the taxpayer that the matter has been referred.

EP or EO Determinations will also refer to EP or EO Technical any request for a determination letter that in its judgment should have the attention of EP or EO Technical.

No-rule areas

.02 If the request involves an issue on which the Service will not issue a letter ruling or determination letter, the request will not be forwarded to EP or EO Technical. EP or EO Determinations will notify the taxpayer that the Service will not issue a letter ruling or a determination letter on the issue. *See* sections 7 and 8 of this revenue procedure for a description of no-rule areas.

Requests for letter rulings

.03 Requests for letter rulings received by EP or EO Technical that, under section 6 of this revenue procedure, may not be acted upon by EP or EO Technical will be forwarded to the Director, EP or EO Examinations. The taxpayer will be notified of this action. If the request is on an issue or in an area of the type discussed in section 8 of this revenue procedure, and the Service decides not to issue a letter ruling or an information letter, EP or EO Technical will notify the taxpayer and will then forward the request to the Director, EP or EO Examinations for association with the related return.

SECTION 16. WHAT ARE THE GENERAL PROCEDURES APPLICABLE TO INFORMATION LETTERS ISSUED BY THE HEADQUARTERS OFFICE?

Will be made available to the public

.01 Information letters that are issued by the headquarters office to members of the public will be made available to the public. These documents provide general statements of well-defined law without applying them to a specific set of facts. *See* section 3.06 of this revenue procedure. Information letters that are issued by the field, however, will not be made available to the public.

The following documents also will not be available for public inspection as part of this process:

(1) letters that merely transmit Service publications or other publicly available material, without significant legal discussion;

(2) responses to taxpayer or third party contacts that are inquiries with respect to a pending request for a letter ruling, technical advice memorandum, or Chief Counsel Advice (whose public inspection is subject to § 6110); and

(3) responses to taxpayer or third party communications with respect to any investigation, audit, litigation, or other enforcement action.

Deletions made under the Freedom of Information Act

.02 Before any information letter is made available to the public, the headquarters office will delete any name, address, and other identifying information as appropriate under the Freedom of Information Act ("FOIA") (for example, FOIA personal privacy exemption of 5 U.S.C. § 552(b)(6) and tax details exempt pursuant to § 6103, as incorporated into FOIA by 5 U.S.C. § 552(b)(3). Because information letters do not constitute written determinations (including Chief Counsel Advice) as defined in § 6110, these documents are not subject to public inspection under § 6110.

Effect of information letters

.03 Information letters are advisory only and have no binding effect on the Service. *See* section 3.06 of this revenue procedure. If the headquarters office issues an information letter in response to a request for a letter ruling that does not meet the requirements of this revenue procedure, the information letter is not a substitute for a letter ruling.

SECTION 17. WHAT IS THE EFFECT OF THIS REVENUE PROCEDURE ON OTHER DOCUMENTS?

Rev. Proc. 2012–4 is superseded.

SECTION 18. EFFECTIVE DATE

This revenue procedure is effective January 2, 2013.

SECTION 19. PAPERWORK REDUCTION ACT

The collections of information contained in this revenue procedure have been reviewed and approved by the Office of Management and Budget in accordance with the Paperwork Reduction Act (44 U.S.C. § 3507) under control number 1545–1520.

An agency may not conduct or sponsor, and a person is not required to respond to, a collection of information unless the collection of information displays a valid OMB control number.

The collections of information in this revenue procedure are in sections 7.07, 9.02, 9.03, 9.04, 9.05, 9.06, 10.02, 10.03, 11.03, 11.04(1)–(5), 11.06, 12.01, 12.06, 12.07, 13.09(1), 14.02(1), and in Appendices B, C, D and E. This information is required to evaluate and process the request for a letter ruling or determination letter. In addition, this information will be used to help the Service delete certain information from the text of the letter ruling or determination letter before it is made available for public inspection, as required by § 6110. The collections of information are required to obtain a letter ruling or determination letter. The likely respondents are businesses or other for-profit institutions.

The estimated total annual reporting and/or recordkeeping burden is 12,650 hours.

The estimated annual burden per respondent/recordkeeper varies from 15 minutes to 16 hours, depending on individual circumstances and the type of request involved, with an estimated average burden of 6.01 hours. The estimated number of respondents and/or recordkeepers is 2,103.

The estimated annual frequency of responses is one request per applicant, except that a taxpayer requesting a letter ruling may also request a presubmission conference.

Books or records relating to a collection of information must be retained as long as their contents may become material in the administration of any internal revenue law. Generally, tax returns and tax return information are confidential, as required by § 6103.

DRAFTING INFORMATION

The principal author of this revenue procedure is Eric D. Slack of the Employee Plans, Tax Exempt and Government Entities Division. For further information regarding how this revenue procedure applies to employee plans and exempt organizations matters, contact the Exempt Organizations and Employee Plans Customer Assistance Center at 877–829–5500. For employee plans matters, Mr. Slack can be emailed at *RetirementPlanQuestions@irs.gov*. For exempt organizations matters, Mr. Dave Rifkin can be emailed at *tege.eo.ra@irs.gov*. Please put "Question about Rev. Proc. 2013–4" in the subject line.

INDEX

References are to sections in Rev. Proc. 2013–4

— additional information . . . . sec. 9.02(9), 9.03, 11.03, 11.04

— closing agreement . . . . sec. 3.03, 6.06(4), 9.02(4), 9.02(15), 13.04

— conference . . . . sec. 9.02(9), 9.03(5), 12.01–.09, 13.09(2), 14.02(2)

— disclose . . . . sec. 9.02(9)

— exempt organization . . . . : . . . . sec. 6.01

— expedited handling . . . . sec. 9.03(3)

— extension . . . . sec. 6.02, 6.04, 11.04, 12.01, 12.06

— fax . . . . sec. 9.03(4), 11.04

— fee . . . . sec. 9.02(14), 11.04(5)

— hand delivered . . . . 9.04(1)

— information letter . . . . sec. 3.06, 8.01, 15.03

— no rule . . . . sec. 8, 15.02

— perjury statement . . . . sec. 9.02(13), 11.04, 11.06

— power of attorney . . . . sec. 9.02(12), 9.03(2)

— reliance . . . . sec. 3.09, 11.02, 12.07, 13, 14

— representatives . . . . sec. 3.09, 9.02(10)–(11), 9.03(2)

— retroactive . . . . sec. 11.02, 12.04, 12.07, 13, 14

— revenue ruling . . . . sec. 3.07, 13.04, 13.09(1)

— section 6110 . . . . sec. 9.02(9), 13.02

— status . . . . sec. 9.07

— technical advice . . . . sec. 7.08, 13.03, 13.09(1), 14

— telephone . . . . sec. 9.02(1), 11.04, 12.01, 12.08

— where to send . . . . sec. 9.04

— withdraw . . . . sec. 9.08

APPENDIX A

SAMPLE FORMAT FOR A LETTER RULING REQUEST

(Insert the date of request)

[for Employee Plans]
Internal Revenue Service
Attention: EP Letter Rulings
P.O. Box 27063
McPherson Station
Washington, D.C. 20038

[for Exempt Organizations]
Internal Revenue Service
Attention: EO Letter Rulings
P.O. Box 27720
McPherson Station
Washington, D.C. 20038

Dear Sir or Madam:

(Insert the name of the taxpayer) (the "Taxpayer") requests a ruling on the proper treatment of *(insert the subject matter of the letter ruling request)* under § *(insert the number)* of the Internal Revenue Code.

[If the taxpayer is requesting expedited handling, the letter ruling request must contain a statement to that effect. This statement must explain the need for expeditious handling. See section 9.03(3).]

A. STATEMENT OF FACTS

1. Taxpayer Information

[Provide the statements required by sections 9.02(1)(a), (b), and (c) of Rev. Proc. 2013–4, 2013–1 I.R.B. 126. (Hereafter, all references are to Rev. Proc. 2013–4 unless otherwise noted.)]

For example, a taxpayer that maintains a qualified employee retirement plan and files an annual Form 5500 series of returns may include the following statement to satisfy sections 9.02(1)(a), (b), and (c):

The Taxpayer is a construction company with principal offices located at 100 Whatever Drive, Wherever, Maryland 12345, and its telephone number is (123) 456–7890. The Taxpayer's federal employer identification number is 00–1234567. The Taxpayer uses the Form 5500 series of returns on a calendar year basis to report its qualified employee retirement plan and trust.

2. Detailed Description of the Transaction.

[The ruling request must contain a complete statement of the facts relating to the transaction that is the subject of the letter ruling request. This statement must include a detailed description of the transaction, including material facts in any accompanying documents, and the business reasons for the transaction. See sections 9.02(1)(b), 9.02(1)(c), and 9.02(2).]

B. RULING REQUESTED

[The ruling request should contain a concise statement of the ruling requested by the taxpayer.]

C. STATEMENT OF LAW

[The ruling request must contain a statement of the law in support of the taxpayer's views or conclusion, including any authorities believed to be contrary to the position advanced in the ruling request. This statement must also identify any pending legislation that may affect the proposed transaction. See sections 9.02(6), 9.02(7), and 9.02(8).]

D. ANALYSIS

[The ruling request must contain a discussion of the facts and an analysis of the law. See sections 9.02(3), 9.02(6), 9.02(7), and 9.02(8).]

E. CONCLUSION

[The ruling request should contain a statement of the taxpayer's conclusion on the ruling requested.]

F. PROCEDURAL MATTERS

1. Rev. Proc. 2013–4 statements

a.   [The statement required by section 9.02(4).]

b.   [The statement required by section 9.02(5).]

c.   [The statement required by section 9.02(6) regarding whether the law in connection with the letter ruling request is uncertain and whether the issue is adequately addressed by relevant authorities.]

d.   [The statement required by section 9.02(7) when the taxpayer determines that there are no contrary authorities.]

e.   [If the taxpayer wants to have a conference on the issues involved in the letter ruling request, the ruling request should contain a statement to that effect. See section 9.03(5).]

f.   [If the taxpayer is requesting the letter ruling to be issued by fax, the ruling request should contain a statement to that effect. See section 9.03(4).]

g.   [If the taxpayer is requesting separate letter rulings on multiple issues, the letter ruling request should contain a statement to that effect. See section 9.03(1).]

2. Administrative

a.   A Power of Attorney is enclosed. [See sections 9.02(12) and 9.03(2).]

b.   The deletions statement and checklist required by Rev. Proc. 2013–4 are enclosed. [See sections 9.02(9) and 9.02(17).]

c.   The required user fee is enclosed. [See section 9.02(14).]

Very truly yours,

(*Insert the name of the taxpayer or the taxpayer's authorized representative*)

By:

_____ ____

Signature   Date

Typed or printed name
of person signing request

DECLARATION: [See section 9.02(13).]

Under penalties of perjury, I declare that I have examined this request, including accompanying documents, and to the best of my knowledge and belief, the request contains all the relevant facts relating to the request and such facts are true, correct, and complete.

(*Insert the name of the taxpayer*)

By:

_____   _____ _____

Signature   Title   Date

_____

Typed or printed name of
person signing declaration

APPENDIX B

CHECKLIST

IS YOUR RULING REQUEST COMPLETE?

INSTRUCTIONS

The Service will be able to respond more quickly to your letter ruling request if it is carefully prepared and complete. To ensure that your request is in order, use this checklist. Complete the four items of information requested before the checklist. Answer each question by circling "Yes," "No," or "N/A." When a question contains a place for a page number, insert the page number (or numbers) of the request that gives the information called for by a yes answer to a question. **Sign and date the checklist (as taxpayer or authorized representative) and place it on top of your request.**

If you are an authorized representative submitting a request for a taxpayer, you must include a completed checklist with the request, or the request will either be returned to you or substantive consideration of it will be deferred until a completed checklist is submitted. **If you are a taxpayer preparing your own request without professional assistance, an incomplete checklist will not be cause for returning your request or deferring substantive consideration of the request.** However, you should still complete as much of the checklist as possible and submit it with your request.

TAXPAYER'S NAME _____

TAXPAYER'S I.D. No. _____

ATTORNEY/P.O.A. _____

PRIMARY CODE SECTION _____

CIRCLE ONE	ITEM
Yes No N/A	1. Does your request involve an issue under the jurisdiction of the Commissioner, Tax Exempt and Government Entities Division? See section 5 of Rev. Proc. 2013–4, 2013–1 I.R.B. 126, for issues under the jurisdiction of other offices. (Hereafter, all references are to Rev. Proc. 2013–4 unless otherwise noted.)
Yes No N/A	2. If your request involves a matter on which letter rulings are not ordinarily issued, have you given compelling reasons to justify the issuance of a private letter ruling? Before preparing your request, you may want to call the office responsible for substantive interpretations of the principal Internal Revenue Code section on which you are seeking a letter ruling to discuss the likelihood of an exception. The appropriate office to call for this information may be obtained by calling (202) 283–9660 (Employee Plans matters), or (202) 283–0289 (Exempt Organizations matters) (not toll-free calls).
Yes No N/A Page _____	3. If the request involves an employee plans qualification matter under § 401(a), § 409, or § 4975(e)(7), have you demonstrated that the request satisfies the three criteria in section 6.03 for a headquarters office ruling?
Yes No N/A Page _____	4. If the request deals with a completed transaction, have you filed the return for the year in which the transaction was completed? See sections 6.01 and 6.02.
Yes No	5. Are you requesting a letter ruling on a hypothetical situation or question? See section 8.03.
Yes No	6. Are you requesting a letter ruling on alternative plans of a proposed transaction? See section 8.03.
Yes No	7. Are you requesting the letter ruling for only part of an integrated transaction? See section 8.04.
Yes No	8. Have you submitted another letter ruling request for the transaction covered by this request?
Yes No	9. Are you requesting the letter ruling for a business, trade, industrial association, or similar group concerning the application of tax law to its members? See section 6.07.

Yes No Pages ———	10. Have you included a complete statement of all the facts relevant to the transaction? See section 9.02(1).
Yes No N/A	11. Have you submitted with the request true copies of all wills, deeds, plan documents, and other documents relevant to the transaction, and labeled and attached them in alphabetical sequence? See section 9.02(2).
Yes No Page ———	12. Have you included, rather than merely by reference, all material facts from the documents in the request? Are they accompanied by an analysis of their bearing on the issues that specifies the document provisions that apply? See section 9.02(3).
Yes No Page ———	13. Have you included the required statement regarding whether the same issue in the letter ruling request is in an earlier return of the taxpayer or in a return for any year of a related taxpayer? See section 9.02(4).
Yes No Page ———	14. Have you included the required statement regarding whether the Service previously ruled on the same or similar issue for the taxpayer, a related taxpayer, or a predecessor? See section 9.02(5).
Yes No Page ———	15. Have you included the required statement regarding whether the taxpayer, a related taxpayer, a predecessor, or any representatives previously submitted the same or similar issue but withdrew it before the letter ruling was issued? See section 9.02(5).
Yes No Page ———	16. Have you included the required statement regarding whether the law in connection with the request is uncertain and whether the issue is adequately addressed by relevant authorities? See section 9.02(6).
Yes No Pages ———	17. Have you included the required statement of relevant authorities in support of your views? See section 9.02(6).
Yes No N/A Pages ———	18. Does your request discuss the implications of any legislation, tax treaties, court decisions, regulations, notices, revenue rulings, or revenue procedures you determined to be contrary to the position advanced? See section 9.02(7), which states that taxpayers are encouraged to inform the Service of such authorities.
Yes No N/A Page ———	19. If you determined that there are no contrary authorities, have you included a statement to this effect in your request? See section 9.02(7).
Yes No N/A Page ———	20. Have you included in your request a statement identifying any pending legislation that may affect the proposed transaction? See section 9.02(8).
Yes No	21. Is the request accompanied by the deletions statement required by § 6110? See section 9.02(9).
Yes No N/A Page ———	22. Have you (or your authorized representative) signed and dated the request? See section 9.02(10).
Yes No N/A	23. If the request is signed by your representative, or if your representative will appear before the Service in connection with the request, is the request accompanied by a properly prepared and signed power of attorney with the signatory's name typed or printed? See section 9.02(12).
Yes No N/A Page ———	24. Have you included, signed and dated, the penalties of perjury statement in the form required by section 9.02(13)?
Yes No N/A	25. Have you included the correct user fee with the request and made your check or money order payable to the United States Treasury? See section 9.02(14) and Rev. Proc. 2013–8, page 237, this Bulletin for the correct amount and additional information on user fees.
Yes No N/A	26. Are you submitting your request in duplicate if necessary? See section 9.02(15).
Yes No N/A Pages ———	27. If you are requesting separate letter rulings on different issues involving one factual situation, have you included a statement to that effect in each request? See section 9.03(1).
Yes No N/A Page ———	28. If you have more than one representative, have you designated whether the representatives listed on the power of attorney are to receive a copy of the letter ruling? See section 9.03(2).
Yes No N/A	29. If you want your letter ruling request to be processed ahead of the regular order or by a specific date, have you requested expedited handling in the form required by section 9.03(3) and stated a compelling need for such action in the request?

Yes No N/A
Page _____

30. If you want to have a conference on the issues involved in the request, have you included a request for conference in the ruling request? See section 9.03(5).

Yes No N/A

31. If your request is covered by any of the guideline revenue procedures or other special requirements listed in section 10 of Rev. Proc. 2013–4, have you complied with all of the requirements of the applicable revenue procedure?

Yes No N/A
Page _____

32. If you are requesting relief under § 7805(b) (regarding retroactive effect), have you complied with all of the requirements in section 13.09?

Yes No N/A

33. Have you addressed your request to the appropriate office listed in section 9.04? Improperly addressed requests may be delayed (sometimes for over a week) in reaching the appropriate office for initial processing.

_____   _____   _____

Signature   Title or authority   Date

_____

Typed or printed name of
person signing checklist

Appendix G

Revenue Procedure 2013-6, Procedure for Requesting Private Letter Rulings, 2013-1 CB 198

26 CFR 601.201: Rulings and determination letters.

Rev. Proc. 2013–6

TABLE OF CONTENTS

SECTION 1. WHAT IS THE PURPOSE OF THIS REVENUE PROCEDURE? 201
  .01 Purpose of revenue procedure 201
  .02 Organization of revenue procedure 201

SECTION 2. WHAT CHANGES HAVE BEEN MADE TO THIS PROCEDURE? 201
  .01 In general 201
  .02 Other changes 201
  .03 Other guidance 201

PART I. PROCEDURES FOR DETERMINATION LETTER REQUESTS

SECTION 3. ON WHAT ISSUES MAY TAXPAYERS REQUEST WRITTEN GUIDANCE UNDER THIS
      PROCEDURE? 202
  .01 Types of requests 202
  .02 Areas in which determination letters will not be issued 202
  .03 Submission period for applications 203

SECTION 4. ON WHAT ISSUES MUST WRITTEN GUIDANCE BE REQUESTED UNDER DIFFERENT
      PROCEDURES? 204
  .01 Tax Exempt and Government Entities 204
  .02 Chief Counsel's revenue procedure 204

SECTION 5. WHAT IS THE GENERAL SCOPE OF A DETERMINATION LETTER? 204
  .01 Scope of this section 204
  .02 Scope of determination letters 204
  .03 Nondiscrimination in amount requirement 204
  .04 Governmental plans under § 414(d).. 204
  .05 Church plans under § 414(e) 204
  .06 Tax treatment of certain contributions of § 414(h) 205
  .07 Other limits on scope of determination letter 205
  .08 Affiliated service groups, leased employees and partial terminations 205
  .09 Publication 794 205

SECTION 6. WHAT IS THE GENERAL PROCEDURE FOR REQUESTING DETERMINATION LETTERS? 205
  .01 Scope 205
  .02 Qualified trusteed plans 205
  .03 Qualified nontrusteed annuity plans 205
  .04 Complete information required 205
  .05 Complete copy of plan and trust instrument required 206
  .06 Section 9 of Rev. Proc. 2013–4 applies... 206
  .07 Separate application for each single § 414(l) plan... 206
  .08 Prior letters 206
  .09 User fees 206
  .10 Interested party notification and comment 206
  .11 Contrary authority must be distinguished 206
  .12 Employer/employee relationship 206
  .13 Incomplete applications returned 207
  .14 Effect of failure to disclose material fact... 207
  .15 Where to file requests 207
  .16 Submission of related plans... 207
  .17 Withdrawal of requests... 207
  .18 Right to status conference 208
  .19 How to request status conference 208

SECTION 7. INITIAL QUALIFICATION, ETC... 208
   .01 Scope 208
   .02 Forms 208
   .03 Timing 209
   .04 Application must include copy of plan and amendments 209
   .05 Restatements required 209
   .06 Controlled group, etc.. 209
   .07 § 414(x) combined plans 209

SECTION 8. EMPLOYER RELIANCE ON M&P AND VOLUME SUBMITTER PLANS 209
   .01 Scope 209
   .02 Modifications to Revenue Procedure 2011–49.................................... 209
   .03 Reliance equivalent to determination letter..................................... 210

SECTION 9. DETERMINATION LETTER FILING PROCEDURES FOR VOLUME SUBMITTER PLANS ... 210
   .01 Scope 210
   .02 Determination letter for adoption of volume submitter plan 211
   .03 Timing of determination letter applications for adopting employers of pre-approved plans 212

SECTION 10. MULTIPLE EMPLOYER PLANS 212
   .01 Scope 212
   .02 Options to file for the plan only or for both the plan and employers maintaining the plan 212
   .03 Where to file 212
   .04 Determination letter sent to each employer who files Form 5300 212
   .05 Addition of employers 212

SECTION 11. RESERVED 213

SECTION 12. TERMINATION OR DISCONTINUANCE OF CONTRIBUTIONS; NOTICE OF MERGERS, CONSOLIDATIONS, ETC. 213
   .01 Scope 213
   .02 Forms 213
   .03 Supplemental information 213
   .04 Compliance with Title IV of ERISA 214
   .05 Termination prior to time for amending for change in law 214
   .06 Restatement not required for terminating plan 214

SECTION 13. GROUP TRUSTS 214
   .01 Scope 214
   .02 Required information 214
   .03 Forms.. 214

SECTION 14. AFFILIATED SERVICE GROUPS; LEASED EMPLOYEES 215
   .01 Scope 215
   .02 Employer must request the determination under § 414(m) or § 414(n)......... 215
   .03 Forms.. 215
   .04 Employer is responsible for determining status under § 414(m) and § 414(n)... 215
   .05 Pre-approved plans 215
   .06 Required information for § 414(m) determination 215
   .07 Required information for § 414(n) determination 216

SECTION 15. WAIVER OF MINIMUM FUNDING 216
   .01 Scope 216
   .02 Applicability of Rev. Proc. 2004–15 216
   .03 Waiver request submitted to EP Technical 217
   .04 Waiver and determination letter request submitted to EP Technical 217
   .05 Handling of the request 217
   .06 When waiver request should be submitted 218

SECTION 16. SECTION 401(h) AND § 420 DETERMINATION LETTERS 218

.01 Scope 218
.02 Required information for § 401(h) determination 218
.03 Required information for § 420 determination 218

PART II. INTERESTED PARTY NOTICE AND COMMENT

SECTION 17. WHAT RIGHTS TO NOTICE AND COMMENT DO INTERESTED PARTIES HAVE? 219
.01 Rights of interested parties 219
.02 Comments by interested parties 220
.03 Requests for DOL to submit comments 220
.04 Right to comment if DOL declines to comment 221
.05 Confidentiality of comments 221
.06 Availability of comments 221
.07 When comments are deemed made 221

SECTION 18. WHAT ARE THE GENERAL RULES FOR NOTICE TO INTERESTED PARTIES? 222
.01 Notice to interested parties 222
.02 Time when notice must be given 222
.03 Content of notice 222
.04 Procedures for making information available to interested parties 223
.05 Information to be available to interested parties 223
.06 Special rules if there are fewer than 26 participants 223
.07 Information described in § 6104(a)(1)(D) should not be included 224
.08 Availability of additional information to interested parties 224
.09 Availability of notice to interested parties... 224

PART III. PROCESSING DETERMINATION LETTER REQUESTS

SECTION 19. HOW DOES THE SERVICE HANDLE DETERMINATION LETTER REQUESTS 225
.01 Oral advice 225
.02 Conferences 225
.03 Determination letter based solely on administrative record 225
.04 Notice of final determination 226
.05 Issuance of the notice of final determination 226

SECTION 20. EXHAUSTION OF ADMINISTRATIVE REMEDIES... 226
.01 In general 226
.02 Steps for exhausting administrative remedies 226
.03 Applicant's request for § 7805(b) relief... 226
.04 Interested parties 227
.05 Deemed exhaustion of administrative remedies 227
.06 Service must act on appeal 227
.07 Service must act on § 7805(b) request.. 227
.08 Effect of technical advice request 227

SECTION 21. WHAT EFFECT WILL AN EMPLOYEE PLAN DETERMINATION LETTER HAVE? 227
.01 Scope of reliance on determination letter 227
.02 Sections 13 and 14 of Rev. Proc. 2013–4 applicable 227
.03 Effect of subsequent publication of revenue ruling, etc. 227
.04 Determination letter does not apply to taxability issues 228

SECTION 22. EFFECT ON OTHER REVENUE PROCEDURES 228

SECTION 23. EFFECTIVE DATE 228

DRAFTING INFORMATION... 228

EXHIBIT 229

APPENDIX §§ 401(h) AND 420 DETERMINATION LETTERS... 231

8

8

8

SECTION 1. WHAT IS THE PURPOSE OF THIS REVENUE PROCEDURE?

Purpose of revenue procedure

.01 This revenue procedure sets forth the procedures of the Internal Revenue Service for issuing determination letters on the qualified status of pension, profit-sharing, stock bonus, annuity, and employee stock ownership plans (ESOPs) under §§ 401, 403(a), 409 and 4975(e)(7) of the Internal Revenue Code of 1986, and the status for exemption of any related trusts or custodial accounts under § 501(a). Also see Rev. Proc. 2007–44, 2007–2 C.B. 54, as modified by Rev. Proc. 2008–56, 2008–2 C.B. 826, and Rev. Proc. 2009–36, 2009–2 C.B. 304, which contains a description of the determination letter program, including when to submit a request for a determination letter within the 5-year and 6-year staggered remedial amendment cycles, that apply to individually designed and pre-approved (Master & Prototype and Volume Submitter (VS)) plans. Also see Rev. Proc. 2011–49, 2011–44 I.R.B. 608, for procedures for pre-approved plans.

This revenue procedure is effective February 1, 2013.

Organization of revenue procedure

.02 Part I of this revenue procedure contains instructions for requesting determination letters for various types of plans and transactions. Part II contains procedures for providing notice to interested parties and for interested parties to comment on determination letter requests. Part III contains procedures concerning the processing of determination letter requests and describes the effect of a determination letter.

SECTION 2. WHAT CHANGES HAVE BEEN MADE TO THIS PROCEDURE?

In general

.01 This revenue procedure is a general update of Rev. Proc. 2012-6, 2012-1 I.R.B 197, which contains the Service's general procedures for employee plans determination letter requests.

Other changes

.02 In addition to minor revisions, such as updating references, the following changes have been made:

(1) Section 5.09 is modified to include an electronic reference to Publication 794;

(2) Sections 7.02(7), 12.02(7) and 13.03(2) are revised to include Form 8821;

(3) Section 7.04 clarifies documents to submit with a determination letter application;

(4) Section 7.05 is revised to eliminate the definition of "working copy";

(5) Section 12.02(3) is revised to state that sample calculations are to be submitted along with Form 6088.

(6) Exhibit: Sample Notice to Interested Parties is revised to change the address.

Other guidance

.03 Other guidance affecting this revenue procedure:

(1) Rev. Proc. 2011–49, 2011–44 I.R.B. 608 describes the procedures for the "pre-approval" of plans under the master and prototype (M&P) program and the VS program. Rev. Proc. 2007–44 describes a system of remedial amendment cycles that applies to pre-approved plans and individually designed plans, and the deadlines to submit applications for opinion, advisory and determination letters. The Service issues a Cumulative List every year identifying changes affecting plan qualification requirements to be used by plans whose remedial amendment cycle begins in the month of February following the publication of the Cumulative List.

(2) The 2012 Cumulative List is contained in Notice 2012–76, 2012–52 I.R.B. 775.

PART I. PROCEDURES FOR DETERMINATION LETTER REQUESTS

**SECTION 3. ON WHAT ISSUES
MAY TAXPAYERS REQUEST
WRITTEN GUIDANCE UNDER
THIS PROCEDURE?**

Types of requests

.01 Determination letters may be requested on completed and proposed transactions as set forth in the table below:

	TYPE OF REQUEST	FORMS	REV. PROC. SECTION
1.	**Initial Qualification, etc.**		
a.	Individually-designed plans (including collectively bargained plans) and partial terminations	5300	7
b.	ESOPs	5300, 5309	7
c.	Adoptions of volume submitter plans (where the employer has made limited modifications to the language of the approved specimen plan)	5307	9
d.	Multiple employer plans	5300	10
e.	Group trusts	5316	13
f.	§ 414(x) combined plans	5300	7
2.	**Termination**		
a.	In general	5310, 6088	12
b.	Multiemployer plan covered by PBGC insurance	5300, 6088	12

Note: Form 5310–A, *Notice of Plan Merger, Consolidation, Spinoff or Transfer of Plan Assets or Liabilities – Notice of Qualified Separate Lines of Business* generally must be filed not less than 30 days before the merger, consolidation or transfer of assets and liabilities. The filing of Form 5310–A will not result in the issuance of a determination letter.

	TYPE OF REQUEST	FORMS	REV. PROC. SECTION
3.	**Special Procedures**		
a.	Affiliated service group status (§ 414(m)), leased employees (§ 414(n)), partial termination	5300	14
b.	Minimum funding waiver	5300	15
c.	Section 401(h) determination letters	5300	16
d.	Section 420 determination letters including other matters under § 401(a)	5300, Cover letter, Checklist	16
e.	Section 420 determination letters excluding other matters under § 401(a)	Cover letter, Checklist	16

Areas in which determination letters will not be issued

.02 Determination letters issued in accordance with this revenue procedure do not include determinations on the following issues within the jurisdiction of the Commissioner, TE/GE:

(1) Issues involving §§ 72, 79, 105, 125, 127, 129, 402, 403 (other than 403(a)), 404, 409(l), 409(m), 412, 414(h)(2), 415(m), 457, 511 through 515, and 4975 (other than 4975(e)(7)), un-

less these determination letters are authorized under section 7 of Rev. Proc. 2013–4, page 126, this Bulletin.

(2) Plans or plan amendments for which automatic approval is granted pursuant to section 19.01 of Rev. Proc. 2011–49.

(3) Plan amendments described below (these amendments will, to the extent provided, be deemed not to alter the qualified status of a plan under § 401(a)).

(a) An amendment solely to permit a trust forming part of a plan to participate in a pooled fund arrangement described in Rev. Rul. 81–100, 1981–1 C.B. 326, as clarified and modified by Rev. Rul. 2004–67, 2004–2 C.B. 28; , and Rev. Rul. 2011–1, 2011–2 I.R.B. 251;

(b) An amendment that merely adjusts the maximum limitations under § 415 to reflect annual cost-of-living increases under § 415(d), other than an amendment that adds an automatic cost-of-living adjustment provision to the plan; and

(c) An amendment solely to include language pursuant to § 403(c)(2) of Title I of the Employee Retirement Income Security Act of 1974 (ERISA) concerning the reversion of employer contributions made as a result of mistake of fact.

(4) This section applies to determination letter requests with respect to plans that combine an ESOP (as defined in § 4975(e)(7) of the Code) with retiree medical benefit features described in § 401(h) (HSOPs).

(a) In general, determination letters will not be issued with respect to plans that combine an ESOP with an HSOP with respect to:

(i)   whether the requirements of § 4975(e)(7) are satisfied;

(ii) whether the requirements of § 401(h) are satisfied; or

(iii) whether the combination of an ESOP with an HSOP in a plan adversely affects its qualification under § 401(a).

(b) A plan is considered to combine an ESOP with an HSOP if it contains ESOP provisions and § 401(h) provisions.

(c) However, an arrangement will not be considered covered by section 3.02(4) of this revenue procedure if, under the provisions of the plan, the following conditions are satisfied:

(i)   No individual accounts are maintained in the § 401(h) account (except as required by § 401(h)(6));

(ii) No employer securities are held in the § 401(h) account;

(iii) The § 401(h) account does not contain the proceeds (directly or otherwise) of an exempt loan as defined in § 54.4975–7(b)(1)(iii) of the Pension Excise Tax Regulations; and

(iv) The amount of actual contributions to provide § 401(h) benefits (when added to actual contributions for life insurance protection under the plan) does not exceed 25 percent of the sum of: (1) the amount of cash contributions actually allocated to participants' accounts in the plan and (2) the amount of cash contributions used to repay principal with respect to the exempt loan, both determined on an aggregate basis since the inception of the § 401(h) arrangement.

Submission period for applications   .03 The Service will accept applications for determination letters for the second Cycle C submission period from February 1, 2013 to January 31, 2014. The Service will also accept opinion and advisory letter applications for defined benefit plans that are Master and Prototype (M&P) or Volume Submitter (VS) plans beginning on February 1, 2013. The Service's review will take into account the qualification requirements, and other items identified on the 2012 Cumulative List in Notice 2012–76.

SECTION 4. ON WHAT ISSUES MUST WRITTEN GUIDANCE BE REQUESTED UNDER DIFFERENT PROCEDURES?

TE/GE

.01 Other procedures for obtaining rulings, determination letters, opinion letters, etc., on matters within the jurisdiction of the Commissioner, TE/GE are contained in the following revenue procedures:

(1) Employee Plans Technical (EP Technical) letter rulings, information letters, etc.: *See* Rev. Proc. 2013–4, page 126, this Bulletin.

(2) M&P and VS plans: *See*, Rev. Proc. 2011–49.

(3) Technical advice requests: *See* Rev. Proc. 2013–5, page 170, this Bulletin.

Chief Counsel's revenue procedure

.02 For the procedures for obtaining letter rulings, determination letters, etc., on matters within the jurisdiction of the Division Counsel/Associate Chief Counsel (Tax Exempt and Government Entities), or within the jurisdiction of other offices of Chief Counsel, see Rev. Proc. 2013–1, page 1, this Bulletin.

SECTION 5. WHAT IS THE GENERAL SCOPE OF A DETERMINATION LETTER?

Scope of this section

.01 This section delineates, generally, the scope of an employee plan determination letter. This section also identifies certain qualification requirements that are not considered by the Service in its review of a plan and with respect to which determination letters do not provide reliance. This section applies to all determination letters other than letters relating to the qualified status of group trusts; and certain letters relating solely to the requirements of § 420, regarding the transfer of assets in a defined benefit plan to a health benefit account described in § 401(h). For additional information pertaining to the scope of reliance on a determination letter, see sections 8, 9 and 21 of this revenue procedure.

Scope of determination letters

.02 In general, employee plans are reviewed by the Service for compliance with the form requirements (that is, those plan provisions that are required as a condition of qualification under § 401(a)). For terminating plans, the requirements are those that apply as of the date of termination. See Rev. Proc. 2007–44 for further details on the scope of the Service's review of determination letter applications.

Nondiscrimination in amount requirement

.03 Generally, a plan will not be reviewed for, and a determination letter may not be relied on with respect to, whether a plan satisfies the nondiscrimination requirements of § 401(a)(4), the minimum participation requirements of § 401(a)(26), or the minimum coverage requirements of § 410(b). However, if the applicant elects, a plan will be reviewed for, and a determination letter may be relied on with respect to whether the terms of the plan satisfy one of the design-based safe harbors in §§ 1.401(a)(4)–2(b) and 1.401(a)(4)–3(b) of the regulations (relating to nondiscrimination in amount of contributions and benefits.) A plan will also be reviewed for, and a determination letter may be relied on with respect to, whether a plan's terms satisfy the applicable requirements of sections 401(k) and 401(m).

Governmental plans under § 414(d)

.04 A plan will not be reviewed for and a determination letter does not constitute a ruling or determination as to whether the plan is a governmental plan within the meaning of § 414(d). If a determination letter applicant indicates on the application that the plan is a governmental plan within the meaning of § 414(d), the determination letter issued for the plan is predicated on that representation.

Church plans under § 414(e)

.05 A plan will not be reviewed for and a determination letter does not constitute a ruling or determination as to whether the plan is a church plan within the meaning of § 414(e). If a determination letter applicant indicates on the application that the plan is a church plan within the meaning of § 414(e), the determination letter issued for the plan is predicated on that representation.

Tax treatment of certain contributions of § 414(h)

.06 A plan will not be reviewed for and a determination letter may not be relied on with respect to whether contributions to the plan satisfy § 414(h). A determination letter does not express an opinion on whether contributions made to a plan treated as a governmental plan defined in § 414(d) constitute employer contributions under § 414(h)(2).

Other limits on scope of determination letter

.07 A favorable determination letter does not provide reliance for purposes of § 404, § 412, § 430, and §432 with respect to whether an interest rate (or any other actuarial assumption) is reasonable. A favorable determination letter does not constitute a determination with respect to whether any requirements of § 414(r), relating to whether an employer is operating qualified separate lines of business, are satisfied.

Affiliated service groups, leased employees and partial terminations

.08 Applicants may elect that the letter include a determination as to whether:

(1) the employer is a member of an affiliated service group within the meaning of § 414(m),

(2) leased employees are deemed employees of the employer under the meaning of § 414(n), and/or

(3) a partial termination has occurred with respect to the plan, and if so, its impact on plan qualification.

Publication 794

.09 Publication 794, *Favorable Determination Letter*, contains other information regarding the scope of a determination letter, including the requirement that all information submitted with the application be retained as a condition of reliance. In addition, the specific terms of each letter may further define its scope and the extent to which it may be relied upon. Publication 794 can also be found at *http://www.irs.gov/Forms-&-Pubs*.

SECTION 6. WHAT IS THE GENERAL PROCEDURE FOR REQUESTING DETERMINATION LETTERS?

Scope

.01 This section contains procedures that are generally applicable to all determination letter requests. Additional procedures for specific requests are contained in sections 7 through 16.

Qualified trusteed plans

.02 A trust created or organized in the United States and forming part of a pension, profit-sharing, stock bonus or annuity plan of an employer for the exclusive benefit of its employees or their beneficiaries that meets the requirements of § 401(a) is a qualified trust and is exempt from federal income tax under § 501(a) unless the exemption is denied under § 502, relating to feeder organizations, or § 503, relating to prohibited transactions, if, in the latter case, the plan is one described in § 503(a)(1)(B).

Qualified nontrusteed annuity plans

.03 A nontrusteed annuity plan that meets the applicable requirements of § 401(a) and other additional requirements as provided under § 403(a) and § 404(a)(2) (relating to deductions of employer contributions for the purchase of retirement annuities) qualifies for the special tax treatment under § 404(a)(2), and the other sections of the Code, if the additional provisions of such other sections are also met.

Complete information required

.04 An applicant requesting a determination letter must file the material required by this revenue procedure with Employee Plans Determinations (EP Determinations) at the address in section 6.15. The filing of the application, when accompanied by all information and documents required by this revenue procedure, will generally serve to provide the Service with the information required to make the requested determination. However, in making the determination, the Service may require the submission of additional information. Information submitted to the Service in connection with an application for determination may be subject to public inspection to the extent provided by § 6104. The applicant must include Employee Plans Compliance Resolution System documentation for any closing agreement or compliance statement (including Appendix D or F) issued or applied for during the current 5-year or 6-year remedial amendment cycle, if any, with the determination letter application.

Complete copy of plan and trust instrument required

.05 All changes made to the most recently approved version of the plan may be, but are not required to be, redlined or highlighted. The determination letter application must also include a copy of the signed and dated timely required interim and other plan amendments made to the date of the application (other than such amendments adopted on behalf of the employer by the practitioner that sponsors the employer's VS plan), as provided in section 7.04 (even if these amendments are dated earlier than a previous determination letter issued with respect to the plan) to show that the conditions for eligibility for the applicable remedial amendment period are satisfied.

In order for documents to be properly scanned, documents submitted should not be stapled or bound and the application form should be prepared using Courier 10 point font.

Section 9 of Rev. Proc. 2013–4 applies

.06 Section 9 of Rev. Proc. 2013–4 is generally applicable to requests for determination letters under this revenue procedure.

Separate application for each single § 414(l) plan

.07 A separate application is required for each single plan within the meaning of § 414(l). This requirement does not pertain to applications regarding the qualified status of group trusts.

Prior letters

.08 If the plan has received a favorable determination letter in the past, the application must include a copy of the latest determination letter. If a prior determination letter is not available, an explanation must be included with the application, and the employer must include a copy of the prior plan or adoption agreement, including the opinion or advisory letter, if applicable.

If the submitted plan is the result of a merger of two or more plans, include a copy of the prior determination letter for all the plans that combined to result in the merged plan. If a prior determination letter is not available for any such plan involved in a merger, an explanation must be included with the application, and the employer must include a copy of the prior plan document and adoption agreement, including the opinion or advisory letter, if applicable. For each plan involved in a merger, provide all of the amendments adopted after the date of the most recent determination, opinion or advisory letter for each of the merged plans, as well as the prior plan document.

User fees

.09 The appropriate user fee, if applicable, must be paid according to the procedures of Rev. Proc. 2013–8, page 237, this Bulletin. Form 8717, *User Fee for Employee Plan Determination Letter Request*, must accompany each determination letter request by an authorized representative. If the criteria for the user fee exemption are met in accordance with Notice 2011–86, 2011–45 I.R.B. 698, the certification on Form 8717 must be signed. Stamped signatures are not acceptable.

Interested party notification and comment

.10 Before filing an application, the applicant requesting a determination letter must satisfy the requirements of section 3001(a) of ERISA, and § 7476(b)(2) of the Code and the regulations thereunder, which provide that an applicant requesting a determination letter on the qualified status of certain retirement plans must notify interested parties of such application. The general rules of the Service with respect to notifying interested parties of requests for determination letters relating to the qualification of plans involving §§ 401 and 403(a) are set out below in sections 17 and 18 of this revenue procedure.

Contrary authority must be distinguished

.11 If the application for determination involves an issue where contrary authorities exist, failure to disclose or distinguish such significant contrary authorities may result in requests for additional information, which will delay action on the application.

Employer/employee relationship

.12 The Service ordinarily does not make determinations regarding the existence of an employer-employee relationship as part of its determination on the qualification of a plan, but relies on the applicant's representations or assumptions, stated or implicit, regarding the existence of such a relationship. The Service will, however, make a determination regarding the existence of an employer-employee relationship when so requested by the applicant. In such cases, the application with respect to the qualification of the plan should be filed in accordance with the provisions of this revenue procedure, contain the information and documents in the instructions to the application, and be accompanied by a completed Form SS–8, *Determination of Worker Status for Purposes of Federal Employment Taxes and Income Tax Withholding*, and any information and copies of documents the organization deems appropriate to establish its status. The Service may, in addition, require further information that it considers necessary to determine the employment status of the individuals involved or the qualification of the plan. After the employer-employee relationships have been determined, EP Determinations may issue a determination letter as to the qualification of the plan.

Incomplete applications returned

.13 If an applicant requesting a determination letter does not comply with all the required provisions of this revenue procedure, EP Determinations, in its discretion, may return the application and point out to the applicant those provisions which have not been met. The failure to provide information required by an application, including any supplemental information required by the instructions for the application, may result in the application being returned to the applicant as incomplete. The request may also be returned pursuant to Rev. Proc. 2013–8 if the correct user fee is not attached. If such a request is returned to the applicant, the 270-day period described in § 7476(b)(3) will not begin to run until such time as the provisions of this section have been satisfied. Applications must be submitted with the current version of an application form. If an application is not submitted with the current version of the appropriate application form, the application will be returned.

Effect of failure to disclose material fact

.14 The Service may determine, based on the application form, the extent of review of the plan document. A failure to disclose a material fact or misrepresentation of a material fact on the application may adversely affect the reliance that would otherwise be obtained through issuance by the Service of a favorable determination letter. Similarly, failure to accurately provide any of the information called for on any form required by this revenue procedure may result in no reliance.

Where to file requests

.15 Requests for determination letters are to be addressed to EP Determinations at the following address:

> Internal Revenue Service
> P.O. Box 12192
> Covington, KY 41012–0192

Requests shipped by Express Mail or a delivery service should be sent to:

> Internal Revenue Service
> 201 West Rivercenter Blvd.
> Attn: Extracting Stop 312
> Covington, KY 41011

Determination letter applications will not be accepted via fax.

Submission of related plans

.16 If applications for two or more plans of the same employer are submitted together, each application should include a cover letter that identifies the name of the employer and the plan numbers and employer identification numbers of all the related plans submitted together. The Service will determine whether these applications will be worked simultaneously.

Withdrawal of requests

.17 The applicant's request for a determination letter may be withdrawn by a written request at any time prior to the issuance of a final adverse determination letter. If an appeal to a proposed adverse determination letter is filed, a request for a determination letter may be withdrawn at any time prior to the forwarding of the proposed adverse action to the Chief, Appeals Office. In the case of a withdrawal, the Service will not issue a determination of any type. A failure to issue a determination letter as a result of a withdrawal will not be considered a failure of the Secretary or his delegate to make a determination within the meaning of § 7476. However, the Service may consider the information submitted in connection with the withdrawn request in a subsequent examination. Generally, the user fee will not be refunded if the application is withdrawn.

Right to status conference

.18 An applicant for a determination letter has the right to a have a conference with the EP Determinations Manager concerning the status of the application if the application has been pending at least 270 days. The status conference may be by phone or in person, as mutually agreed upon. During the conference, any issues relevant to the processing of the application may be addressed, but the conference will not involve substantive discussion of technical issues. No tape, stenographic, or other verbatim recording of a status conference may be made by any party. Subsequent status conferences may also be requested if at least 90 days have passed since the last preceding status conference.

How to request status conference

.19 A request for a status conference with the EP Determinations Manager is to be made in writing and is to be sent to the specialist assigned to review the application or, if the applicant does not know who is reviewing the application, to the EP Determinations Manager at the address in section 6.15. If, pursuant to section 15, the application for a determination letter has been submitted to Employee Plans Technical (EP Technical) together with a request for a waiver of minimum funding, the request for a status conference should be sent to the address in section 15.03. In this case, the right to a status conference will be with the EP Technical Manager or designee.

SECTION 7. WHEN DETERMINATION LETTERS ARE ISSUED

Requesting Determination Letters

.01 This section 7 contains the procedures for requesting determination letters for individually designed plans in the following circumstances:

(1) Initial qualification.

(2) Amendment and restatement subsequent to initial qualification.

(3) Plan termination.

Forms

.02 A determination letter request for the items listed in section 7.01 is made by filing the appropriate form according to the instructions to the form and any prevailing revenue procedures, notices, and announcements.

(1) Form 5300, *Application for Determination for Employee Benefit Plan*, must be filed to request a determination letter for individually designed plans, including collectively bargained plans and M&P plans that have made modifications.

(2) Form 5309, *Application for Determination of Employee Stock Ownership Plan*, must be filed as an attachment with a Form 5300, in order to request a determination whether the plan is an ESOP under § 409 or § 4975(e)(7).

(3) Form 5310, *Application for Determination for Terminating Plan* (Also see section 12 of this revenue procedure for additional requirements pertaining to applications for determination upon plan termination.)

(4) Form 8905, *Certification of Intent to Adopt a Pre-approved Plan*, executed before the end of the employer's 5-year remedial amendment cycle as determined under Part III of Rev. Proc. 2007–44, if applicable.

(5) Form 8717, *User Fee for Employee Plan Determination Letter Request*.

(6) Form 2848, *Power of Attorney and Declaration of Representative*.

(7) Form 8821, *Tax Information Authorization*.

Timing

.03 All determination letter submissions must be submitted timely under the procedures set forth in Rev. Proc. 2007–44. The timing of the submission period for any particular individually designed plan within staggered remedial amendment cycles will depend on the plan's particular cycle. The second submission period for Cycle C individually designed plans will begin February 1, 2013 and will end on January 31, 2014. Generally, an off-cycle application will not be reviewed until all on-cycle plans have been reviewed and processed. Section 14.02, (1)–(3) of Rev. Proc. 2007–44 lists the types of applications that may be submitted off-cycle and given the same priority as on cycle applications.

Applicants are reminded that an off-cycle application will not be converted to an on-cycle application once the on-cycle submission period begins if the off-cycle application has not been processed. Generally, if an off-cycle application is not reviewed before the beginning of the on-cycle period, the application will be returned with the user fee.

Application must include copy of plan and amendments

.04 The plan, all interim and other plan amendments adopted or effective during the plan's current remedial amendment cycle must be included in the application package along with a copy of the restated plan and trust instrument. If the plan did not receive a favorable determination letter, all plan documents and amendments for the cumulative list applicable for the plan's prior submission period must be submitted. If the plan relied upon an opinion or advisory letter with respect to its prior remedial amendment cycle, the plan, adoption agreements and all applicable amendments for the plan's prior submission period must also be submitted.

In general, a determination letter may not be relied upon for any period preceding the beginning of the remedial amendment cycle for which the letter is issued. Thus, for example, if an application for a determination letter includes a plan amendment that was effective before the beginning of the plan's current remedial amendment cycle, the determination letter may not be relied upon with respect to the effect of the amendment for the period preceding the beginning of the cycle.

The Service has the discretion to request copies of any amendments during its review of a plan.

Restatements required

.05 Individually designed plans must be restated when they are submitted for determination letter applications.

Controlled group elections pursuant to Revenue Procedure 2007–44.

.06 If, pursuant to Rev. Proc. 2007–44, an election has been made for related entities (as described under section 10 of that revenue procedure) to be on the same cycle, each application must include a cover letter that identifies the name of each member of the controlled group and/or employer within the affiliated service group, and the plan numbers and employer identification numbers of all the related plans submitted together. When a controlled group election has been made for multiple plans to be on the same cycle, the Service will determine whether these applications will be worked simultaneously.

§ 414(x) combined plans

.07 The Service will consider § 414(x) in issuing determination letters for individually designed plans that consist of a defined benefit plan and a qualified cash or deferred arrangement. A § 414(x) combined plan sponsor must submit two Forms 5300 and two applicable user fees.

SECTION 8. EMPLOYER RELIANCE ON M&P AND VOLUME SUBMITTER PLANS

Scope

.01 Rev. Proc. 2011–49 describes the procedures for requesting opinion letters and advisory letters on M&P and VS plans and the extent to which adopting employers of such plans may rely on favorable opinion or advisory letters without having to request individual determination letters.

Modifications to Revenue Procedure 2011–49

.02 Rev. Proc. 2011–49 is hereby modified as follows with respect to determination letter applications filed on or after May 1, 2012:

(1) An adopting employer of an M&P plan (whether standardized or nonstandardized) may not apply for a determination letter for the plan on Form 5307.

(2) An adopting employer of a VS plan may not apply for a determination letter for the plan on Form 5307 unless the employer has modified the terms of the approved plan and the modifications are not so extensive as to cause the plan to be treated as an individually designed plan.

(3) An application for a determination letter for an M&P or VS plan that is filed on Form 5300 is treated as an application for an individually designed plan, requiring the plan to be restated to take into account the Cumulative List in effect when the application is filed, unless the employer is filing the application solely for one or more of the following reasons:

(a) The employer has modified the terms of the M&P plan by adding overriding language necessary to coordinate the application of the limitations of section 415 or the requirements of section 416 because the employer maintains multiple plans.

(b) The plan is a pension plan and the normal retirement age under the plan is lower than 62. In this case, a determination letter is required for reliance that the plan's normal retirement age satisfies the requirements of section 1.401(a)–1(b)(2) of the regulations.

(c) The employer seeks a determination as to whether there has been a partial termination of the plan, the employer is a member of an affiliated service group under section 414(m), or the employer is a recipient of services of leased employees under section 414(n).

(d) The plan is a multiple employer plan.

(e) The employer is required to obtain a determination letter to comply with published procedures of the Service (for example, in conjunction with a request for a minimum funding waiver).

In the situations described in subparagraphs (a) through (e), the plan does not have to be restated for the Cumulative List in effect when the application is filed and will be reviewed on the basis of the Cumulative List that was considered in issuing the opinion or advisory letter for the plan. An employer that submits an application for a determination letter for an M&P or VS plan on Form 5300 for one or more of the reasons described in subparagraphs (a) through (e) should identify the reason in a cover letter to the application and include a copy of the opinion or advisory letter.

Section 9 of this revenue procedure describes the procedures for requesting determination letters on VS plans where the employer has made limited modifications to the language of the approved specimen plan.

Reliance equivalent to determination letter

.03 If an employer can rely on a favorable opinion or advisory letter pursuant to Section 19 of Rev. Proc. 2011–49, as modified by this revenue procedure, the opinion or advisory letter shall be equivalent to a favorable determination letter. For example, the favorable opinion or advisory letter shall be treated as a favorable determination letter for purposes of section 21 of this revenue procedure, regarding the effect of a determination letter, and section 5.01(4) of Rev. Proc. 2008–50, 2008–35 I.R.B. 464, as updated, regarding the definition of "favorable letter" for purposes of the Employee Plans Compliance Resolution System.

SECTION 9. DETERMINATION LETTER FILING PROCEDURES FOR VOLUME SUBMITTER PLANS

Scope

.01 This section contains procedures for requesting determination letters for adopting employers of VS plans where the employer has made limited modifications to the approved specimen plan.

Determination letter for adoption of volume submitter plan

.02 An application filed on Form 5307, must include any interim plan amendments unless the VS plan authorizes the practitioner to amend on behalf of the adopting employer. The Service may, however, request evidence of adoption of interim amendments during the course of its review of a particular plan. With respect to determination letters for adopting employers of VS plans:

(1) An application for a determination letter for an employer's adoption of an approved VS plan where the employer has made limited modifications to the language of the approved specimen plan must be sent to the address provided in section 6.15. For VS plans involved in plan mergers, see section 6.08 of this procedure.

(2) The application for a determination letter must include the following:

(a) Form 8717, *User Fee for Employee Plan Determination Letter Request*;

(b) Form 5307, *Application for Determination for Adopters of Modified Volume Submitter (VS) Plans*;

(c) Form 2848, *Power of Attorney and Declaration of Representative*, or other written authorization allowing the VS practitioner to act as a representative of the employer with respect to the request for a determination letter;

(d) Form 8905, *Certification of Intent to Adopt a Pre-approved Plan*, executed before the end of the employer's 5-year remedial amendment cycle as determined under Part III of Rev. Proc. 2007–44, if applicable;

(e) A copy of the most recent advisory letter for the practitioner's VS specimen plan;

(f) A complete copy of the plan and trust instrument, if applicable, and a copy of the completed adoption agreement;

(g) A written representation (signature optional) made by the VS practitioner which explains how the plan and trust instrument differ from the approved specimen plan, describing the location, nature and effect of each deviation from the language of the approved specimen plan;

(h) A copy of the plan's latest favorable determination letter, if applicable;

(i) Applications filed on Form 5307 for VS plans where the employer has made modifications to the language of the approved specimen plan that do not authorize the practitioner to amend on behalf of the adopting employer must include any interim amendments that were adopted for qualification changes on the applicable Cumulative List used in reviewing and approving the underlying VS plan; and

(j) Any other information or material that may be required by the Service.

(3) Deviations from the language of the approved specimen plan will be evaluated based on the extent and complexities of the changes. If the changes are determined not to be compatible with the VS program, the Service may require the applicant to file Form 5300 and pay the higher user fee. *See also*, Rev. Proc. 2007–44, section 19.

(4) An employer will not be treated as having adopted a VS plan if the employer has signed or otherwise adopted the plan prior to the date on the VS specimen plan's advisory letter. In this case, the determination letter application for the employer's plan may not be filed on Form 5307 and will not be eligible for a reduced user fee. A determination letter application for a VS plan must be based on the approved VS specimen plan with any applicable modifications. *See* section 19.03 in Rev. Proc. 2011–49.

Timing of determination letter applications for adopting employers of pre-approved plans

.03 In accordance with Part IV of Rev. Proc. 2007–44, adopting employers of M&P and volume submitter plans have a six-year remedial amendment cycle. The Service's announced deadline for an adopting employer to adopt the approved M&P or volume submitter plan will be the approximate two-year window at the end of the plan's remedial amendment cycle with respect to all disqualifying provisions for which the remedial amendment period would otherwise end during the cycle. An adopting employer of an M&P or a volume submitter plan who must obtain a determination letter for reliance must not submit such determination letter application until the Service's announced deadline for employers to adopt a pre-approved plan and, if necessary, file a determination letter application, as described in Part IV of Rev. Proc. 2007–44. See section 17 of Rev. Proc. 2007–44 for the eligibility requirements that must be satisfied in order to be considered an adopting employer of an M&P plan or a volume submitter plan and thus eligible for the six-year remedial amendment cycle.

Applications submitted prior to the Service's announced two-year window deadline for an adopting employer to adopt the approved master and prototype (M&P) or volume submitter (VS) plan will be returned to the applicant.

SECTION 10. MULTIPLE EMPLOYER PLANS

Scope

.01 This section contains procedures for applications filed with respect to plans described in § 413(c). A plan is not described in § 413(c) if all the employers maintaining the plan are members of the same controlled group or affiliated service group under § 414(b), (c) or (m).

Options to file for the plan only or for both the plan and employers maintaining the plan

.02 A determination letter applicant for a multiple employer plan can request either (1) a letter for the plan in the name of the controlling member or (2) a letter for the plan in the name of the controlling member and a letter for each employer maintaining the plan with respect to whom a separate Form 5300 is filed.

(1) An applicant requesting a letter for the plan submits one Form 5300 application for the plan in the name of the controlling member, either including or omitting the design-based safe harbor questions. The user fee for a single employer plan will apply. An employer maintaining a multiple employer plan can rely on a favorable determination letter issued for the plan except with respect to the requirements of §§ 401(a)(4), 401(a)(26), 401(l), 410(b) and 414(s), and, if the employer maintains or has ever maintained another plan, §§ 415 and 416.

(2) An applicant requesting a letter for the plan and for an employer maintaining the plan must submit the filing required in (1) above as well as a separate Form 5300 application, completed through line 8, and, if applicable, a completed adoption agreement, for each employer requesting a separate letter. The user fee for the application will be determined under the user fee schedules for multiple employer plans in section 6.05 of Rev. Proc. 2013–8.

Where to file

.03 The complete application, including all Forms 5300 (and, if applicable, adoption agreements) for employers maintaining the plan who request separate letters must be filed as one submission with EP Determinations. The application is to be sent to the address in section 6.15.

Determination letter sent to each employer who files Form 5300

.04 The Service will mail a determination letter to each employer maintaining the plan for whom a separate Form 5300 has been filed.

Addition of employers

.05 An employer may continue to rely on a favorable determination letter after another employer commences participation in the plan, regardless of whether the first employer's reliance is based on its own letter or the letter issued for the plan and regardless of whether an application for a determination letter for the new employer is filed. An application for a determination letter that takes into account the addition of such other employer should include a completed Form 5300 for the plan in the name of the controlling member on the Form 5300 filed pursuant to section 10.02 above, and a supplemental Form 5300 (and, if applicable, adoption agreement) for each new employer who desires a separate determination letter. The Service will send the determination letter only to the applicant and the new employers. However, a new employer that joins a multiple employer plan after the existing multiple employer plan was timely submitted in Cycle B (the applicable cycle as described in section 10 of Rev. Proc. 2007–44), will be subject to the rules under Rev. Proc. 2007–44, including the off-cycle filing rules under section 14 of that revenue procedure.

SECTION 11. RESERVED   Reserved

SECTION 12. TERMINATION OR DISCONTINUANCE OF CONTRIBUTIONS; NOTICE OF MERGERS, CONSOLIDATIONS, ETC.

Scope

.01 This section contains procedures for requesting determination letters involving plan termination or discontinuance of contributions. This section also contains procedures regarding required notice of merger, consolidation, or transfer of assets or liabilities.

Forms

.02 Required Forms

(1) Form 5310, *Application for Determination for Terminating Plan*, is filed by plans other than multiemployer plans covered by the insurance program of the Pension Benefit Guaranty Corporation (PBGC).

(2) Form 5300, *Application for Determination of Employee Benefit Plan*, is filed in the case of a multiemployer plan covered by PBGC insurance.

(3) Form 6088, *Distributable Benefits from Employee Pension Benefit Plans*, is also required of a sponsor or plan administrator of a defined benefit plan or an underfunded defined contribution plan who files an application for a determination letter regarding plan termination. For collectively bargained plans, a Form 6088 is required only if the plan benefits employees who are not collectively bargained employees within the meaning of § 1.410(b)–6(d). A separate Form 6088 is required for each employer employing such employees. See Instructions for Form 6088 for information required to be submitted along with the form, including calculations.

(4) Form 5310–A, *Notice of Plan Merger or Consolidation, Spinoff, or Transfer of Plan Assets or Liabilities — Notice of Qualified Separate Lines of Business*, if required, generally must be filed not later than 30 days before merger, consolidation or transfer of assets and liabilities. The filing of Form 5310–A will not result in the issuance of a determination letter.

(5) Form 8905, *Certification of Intent to Adopt a Pre-approved Plan*, must be filed to establish the employer's eligibility for the 6-year remedial amendment cycle where the employer executed the form by the end of the employer's 5-year remedial amendment cycle as determined under Part III of Rev. Proc. 2007–44.

(6) Form 8717, *User Fee for Employee Plan Determination Letter Request*.

(7) Form 2848, *Power of Attorney and Declaration of Representative*, or other written authorization allowing the VS practitioner to act as a representative of the employer with respect to the request for a determination letter. If applicable, submit Form 8821, *Tax Information Authorization*.

Supplemental information

.03 The application for a determination letter involving plan termination must also include any supplemental information or schedules required by the forms or form instructions. For example, the application must include copies of all records of actions taken to terminate the plan (such as a resolution of the board of directors) and a schedule providing certain information regarding employees who separated from vesting service with less than 100% vesting.

In cases involving the termination of plans that contain a § 401(h) feature, the cover letter of the submission must reference the § 401(h) feature and make clear that this feature is part of the termination application. The cover letter must specifically state the location of plan provisions that relate to the § 401(h) feature.

Compliance with Title IV of ERISA	.04 In the case of plans subject to Title IV of ERISA, a favorable determination letter issued in connection with a plan's termination is conditioned on approval that the termination is a valid termination under Title IV of ERISA. Notification by PBGC that a plan may not be terminated will be treated as a material change of fact.
Termination prior to time for amending for change in law	.05 A plan that terminates after the effective date of a change in law, but prior to the date that amendments are otherwise required, must be amended to comply with the applicable provisions of law from the date on which such provisions become effective with respect to the plan. Because such a terminated plan would no longer be in existence by the required amendment date and therefore could not be amended on that date, such plan must be amended in connection with the plan termination to comply with those provisions of law that become effective with respect to the plan on or before the date of plan termination. (Such amendments include any amendments made after the date of plan termination that were required in order to obtain a favorable determination letter.) In addition, annuity contracts distributed from such terminated plans also must meet all the applicable provisions of any change in law. See also section 8 of Rev. Proc. 2007–44.
	An application will be deemed to be filed in connection with plan termination if it is filed no later than the later of (i) one year from the effective date of the termination, or (ii) one year from the date on which the action terminating the plan is adopted. However, in no event can the application be filed later than twelve months from the date of distribution of substantially all plan assets in connection with the termination of the plan.
Restatement not required for terminating plan	.06 A terminating plan generally does not have to be restated. However, see section 7.05 and .05 of this section above.

SECTION 13. GROUP TRUSTS

Scope	.01 This section provides special procedures for requesting a determination letter on the qualified status of a group trust under Rev. Rul. 81–100, as clarified and modified by Rev. Rul. 2004–67 and Rev. Rul. 2011–1, 2011–2 I.R.B. 251.
Required information	.02 A request for a determination letter on the status of a group trust is made by submitting a Form 5316, *Application for Group or Pooled Trust Ruling*, demonstrating how the group trust satisfies the criteria listed in Rev. Rul. 2011–1, together with the trust instrument and related documents. Rev. Rul. 2004–67 extends the ability to participate in group trusts to eligible governmental plans under § 457(b) and clarifies the ability of certain individual retirement accounts under § 408 to participate. Rev. Rul. 2011–1 extends the ability to participate in group trusts to custodial accounts under § 403(b)(7), retirement income accounts under § 403(b)(9), and governmental retiree benefit plans under § 401(a)(24). There are two model amendments in Rev. Rul. 2011–1. Amendment 1 is for a group trust that received a determination letter from the Service prior to January 10, 2011, that the group trust satisfies Rev. Rul. 81–100, but that does not satisfy the separate account requirement of paragraph (6) of the Holding of Rev. Rul. 2011–1. Amendment 2 is for a group trust that received a determination letter from the Service prior to January 10, 2011, that the group trust satisfies Rev. Rul. 81–100, as modified by Rev. Rul. 2004–67, and that intends to permit custodial accounts under § 403(b)(7), retirement income accounts under § 403(b)(9), or § 401(a)(24) governmental retirement plans to participate in the group trust.
Forms	.03 Required Forms
	(1) Form 8717, *User Fee for Employee Plan Determination Letter Request.*.
	(2) Form 2848, *Power of Attorney and Declaration of Representative*, or other written authorization allowing the VS practitioner to act as a representative of the employer with respect to the request for a determination letter. If applicable, submit Form 8821, *Tax Information Authorization*.
	(3) Form 5316, *Application for Group or Pooled Trust Ruling*.

**SECTION 14. AFFILIATED
SERVICE GROUPS; LEASED
EMPLOYEES**

Scope

.01 This section provides procedures for determination letter requests on affiliated service group status under § 414(m), and whether an employee is a leased employee and is deemed to be an employee of the recipient employer for qualification purposes under § 414(n).

**Employer must request the
determination under § 414(m) or
§ 414(n)**

.02 Generally, a determination letter will indicate whether the employer is a member of an affiliated service group under § 414(m) or whether an employee is a leased employee and is deemed to be an employee of the recipient employer under § 414(n) only if the employer requests such determination, and submits with the determination letter application the information specified in section 14.06 or section 14.07 below.

Forms

.03 Form 5300 is submitted for a request on affiliated service group status or leased employee status. Form 5307 cannot be used for this purpose.

**Employer is responsible for
determining status under § 414(m)
and § 414(n)**

.04 An employer is responsible for determining at any particular time whether it is a member of an affiliated service group and, if so, whether its plan(s) continues to meet the requirements of § 401(a) taking into account § 414(m). An employer or plan administrator is also responsible for taking action relative to the employer's qualified plan if that employer becomes, or ceases to be, a member of an affiliated service group. An employer that is the recipient of services of leased employees within the meaning of § 414(n) is also responsible for determining at any particular time whether a leased employee is deemed to be an employee of the recipient for qualified plan purposes.

Pre-approved plans

.05 An employer that has adopted a pre-approved plan and wants a determination with respect to § 414(m) or § 414(n) must submit the information required by section 14.06 or section 14.07 of this revenue procedure and any other materials necessary to make a determination along with Form 5300. When an employer requests a determination regarding affiliated service group status or leased employees, the plan will be reviewed on the basis of the Cumulative List that was used to review the underlying pre-approved plan.

**Required information for § 414(m)
determination**

.06 A determination letter will be issued with respect to § 414(m) only if the employer requests such a determination and the application includes:

(1) A description of the nature of the business of the employer, specifically whether it is a service organization or an organization whose principal business is the performance of management functions for another organization, including the reasons therefor;

(2) The identification of other members (or possible members) of the affiliated service group;

(3) A description of the business of each member (or possible member) of the affiliated service group, describing the type of organization (corporation, partnership, etc.) and indicating whether the member is a service organization or an organization whose principal business is the performance of management functions for the other group member(s);

(4) The ownership interests between the employer and the members (or possible members) of the affiliated service group (including ownership interests as described in § 414(m)(2)(B)(ii) or § 414(m)(6)(B));

(5) A description of services performed for the employer by the members (or possible members) of the affiliated service group, or vice versa (including the percentage of each member's (or possible member's) gross receipts and service receipts provided by such services, if available, and data as to whether such services are a significant portion of the member's business) and whether, as of December 13, 1980, it was not unusual for the services to be performed by employees of organizations in that service field in the United States;

(6) A description of how the employer and the members (or possible members) of the affiliated service group associate in performing services for other parties;

(7) In the case of a management organization under § 414(m)(5):

(a) A description of the management functions, if any, performed by the employer for the member(s) (or possible member(s)) of the affiliated service group, or received by the employer from any other members (or possible members) of the group (including data explaining whether the management functions are performed on a regular and continuous basis) and whether or not it is unusual for such management functions to be performed by employees of organizations in the employer's business field in the United States;

(b) If management functions are performed by the employer for the member (or possible members) of the affiliated service group, a description of what part of the employer's business constitutes the performance of management functions for the member (or possible member) of the group (including the percentage of gross receipts derived from management activities as compared to the gross receipts from other activities);

(8) A copy of any ruling issued by the headquarters office on whether the employer is an affiliated service group; a copy of any prior determination letter that considered the effect of § 414(m); and, if known, a copy of any such ruling or determination letter issued to any other member (or possible member) of the same affiliated service group, accompanied by a statement as to whether the facts upon which the ruling or determination letter was based have changed.

Required information for § 414(n) determination

.07 A determination letter will be issued with respect to § 414(n) only if the employer requests such a determination and the application includes:

(1) A description of the nature of the business of the recipient organization;

(2) A copy of the relevant leasing agreement(s);

(3) A description of the function of all leased employees within the trade or business of the recipient organization (including data as to whether all leased employees are performing services on a substantially full-time basis);

(4) A description of facts and circumstances relevant to a determination of whether such leased employees' services are performed under primary direction or control by the recipient organization (including whether the leased employees are required to comply with instructions of the recipient about when, where, and how to perform the services, whether the services must be performed by particular persons, whether the leased employees are subject to the supervision of the recipient, and whether the leased employees must perform services in the order or sequence set by the recipient);

(5) If the recipient organization is relying on any qualified plan(s) maintained by the employee leasing organization for purposes of qualification of the recipient organization's plan, a description of such plan(s) (including a description of the contributions or benefits provided for all leased employees which are attributable to services performed for the recipient organization, plan eligibility, and vesting.)

SECTION 15. WAIVER OF MINIMUM FUNDING

Scope

.01 This section provides procedures with respect to defined contribution plans for requesting a waiver of the minimum funding standard account and requesting a determination letter on any plan amendment required for the waiver.

Applicability of Rev. Proc. 2004–15

.02 The procedures in Rev. Proc. 2004–15, 2004–1 C.B. 490, apply to the request for a waiver of the minimum funding requirement. Section 2 of that revenue procedure contains the procedures for obtaining waivers of the minimum funding standards in the instance of defined benefit plans. In order to provide maximum flexibility in requesting a waiver for a defined contribution pension plan, section 3 of that revenue procedure contains three alternative methods as described more fully in Rev. Proc. 2004–15.

Waiver request submitted to EP Technical

.03 The first two alternatives involve (1) a waiver ruling only, without submission of a plan amendment, and (2) a waiver ruling only, with submission of a plan amendment. Under these first two procedures, requests for waivers must be submitted to:

> Employee Plans
> Internal Revenue Service
> Commissioner, TE/GE
> Attention: SE:T:EP:RA
> P.O. Box 27063
> McPherson Station
> Washington, D.C. 20038

In both cases, the applicant must satisfy the requirements of section 2 of Rev. Proc. 2004–15, other than the parts applicable only to defined benefit plans.

If a plan amendment is not submitted or is not already part of a plan, the Service will supply an amendment which will, if adopted, satisfy section 3 of Rev. Rul. 78–223, 1978–1 C.B. 125. The waiver will be conditioned upon the plan being amended by adoption of that amendment, within a reasonable period of time, and will contain a caveat stating that the ruling is not a ruling as to the effect the plan provision may have on the qualified status of the plan. The applicant may request reconsideration within 60 days of the date of the letter if the amendment is inappropriate, by submitting a letter to the above address.

If the request for the waiver is submitted along with a plan amendment, the plan provisions necessary to satisfy section 3 of Rev. Rul. 78–223 must be included. All waivers issued pursuant to this alternative will contain a caveat indicating that the ruling is not a ruling as to the effect any plan provision may have on the qualified status of the plan.

Waiver and determination letter request submitted to EP Technical

.04 The third alternative is a request for a waiver ruling and a determination letter request. Both requests must be submitted by the applicant to EP Technical at the address set forth in section 15.03 where it will be treated as if it had been submitted as a request for technical advice from the Determinations Manager. The request must:

(1) satisfy all the procedural requirements of 3.03 of Rev. Proc. 2004–15;

(2) include a completed Form 5300 and all necessary documents, plan amendments and information required by the Form 5300 and Rev. Proc. 2004–15 for approval;

(3) indicate which Area Office has audit jurisdiction over the return; and

(4) submit the user fee for both requests to EP Technical.

In addition, the procedures for notice and comment by interested parties, contained in sections 17, 18 and 19 of this revenue procedure, and the notice and comment procedures provided in section 2.02 of Rev. Proc. 2004–15 must be satisfied. Comments will be forwarded to the Determinations Office that is considering the determination letter request for the plan amendments.

Handling of the request

.05 The waiver request described in section 15.04 above will be handled by EP Technical as follows:

(1) The waiver request and supporting documents will be forwarded to EP Technical, SE:T:EP:RA:T, which will treat the request as a technical advice on the qualification issue with respect to the plan provisions necessary to satisfy section 3 of Rev. Rul. 78–223.

(2) The appropriate Determinations Office will be notified of the request. In order not to delay the processing of the request, all materials relating to the determination letter request will be forwarded by EP Technical to the Determinations Manager for consideration while the technical advice request is completed.

(3) EP Technical will consider both issues. If a waiver is to be granted and if EP Technical believes that qualification of the plan is not adversely affected by the plan amendment, the mandatory technical advice memorandum will be issued to the Determinations Manager. The Determinations Manager must decide within 10 working days from the date of the technical advice memorandum either to furnish the applicant with the technical advice memorandum and with a favorable advance determination letter, or to ask for reconsideration of the technical advice memorandum. This request must be in writing. An initial written notice of intent to make this request may be submitted within 10 working days of the date of the technical advice memorandum and followed by a written request within 30 working days from the date of such written notice. If the Determinations Manager does not ask for reconsideration of the technical advice memorandum within 10 working days, EP Technical will issue the waiver ruling. This ruling will not contain the caveat described in section 3.02 of Rev. Proc. 2004–15.

When waiver request should be submitted

.06 In the case of a plan other than a multiemployer plan, all waiver requests must be submitted to the Service no later than the 15th day of the third month following the close of the plan year for which the waiver is requested. The Service may not extend this statutory deadline. A request for a waiver with respect to a multiemployer plan generally must be submitted no later than the close of the plan year following the plan year for which the waiver is requested.

In seeking a waiver with respect to a plan year that has not yet ended, the applicant may have difficulty in furnishing sufficient current evidence in support of the request. For this reason it is generally advisable that such advance request be submitted no earlier than 180 days prior to the end of the plan year for which the waiver is requested.

SECTION 16. SECTION 401(h) AND § 420 DETERMINATION LETTERS

Scope

.01 This section provides procedures for requesting determination letters (i) with respect to whether the requirements of § 401(h) are satisfied in a plan with retiree medical benefit features and (ii) on plan language that permits, pursuant to § 420, the transfer of assets in a defined benefit plan to a health benefit account described in § 401(h).

Required information for § 401(h) determination

.02 EP Determinations will issue a determination letter that considers whether the requirements of § 401(h) are satisfied in a plan with retiree medical benefit features only if the plan sponsor requests such a determination and the sponsor's application includes, in addition to the application forms and any other material required by this revenue procedure, a cover letter that requests consideration of § 401(h). The cover letter must specifically state that consideration is being requested with regard to § 401(h) in addition to other matters under § 401(a) and must specifically state the location of plan provisions that satisfy the requirements of § 401(h). Part I of the checklist in the Appendix of this revenue procedure may be used to identify the location of relevant plan provisions.

Required information for § 420 determination

.03 EP Determinations will consider the qualified status of certain plan language designed to comply with § 420 only if the plan sponsor requests such consideration with Form 5300 in a cover letter. The cover letter must specifically state (i) whether consideration is being requested only with regard to § 420, or (ii) whether consideration is being requested with regard to § 420 in addition to other matters under § 401(a). (If consideration of other matters under § 401(a) is being requested, the application forms and other material required by this revenue procedure must also be submitted.) The cover letter must specifically state the location of plan provisions that satisfy each of the following requirements. Parts I and II of the checklist in the Appendix of this revenue procedure may be used to identify the location of relevant plan provisions.

(1) The plan must include a health benefits account as described in § 401(h).

(2) The plan must provide that transfers shall be limited to transfers of "excess assets" as defined in § 420(e)(2).

(3) The plan must provide that only one transfer may be made in a taxable year. However, for purposes of determining whether the rule in the preceding sentence is met, a plan may provide that a transfer will not be taken into account if it is a transfer that:

(a) Is made after the close of the taxable year preceding the employer's first taxable year beginning after December 31, 1990, and before the earlier of (i) the due date (including extensions) for the filing of the return of tax for such preceding year, or (ii) the date such return is filed; and

(b) Does not exceed the expenditures of the employer for qualified current retiree health liabilities for such preceding taxable year.

(4) The plan must provide that the amount transferred shall not exceed the amount which is reasonably estimated to be the amount the employer will pay out (whether directly or through reimbursement) of the health benefit account during the taxable year of the transfer for "qualified current retiree health liabilities," as defined in § 420(e)(1).

(5) The plan must provide that no transfer will be made after December 31, 2013.

(6) The plan must provide that any assets transferred, and any income allocable to such assets, shall be used only to pay qualified current retiree health liabilities for the taxable year of transfer.

(7) The plan must provide that any amounts transferred to a health benefits account (and income attributable to such amounts) which are not used to pay qualified current retiree health liabilities shall be transferred back to the defined benefit portion of the plan.

(8) The plan must provide that the amounts paid out of a health benefits account will be treated as paid first out of transferred assets and income attributable to those assets.

(9) The plan must provide that the accrued pension benefits for participants and beneficiaries must become nonforfeitable as if the plan had terminated immediately prior to the transfer (or in the case of a participant who separated during the 1-year period ending on the date of transfer immediately before such separation). In the case of a transfer described in § 420(b)(4) that relates to a prior year, the plan must provide that the accrued benefit of a participant who separated from service during the taxable year to which such transfer relates will be recomputed and treated as nonforfeitable immediately before such separation.

(10) The plan must provide that a transfer will be permitted only if each group health plan or arrangement under which health benefits are provided contains provisions satisfying § 420(c)(3). The plan must define "applicable employer cost", "cost maintenance period", and "benefit maintenance period", as applicable, consistent with § 420(c)(3), as amended. If applicable, the provisions of the plan must also reflect the transition rule in § 535(c)(2) of the Tax Relief Extension Act of 1999 (TREA '99). The plan may provide that § 420(c)(3) is satisfied separately with respect to individuals eligible for benefits under Title XVIII of the Social Security Act at any time during the taxable year and with respect to individuals not so eligible.

(11) The plan must provide that transferred assets cannot be used for key employees (as defined in § 416(i)(1)).

PART II. INTERESTED PARTY NOTICE AND COMMENT

SECTION 17. WHAT RIGHTS TO NOTICE AND COMMENT DO INTERESTED PARTIES HAVE?

Rights of interested parties   .01 Persons who qualify as interested parties under § 1.7476–1(b), have the following rights:

(1) To receive notice, in accordance with section 18 below, that an application for an advance determination will be filed regarding the qualification of plans described in §§ 401, 403(a), 409 and/or 4975(e)(7);

(2) To submit written comments with respect to the qualification of such plans to the Service;

(3) To request the Department of Labor to submit a comment to the Service on behalf of the interested parties; and

(4) To submit written comments to the Service on matters with respect to which the Department of Labor was requested to comment but declined.

Comments by interested parties

.02 Comments submitted by interested parties must be received by EP Determinations by the 45th day after the day on which the application for determination is received by EP Determinations. (However, see sections 17.03 and 17.04 for filing deadlines where the Department of Labor has been requested to comment.) Such comments must be in writing, signed by the interested parties or by an authorized representative of such parties (as provided in section 9.02(11) of Rev. Proc. 2013–4), addressed to EP Determinations at the address in section 6.17, and contain the following information:

(1) The names of the interested parties making the comments;

(2) The name and taxpayer identification number of the applicant for a determination;

(3) The name of the plan, the plan identification number, and the name of the plan administrator;

(4) Whether the parties submitting the comment are:

(a) Employees eligible to participate under the plan,

(b) Employees with accrued benefits under the plan, or former employees with vested benefits under the plan,

(c) Beneficiaries of deceased former employees who are eligible to receive or are currently receiving benefits under the plan,

(d) Employees not eligible to participate under the plan.

(5) The specific matters raised by the interested parties on the question of whether the plan meets the requirements for qualification involving §§ 401 and 403(a), and how such matters relate to the interests of the parties making the comment; and

(6) The address of the interested party submitting the comment (or if a comment is submitted jointly by more than one party, the name and address of a designated representative) to which all correspondence, including a notice of the Service's final determination with respect to qualification, should be sent. (The address designated for notice by the Service will also be used by the Department of Labor in communicating with the parties submitting a request for comment.) The designated representative may be one of the interested parties submitting the comment or an authorized representative. If two or more interested parties submit a single comment and one person is not designated in the comment as the representative for receipt of correspondence, a notice of determination mailed to any interested party who submitted the comment shall be notice to all the interested parties who submitted the comment for purposes of § 7476(b)(5) of the Code.

Requests for DOL to submit comments

.03 A request to the Department of Labor to submit to EP Determinations a comment pursuant to section 3001(b)(2) of ERISA must be made in accordance with the following procedures.

(1) The request must be received by the Department of Labor by the 25th day after the day the application for determination is received by EP Determinations. However, if the parties requesting the Department to submit a comment wish to preserve the right to comment to EP

Determinations in the event the Department declines to comment, the request must be received by the Department by the 15th day after the day the application for determination is received by EP Determinations.

(2) The request to the Department of Labor to submit a comment to EP Determinations must:

(a) Be in writing;

(b) Be signed as provided in section 17.02 above;

(c) Contain the names of the interested parties requesting the Department to comment and the address of the interested party or designated representative to whom all correspondence with respect to the request should be sent. See also section 17.02(6) above;

(d) Contain the information prescribed in section 17.02(2), (3), (4), (5) and (6) above;

(e) Indicate that the application was or will be submitted to EP Determinations at the address in section 6.17;

(f) Contain a statement of the specific matters upon which the Department's comment is sought, as well as how such matters relate to the interested parties making the request; and

(g) Be addressed as follows:

> Deputy Assistant Secretary
> Employee Benefits Security Administration
> U.S. Department of Labor
> 200 Constitution Avenue, N.W.
> Washington, D.C. 20210
> Attention: 3001 Comment Request

Right to comment if DOL declines to comment

.04 If a request described in 17.03 is made and the Department of Labor notifies the interested parties making the request that it declines to comment on a matter concerning qualification of the plan which was raised in the request, the parties submitting the request may still submit a comment to EP Determinations on such matter. The comment must be received by the later of the 45th day after the day the application for determination is received by EP Determinations or the 15th day after the day on which notification is given by the Department that it declines to submit a comment on such matter. (See section 17.07 for the date of notification.) In no event may the comment be received later than the 60th day after the day the application for determination was received. Such a comment must comply with the requirements of section 17.02 and include a statement that the comment is being submitted on matters raised in a request to the Department upon which the Department declined to comment.

Confidentiality of comments

.05 For rules regarding the confidentiality of contents of written comments submitted by interested parties to the Service pursuant to section 17.02 or 17.04, see § 601.201(o)(5) of the Statement of Procedural Rules.

Availability of comments

.06 For rules regarding the availability to the applicant of copies of all comments on the application submitted pursuant to section 17.01(1), (2), (3) and (4) of this revenue procedure, see § 601.201(o)(5) of the Statement of Procedural Rules.

When comments are deemed made

.07 An application for an advance determination, a comment to EP Determinations, or a request to the Department of Labor shall be deemed made when it is received by EP Determinations, or the Department. Notification by the Department that it declines to comment shall be deemed given when it is received by the interested party or designated representative. The notice described in section 18.01 below shall be deemed given when it is posted or sent to the person in the manner described in § 1.7476–2. In the case of an application, comment, request, notification, or notice that is sent by mail or a private delivery service that has been designated under § 7502(f), the date as of which it shall be deemed received will be determined under § 7502. However, if such an application, comment, request, notification, or notice is not received within a reasonable period from the date determined under § 7502, the immediately preceding sentence shall not apply.

SECTION 18. WHAT ARE THE GENERAL RULES FOR NOTICE TO INTERESTED PARTIES?

Notice to interested parties

.01 Notice that an application for an advance determination regarding the qualification of a plan that is described in §§ 401, 403(a), 409 and 4975(e)(7) and that is subject to § 410 is to be made must be given to all interested parties in the manner prescribed in § 1.7476–2(c) and in accordance with the requirements of this section. A notice to interested parties is deemed to be provided in a manner that satisfies § 1.7476–2(c) if the notice is delivered using an electronic medium under a system that satisfies the requirements of § 1.402(f)–1 Q&A–5.

Time when notice must be given

.02 Notice must be given not less than 10 days nor more than 24 days prior to the day the application for a determination is made. If, however, an application is returned to the applicant for failure to adequately satisfy the notification requirements with respect to a particular group or class of interested parties, the applicant need not cause notice to be given to those groups or classes of interested parties with respect to which the notice requirement was already satisfied merely because, as a result of the resubmission of the application, the time limitations of this subsection would not be met.

Content of notice

.03 The notice referred to in section 18.01 shall contain the following information:

(1) A brief description identifying the class or classes of interested parties to whom the notice is addressed (*e.g.*, all present employees of the employer, all present employees eligible to participate);

(2) The name of the plan, the plan identification number, and the name of the plan administrator;

(3) The name and taxpayer identification number of the applicant for a determination;

(4) That an application for a determination as to the qualified status of the plan is to be made to the Service at the address in section 6.17, and stating whether the application relates to an initial qualification, a plan amendment, termination, or a partial termination;

(5) A description of the class of employees eligible to participate under the plan;

(6) Whether or not the Service has issued a previous determination as to the qualified status of the plan;

(7) A statement that any person to whom the notice is addressed is entitled to submit, or request the Department of Labor to submit, to EP Determinations, a comment on the question of whether the plan meets the requirements of § 401 or 403(a); that two or more such persons may join in a single comment or request; and that if such persons request the Department of Labor to submit a comment and the Department of Labor declines to do so with respect to one or more matters raised in the request, the persons may still submit a comment to EP Determinations with respect to the matters on which the Department declines to comment. The Pension Benefit Guaranty Corporation (PBGC) may also submit comments. In every instance where there is either a final adverse termination or a distress termination, the Service formally notifies the PBGC for comments;

(8) The specific dates by which a comment to EP Determinations or a request to the Department of Labor must be received in order to preserve the right of comment (see section 17 above);

(9) The number of interested parties needed in order for the Department of Labor to comment; and

(10) Except to the extent that the additional informational material required to be made available by sections 18.05 through 18.09 are included in the notice, a description of a reasonable procedure whereby such additional informational material will be available to interested parties (see section 18.04). (Examples of notices setting forth the above information, in a case in which the additional information required by sections 18.05 through 18.09 will be made available at places accessible to the interested parties, are set forth in the Exhibit attached to this revenue procedure.)

Procedures for making information available to interested parties

.04 The procedure referred to in section 18.03(10), whereby the additional informational material required by sections 18.05 through 18.09 will (to the extent not included in the notice) be made available to interested parties, may consist of making such material available for inspection and copying by interested parties at a place or places reasonably accessible to such parties, or supplying such material by using a method of delivery or a combination thereof that is reasonably calculated to ensure that all interested parties will have access to the materials, provided such procedure is immediately available to all interested parties, is designed to supply them with such additional informational material in time for them to pursue their rights within the time period prescribed, and is available until the earlier of: 1) the filing of a pleading commencing a declaratory judgment action under § 7476 with respect to the qualification of the plan; or 2) the 92nd day after the day the notice of final determination is mailed to the applicant. Reasonable charges to interested parties for copying and/or mailing such additional informational material are permissible.

Information to be available to interested parties

.05 Unless provided in the notice, or unless section 18.06 applies, there shall be made available to interested parties under a procedure described in section 18.04:

(1) An updated copy of the plan and the related trust agreement (if any); and

(2) The application for determination.

Special rules if there are fewer than 26 participants

.06 If there would be fewer than 26 participants in the plan, as described in the application (including, as participants, former employees with vested benefits under the plan, beneficiaries of deceased former employees currently receiving benefits under the plan, and employees who would be eligible to participate upon making mandatory employee contributions, if any), then in lieu of making the materials described in section 18.05 available to interested parties who are not participants (as described above), there may be made available to such interested parties a document containing the following information:

(1) A description of the plan's requirements respecting eligibility for participation and benefits and the plan's benefit formula;

(2) A description of the provisions providing for nonforfeitable benefits;

(3) A description of the circumstances which may result in ineligibility, or denial or loss of benefits;

(4) A description of the source of financing of the plan and the identity of any organization through which benefits are provided;

(5) A description of any optional forms of benefits described in § 411(d)(6) which have been reduced or eliminated by plan amendment; and

(6) Any coverage schedule or other demonstration submitted with the application to show that the plan meets the requirements of §§ 401(a)(4) and 410(b).

However, once an interested party or designated representative receives a notice of final determination, the applicant must, upon request, make available to such interested party (whether or not the plan has fewer than 26 participants) an updated copy of the plan and related trust agreement (if any) and the application for determination.

Information described in § 6104(a)(1)(D) should not be included

.07 Information of the type described in § 6104(a)(1)(D) should not be included in the application, plan, or related trust agreement submitted to the Service. Accordingly, such information should not be included in any of the material required by section 18.05 or 18.06 to be available to interested parties.

Availability of additional information to interested parties

.08 Unless provided in the notice, there shall be made available to interested parties under a procedure described in section 18.04, any additional document dealing with the application which is submitted by or for the applicant to the Service, or furnished by the Service to the applicant; provided, however, if there would be fewer than 26 participants in the plan as described in the application (including, as participants, former employees with vested benefits under the plan, beneficiaries of deceased former employees currently receiving benefits under the plan, and employees who would be eligible to participate upon making mandatory employee contributions, if any), such additional documents need not be made available to interested parties who are not participants (as described above) until they, or their designated representative, receive a notice of final determination. The applicant may also withhold from such inspection and copying information described in § 6104(a)(1)(C) and (D) which may be contained in such additional documents.

Availability of notice to interested parties

.09 Unless provided in the notice, there shall be made available to all interested parties under a procedure described in section 18.04 the material described in sections 17.02 through 17.07 above.

PART III. PROCESSING DETERMINATION LETTER REQUESTS

SECTION 19. HOW DOES THE SERVICE HANDLE DETERMINATION LETTER REQUESTS

Oral advice

.01 Oral advice.

(1) The Service does not issue determination letters on oral requests. However, personnel in EP Determinations ordinarily will discuss with taxpayers or their representatives inquiries regarding: substantive tax issues; whether the Service will issue a determination letter on particular issues; and questions relating to procedural matters about submitting determination letter requests. Any discussion of substantive issues will be at the discretion of the Service on a time available basis, will not be binding on the Service, and cannot be relied upon as a basis of obtaining retroactive relief under the provisions of § 7805(b). A taxpayer may seek oral technical assistance from a taxpayer service representative when preparing a return or report, under established procedures. Oral advice is advisory only, and the Service is not bound to recognize it in the examination of the taxpayer's return.

(2) The advice or assistance furnished, whether requested by personal appearance, telephone, or correspondence will be limited to general procedures, or will direct the inquirer to source material, such as pertinent Code provisions, regulations, revenue procedures, and revenue rulings that may aid the inquirer in resolving the question or problem.

Conferences

.02 EP Determinations may grant a conference upon written request from a taxpayer or his representative, provided the request shows that a substantive plan, amendment, etc., has been developed for submission to the Service, but that special problems or issues are involved, and EP Determinations concludes that a conference would be warranted in the interest of facilitating review and determination when the plan, etc., is formally submitted. See section 6.18 regarding the right to a status conference on applications pending for at least 270 days.

Determination letter based solely on administrative record

.03 Administrative Record

(1) In the case of a request for a determination letter, the determination of EP Determinations or the appeals office on the qualification or non-qualification of the retirement plan shall be based solely upon the facts contained in the administrative record. The administrative record shall consist of the following:

(a) The request for determination, the retirement plan and any related trust instruments, and any written modifications or amendments made by the applicant during the proceedings within the Service;

(b) All other documents submitted to the Service by, or on behalf of, the applicant with respect to the request for determination;

(c) All written correspondence between the Service and the applicant with respect to the request for determination and any other documents issued to the applicant from the Service;

(d) All written comments submitted to the Service pursuant to sections 17.01(2), (3), and (4) above, and all correspondence relating to comments submitted between the Service and persons (including PBGC and the Department of Labor) submitting comments pursuant to sections 17.01(2), (3), and (4) above; and

(e) In any case in which the Service makes an investigation regarding the facts as represented or alleged by the applicant in the request for determination or in comments submitted pursuant to sections 17.01(2), (3), and (4) above, a copy of the official report of such investigation.

(2) The administrative record shall be closed upon the earlier of the following events:

(a) The date of mailing of a notice of final determination by the Service with respect to the application for determination; or

(b) The filing of a petition with the United States Tax Court seeking a declaratory judgment with respect to the retirement plan.

(3) Any oral representation or modification of the facts as represented or alleged in the application for determination or in a comment filed by an interested party, which is not reduced to writing shall not become a part of the administrative record and shall not be taken into account in the determination of the qualified status of the retirement plan by EP Determinations or the appeals office.

Notice of final determination

.04 In the case of final determination, the notice of final determination:

(1) Shall be the letter issued by EP Determinations or the appeals office which states that the applicant's plan satisfies the qualification requirements of the Code. The favorable determination letter will be sent by certified or registered mail where either an interested party, the Department of Labor, or the PBGC has commented on the application for determination.

(2) Shall be the letter issued, by certified or registered mail, by EP Determinations or the appeals office subsequent to a letter of proposed determination, stating that the applicant's plan fails to satisfy the qualification requirements of the Code.

Issuance of the notice of final determination

.05 EP Determinations or the appeals office will send the notice of final determination to the applicant, to the interested parties who have previously submitted comments on the application to the Service (or to the persons designated by them to receive such notice), to the Department of Labor in the case of a comment submitted by the Department, and to PBGC if it has filed a comment.

SECTION 20. EXHAUSTION OF ADMINISTRATIVE REMEDIES

In general

.01 For purposes of § 7476(b)(3), a petitioner shall be deemed to have exhausted the administrative remedies available within the Service upon the completion of the steps described in sections 20.02, 20.03, 20.04, or 20.05 subject, however, to sections 20.06 and 20.07. If applicants, interested parties, or the PBGC do not complete the applicable steps described below, they will not have exhausted their respective available administrative remedies as required by § 7476(b)(3) and will, thus, be precluded from seeking declaratory judgment under § 7476 except to the extent that section 20.05 or 20.08 applies.

Steps for exhausting administrative remedies

.02 In the case of an applicant, with respect to any matter relating to the qualification of a plan, the steps referred to in section 20.01 are:

(1) Filing a completed application with EP Determinations pursuant to this revenue procedure;

(2) Complying with the requirements pertaining to notice to interested parties as set forth in this revenue procedure and § 1.7476–2 of the regulations; and,

(3) Appealing to the appropriate appeals office pursuant to paragraph 601.201(o)(6) of the Statement of Procedural Rules, in the event a notice of proposed adverse determination is issued by EP Determinations.

Applicant's request for § 7805(b) relief

.03 Consideration of relief under § 7805(b) will be included as one of the applicant's steps in exhausting administrative remedies only if the applicant requests EP Determinations to seek technical advice from EP Technical on the applicability of such relief. The applicant's request must be made in writing according to the procedures for requesting technical advice (*see* section 19 of Rev. Proc. 2013–5).

Interested parties

.04 In the case of an interested party or the PBGC, the steps referred to in section 20.01 are, with respect to any matter relating to the qualification of the plan, submitting to EP Determinations a comment raising such matter in accordance with section 17.01(2) above, or requesting the Department of Labor to submit to EP Determinations a comment with respect to such matter in accordance with section 17.01(3) and, if the Department of Labor declines to comment, submitting the comment in accordance with section 17.01(4) above, so that it may be considered by the Service through the administrative process.

Deemed exhaustion of administrative remedies

.05 An applicant, an interested party, or the PBGC shall in no event be deemed to have exhausted administrative remedies prior to the earlier of:

(1) The completion of those steps applicable to each as set forth in sections 20.01, 20.02, 20.03 or 20.04, which constitute their administrative remedies; or,

(2) The expiration of the 270-day period described in § 7476(b)(3), which period shall be extended in a case where there has not been a completion of all the steps referred to in section 20.02 and the Service has proceeded with due diligence in processing the application for determination.

Service must act on appeal

.06 The step described in section 20.02(3) will not be considered completed until the Service has had a reasonable time to act upon the appeal.

Service must act on § 7805(b) request

.07 Where the applicant has requested EP Determinations to seek technical advice on the applicability of § 7805(b) relief, the applicant's administrative remedies will not be considered exhausted until EP Technical has had a reasonable time to act upon the request for technical advice.

Effect of technical advice request

.08 The step described in section 20.02(3) will not be available or necessary with respect to any issue on which technical advice has been obtained from EP Technical.

SECTION 21. WHAT EFFECT WILL AN EMPLOYEE PLAN DETERMINATION LETTER HAVE?

Scope of reliance on determination letter

.01 A determination letter issued pursuant to this revenue procedure contains only the opinion of the Service as to the qualification of the particular plan involving the provisions of §§ 401 and 403(a) and the status of a related trust, if any, under § 501(a). Such a determination letter is based on the facts and demonstrations presented to the Service in connection with the application for the determination letter and may not be relied upon after a change in material fact or the effective date of a change in law, except as provided. The Service may determine, based on the application form, the extent of review of the plan document. Failure to disclose a material fact or misrepresentation of a material fact adversely affects the reliance that would otherwise be obtained through the issuance by the Service of a favorable determination letter. Similarly, failure to accurately provide any of the information called for on any form required by this revenue procedure may result in no reliance. Applicants are advised to retain copies of all supporting data submitted with their applications. Failure to do so may limit the scope of reliance.

Sections 13 and 14 of Rev. Proc. 2013–4 applicable

.02 Except as otherwise provided in this section, determination letters are governed, generally, by the provisions of sections 13 and 14 of Rev. Proc. 2013–4.

Effect of subsequent publication of revenue ruling, etc.

.03 The prior qualification of a plan as adopted by an employer will not be considered to be adversely affected by the publication of a revenue ruling, a revenue procedure, or an administrative pronouncement within the meaning of § 1.6661–3(b)(2) of the regulations where:

(1) The plan was the subject of a favorable determination letter and the request for that letter contained no misstatement or omission of material facts;

(2) The facts subsequently developed are not materially different from the facts on which the determination letter was based;

(3) There has been no change in the applicable law; and

(4) The employer that established the plan acted in good faith in reliance on the determination letter.

However, all such plans must be amended to comply with the published guidance for subsequent years, in accordance with the rules set forth in Rev. Proc. 2007–44. See, in particular, Part II of that revenue procedure.

Determination letter does not apply to taxability issues

.04 While a favorable determination letter may serve as a basis for determining deductions for employer contributions thereunder, it is not to be taken as an indication that contributions are necessarily deductible as made. This latter determination can be made only upon an examination of the employer's tax return, in accordance with the limitations, and subject to the conditions of, § 404.

SECTION 22. EFFECT ON OTHER REVENUE PROCEDURES

Rev. Proc. 2012–6 is superseded. Rev. Proc. 2011–49 is modified.

SECTION 23. EFFECTIVE DATE

This revenue procedure is effective February 1, 2013.

SECTION 24. PAPERWORK REDUCTION ACT

The collections of information contained in this revenue procedure have been reviewed and approved by the Office of Management and Budget in accordance with the Paperwork Reduction Act (44 U.S.C. 3507) under control number 1545–1520.

An agency may not conduct or sponsor, and a person is not required to respond to, a collection of information unless the collection of information displays a valid OMB control number.

The collections of information in this revenue procedure are in sections 6.05, 6.16, 6.18, 6.19, 6.20, 7.04, 13, 14, 15, 16, 19.02, and 21.04. This information is required to determine plan qualification. This information will be used to determine whether a plan is entitled to favorable tax treatment. The collections of information are mandatory. The likely respondents are businesses or other for-profit institutions.

The estimated total annual reporting and/or recordkeeping burden is 163,186 hours.

The estimated annual burden per respondent/recordkeeper varies from 1 hour to 40 hours, depending on individual circumstances, with an estimated average of 2.02 hours. The estimated number of respondents and/or recordkeepers is 80,763.

The estimated annual frequency of responses (used for reporting requirements only) is once every three years.

Books or records relating to a collection of information must be retained as long as their contents may become material in the administration of any internal revenue law. Generally tax returns and tax return information are confidential, as required by 26 U.S.C. 6103.

DRAFTING INFORMATION

The principal author of this revenue procedure is Eric Slack of the Employee Plans, Tax Exempt and Government Entities Division. For further information regarding this revenue procedure, please contact the Employee Plans taxpayer assistance telephone service at 1–877–829–5500 (a toll-free number) or Mr. Slack at *RetirementPlanQuestions@irs.gov*.

EXHIBIT: SAMPLE NOTICE   The Exhibit set forth below, may be used to satisfy the requirements of section 18 of this
TO INTERESTED PARTIES   revenue procedure.

EXHIBIT: SAMPLE NOTICE TO INTERESTED PARTIES

1.   Notice To: _____ [describe class or classes of interested parties]

An application is to be made to the Internal Revenue Service for an advance determination on the qualification of the following
employee pension benefit plan:

2.   _____

       (name of plan)

3.   _____

       (plan number)

4.   _____

       (name and address of applicant)

5.   _____

       (applicant EIN)

6.   _____

       (name and address of plan administrator)

7.   The application will be filed on _____ for an advance determination as to whether the plan meets
the qualification requirements of § 401 or 403(a) of the Internal Revenue Code of 1986, with respect to the plan's
_____ [initial qualification, amendment, termination, or partial termination].
The application will be filed with:

          Internal Revenue Service
          EP Determinations
          Attn: Customer Service Manager
          P.O. Box 2508
          Cincinnati, OH 45202

8.   The employees eligible to participate under the plan are:

9.   The Internal Revenue Service _____ [has/has not] previously issued a determination letter with
respect to the qualification of this plan.

RIGHTS OF INTERESTED PARTIES

10.   You have the right to submit to EP Determinations, at the above address, either individually or jointly with other interested
parties, your comments as to whether this plan meets the qualification requirements of the Internal Revenue Code.

     You may instead, individually or jointly with other interested parties, request the Department of Labor to submit, on your
behalf, comments to EP Determinations regarding qualification of the plan. If the Department declines to comment on all
or some of the matters you raise, you may, individually, or jointly if your request was made to the Department jointly,
submit your comments on these matters directly to EP Determinations.

REQUESTS FOR COMMENTS BY THE DEPARTMENT OF LABOR

11.   The Department of Labor may not comment on behalf of interested parties unless requested to do so by the lesser of 10 employees or 10 percent of the employees who qualify as interested parties. The number of persons needed for the Department to comment with respect to this plan is _____. If you request the Department to comment, your request must be in writing and must specify the matters upon which comments are requested, and must also include:

(1) the information contained in items 2 through 5 of this Notice; and

(2) the number of persons needed for the Department to comment.

A request to the Department to comment should be addressed as follows:

> Deputy Assistant Secretary
> Employee Benefits Security Administration
> ATTN: 3001 Comment Request
> U.S. Department of Labor,
> 200 Constitution Avenue, N.W.
> Washington, D.C. 20210

COMMENTS TO THE INTERNAL REVENUE SERVICE

12.   Comments submitted by you to EP Determinations must be in writing and received by it by _____. However, if there are matters that you request the Department of Labor to comment upon on your behalf, and the Department declines, you may submit comments on these matters to EP Determinations to be received by it within 15 days from the time the Department notifies you that it will not comment on a particular matter, or by _____, whichever is later, but not after _____. A request to the Department to comment on your behalf must be received by it by _____ if you wish to preserve your right to comment on a matter upon which the Department declines to comment, or by _____ if you wish to waive that right.

ADDITIONAL INFORMATION

13.   Detailed instructions regarding the requirements for notification of interested parties may be found in sections 17 and 18 of Rev. Proc. 2013–6. Additional information concerning this application (including, where applicable, an updated copy of the plan and related trust; the application for determination; any additional documents dealing with the application that have submitted to the Service; and copies of section 17 of Rev. Proc. 2013–6 are available at _____ during the hours of _____ for inspection and copying. (There is a nominal charge for copying and/or mailing.)

APPENDIX

Checklist   As part of a § 401(h) or § 420 determination letter request described in section 16 of this revenue procedure the following checklist may be completed and attached to the determination letter request. If the request relates to § 401(h) but not to § 420, complete Part I only. If the request relates to § 420, complete Parts I and II.

PART I

		CIRCLE	SECTION

1. Does the Plan contain a medical benefits account within the meaning of § 401(h) of the Code? If the medical benefits account is a new provision, items "a" through "h" should be completed.   Yes No

   a. Does the medical benefits account specify the medical benefits that will be available and contain provisions for determining the amount that will be paid?   Yes No   _____

   b. Does the medical benefits account specify who will benefit?   Yes No   _____

   c. Does the medical benefits account indicate that such benefits, when added to any life insurance protection in the Plan, will be subordinate to retirement benefits? (This requirement will not be satisfied unless the amount of actual contributions to provide § 401(h) benefits (when added to actual contributions for life insurance protection under the Plan) does not exceed 25 percent of the total actual contributions to the Plan (other than contributions to fund past service credits), determined on an aggregate basis since the inception of the § 401(h) arrangement.)   Yes No

   d. Does the medical benefits account maintain separate accounts with respect to contributions to key employees (as defined in § 416(i)(1) of the Code) to fund such benefits?   Yes No   _____

   e. Does the medical benefits account state that amounts contributed must be reasonable and ascertainable?   Yes No   _____

   f. Does the medical benefits account provide for the impossibility of diversion prior to satisfaction of liabilities (other than item "7" below)?   Yes No   _____

   g. Does the medical benefits account provide for reversion upon satisfaction of all liabilities (other than item "7" below)?   Yes No   _____

   h. Does the medical benefits account provide that forfeitures must be applied as soon as possible to reduce employer contributions to fund the medical benefits?   Yes No   _____

PART II

2. Does the Plan limit transfers to "Excess Assets" as defined in § 420(e)(2) of the Code?   Yes No   _____

3. Does the Plan provide that only one transfer may be made in a taxable year (except with regard to transfers relating to prior years pursuant to § 420(b)(4) of the Code)?   Yes No   _____

4. Does the Plan provide that the amount transferred shall not exceed the amount reasonably estimated to be paid for qualified current retiree health liabilities?   Yes No   _____

5. Does the Plan provide that no transfer will be made after December 31, 2013?   Yes No   _____

6. Does the Plan provide that transferred assets and income attributable to such assets shall be used only to pay qualified current retiree health liabilities for the taxable year of transfer?   Yes No   _____

7. Does the Plan provide that any amounts transferred (plus income) that are not used to pay qualified current retiree health liabilities shall be transferred back to the defined benefit portion of the Plan?   Yes No   _____

8. Does the Plan provide that amounts paid out of a health benefits account will be treated as paid first out of transferred assets and income attributable to those assets?   Yes No   _____

9. Does the Plan provide that participants' accrued benefits become nonforfeitable on a termination basis (i) immediately prior to transfer, or (ii) in the case of a participant who separated within 1 year before the transfer, immediately before such separation?   Yes No   _____

10. In the case of transfers described in § 420(b)(4) of the Code relating to 1990, does the Plan provide that benefits will be recomputed and become nonforfeitable for participants who separated from service in such prior year as described in § 420(c)(2)?   Yes No   _____

11. Does the Plan provide that transfers will be permitted only if each group health plan or arrangement contains provisions satisfying § 420(c)(3) of the Code, as amended?   Yes No   _____

12. Does the Plan define "applicable employer cost", "cost maintenance period" and "benefit maintenance period", as needed, consistently with § 420(c)(3) of the Code, as amended?   Yes No   _____

13. Do the Plan's provisions reflect the transition rule in section 535(c)(2) of TREA'99, if applicable?   Yes No   _____

14. Does the Plan provide that transferred assets cannot be used for key employees?   Yes No   _____

_____

Appendix H

Sample Summary Plan Description, DOL Regs. §2520.102-3t(2)

As a participant in (name of plan) you are entitled to certain rights and protections under the Employee Retirement Income Security Act of 1974 (ERISA). ERISA provides that all plan participants shall be entitled to:

Receive Information About Your Plan and Benefits

- Examine, without charge, at the plan administrator's office and at other specified locations, such as worksites and union halls, all documents governing the plan, including insurance contracts and collective bargaining agreements, and a copy of the latest annual report (Form 5500 Series) filed by the plan with the U.S. Department of Labor and available at the Public Disclosure Room of the Pension and Welfare Benefit Administration.

- Obtain, upon written request to the plan administrator, copies of documents governing the operation of the plan, including insurance contracts and collective bargaining agreements, and copies of the latest annual report (Form 5500 Series) and updated summary plan description. The administrator may make a reasonable charge for the copies.

- Receive a summary of the plan's annual financial report. The plan administrator is required by law to furnish each participant with a copy of this summary annual report.

- Obtain a statement telling you whether you have a right to receive a pension at normal retirement age (age * * *) and if so, what your benefits would be at normal retirement age if you stop working under the plan now. If you do not have a right to a pension, the statement will tell you how many more years you have to work to get a right to a pension. This statement must be requested in writing and is not required to be given more than once every twelve (12) months. The plan must provide the statement free of charge.

Continue Group Health Plan Coverage

- Continue health care coverage for yourself, spouse or dependents if there is a loss of coverage under the plan as a result of a qualifying event. You or your dependents may have to pay for such coverage. Review this summary plan description and the documents governing the plan on the rules governing your COBRA continuation coverage rights.

- Reduction or elimination of exclusionary periods of coverage for preexisting conditions under your group health plan, if you have creditable coverage from another plan. You should be provided a certificate of creditable coverage, free of charge, from your group health plan or health insurance issuer when you lose coverage under the plan, when you become entitled to elect COBRA continuation coverage, when your COBRA continuation coverage ceases, if you request it before losing coverage, or if you request it up to 24 months after losing coverage. Without evidence of creditable coverage, you may be subject to a preexisting condition exclusion for 12 months (18 months for late enrollees) after your enrollment date in your coverage.

Prudent Actions by Plan Fiduciaries

In addition to creating rights for plan participants, ERISA imposes duties upon the people who are responsible for the operation of the employee benefit plan. The people who operate your plan, called "fiduciaries" of the plan, have a duty to do so prudently and in the interest of you and other plan participants and beneficiaries. No one, including your employer, your union, or any other person, may fire you or otherwise discriminate against you in any way to prevent you from obtaining a (pension, welfare) benefit or exercising your rights under ERISA.

Enforce Your Rights

If your claim for a (pension, welfare) benefit is denied or ignored, in whole or in part, you have a right to know why this was done, to obtain copies of documents relating to the decision without charge, and to appeal any denial, all within certain time schedules.

Under ERISA, there are steps you can take to enforce the above rights. For instance, if you request a copy of plan documents or the latest annual report from the plan and do not receive them within 30 days, you may file suit in a Federal court. In such a case, the court may require the plan administrator to provide the materials and pay you up to $110 a day until you receive the materials, unless the materials were not sent because of reasons beyond the control of the administrator. If you have a claim for benefits which is denied or ignored, in whole or in part, you may file suit in a state or Federal court. In addition, if you disagree with the plan's decision or lack thereof concerning the qualified status of a domestic relations order or a medical child support order, you may file suit in Federal court. If it should happen that plan fiduciaries misuse the plan's money, or if you are discriminated against for asserting your rights, you may seek assistance from the U.S. Department of Labor, or you may file suit in a Federal court. The court will decide who should pay court costs and legal fees. If you are successful the court may order the person you have sued to pay these costs and fees. If you lose, the court may order you to pay these costs and fees, for example, if it finds your claim is frivolous.

Assistance with Your Questions

If you have any questions about your plan, you should contact the plan administrator. If you have any questions about this statement or about your rights under ERISA, or if you need assistance in obtaining documents from the plan administrator, you should contact the nearest office of the Employee Benefits Security Administration, U.S. Department of Labor, listed in your telephone directory or the Division of Technical Assistance and Inquiries, Employee Benefits Security Administration, U.S. Department of Labor, 200 Constitution Avenue N.W., Washington, D.C. 20210. You may also obtain certain publications about your rights and responsibilities under ERISA by calling the publications hotline of the Employee Benefits Security Administration.

Appendix I

Sample Summary Annual Report, DOL Regs. §2520.104-10(d)(3)

Summary Annual Report for (name of plan)

This is a summary of the annual report for (name of plan and EIN) for (period covered by this report). The annual report has been filed with the Pension and Welfare Benefits Administration, as required under the Employee Retirement Income Security Act of 1974 (ERISA).

Basic Financial Statement

Benefits under the plan are provided by (indicate funding arrangements). Plan expenses were ($). These expenses included ($) in administrative expenses and ($) in benefits paid to participants and beneficiaries, and ($) in other expenses. A total of () persons were participants in or beneficiaries of the plan at the end of the plan year, although not all of these persons had yet earned the right to receive benefits.

[If the plan is funded other than solely by allocated insurance contracts:]

The value of plan assets, after subtracting liabilities of the plan, was ($) as of (the end of the plan year), compared to ($) as of (the beginning of the plan year). During the plan year the plan experienced an (increase) (decrease) in its net assets of ($) This (increase) (decrease) includes unrealized appreciation or depreciation in the value of plan assets; that is, the difference between the value of the plan's assets at the end of the year and the value of the assets at the beginning of the year or the cost of assets acquired during the year. The plan had total income of ($), including employer contributions of ($), employee contributions of ($), (gains) (losses) of ($), from the sale of assets, and earnings from investments of ($).

[If any funds are used to purchase allocated insurance contracts:]

The plan has (a) contract(s) with (name of insurance carrier(s)) which allocate(s) funds toward (state whether individual policies, group deferred annuities, or other). The total premiums paid for the plan year ending (date) were ($).

Minimum Funding Standards

[If the plan is a defined benefit plan:]

An actuary's statement shows that (enough money was contributed to the plan to keep it funded in accordance with the minimum funding standards of ERISA) (not enough money was contributed to the plan to keep it funded in accordance with the minimum funding standards of ERISA. The amount of the deficit was $).

[If the plan is a defined contribution plan covered by funding requirements:]

(Enough money was contributed to the plan to keep it funded in accordance with the minimum funding standards of ERISA) (Not enough money was contributed to the plan to keep it funded in accordance with the minimum funding standards of ERISA. The amount of the deficit was $).

Your Rights to Additional Information

You have the right to receive a copy of the full annual report, or any part thereof, on request. The items listed below are included in that report: [Note—list only those items that are actually included in the latest annual report]

1. an accountant's report;

2. financial information and information on payments to service providers;

3. assets held for investment;

4. fiduciary information, including non-exempt transactions between the plan and parties-in-interest (that is, persons who have certain relationships with the plan);

5. loans or other obligations in default or classified as uncollectible;

6. leases in default or classified as uncollectible;

7. transactions in excess of five percent of the plan assets;

8. insurance information including sales commissions paid by insurance carriers;

9. information regarding any common or collective trusts, pooled separate accounts, master trusts, or 103-12 investment entities in which the plan participates, and

10. actuarial information regarding the funding of the plan.

To obtain a copy of the full annual report, or any part thereof, write or call the office of (name), who is (state title: e.g., the plan administrator), (business address and telephone number). The charge to cover copying costs will be ($) for the full annual report, or ($) per page for any part thereof.

You also have the right to receive from the plan administrator, on request and at no charge, a statement of the assets and liabilities of the plan and accompanying notes, or a statement of income and expenses of the plan and accompanying notes, or both. If you request a copy of the full annual report from the plan administrator, these two statements and accompanying notes will be included as part of that report. The charge to cover copying costs given above does not include a charge for the copying of these portions of the report because these portions are furnished without charge.

You also have the legally protected right to examine the annual report at the main office of the plan (address), (at any other location where the report is available for examination), and at the U.S. Department of Labor in Washington, D.C., or to obtain a copy from the U.S. Department of Labor upon payment of copying costs. Requests to the Department should be addressed to: Public Disclosure Room, Room N-1513, Employee Benefits Security Administration, U.S. Department of Labor, 200 Constitution Avenue, N.W., Washington, D.C. 20210.

Appendix J

Model Section 402(f) Notice for Payments from a Designated Roth Account from Notice 2009-68, IRB 2009-39

<u>**YOUR ROLLOVER OPTIONS**</u>

You are receiving this notice because all or a portion of a payment you are receiving from the [INSERT NAME OF PLAN] (the "Plan") is eligible to be rolled over to a Roth IRA or designated Roth account in an employer plan. This notice is intended to help you decide whether to do a rollover.

This notice describes the rollover rules that apply to payments from the Plan that are from a designated Roth account. If you also receive a payment from the Plan that is not from a designated Roth account, you will be provided a different notice for that payment, and the Plan administrator or the payor will tell you the amount that is being paid from each account.

Rules that apply to most payments from a designated Roth account are described in the "General Information About Rollovers" section. Special rules that only apply in certain circumstances are described in the "Special Rules and Options" section.

GENERAL INFORMATION ABOUT ROLLOVERS

How can a rollover affect my taxes?

After-tax contributions included in a payment from a designated Roth account are not taxed, but earnings might be taxed. The tax treatment of earnings included in the payment depends on whether the payment is a qualified distribution. If a payment is only part of your designated Roth account, the payment will include an allocable portion of the earnings in your designated Roth account.

If the payment from the Plan is not a qualified distribution and you do not do a rollover to a Roth IRA or a designated Roth account in an employer plan, you will be taxed on the earnings in the payment. If you are under age 59½, a 10% additional income tax on early distributions will also apply to the earnings (unless an exception applies). However, if you do a rollover, you will not have to pay taxes currently on the earnings and you will not have to pay taxes later on payments that are qualified distributions.

If the payment from the Plan is a qualified distribution, you will not be taxed on any part of the payment even if you do not do a rollover. If you do a rollover, you will not be taxed on the amount you roll over and any earnings on the amount you roll over will not be taxed if paid later in a qualified distribution.

A qualified distribution from a designated Roth account in the Plan is a payment made after you are age 59½ (or after your death or disability) and after you have had a designated Roth account in the Plan for at least 5 years. In applying the 5-year rule, you count from January 1 of the year your first contribution was made to the designated Roth account. However, if you did a direct rollover to a designated Roth account in the Plan from a designated Roth account in another employer plan, your participation will count from January 1 of the year your first contribution was made to the designated Roth account in the Plan or, if earlier, to the designated Roth account in the other employer plan.

Where may I roll over the payment?

You may roll over the payment to either a Roth IRA (a Roth individual retirement account or Roth individual retirement annuity) or a designated Roth account in an employer plan (a tax-qualified plan or Section 403(b) plan) that will accept the rollover. The rules of the Roth IRA or employer plan that holds the rollover will determine your investment options, fees, and rights to payment from the Roth IRA or employer plan (for example, no spousal consent rules apply to Roth IRAs and Roth IRAs may not provide loans). Further, the amount rolled over will become subject to the tax rules that apply to the Roth IRA or the designated Roth account in the employer plan. In general, these tax rules are similar to those described elsewhere in this notice, but differences include:

- If you do a rollover to a Roth IRA, all of your Roth IRAs will be considered for purposes of determining whether you have satisfied the 5-year rule (counting from January 1 of the year for which your first contribution was made to any of your Roth IRAs).

- If you do a rollover to a Roth IRA, you will not be required to take a distribution from the Roth IRA during your lifetime and you must keep track of the aggregate amount of the after-tax contributions in all of your Roth IRAs (in order to determine your taxable income for later Roth IRA payments that are not qualified distributions).

- Eligible rollover distributions from a Roth IRA can only be rolled over to another Roth IRA.

How do I do a rollover?

There are two ways to do a rollover. You can either do a direct rollover or a 60-day rollover.

If you do a direct rollover, the Plan will make the payment directly to your Roth IRA or designated Roth account in an employer plan. You should contact the Roth IRA sponsor or the administrator of the employer plan for information on how to do a direct rollover.

If you do not do a direct rollover, you may still do a rollover by making a deposit within 60 days into a Roth IRA, whether the payment is a qualified or nonqualified distribution. In addition, you can do a rollover by making a deposit within 60 days into a designated Roth account in an employer plan if the payment is a nonqualified distribution and the rollover does not exceed the amount of the earnings in the payment. You cannot do a 60-day rollover to an employer plan of any part of a qualified distribution. If you receive a distribution that is a nonqualified distribution and you do not roll over an amount at least equal to the earnings allocable to the distribution, you will be taxed on the amount of those earnings not rolled over, including the 10% additional income tax on early distributions if you are under age 59½ (unless an exception applies).

If you do a direct rollover of only a portion of the amount paid from the Plan and a portion is paid to you, each of the payments will include an allocable portion of the earnings in your designated Roth account.

If you do not do a direct rollover and the payment is not a qualified distribution, the Plan is required to withhold 20% of the earnings for federal income taxes (up to the amount of cash and property received other than employer stock). This means that, in order to roll over the entire payment in a 60-day rollover to a Roth IRA, you must use other funds to make up for the 20% withheld.

How much may I roll over?

If you wish to do a rollover, you may roll over all or part of the amount eligible for rollover. Any payment from the Plan is eligible for rollover, except:

- Certain payments spread over a period of at least 10 years or over your life or life expectancy (or the lives or joint life expectancy of you and your beneficiary)

- Required minimum distributions after age 70½ (or after death)

- Hardship distributions

- ESOP dividends

- Corrective distributions of contributions that exceed tax law limitations

- Loans treated as deemed distributions (for example, loans in default due to missed payments before your employment ends)

- Cost of life insurance paid by the Plan

- Contributions made under special automatic enrollment rules that are withdrawn pursuant to your request within 90 days of enrollment

- Amounts treated as distributed because of a prohibited allocation of **S** corporation stock under an ESOP (also, there will generally be adverse tax consequences if **S** corporation stock is held by an IRA).

The Plan administrator or the payor can tell you what portion of a payment is eligible for rollover.

If I don't do a rollover, will I have to pay the 10% additional income tax on early distributions?

If a payment is not a qualified distribution and you are under age 59½, you will have to pay the 10% additional income tax on early distributions with respect to the earnings allocated to the payment that you do not roll over (including amounts withheld for income tax), unless one of the exceptions listed below applies. This tax is in addition to the regular income tax on the earnings not rolled over.

The 10% additional income tax does not apply to the following payments from the Plan:

- Payments made after you separate from service if you will be at least age 55 in the year of the separation

- Payments that start after you separate from service if paid at least annually in equal or close to equal amounts over your life or life expectancy (or the lives or joint life expectancy of you and your beneficiary)

- Payments made due to disability

- Payments after your death

- Payments of ESOP dividends

- Corrective distributions of contributions that exceed tax law limitations

- Cost of life insurance paid by the Plan

- Contributions made under special automatic enrollment rules that are withdrawn pursuant to your request within 90 days of enrollment

- Payments made directly to the government to satisfy a federal tax levy

- Payments made under a qualified domestic relations order (QDRO)

- Payments up to the amount of your deductible medical expenses

- Certain payments made while you are on active duty if you were a member of a reserve component called to duty after September 11, 2001 for more than 179 days

- Payments of certain automatic enrollment contributions requested to be withdrawn within 90 days of the first contribution.

If I do a rollover to a Roth IRA, will the 10% additional income tax apply to early distributions from the IRA?

If you receive a payment from a Roth IRA when you are under age 59½, you will have to pay the 10% additional income tax on early distributions on the earnings paid from the Roth IRA, unless an exception applies or the payment is a qualified distribution. In general, the exceptions to the 10% additional income tax for early distributions from a Roth IRA listed above are the same as the exceptions for early distributions from a plan. However, there are a few differences for payments from a Roth IRA, including:

- There is no special exception for payments after separation from service.

- The exception for qualified domestic relations orders (QDROs) does not apply (although a special rule applies under which, as part of a divorce or separation agreement, a tax-free transfer may be made directly to a Roth IRA of a spouse or former spouse).

- The exception for payments made at least annually in equal or close to equal amounts over a specified period applies without regard to whether you have had a separation from service.

- There are additional exceptions for (1) payments for qualified higher education expenses, (2) payments up to $10,000 used in a qualified first-time home purchase, and (3) payments after you have received unemployment compensation for 12 consecutive weeks (or would have been eligible to receive unemployment compensation but for self-employed status).

Will I owe State income taxes?

This notice does not describe any State or local income tax rules (including withholding rules).

SPECIAL RULES AND OPTIONS

If you miss the 60-day rollover deadline

Generally, the 60-day rollover deadline cannot be extended. However, the IRS has the limited authority to waive the deadline under certain extraordinary circumstances, such as when external events prevented you from completing the rollover by the 60-day rollover deadline. To apply for a waiver, you must file a private letter ruling request with the IRS. Private letter ruling requests require the payment of a nonrefundable user fee. For more information, see IRS Publication 590, Individual Retirement Arrangements (IRAs).

If your payment includes employer stock that you do not roll over

If you receive a payment that is not a qualified distribution and you do not roll it over, you can apply a special rule to payments of employer stock (or other employer securities) that are paid in a lump sum after separation from service (or after age 59½, disability, or the participant's death). Under the special rule, the net unrealized appreciation on the stock included in the earnings in the payment will not be taxed when distributed to you from the Plan and will be taxed at capital gain rates when you sell the stock. If you do a rollover to a Roth IRA for a nonqualified distribution that includes employer stock (for example, by selling the stock and rolling over the proceeds within 60 days of the distribution), you will not have any taxable income and the special rule relating to the distributed employer stock will not apply to any subsequent payments from the Roth IRA or employer plan. Net unrealized appreciation is generally the increase in the value of the employer stock after it was acquired by the Plan. The Plan administrator can tell you the amount of any net unrealized appreciation.

If you receive a payment that is a qualified distribution that includes employer stock and you do not roll it over, your basis in the stock (used to determine gain or loss when you later sell the stock) will equal the fair market value of the stock at the time of the payment from the Plan.

If you have an outstanding loan that is being offset

If you have an outstanding loan from the Plan, your Plan benefit may be offset by the amount of the loan, typically when your employment ends. The loan offset amount is treated as a distribution to you at the time of the offset and, if the distribution is a nonqualified distribution, the earnings in the loan offset will be taxed (including the 10% additional income tax on early distributions, unless an exception applies) unless you do a 60-day rollover in the amount of the earnings in the loan offset to a Roth IRA or designated Roth account in an employer plan.

If you receive a nonqualified distribution and you were born on or before January 1, 1936

If you were born on or before January 1, 1936, and receive a lump sum distribution that is not a qualified distribution and that you do not roll over, special rules for calculating the amount of the tax on the earnings in the payment might apply to you. For more information, see IRS Publication 575, Pension and Annuity Income.

If you receive a nonqualified distribution, are an eligible retired public safety officer, and your pension payment is used to pay for health coverage or qualified long-term care insurance

If the Plan is a governmental plan, you retired as a public safety officer, and your retirement was by reason of disability or was after normal retirement age, you can exclude from your taxable income nonqualified distributions paid directly as premiums to an accident or health plan (or a qualified long-term care insurance contract) that your employer maintains for you, your spouse, or your dependents, up to a maximum of $3,000 annually. For this purpose, a public safety officer is a law enforcement officer, firefighter, chaplain, or member of a rescue squad or ambulance crew.

If you are not a plan participant

Payments after death of the participant. If you receive a distribution after the participant's death that you do not roll over, the distribution will generally be taxed in the same manner described elsewhere in this notice. However, whether the payment is a qualified distribution generally depends on when the participant first made a contribution to the designated Roth account in the Plan. Also, the 10% additional income tax on early distributions and the special rules for public safety officers do not apply, and the special rule described under the section "If you receive a nonqualified distribution and you were born on or before January 1, 1936" applies only if the participant was born on or before January 1, 1936.

If you are a surviving spouse. If you receive a payment from the Plan as the surviving spouse of a deceased participant, you have the same rollover options that the participant would have had, as described elsewhere in this notice. In addition, if you choose to do a rollover to a Roth IRA, you may treat the Roth IRA as your own or as an inherited Roth IRA.

A Roth IRA you treat as your own is treated like any other Roth IRA of yours, so that you will not have to receive any required minimum distributions during your lifetime and earnings paid to you in a nonqualified distribution before you are age 59½ will be subject to the 10% additional income tax on early distributions (unless an exception applies).

If you treat the Roth IRA as an inherited Roth IRA, payments from the Roth IRA will not be subject to the 10% additional income tax on early distributions. An inherited Roth IRA is subject to required minimum distributions. If the participant had started taking required minimum distributions from the Plan, you will have to receive required minimum distributions from the inherited Roth IRA. If the participant had not started taking required minimum distributions, you will not have to start receiving required minimum distributions from the inherited Roth IRA until the year the participant would have been age 70½.

If you are a surviving beneficiary other than a spouse. If you receive a payment from the Plan because of the participant's death and you are a designated beneficiary other than a surviving spouse, the only rollover option you have is to do a direct rollover to an inherited Roth IRA. Payments from the inherited Roth IRA, even if made in a nonqualified distribution, will not be subject to the 10% additional income tax on early distributions. You will have to receive required minimum distributions from the inherited Roth IRA.

Payments under a qualified domestic relations order. If you are the spouse or a former spouse of the participant who receives a payment from the Plan under a qualified domestic relations order (QDRO), you generally have the same options the participant would have (for example, you may roll over the payment as described in this notice).

If you are a nonresident alien

If you are a nonresident alien and you do not do a direct rollover to a U.S. IRA or U.S. employer plan, instead of withholding 20%, the Plan is generally required to withhold 30% of the payment for federal income taxes. If the amount withheld exceeds the amount of tax you owe (as may happen if you do a 60-day rollover), you may request an income tax refund by filing Form 1040NR and attaching your Form 1042-S. See Form W-8BEN for claiming that you are entitled to a reduced rate of withholding under an income tax treaty. For more information, see also IRS Publication 519, U.S. Tax Guide for Aliens, and IRS Publication 515, Withholding of Tax on Nonresident Aliens and Foreign Entities.

Other special rules

If a payment is one in a series of payments for less than 10 years, your choice whether to make a direct rollover will apply to all later payments in the series (unless you make a different choice for later payments).

If your payments for the year (only including payments from the designated Roth account in the Plan) are less than $200, the Plan is not required to allow you to do a direct rollover and is not required to withhold for federal income taxes. However, you can do a 60-day rollover.

Unless you elect otherwise, a mandatory cashout from the designated Roth account in the Plan of more than $1,000 will be directly rolled over to a Roth IRA chosen by the Plan administrator or the payor. A mandatory cashout is a payment from a plan to a participant made before age 62 (or normal retirement age, if later) and without consent, where the participant's benefit does not exceed $5,000 (not including any amounts held under the plan as a result of a prior rollover made to the plan).

You may have special rollover rights if you recently served in the U.S. Armed Forces. For more information, see IRS Publication 3, Armed Forces' Tax Guide.

FOR MORE INFORMATION

You may wish to consult with the Plan administrator or payor, or a professional tax advisor, before taking a payment from the Plan. Also, you can find more detailed information on the federal tax treatment of payments from employer plans in: IRS Publication 575, Pension and Annuity Income; IRS Publication 590, Individual Retirement Arrangements (IRAs); and IRS Publication 571, Tax-Sheltered Annuity Plans (403(b) Plans). These publications are available from a local IRS office, on the web at *www.irs.gov*, or by calling 1-800-TAX-FORM.

Appendix K

Model Section 402(f) Notice for Payments NOT from a Designated Roth Account from Notice 2009-68, IRB 2009-39

YOUR ROLLOVER OPTIONS

You are receiving this notice because all or a portion of a payment you are receiving from the [INSERT NAME OF PLAN] (the "Plan") is eligible to be rolled over to an IRA or an employer plan. This notice is intended to help you decide whether to do such a rollover.

This notice describes the rollover rules that apply to payments from the Plan that are *not* from a designated Roth account (a type of account with special tax rules in some employer plans). If you also receive a payment from a designated Roth account in the Plan, you will be provided a different notice for that payment, and the Plan administrator or the payor will tell you the amount that is being paid from each account.

Rules that apply to most payments from a plan are described in the "General Information About Rollovers" section. Special rules that only apply in certain circumstances are described in the "Special Rules and Options" section.

GENERAL INFORMATION ABOUT ROLLOVERS

How can a rollover affect my taxes?

You will be taxed on a payment from the Plan if you do not roll it over. If you are under age 59½ and do not do a rollover, you will also have to pay a 10% additional income tax on early distributions (unless an exception applies). However, if you do a rollover, you will not have to pay tax until you receive payments later and the 10% additional income tax will not apply if those payments are made after you are age 59½ (or if an exception applies).

Where may I roll over the payment?

You may roll over the payment to either an IRA (an individual retirement account or individual retirement annuity) or an employer plan (a tax-qualified plan, Section 403(b) plan, or governmental Section 457(b) plan) that will accept the rollover. The rules of the IRA or employer plan that holds the rollover will determine your investment options, fees, and rights to payment from the IRA or employer plan (for example, no spousal consent rules apply to IRAs and IRAs may not provide loans). Further, the amount rolled over will become subject to the tax rules that apply to the IRA or employer plan.

How do I do a rollover?

There are two ways to do a rollover. You can do either a direct rollover or a 60-day rollover.

If you do a direct rollover, the Plan will make the payment directly to your IRA or an employer plan. You should contact the IRA sponsor or the administrator of the employer plan for information on how to do a direct rollover.

If you do not do a direct rollover, you may still do a rollover by making a deposit into an IRA or eligible employer plan that will accept it. You will have 60 days after you receive the payment to make the deposit. If you do not do a direct rollover, the Plan is required to withhold 20% of the payment for federal income taxes (up to the amount of cash and property received other than employer stock). This means that, in order to roll over the entire payment in a 60-day rollover, you must use other funds to make up for the 20% withheld. If you do not roll over the entire amount of the payment, the portion not rolled over will be taxed and will be subject to the 10% additional income tax on early distributions if you are under age 59½ (unless an exception applies).

How much may I roll over?

If you wish to do a rollover, you may roll over all or part of the amount eligible for rollover. Any payment from the Plan is eligible for rollover, except:

- Certain payments spread over a period of at least 10 years or over your life or life expectancy (or the lives or joint life expectancy of you and your beneficiary)

- Required minimum distributions after age 70½ (or after death)

- Hardship distributions

- ESOP dividends

- Corrective distributions of contributions that exceed tax law limitations

- Loans treated as deemed distributions (for example, loans in default due to missed payments before your employment ends)

- Cost of life insurance paid by the Plan

- Contributions made under special automatic enrollment rules that are withdrawn pursuant to your request within 90 days of enrollment

- Amounts treated as distributed because of a prohibited allocation of S corporation stock under an ESOP (also, there will generally be adverse tax consequences if you roll over a distribution of S corporation stock to an IRA).

The Plan administrator or the payor can tell you what portion of a payment is eligible for rollover.

If I don't do a rollover, will I have to pay the 10% additional income tax on early distributions?

If you are under age 59½, you will have to pay the 10% additional income tax on early distributions for any payment from the Plan (including amounts withheld for income tax) that you do not roll over, unless one of the exceptions listed below applies. This tax is in addition to the regular income tax on the payment not rolled over.

The 10% additional income tax does not apply to the following payments from the Plan:

- Payments made after you separate from service if you will be at least age 55 in the year of the separation

- Payments that start after you separate from service if paid at least annually in equal or close to equal amounts over your life or life expectancy (or the lives or joint life expectancy of you and your beneficiary)

- Payments from a governmental defined benefit pension plan made after you separate from service if you are a public safety employee and you are at least age 50 in the year of the separation

- Payments made due to disability

- Payments after your death

- Payments of ESOP dividends

- Corrective distributions of contributions that exceed tax law limitations

- Cost of life insurance paid by the Plan

- Contributions made under special automatic enrollment rules that are withdrawn pursuant to your request within 90 days of enrollment

- Payments made directly to the government to satisfy a federal tax levy

- Payments made under a qualified domestic relations order (QDRO)

- Payments up to the amount of your deductible medical expenses

- Certain payments made while you are on active duty if you were a member of a reserve component called to duty after September 11, 2001 for more than 179 days

- Payments of certain automatic enrollment contributions requested to be withdrawn within 90 days of the first contribution.

If I do a rollover to an IRA, will the 10% additional income tax apply to early distributions from the IRA?

If you receive a payment from an IRA when you are under age 59½, you will have to pay the 10% additional income tax on early distributions from the IRA, unless an exception applies. In general, the exceptions to the 10% additional income tax for early distributions from an IRA are the same as the exceptions listed above for early distributions from a plan. However, there are a few differences for payments from an IRA, including:

- There is no exception for payments after separation from service that are made after age 55.

- The exception for qualified domestic relations orders (QDROs) does not apply (although a special rule applies under which, as part of a divorce or separation agreement, a tax-free transfer may be made directly to an IRA of a spouse or former spouse).

- The exception for payments made at least annually in equal or close to equal amounts over a specified period applies without regard to whether you have had a separation from service.

- There are additional exceptions for (1) payments for qualified higher education expenses, (2) payments up to $10,000 used in a qualified first-time home purchase, and (3) payments after you have received unemployment compensation for 12 consecutive weeks (or would have been eligible to receive unemployment compensation but for self-employed status).

Will I owe State income taxes?

This notice does not describe any State or local income tax rules (including withholding rules).

SPECIAL RULES AND OPTIONS

If your payment includes after-tax contributions

After-tax contributions included in a payment are not taxed. If a payment is only part of your benefit, an allocable portion of your after-tax contributions is generally included in the payment. If you have pre-1987 after-tax contributions maintained in a separate account, a special rule may apply to determine whether the after-tax contributions are included in a payment.

You may roll over to an IRA a payment that includes after-tax contributions through either a direct rollover or a 60-day rollover. You must keep track of the aggregate amount of the after-tax contributions in all of your IRAs (in order to determine your taxable income for later payments from the IRAs). If you do a direct rollover of only a portion of the amount paid from the Plan and a portion is paid to you, each of the payments will include an allocable portion of the after-tax contributions. If you do a 60-day rollover to an IRA of only a portion of the payment made to you, the after-tax contributions are treated as rolled over last. For example, assume you are receiving a complete distribution of your benefit which totals $12,000, of which $2,000 is after-tax contributions. In this case, if you roll over $10,000 to an IRA in a 60-day rollover, no amount is taxable because the $2,000 amount not rolled over is treated as being after-tax contributions.

You may roll over to an employer plan all of a payment that includes after-tax contributions, but only through a direct rollover (and only if the receiving plan separately accounts for after-tax contributions and is not a governmental Section 457(b) plan). You can do a 60-day rollover to an employer plan of part of a payment that includes after-tax contributions, but only up to the amount of the payment that would be taxable if not rolled over.

If you miss the 60-day rollover deadline

Generally, the 60-day rollover deadline cannot be extended. However, the IRS has the limited authority to waive the deadline under certain extraordinary circumstances, such as when external events prevented you from completing the rollover by the 60-day rollover deadline. To apply for a waiver, you must file a private letter ruling request with the IRS. Private letter ruling requests require the payment of a nonrefundable user fee. For more information, see IRS Publication 590, Individual Retirement Arrangements (IRAs).

If your payment includes employer stock that you do not roll over

If you do not do a rollover, you can apply a special rule to payments of employer stock (or other employer securities) that are either attributable to after-tax contributions or paid in a lump sum after separation from service (or after age 59½, disability, or the participant's death). Under the special rule, the net unrealized appreciation on the stock will not be taxed when distributed from the Plan and will be taxed at capital gain rates when you sell the stock. Net unrealized appreciation is generally the increase in the value of employer stock after it was acquired by the Plan. If you do a rollover for a payment that includes employer stock (for example, by selling the stock and rolling over the proceeds within 60 days of the payment), the special rule relating to the distributed employer stock will not apply to any subsequent payments from the IRA or employer plan. The Plan administrator can tell you the amount of any net unrealized appreciation.

If you have an outstanding loan that is being offset

If you have an outstanding loan from the Plan, your Plan benefit may be offset by the amount of the loan, typically when your employment ends. The loan offset amount is treated as a distribution to you at the time of the offset and will be taxed (including the 10% additional income tax on early distributions, unless an exception applies) unless you do a 60-day rollover in the amount of the loan offset to an IRA or employer plan.

If you were born on or before January 1, 1936

If you were born on or before January 1, 1936 and receive a lump sum distribution that you do not roll over, special rules for calculating the amount of the tax on the payment might apply to you. For more information, see IRS Publication 575, Pension and Annuity Income.

If your payment is from a governmental Section 457(b) plan

If the Plan is a governmental Section 457(b) plan, the same rules described elsewhere in this notice generally apply, allowing you to roll over the payment to an IRA or an employer plan that accepts rollovers. One difference is that, if you do not do a rollover, you will not have to pay the 10% additional income tax on early distributions from the Plan even if you are under age 59½ (unless the payment is from a separate account holding rollover contributions that were made to the Plan from a tax-qualified plan, a Section 403(b) plan, or an IRA). However, if you do a rollover to an IRA or to an employer plan that is not a governmental Section 457(b) plan, a later distribution made before age 59½ will be subject to the 10% additional income tax on early distributions (unless an exception applies). Other differences are that you cannot do a rollover if the payment is due to an "unforeseeable emergency" and the special rules under "If your payment includes employer stock that you do not roll over" and "If you were born on or before January 1, 1936" do not apply.

If you are an eligible retired public safety officer and your pension payment is used to pay for health coverage or qualified long-term care insurance

If the Plan is a governmental plan, you retired as a public safety officer, and your retirement was by reason of disability or was after normal retirement age, you can exclude from your taxable income plan payments paid directly as premiums to an accident or health plan (or a qualified long-term care insurance contract) that your employer maintains for you, your spouse, or your dependents, up to a maximum of $3,000 annually. For this purpose, a public safety officer is a law enforcement officer, firefighter, chaplain, or member of a rescue squad or ambulance crew.

If you roll over your payment to a Roth IRA

You can roll over a payment from the Plan made before January 1, 2010 to a Roth IRA only if your modified adjusted gross income is not more than $100,000 for the year the payment is made to you and, if married, you file a joint return. These limitations do not apply to payments made to you from the Plan after 2009. If you wish to roll over the payment to a Roth IRA, but you are not eligible to do a rollover to a Roth IRA until after 2009, you can do a rollover to a traditional IRA and then, after 2009, elect to convert the traditional IRA into a Roth IRA.

If you roll over the payment to a Roth IRA, a special rule applies under which the amount of the payment rolled over (reduced by any after-tax amounts) will be taxed. However, the 10% additional income tax on early distributions will not apply (unless you take the amount rolled over out of the Roth IRA within 5 years, counting from January 1 of the year of the rollover). For payments from the Plan during 2010 that are rolled over to a Roth IRA, the taxable amount can be spread over a 2-year period starting in 2011.

If you roll over the payment to a Roth IRA, later payments from the Roth IRA that are qualified distributions will not be taxed (including earnings after the rollover). A qualified distribution from a Roth IRA is a payment made after you are age 59½ (or after your death or disability, or as a qualified first-time homebuyer distribution of up to $10,000) and after you have had a Roth IRA for at least 5 years. In applying this 5-year rule, you count from January 1 of the year for which your first contribution was made to a Roth IRA. Payments from the Roth IRA that are not qualified distributions will be taxed to the extent of earnings after the rollover, including the 10% additional income tax on early distributions (unless an exception applies). You do not have to take required minimum distributions from a Roth IRA during your lifetime. For more information, see IRS Publication 590, Individual Retirement Arrangements (IRAs).

You cannot roll over a payment from the Plan to a designated Roth account in an employer plan.

If you are not a plan participant

Payments after death of the participant. If you receive a distribution after the participant's death that you do not roll over, the distribution will generally be taxed in the same manner described elsewhere in this notice. However, the 10% additional income tax on early distributions and the special rules for public safety officers do not apply, and the special rule described under the section "If you were born on or before January 1, 1936" applies only if the participant was born on or before January 1, 1936.

If you are a surviving spouse. If you receive a payment from the Plan as the surviving spouse of a deceased participant, you have the same rollover options that the participant would have had, as described elsewhere in this notice. In addition, if you choose to do a rollover to an IRA, you may treat the IRA as your own or as an inherited IRA.

An IRA you treat as your own is treated like any other IRA of yours, so that payments made to you before you are age 59½ will be subject to the 10% additional income tax on early distributions (unless an exception applies) and required minimum distributions from your IRA do not have to start until after you are age 70½.

If you treat the IRA as an inherited IRA, payments from the IRA will not be subject to the 10% additional income tax on early distributions. However, if the participant had started taking required minimum distributions, you will have to receive required minimum distributions from the inherited IRA. If the participant had not started taking required minimum distributions from the Plan, you will not have to start receiving required minimum distributions from the inherited IRA until the year the participant would have been age 70½.

If you are a surviving beneficiary other than a spouse. If you receive a payment from the Plan because of the participant's death and you are a designated beneficiary other than a surviving spouse, the only rollover option you have is to do a direct rollover to an inherited IRA. Payments from the inherited IRA will not be subject to the 10% additional income tax on early distributions. You will have to receive required minimum distributions from the inherited IRA.

Payments under a qualified domestic relations order. If you are the spouse or former spouse of the participant who receives a payment from the Plan under a qualified domestic relations order (QDRO), you generally have the same options the participant would have (for example, you may roll over the payment to your own IRA or an eligible employer plan that will accept it). Payments under the QDRO will not be subject to the 10% additional income tax on early distributions.

If you are a nonresident alien

If you are a nonresident alien and you do not do a direct rollover to a U.S. IRA or U.S. employer plan, instead of withholding 20%, the Plan is generally required to withhold 30% of the payment for federal income taxes. If the amount withheld exceeds the amount of tax you owe (as may happen if you do a 60-day rollover), you may request an income tax refund by filing Form 1040NR and attaching your Form 1042-S. See Form W-8BEN for claiming that you are entitled to a reduced rate of withholding under an income tax treaty. For more information, see also IRS Publication 519, U.S. Tax Guide for Aliens, and IRS Publication 515, Withholding of Tax on Nonresident Aliens and Foreign Entities.

Other special rules

If a payment is one in a series of payments for less than 10 years, your choice whether to make a direct rollover will apply to all later payments in the series (unless you make a different choice for later payments).

If your payments for the year are less than $200 (not including payments from a designated Roth account in the Plan), the Plan is not required to allow you to do a direct rollover and is not required to withhold for federal income taxes. However, you may do a 60-day rollover.

Unless you elect otherwise, a mandatory cashout of more than $1,000 (not including payments from a designated Roth account in the Plan) will be directly rolled over to an IRA chosen by the Plan administrator or the payor. A mandatory cashout is a payment from a plan to a participant made before age 62 (or normal retirement age, if later) and without consent, where the participant's benefit does not exceed $5,000 (not including any amounts held under the plan as a result of a prior rollover made to the plan).

You may have special rollover rights if you recently served in the U.S. Armed Forces. For more information, see IRS Publication 3, Armed Forces' Tax Guide.

FOR MORE INFORMATION

You may wish to consult with the Plan administrator or payor, or a professional tax advisor, before taking a payment from the Plan. Also, you can find more detailed information on the federal tax treatment of payments from employer plans in: IRS Publication 575, Pension and Annuity Income; IRS Publication 590, Individual Retirement Arrangements (IRAs); and IRS Publication 571, Tax-Sheltered Annuity Plans (403(b) Plans). These publications are available from a local IRS office, on the web at *www.irs.gov*, or by calling 1-800-TAX-FORM.

* * *

Appendix L1

Operational Failures and Correction Methods; Appendix A to Rev. Proc. 2013-12, 2013-4 IRB 313

.01 *General rule.* (i) This appendix sets forth Operational Failures and Correction Methods relating to Qualified Plans. In each case, the method described corrects the Operational Failure identified in the headings below. Corrective allocations and distributions should reflect Earnings and actuarial adjustments in accordance with section 6.02(4) of this revenue procedure. The correction methods in this appendix are acceptable to correct Qualification Failures under VCP, and to correct Qualification Failures under SCP that occurred notwithstanding that the plan has established practices and procedures reasonably designed to promote and facilitate overall compliance with the Code, as provided in section 4.04 of this revenue procedure. To the extent a failure listed in this appendix could occur under a 403(b) Plan, a SEP, or a SIMPLE IRA Plan, the correction method listed for such failure may similarly be used to correct the failure.

(ii) Correction methods permitted in Appendix A and Appendix B are deemed to be reasonable and appropriate methods of correcting a failure. As provided in section 6.02(2), there may be more than one reasonable and appropriate correction of a failure. Any correction method used that is not described in Appendix A or Appendix B would need to satisfy the correction principles of section 6.02. For example, the sponsor of a 403(b) Plan that failed to satisfy the universal availability requirement of §403(b)(12)(A)(ii) might propose to determine the missed deferral for an excluded employee using a percentage based on the average deferrals for all employees in the plan instead of using the rule for calculating missed deferrals set out in .05(6)(b). In doing so, the proposed correction method would fall outside Appendix A, and the Plan Sponsor would need to satisfy the general correction principles of section 6.02 and other applicable rules in this revenue procedure.

. 02 *Failure to properly provide the minimum top-heavy benefit under §416 to non-key employees.* In a defined contribution plan, the permitted correction method is to properly contribute and allocate the required top-heavy minimums to the plan in the manner provided for in the plan on behalf of the non-key employees (and any other employees required to receive top-heavy allocations under the plan). In a defined benefit plan, the minimum required benefit must be accrued in the manner provided in the plan.

.03 *Failure to satisfy the ADP test set forth in §401(k)(3), the ACP test set forth in §401(m)(2), or, for plan years beginning on or before December 31, 2001, the multiple use test of §401(m)(9).* The permitted correction method is to make qualified nonelective contributions (QNECs) (as defined in §1.401(k)-6) on behalf of the nonhighly compensated employees to the extent necessary to raise the actual deferral percentage or actual contribution percentage of the nonhighly compensated employees to the percentage needed to pass the test or tests. For purposes of correcting a failed ADP, ACP, or multiple use test, any amounts used to fund QNECs must satisfy the definition of QNEC in §1.401(k)-6. The contributions must be made on behalf of all eligible nonhighly compensated employees (to the extent permitted under §415) and must be the same percentage of compensation. QNECs contributed to satisfy the ADP test need not be taken into account for determining additional contributions (e.g., a matching contribution), if any. For purposes of this section .03, employees who would have received a matching contribution had they made elective deferrals must be counted as eligible employees for the ACP test, and the plan must satisfy the ACP test. Under this correction method, a plan may not be treated as two separate plans, one covering otherwise excludable employees and the other covering all other employees (as permitted in §1.410(b)-6(b)(3)), in order to reduce the number of employees eligible to receive QNECs. Likewise, under this correction method, the plan may not be restructured into component plans in order to reduce the number of employees eligible to receive QNECs.

.04 *Failure to distribute elective deferrals in excess of the §402(g) limit (in contravention of §401(a)(30)).* The permitted correction method is to distribute the excess deferral to the employee and to report the amount as taxable in the year of deferral and in the year distributed. The inclusion of the deferral and the distribution in gross income applies whether or not any portion of the excess deferral is attributable to a designated Roth contribution (see §402A(d)(3)). In accordance with §1.402(g)-1(e)(1)(ii), a distribution to a highly compensated employee is included in the ADP test and a distribution to a nonhighly compensated employee is not included in the ADP test.

.05 *Exclusion of an eligible employee from all contributions or accruals under the plan for one or more plan years.*

(1) *Improperly excluded employees: employer provided contributions or benefits.* For plans with employer provided contributions or benefits (which are neither elective deferrals under a qualified cash or deferred arrangement under §401(k) nor matching or after-tax employee contributions that are subject to §401(m)), the permitted correction method is to make a contribution to the plan on behalf of the employees excluded from a defined contribution plan or to provide benefit accruals for the employees excluded from a defined benefit plan.

(2) *Improperly excluded employees: contributions subject to §401(k) or 401(m).* (a) For plans providing benefits subject to §401(k) or 401(m), the corrective contribution for an improperly

excluded employee is described in the following paragraphs of this section .05(2). (See Examples 3 through 12 of Appendix B.)

(b) If the employee was not provided the opportunity to elect and make elective deferrals (other than designated Roth contributions) to a §401(k) plan that does not satisfy §401(k)(3) by applying the safe harbor contribution requirements of§401(k)(12) or 401(k)(13), the employer must make a QNEC to the plan on behalf of the employee that replaces the "missed deferral opportunity." The missed deferral opportunity is equal to 50% of the employee's "missed deferral." The missed deferral is determined by multiplying the actual deferral percentage for the year of exclusion (whether or not the plan is using current or prior year testing) for the employee's group in the plan (either highly compensated or nonhighly compensated) by the employee's compensation for that year. The employee's missed deferral amount is reduced further to the extent necessary to ensure that the missed deferral does not exceed applicable plan limits, including the annual deferral limit under §402(g) for the calendar year in which the failure occurred. Under this correction method, a plan may not be treated as two separate plans, one covering otherwise excludable employees and the other covering all other employees (as permitted in §1.410(b)-6(b)(3)) in order to reduce the applicable ADP, the corresponding missed deferral, and the required QNEC. Likewise, restructuring the plan into component plans is not permitted in order to reduce the applicable ADP, the corresponding missed deferral, and the required QNEC. The QNEC required for the employee for the missed deferral opportunity for the year of exclusion is adjusted for Earnings to the date the corrective QNEC is made on behalf of the affected employee.

(c) If the employee should have been eligible for but did not receive an allocation of employer matching contributions under a non-safe harbor plan because he or she was not given the opportunity to make elective deferrals, the employer must make a corrective employer nonelective contribution on behalf of the affected employee. The corrective employer nonelective contribution is equal to the matching contribution the employee would have received had the employee made a deferral equal to the missed deferral determined under section .05(2)(b). The corrective employer nonelective contribution must be adjusted for Earnings to the date the corrective contribution is made on behalf of the affected employee.

(d) (i) If the employee was not provided the opportunity to elect and make elective deferrals (other than designated Roth contributions) to a safe harbor §401(k) plan that uses a rate of matching contributions to satisfy the safe harbor requirements of §401(k)(12), then the missed deferral is deemed equal to the greater of 3% of compensation or the maximum deferral percentage for which the employer provides a matching contribution rate that is at least as favorable as 100% of the elective deferral made by the employee. If the employee was not provided the opportunity to elect and make elective deferrals (other than Roth contributions) to a safe harbor §401(k) plan that uses nonelective contributions to satisfy the safe harbor requirements of §401(k)(12), then the missed deferral is deemed equal to 3% of compensation. In either event, this estimate of the missed deferral replaces the estimate based on the ADP test in a traditional §401(k) plan. The required QNEC on behalf of the excluded employee is equal to (i) 50% of the missed deferral, plus (ii) either (A) an amount equal to the contribution that would have been required as a matching contribution based on the missed deferral in the case of a safe harbor §401(k) plan that uses a rate of matching contributions to satisfy the safe harbor requirements of §401(k)(12) or (B) the nonelective contribution that would have been made on behalf of the employee in the case of a safe harbor §401(k) plan that uses nonelective contributions to satisfy the safe harbor requirements of §401(k)(12). The QNEC required to replace the employee's missed deferral opportunity and the corresponding matching or nonelective contribution is adjusted for Earnings to the date the corrective QNEC is made on behalf of the employee.

(ii) If the employee was not provided the opportunity to make an affirmative election with respect to elective deferrals (other than designated Roth contributions) to a safe harbor §401(k) plan that uses an automatic contribution arrangement to satisfy the safe harbor requirements of §401(k)(13) and the failure occurs for a period that does not extend past the last day of the first plan year which begins after the date on which the first deferral would have been made (but for the failure), then the missed deferral is deemed to equal 3% of the employee's compensation under the plan. If the failure occurs for a plan year or plan years subsequent to the period described in the prior sentence, then the missed deferral for each subsequent plan year is equal to the qualified percentage specified in the plan document to comply with §401(k)(13)(C)(iii). The missed deferral determined in accordance with this section .05(2)(d)(ii) replaces the estimate based on the ADP test in a traditional §401(k) plan. The required corrective employer contribution on behalf of the excluded employee is equal to (i) the missed deferral opportunity, which is an amount equal to 50% of the missed deferral, plus (ii) an amount equal to either the matching contribution that would apply under §401(k)(13) based on the missed deferral or the nonelective contribution that would have been made on behalf of the employee under §401(k)(13), whichever applies under the plan. The employer contribution for the missed deferral opportunity must be a QNEC. The corrective employer contribution consisting of the QNEC required to replace the employee's missed deferral opportunity and the corresponding matching or nonelective contribution is adjusted for Earnings to the date the corrective employer contribution is made on behalf of the employee.

(iii) In the case of a failure to make the required nonelective contribution for a plan year under a safe harbor §401(k) plan that uses the nonelective contribution under §401(k)(12)(C) to satisfy the safe harbor requirements of §401(k)(12) or that uses the nonelective contribution under §401(k)(13)(D)(i)(I) to satisfy the safe harbor requirements of §401(k)(13), the nonelective contribution (which must be a QNEC in the case of a plan that uses §401(k)(12) to satisfy ADP) required to be made on behalf of the employee is equal to 3% of the employee's compensation during the period of the failure. For this purpose, the period of the failure for any plan year ends at the end of the plan year or, if earlier, the later of June 18, 2009 or the date 30 days after notice was provided to employees as required under applicable Treasury Regulations (see §1.401(k)-3(g)(ii) of the proposed regulations, at 74 FR 23134).

(e) If the employee should have been eligible to elect and make after-tax employee contributions (other than designated Roth contributions), the employer must make a QNEC to the plan on behalf of the employee that is equal to the "missed opportunity for making after-tax employee contributions." The missed opportunity for making after-tax employee contributions is equal to 40% of the employee's "missed after-tax contributions." The employee's missed after-tax contributions are equal to the actual contribution percentage (ACP) for the employee's group (either highly compensated or nonhighly compensated) times the employee's compensation, but with the resulting amount not to exceed applicable plan limits. If the ACP consists of both matching and after-tax employee contributions, then, in lieu of basing the employee's missed after-tax employee contributions on the ACP for the employee's group, the employer is permitted to determine separately the portion of the ACP that is attributable to after-tax employee contributions for the employee's group (either highly compensated or nonhighly compensated), multiplied by the employee's compensation for the year of exclusion. The QNEC must be adjusted for Earnings to the date the corrective QNEC is made on behalf of the affected employee.

(f) If the employee was improperly excluded from an allocation of employer matching contributions because he or she was not given the opportunity to make after-tax employee contributions (other than designated Roth contributions), the employer must make a corrective employer nonelective contribution on behalf of the affected employee. The corrective employer nonelective contribution is equal to the matching contribution the employee would have received had the employee made an after-tax employee contribution equal to the missed after-tax employee contribution determined under section .05(2)(e). The corrective employer nonelective contribution must be adjusted for Earnings to the date the corrective contribution is made on behalf of the affected employee.

(g) The methods for correcting the failures described in this section .05(2) do not apply until after the correction of other qualification failures. Thus, for example, if, in addition to the failure of excluding an eligible employee, the plan also failed the ADP or ACP test, the correction methods described in section .05(2)(b) through (f) cannot be used until after correction of the ADP or ACP test failures. For purposes of this section .05(2), in order to determine whether the plan passed the ADP or ACP test, the plan may rely on a test performed with respect to those eligible employees who were provided with the opportunity to make elective deferrals or after-tax employee contributions and receive an allocation of employer matching contributions, in accordance with the terms of the plan, and may disregard the employees who were improperly excluded.

(3) *Improperly excluded employees: designated Roth contributions.* For employees who were improperly excluded from plans that (i) are subject to §401(k) (as described in section .05(2)) and (ii) provide for the optional treatment of elective deferrals as designated Roth contributions, the correction is the same as described under section .05(2). Thus, for example, the corrective employer contribution required to replace the missed deferral opportunity is made in accordance with the method described in section .05(2)(b) in the case of a §401(k) plan that is not a

safe harbor §401(k) plan or .05(2)(d) in the case of a safe harbor §401(k) plan. However, none of the corrective contributions made by the employer may be treated as designated Roth contributions (and may not be included in an employee's gross income) and thus may not be contributed or allocated to a Roth account (as described in §402A(b)(2)). The corrective employer contribution must be allocated to an account established for receiving a QNEC or any other employer contribution in which the employee is fully vested and subject to the withdrawal restrictions that apply to elective deferrals.

(4) *Improperly excluded employees: catch-up contributions only.* (a) *Correction for missed catch-up contributions.* If an eligible employee was not provided the opportunity to elect and make catch-up contributions to a §401(k) plan, the employer must make a QNEC to the plan on behalf of the employee that replaces the "missed deferral opportunity" attributable to the failure to permit an eligible employee to make a catch-up contribution pursuant to §414(v). The missed deferral opportunity for catch-up contributions is equal to 50% of the employee's missed deferral attributable to catch-up contributions. For this purpose, the missed deferral attributable to catch-up contributions is one half of the applicable catch-up contribution limit for the year in which the employee was improperly excluded. Thus, for example if an eligible employee was improperly precluded from electing and making catch-up contributions in 2006, the missed deferral attributable to catch-up contributions is $2,500, which is one half of $5,000, the 2006 catch-up contribution limit for a §401(k) plan. The eligible employee's missed deferral opportunity is $1,250 (i.e., 50% of the missed deferral attributable to catch-up contributions of $2,500). The QNEC required to replace the missed deferral opportunity for the year of exclusion is adjusted for Earnings to the date the corrective QNEC is made on behalf of the affected employee. For purposes of this correction, an eligible employee, pursuant to §414(v)(5), refers to any participant who (i) would have attained age 50 by the end of the plan's taxable year and (ii) in the absence of the plan's catch-up provision, could not make additional elective deferrals on account of the plan or statutory limitations described in §414(v)(3) and §1.414(v)-1(b)(1).

(b) *Correction for missed matching contributions on catch-up contributions.* If an employee was precluded from making catch-up contributions under this section .05(4), the Plan Sponsor should ascertain whether the affected employee would have been entitled to an additional matching contribution on account of the missed deferral. If the employee would have been entitled to an additional matching contribution, then the employer must make a corrective employer nonelective contribution for the matching contribution on behalf of the affected employee. The corrective employer nonelective contribution is equal to the additional matching contribution the employee would have received had the employee made a deferral equal to the missed deferral determined under paragraph (a) of this section .05(4). The corrective employer nonelective contribution must be adjusted for Earnings to the date the corrective contribution is made on behalf of the affected employee. If in addition to the failure to provide matching contributions under this section .05(4)(b), the plan also failed the ACP test, the correction methods described in this section cannot be used until after correction of the ACP test failure. For purposes of this section, in order to determine whether the plan passed the ACP test the plan may rely on a test performed with respect to those eligible employees who were provided with the opportunity to make elective deferrals or after-tax employee contributions and receive an allocation of employer matching contributions, in accordance with the terms of the plan, and may disregard any employer matching contribution that was not made on account of the plan's failure to provide an eligible employee with the opportunity to make a catch-up contribution.

(5) *Failure to implement an employee election.* (a) *Missed opportunity for elective deferrals.* For eligible employees who filed elections to make elective deferrals under the Plan which the Plan Sponsor failed to implement on a timely basis, the Plan Sponsor must make a QNEC to the plan on behalf of the employee to replace the "missed deferral opportunity." The missed deferral opportunity is equal to 50% of the employee's "missed deferral." The missed deferral is determined by multiplying the employee's elected deferral percentage by the employee's compensation. If the employee elected a dollar amount for an elective deferral, the missed deferral would be the specified dollar amount. The employee's missed deferral amount is reduced further to the extent necessary to ensure that the missed deferral does not exceed applicable plan limits, including the annual deferral limit under §402(g) for the calendar year in which the failure occurred. The QNEC must be adjusted for Earnings to the date the corrective QNEC is made on behalf of the affected employee.

(b) *Missed opportunity for after-tax employee contributions.* For eligible employees who filed elections to make after-tax employee contributions under the Plan which the Plan Sponsor failed to implement on a timely basis, the Plan Sponsor must make a QNEC to the plan on behalf of the employee to replace the employee's missed opportunity for after-tax employee contributions. The missed opportunity for making after-tax employee contributions is equal to 40% of the employee's "missed after-tax contributions." The missed after-tax employee contribution is determined by multiplying the employee's elected after-tax employee contribution percentage by the employee's compensation. The QNEC must be adjusted for Earnings to the date the corrective QNEC is made on behalf of the affected employee.

(c) *Missed opportunity affecting matching contributions.* In the event of failure described in paragraph (a) or (b) of this section .05(5), if the employee would have been entitled to an additional matching contribution had either the missed deferral or after-tax employee contribution been made, then the Plan Sponsor must make a corrective employer nonelective contribution for the matching contribution on behalf of the affected employee, or a corrective QNEC in the case of a safe harbor plan under §401(k)(12). The corrective employer nonelective contribution or QNEC is equal to the matching contribution the employee would have received had the employee made a deferral equal to the missed deferral determined under this paragraph. The corrective employer nonelective contribution or QNEC must be adjusted for Earnings to the date the corrective contribution or QNEC is made on behalf of the affected employee.

(d) *Coordination with correction of other Qualification Failures.* The method for correcting the failures described in this section .05(5) does not apply until after the correction of other qualification failures. Thus, for example, if in addition to the failure to implement an employee's election, the plan also failed the ADP test or ACP test, the correction methods described in section .05(5)(a), (b), or (c) cannot be used until after correction of the ADP or ACP test failures. For purposes of this section .05(5), in order to determine whether the plan passed the ADP or ACP test the plan may rely on a test performed with respect to those eligible employees who were not impacted by the Plan Sponsor's failure to implement employee elections and received allocations of employer matching contributions, in accordance with the terms of the plan, and may disregard employees whose elections were not properly implemented.

(6) *Failure of a 403(b) Plan to satisfy the universal availability requirement of §403(b)(12)(A)(ii).* (a) Subject to the specific rules in this section .05(6), the correction methods set forth in this section .05 (and section 2.02 of Appendix B) for a Qualified Plan also apply to a 403(b) Plan that has a similar failure.

(b) If the employee was not provided the opportunity to elect and make elective deferrals to a 403(b) Plan, then, in lieu of determining the missed deferral based on the actual deferral percentage as described in section .05(2)(b), the missed deferral is deemed equal to the greater of 3% of compensation or the maximum deferral percentage for which the Plan Sponsor provides a matching contribution rate that is at least as favorable as 100% of the elective deferral made by the employee.

(7) *Improper exclusion of an eligible employee from a SIMPLE IRA plan subject to the requirements of §408(p).* (a) Subject to the specific rules in this section .05(7), the correction methods set forth in this section .05 for a Qualified Plan also apply to a SIMPLE IRA plan that has a similar failure.

(b) If the employee was not provided the opportunity to elect and make elective deferrals to a SIMPLE IRA plan, then, in lieu of determining the missed deferral based on the actual deferral percentage as described in section .05(2)(b), the missed deferral is deemed to be 3% of compensation.

.06 *Failure to timely pay the minimum distribution required under §401(a)(9).* In a defined contribution plan, the permitted correction method is to distribute the required minimum distributions (with Earnings from the date of the failure to the date of the distribution). The amount required to be distributed for each year in which the initial failure occurred should be determined by dividing the adjusted account balance on the applicable valuation date by the applicable distribution period. For this purpose, adjusted account balance means the actual account balance, determined in accordance with §1.401(a)(9)-5, Q&A-3, reduced by the amount of the total missed minimum distributions for prior years. In a defined benefit plan, the permitted correction method is to distribute the required minimum distributions, plus an interest payment based on the plan's actuarial equivalence factors in effect on the date that the distribution should have been made. See section 6.02(4)(d) of this revenue procedure. If this correction is made at the time the plan is subject to a restriction on single-sum payments pursuant to §436(d), the Plan Sponsor must contribute to the plan the applicable amount under section 6.02(4)(e)(ii)(A) as part of the correction.

.07 *Failure to obtain participant or spousal consent for a distribution subject to the participant and spousal consent rules under §§401(a)(11), 411(a)(11), and 417.* (1) The permitted correction method is to give each affected participant a choice between providing informed consent for the distribution actually made or receiving a qualified joint and survivor annuity. In the event that participant or spousal consent is required but cannot be obtained, the participant must receive a qualified joint and survivor annuity based on the monthly amount that would have been provided under the plan at his or her retirement date. This annuity may be actuarially reduced to take into account distributions already received by the participant. However, the portion of the qualified joint and survivor annuity payable to the spouse upon the death of the participant may not be actuarially reduced to take into account prior distributions to the participant. Thus, for example, if, in accordance with the automatic qualified joint and survivor annuity option under a plan, a married participant who retired would have received a qualified joint and survivor annuity of $600 per month payable for life with $300 per month payable to the spouse for the spouse's life beginning upon the participant's death, but instead received a single-sum distribution equal to the actuarial present value of the participant's accrued benefit under the plan, then the $600 monthly annuity payable during the participant's lifetime may be actuarially reduced to take the single-sum distribution into account. However, the spouse must be entitled to receive an annuity of $300 per month payable for life beginning at the participant's death.

(2) An alternative permitted correction method is to give each affected participant a choice between (i) providing informed consent for the distribution actually made, (ii) receiving a qualified joint and survivor annuity (both (i) and (ii) of this section .07(2) are described in section .07(1) of this Appendix A), or (iii) a single-sum payment to the participant's spouse equal to the actuarial present value of that survivor annuity benefit (calculated using the applicable interest rate and mortality table under §417(e)(3)). For example, assuming the actuarial present value of a $300 per month annuity payable to the spouse for the spouse's life beginning upon the participant's death was $7,837 (calculated using the applicable interest rate and applicable mortality table under §417(e)(3)), the single-sum payment to the spouse under clause (iii) of this section .07(2) is equal to $7,837. If the single-sum payment is made to the spouse, then the payment is treated in the same manner as a distribution under §402(c)(9) for purposes of rolling over the payment to an IRA or other eligible retirement plan. If correction is made at the time the plan is subject to a restriction on single-sum payments pursuant to §436(d), then the alternative permitted correction in this section .07(2) is available only if the Plan Sponsor (or other person) contributes to the plan the applicable amount under section 6.02(4)(e)(ii)(A) as part of the correction.

.08 *Failure to satisfy the §415 limits in a defined contribution plan.* For limitation years beginning before January 1, 2009, the permitted correction for failure to limit annual additions (other than elective deferrals and after-tax employee contributions) allocated to participants in a defined contribution plan as required in §415 (even if the excess did not result from the allocation of forfeitures or from a reasonable error in estimating compensation) is to place the excess annual additions into an unallocated account, similar to the suspense account described in §1.415-6(b)(6)(iii) (as it appeared in the April 1, 2007 edition of 26 CFR part 1) prior to amendments made by the final regulations under §415, to be used as an employer contribution, other than elective deferrals, in the succeeding year(s). While such amounts remain in the unallocated account, the Plan Sponsor is not permitted to make additional contributions to the plan. The permitted correction for failure to limit annual additions that are elective deferrals or after-tax employee contributions (even if the excess did not result from a reasonable error in determining compensation, the amount of elective deferrals or after-tax employee contributions that could be made with respect to an individual under the §415 limits) is to distribute the elective deferrals or after-tax employee contributions using a method similar to that described under §1.415-6(b)(6)(iv) (as it appeared in the April 1, 2007 edition of 26 CFR part 1) prior to amendments made by the final regulations under §415. Elective deferrals and after-tax employee contributions that are matched may be returned to the employee, provided that the matching contributions relating to such contributions are forfeited (which will also reduce excess annual additions for the affected individuals). The forfeited matching contributions are to be placed into an unallocated account to be used as an employer contribution, other than elective deferrals, in succeeding periods. For limitation years beginning on or after January 1, 2009, the failure to limit annual additions allocated to participants in a defined contribution plan as required in §415 is corrected in accordance with section 6.06(2) and (3).

.09 *Orphan Plans; orphan contracts and other assets.* (1) *Orphan Plans.* If (a) a plan has one or more failures (whether a Qualification Failure or a 403(b) Failure) that result from the Plan Sponsor having ceased to exist, the Plan Sponsor no longer maintaining the plan, or similar reasons and (b) the plan is an Orphan Plan, as defined in section 5.03 (i.e., is not a plan to which ERISA applies), the permitted correction is to terminate the plan and distribute plan assets to participants and beneficiaries. This correction must satisfy four conditions. First, the correction must comply with conditions, standards, and procedures substantially similar to those set forth in section 2578.1 of the Department of Labor regulations (relating to abandoned plans). Second, the qualified termination administrator, as defined in 2578.1(g) of the Department of Labor regulations, based on plan records located and updated in accordance with the Department of Labor regulations, must have reasonably determined whether, and to what extent, the survivor annuity requirements of §§401(a)(11) and 417 apply to any benefit payable under the plan and take reasonable steps to comply with those requirements (if applicable). Third, each participant and beneficiary must have been provided a nonforfeitable right to his or her accrued benefits as of the date of deemed termination under the Department of Labor regulations, subject to income, expenses, gains, and losses between that date and the date of distribution. Fourth, participants and beneficiaries must receive notification of their rights under §402(f). In addition, notwithstanding correction under this revenue procedure, the Service reserves the right to pursue appropriate remedies under the Code against any party who is responsible for the plan, such as the Plan Sponsor, plan administrator, or owner of the business, even in its capacity as a participant or beneficiary under the plan. However, with respect to the first through third conditions above, notice need not be furnished to the Department of Labor, and notices furnished to the Plan Sponsor, participants, or beneficiaries need not indicate that the procedures followed or notices furnished actually comply with, or are required under, Department of Labor regulations.

(2) *403(b) Failures for orphan contracts or other assets.* (a) *Former employees or beneficiaries.* In any case in which a 403(b) Failure results from the Plan Sponsor having ceased involvement with respect to specific assets (including an insurance annuity contract) held under a defined contribution plan on behalf of a participant who is a former employee or on behalf of a beneficiary, a permitted correction is to distribute those plan assets to the participant or beneficiary. Compliance with the distribution rules of section 2578.1(d)(2)(vii) of the Department of Labor regulations satisfies this paragraph .09(2))

(b) *Failures Relating to Information Sharing Agreements.* In any case in which a 403(b) Failure results from a contract issued in an exchange not being part of a 403(b) Plan due to the failure to have an information sharing agreement pursuant to §1.403(b)-10(b)(2)(i)(C), a permitted correction is for the assets held under the contract to be transferred to another vendor to which contributions are being made under the plan in order to become a contract which is held under the plan without regard to the special rules in §1.403(b)-10(b).

Appendix L2

Correction Methods and Examples; Earnings Adjustment Methods and Examples; Appendix B to Rev. Proc. 2013-12, 2013-4 IRB 313

SECTION 1. PURPOSE, ASSUMPTIONS FOR EXAMPLES AND SECTION REFERENCES

.01 *Purpose.* (1) This appendix sets forth correction methods relating to Operational Failures under Qualified Plans. This appendix also sets forth Earnings adjustment methods. In each case, the method described corrects the Operational Failure identified in the headings below. Corrective allocations and distributions should reflect Earnings and actuarial adjustments in accordance with section 6.02(4) of this revenue procedure. The correction methods in this appendix are acceptable to correct Qualification Failures under VCP, and to correct Qualification Failures under SCP that occurred notwithstanding that the plan has established practices and procedures reasonably designed to promote and facilitate overall compliance with the Code, as provided in section 4.04 of this revenue procedure.

(2) To the extent a failure listed in this appendix could occur under a 403(b) Plan, SEP, or SIMPLE IRA Plan, the correction method listed for such failure may similarly be used to correct the failure.

.02 *Assumptions for Examples.* Unless otherwise specified, for ease of presentation, the examples assume that:

(1) the plan year and the §415 limitation year are the calendar year;

(2) the Plan Sponsor maintains a single plan intended to satisfy §401(a) and has never maintained any other plan;

(3) in a defined contribution plan, the plan provides that forfeitures are used to reduce future employer contributions;

(4) the Qualification Failures are Operational Failures and the eligibility and other requirements for SCP, VCP, or Audit CAP, whichever applies, are satisfied; and

(5) there are no Qualification Failures other than the described Operational Failures, and if a corrective action would result in any additional Qualification Failure, appropriate corrective action is taken for that additional Qualification Failure in accordance with EPCRS.

.03 *Designated Roth contributions.* The examples in this Appendix B generally do not identify whether the plan offers designated Roth contributions. The results in the examples, including corrective contributions, would be the same whether or not the plan offered designated Roth contributions.

.04 *Section references.* References to section 2 and section 3 are references to section 2 and 3 in this appendix.

SECTION 2. CORRECTION METHODS AND EXAMPLES

.01 *ADP/ACP Failures.* (1) *Correction Methods.* (a) *Appendix A Correction Method.* Appendix A.03 sets forth a correction method for a failure to satisfy the actual deferral percentage ("ADP"), actual contribution percentage ("ACP"), or, for plan years beginning on or before December 31, 2001, multiple use test set forth in §§401(k)(3), 401(m)(2), and 401(m)(9), respectively.

(b) *One-to-One Correction Method.* (i) *General.* In addition to the correction method in Appendix A, a failure to satisfy the ADP test or ACP test may be corrected by using the one-to-one correction method set forth in this section 2.01(1)(b). Under the one-to-one correction method, an excess contribution amount is determined and assigned to highly compensated employees as provided in paragraph (1)(b)(ii) below. That excess contribution amount (adjusted for Earnings) is either distributed to the highly compensated employees or forfeited from the highly compensated employees' accounts as provided in paragraph (1)(b)(iii) below. That same dollar amount (i.e., the excess contribution amount, adjusted for Earnings) is contributed to the plan and allocated to nonhighly compensated employees as provided in paragraph (1)(b)(iv) below. Under this correction method, a plan may not be treated as two separate plans, one covering otherwise excludable employees and the other covering all other employees (as permitted in §1.410(b)- 6(b)(3)). Likewise, restructuring the plan into component plans is not permitted. This correction method may also be used to correct a failure to satisfy the multiple use test for plan years beginning on or before December 31, 2001.

(ii) *Determination of the Excess Contribution Amount.* The excess contribution amount for the year is equal to the excess of (A) the sum of the excess contributions (as defined in §401(k)(8)(B)), the excess aggregate contributions (as defined in§401(m)(6)(B)), and for plan years beginning on or before December 31, 2001 the amount treated as excess contributions or excess aggregate contributions under the multiple use test for the year, as assigned to each highly compensated employee in accordance with § §401(k)(8)(C) and 401(m)(6)(C), over (B) previous corrections that complied with § §401(k)(8) and 401(m)(6), and, for plan years beginning on or before December 31, 2001, the multiple use test.

(iii) *Distributions and Forfeitures of the Excess Contribution Amount.* (A) The portion of the excess contribution amount assigned to a particular highly compensated employee under paragraph (1)(b)(ii) is adjusted for Earnings from the end of the plan year of the year of the failure through the date of correction. The amount assigned to a particular highly compensated employee, as adjusted, is distributed or, to the extent the amount was forfeitable as of the close of the plan year of the failure, is forfeited. If the amount is forfeited, it is used in accordance with the plan provisions relating to forfeitures that were in effect for the year of the failure. If the amount so assigned to a particular highly compensated employee has been previously distributed, the amount is an Excess Amount within the meaning of section 5.01(3) of this revenue procedure. Thus, pursuant to section 6.06 of this revenue procedure, the Plan Sponsor must notify the employee that the Excess Amount is not eligible for favorable tax treatment accorded to distributions from qualified plans (and, specifically, is not eligible for tax-free rollover).

(B) If any matching contributions (adjusted for Earnings) are forfeited in accordance with §411(a)(3)(G), the forfeited amount is used in accordance with the plan provisions relating to forfeitures that were in effect for the year of the failure.

(C) If a payment was made to an employee and that payment is a forfeitable match described in either paragraph (1)(b)(iii)(A) or (B), then it is an Overpayment defined in section 5.01(6) of this revenue procedure that must be corrected (see sections 2.04 and 2.05 below).

(iv) *Contribution and Allocation of Equivalent Amount.* (A) The Plan Sponsor makes a contribution to the plan that is equal to the aggregate amounts distributed and forfeited under paragraph (1)(b)(iii)(A) (i.e., the excess contribution amount adjusted for Earnings, as provided in paragraph (1)(b)(iii)(A), which does not include any matching contributions forfeited in accordance with §411(a)(3)(G) as provided in paragraph (1)(b)(iii)(B)). The contribution must be a QNEC as defined in§1.401(k)-6.

(B) *(1)* This paragraph (1)(b)(iv)(B) *(1)* applies to a plan that uses the current year testing method described in §1.401(k)-2(a)(2), 1.401(m)-2(a)(2), and, for periods prior to the effective date of those regulations, Notice 98-1, 1998-1 C.B. 327. The contribution made under paragraph (1)(b) (iv)(A) is allocated to the account balances of those individuals who were either (I) the eligible employees for the year of the failure who were nonhighly compensated employees for that year or (II) the eligible employees for the year of the failure who were nonhighly compensated employees for that year and who also are nonhighly compensated employees for the year of correction. Alternatively, the contribution is allocated to account balances of eligible employees described in (I) or (II) of the preceding sentence, except that the allocation is made only to the account balances of those employees who are employees on a date during the year of the correction that is no later than the date of correction. Regardless of which of these four options (described in the two preceding sentences) the Plan Sponsor selects, eligible employees must receive a uniform allocation (as a percentage of compensation) of the contribution. (See Examples 1 and 2.) Under the one-to-one correction method, the amount allocated to the account balance of an employee (i.e., the employee's share of the total amount contributed under paragraph (1)(b)(iv)(A)) is not further adjusted for Earnings and is treated as an annual addition under §415 for the year of the failure for the employee for whom it is allocated.

(2) This paragraph (1)(b)(iv)(B) *(2)* applies to a plan that uses the prior year testing method described in § §1.401(k)-2(a)(2) and 1.401(m)-2(a)(2) and, for periods prior to the effective date of those regulations, Notice 98-1. Paragraph (1)(b)(iv)(B)(*1*) is applied by substituting "the year prior to the year of the failure" for "the year of the failure."

(2) *Examples.*

Example 1:

Employer A maintains a profit-sharing plan with a cash or deferred arrangement that is intended to satisfy §401(k) using the current year testing method. The plan does not provide for matching contributions or after-tax employee contributions. In 2007, it was discovered that the ADP test for 2005 was not performed correctly. When the ADP test was performed correctly, the test was not satisfied for 2005. For 2005, the ADP for highly compensated employees was 9% and the ADP for nonhighly compensated employees was 4%. Accordingly, the ADP for highly compensated employees exceeded the ADP for non-highly compensated employees by more than two percentage points (in violation of §401(k) (3)). There were two highly compensated employees eligible under the §401(k) plan during 2005, Employee P and Employee Q. Employee P made elective deferrals of $10,000, which is equal to 10% of Employee P's compensation of $100,000 for 2005. Employee Q made elective deferrals of $9,500, which is equal to 8% of Employee Q's compensation of $118,750 for 2005.

Correction:

On June 30, 2007, Employer A uses the one-to-one correction method to correct the failure to satisfy the ADP test for 2005. Accordingly, Employer A calculates the dollar amount of the excess contributions for the two highly compensated employees in the manner described in §401(k) (8)(B). The amount of the excess contribution for Employee P is $4,000 (4% of $100,000) and the amount of the excess contribution for Employee Q is $2,375 (2% of $118,750), or a total of $6,375. In accordance with §401(k)(8)(C), $6,375, the excess contribution amount, is assigned $3,437.50 to Employee P and $2,937.50 to Employee Q. It is determined that the Earnings on the assigned amounts through June 30, 2007 are $687 and $587 for Employees P and Q, respectively. The assigned amounts and the Earnings are distributed to Employees P and Q. Therefore, Employee P receives $4,124.50 ($3,437.50 + $687) and Employee Q receives $3,524.50 ($2,937.50 + $587). In addition, on the same date, Employer A makes a corrective contribution to the §401(k) plan equal to $7,649 (the sum of the $4,124.50 distributed to Employee P and the $3,524.50 distributed to Employee Q). The corrective contribution is allocated to the account balances of eligible nonhighly compensated employees for 2005, pro rata based on their compensation for 2005 (subject to §415 for 2005).

Example 2:

The facts are the same as in Example 1, except that for 2005 the plan also provides for (1) after-tax employee contributions and (2) matching contributions equal to 50% of the sum of an employee's elective deferrals and after-tax employee contributions that do not exceed 10% of the employee's compensation. The plan provides that matching contributions are subject to the plan's 20% per year of service vesting schedule and that matching contributions are forfeited and used to reduce employer contributions if associated elective deferrals or after-tax employee contributions are distributed to correct an ADP or ACP test failure. For 2005, nonhighly compensated employees made after-tax employee contributions and no highly compensated employee made any after-tax employee contributions. Employee P received a matching contribution of $5,000 (50% of $10,000) and Employee Q received a matching contribution of $4,750 (50% of $9,500). Employees P and Q were 100% vested in 2005. It was determined that the plan satisfied the requirements of the ACP test for 2005.

Correction:

The same corrective actions are taken as in Example 1. In addition, in accordance with the plan's terms, corrective action is taken to forfeit Employee P's and Employee Q's matching contributions associated with their distributed excess contributions. Employee P's distributed excess contributions and associated matching contributions are $3,437.50 and $1,718.75, respectively. Employee Q's distributed excess contributions and associated matching contributions are $2,937.50 and $1,468.75, respectively. Thus, $1,718.75 is forfeited from Employee P's account and $1,468.75 is forfeited from Employee Q's account. In addition, the Earnings on the forfeited amounts are also forfeited. It is determined that the respective Earnings on the forfeited amount for Employee P is $250 and for Employee Q is $220. The total amount of the forfeitures of $3,657.50 (Employee P's $1,718.75 + $250 and Employee Q's $1,468.75 + $220) is used to reduce contributions for 2007 and subsequent years.

.02 Exclusion of Otherwise Eligible Employees. (1) *Exclusion of Eligible Employees in a§ 401(k) or (m) Plan.* (a) *Correction Method.* (i) *Appendix A Correction Method for Full Year Exclusion.* Appendix A, section .05(2) sets forth the correction method for the exclusion of an eligible employee from electing and making elective deferrals (other than designated Roth contributions) and after-tax employee contributions to a plan that provides benefits that are subject to the requirements of§401(k) or 401(m) for one or more full plan years. (See Example 3.) Appendix A,

section .05(2) also specifies the method for determining missed elective deferrals and the corrective contributions for employees who were improperly excluded from electing and making elective deferrals to a safe harbor §401(k) plan for one or more full plan years. (See Examples 8, 9, and 10.) Appendix A, section .05(3) sets forth the correction method for the exclusion of an eligible employee from electing and making elective deferrals in a plan that (i) is subject to §401(k) and (ii) provides employees with the opportunity to make designated Roth contributions. Appendix A, section .05(4) sets forth the correction method for the situation where an eligible employee was permitted to make an elective deferral, but was not provided with the opportunity to make catch-up contributions under the terms of the plan and §414(v), and correction is being made by making a QNEC on behalf of the excluded employee. (See Example 11.) Appendix A, section .05(5) sets forth the correction method for the failure by a plan to implement an employee's election with respect to elective deferrals (including designated Roth contributions) or after-tax employee contributions. (See Example 12.) In section 2.02(1)(a)(ii) below, the correction methods for (I) the exclusion of an eligible employee from all contributions (including designated Roth contributions) under a§401(k) or (m) plan for a full year, as described in Appendix A, sections .05(2) and .05(3), (II) the exclusion of an eligible employee who was permitted to make elective deferrals, but was not permitted to make catch-up contributions for a full plan year as described in Appendix A, section .05(4), and (III) the exclusion of an eligible employee on account of the failure to implement an employee's election to make elective deferrals or after-tax employee contributions to the plan as described in Appendix A, section .05(5) are expanded to include correction for the exclusion from these contributions (including designated Roth contributions) under a §401(k) or (m) plan for a partial plan year. This correction for a partial year exclusion may be used in conjunction with the correction for a full year exclusion.

(ii) *Expansion of Correction Method to Partial Year Exclusion.* (A) *In General.* The correction method in Appendix A, section .05, is expanded to cover an employee who was improperly excluded from electing and making elective deferrals (including designated Roth contributions) or after-tax employee contributions for a portion of a plan year or from receiving matching contributions (on either elective deferrals or after-tax employee contributions) for a portion of a plan year. In such a case, a permitted correction method for the failure is for the Plan Sponsor to satisfy this section 2.02(1)(a)(ii). The Plan Sponsor makes a QNEC on behalf of the excluded employee. The method and examples described to correct the failure to include otherwise eligible employees do not apply until after correction of other qualification failures. Thus, for example, in the case of a §401(k) plan that does not apply the safe harbor contribution requirements of §401(k)(12) or 401(k)(13) the correction for improperly excluding an employee from making elective deferrals, as described in the narrative and the examples in this section cannot be used until after correction of the ADP test failure. (See Appendix A, section .05(2)(g).)

(B) *Elective Deferral Failures. (1)* The appropriate QNEC for the failure to allow an employee to elect and make elective deferrals (including designated Roth contributions) for a portion of the plan year is equal to the missed deferral opportunity which is an amount equal to 50% of the employee's missed deferral. The employee's missed deferral is determined by multiplying the ADP of the employee's group (either highly or nonhighly compensated), determined prior to correction under this section 2.02(1)(a)(ii), by the employee's plan compensation for the portion of the year during which the employee was improperly excluded. In a safe harbor §401(k) plan, the employee's missed deferral is determined by multiplying 3% (or, if greater, whatever percentage of the participant's compensation which, if contributed as an elective deferral, would have been matched at a rate of 100% or more) by the employee's plan compensation for the portion of the year during which the employee was improperly excluded. The missed deferral for the portion of the plan year during which the employee was improperly excluded from being eligible to make elective deferrals is reduced to the extent that (i) the sum of the missed deferral (as determined in the preceding two sentences of this paragraph) and any elective deferrals actually made by the employee for that year would exceed (ii) the maximum elective deferrals permitted under the plan for the employee for that plan year (including the §402(g) limit). The corrective contribution is adjusted for Earnings. For purposes of correcting other failures under this revenue procedure (including determination of any required matching contribution) after correction has occurred under this section 2.02(1)(a)(ii)(B), the employee is treated as having made pre-tax elective deferrals equal to the employee's missed deferral for the portion of the year during which the employee was improperly excluded. (See Examples 4 and 5.)

(2) The appropriate corrective contribution for the plan's failure to implement an employee's election with respect to elective deferrals is equal to the missed deferral opportunity which is an amount equal to 50% of the employee's missed deferral. Corrective contributions are adjusted for Earnings. The missed deferral is determined by multiplying the employee's deferral percentage by the employee's plan compensation for the portion of the year during which the employee was improperly excluded. If the employee elected a fixed dollar amount that can be attributed to the period of exclusion, then the flat dollar amount for the period of exclusion may be used for this purpose. If the employee elected a fixed dollar amount to be deferred for the entire plan year, then that dollar amount is multiplied by a fraction. The fraction is equal to the number of months, including partial months where applicable, during which the eligible employee was excluded from making elective deferral contributions divided by 12. The missed deferral for the portion of the plan year during which the eligible employee was improperly excluded from making elective deferrals is reduced to the extent that (i) the sum of the missed deferral (as determined in the preceding three sentences) and any elective deferrals actually made by the employee for that year would exceed (ii) the maximum elective deferrals permitted under the plan for the employee for that plan year (including the §402(g) limit). The corrective contribution is adjusted for Earnings. The requirements relating to the passage of the ADP test before this correction method can be used, as described in Appendix A, section .05(5)(d), still apply.

(C) *After-Tax Employee Contribution Failures. (1)* The appropriate corrective contribution for the failure to allow employees to elect and make after-tax employee contributions for a portion of the plan year is equal to the missed after-tax employee contributions opportunity, which is an amount equal to 40% of the employee's missed after-tax employee contributions.

The employee's missed after-tax employee contributions are determined by multiplying the ACP of the employee's group (either highly or nonhighly compensated), determined prior to correction under this section 2.02(1)(a)(ii)(C), by the employee's plan compensation for the portion of the year during which the employee was improperly excluded. If the ACP consists of both matching and after-tax employee contributions, then, for purposes of the preceding sentence, in lieu of basing the missed after-tax employee contributions on the ACP for the employee's group (either highly compensated or nonhighly compensated), the Plan Sponsor is permitted to determine separately the portions of the ACP that are attributable to matching contributions and after-tax employee contributions and base the missed after-tax employee contributions on the portion of the ACP that is attributable to after-tax employee contributions. The missed after-tax employee contribution is reduced to the extent that (i) the sum of that contribution and the actual total after-tax employee contributions made by the employee for the plan year would exceed (ii) the sum of the maximum after-tax employee contributions permitted under the plan for the employee for the plan year. The corrective contribution is adjusted for Earnings. The requirements relating to the passage of the ACP test before this correction method can be used, as described in Appendix A, section .05(2)(g), still apply.

(2) The appropriate corrective contribution for the plan's failure to implement an employee's election with respect to after-tax employee contributions for a portion of the plan year is equal to the missed after-tax employee contributions opportunity, which is an amount equal to 40% of the employee's missed after-tax employee contributions. Corrective contributions are adjusted for Earnings. The missed after-tax employee contribution is determined by multiplying the employee's elected after-tax employee contribution percentage by the employee's plan compensation for the portion of the year during which the employee was improperly excluded. If the employee elected a flat dollar amount that can be attributed to the period of exclusion, then the flat dollar amount for the period of exclusion may be used for this purpose. If the employee elected a flat dollar amount to be contributed for the entire plan year, then that dollar amount is multiplied by a fraction. The fraction is equal to the number of months, including partial months where applicable, during which the eligible employee was excluded from making after-tax employee contributions divided by 12. The missed after-tax employee contribution is reduced to the extent that (i) the sum of that contribution and the actual total after-tax employee contributions made by the employee for the plan year would exceed (ii) the sum of the maximum after-tax employee contributions permitted under the plan for the employee for the plan year. The requirements relating to the passage of the ACP test before this correction method can be used, as described in Appendix A, section .05(5)(d), still apply.

(D) *Matching Contribution Failures. (1)* The appropriate corrective contribution for the failure to make matching contributions for an employee because the employee was precluded from making elective deferrals (including designated Roth contributions) or after-tax employee contributions for a portion of the plan year is equal to the matching contribution that would have been made for the employee if (1) the employee's elective deferrals for that portion of the plan year had equaled the employee's missed deferrals (determined under section 2.02(1)(a)(i)(B)) or (2) the employee's after-tax contribution for that portion of the plan year had equaled the employee's missed after-tax employee contribution (determined under section 2.02(1)(a)(ii) (C)). This matching contribution is reduced to the extent that (i) the sum of this contribution and other matching contributions actually made on behalf of the employee for the plan year would exceed (ii) the maximum matching contribution permitted if the employee had made the maximum matchable contributions permitted under the plan for the plan year. The corrective contribution is adjusted for Earnings. The requirements relating to the passage of the ACP test before this correction method can be used, as described in Appendix A, section .05(2)(g), still apply.

(2) The appropriate corrective contribution for the failure to make matching contributions for an employee because of the failure by the plan to implement an employee's election with respect to elective deferrals (including designated Roth contributions) or, where applicable, after-tax employee contributions for a portion of the plan year is equal to the matching contribution that would have been made for the employee if the employee made the elective deferral as determined under section 2.02(1)(a)(ii)(B)(2), or where applicable, the after-tax employee contribution determined under section 2.02(1)(a)(ii)(C)(2). This matching contribution is reduced to the extent that (i) the sum of this contribution and other matching contributions actually made on behalf of the employee for the plan year would exceed (ii) the maximum matching contribution permitted if the employee had made the maximum matchable contributions permitted under the plan for the plan year. The corrective contribution is adjusted for Earnings. The requirements relating to the passage of the ACP test before this correction method can be used, as described in Appendix A, section .05(5)(d), still apply.

(E) *Use of Prorated Compensation.* For purposes of this paragraph (1)(a)(ii), for administrative convenience, in lieu of using the employee's actual plan compensation for the portion of the year during which the employee was improperly excluded, a pro rata portion of the employee's plan compensation that would have been taken into account for the plan year, if the employee had not been improperly excluded, may be used.

(F) *Special Rule for Brief Exclusion from Elective Deferrals and After-Tax Employee Contributions.* An Plan Sponsor is not required to make a corrective contribution with respect to elective deferrals (including designated Roth contributions) or after-tax employee contributions, as provided in sections 2.02(1)(a)(ii)(B) and (C), but is required to make a corrective contribution with respect to any matching contributions, as provided in section 2.02(1)(a)(ii)(D), for an employee for a plan year if the employee has been provided the opportunity to make elective deferrals or after-tax employee contributions under the plan for a period of at least the last 9 months in that plan year and during that period the employee had the opportunity to make elective deferrals or after-tax employee contributions in an amount not less than the maximum amount that would have been permitted if no failure had occurred. (See Examples 6 and 7.)

(b) *Examples.*

Example 3:

Employer B maintains a §401(k) plan. The plan provides for matching contributions for eligible employees equal to 100% of elective deferrals that do not exceed 3% of an employee's compensation. The plan allows employees to make after-tax employee contributions up to a maximum of the lesser of 2% of compensation or $1,000. The after-tax employee contributions are not matched. The plan provides that employees who complete one year of service are eligible to participate in the plan on the next designated entry date. The entry dates are January 1, and July 1. In 2007, it is discovered that Employee V, an NHCE with compensation of $30,000, was excluded from the plan for the 2006 plan year even though she satisfied the plan's eligibility requirements as of January 1, 2006.

For the 2006 plan year, the relevant employee and contribution information is as follows:

	Compensation	Elective deferral	Match	After-Tax Employee Contribution
Highly Compensated Employees (HCEs):				
R	$200,000	$6,000	$6,000	$0
S	$150,000	$12,000	$4,500	$1,000
Nonhighly Compensated Employees (NHCEs):				
T	$80,000	$12,000	$2,400	$1,000
U	$50,000	$500	$500	$0

HCEs:	NHCEs:
ADP - 5.5%	ADP - 8%
ACP - 3.33%	ACP -2.63%
ACP attributable to matching contributions - 3%	ACP attributable to matching contributions - 2%
ACP attributable to after-tax employee contributions - 0.33%	ACP attributable to after-tax employee contributions - 0.63%

Correction:

Employer B uses the correction method for a full year exclusion, described in Appendix A, section .05(2), to correct the failure to include Employee V in the plan for the full plan year beginning January 1, 2006. Employer B calculates the corrective QNEC to be made on behalf of Employee V as follows:

Elective deferrals: Employee V was eligible to, but was not provided with the opportunity to, elect and make elective deferrals in 2006. Thus, Employer B must make a QNEC to the plan on behalf of Employee V equal to the missed deferral opportunity for Employee V, which is 50% of Employee V's missed deferral. The QNEC is adjusted for Earnings. The missed deferral for Employee V is determined by using the ADP for NHCEs for 2006 and multiplying that percentage by Employee V's compensation for 2006. Accordingly, the missed deferral for Employee V on account of the employee's improper exclusion from the plan is $2,400 (8% x $30,000). The missed deferral opportunity is $1,200 (i.e., 50% x $2,400). Thus, the required corrective contribution for the failure to provide Employee V with the opportunity to make elective deferrals to the plan is $1,200 (plus Earnings). The corrective contribution is made to a pre-tax QNEC account for Employee V (not to a designated Roth contributions account even if the plan offers designated Roth contributions, as provided in section .05(3) of Appendix A).

Matching contributions: Employee V should have been eligible for, but did not receive, an allocation of employer matching contributions because Employee V was not provided the opportunity to make elective deferrals in 2006. Thus, Employer B must make a corrective employer nonelective contribution to the plan on behalf of Employee V that is equal to the matching contribution Employee V would have received had the missed deferral been made. The corrective employer nonelective contribution is adjusted for Earnings. Under the terms of the plan, if Employee V had made an elective deferral of $2,400 or 8% of compensation ($30,000), the employee would have been entitled to a matching contribution equal to 100% of the first 3% of Employee V's compensation ($30,000) or $900. Accordingly, the contribution required to replace the missed employer matching contribution is $900 (plus Earnings).

After-tax employee contributions: Employee V was eligible to, but was not provided with the opportunity to, elect and make after-tax employee contributions in 2006. Employer B must make a QNEC to the plan equal to the missed opportunity for making after-tax employee contributions for Employee V, which is 40% of Employee V's missed after-tax employee contribution. The QNEC is adjusted for Earnings. The missed after-tax employee contribution for Employee V is estimated by using the ACP for NHCEs (to the extent that the ACP is attributable to after-tax employee contributions) for 2006 and multiplying that percentage by Employee V's compensation for 2006. Accordingly, the missed after-tax employee contribution for Employee V, on account of the employee's improper exclusion from the plan is $189 (0.63% x $30,000). The missed opportunity to make after-tax employee contributions to the plan is $76 (40% x $189). Thus, the required corrective contribution for the failure to provide Employee V with the opportunity to make the $189 after-tax employee contribution to the plan is $76 (plus Earnings).

The total required corrective contribution, before adjustments for Earnings, on behalf of Employee V is $2,176 ($1,200 for the missed deferral opportunity plus $900 for the missed matching contribution plus $76 for the missed opportunity to make after-tax employee contributions). The required corrective contribution is further adjusted for Earnings. The corrective contribution for the missed deferral opportunity ($1,200), the missed opportunity for after-tax employee contributions ($76), and related Earnings must be made in the form of a QNEC.

Example 4:

Employer C maintains a §401(k) plan. The plan provides for matching contributions for each payroll period that are equal to 100% of an employee's elective deferrals that do not exceed 2% of the eligible employee's plan compensation during the payroll period. The plan provides for after-tax employee contributions. The after-tax employee contribution cannot exceed $1,000 for the plan year. The plan provides that employees who complete one year of service are eligible to participate in the plan on the next January 1 or July 1 entry date. Employee X, a nonhighly compensated employee, who met the eligibility requirements and should have entered the plan on January 1, 2006, was not offered the opportunity to elect to have elective contributions made on his behalf to the plan. In August of 2006, the error was discovered and Employer C offered Employee X the opportunity to make elective deferrals and after-tax employee contributions as of September 1, 2006. Employee X made elective deferrals equal to 4% of the employee's plan compensation for each payroll period from September 1, 2006 through December 31, 2006 (resulting in elective deferrals of $400). Employee X's plan compensation for 2006 was $36,000 ($26,000 for the first eight months and $10,000 for the last four months). Employer C made matching contributions equal to $200 on behalf of Employee X, which is 2% of Employee X's plan compensation for each payroll period from September 1, 2006 through December 31, 2006 ($10,000). After being allowed to participate in the plan, Employee X made $250 of after-tax employee contributions for the 2006 plan year. The ADP for nonhighly compensated employees for 2006 was 3% and the ACP for nonhighly compensated employees for 2006 was 2.3%. The ACP attributable to matching contributions for nonhighly compensated employees for 2006 was 1.8%. The ACP attributable to employee contributions for nonhighly compensated employees for 2006 was 0.5%.

Correction:

In accordance with section 2.02(1)(a)(ii), Employer C uses the correction method described in Appendix A, section .05, to correct for the failure to provide Employee X the opportunity to elect and make elective deferrals and after-tax employee contributions, and, as a result, the failure of Employee X to receive matching contributions for a portion of the plan year (January 1, 2006 through August 31, 2006). Thus, Employer C makes a corrective contribution on behalf of Employee X that satisfies the requirements of section 2.02(1)(a)(ii). Employer C elects to utilize the provisions of section 2.02(1)(a)(ii)(E) to determine Employee X's compensation for the portion of the year in which Employee X was not provided the opportunity to make elective deferrals and after-tax employee contributions. Thus, for administrative convenience, in lieu of using actual plan compensation of $26,000 for the period Employee X was excluded, Employee X's annual plan compensation is prorated for the 8-month period that the employee was excluded from participating in the plan. The corrective contribution is determined as follows:

(1) *Corrective contribution for missed deferral*: Employee X was eligible to, but was not provided with the opportunity to, elect and make elective deferrals from January 1 through August 31 of 2006. Employer C must make a QNEC to the plan on behalf of Employee X equal to Employee X's missed deferral opportunity for that period, which is 50% of Employee X's missed deferral. The corrective contribution is adjusted for Earnings. Employee X's missed deferral is determined by multiplying the 3% ADP for nonhighly compensated employees by $24,000 (8/12ths of the employee's 2006 compensation of $36,000). Accordingly, the missed deferral is $720. The missed deferral is not reduced because when this amount is added to the amount already deferred, no plan limit (including §402(g)) was exceeded. Accordingly, the required QNEC is $360 (i.e. 50% multiplied by the missed deferral amount of $720). The required QNEC is adjusted for Earnings.

(2) *Corrective contribution for missed matching contribution*: Under the terms of the plan, if Employee X had made an elective deferral of $720 or 3% of compensation for the period of exclusion ($24,000), the employee would have been entitled to a matching contribution equal to 2% of $24,000 or $480. The missed matching contribution is not reduced because no plan limit is exceeded when this amount is added to the matching contribution already contributed for the 2006 plan year. Accordingly, the required corrective employer contribution is $480. The required corrective employer contribution is adjusted for Earnings.

(3) *Corrective contribution for missed after-tax employee contribution*: Employee X was eligible to, but was not provided with the opportunity to elect and make after-tax employee contributions from January 1 through August 31 of 2006. Employer C must make a QNEC to the plan on behalf of Employee X equal to the missed opportunity to make after-tax employee contributions. The missed opportunity to make after-tax employee contributions is equal to 40% of Employee X's missed after-tax employee contributions. The QNEC is adjusted for Earnings. The missed after-tax employee contribution amount is equal to the 0.5% ACP attributable to employee contributions for nonhighly compensated employees multiplied by $24,000 (8/12ths of the employee's 2006 plan compensation of $36,000). Accordingly, the missed after-tax employee contribution amount is $120. The missed after-tax employee contribution is not reduced because the sum of $120 and the previously made after-tax employee contribution of $250 is less than the overall plan limit of $1,000. Therefore, the required QNEC is $48 (i.e., 40% multiplied by the missed after-tax employee contribution of $120). The QNEC is adjusted for Earnings.

The total required corrective contribution, before adjustments for Earnings, on behalf of Employee X is $888 ($360 for the missed deferral opportunity plus $480 for the missed matching contribution plus $48 for the missed opportunity to make after-tax employee contributions). The corrective contribution for the missed deferral opportunity ($360), the missed opportunity for after-tax employee contributions ($48), and related Earnings must be made in the form of a QNEC.

Example 5:

The facts (including the ADP and ACP results) are the same as in Example 4, except that it is now determined that Employee X, after being included in the plan in 2006, made after-tax employee contributions of $950.

Correction:

The correction is the same as in Example 4, except that the QNEC required to replace the missed after-tax employee contribution is re-calculated to take into account applicable plan limits in accordance with the provisions of section 2.02(1)(a)(ii)(C). The QNEC is determined as follows:

The missed after-tax employee contribution amount is equal to the 0.5% ACP attributable to after-tax employee contributions for nonhighly compensated employees multiplied by $24,000 (8/12ths of the employee's 2006 plan compensation of $36,000). The missed after-tax employee contribution amount, based on this calculation, is $120. However, the sum of this amount ($120) and the previously made after-tax employee contribution ($950) is $1,070. Because the plan limit for after-tax employee contributions is $1,000, the missed after-tax employee contribution needs to be reduced by $70, to ensure that the total after-tax employee contributions comply with the plan limit. Accordingly, the missed after-tax employee contribution is $50 ($120 minus $70) and the required QNEC is $20 (i.e. 40% multiplied by the missed after-tax employee contribution of $50). The QNEC is adjusted for Earnings.

Example 6:

Employer D sponsors a §401(k) plan. The plan has a one year of service eligibility requirement and provides for January 1 and July 1 entry dates. Employee Y, who should have been provided the opportunity to elect and make elective deferrals for the plan year beginning on January 1, 2006, was not provided the opportunity to elect and make elective deferrals until July 1, 2006. Employee Y made $5,000 in elective deferrals to the plan in 2006. Employee Y was a highly compensated employee with compensation for 2006 of $200,000. Employee Y's compensation from January 1 through June 30, 2006 was $130,000. The ADP for highly compensated employees for 2006 was 10%. The ADP for nonhighly compensated employees for 2006 was 8%. The §402(g) limit for deferrals made in 2006 was $15,000.

Correction:

QNEC for missed deferral: Employee Y's missed deferral is equal to the 10% ADP for highly compensated employees multiplied by $130,000 (compensation earned for the portion of the year in which Employee Y was erroneously excluded, i.e., January 1, 2006 through June 30, 2006). The missed deferral amount, based on this calculation is $13,000. However, the sum of this amount ($13,000) and the previously made elective contribution ($5,000) is $18,000. The

2006 §402(g)limit for elective deferrals is $15,000. In accordance with the provisions of section 2.02(1)(a)(ii)(B), the missed deferral needs to be reduced by $3,000 to ensure that the total elective contribution complies with the applicable §402(g) limit. Accordingly, the missed deferral is $10,000 ($13,000 minus $3,000) and the required QNEC is $5,000 (i.e., 50% multiplied by the missed deferral of $10,000). The QNEC is adjusted for Earnings.

Example 7:

Employer E maintains a §401(k) plan. The plan provides for matching contributions for each payroll period that are equal to 100% of an employee's elective deferrals that do not exceed 2% of the eligible employee's plan compensation during the payroll period. The plan also provides that the annual limit on matching contributions is $750. The plan provides for after-tax employee contributions. The after-tax employee contribution cannot exceed $1,000 during a plan year. The plan provides that employees who complete one year of service are eligible to participate in the plan on the next January 1 or July 1 entry date. Employee Z, a nonhighly compensated employee who met the eligibility requirements and should have entered the plan on January 1, 2006, was not offered the opportunity to elect to have elective contributions made on his behalf to the plan. In March of 2006, the error was discovered and Employer E offered the employee an election opportunity as of April 1, 2006. Employee Z had the opportunity to make the maximum elective deferrals and/or after-tax employee contributions that could have been made under the terms of the plan for the entire 2006 plan year. The employee made elective deferrals equal to 3% of the employee's plan compensation for each payroll period from April 1, 2006 through December 31, 2006 (resulting in elective deferrals of $960). The employee's plan compensation for 2006 was $40,000 ($8,000 for the first three months and $32,000 for the last nine months). Employer E made matching contributions equal to $640 for the excluded employee, which is 2% of the employee's plan compensation for each payroll period from April 1, 2006 through December 31, 2006 ($32,000). After being allowed to participate in the plan, the employee made $500 in after-tax employee contributions. The ADP for nonhighly compensated employees for 2006 was 3% and the ACP for nonhighly compensated employees for 2006 was 2.3%. The portion of the ACP attributable to matching contributions for nonhighly compensated employees for 2006 was 1.8%. The portion of the ACP attributable to after-tax employee contributions for nonhighly compensated employees for 2006 was 0.5%.

Correction:

Employer E uses the correction method for partial year exclusions, pursuant to section 2.02(1)(a)(ii), to correct the failure to include an eligible employee in the plan. Because Employee Z was given an opportunity to make elective deferrals and after-tax employee contributions to the plan for at least the last 9 months of the plan year (and the amount of the elective deferrals or after-tax employee contributions that the employee had the opportunity to make was not less than the maximum elective deferrals or after-tax employee contributions that the employee could have made if the employee had been given the opportunity to make elective deferrals and after-tax employee contributions on January 1, 2006), under the special rule set forth in section 2.02(1)(a)(ii)(F), Employer E is not required to make a QNEC for the failure to provide the employee with the opportunity to make either elective deferrals or after-tax employee contributions. The employer only needs to make a corrective employer nonelective contribution for the failure to provide the employee with the opportunity to receive matching contributions on deferrals that could have been made during the first 3 months of the plan year. The calculation of the corrective employer contribution required to correct this failure is shown as follows:

The missed matching contribution is determined by calculating the matching contribution that the employee would have received had the employee been provided the opportunity to make elective deferrals during the period of exclusion, i.e., January 1, 2006 through March 31, 2006. Assuming that the employee elected to defer an amount equal to 3% of compensation (which is the ADP for the nonhighly compensated employees for the plan year), then, under the terms of the plan, the employee would have been entitled to a matching contribution of 2% of compensation. Pursuant to the provisions of section 2.02(1)(a)(ii)(E), Employer E determines compensation by prorating Employee Z's annual compensation for the portion of the year that Employee Z was not given the opportunity to make elective deferrals or after-tax employee contributions. Accordingly, the missed matching contribution for the period of exclusion is obtained by multiplying 2% by Employee Z's compensation of $10,000 (3/12ths of the employee's 2006 plan compensation of $40,000). Based on this calculation, the missed matching contribution is $200. However, when this amount is added to the matching contribution already received ($640), the total ($840) exceeds the $750 plan limit on matching contributions by $90. Accordingly, pursuant to section 2.02(1)(a)(ii)(D), the missed matching contribution figure is reduced to $110 ($200 minus $90). The required corrective employer contribution is $110. The corrective contribution is adjusted for Earnings.

Example 8:

Employer G maintains a safe harbor §401(k) plan that requires matching contributions that satisfy the requirements of §401(k)(12), which are equal to: 100% of elective deferrals that do not exceed 3% of an employee's compensation and 50% of elective deferrals that exceed 3% but do not exceed 5% of an employee's compensation. Employee M, a nonhighly compensated employee who met the eligibility requirements and should have entered the plan on January 1, 2006, was not offered the opportunity to defer under the plan and was erroneously excluded for all of 2006. Employee M's compensation for 2006 was $20,000.

Correction:

In accordance with the provisions of section 2.02(1)(a)(ii)(B), Employee M's missed deferral on account of exclusion from the safe harbor §401(k) plan is 3% of compensation. Thus, the missed deferral is equal to 3% multiplied by $20,000, or $600. Accordingly, the required QNEC for Employee M's missed deferral opportunity in 2006 is $300, i.e., 50% of $600. The missed matching contribution, based on the missed deferral of $600, is $600. The required corrective contribution for Employee M's missed matching contribution is $600. Since the matching contribution is required to satisfy the requirements of §401(k)(12), the corrective contribution must be made in the form of a QNEC. The total QNEC, before adjustments for Earnings, on behalf of Employee M is $900 (i.e., $300 for the missed deferral opportunity, plus $600 for the missed matching contribution). The QNEC is adjusted for Earnings.

Example 9:

Same facts as Example 8, except that the plan provides for matching contributions equal to 100% of elective deferrals that do not exceed 4% of an employee's compensation.

Correction:

In accordance with the provisions of section 2.02(1)(a)(ii)(B), Employee M's missed deferral on account of exclusion from the safe harbor §401(k) plan is 4% of compensation. The missed deferral is 4% of compensation because the plan provides for a 100% match for deferrals up to that level of compensation. (See Appendix A, section .05(2)(d).) Therefore, in this case, Employee M's missed deferral is equal to 4% multiplied by $20,000, or $800. The QNEC for Employee M's missed deferral opportunity in 2006 is $400, i.e., 50% multiplied by $800. The missed matching contribution, based on the missed deferral of $800, is $800. Thus, the required corrective contribution for Employee M's missed matching contribution is $800. Since the matching contribution is required to satisfy the requirements of §401(k)(12), the corrective contribution must be made in the form of a QNEC. The total QNEC, before adjustments for Earnings, on behalf of Employee M is $1,200 (i.e., $400 for the missed deferral opportunity plus $800 for the missed matching contribution). The QNEC is adjusted for Earnings.

Example 10:

Same facts as Example 8, except that the plan uses a rate of nonelective contributions to satisfy the requirements of §401(k)(12) and provides for a nonelective contribution equal to 3% of compensation.

Correction:

In accordance with the provisions of section 2.02(1)(a)(ii)(B), Employee M's missed deferral on account of exclusion from the safe harbor §401(k) plan is 3% of compensation. Thus, the missed deferral is equal to 3% multiplied by $20,000, or $600. Thus, the QNEC for Employee M's missed deferral opportunity in 2006 is $300 (50% of $600). The required nonelective contribution, based on the plan's formula of 3% of compensation for nonelective contributions, is $600. Since the nonelective contribution is required to satisfy the requirements of §401(k)(12), the corrective contribution is made in the form of a QNEC. The total required QNEC, before adjustments for Earnings, on behalf of Employee M is $900 (i.e., $300 for the missed deferral opportunity, plus $600 for the missed nonelective contribution). The QNEC is adjusted for Earnings.

Example 11:

Employer H maintains a §401(k) plan. The plan limit on deferrals is the lesser of the deferral limit under §401(a)(30) or the limitation under §415. The plan also provides that eligible participants (as defined in §414(v)(5)) may make contributions in excess of the plan's deferral limits, up to the limitations on catch-up contributions for the year. The plan also provides for a 60% matching contribution on elective deferrals. The deferral limit under §401(a)(30) for 2006 is $15,000. The limitation on catch-up contributions under the terms of the plan and §414(v)(2)(B)(i) is $5,000. Employee R, age 55, was provided with the opportunity to make elective deferrals up to the plan limit, but was not provided the option to make catch-up contributions. Employee R is a nonhighly compensated employee who earned $60,000 in compensation and made elective deferrals totaling $15,000 in 2006.

Correction:

In accordance with the provisions of Appendix A, section .05(4), Employee R's missed deferral on account of the plan's failure to offer the opportunity to make catch-up contributions is $2,500 (or one half of the limitation on catch-up contributions for 2006). The missed deferral opportunity is $1,250 (or 50% of $2,500). Thus, the required QNEC for Employee R's missed deferral opportunity relating to catch-up contributions in 2006 is $1,250 adjusted for Earnings. In addition, Employee R was entitled to an additional matching contribution, under the terms of the plan, equal to 60% of the missed deferral that is attributable to the catch-up contribution that the employee would have made had the failure not occurred. In this case, the missed deferral is $2,500 and the corresponding matching contribution is $1,500 (i.e., 60% of $2,500). Thus, the required corrective contribution for the additional matching contribution that should have been made on behalf of Employee R is $1,500 adjusted for Earnings.

Example 12:

Employer K maintains a §401(k) plan. The plan provides for matching contributions for eligible employees equal to 100% of elective deferrals that do not exceed 3% of an employee's compensation. On January 1, 2006, Employee T made an election to contribute 10% of compensation for the 2006 plan year. However, Employee T's election was not processed, and the required amounts were not withheld from Employee T's salary in 2006. Employee T's salary was $30,000 in 2006.

Correction:

Employer K uses the correction method described in Appendix A, section .05(5), to correct the failure to implement Employee T's election to make elective deferrals under the plan for the full plan year beginning January 1, 2006. Employer K calculates the corrective QNEC to be made on behalf of Employee T as follows:

(1) *Elective deferrals*: Employee T's election to make elective deferrals, pursuant to an election, in 2006 was not implemented. Thus, pursuant to section .05(5)(a) of Appendix A, Employer K must make a QNEC to the plan on behalf of Employee T equal to the missed deferral opportunity for Employee T, which is 50% of Employee T's missed deferral. The QNEC is adjusted for Earnings. The missed deferral for Employee T is determined by using T's elected deferral percentage (10%) for 2006 and multiplying that percentage by Employee T's compensation for 2006 ($30,000). Accordingly, the missed deferral for Employee V, on account of the employee's improper exclusion from the plan is $3,000 (10% x $30,000). The missed deferral opportunity is $1,500 (i.e., 50% x $3,000). Thus, the required QNEC for the failure to provide Employee V with the opportunity to make elective deferrals to the plan is $1,500 (adjusted for Earnings).

(2) *Matching contributions*: Employee T should have been eligible for but did not receive an allocation of employer matching contributions because no elective deferrals were made on behalf of Employee T in 2006. Thus, pursuant to section .05(5)(c) of Appendix A, Employer K must make a corrective employer nonelective contribution to the plan on behalf of Employee T that is equal to the matching contribution Employee T would have received had the missed deferral been made. The corrective employer nonelective contribution is adjusted for Earnings. Under the terms of the plan, if Employee T had made an elective deferral of $3,000 or 10% of compensation ($30,000), the employee would have been entitled to a matching contribution equal to 100% of the first 3% of Employee T's compensation ($30,000) or $900. Accordingly, the contribution required to replace the missed employer matching contribution is $900 (adjusted for Earnings).

The total required corrective contribution, before adjustments for Earnings, on behalf of Employee T is $2,400 ($1,500 for the missed deferral opportunity plus $900 for the missed matching contribution). The corrective contribution for the missed deferral opportunity ($1,500) and related Earnings must be made in the form of a QNEC.

(2) *Exclusion of Eligible Employees In a Profit-Sharing Plan*. (a) *Correction Methods*. (i) *Appendix A Correction Method*. Appendix A, section .05, sets forth the correction method for correcting the failure to make a contribution on behalf of the employees improperly excluded from a defined contribution plan or to provide benefit accruals for the employees improperly excluded from a defined benefit plan. In the case of a defined contribution plan, the correction method is to make a contribution on behalf of the excluded employee. Section 2.02(2)(a)(ii) of this Appendix B clarifies the correction method in the case of a profit-sharing or stock bonus plan that provides for nonelective contributions (within the meaning of §1.401(k)-6).

(ii) *Additional Requirements for Appendix A Correction Method as applied to Profit-Sharing Plans*. To correct for the exclusion of an eligible employee from nonelective contributions in a profit-sharing or stock bonus plan under the Appendix A correction method, an allocation amount is determined for each excluded employee on the same basis as the allocation amounts were determined for the other employees under the plan's allocation formula (e.g., the same ratio of allocation to compensation), taking into account all of the employee's relevant factors (e.g., compensation) under that formula for that year. The Plan Sponsor makes a corrective contribution on behalf of the excluded employee that is equal to the allocation amount for the excluded employee. The corrective contribution is adjusted for Earnings. If, as a result of excluding an employee, an amount was improperly allocated to the account balance of an eligible employee who shared in the original allocation of the nonelective contribution, no reduction is made to the account balance of the employee who shared in the original allocation on account of the improper allocation. (See Example 15.)

(iii) *Reallocation Correction Method.* (A) *In General.* Subject to the limitations set forth in section 2.02(2)(a)(iii)(F) below, in addition to the Appendix A correction method, the exclusion of an eligible employee for a plan year from a profit-sharing or stock bonus plan that provides for nonelective contributions may be corrected using the reallocation correction method set forth in this section 2.02(2)(a)(iii). Under the reallocation correction method, the account balance of the excluded employee is increased as provided in paragraph (2)(a)(iii)(B) below, the account balances of other employees are reduced as provided in paragraph (2)(a)(iii)(C) below, and the increases and reductions are reconciled, as necessary, as provided in paragraph (2)(a)(iii)(D) below. (See Examples 16 and 17.)

(B) *Increase in Account Balance of Excluded Employee.* The account balance of the excluded employee is increased by an amount that is equal to the allocation the employee would have received had the employee shared in the allocation of the nonelective contribution. The amount is adjusted for Earnings.

(C) *Reduction in Account Balances of Other Employees.* (1) The account balance of each employee who was an eligible employee who shared in the original allocation of the nonelective contribution is reduced by the excess, if any, of (I) the employee's allocation of that contribution over (II) the amount that would have been allocated to that employee's account had the failure not occurred. This amount is adjusted for Earnings taking into account the rules set forth in section 2.02(2)(a)(iii)(C)(2) and (3) below. The amount after adjustment for Earnings is limited in accordance with section 2.02(2)(a)(iii)(C)(4) below.

(2) This paragraph (2)(a)(iii)(C)(2) applies if most of the employees with account balances that are being reduced are nonhighly compensated employees. If there has been an overall gain for the period from the date of the original allocation of the contribution through the date of correction, no adjustment for Earnings is required to the amount determined under section 2.02(2)(a)(iii)(C)(1) for the employee. If the amount for the employee is being adjusted for Earnings and the plan permits investment of account balances in more than one investment fund, for administrative convenience, the reduction to the employee's account balance may be adjusted

by the lowest rate of return of any fund for the period from the date of the original allocation of the contribution through the date of correction.

(3) If an employee's account balance is reduced and the original allocation was made to more than one investment fund or there was a subsequent distribution or transfer from the fund receiving the original allocation, then reasonable, consistent assumptions are used to determine the Earnings adjustment.

(4) The amount determined in section 2.02(2)(a)(iii)(C)(*1*) for an employee after the application of section 2.02(2)(a)(iii)(C)(*2*) and (*3*) may not exceed the account balance of the employee on the date of correction, and the employee is permitted to retain any distribution made prior to the date of correction.

(D) *Reconciliation of Increases and Reductions.* If the aggregate amount of the increases under section 2.02(2)(a)(iii)(B) exceeds the aggregate amount of the reductions under section 2.02(2)(a)(iii)(C), the Plan Sponsor makes a corrective contribution to the plan for the amount of the excess. If the aggregate amount of the reductions under section 2.02(2)(a)(iii)(C) exceeds the aggregate amount of the increases under section 2.02(2)(a)(iii)(B), then the amount by which each employee's account balance is reduced under section 2.02(2)(a)(iii)(C) is decreased on a pro rata basis.

(E) *Reductions Among Multiple Investment Funds.* If an employee's account balance is reduced and the employee's account balance is invested in more than one investment fund, then the reduction may be made from the investment funds selected in any reasonable manner.

(F) *Limitations on Use of Reallocation Correction Method.* If any employee would be permitted to retain any distribution pursuant to section 2.02(2)(a)(iii)(C)(*4*), then the reallocation correction method may not be used unless most of the employees who would be permitted to retain a distribution are nonhighly compensated employees.

(b) *Examples.*

Example 13:

Employer D maintains a profit-sharing plan that provides for discretionary nonelective employer contributions. The plan provides that the employer's contributions are allocated to account balances in the ratio that each eligible employee's compensation for the plan year bears to the compensation of all eligible employees for the plan year and, therefore, the only relevant factor for determining an allocation is the employee's compensation. The plan provides for self-directed investments among four investment funds and daily valuations of account balances. For the 2006 plan year, Employer D made a contribution to the plan of a fixed dollar amount. However, five employees who met the eligibility requirements were inadvertently excluded from participating in the plan. The contribution resulted in an allocation on behalf of each of the eligible employees, other than the excluded employees, equal to 10% of compensation. Most of the employees who received allocations under the plan for the year of the failure were nonhighly compensated employees. No distributions have been made from the plan since 2006. If the five excluded employees had shared in the original allocation, the allocation made on behalf of each employee would have equaled 9% of compensation. The excluded employees began participating in the plan in the 2007 plan year.

Correction:

Employer D uses the Appendix A correction method to correct the failure to include the five eligible employees. Thus, Employer D makes a corrective contribution to the plan. The amount of the corrective contribution on behalf of the five excluded employees for the 2006 plan year is equal to 10% of compensation of each excluded employee, the same allocation that was made for other eligible employees, adjusted for Earnings. The excluded employees receive an allocation equal to 10% of compensation (adjusted for Earnings) even though, had the excluded employees originally shared in the allocation for the 2006 contribution, their account balances, as well as those of the other eligible employees, would have received an allocation equal to only 9% of compensation.

Example 14:

The facts are the same as in Example 13.

Correction:

Employer D uses the reallocation correction method to correct the failure to include the five eligible employees. Thus, the account balances are adjusted to reflect what would have resulted from the correct allocation of the employer contribution for the 2006 plan year among all eligible employees, including the five excluded employees. The inclusion of the excluded employees in the allocation of that contribution would have resulted in each eligible employee, including each excluded employee, receiving an allocation equal to 9% of compensation. Accordingly, the account balance of each excluded employee is increased by 9% of the employee's 2006 compensation, adjusted for Earnings. The account balance of each of the eligible employees other than the excluded employees is reduced by 1% of the employee's 2006 compensation, adjusted for Earnings. Employer D determines the adjustment for Earnings using the rate of return of each eligible employee's excess allocation (using reasonable, consistent assumptions). Accordingly, for an employee who shared in the original allocation and directed the investment of the allocation into more than one investment fund or who subsequently transferred a portion of a fund that had been credited with a portion of the 2006 allocation to another fund, reasonable, consistent assumptions are followed to determine the adjustment for Earnings. It is determined that the total of the initially determined reductions in account balances exceeds the total of the required increases in account balances. Accordingly, these initially determined reductions are decreased pro rata so that the total of the actual reductions in account balances equals the total of the increases in the account balances, and Employer D does not make any corrective contribution. The reductions from the account balances are made on a pro rata basis among all of the funds in which each employee's account balance is invested.

Example 15:

The facts are the same as in Example 13.

Correction:

The correction is the same as in Example 14, except that, because most of the employees whose account balances are being reduced are nonhighly compensated employees, for administrative convenience, Employer D uses the rate of return of the fund with the lowest rate of return for the period of the failure to adjust the reduction to each account balance. It is determined that the aggregate amount (adjusted for Earnings) by which the account balances of the excluded employees is increased exceeds the aggregate amount (adjusted for Earnings) by which the other employees' account balances are reduced. Accordingly, Employer D makes a contribution to the plan in an amount equal to the excess. The reduction from account balances is made on a pro rata basis among all of the funds in which each employee's account balance is invested.

.03 *Vesting Failures.* (1) *Correction Methods.* (a) *Contribution Correction Method.* A failure in a defined contribution plan to apply the proper vesting percentage to an employee's account balance that results in forfeiture of too large a portion of the employee's account balance may be corrected using the contribution correction method set forth in this paragraph. The Plan Sponsor makes a corrective contribution on behalf of the employee whose account balance was improperly forfeited in an amount equal to the improper forfeiture. The corrective contribution is adjusted for Earnings. If, as a result of the improper forfeiture, an amount was improperly allocated to the account balance of another employee, no reduction is made to the account balance of that employee. (See Example 16.)

(b) *Reallocation Correction Method.* In lieu of the contribution correction method, in a defined contribution plan under which forfeitures of account balances are reallocated among the account balances of the other eligible employees in the plan, a failure to apply the proper vesting percentage to an employee's account balance which results in forfeiture of too large a portion of the employee's account balance may be corrected under the reallocation correction method set forth in this paragraph. A corrective reallocation is made in accordance with the reallocation correction method set forth in section 2.02(2)(a)(iii), subject to the limitations set forth in section 2.02(2)(a)(iii)(F). In applying section 2.02(2)(a)(iii)(B), the account balance of the employee who incurred the improper forfeiture is increased by an amount equal to the amount of the improper forfeiture and the amount is adjusted for Earnings. In applying section 2.02(2)(a)(iii)(C)(*1*), the account balance of each employee who shared in the allocation of the improper forfeiture is reduced by the amount of the improper forfeiture that was allocated to that employee's account. The Earnings adjustments for the account balances that are being reduced are determined in accordance with sections 2.02(2)(a)(iii)(C)(*2*) and (*3*) and the reductions after adjustments for Earnings are limited in accordance with section 2.02(2)(a)(iii)(C)(*4*). In accordance with section 2.02(2)(a)(iii)(D), if the aggregate amount of the increases exceeds the aggregate amount of the reductions, the Plan Sponsor makes a corrective contribution to the plan for the amount of the excess. In accordance with section 2.02(2)(a)(iii)(D), if the aggregate amount of the reductions exceeds the aggregate amount of the increases, then the amount by which each employee's account balance is reduced is decreased on a pro rata basis. (See Example 17.)

(2) *Examples.*

Example 16:

Employer E maintains a profit-sharing plan that provides for nonelective contributions. The plan provides for self-directed investments among four investment funds and daily valuation of account balances. The plan provides that forfeitures of account balances are reallocated among the account balances of other eligible employees on the basis of compensation. During the 2006 plan year, Employee R terminated employment with Employer E and elected and received a single-sum distribution of the vested portion of his account balance. No other distributions have been made since 2006. However, an incorrect determination of Employee R's vested percentage was made resulting in Employee R receiving a distribution of less than the amount to which he was entitled under the plan. The remaining portion of Employee R's account balance was forfeited and reallocated (and these reallocations were not affected by the limitations of §415). Most of the employees who received allocations of the improper forfeiture were nonhighly compensated employees.

Correction:

Employer E uses the contribution correction method to correct the improper forfeiture. Thus, Employer E makes a contribution on behalf of Employee R equal to the incorrectly forfeited amount (adjusted for Earnings) and Employee R's account balance is increased accordingly and subsequently distributed to Employee R. No reduction is made from the account balances of the employees who received an allocation of the improper forfeiture.

Example 17:

The facts are the same as in Example 16.

Correction:

Employer E uses the reallocation correction method to correct the improper forfeiture. Thus, Employee R's account balance is increased by the amount that was improperly forfeited (adjusted for Earnings) and such increase will be distributed to Employee R. The account of each employee who shared in the allocation of the improper forfeiture is reduced by the amount of the improper forfeiture that was allocated to that employee's account (adjusted for Earnings). Because most of the employees whose account balances are being reduced are nonhighly compensated employees, for administrative convenience, Employer E uses the rate of return of the fund with the lowest rate of return for the period of the failure to adjust the reduction to each account balance. It is determined that the amount (adjusted for Earnings) by which the account balance of Employee R is increased exceeds the aggregate amount (adjusted for Earnings) by which the other employees' account balances are reduced. Accordingly, Employer E makes a contribution to the plan in an amount equal to the excess. The reduction from the account balances is made on a pro rata basis among all of the funds in which each employee's account balance is invested.

.04 *§415 Failures.* (1) *Failures Relating to a §415(b) Excess.* (a) *Correction Methods.* (i) *Return of Overpayment Correction Method.* Overpayments as a result of amounts being paid in excess of the limits of §415(b) may be corrected using the return of Overpayment correction method set forth in this paragraph (1)(a)(i). The Plan Sponsor takes reasonable steps to have the Overpayment (with appropriate interest) returned by the recipient to the plan and reduces future benefit payments (if any) due to the employee to reflect §415(b). To the extent the amount returned by the recipient is less than the Overpayment, adjusted for Earnings at the plan's earnings rate, then the Plan Sponsor or another person contributes the difference to the plan. In addition, in accordance with section 6.06 of this revenue procedure, the Plan Sponsor must notify the recipient that the Overpayment was not eligible for favorable tax treatment accorded to distributions from qualified plans (and, specifically, was not eligible for tax-free rollover). (See Examples 20 and 21.)

(ii) *Adjustment of Future Payments Correction Method.* (A) *In General.* In addition to the return of overpayment correction method, in the case of plan benefits that are being distributed in the form of periodic payments, Overpayments as a result of amounts being paid in excess of the limits in §415(b) may be corrected by using the adjustment of future payments correction method set forth in this paragraph (1)(a)(ii). Future payments to the recipient are reduced so that they do not exceed the §415(b) maximum limit and an additional reduction is made to recoup the Overpayment (over a period not longer than the remaining payment period) so that the actuarial present value of the additional reduction is equal to the Overpayment plus interest at the interest rate used by the plan to determine actuarial equivalence. (See Examples 18 and 19.)

(B) *Joint and Survivor Annuity Payments.* If the employee is receiving payments in the form of a joint and survivor annuity, with the employee's spouse to receive a life annuity upon the employee's death equal to a percentage (e.g., 75%) of the amount being paid to the employee, the reduction of future annuity payments to reflect §415(b) reduces the amount of benefits payable during the lives of both the employee and spouse, but any reduction to recoup Overpayments made to the employee does not reduce the amount of the spouse's survivor benefit. Thus, the spouse's benefit will be based on the previous specified percentage (e.g., 75%) of the maximum permitted under §415(b), instead of the reduced annual periodic amount payable to the employee.

(C) *Overpayment Not Treated as an Excess Amount.* An Overpayment corrected under this adjustment of future payment correction method is not treated as an Excess Amount as defined in section 5.01(3) of this revenue procedure.

(b) *Examples.*

Example 18:

Employer F maintains a defined benefit plan funded solely through employer contributions. The plan provides that the benefits of employees are limited to the maximum amount permitted under §415(b), disregarding cost-of-living adjustments under §415(d) after benefit payments have commenced. At the beginning of the 2006 plan year, Employee S retired and started receiving an annual straight life annuity of $185,000 from the plan. Due to an administrative error, the annual amount received by Employee S for 2006 included an Overpayment of $10,000 (because the §415(b)(1)(A) limit for 2006 was $175,000). This error was discovered at the beginning of 2007.

Correction:

Employer F uses the adjustment of future payments correction method to correct the failure to satisfy the limit in §415(b). Future annuity benefit payments to Employee S are reduced so that they do not exceed the §415(b) maximum limit, and, in addition, Employee S's future benefit payments from the plan are actuarially reduced to recoup the Overpayment. Accordingly, Employee S's future benefit payments from the plan are reduced to $175,000 and further reduced by $1,000 annually for life, beginning in 2007. The annual benefit amount is reduced by $1,000 annually for life because, for Employee S, the actuarial present value of a benefit of $1,000 annually for life commencing in 2007 is equal to the sum of $10,000 and interest at the rate used by the plan to determine actuarial equivalence beginning with the date of the first Overpayment and ending with the date the reduced annuity payment begins. Thus, Employee S's remaining benefit payments are reduced so that Employee S receives $174,000 for 2007, and for each year thereafter.

Example 19:

The facts are the same as in Example 18.

Correction:

Employer F uses the adjustments of future payments correction method to correct the §415(b) failure, by recouping the entire excess payment made in 2006 from Employee S's remaining benefit payments for 2007. Thus, Employee S's annual annuity benefit for 2007 is reduced to $164,400 to reflect the excess benefit amounts (increased by interest) that were paid from the plan to Employee S during the 2006 plan year. Beginning in 2008, Employee S begins to receive annual benefit payments of $175,000.

Example 20:

The facts are the same as in Example 18, except that the benefit was paid to Employee S in the form of a single-sum distribution in 2006, which exceeded the maximum §415(b) limits by $110,000.

Correction:

Employer F uses the return of overpayment correction method to correct the §415(b) failure. Thus, Employer F notifies Employee S of the $110,000 Overpayment and that the Overpayment was not eligible for favorable tax treatment accorded to distributions from qualified plans (and, specifically, was not eligible for tax-free rollover). The notice also informs Employee S that the Overpayment (with interest at the rate used by the plan to calculate the single-sum payment) is owed to the plan. Employer F takes reasonable steps to have the Overpayment (with interest at the rate used by the plan to calculate the single-sum payment) paid to the plan. Employee S pays the $110,000 (plus the requested interest) to the plan. It is determined that the plan's rate of return for the relevant period was 2 percentage points more than the rate used by the plan to calculate the single-sum payment. Accordingly, Employer F contributes the difference to the plan.

Example 21:

The facts are the same as in Example 20.

Correction:

Employer F uses the return of overpayment correction method to correct the §415(b) failure. Thus, Employer F notifies Employee S of the $110,000 Overpayment and that the Overpayment was not eligible for favorable tax treatment accorded to distributions from qualified plans (and, specifically, was not eligible for tax-free rollover). The notice also informs Employee S that the Overpayment (with interest at the rate used by the plan to calculate the single-sum payment) is owed to the plan. Employer F takes reasonable steps to have the Overpayment (with interest at the rate used by the plan to calculate the single-sum payment) paid to the plan. As a result of Employer F's recovery efforts, some, but not all, of the Overpayment (with interest) is recovered from Employee S. It is determined that the amount returned by Employee S to the plan is less than the Overpayment adjusted for Earnings at the plan's rate of return. Accordingly, Employer F contributes the difference to the plan.

(2) *Failures Relating to a §415(c) Excess.* (a) *Correction Methods.* (i) *Appendix A Correction Method.* Appendix A, section .08, sets forth the correction method for correcting the failure to satisfy the §415(c) limits on annual additions.

(ii) *Forfeiture Correction Method.* In addition to the Appendix A correction method, the failure to satisfy §415(c) with respect to a nonhighly compensated employee (A) who in the limitation year of the failure had annual additions consisting of both (I) either elective deferrals or after-tax employee contributions or both and (II) either matching or nonelective contributions or both, (B) for whom the matching and nonelective contributions equal or exceed the portion of the employee's annual addition that exceeds the limits under §415(c) ("§415(c) excess") for the limitation year, and (C) who has terminated with no vested interest in the matching and nonelective contributions (and has not been reemployed at the time of the correction), may be corrected by using the forfeiture correction method set forth in this paragraph. The §415(c) excess is deemed to consist solely of the matching and nonelective contributions. If the employee's §415(c) excess (adjusted for Earnings) has previously been forfeited, the §415(c) failure is deemed to be corrected. If the §415(c) excess (adjusted for Earnings) has not been forfeited, that amount is placed in an unallocated account, as described in section 6.06(2) of this revenue procedure, to be used to reduce employer nonelective contributions in succeeding year(s) (or if the amount would have been allocated to other employees who were in the plan for the year of the failure if the failure had not occurred, then that amount is reallocated to the other employees in accordance with the plan's allocation formula). Note that while this correction method will permit more favorable tax treatment of elective deferrals for the employee than the Appendix A correction method, this correction method could be less favorable to the employee in certain cases, for example, if the employee is subsequently reemployed and becomes vested. (See Examples 22 and 23.)

(iii) *Return of Overpayment Correction Method.* A failure to satisfy §415(c) that includes a distribution of the §415(c) excess attributable to nonelective contributions and matching contributions may be corrected using the return of Overpayment correction method set forth in section 6.06(3) of this revenue procedure.

(b) *Examples.*

Example 22:

Employer G maintains a §401(k) plan. The plan provides for nonelective employer contributions, elective deferrals, and after-tax employee contributions. The plan provides that the nonelective contributions vest under a 5-year cliff vesting schedule. The plan provides that when an employee terminates employment, the employee's nonvested account balance is forfeited five years after a distribution of the employee's vested account balance and that forfeitures are used to reduce employer contributions. For the 1998 limitation year, the annual additions made on behalf of two nonhighly compensated employees in the plan, Employees T and U, exceeded the limit in §415(c). For the 1998 limitation year, Employee T had §415 compensation of $60,000, and, accordingly, a §415(c)(1)(B) limit of $15,000. Employee T made elective deferrals and after-tax employee contributions. For the 1998 limitation year, Employee U had §415 compensation of $40,000, and, accordingly, a §415(c)(1)(B) limit of $10,000. Employee U made elective deferrals. Also, on January 1, 1999, Employee U, who had three years of service with Employer G, terminated his employment and received his entire vested account balance (which consisted of his elective deferrals). The annual additions for Employees T and U consisted of:

	T	U
Nonelective Contributions	$7,500	$4,500
Elective Deferrals	$10,000	$5,800
After-tax Contributions	$500	$0
Total Contributions	$18,000	$10,300
§415(c) Limit	$15,000	$10,000
§415(c) Excess	$3,000	$300

Correction:

Employer G uses the Appendix A correction method to correct the §415(c) excess with respect to Employee T (i.e., $3,000). Thus, a distribution of plan assets (and corresponding reduction of the account balance) consisting of $500 (adjusted for Earnings) of after-tax employee contributions and $2,500 (adjusted for Earnings) of elective deferrals is made to Employee T. Employer G uses the forfeiture correction method to correct the §415(c) excess with respect to Employee U. Thus, the §415(c) excess is deemed to consist solely of the nonelective contributions. Accordingly, Employee U's nonvested account balance is reduced by $300 (adjusted for Earnings) which is placed in an unallocated account, as described in section 6.06(2) of this revenue procedure, to be used to reduce employer contributions in succeeding year(s). After correction, it is determined that the ADP and ACP tests for 1998 were satisfied.

Example 23:

Employer H maintains a §401(k) plan. The plan provides for nonelective employer contributions, matching contributions, and elective deferrals. The plan provides for matching contributions that are equal to 100% of an employee's elective deferrals that do not exceed 8% of the employee's plan compensation for the plan year. For the 1998 limitation year, Employee V had §415 compensation of $50,000, and, accordingly, a §415(c)(1)(B) limit of $12,500. During that limitation year, the annual additions for Employee V totaled $15,000, consisting of $5,000 in elective deferrals, a $4,000 matching contribution (8% of $50,000), and a $6,000 nonelective employer contribution. Thus, the annual additions for Employee V exceeded the §415(c) limit by $2,500.

Correction:

Employer H uses the Appendix A correction method to correct the §415(c) excess with respect to Employee V (i.e., $2,500). Accordingly, $1,000 of the unmatched elective deferrals (adjusted for Earnings) are distributed to Employee V. The remaining $1,500 excess is apportioned equally between the elective deferrals and the associated matching employer contributions, so Employee V's account balance is further reduced by distributing to Employee V $750 (adjusted for Earnings) of the elective deferrals and forfeiting $750 (adjusted for Earnings) of the associated employer matching contributions. The forfeited matching contributions are placed in an unallocated account, as described in section 6.06(2) of this revenue procedure, to be used to reduce employer contributions in succeeding year(s). After correction, it is determined that the ADP and ACP tests for 1998 were satisfied.

.05 *Correction of Other Overpayment Failures.* An Overpayment, other than one described in section 2.04(1) (relating to a §415(b) excess) or section 2.04(2) (relating to a §415(c) excess), may be corrected in accordance with this section 2.05. An Overpayment from a defined benefit plan is corrected in accordance with the rules in section 2.04(1). An Overpayment from a defined contribution plan is corrected in accordance with the rules in section 2.04(2)(a)(iii).

.06 *Section 401(a)(17) Failures.* (1) *Reduction of Account Balance Correction Method.* The allocation of contributions or forfeitures under a defined contribution plan for a plan year on the basis of compensation in excess of the limit under §401(a)(17) for the plan year may be corrected using the reduction of account balance correction method set forth in section 6.06(2) of this revenue procedure.

(2) *Example.*

Example 24:

Employer J maintains a money purchase pension plan. Under the plan, an eligible employee is entitled to an employer contribution of 8% of the employee's compensation up to the §401(a)(17) limit ($220,000 for 2006). During the 2006 plan year, an eligible employee, Employee W, inadvertently was credited with a contribution based on compensation above the §401(a)(17) limit. Employee W's compensation for 2006 was $250,000. Employee W received a contribution of $20,000 for 2006 (8% of $250,000), rather than the contribution of $17,600 (8% of $220,000) provided by the plan for that year, resulting in an improper allocation of $2,400.

Correction:

The §401(a)(17) failure is corrected using the reduction of account balance method by reducing Employee W's account balance by $2,400 (adjusted for Earnings) and crediting that amount to an unallocated account, as described in section 6.06(2) of this revenue procedure, to be used to reduce employer contributions in succeeding year(s).

.07 *Correction by Amendment.* (1) *Section 401(a)(17) Failures.* (a) *Contribution Correction Method.* In addition to the reduction of account balance correction method under section 6.06(2) of this revenue procedure, a Plan Sponsor may correct a §401(a)(17) failure for a plan year under a defined contribution plan by using the contribution correction method set forth in this paragraph. The Plan Sponsor contributes an additional amount on behalf of each of the other employees (excluding each employee for whom there was a §401(a)(17) failure) who received an allocation for the year of the failure, and amends the plan (as necessary) to provide for the additional allocation. The amount contributed for an employee is equal to the employee's plan compensation for the year of the failure multiplied by a fraction, the numerator of which is the improperly allocated amount made on behalf of the employee with the largest improperly allocated amount, and the denominator of which is the limit under §401(a)(17) applicable to the year of the failure. The resulting additional amount for each of the other employees is adjusted for Earnings. (See Example 25.)

(b) *Example.*

Example 25:

The facts are the same as in Example 24.

Correction:

Employer J corrects the failure under VCP using the contribution correction method by (1) amending the plan to increase the contribution percentage for all eligible employees (other than Employee W) for the 2003 plan year and (2) contributing an additional amount (adjusted for Earnings) for those employees for that plan year. To determine the increase in the plan's contribution percentage (and the additional amount contributed on behalf of each eligible employee), the improperly allocated amount ($2,400) is divided by the §401(a)(17) limit for 2006 ($220,000). Accordingly, the plan is amended to increase the contribution percentage by 1.09 percentage points ($2,400/$220,000) from 8% to 9.09%. In addition, each eligible employee for the 2006 plan year (other than Employee W) receives an additional contribution of 1.09% multiplied by that employee's plan compensation for 2006. This additional contribution is adjusted for Earnings.

(2) *Hardship Distribution Failures and Plan Loan Failures.* (a) *Plan Amendment Correction Method.* The Operational Failure of making hardship distributions to employees under a plan that does not provide for hardship distributions may be corrected using the plan amendment correction method set forth in this paragraph. The plan is amended retroactively to provide for the hardship distributions that were made available. This paragraph does not apply unless (i) the amendment satisfies §401(a), and (ii) the plan as amended would have satisfied the qualification requirements of §401(a) (including the requirements applicable to hardship distributions under §401(k), if applicable) had the amendment been adopted when hardship distributions were first made available. (See Example 26.) The Plan Amendment Correction Method is also available

for the Operational Failure of permitting plan loans to employees under a plan that does not provide for plan loans. The plan is amended retroactively to provide for the plan loans that were made available. This paragraph does not apply unless (i) the amendment satisfies §401(a), and (ii) the plan as amended would have satisfied the qualification requirements of §401(a) (and the requirements applicable to plan loans under §72(p)) had the amendment been adopted when plan loans were first made available.

(b) *Example*.

Example 26:

Employer K, a for-profit corporation, maintains a §401(k) plan. Although plan provisions in 2005 did not provide for hardship distributions, beginning in 2005 hardship distributions of amounts allowed to be distributed under §401(k) were made currently and effectively available to all employees (within the meaning of §1.401(a)(4)-4). The standard used to determine hardship satisfied the deemed hardship distribution standards in §1.401(k)-1(d). Hardship distributions were made to a number of employees during the 2005 and 2006 plan years, creating an Operational Failure. The failure was discovered in 2007.

Correction:

Employer K corrects the failure under VCP by adopting a plan amendment, effective January 1, 2005, to provide a hardship distribution option that satisfies the rules applicable to hardship distributions in §1.401(k)-1(d). The amendment provides that the hardship distribution option is available to all employees. Thus, the amendment satisfies §401(a), and the plan as amended in 2005 would have satisfied §401(a) (including §1.401(a)(4)-4 and the requirements applicable to hardship distributions under §401(k)) if the amendment had been adopted in 2005.

(3) *Early Inclusion of Otherwise Eligible Employee Failure*. (a) *Plan Amendment Correction Method*. The Operational Failure of including an otherwise eligible employee in the plan who either (i) has not completed the plan's minimum age or service requirements, or (ii) has completed the plan's minimum age or service requirements but became a participant in the plan on a date earlier than the applicable plan entry date, may be corrected by using the plan amendment correction method set forth in this paragraph. The plan is amended retroactively to change the eligibility or entry date provisions to provide for the inclusion of the ineligible employee to reflect the plan's actual operations. The amendment may change the eligibility or entry date provisions with respect to only those ineligible employees that were wrongly included, and only to those ineligible employees, provided (i) the amendment satisfies §401(a) at the time it is adopted, (ii) the amendment would have satisfied §401(a) had the amendment been adopted at the earlier time when it is effective, and (iii) the employees affected by the amendment are predominantly nonhighly compensated employees. For a defined benefit plan, a contribution may have to be made to the plan for a correction that is accomplished through a plan amendment if the plan is subject to the requirements of §436(c) at the time of the amendment, as described in section 6.02(4)(e)(ii).

(b) *Example.*

Example 27:

Employer L maintains a §401(k) plan applicable to all of its employees who have at least six months of service. The plan is a calendar year plan. The plan provides that Employer L will make matching contributions based upon an employee's salary reduction contributions. In 2007, it is discovered that all four employees who were hired by Employer L in 2006 were permitted to make salary reduction contributions to the plan effective with the first weekly paycheck after they were employed. Three of the four employees are nonhighly compensated. Employer L matched these employees' salary reduction contributions in accordance with the plan's matching contribution formula. Employer L calculates the ADP and ACP tests for 2006 (taking into account the salary reduction and matching contributions that were made for these employees) and determines that the tests were satisfied.

Correction:

Employer L corrects the failure under SCP by adopting a plan amendment, effective for employees hired on or after January 1, 2006, to provide that there is no service eligibility requirement under the plan and submitting the amendment to the Service for a determination letter.

SECTION 3. EARNINGS ADJUSTMENT METHODS AND EXAMPLES

.01 *Earnings Adjustment Methods.* (1) *In general.* (a) Under section 6.02(4)(a) of this revenue procedure, whenever the appropriate correction method for an Operational Failure in a defined contribution plan includes a corrective contribution or allocation that increases one or more employees' account balances (now or in the future), the contribution or allocation is adjusted for Earnings and forfeitures. This section 3 provides Earnings adjustment methods (but not forfeiture adjustment methods) that may be used by a Plan Sponsor to adjust a corrective contribution or allocation for Earnings in a defined contribution plan. Consequently, these Earnings adjustment methods may be used to determine the Earnings adjustments for corrective contributions or allocations made under the correction methods in section 2 and under the correction methods in Appendix A. If an Earnings adjustment method in this section 3 is used to adjust a corrective contribution or allocation, that adjustment is treated as satisfying the Earnings adjustment requirement of section 6.02(4)(a) of this revenue procedure. Other Earnings adjustment methods, different from those illustrated in this section 3, may also be appropriate for adjusting corrective contributions or allocations to reflect Earnings.

(b) Under the Earnings adjustment methods of this section 3, a corrective contribution or allocation that increases an employee's account balance is adjusted to reflect an "earnings amount" that is based on the Earnings rate(s) (determined under section 3.01(3)) for the period of the failure (determined under section 3.01(2)). The Earnings amount is allocated in accordance with section 3.01(4).

(c) The rule in section 6.02(5)(a) of this revenue procedure permitting reasonable estimates in certain circumstances applies for purposes of this section 3. For this purpose, a determination of Earnings made in accordance with the rules of administrative convenience set forth in this section 3 is treated as a precise determination of Earnings. Thus, if the probable difference between an approximate determination of Earnings and a determination of Earnings under this section 3 is insignificant and the administrative cost of a precise determination would significantly exceed the probable difference, reasonable estimates may be used in calculating the appropriate Earnings.

(d) This section 3 does not apply to corrective distributions or corrective reductions in account balances. Thus, for example, while this section 3 applies in increasing the account balance of an improperly excluded employee to correct the exclusion of the employee under the reallocation correction method described in section 2.02(2)(a)(iii)(B), this section 3 does not apply in reducing the account balances of other employees under the reallocation correction method. (See section 2.02(2)(a)(iii)(C) for rules that apply to the Earnings adjustments for such reductions.) In addition, this section 3 does not apply in determining Earnings adjustments under the one-to-one correction method described in section 2.01(1)(b)(iii).

(2) *Period of the Failure.* (a) *General Rule.* For purposes of this section 3, the "period of the failure" is the period from the date that the failure began through the date of correction. For example, in the case of an improper forfeiture of an employee's account balance, the beginning of the period of the failure is the date as of which the account balance was improperly reduced. See section 6.02(4)(f) of this revenue procedure.

(b) *Rules for Beginning Date for Exclusion of Eligible Employees from Plan.* (i) *General Rule.* In the case of an exclusion of an eligible employee from a plan contribution, the beginning of the period of the failure is the date on which contributions of the same type (e.g., elective deferrals, matching contributions, or discretionary nonelective employer contributions) were made for other employees for the year of the failure. In the case of an exclusion of an eligible employee from an allocation of a forfeiture, the beginning of the period of the failure is the date on which forfeitures were allocated to other employees for the year of the failure.

(ii) *Exclusion from a §401(k) or (m) Plan.* For administrative convenience, for purposes of calculating the Earnings rate for corrective contributions for a plan year (or the portion of the plan year) during which an employee was improperly excluded from making periodic elective deferrals or after-tax employee contributions, or from receiving periodic matching contributions, the Plan Sponsor may treat the date on which the contributions would have been made as the midpoint of the plan year (or the midpoint of the portion of the plan year) for which the failure occurred. Alternatively, in this case, the Plan Sponsor may treat the date on which the contributions would have been made as the first date of the plan year (or the portion of the plan year) during which an employee was excluded, provided that the Earnings rate used is one half of the Earnings rate applicable under section 3.01(3) for the plan year (or the portion of the plan year) for which the failure occurred.

(3) *Earnings Rate.* (a) *General Rule.* For purposes of this section 3, the Earnings rate generally is based on the investment results that would have applied to the corrective contribution or allocation if the failure had not occurred.

(b) *Multiple Investment Funds.* If a plan permits employees to direct the investment of account balances into more than one investment fund, the Earnings rate is based on the rate applicable to the employee's investment choices for the period of the failure. For administrative convenience, if most of the employees for whom the corrective contribution or allocation is made are nonhighly compensated employees, the rate of return of the fund with the highest rate of return under the plan for the period of the failure may be used to determine the Earnings rate for all corrective contributions or allocations. If the employee had not made any applicable investment choices, the Earnings rate may be based on the rate of return under the plan as a whole (i.e., the average of the rates earned by all of the funds in the valuation periods during the period of the failure weighted by the portion of the plan assets invested in the various funds during the period of the failure).

(c) *Other Simplifying Assumptions.* For administrative convenience, the Earnings rate applicable to the corrective contribution or allocation for a valuation period with respect to any investment fund may be assumed to be the actual Earnings rate for the plan's investments in that fund during that valuation period. For example, the Earnings rate may be determined without regard to any special investment provisions that vary according to the size of the fund. Further, the Earnings rate applicable to the corrective contribution or allocation for a portion of a valuation period may be a pro rata portion of the Earnings rate for the entire valuation period, unless the application of this rule would result in either a significant understatement or overstatement of the actual Earnings during that portion of the valuation period.

(4) *Allocation Methods.* (a) *In General.* For purposes of this section 3, the Earnings amount generally may be allocated in accordance with any of the methods set forth in this paragraph (4). The methods under paragraph (4)(c), (d), and (e) are intended to be particularly helpful where corrective contributions are made at dates between the plan's valuation dates.

(b) *Plan Allocation Method.* Under the plan allocation method, the Earnings amount is allocated to account balances under the plan in accordance with the plan's method for allocating Earnings as if the failure had not occurred. (See, Example 28.)

(c) *Specific Employee Allocation Method.* Under the specific employee allocation method, the entire Earnings amount is allocated solely to the account balance of the employee on whose behalf the corrective contribution or allocation is made (regardless of whether the plan's allocation method would have allocated the Earnings solely to that employee). In determining the allocation of plan Earnings for the valuation period during which the corrective contribution or allocation is made, the corrective contribution or allocation (including the Earnings amount) is treated in the same manner as any other contribution under the plan on behalf of the employee during that valuation period. Alternatively, where the plan's allocation method does not allocate plan Earnings for a valuation period to a contribution made during that valuation period, plan Earnings for the valuation period during which the corrective contribution or allocation is made may be allocated as if that employee's account balance had been increased as of the last day of the prior valuation period by the corrective contribution or allocation, including only that portion of the Earnings amount attributable to Earnings through the last day of the prior valuation period. The employee's account balance is then further increased as of the last day of the valuation period during which the corrective contribution or allocation is made by that portion of the Earnings amount attributable to Earnings after the last day of the prior valuation period. (See Example 29.)

(d) *Bifurcated Allocation Method.* Under the bifurcated allocation method, the entire Earnings amount for the valuation periods ending before the date the corrective contribution or allocation is made is allocated solely to the account balance of the employee on whose behalf the corrective contribution or allocation is made. The Earnings amount for the valuation period during which the corrective contribution or allocation is made is allocated in accordance with the plan's method for allocating other Earnings for that valuation period in accordance with section 3.01(4)(b). (See Example 30.)

(e) *Current Period Allocation Method.* Under the current period allocation method, the portion of the Earnings amount attributable to the valuation period during which the period of the failure begins ("first partial valuation period") is allocated in the same manner as Earnings for the valuation period during which the corrective contribution or allocation is made in accordance with section 3.01(4)(b). The Earnings for the subsequent full valuation periods ending before the beginning of the valuation period during which the corrective contribution or allocation is made are allocated solely to the employee for whom the required contribution should have been made. The Earnings amount for the valuation period during which the corrective contribution or allocation is made ("second partial valuation period") is allocated in accordance with the plan's method for allocating other Earnings for that valuation period in accordance with section 3.01(4)(b). (See Example 31.)

.02 *Examples.*

Example 28:

Employer L maintains a profit-sharing plan that provides only for nonelective contributions. The plan has a single investment fund. Under the plan, assets are valued annually (the last day of the plan year) and Earnings for the year are allocated in proportion to account balances as of the last day of the prior year, after reduction for distributions during the current year but without regard to contributions received during the current year (the "prior year account balance"). Plan contributions for 1997 were made on March 31, 1998. On April 20, 2000, Employer L determines that an operational failure occurred for 1997 because Employee X was improperly excluded from the plan. Employer L decides to correct the failure by using the Appendix A correction method for the exclusion of an eligible employee from nonelective contributions in a profit-sharing plan.

Under this method, Employer L determines that this failure is corrected by making a contribution on behalf of Employee X of $5,000 (adjusted for Earnings). The Earnings rate under the plan for 1998 was +20%. The Earnings rate under the plan for 1999 was +10%. On May 15, 2000, when Employer L determines that a contribution to correct for the failure will be made on June 1, 2000, a reasonable estimate of the Earnings rate under the plan from January 1, 2000 to June 1, 2000 is +12%.

Earnings Adjustment on the Corrective Contribution:

The $5,000 corrective contribution on behalf of Employee X is adjusted to reflect an earnings amount based on the Earnings rates for the period of the failure (March 31, 1998 through June 1, 2000) and the earnings amount is allocated using the plan allocation method. Employer L determines that a pro rata simplifying assumption may be used to determine the Earnings rate for the period from March 31, 1998 to December 31, 1998, because that rate does not significantly understate or overstate the actual investment return for that period. Accordingly, Employer L determines that the Earnings rate for that period is 15% (9/12 of the plan's 20% Earnings rate for the year). Thus, applicable Earnings rates under the plan during the period of the failure are:

Time Periods	Earnings Rate
3/31/98 - 12/31/98 (First Partial Valuation Period)	+15%
1/1/99 - 12/31/99	+10%
1/1/00 - 6/1/00 (Second Partial Valuation Period)	+12%

If the $5,000 corrective contribution had been contributed for Employee X on March 31, 1998, (1) Earnings for 1998 would have been increased by the amount of the Earnings on the additional $5,000 contribution from March 31, 1998 through December 31, 1998 and would have been allocated as 1998 Earnings in proportion to the prior year (December 31, 1997) account balances, (2) Employee X's account balance as of December 31, 1998 would have been increased by the additional $5,000 contribution, (3) Earnings for 1999 would have been increased by the 1999 Earnings on the additional $5,000 contribution (including 1998 Earnings thereon) allocated in proportion to the prior year (December 31, 1998) account balances along with other 1999 Earnings, and (4) Earnings for 2000 would have been increased by the Earnings on the additional $5,000 (including 1998 and 1999 Earnings thereon) from January 1 to June 1, 2000 and would be allocated in proportion to the prior year (December 31, 1999) account balances along with other 2000 Earnings. Accordingly, the $5,000 corrective contribution is adjusted to reflect an Earnings amount of $2,084 ($5,000[(1.15)(1.10)(1.12)-1]) and the earnings amount is allocated to the account balances under the plan allocation method as follows:

(a) Each account balance that shared in the allocation of Earnings for 1998 is increased, as of December 31, 1998, by its appropriate share of the Earnings amount for 1998, $750 ($5,000(.15)).

(b) Employee X's account balance is increased, as of December 31, 1998, by $5,000.

(c) The resulting December 31, 1998 account balances will share in the 1999 Earnings, including the $575 for 1999 Earnings included in the corrective contribution ($5,750(.10)), to determine the account balances as of December 31, 1999. However, each account balance other than Employee X's account balance has already shared in the 1999 Earnings, excluding the $575. Accordingly, Employee X's account balance as of December 31, 1999 will include $500 of the 1999 portion of the earnings amount based on the $5,000 corrective contribution allocated to Employee X's account balance as of December 31, 1998 ($5,000(.10)). Then each account balance that originally shared in the allocation of Earnings for 1999 (i.e., excluding the $5,500 additions to Employee X's account balance) is increased by its appropriate share of the remaining 1999 portion of the earnings amount, $75.

(d) The resulting December 31, 1999 account balances (including the $5,500 additions to Employee X's account balance) will share in the 2000 portion of the earnings amount based on the estimated January 1, 2000 to June 1, 2000 Earnings included in the corrective contribution equal to $759 ($6,325(.12)). (See Table 1.)

Table 1 Calculation and Allocation of the Corrective Amount Adjusted for Earnings			
	Earnings Rate	Amount	Allocated to
Corrective Contribution		$5,000	Employee X
First Partial Valuation Period Earnings	15%	$750[1]	All 12/31/1997 Account Balances[4]
1999 Earnings	10%	$575[2]	Employee X ($500)/All 12/31/1998 Account Balances ($75)[4]
Second Partial Valuation Period Earnings	12%	$759[3]	All 12/31/1999 Account Balances (including Employee X's $5,500)[4]
Total Amount Contributed		$7,084	

[1]$5,000 × 15%
[2]$5,750($5,000 + $750) × 10%
[3]$6,325($5,000 + $750 + $575) × 12%
[4]After reduction for distributions during the year for which Earnings are being determined but without regard to contributions received during the year for which Earnings are being determined.

Example 29:

The facts are the same as in Example 28.

Earnings Adjustment on the Corrective Contribution:

The earnings amount on the corrective contribution is the same as in Example 28, but the earnings amount is allocated using the specific employee allocation method. Thus, the entire earnings amount for all periods through June 1, 2000 (i.e., $750 for March 31, 1998 to December 31, 1998, $575 for 1999, and $759 for January 1, 2000 to June 1, 2000) is allocated to Employee X. Accordingly, Employer L makes a contribution on June 1, 2000 to the plan of $7,084 ($5,000(1.15)(1.10)(1.12)). Employee X's account balance as of December 31, 2000 is increased by $7,084. Alternatively, Employee X's account balance as of December 31, 1999 is increased by $6,325 ($5,000(1.15)(1.10)), which shares in the allocation of Earnings for 2000, and Employee X's account balance as of December 31, 2000 is increased by the remaining $759. (See Table 2.)

Example 30:

The facts are the same as in Example 28.

Earnings Adjustment on the Corrective Contribution:

The earnings amount on the corrective contribution is the same as in Example 28, but the earnings amount is allocated using the bifurcated allocation method. Thus, the Earnings for the first partial valuation period (March 31, 1998 to December 31, 1998) and the Earnings for 1999 are allocated to Employee X. Accordingly, Employer L makes a contribution on June 1, 2000 to the plan of

Table 2 Calculation and Allocation of the Corrective Amount Adjusted for Earnings			
	Earnings Rate	**Amount**	**Allocated to**
Corrective Contribution		$5,000	Employee X
First Partial Valuation Period Earnings	15%	$750[1]	Employee X
1999 Earnings	10%	$575[2]	Employee X
Second Partial Valuation Period Earnings	12%	$759[3]	Employee X
Total Amount Contributed		$7,084	

[1]$5,000 × 15%
[2]$5,750($5,000 + $750) × 10%
[3]$6,325($5,000 + $750 + $575) x 12%

Table 3	Calculation and Allocation of the Corrective Amount Adjusted for Earnings		
	Earnings Rate	Amount	Allocated to
Corrective Contribution		$5,000	Employee X
First Partial Valuation Period Earnings	15%	$750[1]	Employee X
1999 Earnings	10%	$575[2]	Employee X
Second Partial Valuation Period Earnings	12%	$759[3]	12/31/99 Account Balances (including Employee X's $6,325)[4]
Total Amount Contributed		$7,084	

[1] $5,000 × 15%
[2] $5,750($5,000 + $750) × 10%
[3] $6,325($5,000 + $750 + $575) x 12%
[4] After reduction for distributions during the 2000 year but without regard to contributions received during the 2000 year.

$7,084 ($5,000(1.15)(1.10)(1.12)). Employee X's account balance as of December 31, 1999 is increased by $6,325 ($5,000(1.15)(1.10)); and the December 31, 1999 account balances of employees (including Employee X's increased account balance) will share in estimated January 1, 2000 to June 1, 2000 Earnings on the corrective contribution equal to $759 ($6,325(.12)). (See, Table 3.)

Example 31:

The facts are the same as in Example 28.

Earnings Adjustment on the Corrective Contribution:

The earnings amount on the corrective contribution is the same as in Example 28, but the earnings amount is allocated using the current period allocation method. Thus, the Earnings for the first partial valuation period (March 31, 1998 to December 31, 1998) are allocated as 2000 Earnings. Accordingly, Employer L makes a contribution on June 1, 2000 to the plan of $7,084 ($5,000 (1.15)(1.10)(1.12)). Employee X's account balance as of December 31, 1999 is increased by the sum of $5,500 ($5,000(1.10)) and the remaining 1999 Earnings on the corrective contribution equal to $75 ($5,000(.15)(.10)). Further, both (1) the estimated March 31, 1998 to December 31, 1998 Earnings on the corrective contribution equal to $750 ($5,000(.15)) and (2) the estimated January 1, 2000 to June 1, 2000 Earnings on the corrective contribution equal to $759 ($6,325(.12)) are treated in the same manner as 2000 Earnings by allocating these amounts to the December 31, 2000 account balances of employees in proportion to account balances as of December 31, 1999 (including Employee X's increased account balance). (See, Table 4.) Thus, Employee X is allocated the Earnings for the full valuation period during the period of the failure.

Table 4	Calculation and Allocation of the Corrective Amount Adjusted for Earnings		
	Earnings Rate	Amount	Allocated to
Corrective Contribution		$5,000	Employee X
First Partial Valuation Period Earnings	15%	$750[1]	12/31/99 Account Balances (including Employee X's $5,575)[4]
1999 Earnings	10%	$575[2]	Employee X
Second Partial Valuation Period Earnings	12%	$759[3]	12/31/99 Account Balances (including Employee X's $5,575)[4]
Total Amount Contributed		$7,084	

[1] $5,000 × 15%
[2] $5,750 ($5,000 + $750) × 10%
[3] $6,325 ($5,000 + $750 + $575) x 12%
[4] After reduction for distributions during the year for which Earnings are being determined but without regard to contributions received during the year for which Earnings are being determined.

Index

A

A Organization 210-211
Actual Contribution Percentage (ACP)
    test 59, 88, 214
Actual Deferral Percentage (ADP)
    test for elective deferrals 53, 88
actuarial interest of a beneficiary of a trust estate ...203
additional employer contributions.........................84
additional rules 84
    for the use of safe harbors 24
adoption agreement 75
affiliated service group 38, 208
    rules...208
after-tax contributions... 1
    Roth contribution...264
age-based allocation rates 99
aggregation or disaggregation of plans..................61
aggregation rule 38
allocation methods...20
    and plan terminations.....................................201
The American Taxpayer Relief Act of 2012........111
Arizona Governing Committee v. Norris..............196
Audit Closing Agreement Program
    (Audit CAP) 254-255, 257
auditing plans..26
automatic enrollment and escalation.....................74
automatic rollover 155
    to IRA safe harbor requirements 156-157
average benefit test 50
Average Deferral Percentage (ADF) test 14, 16
average surrender factor...195

B

B Organization...210-211
basic plan document...75-76
benefit payments 121
benefits of insurance in plan.................................185
broadly available allocation rates...........................99
brother-sister controlled group..............................203

C

carve out all HCE 101
Cash or Deferred Arrangements
    (CODA)... 1-2
closing of administrative record 226
Code Section 401(k) 2
combined group..205
common 401(k) plan compliance errors.............252
common plan design factors 73
comparison of Roth IRAs and Roth 401(k)
    plan...108
compensation for the overall limit 42
compensation 22
    in general...36
    when it is paid 40
complete discontinuance 216
    of contributions.. 30, 215
compliance procedures...254
complying
    with nondiscrimination rules...........................47
    with the incidental benefit rule 187
computing the ADP 54
contribution.. 19
    limits 20, 35
    requirement 80
control over the plan or its assets.........................164
controlled group rules 201
controlling interest 204
correction procedures under IRS' EPCRS
    and EBSA's programs 259
coverage requirement 14, 48
cross-testing...98
current employees 49
custom designed plans 77

D

DB/k
    other rules 94
    plan offers...91

DB/k (cont'd)
    requirements for the 401(k) portion 93
    vesting requirements 94
deductible employer contributions 7
Defined Benefit (DB)plan 4
disability, definition of 153
Delinquent Filer Voluntary Compliance
    Program (DFVCP) 257-258
Department of Labor (DOL) 7
designated beneficiary 124
designated Roth contribution 109-110
designating Roth account in 401(k) plan 108
designing
    the plan 73
    using safe harbor 401(k) plans 79
    with eligibility requirements 78
    with section 414(x) combination defined
        benefit and 401(k) plans (DB/k) 91
determination letter 221, 223, 254
    process 224
determining cost or basis 141-142
DFVCP 261
disabled employee 116
disadvantages of insurance plan 186
disaggregated 62
disclosure 7
    requirements 236
discretionary authority 164
disqualifying provisions 229
distribution
    due to the participants disability 153
    to a beneficiary due to the employee's death ...114
    to unemployed individuals for health
        insurance premiums 154
division of assets as part of a divorce 146
documentation error correction 259
DOL 257
    correction programs 257
    DFVCP 267
    Regulation Section 2550.404c-1(b)(3) 177
Domestic Relations Order (DRO) 146
    review 149

E

effect of a determination letter 222

elective deferral
    and the matching contribution 47
    distributions 122
    on a pre-tax basis 107
eligibility 74
eligible automatic contribution
    arrangements 89
eligible employers 11-12
employee
    contributions 26, 60
    elections requirement 97
    elective contributions 14
    elective deferrals 19
    nonelective contributions 16
Employee Plans Compliance Resolution
    System (ERCRS) 255
Employee Retirement Income Security Act
    of 1974 (ERISA) 2, 230
employer
    bankruptcy 4
    contributions 19, 26, 87
    deductions 97
    securities 180
enforcement responsibility 7
EPCRS 254, 261, 263
    VCP submissions 265
EPCRS 263
equivalent accrual rate 99
ERISA 163
    fiduciary, who is a fiduciary 250
    IRS reporting 221
    Section 404(c) plans 168
    Section 404(c) 167, 169
    Section 404(c)(5) 177
errors and violations not covered 259
excess benefit plans linked to the 401(k) plan 252
excess contributions 43, 263
excess deferral 114
excludable employees 12, 22, 49
exclusive benefit of employees 9

F

facts-and-circumstances test 9, 51, 83
failed plans 16
fee disclosures 198

fiduciaries.....................................8, 165, 167, 177, 250
    requirements..7
    responsibilities... 163, 196
financial hardship distribution 264
First Service Organization (FSO) 208-211
five-year participation period 113
Form
    5300 Schedule Q, Elective Deferral Requests...216
    5310 Application for Determination
        upon Termination 216
    5500.. 230-235
        annual return/report of employee
            benefit plan 217
        insurance information 233
        service provider information..................... 233
    5500-SF Short Form Annual Return/
        Report of Small Employee Benefit Plan ...217
    8717 User Fee for Employee Plan
        Determination Letter Request........... 216, 224
formal requirements 8
former employees.. 22, 49
fundamentals..7

G

general nondiscrimination test 25, 48
governmental entities 13
graduated vesting..30

H

hardship
    distribution 117
    withdrawals.. 75, 134
HCE 93, 100
Highly Compensated Employees
    (HCEs)................ 13-14, 21, 47, 53, 201, 212, 267
hybrid plans...94

I

income beneficiary...207
income tax
    consequences..188
    on value of life insurance protection...............189

indefinite impairment...153
independent contractors and leased
    employees...9
independent fiduciary 197
information provided to participants
    and beneficiaries...235
in-plan Roth rollover 111
    requirements...111
    tax consequences 112
Internal Revenue Code section 401(a) 1
Internal Revenue Service (IRS)...................................7
Interpolated Terminal Reserve..................... 194-195
investment
    advice for a fee..164
    fee disclosures..259
    manager..166
    risk..4
investment-related information.............................171
issues
    participation 7
    funding..7
    vesting..7
IRS and DOL
    audit programs...251
    reporting requirements 230
IRS
    correction programs 253
    EPCRS 253
    reporting requirements 216
    Uniform Lifetime Table...................................127

J

joint and survivor annuity 144
joint life expectancy 127

L

life insurance
    in 401(k) plans 185
    options at retirement or termination 191-196
lifetime RMDs... 124, 127
limits on fiduciary responsibility............................166
loan repayments...264
loans or hardship withdrawal.......................................4

M

making contributions 26
management organization 212
mandatory and discretionary plan
     amendments 260
mass submitter 76
Master and Prototype (M&P) plans 75
matching contribution 16, 58-59, 74
Matz v. Household international Tax
     Reduction Investment Plan 215
maximum ADP for HCE 57
medical expenses incurred 154
minimum participation standards 78
missed deferral opportunity for excluded
     employees 262
missed or late contributions 262
Model Investment Option Comparative
     Chart 198
multiple employers 201
multiple limits 35

N

negative tax consequences 249
Net Unrealized Appreciation (NUA) 141
new comparability 98
NHCE 87, 93, 101
1996 Defense of Marriage Act (DOMA) 143
nondiscrimination test 13, 109
     for the profit sharing portion 59
nonelective contribution 59
Nonhighly Compensated Employees
     (NHCE) 24, 51, 201, 214
nonqualified distributions 114
nonqualified deferred compensation plans
     and error corrections 266
     associated ot linked to a qualified
     401(k) plan 267
nonresident alien employee 12
normal retirement
     age 29
     benefit 29
notice concerning distributions 242
notice requirement 59, 82, 97

O

obtaining a determination letter 222
open architecture 401(k) 167
operational error corrections 261
opportunity to exercise control 168
overpayments 263

P

parent-subsidiary controlled group 202
partial termination 215
participant death 130-134
participant or beneficiary control 167
participant's compensation 37
Pension Protection Act of 2006 180
per-employee limit 36
     under Section 415 37
permanent plan 8
plan amendments 229
plan
     cashouts and automatic rollovers 155
     fiduciary 196
     investments 163
     limit violations 263
     loans 75, 137
     mergers 201, 212,
     terminations 214
pre-ERISA money purchase plan 11
Premiums, Earnings, and Reasonable
     Charges (PERC) 194
preretirement survivor annuity 144
pre-tax
     basis 123
     contributions 2
     employee contributions 7
     nonqualified Section 409A technique 101
preventing and fixing broken 401(k)
     plans 249
profit-sharing or stock bonus plan 11
Prohibited Transaction
     Exemption (PTE) 179
prohibited transaction 196, 250, 259
providing investment advice to plan
     participants 174

Q

QACA..87
   minimum contribution percentages................86
Qualified Automatic Contribution
   Arrangement (QACA)..74
qualified automatic contributions
   with safe harbor contributions.........................85
qualified change in investment options.......173-174
Qualified Default Investment Alternative
   (QDIA) 74, 89, 177-178, 182
qualified distributions..113
Qualified Domestic Relations Order
   (QDRO).. 111, 146
Qualified Joint and Survivor Annuity
   (QJSA) 144
Qualified Matching Contributions (QMACs) 57
Qualified Nonelective Contributions
   (QNECs) 57, 262
qualified plan.. 1, 10, 123
Qualified Preretirement Survivor
   Annuity (QPSA) 144
qualified Roth contribution program..................108

R

ratio percentage test 50
RBD...130
recipient organization...............................212
regulatory matters 221
remedial amendments....................................229
report 7
   and recordkeeping requirements....................117
   of rollover to the IRS....................................117
Required Beginning Date (RBD).........................123
required minimum distributions.........................123
restrictions on investment in employer
   securities...181
Retirement Equity Act of 1984 (REA)................142
Revenue Act of 1978 2
Revenue
   Procedure 2013-12..262
   Procedure 2013-16..224
   Ruling 2013-17...143
   Ruling 72-509...10

revocation or modification of determination
   letter 223
rollover contribution...115
Roth
   option...107
   separate accounting requirement 110
   violations...264
Roth 401(k)...74
   conversions 110
   distributions...112
   feature 108
rural cooperative plan...11

S

safe harbor 15-16, 40
   401(k)...101
   correction methods....................................256
   discrimination test..22
   plans...75
   provisions...83
   test 51
   for determining the fair market value
      of life insurance policies 193
same-sex marriages.....................................143
satisfying the ACP test...............................60
seasoned money..188
Section 1563(a) 202
Section 318 attribution rules 21
Section 401(a)(31)..155
Section 401(k)(12) safe harbor..............................79
section 401(k)(13)
   plans...85
   safe harbor 79
Section 402(a)(8) 2
Section 402(f) notice
   content of 243
Section 402(g) maximum annual amount
   permitted..263
Section 409A
   nonqualified deferred compensation plans..252
      correction programs for 267
Section 410(k)(12) plans 80
Section 411(d)(6) protected benefits 212, 214
Section 414(x) safe harbor 79

Section 415(c)(3) 40
Section 72(t) early distribution
    penalty and exceptions 152
self-correction of Section 415(c) failures 256
Self-Correction Program (SCP) 253-254, 256
self-employed individuals 12, 37, 39, 42
separate accounts for each participant 20
SIMPLE 401(k)
    contributions 97
    plan year 97
    plans 36, 79, 95
    vesting requirement 97
Small Business Jobs Act of 2010 111
small employer 91
sole designated beneficiary 129
special tax treatment 221
spousal rights in 401(k) plan distributions 142
state and local governments 11
Summary Annual Report (SAR) 242
Summary Plan Description (SPD) 10, 237, 241
    content of 239
Summary of Material Modifications (SMM) 241
    time for providing and SMM 241

T

tax
    benefits of 401(k) plans 7
    deferred growth 7, 123
    exempt
        educational institutions 12
        entities 13
        organizations 11
    of distributions under QDROs 150
    treatment of rollovers 115
techniques for increasing NHCE participation ... 101
terminating a 401(k) plan 214
three-year cliff 30
thrift savings plans 1
timely
    deposits 26
    remittance 262

Title VII of Civil Rights Act 196
too early participation opportunity 262
top hat
    excess benefit 266
    nonqualified deferred compensation
        plan 267
    plan 252
    rules 61
Traditional or QACA safe harbor 88
Treasury Regulation Section 35.3405-1T 151
treatment of excess contributions 42
trust
    as defined beneficiary 125
    or custodial agreement 75
types of plan documents 75

U

ultimate deposit deadline 26
uniform points allocation formula 22, 23
union employees 12
unisex rates requirement 196

V

VCP submission 261
vesting 27, 75
VFCP 261
Volume Submitter (VS) plans 77
Voluntary Contribution Program (VCP) 253-256
Voluntary Fiduciary Correction Program
    (VFCP) 257-259

W

Windsor ruling 143
witholdings on distributions 150

Y

year of service 31